Performance Appraisal and Management

Sara Miller McCune founded SAGE Publishing in 1965 to support the dissemination of usable knowledge and educate a global community. SAGE publishes more than 1000 journals and over 800 new books each year, spanning a wide range of subject areas. Our growing selection of library products includes archives, data, case studies and video. SAGE remains majority owned by our founder and after her lifetime will become owned by a charitable trust that secures the company's continued independence.

Los Angeles | London | New Delhi | Singapore | Washington DC | Melbourne

Performance Appraisal and Management

Kevin R. Murphy
University of Limerick, Ireland

Jeanette N. Cleveland
Colorado State University, USA

Madison E. Hanscom
Colorado State University, USA

Los Angeles | London | New Delhi
Singapore | Washington DC | Melbourne

FOR INFORMATION:

SAGE Publications, Inc.
2455 Teller Road
Thousand Oaks, California 91320
E-mail: order@sagepub.com

SAGE Publications Ltd.
1 Oliver's Yard
55 City Road
London, EC1Y 1SP
United Kingdom

SAGE Publications India Pvt. Ltd.
B 1/I 1 Mohan Cooperative Industrial Area
Mathura Road, New Delhi 110 044
India

SAGE Publications Asia-Pacific Pte. Ltd.
3 Church Street
#10-04 Samsung Hub
Singapore 049483

Acquisitions Editor: Maggie Stanley
Editorial Assistant: Alissa Nance
Production Editor: Nevair Kabakian
Copy Editor: Terri Lee Paulsen
Typesetter: Hurix Digital
Proofreader: Laura Webb
Indexer: Judy Hunt
Cover Designer: Dally Verghese
Marketing Manager: Amy Lammers

Printed in the United States of America

Library of Congress Cataloging-in-Publication Data

Names: Murphy, Kevin R., 1952- author. | Cleveland, Jeanette, author. | Hanscom, Madison E., author.

Title: Performance appraisal and management / Kevin R. Murphy, Colorado State University, USA, Pennsylvania State University, USA, Jeanette N. Cleveland, Colorado State University, USA, Madison E. Hanscom, Colorado State University, USA.

Description: Thousand Oaks, California : SAGE, [2019] | Includes bibliographical references and index.

Identifiers: LCCN 2017048316 | ISBN 9781506352909 (pbk. : alk. paper)

Subjects: LCSH: Employees—Rating of. | Performance standards.

Classification: LCC HF5549.5.R3 M8624 2019 | DDC 658.3/125—dc23 LC record available at https://lccn.loc.gov/2017048316

This book is printed on acid-free paper.

18 19 20 21 22 10 9 8 7 6 5 4 3 2 1

BRIEF CONTENTS

DETAILED CONTENTS

SECTION III: CHALLENGES IN IMPLEMENTING AND EVALUATING PERFORMANCE APPRAISAL SYSTEMS 183

Chapter 9 • Giving and Receiving Feedback 185

PREFACE

Performance appraisal is a task we all love to hate. Managers often do not like to give performance appraisals, and employees often do not want to receive them. Further, the business press has talked about the coming doom of performance appraisal for years. Yet, performance appraisal continues to serve critically important functions in organizations, and some form of performance appraisal is practiced in virtually all large organizations and in many smaller ones. This book was written to explore why performance appraisal presents so many challenges in organizations, and how performance appraisals can be improved.

The current book started as a simple revision of a 1995 book by Murphy and Cleveland (*Understanding Performance Appraisal: Social, Organizational and Goal-Oriented Perspectives*), also published by SAGE. As we started to read and review the substantial body of research published since 1995, we realized that something more than a simple revision was needed. In the last 20 years, an increasing number of researchers and practitioners have become dissatisfied with performance appraisal and have tried (with uneven success) to devise replacements. Performance management has emerged as an important set of ideas in human resource management, and some proponents of this method have suggested that it is a good replacement for traditional performance appraisal. As we read this literature, we tried to understand *why* performance appraisal is often seen as a problem rather than as an opportunity to improve organizations, and to understand what sorts of responses organizations might make to the challenges of developing, implementing, and (most importantly) benefiting from performance appraisal systems.

Like our 1995 book, the current book is based first and foremost on empirical research. This book includes approximately 900 references, the majority of these being research studies published in a wide array of journals. All three of the authors are industrial and organizational psychologists, and we are strong proponents of the scientist–practitioner model, which recognizes the ways science contributes to practice but also the way that the practical process of designing and implementing performance appraisal systems brings to light new scientific questions and useful insights into their solution. We have tried to bring together research from a number of disciplines, ranging from ethics to psychology to economics to help the reader understand the challenges and opportunities that performance appraisal entails.

This book is designed to be useful to a number of audiences. We believe this book will be useful to students in psychology, management, and human resource management courses as well as performance appraisal researchers and practitioners. The book does rely upon and cite a substantial body of research, yet we do not assume any prior knowledge of the field or of the research methods that are used in studying performance appraisal. We hope this book will give its readers a clear understanding of why performance appraisals can be so challenging in organizations (and, frankly, why they fail in many organizations) and a realistic appreciation for ways the performance appraisal process can be improved in organizations.

Kevin R. Murphy, Jeanette N. Cleveland, and Madison E. Hanscom
Castletroy, Ireland
October 26, 2017

ACKNOWLEDGMENTS

Numerous colleagues helped us in preparing this book, but we want to single out those whose contributions were especially noteworthy. First, Miranda Nabkel helped tremendously in organizing and checking our reference section. Second, Angelo DeNisi gave us insightful and constructive feedback on our early draft of our chapter on performance management. We are deeply indebted to both Miranda and Angelo. In addition, we want to thank both undergraduate and graduate psychology students in Dr. Cleveland's Performance Appraisal seminar during fall 2015 who highlighted areas for updating chapters from the 1995 performance appraisal book including the following master's and doctoral students: Kemol Anderson, Rebecca Brossoit, Dorey Chaffee, Lauren Cotter, Lena-Alyeska Huebner, Megan Naude, and Samantha Stelman.

We would also like to thank the following reviewers who provided insightful feedback and helpful suggestions on the manuscript: Uma J. Iyer, Austin Peay State University; Mo Cayer, University of New Haven; Brent E. Winston, Regent University; Ann Membel, Regis University; Rumaisa Shaukat, University of Ottawa; Deb Armstrong, University of New Brunswick; Tara S. Behrend, George Washington University; Sean Valentine, University of North Dakota; Cort W. Rudolph, Saint Louis University; Christine R. Day, Eastern Michigan University; Jennifer E. Fairweather, Regis University; Jing Zhang, California State University, San Bernadino; Michele A. Paludi, Excelsior College; and Eric S. Ecklund, Saint Francis University.

ABOUT THE AUTHORS

Kevin R. Murphy

Kevin Murphy holds the Kemmy Chair of Work and Employment Studies, Kemmy Business School, University of Limerick, Ireland. He earned his PhD in psychology from Penn State in 1979, and has served on the faculties of Rice University, New York University, Penn State, and Colorado State University. He is a Fellow of the American Psychological Association, the Society for Industrial and Organizational Psychology, and the American Psychological Society, and he is the recipient of the Society for Industrial and Organizational Psychology's 2004 Distinguished Scientific Contribution Award.

He has served as president of the Society for Industrial and Organizational Psychology and editor of *Journal of Applied Psychology* (1991–2002), and is editor of *Industrial and Organizational Psychology: Perspectives on Science and Practice*. He served as chair of the Department of Defense Advisory Committee on Military Personnel Testing, and has also served on five National Academy of Sciences committees dealing with problems in the workplace.

He is the author of over 180 articles and book chapters, and author or editor of 11 books, in areas ranging from psychometrics and statistical analysis to individual differences, performance assessment, gender, and honesty in the workplace.

Jeanette N. Cleveland

Jeanette N. Cleveland is a professor of Industrial & Organizational Psychology at Colorado State University. She earned her BS from Occidental College and MS and PhD from The Pennsylvania State University. She has held faculty positions at Baruch College, The Pennsylvania State University, and has served as an external examiner for University of Limerick, Ireland.

She has served as elected program chair for the Human Resources and Gender & Diversity in Organizations Divisions, division chair for HR and GDO, and prior to this to the executive committees for these divisions of the Academy of Management. In addition, she served as chair/cochair for the HR Doctoral & Junior Faculty Consortium, scholarly achievement award, Best Paper Award, and the GDO Dissertation Award, also for the Academy of Management. She is an elected Fellow of the Society for Industrial and Organizational Psychology (Division 14) and the American Psychological Association.

Her research interests include personal and contextual variables regarding work attitudes and performance decisions, workforce diversity issues including older workers and women, and work and family issues. She has served as consulting editor for *Journal of Organizational Behavior* and has or is currently serving on the editorial boards of *Journal of Applied Psychology, Personnel Psychology, Academy of Management Journal, Journal of Vocational Behavior, Human Resource Management Review, Journal of Management*, and *International Journal of Management Reviews*. She is the coeditor for the Applied Psychology Series for Taylor and Francis. Her books include *Understanding Performance Appraisal:*

Social, Organizational and Goal Perspectives (with K. Murphy) and *Women and Men in Organizations: Sex and Gender Issues* (with M. Stockdale and K. Murphy, 2000).

Madison E. Hanscom

Madison E. Hanscom is a doctoral student in the Industrial and Organizational Psychology doctoral program at Colorado State University. In addition to working on her PhD, Madison is a trainee in occupational health psychology through the Mountains and Plains Education and Research Center. She earned her Bachelor of Science in Psychology from Kennesaw State University in 2014.

INTRODUCTION

1 PERFORMANCE APPRAISAL: RESEARCH AND PRACTICE

PERFORMANCE APPRAISAL: HISTORICAL DEVELOPMENT AND PRESENT STATUS

Performance appraisal can be described as the Henny Youngman of human resource management—it gets no respect. Consider the following quotes:

> Performance appraisals are often described as the "job managers love to hate." (Pettijohn, Parker, Pettijohn, & Kent, 2001, p. 754)

> Nobody wants to get one. Nobody wants to give one. (Ford, 2004, p. 550)

> Performance appraisal (PA) continues to be one of the most persistent problems in organizations. (Gordon & Stewart, 2009, p. 473)

> Performance appraisal is, in practice, more of an organizational curse than a panacea. (Taylor, 1985, p. 185)

> One important component of performance management—that is, the performance review—is dreaded. (Adler et al., 2016, p. 220)

Dissatisfaction with performance appraisal appears to be increasing; many large organizations (e.g., Accenture, Deloitte, Microsoft, GAP, Medtronic) have abandoned or substantially curtailed their use of formal performance appraisal systems (Buckingham & Goodall, 2015; Capelli & Tavis, 2016; Culbert & Rout, 2010; Cunningham, 2015). Deloitte, for example, has replaced traditional appraisal systems with systems that ask team leaders a handful of simple questions about each team member (e.g., "Given what I know of this person's performance, I would always want him or her on my team"). However, getting rid of performance appraisal is not a simple matter, and the decision to do away with the whole uncomfortable business of conducting annual appraisals, giving performance feedback on the basis of these appraisals, and then using them to help make high-stakes decisions (e.g., promotion, salary increase) may cause more problems than it solves.[1] As Starbuck (2004) notes, "We should distrust performance measures, but we cannot ignore them because they are powerful motivators that can produce dramatic improvements in human and organizational performance" (p. 337).

In this book, we explore in depth four points:

- Why so many employees, supervisors, and managers are dissatisfied with performance appraisal

- Why performance appraisal so often fails, or appears to fail, in organizations

- Why performance appraisal is still necessary, and why attempts to replace it with more unstructured and informal approaches have the potential for disaster

- How the benefits of performance appraisal can be salvaged by changing the ways organizations and their members think about and use performance appraisal

Our approach is strongly anchored in scientific theory and empirical research. In the past 75 to 100 years, researchers in the organizational sciences have studied performance appraisal in depth, and have published hundreds if not thousands of relevant and useful studies, but this academic research has had a disappointingly small impact on the way performance appraisal is conducted and used in organizations (Banks & Murphy, 1985; Ilgen, Barnes-Farrell & McKellin, 1993; Murphy & DeNisi, 2008). The aim of this book is to pull together this body of research to help both researchers and the users of performance appraisal in organizations understand why performance appraisal is such a frustrating experience and how it could be improved. The authors of this book are all industrial/organizational psychologists, and we are strong proponents of the Scientist–Practitioner model that characterizes this field. In this book, we take a detailed look at the underlying science and use the results of this work to try and improve the practice of performance appraisal in organizations.

Is Performance Appraisal in Crisis?

There is a long history of research on performance rating and performance appraisal (for reviews, see Bernardin & Beatty, 1984; DeCotiis & Petit, 1978; DeNisi, 2006; DeNisi, Cafferty, & Meglino, 1984; DeNisi & Murphy 2017; Ilgen & Feldman, 1983; Landy & Farr, 1983; Milkovich & Wigdor, 1991; Murphy & Cleveland, 1991, 1995; Wherry & Bartlett, 1982), and while different reviews highlight different strengths and weakness of the methods that are used in organization to measure job performance via rating scales or other similar measures, it is fair to say that none of these reviews lead to the conclusion that performance rating is particularly successful either as a tool for accurately measuring employee performance or as a component of a broader program of performance management. Nearly a century of research on performance appraisal (see, for example, Austin & Villanova, 1992) suggests that there is a longstanding history of problems with performance evaluation in organization and little reason to believe that these problems will be solved simply.

Doubts about performance appraisal are not confined to academics. Performance appraisals have a very high failure rate; up to 90% of appraisal systems in organizations are likely to be viewed as ineffective (Pulakos, Mueller-Hanson, Arad, & Moye 2015; Smith, Hornsby, & Shirmeyer, 1996). Performance management systems do not seem to fare much better; the conclusion that performance management is broken is shared among many researchers (Pulakos & O'Leary, 2011; Pulakos et al., 2015). Stories about the demise of performance appraisal are increasingly common in the business press (Buckingham & Goodall, 2015; Capelli & Tavis, 2016).

On the other hand, nearly every organization uses performance appraisals and performance ratings[2] and there is little sign this is changing, at least in the short term (see Lawler, Benson, & McDermott, 2012; Mercer, 2013). A recent survey of more than 1000 organizations in more than 50 countries reported that: (1) the vast majority of organizations set individual goals (95%) and conduct formal year-end review discussions (94%), (2) most have overall performance ratings (89%), (3) most evaluate competencies/behaviors (86%), (4) most include an employee self-assessment (82%), and (5) most link individual ratings and compensation decisions (89%). More than half (57%) of the organizations globally use a 5-point rating scale (Mercer, 2013), and performance rating (as opposed to some other method of measurement, such as full or partial ranking) is so dominant in the field that we will use the terms "rater" and "ratee" throughout this book to designate the person or persons who have the responsibility for evaluating the performance of some group of employees and the targets of those evaluations, respectively.

Performance ratings are the basis for pay-for-performance systems in many organizations, and it is fair to say that billions of dollars in compensation and rewards are riding on the backs of performance ratings. Performance ratings can have long and lasting effects on employees' lives and careers in organizations, affecting staffing, promotion, and termination decisions as well as affecting access to other development opportunities. There is little evidence that organizations that attempt to get rid of performance appraisal are likely successful in replacing it with anything better, and as we will show in many of the chapters that follow, they may be running severe and unexpected risks.

While there is widespread disappointment and skepticism about performance appraisal, we do not believe that successful performance appraisal is a lost cause. This book lays out, often in considerable detail, the litany of reasons for the failure of performance appraisal, as it is currently designed and implemented, and the many frustrations encountered in attempting to improve appraisals in organizations. Nevertheless, we are optimistic that is it possible to

- make good judgments about who is performing well or poorly and what aspects of performance represent strengths and weaknesses for particular workers,

- use information about current performance to inform important decisions in organizations, and

- develop and administer performance appraisal systems that accomplish worthwhile goals in organizations.

In the chapters that follow, we show how research on performance appraisal can shed light on the success and failure of appraisals in organizations and can open new avenues for reforming the practice of performance appraisal. Chapters 2 through 12 focus on the challenges inherent in performance appraisal; the final two chapters in this book focus on how we can learn what we have learned over nearly a century of research on performance appraisal (DeNisi & Murphy, 2017) to improve performance appraisal in organizations.

To help provide some context for understanding how performance appraisal systems are designed and why, and to understand why these systems seem to fail so often, we start by defining performance appraisal and providing a brief review of the historical context of research and practice in performance appraisal. We pull together major trends in this historical survey with two models that summarize contemporary research and practice, first a simple four-part framework developed by Murphy and Cleveland (1995) and then a more elaborated model of the appraisal process developed by Murphy and DeNisi (2008) that illustrates many of the key themes this book will pursue.

Defining Performance Appraisal

Performance appraisal has a few defining characteristics that help explain the challenges this method faces. In particular, performance appraisal has several characteristics that distinguish it from the sort of simple and immediate performance feedback that is sometimes advocated as part of a performance management system (Aguinis, 2013). In particular, performance appraisal

- is formal and regular—in most organizations, performance appraisal is an annual event that is likely to be tied to the process of salary administration. It is often a required part of the supervisor's job to evaluate his or her subordinates, and this is likely to be done on a regular basis using formally developed tools (e.g., rating scales, information systems);

- is summative—it provides information about performance that has happened over some period of time, most often, providing evaluations of performance over the last year;

- is evaluative—performance appraisal goes beyond simple description, to provide evaluations of the level of performance;

- provides potentially detailed feedback—at a minimum, most performance appraisal systems will provide numerical measures of several aspects of dimensions of performance as well as assessments of overall performance levels, and they often include considerably more detail (e.g., narrative comments, goals for development); and

- has potential consequences for other human resource decisions—performance appraisals are often used as one basis for making decisions about salary, promotions, layoffs, and the like.

Performance appraisal has three main components. First, there is an assessment or evaluation of performance. It is important to note that we are not using the term "measurement" here. That is, performance appraisal systems do *not* provide objective measures of performance; as we will note in Chapter 3, there is a long history of trying to develop objective measures of job performance, and it is a history of failure. Rather than being an objective measure of performance, the type of performance appraisals that are conducted in organizations provide an *evaluation* of performance—that is, someone's judgment about whether your performance is good or bad. In many of the chapters that follow, we will discuss efforts to develop tools and techniques to help ensure that these judgments are fair, consistent, and related to the behaviors the person being evaluated has demonstrated on the job and the effectiveness of these behaviors, but one of the defining features of performance appraisal is that it relies on informed judgments about performance, not on objective measures.

Second, performance appraisal normally involves feedback. This feedback might be something as simple as a set of numeric ratings that represent your supervisor's evaluation, but it often goes a good deal further, providing information about both what the worker has done well and what he or she needs to do better (and perhaps how to do things better). When it is done well, feedback provides employees with clear direction and help in improving performance, as well as a better understanding of the standards that are used in evaluating job performance. When done poorly, feedback can be a demotivating source of stress.

Third, organizations use the results of performance appraisals to help in making high-stakes decisions about employees. The results of performance appraisals are routinely used in making compensation decisions (Mercer, 2013). There is not always an automatic link between a good performance evaluation and a raise, but a poor performance evaluation is very likely to have negative financial consequences for an employee. As we will discuss in several later chapters, the links between performance ratings and organizational rewards (e.g., raises, promotions, developmental opportunities) and sanctions such (e.g., layoffs, performance improvement programs) are a powerful factor in explaining why so many employees receive performance ratings that seem to be inflated.

In sum, performance appraisal is a substantial and important undertaking in organizations. The process of compiling information, making evaluations, providing performance feedback, and using performance evaluations to make decisions about promotions, compensation, and the like consumes a tremendous amount of time and energy in organizations (Buckingham & Goodall, 2015; Pulakos, Mueller-Hanson, Arad, & Moye, 2015). From the employee's perspective, the annual appraisal is likely to be an important and potentially stressful event. Ratings and evaluative comments an employee receives can have important consequences, and even when they do not lead directly to raises, promotions, layoffs, and the like, receiving judgments from your superiors about whether your performance is good or bad can be a stressful and unhappy experience. As we will show in several of the chapters that follow, there are predictable differences in the way *you* evaluate your own job performance and the way *others* evaluate that same performance, and these differences create serious problems for performance appraisal systems.

Researchers and practitioners have been trying for decades to come up with viable alternatives to traditional performance appraisals, with little success. The frequent failure of performance appraisal systems in organizations seems to be leading some organizations to replace performance appraisal with some sort of simple and informal system, but we think this is a serious mistake. Performance appraisal fulfills many important functions in organizations, and the emphasis should be on improving performance appraisal systems rather than on jettisoning them.

The Value of Cross-Cultural Perspectives

The authors of this book are all psychologists who have been trained and have worked in the United States. The great majority of the research cited in this book, and indeed the great majority of research on performance appraisal, is American as well. Nevertheless, we firmly believe that there is a good deal to be learned by paying careful attention to cross-national and cross-cultural studies of performance appraisal. First, performance appraisal is not designed or used in the same way everywhere in the world. Many of the assumptions that are built into performance appraisal systems in American organizations (e.g., that it is a good idea to link financial rewards with individual performance) are far from universal, and thinking about performance appraisal from different perspectives can open our eyes to new ways of thinking about performance appraisal. Chapter 7, which covers the effects of the social, national, and organizational contexts in which performance appraisals are conducted on the design, implementation, and use of appraisal systems, deals most explicitly with cross-cultural and cross-national comparisons of the assumptions behind and the design of performance appraisal systems.

Second, although most of the research we discuss in this book deals with American approaches to performance appraisal, there is real value in considering how other nations and cultures try to solve the problems of evaluating performance, providing useful feedback, and using information about job performance to inform effective human resource management practices. Throughout this book, we have tried to draw useful lessons from our longstanding collaborations with colleagues in different nations and from research from other countries and other cultural perspectives. One of the benefits of such cross-cultural and cross-national collaborations is that they often challenge deep-seated assumptions about how organizations should be structured and run, opening new possibilities for the design of performance appraisal systems. We discuss some of these possibilities in Chapters 13 and 14.

Historical Context

Although the interest in and use of performance appraisal has increased over the last 100 years (DeNisi & Murphy, 2017), the practice of formally evaluating employees has existed for centuries. As early as the third century AD, Sin Yu, an early Chinese philosopher, criticized a biased rater employed by the Wei dynasty on the grounds that "the Imperial Rater of Nine Grades seldom rates men according to their merits but always according to his likes and dislikes" (Patten, 1977, p. 352). In 1648, the *Dublin* (Ireland) *Evening Post* rated legislators using a rating scale based upon personal qualities (Hackett, 1928).

According to Heilbroner (1953), the first industrial application of merit rating probably was made by Robert Owen at his cotton mills in New Lanark, Scotland, in the early 1800s. Wood cubes of different colors indicating different degrees of merit were hung over each employee's work station. As employee performance changed so did the appropriate wood cube. The merit rating or efficiency rating in the Federal Civil Service has been in place since at least 1887 (Petrie, 1950) and perhaps as early as 1842 (Lopez, 1968).

One impetus to the development of performance appraisal in American industry (Patten, 1977) can be traced to the work of industrial psychologists at Carnegie-Mellon University and their early work in salesman selection and man-to-man rating forms based on trait psychology (Scott, Clothier, & Spriegel, 1941). The man-to-man rating form was later used by the Army in World War I to assess the performance of officers (Scott et al., 1941), although formal performance appraisal probably began in the U.S. military in 1813 (Bellows & Estep, 1954) when Army General Lewis Cass submitted to the War Department an evaluation of each of his men using such terms as "a good-natured man" or "knave despised by all."

Although the man-to-man ranking by department is not frequently used in industry or in appraising performance, it can be an effective method for determining the order of layoffs. In fact, in the late 1960s, it was used by many companies that experienced cutbacks in government contracts to make layoff and retention decisions (Patten, 1977). This technique was known as the "totem approach" to manpower cutbacks. After World War I, many of the individuals associated with the work of the man-to-man appraisal secured positions in industry, in part, because business leaders were impressed by the contribution of industrial psychologists to army research. Despite early criticisms (Rudd, 1921), the graphic rating scale increased in popularity and remains predominant today. Figure 1.1 illustrates a number of rating scales that are described in this chapter; Appendix A provides additional examples of rating scales.

FIGURE 1.1 ■ Examples of Rating Scales

Graphic Rating Scale

Planning and Organization

1	2	3	4	5
Poor		Average		Good

Behaviorally Anchored Rating Scale

Planning and Organization

1 – Frequently misses deadlines and fails to complete projects because of poor planning

2

3 – Usually keeps track of priorities and takes appropriate steps to complete projects

4

5 – Always well organized, shows clear evidence of planning ahead for the activities needed to complete projects and be prepared for unforeseen contingencies

Rating Scale Based on Performance Objectives

Planning and Organization

1. Will create detailed and appropriate plans for each step in this year's project

   Failed to meet objective _____ Met objective _____ Exceeded objective _____

2. Will submit orders for necessary materials with sufficient lead time to guarantee on-time delivery

   Failed to meet objective _____ Met objective _____ Exceeded objective _____

3. Will coordinate with other departments to make sure that necessary resources and personnel are available

   Failed to meet objective _____ Met objective _____ Exceeded objective _____

Just prior to and during World War II, the Army again sought assistance from psychologists to improve its rating system. The outcomes of these research efforts included the forced-choice technique and the critical incident approach to merit rating (Flanagan, 1949; Sisson, 1948). Appraisal of industry employees became popular only after World War I, and appraisal of managers was not widely practiced until after World War II.

By the early 1950s, appraisal was an accepted practice in many organizations. In 1962, performance appraisal was conducted in 61% of the organizations surveyed (Spriegel, 1962) and typically, top management was exempt from appraisals (Whisler & Harper, 1962). After the passage of the 1964 Civil Rights Act and the 1966 and 1970 Equal Employment Opportunity Commission (EEOC) Guidelines for regulation of selection procedures, legal considerations exerted strong pressure on organizations to formalize their appraisal systems (DeVries, Morrison, Shullman, & Gerlach, 1986). Federal legislation and the civil rights and women's movement of the 1960s and 1970s created the need for rapid improvements in organizational appraisal practices.

DeVries et al. (1986) pointed out two particular trends in the practice of performance appraisal during the second half of the 20th century. First, performance appraisal methods evolved from assessments of broad traits and essay approaches to behavioral and results-oriented methods, such as Behaviorally Anchored Rating Scales (BARS) and Management-by-Objectives (MBO).[3] A second trend is that the number of uses of performance appraisal in organizations increased (Cleveland, Murphy, & Williams, 1989; DeVries et al., 1986). The earliest use of performance appraisals was as a basis for human resource decisions such as promotions, salary increases, and the like. However, throughout the 1960s and 1970s performance appraisals were increasingly used for employee development and feedback, corporate planning, legal documentation (DeVries et al., 1986), systems maintenance, and research (Cleveland et al., 1989).

Another important development in the 1960s and 1970s was the changing legal context. Starting with the Civil Rights Act of 1964, the possibility that decisions made on the basis of performance appraisals (e.g., raises, promotions) might be challenged on the basis that they discriminated against members of different racial groups, women, older workers, and the like needed to be taken seriously. In particular, the decision of the U.S. Supreme Court in the *Griggs v. Duke Power* (401 U.S. 424) case established the principle that it is the responsibility of the organization that uses tests, assessments, or other instruments (including performance appraisals) that appear to discriminate to demonstrate the validity and business necessity of that assessment. The result has been increasing scrutiny of performance appraisals, and increasing efforts on the part of organizations to make sure that their appraisals are sufficiently reliable and job-related to survive this scrutiny.

In the last 10–20 years, there has been increasing interest in performance management, an approach that includes the systematic evaluation of performance. The relationship between performance appraisal as described in this chapter and performance management is sometimes complex, and in Chapter 2 we explore the relationship between performance appraisal and performance management.

Major Trends in Performance Appraisal Research

DeNisi and Murphy (2017) reviewed 100 years of research on performance appraisal and performance management.[4] Their review and several others (e.g., Murphy & Cleveland, 1991, 1995) suggest that research in performance appraisal can be divided into three phases, in which different issues predominated.

A substantial portion of the research published between 1917 and 1980 was devoted to *measurement*. Many of the studies published during this period were designed to improve the quality of measurement performance appraisals provided, introducing refinements in rating scale formats, new methods of rater training, and development of increasingly sophisticated criteria for evaluating ratings (DeNisi & Murphy, 2017; Landy & Farr, 1980).

SPOTLIGHT 1.1 PERFORMANCE APPRAISAL IS A MULTISTEP PROCESS

Many of the studies cited in this book focus on one part of the performance appraisal process—that is, performance rating. It is important to recognize that the process of completing a performance rating form is only one part of a multistep process. We think performance appraisal is best described as a four-step process. These steps will not always occur in the same sequence, and they might not be repeated every year (performance appraisal is an annual event in most organizations), but they are a useful starting point for understanding the complexity of performance appraisal and the issues organizations need to consider when developing and administering performance appraisal systems. These four steps are:

1. **Conveying standards and articulating expectations**—Performance appraisal works best when there is clarity and agreement about what an employee is expected to do and what represents good, average, and poor performance. In some organizations, supervisors and subordinates will meet to define concrete performance goals, and this step will be an explicit part of each year's performance evaluation. In other organizations, standards and expectations might be a focus on initial training and socialization, and may not be revisited on a regular basis. Some performance management programs will involve frequent discussions of what each employee is expected to do and accomplish, along with frequent feedback about how well these expectations are being met.

2. **Collecting information about performance**—The supervisors or managers who are responsible for evaluating an employee's performance are likely to use a number of methods to collect relevant information, ranging from personally observing the employee doing his or her job to receiving feedback from peers and customers or obtaining information about the employee's success in meeting specific performance goals.

3. **Evaluating performance**—Performance appraisal usually involves making judgments about performance, that is, determining whether performance meets or exceeds expectations. In some appraisal systems, where there are detailed and objective performance goals, the role of judgment may be minimal. If a performance goal states that an employee will make 100 sales each month, a simple count might determine whether or not this goal has been met. It is more common, however, for supervisors or managers to consider a range of information and to make some judgments about whether or not expectations have been met.

4. **Providing feedback and opportunities for comment and review**—Most performance appraisal systems will include a face-to-face meeting between the supervisor and each individual being evaluated that will convey both the supervisor's evaluation of performance (e.g., performance ratings) and feedback about the factors that led to that evaluation and steps the employee can take to maintain or improve performance levels. Employees will often be given an opportunity to comment on their evaluation, and perhaps to provide information that might lead to modifications in the ratings or feedback. This meeting might involve detailed planning for the next year, setting new performance goals, or counseling about ways to improve performance.

When it is done well, performance appraisal can help employees develop a concrete understanding of what is expected of them, a clear sense of how their performance is evaluated and why, and a good sense of how performance can be improved in the future.

Starting in the 1980s the emphasis in performance appraisal shifted to studies of *cognitive processes* (e.g., DeNisi, 2006; DeNisi, Cafferty, & Meglino, 1984; Feldman, 1981). Here, the emphasis was on understanding how raters handled the potentially challenging task of forming judgments about their subordinates' performance levels. Drawing on the growing body of cognitively oriented research in several fields, performance appraisal researchers paid considerable attention to understanding the ways raters observed, made sense of, recalled, and integrated behavioral information when making judgments about their subordinates.

By the 1980s, doubts were growing about the potential contribution of further research on improving performance measurement, especially through the improvement of rating scales, had emerged (Landy & Farr, 1980). By the 1990s similar doubts emerged about the potential contribution of cognitively oriented research to improve performance appraisal in organizations (Banks & Murphy, 1985; Ilgen, Barnes-Farrell, & McKellin, 1993). Rather than focus on attempts to improve measurement or attempts to understand how raters made judgments, researchers started to turn their attention to the *context* in which performance appraisals are carried out (Levy & Williams, 2004; Murphy & Cleveland, 1991, 1995). Research in this tradition has examined the social and organizational factors that influence the way performance appraisals are conducted and used in organizations. For example, whereas the tendency of raters to give high scores to virtually everyone they rate (creating the *Lake Woebegone effect*, where everyone is above average) was conceptualized as a correctable rater error during the *measurement* and *cognitive processes* phases of performance appraisal research, work in the *context-oriented* phase has focused on the cultural and organizational forces that motivate raters to inflate their ratings. Research that takes this perspective suggests that giving high ratings is not necessarily an error, but rather may be a smart response to the various pressures in the rating environment.

The first 75 years of performance appraisal research (1917–1980s) were dedicated largely to understanding *how* we evaluate performance and how we might improve this process. The context-oriented phase of performance appraisal research has focused more strongly on *why* organizations conduct performance appraisals—that is, on the use of evaluations of job performance to provide performance feedback and to drive important decisions in human resource management. It has also focused on the interplay between the social and organizational environments in which appraisals are conducted and the outcomes of performance appraisal. There are some indications that research in performance appraisal is entering a new phase, in which the relationship between performance evaluation in organizations and the broader strategy of performance management will take the forefront. In Chapter 2, we examine this possibility in some detail.

Models of the Performance Appraisal Process

Murphy and Cleveland (1995) proposed a fairly simple and general model designed to highlight the most important issues for understanding performance appraisal. This model, which provides an overarching framework for much of our work over the last 20 years, and which strongly influenced the structure and contents of the current book, is shown in Figure 1.2.

Murphy and Cleveland (1995) noted first that it was useful to separate judgment from rating, and the fact that ratings do not always seem to realistically reflect the performance

FIGURE 1.2   ■   Murphy and Cleveland (1995) Model

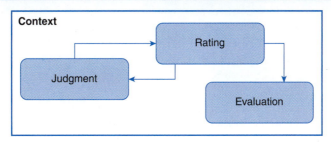

of the people being evaluated does not necessarily mean that raters *cannot* sensibly evaluate their subordinates. Rather, they often have strong motivations to record ratings that do not fully reflect their evaluations of how well their subordinates have performed (Banks & Murphy, 1985). The judgments raters form about their subordinates do have some bearing on the ratings they give, but judgments and ratings are not necessarily identical, and this has clear implications for performance appraisal research and practice that are explored in several of the chapters that follow. Second, evaluations of appraisal systems are largely driven by the ratings and by the consequences of those ratings (e.g., the attitudes and motivation of the people who are rated). Thus, even if raters form sound judgments about who is a good versus a poor performer, if they rate all of their subordinates as excellent (this is not an unusual occurrence), the appraisal system may fail. Third, virtually all of these processes occur within national, social, organizational, and temporal contexts (although some aspects of judgment are essentially universal, such as a bias in favor of people who are agreeable, and may not be influenced by contexts), and the context substantially influences all of these processes.

Since 1995, there has been a substantial body of research dealing with all four of the components of the Murphy and Cleveland (1995) model, and it is clear that this model can and should be elaborated. Murphy and DeNisi (2008) proposed an expanded model of the appraisal process that summarized several decades of research on performance appraisal. This model, shown in Figure 1.3, helps to flesh out the general concepts presented by Murphy and Cleveland in 1995, and it incorporates advances in several lines of research since 1995. According to Murphy and DeNisi (2008), if you wish to understand performance ratings and the success or failure of performance appraisal systems, you need to consider five general factors that influence performance appraisal in organizations: Distal Factors, Proximal Factors, Intervening Factors, Judgment Factors, and Distortion Factors.

The Murphy and DeNisi (2008) model starts with a set of Distal Factors, which operate at a much higher level of analysis than the processes performance appraisal researchers usually study, but are surely important to help us understand the appraisal and performance management process. These include broad cultural factors, legal constraints, and economic environments that all influence the way performance appraisal is implemented and interpreted in organizations. The role of corporate strategy is also important, and the notion of aligning appraisal processes with strategy is an important part of most performance

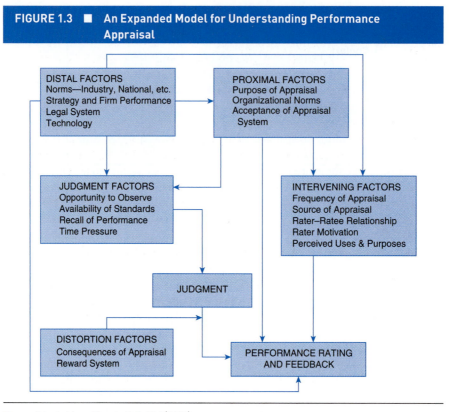

FIGURE 1.3 ■ An Expanded Model for Understanding Performance Appraisal

Source: Adapted from Murphy & DeNisi (2008).

management models (e.g., Aguinis, 2009; Jackson, Schuler, & Jiang, 2014; Pulakos, Mueller-Hanson, O'Leary, & Meyrowitz, 2012). For example, if a firm is competing on the basis of price, appraisals should emphasize efforts by employees to reduce costs. If the organization is attempting to differentiate itself from competitors by offering high quality or excellent customer service, behaviors that support these objectives should be an important part of the performance appraisal process. We would expect the appraisal system in such a firm to look much different than the system in a firm that competes on quality or service.

Technology can impact what is possible and impossible to accomplish in appraisals. For example, computer-based monitoring allows supervisors to have clear information about the specific behaviors exhibited by their subordinates at work, such as response times, time spent with customers, or time spent on unproductive activities (Alder & Ambrose, 2005). Finally, the legal system is extremely important for performance appraisal and performance management. Laws and regulatory policies often constrain what kinds of appraisal systems are possible. In general, the type of distal factors discussed by Murphy and DeNisi (2008) are not easy to change. Nonetheless, we must be aware of how they operate and how they influence performance appraisal and performance management.

Proximal Factors are more under the control of the organization, although not always under the control of the individuals designing appraisals systems. For example, performance appraisal information is used for a variety of purposes in many organizations, and this can affect the ratings that are given. Policies regarding the implementation and use of performance appraisal are often quite difficult to change, if for no other reason than organizational inertia. Organizational norms and acceptance of the appraisal system may be even harder to change—although it is possible. If they hope to create successful performance appraisal systems, firms need to establish something similar to what Bowen and Ostroff (2004) refer to as a performance culture, where employees come to trust appraisals and see them as a tool to help them improve their performance.

In this model, both Proximal and Distal Factors influence a number of Intervening Factors, such as the frequency of appraisal. There Intervening Factors, in turn, can have a direct impact on performance rating and feedback, whereas in this model, Distal Factors have only an indirect effect on these processes. For example, this model suggests that the overall state of the economy (a Distal Factor) would not have a direct effect on performance ratings, but it might have an indirect one by limiting the availability of raises when the economy is tight, or by making more resources available when the economy is growing.

Distal, Proximal, and Intervening Factors are all seen as affecting performance ratings and feedback. But this model also includes a set of Judgment Factors that operate differently. This model assumes (like the Murphy and Cleveland model discussed earlier) that raters form judgments about who is performing well and who is performing poorly, and these judgments might not be influenced by the same set of contextual factors as the ratings they eventually record.

As Murphy and Cleveland (1995) note, judgments are not identical to performance ratings. Rather, there are a wide range of personal, situational, and contextual factors that lead raters to distort the ratings they provide. The processes that lead raters to distort ratings, giving ratings that do not correspond with their own judgment of how well or poorly particular individuals have performed, are central to the failure of performance appraisal systems in organizations.

ORGANIZATION OF THIS BOOK

The two models discussed in the preceding section provide an overarching framework for many of the chapters in this book and provide a starting point for the main arguments this book will make. It is useful here to lay out these main arguments and to make clear what we hope to accomplish by reviewing and synthesizing research on performance appraisal. We first examine why performance appraisal systems fail, then lay out suggestions for improving them.

Understanding Why Performance Appraisal Systems Fail

This book was written to examine two key issues: the frequent failure of performance appraisal systems in organizations and the steps organizations could take to increase the likelihood that their performance appraisal systems will succeed. As we describe in some detail in Chapter 4 and in several of the chapters that follow, there are four key reasons why performance appraisal systems in organizations fail: (1) the genuine difficulty of measuring performance, (2) the contexts in which performance appraisals occur warp the appraisal process and outcomes, (3) organizations attempt to use performance appraisals for multiple conflicting purposes, and (4) raters are motivated to distort performance appraisals.

Measuring and Evaluating Performance Is Difficult

Chapter 3 provides the first glimpse at the inherent difficulty of measuring or evaluating job performance by illustrating the complexity of the construct of "performance" and the many dimensions and facets of job performance. Chapter 5 describes the complex processes involved in obtaining information about and making judgments about performance. Chapter 6 describes the tools (e.g., rating scales, rater training) that have been developed to assist in evaluating performance and in providing performance feedback, as well as reviewing some of the reasons these tools have not been completely successful. Chapters 10 and 11 illustrate why it is so difficult to even evaluate the quality of performance appraisals. Criteria for defining a successful performance appraisal system are often elusive, and the criteria that have been most frequently used for this purpose often ignore critical factors such as the attitudes, beliefs, and reactions of the users of performance appraisal systems.

Context Matters

Chapter 7 examines what we believe to be the single-most important barrier to the success of performance appraisal systems—that is, the contexts in which performance appraisals are conducted. This chapter shows how both Distal Factors (e.g., cross-cultural differences, the legal system, the state of the economy, the technologies used in the workplace) and Proximal Factors (e.g., the climate and culture of an organization) influence the way performance appraisals are designed, conducted, used, and interpreted. Different contextual factors often operate at cross-purposes, and any or all of them can lead to processes and outcomes that are quite different from what the designers of performance appraisal systems intended. Because the context varies across organizations and across time, it is often the case that what works well in one organization or at one point in time will not work in another organization or at another point in time.

The Conflicting Purposes of Performance Appraisal Systems

As Chapter 8 illustrates, organizations often treat performance appraisal as an all-purpose tool, using it as a basis for making high-stakes decisions (e.g., compensation), as a mechanism for providing performance feedback, as a tool for supporting and maintaining other human resource systems, and as a tool for documenting and justifying actions taken on the basis of performance information. There are fundamental conflicts between many of the most important uses of performance appraisal, and organizations that attempt to use the same system for many purposes may find that it does not serve *any* of them well.

The Motivation to Distort

It has long been known that performance ratings are inflated; it is not unusual for 80% of all employees to be rated as "above average." For many years, this was thought to be evidence that supervisors, managers, and other raters were not *able* to accurately evaluate their subordinates. It now seems clear that the problem is that supervisors, managers, and other raters were not *willing* to accurately evaluate the performance of their subordinates.

Chapters 9, 10, and 12 explore why raters are so often motivated to be lenient in their evaluations. These chapters argue that leniency in evaluating performance (i.e., giving high ratings when lower ratings are probably deserved) is not necessarily an error on the part of supervisors and managers, but rather can be a thoughtful strategy to increase the motivation, satisfaction, and performance of the employees they rate.

Can Performance Appraisal Succeed in Organizations?

Despite the many problems noted in Chapters 2–12, we believe performance appraisal *can* succeed in organizations. Indeed, it *must* succeed; none of the alternatives that have been discussed in the recent literature (e.g., Aguinis, 2013; Buckingham & Goodall, 2015) are likely to successfully accomplish all of the things we ask performance appraisal systems to do. In Chapters 13 and 14, we examine how a serious application of the scientist–practitioner model that has allegedly guided work in this area for so many years can open new avenues for improving performance appraisal. This is a model in which research guides practice and in which practice guides research. In other words, this strategy involves taking seriously the insights from scientific research when designing and implementing performance appraisal systems and taking serious the experience of using these systems in organizations to identify important topics for research. Chapters 13 and 14 illustrate what such an approach has to offer in improving performance appraisal systems.

Chapter 14 includes our recommendations for improving performance appraisal systems. First, we examine the rationale for the various uses of performance appraisal in organizations and suggest that a more realistic set of expectations about what performance appraisal systems can and should accomplish is absolutely essential to successful performance appraisal. We explore ways to reduce the motivation to distort and inflate appraisals, and propose a set of principles for the practical, ethical, and successful practice of performance appraisal in organizations.

SUMMARY

Performance appraisal is a formal, summative process of evaluating job performance that has important consequences for individuals and organizations. This chapter examines major trends in research and practice in the area of performance appraisal, and it identifies both the major causes of the failure of performance appraisal systems and potential avenues for making performance appraisal more successful.

The models of the performance appraisal process presented here give some insight into the range of challenges a performance appraisal system faces. First, the task of evaluating performance is a difficult one. The person or persons who are charged with this task must somehow pull together a large amount of information, make sure that the information they have at hand is representative of the employee's behavior, make sense of each piece of information, recall information correctly, and put it together in a systematic way that reflects the many aspects of job performance. Second, there are a number of contextual factors, ranging from broad distal influences (e.g., cultural norms, the legal system) to proximal forces in the organization (e.g., relationships between supervisors and subordinates) that influence job performance and the design, implementation, and use of performance appraisal systems. Third, organizations routinely attempt to use performance appraisal systems for goals and purposes (e.g., development versus salary administration) that are at least partially in conflict. Finally, there are a number of social, political, and contextual influences that push raters to distort performance ratings. Despite the challenges, we believe performance appraisal can and must succeed, and we draw upon almost a century of research to help understand the barriers to success and the ways organizations can overcome these barriers.

EXERCISE: CAN ORGANIZATIONS MANAGE HUMAN RESOURCES WITHOUT PERFORMANCE APPRAISAL?

Dissatisfaction with performance appraisal is widespread, and some organizations are getting rid of their performance appraisal systems. It is useful to think about why most organizations are *not* getting rid of performance appraisal. After all, if appraisal really is an expensive and time-consuming process that does not yield any real benefits, why do organizations continue to use this method?

One way to answer the question above is to think about the range of uses for performance appraisal and to consider how some of the important applications of performance appraisal might be accomplished if your organization decides to abandon performance appraisal. Table1.1 lists some of the major applications of performance appraisal in organizations, along with some of the plausible alternative approaches an organization might try if they decide to abandon performance appraisal.

Table 1.1 is not exhaustive, but it does illustrate that there are often plausible alternatives to relying on performance appraisals to drive important HR functions in organizations. Some of these may not be all that attractive (e.g., decoupling raises and promotions from current performance levels), and others may be feasible only in some jobs (e.g., rely on objective performance measures), but we think that working through how your organization will execute a range of HR functions that depend on information from performance appraisals is an important first step in thinking through whether or not to ditch your performance appraisal system.

TABLE 1.1 ■ Possible Alternatives for Organizations That Abandon Performance Appraisal	
HR Function	**Some Alternatives If Performance Appraisal Is Abandoned**
Annual salary increases	Decouple salary increases from performance
	Use objective performance measures
	Link salary increases to group productivity
Determining individual training needs	Survey managers, supervisors, peers
	Tests and other performance assessments
	Self-ratings of training needs
Promotions	Decouple promotions from current performance
	Use objective performance measures
	Survey managers, supervisors to assess competencies relevant to the future job
Determining organizational training needs	Survey managers, supervisors
	Survey employees
Validating selection systems	Use objective performance measures
	Validate selection measures against group productivity measures

NOTES

1. Stetz and Chmielewski (2016) note that federal law requires the use of performance appraisal in federal workforce of over 4 million employees.

2. There are a variety of performance evaluation methods, and only some of these use what would technically be referred to as "ratings," but we use the term "rater" throughout to designate the person who provides the performance evaluation, and "ratee" to refer to the person being evaluated regardless of the actual scale or form used.

3. However, the older trait-rating scale formats are still prevalent.

4. Their review focused on research published in *Journal of Applied Psychology* (this paper is part of a special issue celebrating the centennial of this important journal), but covered numerous papers published in other journals, as well as important chapters and books.

2

PERFORMANCE MANAGEMENT AND PERFORMANCE APPRAISAL

Why does performance appraisal exist? It is rarely seen as successful or even worthwhile in organizations, and it is useful to ask why so many organizations put themselves through the trouble. In the last 10–15 years, many scholars and practitioners have attempted to answer the question of why you should measure the performance of individual employees by situating performance measurement and performance appraisal in the context of a broader set of ideas labeled "performance management." That is, performance evaluation is important because it is a key tool for improving the performance of individuals, teams, departments, divisions, and organizations and for ensuring that all levels of the organization are working toward the same ends. We will define and describe the ideas that define performance management below, but for now, proponents think of performance management as a method for linking the goals and strategies of organizations with the performance of each member of the organization, while attempting to harmonize the activities of individuals, teams, departments, and divisions to further the key strategic goals of the organization. From this perspective, the careful measurement of individual performance is one part of a larger effort to coordinate the work of virtually every member of the organization toward serving particular strategic goals. That is, proponents of performance management describe it as a method for making sure that the goals, objectives, and plans of individuals, teams, departments, divisions and organizations are all consistent and making sure that these objectives are accomplished.

In this chapter, we first ask why we should study performance appraisal rather than performance management. We will argue that despite the similarities, there are some very important differences between performance appraisal systems and performance management, and that the study of performance appraisal systems continues to be a very important one for organizations and for developing a better understanding of behavior in organizations. To illustrate the similarities and differences between performance appraisal systems and performance management, we describe in some detail the underlying philosophy of performance management, the design and implementation of performance management systems, and the difficulties in evaluating the success or failure of performance management systems. In this section, we will argue that an important difference between performance management and performance appraisal systems is that performance management embodies a top-down approach to human resource management, whereas performance appraisal systems follow a mixed model that includes evaluations from supervisors or managers but that also involves employee input in the form of goal setting, self-evaluation, and systems designed to give employees some voice in both the design and the evaluation of their work. In the sections that follow, we consider the role of performance appraisal in performance management systems, and consider both performance management and performance appraisal in the context of designing effective human resource systems.

WHY STUDY PERFORMANCE APPRAISAL RATHER THAN PERFORMANCE MANAGEMENT?

This book is devoted to developing a better understanding of performance appraisal, in particular of why performance appraisal systems often seem to fail in organizations. In the last 10–20 years, there has been an increasing tendency, particularly in business publications and in schools of business, to argue that performance appraisal is or should be thought of as one component of a broader array of human resource management (HRM) policies that are collectively referred to as "performance management." Some scholars (e.g., Aguinis, 2013) have argued that traditional performance appraisal can *only* be sensibly understood as a component of a broader performance management system, not as a stand-alone topic. This raises the question of why it is worth writing a book about performance appraisal, rather than taking on the broader topic of performance management.

Performance management is clearly an important topic; in a later section of this chapter we discuss some of the unique contributions this approach offers. It is clear that in *some* organizations, performance appraisal or some substitute for traditional performance appraisal (e.g., informal performance feedback that is delivered as needed rather than on an annual basis) is part of a broader strategy of performance management, but we believe there are compelling reasons for studying performance appraisal as a topic on its own. First, despite the attention that companies like Accenture, Deloitte, or Medtronic have received for their efforts to get rid of or replace traditional performance appraisal, formal and regular (usually annual) performance appraisals are still quite common in organizations.[1] Performance management can represent a loose grab bag of activities that varies from organization to organization, but formal performance appraisals are still the norm in many organizations, and the core features of these appraisals are often quite consistent across organizations. Second, even if it is a part of a broader set of activities, performance appraisal is often at the heart of the success or failure of performance management systems, and the issues considered in this book are often pertinent even if a particular organization does not follow the traditional model of annual performance appraisals. Third, there is a very large, long-standing body of research dealing with a range of issues in performance appraisal, whereas serious research on performance management is still in its infancy (DeNisi & Murphy, 2017).

Finally, performance management and performance appraisal involve different assumptions about how organizations should be managed and how the behavior of individual

SPOTLIGHT 2.1 PERFORMANCE APPRAISAL
THE STATE OF THE ART

Gorman, Meriac, Roch, Ray, and Gamble's (2017) survey of Fortune 500 organizations provides a good description of the way large organizations structure, conduct, and use performance appraisals. This survey suggests that performance appraisal is alive and well; the organizations surveyed devote significant resources to their appraisal systems and use performance appraisal as a critical element in a number of human resource decisions.

First, despite the widespread claim in the business press that performance rating is a thing of the past, it is clear that some form of performance rating is still the norm in most organizations. About a quarter of the organizations surveyed rely on multisource rating systems, but in most, the traditional form of appraisal, in which a supervisor or manager evaluates his or her direct reports, using rating scales that tap a variety of performance dimensions,

still dominated. Second, it is still common for organizations to use appraisals for multiple (sometimes conflicting) purposes. Almost two-thirds of the organizations surveyed use performance appraisals for both administrative and developmental purposes.

Gorman et al. (2017) noted that much of the research on performance appraisal, especially studies of actual appraisal practices in organizations, is somewhat dated, and given all of the recent discussions of changes in performance appraisal and performance management, this might be a serious concern. However, the results of their survey suggest that the problems and issues performance appraisal researchers and practitioners have been struggling with since the 1970s are still with us, and that many of the challenges to traditional performance appraisal systems are still quite relevant to current organizational practices.

employees should be evaluated and directed. As we will show in several of the sections that follow, performance management assumes a top-down strategy, in which a handful of top leaders make important decisions about goals, strategies, and about how to accomplish these, and in which the results of these decisions then drive the goals, strategies, and plans of divisions, departments, work groups, and ultimately individual employees. Performance appraisal, in contrast, is often built on a foundation that includes important and influential employee input into the goals that are set, the evaluation of employee behavior, and the outcomes of performance evaluations. We view this more consultative strategy as more likely to succeed in the long term and as more consistent with a number of other developments in the design of work and work organizations, ranging from an increased emphasis on employee engagement to an increased emphasis on less hierarchical, more employee-centric organizations.

PERFORMANCE MANAGEMENT

What is "performance management"? The U.S. Office of Personnel Management (1998) defines performance management to include: (1) planning work and setting expectations, (2) continually monitoring performance, (3) developing the capacity to perform, and (4) periodically rating performance in a summary fashion, and rewarding good performance.[2] Pulakos (2004) notes that (1) planning work and setting expectations involves both identifying the behaviors and the results of those behaviors that are expected or desired, (2) both behaviors and results should be aligned with the broader strategy and goals of the organization, and (3) the main focus of performance management is on improving the employee's effectiveness contribution to the organization. Taking a similar tack, Aguinis (2013) defines performance management as a "continuous process of identifying, measuring and developing the performance of individuals and teams, and aligning performance with the strategic goals of the organization" (p. 2). Performance management has been widely studied in recent years, with numerous reviews of the performance management literature and models of the performance management process appearing within the last decade (Aguinis, 2009, 2013; Den Hartog, Boselie, & Paauwe, 2004; DeNisi & Pritchard, 2006; DeNisi & Smith, 2014; Pritchard, Harrell, DiazGrandos, & Guzman, 2008; Pulakos, 2004, 2009; Pulakos, Mueller-Hanson, O'Leary, & Meyrowitz, 2012). Recent reviews have focused on the apparent shortcomings of performance management, and on potential avenues for improving this process (Pulakos, Hanson, Arad, & Moye, 2015; Pulakos & O'Leary, 2011).

Performance management is related to but distinct from performance appraisal. First, performance management is a broader concept, since it embodies both performance evaluation and the design of jobs, teams, departments, and divisions in such a way that they are all pursuing interlocking goals and strategies. Second, the type of performance evaluation that is used in a performance management program might differ from traditional performance appraisal in many ways (e.g., more frequent, less formal). It might involve different sources of information about performance (e.g., Ledford, Benson, & Lawler [2016] suggest that the newest programs of performance management use crowd sourcing to obtain information about performance). Finally, some performance management programs will include systematic activities (e.g., training, job redesign) to assist employees whose current performance is not meeting standards.

Although performance management programs might entail frequent evaluations of performance, it is still common practice in most organizations to conduct some sort of annual performance appraisal, often linked to salary adjustments (Milkovich & Wigdor, 1991). For example, Pulakos (2009) described a model performance management system that could be established following an eight-step process:

1. Leaders set organizational, division, and department goals.

2. Managers and employees set objectives and discuss behavioral expectations.

3. Managers and employees hold ongoing performance discussions.

4. Employees provide input regarding their own perceptions of their performance.

5. Knowledgeable rating sources provide input on employee performance.

6. Managers rate performance.

7. Managers and employees hold formal review sessions.

8. HR decisions are made, including pay, promotion, and termination.

This performance management system is similar in many ways to a traditional performance appraisal system; the thing that makes this a performance management system rather than a variation of a performance appraisal system is the process of linking the goals pursued by different organizational units described in steps 1–3. Other descriptions of performance management (e.g., Aguinis, 2013) suggest that evaluations have a different focus in performance management than in traditional performance appraisal. In particular, traditional performance appraisal systems have a retrospective focus, looking at what you did over the last year and applying appropriate rewards or sanctions. Performance management, in contrast, can have a prospective focus, using performance feedback as a tool for changing future behavior.[3] That is, rather than evaluating what you did last year, a manager might give feedback about what you are doing right now and use that feedback to try and improve future behavior.

Key Concepts in Performance Management

There are two broad features most performance management systems share, *harmonization* and *enforcement*. First, these systems are designed to explicitly link the goals and strategy of the organization with the goals and activities of every division, department, work team, and employee. Aguinis (2013) notes, "Performance management systems that do not make explicit employee contributions to organizational goals are not true performance management systems" (p. 3). Thus, one hallmark of a successful performance management system is that all levels of the organization are pursuing a set of interlocking goals and each unit (down to the single individual) is pursuing a set of goals that is designed, ultimately, to help the organization accomplish its key goals. Second, they include a variety of mechanisms to ensure that once these goals are set throughout an organization, each individual and each unit of the organization works diligently to achieve their particular goals. In particular, virtually all performance management systems are built around a cycle of evaluating performance, providing feedback, and supporting the improvement of performance. This process might operate on the familiar annual performance cycle, but it is more likely to be a frequent or even continuous process. We use the term "harmonization" to reflect the strong interdependence of the goals pursued at all levels of the organization. More specifically, performance management involves using the highest-level goals and strategy pursued by an organization as a basis for setting concrete performance goals for individuals, teams, departments, and divisions. We use the term "enforcement" because the actions an organization might take to make sure that its members are all pursuing the correct goals can range from what you might call soft power (e.g., providing feedback and encouragement) to more direct efforts to direct the behavior of employees, ranging from salary adjustment to re-assignment and even dismissal.

Performance management can be thought of as an extension or refinement of some of the key ideas of management by objectives (MBO), an approach to managing and evaluating performance that was popular in the 1980s and 1990s. MBO has three main components: goal setting, participation in decision making, and objective measurement (Rodgers & Hunter, 1991). The key idea in MBO was that supervisors and subordinates could work together to both define performance goals and agree on objective metrics by which to measure progress toward accomplishing key goals. Performance management takes what is arguably a less participative approach toward setting goals, one in which the goals of each person, team, and unit in an organization pursue goals that are cascaded down from the top of the organization rather than being set jointly by the employee and his or her supervisor. On the other hand, it takes a less restrictive approach toward evaluating progress, in the sense that evaluations and feedback are ongoing and are not limited to specific objective metrics agreed upon by the rater and the ratee.

Pulakos (2009) notes that a poorly designed or poorly implemented performance management system can decrease employee motivation and productivity, and undermine relationships between employees and managers. She also notes that performance management systems can be designed for a range of different purposes (e.g., for pay and rewards versus employee development, much in the same way as performance appraisal systems), and that systems tailored for one purpose might not be effective when used for other purposes. Like most other systems in organizations, performance management systems work best if there is "buy-in" (i.e., support for the system and its components among leaders, managers, supervisors, and employees).

Proponents of performance management are optimistic about the potential contribution of this approach to the success of organizations and their members. For example, Aguinis (2013) listed 16 potential benefits of performance management systems, including increases in motivation, self-insight, and self-esteem; increased fairness and transparency in administrative actions; increasing clarity regarding organizational goals and job demands; increased employee competence and decreased employee misconduct; better protection from lawsuits; increased commitment to organizations; better communication regarding performance expectations; and more openness to organizational change. Some of these same outcomes might be achieved by improving performance appraisal systems, but proponents of performance management insist that frequent, forward-looking performance feedback has a different effect than a backward-looking annual appraisal, no matter how well done.

Aguinis (2013) documents the increasing international spread of performance management. Other scholars are not so optimistic. For example, Pulakos et al. (2015) report surveys showing that 95% of managers are dissatisfied with their performance management system and that 90% of HR heads believe their performance management system depends on inaccurate information.

It can be hard to determine precisely what "performance management" means, because the programs actually implemented in different organizations can vary so extensively. At its most general level, performance management can encompass many of the activities a firm undertakes to improve an employee's performance, beginning with the evaluation of performance and subsequent feedback to the employee, and continuing through training and administration of rewards (such as pay increases and promotions). It is increasingly common for organizations to adopt or to claim to adopt some form of performance management as a centerpiece of their HR strategy (Aguinis, 2013; Aguinis, Joo, & Gottfredson, 2011), but it is far from clear whether "performance management" means the same thing as you go from one organization to another. We examine the challenges in evaluating performance management systems in more detail in a later section, but in order to fully understand these challenges, it is useful to examine the key steps in implementing a system of performance management.

Implementing Performance Management Systems

The development of performance management systems starts with an assessment of the mission, goals, vision, and strategy of the organization. Virtually all organizations have some form of mission statement, but the relationship between these statements (which are often an embarrassing collection of buzzwords and platitudes) and the actual behavior of the organization are not always clear. For example, consider the description of company mission and goals provided by the Volkswagen Group in 2013, which reads, "The Group's goal is to offer attractive, safe and environmentally sound vehicles which can compete in an increasingly tough market and set world standards in their respective class."[4] Like virtually all mission statements, it includes a claim to represent world-class standards. (A truck stop 20 miles south of us claims to serve the "world's best cinnamon buns." So, not surprisingly, does a restaurant in town.) This statement set a specific goal of offering environmentally sound vehicles that can compete in a tough market, but the relationship between that goal and the actions of the organization seems to have turned out to be quite complicated. At the time this statement was written, Volkswagen was allegedly involved in a large-scale effort to mislead enforcement agencies about the actual environmental soundness of their diesel vehicles, a strategy that in the short term probably helped them to compete but that in retrospect might not look quite so wise. In a similar vein, Lehman Brothers, a company that was allegedly in misleading activities that contributed substantially to a worldwide financial collapse, had a mission statement which read in part:

- We are one firm, defined by our unwavering commitment to our clients, our shareholders, and each other. Our mission is to build unrivaled partnerships with and value for our clients, through the knowledge, creativity, and dedication of our people, leading to superior returns to our shareholders.

- As a trusted partner, we provide comprehensive financial advisory, capital raising and risk management services to corporations and governments worldwide. Extending our global presence and capabilities, we continue to develop innovative and tailored solutions to deliver the full resources of our Firm to our clients.

- Lehman Brothers, an innovator in global finance, serves the financial needs of corporations, governments and municipalities, institutional clients, and high net worth individuals worldwide. Founded in 1850, Lehman Brothers maintains leadership positions in equity and fixed income sales, trading and research, investment banking, private investment management, asset management and private equity.[5]

These honeyed words do not appear to describe the actual behaviors or strategies of this organization, at least during the run-up to the global financial meltdown of the late 2000s.

Mission statements and descriptions of the goals, vision, and strategy of organizations are most likely to be useful in developing performance management systems when they are specific, realistic, and honest. For example, Aguinis (2013) describes the case of a bank that started with a description of organization-level mission, goals, and strategy that (1) laid out a mission of providing a wide range of financial services that would exceed those of their market competitors in value, (2) created a goal of attracting and retaining outstanding staff capable to accomplishing this mission, and (3) described a strategy that involved critically reviewing existing branches and departments to ensure that their activities and capabilities were consistent with these goals and strategies. This type of mission statement could reasonably lead to some concrete statements about the actual strategy, plans, and goals of this organization. In general, consistent, concrete, and realistic descriptions of the mission, goals, and strategies of the organization are the first requirement of a successful performance management system. These missions, goals, and strategies then become the basis for cascading high-level strategy down to smaller and smaller units in the organization.

Although mission statements are often too vague and abstract to provide clear and realistic goals that can be cascaded through an organization, a close examination of the strategy pursued by an organization to compete might be more informative. In general, organizational strategies tend to cluster around three key dimensions: (1) cost, (2) flexibility, and (3) customer service (Dekker, Groot, & Schoute, 2013). Cost-oriented strategies emphasize efficiency in using the firm's resources to deliver products or services at a low cost. Flexibility strategies emphasize developing innovative products and changing products and services as customers' preferences and needs change. Customer service strategies aim at delivering high-quality products and services that match the needs of customers. As Dekker et al. (2013) note, many organizations pursue hybrid strategies that involve some mix of these three dimensions. Organizations that follow a well-defined strategy (e.g., Walmart focuses on managing costs through its interactions with suppliers and its human resource policies) will find it easier to develop a set of cascading goals and methods for achieving them.

Cascading

If a coherent, plausible, and realistic mission and a sensible set of goals and strategies can be defined by an organization, the next challenge is to translate that organization-level plan to goals and strategies for each division and department. This is probably easier for divisions and departments that are close to the core of the strategic plan than for those that provide support roles. Going back to the example of the bank cited earlier, which settled on a strategy of attracting, selecting, and retaining high-quality staff, the implications of this strategy are probably clearer for the human resources department than (for example) the accounting department. Nevertheless, the whole philosophy of performance management implies that each division and department of an organization must start by asking how its activities help the organization accomplish its key goals and implement its core strategy, and to eliminate activities that do not serve these ends.

In theory, this process of harmonizing the activities, goals, and strategies of organizational units with those of the organization as a whole might sound straightforward, but perhaps it is not always so easy. For example, virtually every department has or sponsors activities that are social in nature (e.g., outings, holiday parties). You could make an argument that these support the functioning of the organization by building or maintaining morale, but if this is true, how far should this be pushed? What proportion of a department's time and resources should be devoted to direct versus indirect support for the goals of the organization (here, building morale would be considered indirect support)? Under what conditions should a department undertake actions that do not spring from the current organizational mission, strategy, or plan? If the answer is that they sometimes should, and that this might depend on the judgment of managers or unit leaders (organizational plans and strategies are, after, all subject to change, and they rarely can anticipate all contingencies), what is the difference between an organization that cascades its plans, goals, and strategies and one that does not? The answer is not always obvious.

Next, a link needs to be established between the goals, plans, and strategies of organizational units and the job descriptions of the employees in that unit. Again, this is probably easier for jobs near the core of the strategy than for those at the periphery.

Going back to the Volkswagen Group mission statement, one implication of this mission is that the job descriptions of engineers charged with designing cars should probably emphasize developing technologies that optimized the mix of environmental quality and affordability.[6] Because these two criteria were probably incompatible, at least for the cars in question, cascading the overall corporate strategy down to the engineers who designed the cars probably put them in an untenable position; you can argue that the Volkswagen Group would have been better off revising its overall strategy rather than attempting to enforce incompatible goals on its engineers.

Finally, the cascading process brings members of the organization to the point where they need to form their own performance goals and plans, again with an eye on maximizing the link between what they do as individual employees and overall goals of the organization. This is one point where buy-in is particularly important. Employees who internalize the goals, plans, and strategies of their organization are more likely to develop individual goals and performance plans that are consistent with those higher-level goals, plans, and strategies.

SPOTLIGHT 2.2 CASCADING GOALS
A UNIQUE STRENGTH AND A UNIQUE WEAKNESS OF PERFORMANCE MANAGEMENT

One of the distinctive features of the various performance management systems described by Aguinis (2013), Pulakos (2009), and others is the idea that performance goals should flow from the overall strategy of the organization. That is, most performance management systems start with the assumption that goals should be arranged in a cascading fashion, where the overall strategy and objectives of the organization drive the goals of each division, department, work group, and even each employee. This is a unique strength of performance management, especially when considered in comparison to the way goals are set in traditional performance appraisal systems. Cascading goals helps to focus everyone's attention on *why* they are doing particular things in addition to thinking about *what* people do in the workplace. In contrast, discussions of the ways performance goals are set in more traditional performance appraisal systems focus largely on discussions and negotiation between managers and individual employees. We suspect that these discussions are more often driven by what the employee and supervisor are accustomed to (i.e., the reason why particular goals are set may have more to do with what has been done in the past than with what

the organization is hoping to accomplish) than by the strategy of the firm.

The strategy of cascading goals has the advantage of helping to unify and focus the efforts of all units and members of an organization in a common direction. This is a potentially powerful unifying force, especially if the members of this organization clearly understand and support those goals. On the other hand, if taken too far, this strategy removes individual employees from the equation, defining their jobs, the goals, and metrics they should focus on and the standards for evaluating their performance entirely in terms of a set of strategies designed by a handful of people at the top of the organization. The challenge in traditional performance appraisal systems is for employees and supervisors to be mindful of what their work group, department, division, and so on is trying to accomplish when setting goals and defining standards for evaluating individual employees. The challenge in performance management systems is to give employees and managers sufficient flexibility to define the way they do their work to give them a genuine stake in accomplishing goals they have set, as opposed to goals set by someone higher in the organization.

Employees who have to be encouraged or even coerced into developing performance plans and goals that are driven by the higher-level goals of the organization, but that they do not support, will almost certainly perform at a lower level (Erez & Kanfer, 1983).

Develop a Measurement Approach

The practice of cascading goals, plans, and strategies throughout an organization can be thought of as the aspirational component of performance management. That is, this practice helps to identify what employees, teams, departments, and divisions *should* do. Metrics is where the rubber meets the road; the process of measuring performance and success is what moves what *should* happen toward what *will* happen or what the organization will try to encourage.

Given its emphasis on cascading goals and strategies and harmonizing all levels of an organization to pursue a common set of goals, the literature on performance management is sometimes strangely silent on the development and use of metrics to evaluate the performance of organizations as a whole or the performance of units within the organization (e.g., departments, divisions). For example, two recent, widely cited texts (Aguinis, 2013; Pulakos, 2009) have several chapters devoted primarily to the evaluation of individual performance, but neither deals in any detailed way with questions such as how the performance, effectiveness, or success of organizations should be conceptualized or measured, or how the performance of departments or divisions should be addressed.

Literature in several disciplines (e.g., strategic accounting) has identified a range of metrics that might be used to evaluate the performance of organizational units and perhaps of organizations on the whole. For example, Dekker et al. (2013) describe the use of market performance, cost and resource use, production efficiency, innovation, quality, and individual performance metrics in evaluating the success of a unit, and they note that different classes of measures are likely to be most useful for evaluating the performance of organizational units or organizations that pursue different strategies.

We are skeptical of one of the apparent assumptions of the performance management literature, that if individual members of the organization tailor their jobs and their performance goals to the strategic plans of the organization, and if they are evaluated on these terms and encouraged to increase the effectiveness with which they advance those goals, the organization as a whole will improve and prosper. There is a large literature dealing with aggregation and cross-level inference that suggests we should be cautious in assuming that if individual members of the organization become more effective in their jobs (and if jobs and performance goals are shaped with reference to the overall mission, strategy, and vision of the organization), the organization will become more effective (e.g., Mossholder & Bedian, 1983). There is evidence that changes in individual performance (or the implementation of policies and procedures aimed at increasing individual performance) can have an impact on the performance and success of organizations, but that this effect is neither simple nor certain (Delaney & Huselid, 1996; Huselid, 1995; Pritchard, Jones, Roth, Steubing, & Ekeberg, 1988).

One reason it is difficult to link individual and organizational performance is that adequate measures of organizational performance may not always be easy to obtain, and it may vary depending on the nature of the organization and the strategy it is attempting to pursue. For example, bottom-line financials are almost always relevant, but they may not adequately capture the performance and effectiveness of some organizations (e.g., government agencies, nonprofits, military organizations), and as organizations get more complex and more multinational, assessing organizational performance will become increasingly complicated (Bititci, Garengo, Dörfler, & Nudurupati, 2012).

The Performance of Groups and Teams

When you attempt to aggregate from predictions about the performance of a single individual to predictions about the performance groups, departments, divisions, or organizations, one of the first complications you will face is that much of the work in organizations is characterized by some level of interdependence. That is, your ability to perform your job well, or your department's ability to perform its job well, often depends on how well other individuals or departments are doing *their* jobs. As you aggregate to higher levels, such as organizations, states, or nations, interdependence becomes increasingly common and increasingly complex.

Most work groups or teams demonstrate some level of *task interdependence*, in which any individual member depends (at least in part) on materials, products, ideas, information, or expertise that is possessed or shared by other group members in order to carry out tasks and responsibilities (Van Der Geht, Emans, & Van Der Vriert, 2001). Thus, if one member of a team increases his or her job-relevant knowledge, skills, or abilities, the probability that this increase will lead to an increase in performance depends to a large part on whether other team members will be willing and able to provide the resources necessary to perform well.

Most work groups or teams also demonstrate some level of *goal interdependence*, in the sense that they often share goals and (more importantly) feedback. That is, performance feedback is often provided to groups in relation to group goals or assignments (e.g., a work group is given responsibility for producing 120 units per week and receives feedback about success in reaching this goal each week), and it can be difficult to establish concrete links between feedback to the group and feedback that might be given to individual members of that group.

Interdependence becomes more complex when considering organizations rather than work teams. Thompson (1967) notes that the various departments in an organization might show any of three forms of interdependence: (1) pooled interdependence—where there is little interaction between departments, but where each department's input defines the success of the organization as a whole; (2) sequential interdependence—where one unit must successfully complete its task for the next unit to launch theirs (e.g., assembly lines); or (3) reciprocal interdependence—where departments interact extensively and each depends substantially on the other to complete its assigned tasks and functions. Within a single organization, any or all three of these forms of interdependence might be present.

Interdependence implies that even if one department or section of an organization is able to successfully increase its performance and effectiveness, that increase may not lead to any clear increase in *organizational* effectiveness. For example, suppose there are three departments in an organization that show strong reciprocal interdependence. If one of these departments fails to perform well, it is likely that the organization will underperform even if the other two departments are doing the best job they can.

In theory, a successful performance management program should minimize the effects of interdependence by harmonizing the efforts of individuals, groups, and higher-level units toward a common set of goals. It is true that the poorest-performing department or division might drag down the effectiveness of other departments or divisions, but if they are all at least working in a common direction, it is possible that organizations will be able to minimize the conflicts in the goals, plans, and objectives pursued by different individuals, groups, or units. The question of whether performance management programs do indeed lead to a consistent set of goals and strategies across all levels of an organization is, however, an empirical question that has not, to our knowledge, been adequately answered to date.

Give Feedback and Act on Evaluations

The evaluation of individual performance is a very important component of performance management, but evaluation is only useful if you *do* something with it. Like the performance appraisal literature, the performance management literature suggests three key uses of information about individual performance: (1) improvement and development—using performance feedback to improve subsequent performance by identifying current performance weaknesses and methods of overcoming them; (2) motivation—using performance evaluations to determine rewards and sanctions, which presumably influence the motivation to perform well in the future; and (3) driving personnel actions aimed at resolving recurring performance deficits—replacing ineffective performers, finding new assignments for workers who are not contributing in their current assignments, and providing training or resources to increase the effectiveness of employees.

In both the development and implementation of individual performance measures and their use for the three purposes above, there are scant differences between the suggestions, principles, and findings of research on performance management and comparable research on performance appraisal. Effective performance management requires three essential things: (1) sound and concrete plans, strategies, and goals that are shared and embraced across organizational levels; (2) sound measurement of individual job performance; and (3) smart decisions about how to use those measures to motivate and improve the performance of individuals, which hopefully will translate into better performance for groups, teams, departments, divisions, and entire organizations. Performance measurement is critically important because good measurement is the tool that tells you whether employees are actually doing the things the entire process of cascading goals, objectives, plans, and so on from the top to the bottom of an organization is designed to accomplish. Performance measurement is also the tool that is used to direct rewards and sanctions and a wide range of administrative decisions that are all intended to maximize individual performance, and thereby the performance of each of the levels of an organization.

A substantial portion of this book is devoted to understanding the reasons why performance appraisal systems so often fail (or are seen as failing) in organizations, and virtually all of the issues that will be discussed in Chapters 3–12 are pertinent to understanding whether and why efforts to measure performance, provide feedback, and act on the results of performance measures so often fail to live up to expectations. In general, it hardly matters whether performance measurement efforts are in the form of the traditional annual appraisal, or whether they come in the form of other sorts of performance assessment and feedback often advocated by proponents of performance management (e.g., continuous or frequent performance measurement or feedback), the underlying issues are largely the same. The topics we explore in Chapters 3–12 make it clear that performance measurement is often a challenging task; in Chapters 13 and 14, we explore ways to increase the likelihood that this critical task will be a success.

PERFORMANCE APPRAISAL AND PERFORMANCE MANAGEMENT: SIMILARITIES AND DIFFERENCES

There are some important similarities between performance appraisal and performance management. They are both ultimately concerned with the effectiveness of individuals, work groups, and organizations, and both focus on identifying good performance and on increasing the likelihood that individual employees will be effective in their jobs. They both rely on group leaders, supervisors, or managers to help determine whether employees are performing well and to help them perform better. Some versions of performance management include performance evaluations that are quite similar to traditional performance appraisals (e.g., they might include annual evaluations by one's supervisor or manager, formal ratings, and individual feedback sessions; see, for example, Pulakos, 2009), whereas others are less structured and formal, but still devote considerable time and attention to the evaluation of job performance.

As Table 2.1 illustrates, there are two important differences between performance appraisal and performance management systems: those that involve their orientation in time and those that involve their assumptions about power and influence. First, performance appraisal systems are summative, providing information about how well you performed over the past year (or some other time period). To be sure, this information might be used to create incentives for future performance (e.g., merit raises), but the evaluation is in many respects backward-looking. Performance management, in contrast, often devotes less attention to evaluating what you did over the past year, with a much stronger focus on what you are doing right now, and how it might be improved in the future. In theory, some performance management systems might not include anything like an annual evaluation, and even in those that do include something along these lines, immediate feedback is usually seen as more important than evaluations of past accomplishments or failures.

TABLE 2.1 ■ Comparing Performance Appraisal and Performance Management	
	Critical Differences Between Performance Appraisal and Performance Management
Time orientation	Performance appraisal—the orientation is summative (evaluating performance over the past year or past several months), focusing on an evaluation of what someone has done
	Performance management—the orientation is toward what is happening now (e.g., more immediate feedback) and how future behavior can be corrected or improved
Orientation toward power, authority, and influence	Performance appraisal—the orientation is consultative, with employee input routinely included as an important part of defining work goals and evaluating work performance
	Performance management—the orientation is authoritarian, with an emphasis on top-down design or work goals, plans, and strategies, in which decisions made at the top of the organization are cascaded down to define what each division, department, work group, and individual does and how they should be evaluated

Second, and more important, performance management and performance appraisal systems are built on different ideas about power and influence. Performance management strongly emphasizes top-down planning, in which goals, plans, and objectives cascade down from the top levels of the organization. Taken to its logical conclusion, performance management is a modern extension of Taylorism, in which decisions are made about how people work, what goals they should pursue, and how they should be evaluated at the top of the organization, with no provision and indeed no need for input or decisions from the employees who will actually perform the work. Thus, performance management can be, if taken too literally, authoritarian in its structure.

Performance appraisal, in contrast, has come to include considerable input from employees as a fundamental component of performance appraisal systems. This consultative orientation is not something that was always embraced in performance appraisal systems; appraisal systems were once every bit as authoritarian as many current performance management systems. However, as several chapters in this volume note, contemporary performance appraisal systems almost always include one or more of the following features: (1) performance goals that are set by employees or negotiated between employees and supervisors or managers, (2) self-ratings or some form of self-evaluation, and (3) mechanisms to give employees opportunities to review and comment on or object and appeal to their evaluations. Performance appraisal systems in which evaluations are strictly top-down exercises without any input, sign-off, or review by employees are rare in contemporary organizations.

In our view, the top-down versus consultative difference is critically important. First, there appears to be a strong trend in American organizations away from top-down, Tayloristic systems. Contemporary research and business publications place a good deal of emphasis on topics such as empowerment (Blanchard, Carlos, & Randolph, 2001; Chen, Lam, & Zhong, 2007; Ziguang, Wing, & Jian, 2007), employee-centric organizations (Lee-Hoffmann, 2011; Reeves, 2015; Sharma & Sahoo, 2013), and organizational structures that minimize hierarchy and that involve employees more directly in planning work, setting goals and objectives, and evaluating performance (e.g., Robertson, 2015). The unifying feature of all of these trends is the belief that it is important to give employees the tools and the responsibility to design, plan, manage, and evaluate their own work, and we see this belief as antithetical to performance management, but highly consistent with contemporary performance appraisal. If these trends persist in organizations, it is hard to see how performance management, as currently conceptualized, can survive. Performance appraisal systems, on the other hand, embrace the core assumption behind these trends (i.e., that it is critical to involve and empower employees if organizations hope to succeed).

HUMAN RESOURCE MANAGEMENT, STRATEGIC HRM, AND PERFORMANCE MANAGEMENT

One of the challenges in research on performance management is determining precisely what this term means. The various definitions cited earlier in this chapter (e.g., Aguinis, 2013; Pulakos, 2004; U.S. Office of Personnel Management, 1998) share some commonalities (e.g., aligning individual and team goals with broader organizational strategies, evaluating performance, and providing feedback), but they do not always agree regarding the boundaries of this concept or the relationship between performance management and other management concepts. One way to flesh out the concept of performance management is to describe its relationship to the array of human resource management practices in organizations, as well as its relationship to the broader construct of strategic human resource management.

First, human resource management includes a range of policies and practices that involve bringing people into organizations, preparing them to perform the jobs they have been hired for, evaluating their performance, developing new knowledge and skills, compensating and rewarding job performance, evaluating job performance and providing performance feedback, and assuring the flow of qualified candidates to meet future leadership needs in an organization. Some of the activities that fall under the heading of human resource management are also clearly part of performance management, but others (e.g., recruitment, succession planning) probably are not.

Strategic human resource management (SHRM) is concerned with the relationship between the architecture of HRM activities and firm performance (Becker & Huselid, 2006). Here, architecture is used as a metaphor to describe the system of human resource activities, with the assumption that we need to think about how the entire system of HRM-related activities works rather than thinking about individual components as solutions to particular problems (e.g., using pay increases to motivate performance improvements). The focus of SHRM is on how the human components of organizations can add value to the organization.

SHRM is broader than traditional human resource management, in that it considers a wider array of issues that are likely to influence the ability of an organization to execute its competitive strategy. For example, SHRM involves a careful assessment of what strategies the organization *is* following and what strategies it *should be* following to succeed in its desired niches, as well as the fit between these strategies and the organization's HRM practices (Becker & Huselid, 2006; Schuler & Jackson, 1987). Strategic HRM also involves evaluating key contextual variables, such as the characteristics and capabilities of the available workforce and the culture of the organization, which may have a bearing on the feasibility of implementing particular competitive strategies.

Performance management focuses on a subset of activities and processes that are most tightly related to individual and team performance, starting with the development of goals and performance plans, and continuing through the evaluation of performance and the provision of performance to the point where performance is tied to rewards or other outcomes valued by employees. Performance management also includes the development of capabilities to perform. Figure 2.1 illustrates the span of activities that are part of performance management, human resource management, and strategic human resource management. From this perspective, performance management represents a subset of the range of activities that constitute traditional HRM, which in turn represent a subset of activities that might fall under the heading of strategic HRM.

Performance management can, in turn, be broken down into at least three components: (1) determining *what* individuals and teams should do to contribute to accomplishing key organizational goals (e.g., performance coaching and goal development), (2) determining *how well* they do this and providing timely information regarding performance to individuals and teams (e.g., performance evaluation and feedback), and (3) using this information to improve performance capability, both by increasing motivation (e.g., through rewards) and

FIGURE 2.1 ■ **Human Resource Management, Strategic HRM, and Performance Management**

Strategic HRM
- Evaluating the strategy of the organization
- Assessing workforce characteristics

HRM

Performance Management
- Attracting good candidates
- Selection and placement
- Organizational socialization and job entry
- Coaching and goal development
- Performance evaluation
- Performance feedback
- Rewards and benefits
- Training and career development
- Succession planning
- Development and maintenance of organizational culture

SPOTLIGHT 2.3 IS PERFORMANCE MANAGEMENT SIMPLY MANAGEMENT?

You might wonder why a book that deals with performance appraisal and performance management does not have more chapters devoted specifically to the topic of performance management. There is a two-part answer. First, performance appraisal and performance management share some key concerns (i.e., the process of evaluating peoples' job performance and giving them feedback designed to improve that performance). Most of the research on the underlying steps in this process was developed in the context of performance appraisal, with many key studies being published before performance management emerged as a distinct topic. Second, and more important, we have become convinced that there is less to performance management than meets the eye. In particular, the aspects of performance management that are in any way distinct from performance appraisal are simply long-standing parts of the job description of a manager. In other words, we

are not convinced that there is a meaningful distinction between performance management and management in general.

Consider the essential steps in performance management. They involve: (1) making sure that the activities of your subordinates contribute to the higher-level goals of your department, division, organization, and so on; (2) evaluating the performance of your subordinates; (3) providing performance feedback; and (4) helping to create conditions that support and encourage the performance of your subordinates. We think these are, or should be, parts of the standard job description of a manager. Managers, or at least the good ones, were certainly doing all of these things well before the term "performance management" was invented, and they will continue to do them well after this term has joined the junk heap that contains management buzzwords from the past. Regardless of whether your

(Continued)

(Continued)

organization has a performance management system, it is a good bet that effective supervisors and managers do all of these things, and that these activities take up the great majority of that supervisor's or manager's time. Like Molière Bourgeios Gentleman, who is surprised and delighted to learn that he has been speaking prose all his life without knowing it, we suspect that most managers who read a text on performance management will be surprised and delighted to learn that they have been engaging in performance management all of their working lives without the aid of a performance management program. If they have been managing effectively, they are already engaged in performance management. In this light, a performance management program begins to look more like remedial training for managers and supervisors who do not yet know how to do their jobs.

by increasing knowledge and skills that are relevant to both the current job or project and to future assignments (e.g., through training and career development). Different definitions and discussions of performance management differ substantially on some of the specific details of how these three components should be operationalized (e.g., should performance feedback be frequent and informal?), but these three ideas are present in most variations on the theme of performance management.

CAN PERFORMANCE MANAGEMENT BE SIMPLIFIED?

The performance management processes described in this chapter are complex and time-consuming, and some companies have looked for ways to streamline this process (Vara, 2015). Perhaps the most notable example is Deloitte, a global firm offering consultation, auditing, and financial advisory services; Buckingham and Goodall (2015) describe this system in detail. Like many organizations, Deloitte found themselves devoting a great deal of time and money to performance management; Deloitte's review suggested that they were spending *2 million hours per year* completing forms, holding meetings, and conducting performance reviews.

In re-designing their performance evaluation system, Deloitte abandoned many of the features of the performance management systems described in the literature. They do not use cascading objectives, annual performance reviews, or 360-degree feedback systems. In contrast to other organizations that evaluate multiple aspects of performance each year, Deloitte opted for a radically simplified performance evaluation strategy. At the end of every project (or every quarter for long-term projects) each individual's team leader is asked four simple questions, shown in Table 2.2.

The Deloitte system certainly is simple. Rather than asking peers, supervisors, or others to evaluate performance, this performance review method depends on the opinions of a single team leader. Rather than anchoring evaluations in terms of what the person being evaluated actually *does* in his or her job, this method focuses on general impressions of performance and worth. In theory, this system provides both transparency and recognition of performance (Buckingham & Goodall, 2015). In our view, the Deloitte experience

TABLE 2.2
Deloitte's Four Questions
Given what I know of this person's performance, and if it were my money, I would award this person the highest possible compensation increase and bonus [*measured on a five-point scale from "strongly agree" to "strongly disagree"*].
Given what I know of this person's performance, I would always want him or her on my team [*measured on the same five-point scale*].
This person is at risk for low performance [*yes or no*].
This person is ready for promotion today [*yes or no*].

suggests that performance evaluation systems *can* be simplified. The question is whether they *should* be streamlined to the extent described by Buckingham & Goodall (2015). We believe the answer is clearly no.

Like other organizations, Deloitte uses the results of their performance reviews to drive high-stakes decisions, such as pay increases or promotions. Suppose you are a team member who receives low ratings from your team leader, and therefore does not receive a raise or are denied a promotion. The four questions listed in Table 2.1 do not tell you anything about *what* you are doing well or poorly, only that your team leader is not impressed. Suppose further that ratings like these are used to make a number of decisions about raises or promotions, and at the end of a year you find out that men receive more raises than women, or that older workers do not get promoted, or that white employees receive raises and promotions at a much higher rate than black employees. We should note that we do not know of any reason to believe that these outcomes *are* happening at Deloitte, but suppose this is how things turned out. In our opinion, Deloitte would be in a very difficult position.

The Risk of Over-Simplifying

Federal law, ranging from the Civil Rights Acts of 1964 and 1991 to the Age Discrimination in Employment Act, the Americans with Disabilities Act, and other similar laws all embody a similar set of principles. Businesses are generally free to make decisions about hiring, firing, pay, promotions, and conditions of work *except* when it can be shown that these decisions have a systematically adverse effect on groups of people defined in terms of race and ethnicity, gender, age, religion, national origin, disability, and the like. When decisions about employment or the conditions of work have a systematically adverse effect of this sort, they are forbidden by law *unless* the organization can show that they are job related. For example, if a performance appraisal system leads an organization to give higher raises to men than to women, or to promote younger workers but not older ones or the like, it is up to the organization to demonstrate that this appraisal system does in fact reliably and fairly measure job performance. We do not see how a system like the one described by Buckingham and Goodall (2015) could possibly meet this test. How, for example would Deloitte be able to demonstrate that it is job performance and not simple dislike for particular types of people that is driving these ratings? The usual tools for accomplishing this rely heavily on a demonstration that the appraisal system is tightly linked to the job. For example, if you can show that the job a person occupies requires them to engage in planning, in managing the resources of their work group, and in communicating the results of work to group members and to the organization, an appraisal system that includes well-documented evaluations of planning, resource management, and communication is more likely to survive legal scrutiny than a system that relies entirely on the general impressions of a single rater. We are all for simplicity, but a case can be made that a system like the one described here is overdoing things and that it runs important risks for the organization.

Werner and Bolino (1997) reviewed 46 federal district court, 16 court of appeal, and 2 Supreme Court decisions dealing with discrimination and adverse impact in termination and promotion decisions based on performance appraisals. In reviewing the decisions in those cases, they found that the courts relied heavily upon whether or not (1) performance appraisals are clearly related to the content of the job being performance, and (2) there were due process considerations in appraisals and the decisions based on appraisals. A critical question that is not being considered by organizations that are abandoning performance appraisals is how they will defend against charges of discrimination if they cannot turn to some formal appraisal in their defense? Our review of research and practice in this area suggests that organizations that abandon formal appraisal systems that are based on a careful analysis of the jobs people perform in favor of informal feedback or a few vague questions are practically *begging* for trouble if their appraisal leads to even the appearance of race, sex, or age discrimination.

CAN PERFORMANCE BE MANAGED?

In surveys of employee attitudes, performance management is consistently cited as one of the most unsatisfying and unsatisfactory aspects of their organization (Pulakos, 2009). There are several reasons for this angst. First, there is deep distrust in supervisors' and managers' ability to fairly and accurately evaluate performance. Second, as we lay out in some detail in several chapters that follow, there are numerous structural and contextual features in organizations that make it difficult for managers to provide honest feedback, and smart managers will respond to these pressures by inflating the ratings they assign to most subordinates. Because of skepticism over performance evaluation, regardless of whether this evaluation is in the form of annual performance appraisals or frequent and informal performance feedback, there is also well-founded skepticism among employees that they will receive fair and adequate rewards if they do perform well.

Performance management has become an extremely popular concept. It is widely embraced in business schools in the United States, and it has become a guiding philosophy for human resource management. It might be surprising, therefore, to find out how little evidence there is that performance management actually has a clear effect on the performance or effectiveness of organizations (DeNisi & Murphy, 2017; DeNisi & Smith, 2014). That is, the belief that organizations will become more effective if they install a performance management system is not clearly supported with credible empirical data. We want to be clear here. The data do not show that performance management cannot or does not work; rather, there have not been enough studies in this area to tell with any certainty whether or not different performance management strategies actually work.

One reason why it can be hard to determine whether or not a performance management system works is that the actual goals of the system are not always made explicit, and that they will not necessarily be the same for organizations that pursue different competitive strategies (Dekker et al., 2013). Thus, it might be hard to say with any precision what the behavior of individuals; the effectiveness of teams, departments, and divisions; or the success of organizations should look like if performance management were successful.

Pulakos (2009) notes that organizational-level goals are often lofty and vague, and that it is notoriously difficult and time-consuming to cascade goals from the top of the organization to other organizational levels. Even if an organization is able to devise a coherent strategy and to develop goals for different units that will drive the accomplishment of that strategy, the evaluation of individual performance often represents the Achilles heel of performance management. Regardless of whether this evaluation takes the form of the traditional annual appraisal meeting or the more fluid, frequent, and informal feedback advocated by many proponents of performance management (e.g., Aguinis, 2013), the fundamental problems with evaluating individual performance remain. Supervisors and managers often lack the information they need to make fair and accurate evaluations. If input is sought from multiple sources (e.g., peers, subordinates), it is a safe bet that there will be meaningful disagreements. Even if supervisors and managers have all of the information they need, there are numerous disincentives and few meaningful incentives to provide accurate appraisals. Even if accurate appraisals are somehow obtained, it is a good bet that feedback will not be accepted or acted upon. Finally, organizations routinely shoot themselves in the foot by implementing HR policies in ways that make them almost certain to fail. For example, organizations that claim to pay for performance routinely set aside only small amounts of money for merit pay, making it effectively impossible to fairly reward good performers. For example, the 2012 WorldatWork survey[7] noted that more than two-thirds of the organizations surveyed have some form of pay for performance, but more than three-quarters of these organizations follow merit pay programs in which top performers receive increases that are not much bigger than the increases given to average performers. The small spreads in pay commonly encountered in merit pay systems do not appear to correspond to the differences in performance and productivity of top performers versus average employees (Aguinis & Bradley, 2015; O'Boyle & Aguinis, 2012).

CHALLENGES IN EVALUATING PERFORMANCE MANAGEMENT

There are three challenges to evaluating performance management. The first is definitional. Two firms that claim to have performance management systems in place may or may not employ the same practices. The limits of what is or is not performance management are often unclear. Comparisons between any two different performance management programs can be complex because these programs might differ in multiple ways.

The second challenge involves evidence. Several reviews of performance management research have concluded that there is little clear evidence that performance management works (DeNisi & Smith, 2014; Pulakos & O'Leary, 2011; Pulakos et al., 2015). Part of the problem is that the range of measures that might be used to indicate whether or not performance management is successful is quite large and varied. For example, Bititci et al. (2012) chart the development of models and measures of organizational performance and effectiveness over the last century, and note that while simple measures (e.g., annual profit) were accepted as good indices of organizational effectiveness in the first half of the 20th century, by the 1970s, metrics ranging from sustainability and intellectual property development and use to environmental and social performance were becoming part of the assessment of an organization's effectiveness. As organizations become increasingly globalized, measuring and integrating these metrics into a comprehensive statement about the effectiveness of an organization is becoming increasingly difficult. As a result, the task of empirically linking changes in performance at the individual or even the small-group level with changes in the performance and effectiveness of organizations can be a significant challenge.

The third challenge is disciplinary. Much of the research on performance management comes out of scientific disciplines in which there is a strong premium on developing new theories and models, and very little emphasis on testing whether these theories and models actually work (Edwards, 2010; Kacmar & Whitfield, 2000; Murphy & Russell, 2017). The absence of credible evidence that performance management works is not the same thing as evidence that it does not work, and the lack of confirmatory evidence may in part be explained by the fact that much of the published work in this area is in disciplines that (mistakenly, in our view) put little emphasis on empirically testing key theories or concepts.

Does It Work Versus What Works?

We started this section asking whether performance management works, but this might be the wrong question. Given the wide range of components that are present in performance management programs, the only way to answer this question would be to compare organizations that have performance management systems to organizations that do not have one, and we are not sure there *are* any organizations in which *none* of the components of performance management are present. It might be useful to change questions. Rather than asking whether performance management works, it is probably more useful to ask about the effects of particular components of performance management on the behavior of individuals in organizations and on the effectiveness of organizations (Haines & St-Onge, 2012).

Pulakos et al. (2012, 2015) identified several shortcomings in existing performance management programs; the latter paper as suggested some avenues for improving the practice of performance management. Rather than thinking about performance management as something managers "do" to employees, they suggest that performance management should be thought of as an ongoing series of interactions in which leaders and followers have joint responsibilities. They place considerable emphasis on motivating employees to adopt and commit to goals that are consistent with the overall goals and plans of the organization, and they note that effective motivation often involves giving employees more autonomy, opportunities for mastery, and purpose.[8] They emphasize the value of frequent feedback and experiential learning as ways of enhancing the value of performance management. Levy, Silverman, and Cavanaugh (2015) note that many of these suggestions are already in place in at least some organizations.

It is likely that each of the components of a performance management program has the potential to contribute to improving the performance of individuals and teams. Performance appraisal and performance feedback are frequent sources of complaints, but it is hard to argue that employees and organizations would not benefit if credible information about employee performance was shared with employees. One of the running themes of this book is that performance appraisal and feedback are definitely challenging; in Chapters 13 and 14, we discuss ways of maximizing the value and minimizing the pain of performance appraisals. Similarly, concerted efforts to provide both retrospective evaluations (traditional performance appraisal) and future-looking evaluations (e.g., the sort of frequent and immediate feedback advocated by Aguinis [2013] and others) strike us as potentially valuable. Finally, while the process of cascading goals and strategies is a difficult and time-consuming one, we believe it is very important for overcoming the difficulties often seen in translating improvements in individual performance to improvements at the organizational level. It is unlikely that there is a set of universal best practices for performance management (Becker & Huselid, 2006; Dekker et al., 2013), and one of the significant challenges to performance management researchers will be to identify the conditions under which different possible variations of performance are most likely to be a success.

WHAT IS THE ROLE OF PERFORMANCE APPRAISAL IN PERFORMANCE MANAGEMENT?

In Chapter 1, we outlined the defining features of the traditional forms of performance appraisal: that it is regular, summative, and evaluative and that it provides the basis for feedback and administrative decisions. Some models of performance management (e.g., Pulakos, 2009) include this type of appraisal, but the majority of the descriptions of performance management call for a very different approach to performance evaluation. For example, Aguinis (2013) calls for more frequent, if not continuous evaluations of performance. The assumption here is that summative feedback about what you did well and what you did poorly over the last year is not as valuable for changing behavior as feedback given at the point that behavior occurs.

The suggestion that performance feedback should be more frequent has been echoed by several scholars in this area (e.g., London & Smither, 2002; Steelman, Levy, & Snell, 2004). However, it is important to understand that the feedback that is part of performance management is both quantitatively (i.e., it occurs more often) and qualitatively different from the type of feedback people receive in their annual appraisals. In traditional performance appraisal, performance feedback is the result of a process of collecting, integrating, and evaluating performance relevant in each of the major dimensions of your job. In performance management, feedback is tied to specific tasks or behaviors, and is focused on whether the behavior was effective and how it can be improved. The type of frequent or continuous feedback that characterizes performance management will necessarily be informal and in all likelihood decoupled from administrative decisions (you are unlikely to get salary adjustments on a daily or weekly basis).

The idea that annual summative feedback might not be sufficient and that feedback should be more frequent raises the interesting question of determining the optimal frequency for performance feedback. Very frequent feedback is likely to have the advantage of immediacy, but there is a risk that very frequent feedback will become repetitive, especially if it is feedback about behaviors that are difficult to change in the short run. For example, suppose your mathematical skills are not up to par, making you slow in performing. Less frequent feedback loses this immediacy, but it has the advantage of being based on a potentially large sample of behavior.

Lukas (2010) developed an analytic model to evaluate the optimal frequency of feedback in systems where performance-contingent pay influences employees' decisions to remain with an organization or to leave it. His model suggests that more frequent performance evaluations might not be beneficial. The model incorporates a number of assumptions that are difficult to test, but the results do suggest that more frequent performance feedback might not always be better than less frequent feedback. In particular, frequent feedback about aspects of performance that are difficult to change is likely to feel more like nagging, or even harassment, than like information that is helpful to the employee.

No matter how often it is done, performance evaluation is central to performance management. Given the emphasis on frequent feedback, performance management systems probably place a greater premium than more traditional performance appraisal systems on establishing a culture that makes feedback valuable and acceptable (Levy & Thompson, 2012). Both traditional performance appraisal systems and the more frequent evaluations that are part of most performance management systems function best when there is a high level of trust between supervisors and subordinates. As we will discuss in detail in Chapter 9, it is common for the recipients of performance feedback to believe that they are being unfairly evaluated and for them to reject, or at least resent, the feedback they receive. If feedback is a frequent aspect of day-to-day life in organizations, building trust between supervisors and subordinates is likely to be absolutely critical (Aguinis, 2013).

Regardless of how often it is done, both performance evaluation and performance feedback pose a set of challenges. First, the persons charged with evaluating performance and giving feedback must have the information needed to make sound judgments; the challenges to obtaining and integrating information about subordinate performance discussed in Chapter 5 apply regardless of whether the evaluation is a summative one covering the entire year or an on-the-spot evaluation covering a shorter period of performance. Second, persons charged with evaluating performance and providing feedback must have the tools and training to do the job. Chapters 10 and 11 are based largely on research that assumes the more traditional annual summative appraisal, but many of the issues covered in these chapters will be relevant regardless of the frequency of performance evaluation and feedback. Finally, performance evaluation is a statement of value, and virtually anything a supervisor (or another person involved in evaluation) does that goes beyond a simple count of what the ratee has produced will necessarily be a statement of value (i.e., a judgment of whether it is good or bad or whether it meets, exceeds or fails to meet expectations). This means that performance standards (discussed in Chapter 5) will be an important part of performance evaluation and feedback, regardless of whether it is done continuously or annually. If raters and ratees or different sets of raters have different standards for evaluating performance, they might come to very different judgments about performance, even if they all saw and remembered precisely the same behaviors and outcomes.

This section asks the question, "what is the place of performance appraisal in performance management?" The answer, we believe, is that it is central to the entire enterprise. It may be done in ways that resemble the traditional annual appraisal (which is often coupled with decisions about salary adjustments) or it may be done on a more frequent and informal basis, but it is always done and it must be done well if performance management has any chance of succeeding. Even if you believe that performance management has replaced performance appraisal, we believe you will find all of the issues covered in the chapters that follow to be relevant to understanding how this critically important part of performance management works, and why if often fails to work.

PERFORMANCE APPRAISAL, PERFORMANCE MANAGEMENT, AND INTEGRATED HR INTERVENTIONS

Performance management could be thought of as one variant of a broader strategy of developing sets or clusters of interrelated human resource management activities, all with the goal of increasing performance and effectiveness. There is a significant research literature outside of the boundaries of current performance management research that asks the question of whether systematic efforts to improve the way human resource management functions in organizations actually works, and there are reasons to believe that this broad strategy can be effective.

There is considerable evidence that organizations that adopt bundles of inter-related human resource management practices, all aimed at improving the ability of the organization and its members to execute the core missions of the organizations, can benefit (Huselid, 1995). These bundles of practices (which might or might not include things that are labeled performance management) represent combinations of improvements in selection, training, performance evaluation, employee development, compensation, supervision, and job design, and there is plentiful evidence that adopting these groups of practices can improve the efficiency and performance of organizations (Arthur, 1994; Combs, Ketchen, Hall, & Liu, 2006; Delaney & Huselid, 1996; Huselid, 1995; Youndt, Snell, Dean, & Lepak, 1996). The role of performance appraisal systems in determining the effectiveness of these bundles (if any) is hard to determine (DeNisi & Smith, 2014), but it is likely to be important.

Sometimes, groups of inter-related HR practices are labeled "high-performance work practices," particularly when these practices transfer power and authority to employees. After reviewing 20 years of the literature on the topic and examining 181 articles, Posthuma, Campion, Masimova, and Campion (2013) created nine categories of high-performance work practices: compensation and benefits, job and work design, training and development, recruiting and selection, employee relations, communication, performance appraisal and management, promotions, and turnover, retention, and exit management. Within the performance appraisal and management category, these best practices included appraisals based on objective results or behaviors, appraisals for development, and frequent performance appraisal meetings. However, it is important to keep in mind that empirical evidence that these improvements (whether or not they are framed as part of performance management) actually lead to increases in the performance or effectiveness of organizations is mixed (Cappelli & Neumark, 1999). Becker and Huselid (2006) suggest that the best HRM strategies might depend on the competitive strategy an organization is attempting to follow (see also Dekker et al., 2013). On the whole, there seems to be evidence that high-performance work practices can contribute to organizational effectiveness, but there is also evidence of reverse causation—that is, that effective organizations have the resources and flexibility to adopt these practices (Shin & Konrad, 2017).

It is clear that systematic overhauls to human resource systems that adopt some combination of improvements in selection, training, performance evaluation, employee development, compensation, supervision, and job design can benefit organizations. It is possible that developing a consistent set of performance goals that are harmonized across an organization and pairing these with an improved system for frequent performance feedback could have the same effect, but the evidence to date is simply incomplete. Can improving performance appraisal systems lead to increases in the effectiveness of organizations? The answer might depend largely on how an effective organization is defined.

SUMMARY

The term "performance management" can refer to a wide range of actual policies and practices, but in general they are likely to include attempts to harmonize the goals, plans, and activities of each member of the organization and each unit within the organization so that all activities are aimed at accomplishing critically important organizational goals and then using performance measurement and feedback to enforce and support these goals, plans, and activities. Performance management programs necessarily include some form of performance evaluation, and in that sense, it might be reasonable to think of performance appraisal as simply a component of performance management.

We are not convinced that this is a completely sound approach. Ten different organizations that claim to have performance management systems might end up doing 10 completely different things. There is great enthusiasm for performance management, but we are still far from understanding whether this strategy works or the conditions under which it suc-

ceeds or fails. Performance appraisal, on the other hand, represents a phenomenon that is widespread in organizations and that is widely researched. Thus, at least for now, we see considerable value in studying performance appraisal, regardless of whether it becomes a component of a broader system of performance management.

Despite the efforts of some organizations to get rid of performance appraisal systems, they are only getting rid of some of the surface features of this process, and there is little reason to believe that the informal systems they put into place to replace it will overcome the challenges performance appraisal faces in organizations. Like it or not, performance appraisal is here to stay (albeit sometimes in quite different forms), and the goal of understanding why it succeeds or fails and of finding ways to turn what is often a noxious process dreaded by raters and ratees alike into some sort of a success is one that strikes us as critically important.

ANALYSIS: FROM STRATEGY TO PERFORMANCE GOALS

In this chapter, we noted that a key concept in performance management is the translation of high-level organizational goals and strategies into performance goals for each of the units of an organization. What might this look like in practice?

Suppose you started with a simple taxonomy of strategies organizations follow to gain a competitive advantage. Porter (1985) suggested that competitive strategies could be described in terms of both their scope (broad versus narrow) and their focus (cost versus differentiation). That is, organi-

zations could attempt to gain competitive advantage through broad cost leadership (being broad-based, a low-cost producer), cost focus (being a price leader within a target segment of the economy), broad differentiation (being a unique source of valued goods, often sold at a premium), or focused differentiation (being a niche player, offering unique goods in a target segment of the economy). What sorts of human resource policies would support these four strategies?

Cost-based strategies will probably encourage human resource policies that focus on reducing labor costs. This might be done, for example, by building a labor force that is relatively bottom-heavy (i.e., fewer supervisors or highly paid workers) and minimizing turnover. Differentiation strategies, on the other hand, are likely to focus on talent management, placing a premium on hiring individuals with the skills and knowledge needed to build unique, high-quality products.

How will these strategic goals cascade down to unit-level and individual performance goals? In general, cost-focused strategies are likely to lead to performance goals that center on efficiency, whereas differentiation strategies are more likely to focus on quality and consistency. This might lead to the use of different performance dimensions or difference indicators of success or failure (e.g., reducing waste and scrappage might be an important indicator of successful performance in a manufacturing department of an organization that pursues cost-oriented strategies for gaining competitive advantage). It will probably be easier to translate broad organizational goals and strategies into performance management strategies in departments that are directly involved in the core processes of an organization (e.g., manufacturing, distribution) than in departments that provide staff support (e.g., human resources).

NOTES

1. See, for example, Lawler (2012) and https://www.worldatwork.org/docs/research-and-surveys/Survey-Brief-Compensation-programs-and-practices-2012.pdf.

2. http://www.opm.gov/policy-data-oversight/performance-management/overview-history/

3. Note, however, that the feedback, rewards, and sanctions that are part of traditional performance appraisal are put in place in part to shape the behavior of employees, suggesting that the retrospective-prospective distinction is not as fundamental as it might appear.

4. http://www.strategicmanagementinsight.com/mission-statements/volkswagen-mission-statement.html.

5. http://www.computerworld.co.nz/article/493981/lehman_brothers_company_it_saw_itself/

6. There are a number of more expensive technologies than the ones used by the Volkswagen Group that do produce environmentally sound cars; in the price range Volkswagen was aiming for, it is not clear whether the degree of environmental impact sought was technically feasible.

7. https://www.worldatwork.org/docs/research-and-surveys/Survey-Brief-Compensation-programs-and-practices-2012.pdf

8. In a performance management program with a heavy top-down emphasis, where top management sets the goals and strategy and everyone aligns with this set of goals and strategies, it might be difficult to achieve these outcomes.

3

DEFINING JOB PERFORMANCE

Did Bill Clinton perform well as president of the United States? Your answer might depend on your political affiliation; Democrats will probably have a different answer than Republicans. However, your answer might also depend very much on what you believe "performance as a president" includes. For example, the only time since 1970 when the United States did *not* run a budget deficit was during Clinton's second term. Some people would say this is an indication of effective performance and others would say it was just good luck. He was also the first president in over 100 years to be impeached. Some people would point to that as an indication of poor performance, and others would say it was just pure politics.

One of the reasons it is difficult to accurately evaluate employees' job performance is that "job performance" is a complex, multifaceted construct. Suppose you have three subordinates. Joe always gets his tasks done on time, but is disruptive on the work floor, is often late, and shows little respect for safety rules. Mary does high-quality work, but is rarely timely. Steven is always willing to help others or to do extra work when it is needed. The quality and timeliness of his work is highly variable. Which employee is the best performer? Are any of them a good performer? Are all of them good performers? The answer depends substantially on how job performance is defined.

In this chapter, we examine the meaning and the nature of job performance. We start by considering the common dimensions of job performance (i.e., definitions of what and what is not included under the heading of "job performance"). It is clear that job performance involves more than simple carrying out the list of tasks on a job description; dimensions of job performance that involve interacting with others in the workplace (e.g., organizational citizenship), as well as those that involve potentially dishonest or destructive behavior in the workplace (e.g., counterproductive behavior) are important parts of determining whether a particular employee is effective or ineffective. As jobs become more complex, employees' ability to adapt is also becoming an important part of the definition of job performance. Finally, employees are often faced with choices between ethical and unethical courses of action, and these choices also help to determine whether or not a particular employee is effective in his or her job. In our final section, we consider whether performance should be measured at the individual or at the team level, and also whether we should rely on subjective judgments about performance, or whether the objective measurement of job performance is possible.

DEFINING PERFORMANCE

Job performance is a complex construct, and there have been many disagreements about what *performance* actually means. The most fundamental argument in defining performance is whether to focus on behaviors or results. Consider the following example. You call a stockbroker and ask him or her to purchase 1,000 shares of a particular corporation, hold them for a year, then sell them. Through a series of blunders and clerical errors, the broker buys the wrong shares and sells them after a month, but you end up making money—a lot more money than you would have made if your instructions were followed. Has the stockbroker performed his or her job well? If you focus exclusively on behaviors, the answer is no. The broker is supposed to execute your instructions, and here there was one mistake after another. On the other hand, you are in the market to make money, and your broker certainly did that. If you focus entirely on results, you would have to conclude that your broker did a good job, even if that happened by mistake.

Performance appraisal researchers (e.g., Campbell, 1990) typically prefer to define job performance in terms of behaviors—that is, job performance is something a person *does*. Those behaviors may lead to a variety of results, and these results may or may not be under the control of the individual being evaluated, but the results of the behaviors individuals perform at work are typically not included in the formal definition of job performance. However, as Pulakos and O'Leary (2010) note, it is illogical to completely ignore the results of behaviors. Jobs exist in organizations to produce various outcomes that are important to the organization, and if an individual is executing all of the behaviors required or expected by a job but not producing outcomes that are relevant to the organization, there is a real problem. The problem might reside in the organization rather than in the individual whose performance is being evaluated (e.g., perhaps the organization does not provide the information or resources required to achieve relevant outcomes), but a definition that completely excluded the outcomes of behavior in the workplace might not be a completely useful one. Second, there is evidence that knowing the outcomes of behavior leads to changes in the evaluations of the behavior itself (Martell, Guzzo, & Willis, 1995). That is, behavior that leads to or that appears to lead to valued outcomes is typically evaluated more favorably than a behavior that does not seem to lead to these outcomes.

We prefer to define job performance as *the set of behaviors in the workplace that are relevant to achieving the legitimate goals of the individual, work unit, and organization*. We use the term "legitimate goals" in recognition that individuals, departments, or organizations might pursue a variety of goals in the workplace that are not related to the purpose of the job, the work unit, or the organization. These might include bullying or harassment, jockeying for influence, or organizational misbehavior. Using an example from the recent news, the engineers, managers, and others who helped Volkswagen create and implement software designed to help diesel cars pass emissions tests by cheating rather than building cars that consistently met emissions standards would not be considered to exhibit good job performance, even though their actions might have contributed to the short-term profits of the organization.

There have been two broad approaches to defining what the construct "job performance" actually included. First, there are several general models that attempt to define what it is people do on their jobs and to capture the range of behaviors that constitute job performance. Second, rather than developing comprehensive models of job performance, several researchers have attempted to define and describe the specific aspects or dimensions of job performance.

A GENERAL MODEL OF JOB PERFORMANCE

Campbell and his associates (Campbell, McCloy, Oppler, & Sager, 1993; Campbell & Wiernik, 2015) have developed a model they believe encompasses other existing models of performance in a work role and that specifies what the term "job performance" actually means.[1] In their model, performance represents a set of behaviors in the workplace that are designed to assist work groups and organizations accomplish their goals. They describe performance in most jobs as representing a combination of eight conceptually distinct factors, shown in Table 3.1.

Although the eight factors in this model are distinct, it is important to keep in mind that these factors (as is true for all of the factors discussed here) are likely to be positively intercorrelated. That is, employees who tend to be good at communication also tend to be good at leadership and to be good at carrying out the core tasks of their job. Different individuals might reach comparable levels of performance by different means (e.g., one might excel in technical performance while another is an excellent leader and coworker), but in the end it makes perfect sense to describe workers as being good or poor performers, even though the specific behaviors exhibited by two employees in the same job who are both rated similarly might differ (e.g., one might excel in technical performance but also might engage in counterproductive behaviors, whereas another might be a great team member).

One of the advantages of the Campbell model of job performance is that it aims to pull together diverse streams of research on specific aspects of performance into a single general description of what it means to perform one's job. That is, rather than focusing on one specific aspect of performance (e.g., team leadership), this model attempts to depict the entire domain of job performance. Whether this model will eventually succeed may depend in part on whether the target—i.e., job performance—is a relatively stable phenomenon over time. If job performance is constantly changing in terms of its nature and its determinants, it might not be possible to build a general model that will adequately describe the entire domain of job performance.

TABLE 3.1 ■ The Campbell Model of Job Performance
Technical performance—performance of core job functions
Communication—conveying information to others
Initiative, persistence, and effort—behaviors that indicate exerting effort
Counterproductive work behavior—intentional behaviors that harm others or the organization
Supervisory, management, executive leadership—behaviors that involve leading or structuring the work of others
Management performance—obtaining, preserving, allocating resources to attain organizational goals
Peer/team member leadership performance—providing leadership in the absence of hierarchical relationships
Peer/team member management performance—planning, coordinating, problem solving in the absence of hierarchical relationships

Dynamic criteria. The stability of job performance has been hotly debated, and there is a considerable body of research suggesting that performance changes overtime, and that individuals who are rated as the best performers at one point in time may be rated as average or even below average workers at other points in time (Sturman, Cheramie, & Cashen, 2005). Ployhart and Hakel (1998) provide a thorough review of research on dynamism. They present evidence performance can change over time and that the rate and nature of that change varies from individual to individual.[2] Murphy (1989a) suggested a model for the way job performance and its determinants changes over time and for the factors that could lead to these changes. He noted that in many jobs, there are times when the job is new, or when new tasks are introduced, or when there are significant events in the environment (e.g., an organization changes its product line) that require incumbents to learn new skills and acquire new knowledge. He labeled these *transition* stages and proposed that cognitive abilities would be most important during these transitions. There are other times when incumbents are executing well-learned tasks (labeled *maintenance* stages) when motivation and personality characteristics might be more important determinants of performance. According to this logic, some employees might possess abilities and traits that lead them to excel during transition stages, while others might shine during maintenance stages.

The question that is most important is not *whether* job performance is stable over time (the evidence is compelling that there are some systematic changes in performance over time in many settings), but rather *how much* stability is present. That is, it is entirely possible to conclude that performance is dynamic while at the same time conclude that the highest-ranked performer at any one point in time is likely to still be a relatively good performer at other points in time. That is, the conclusion that performance is dynamic does not mean that personnel selection is pointless or that utility estimates have no meaning.

It is not possible to offer a well-supported answer to the question of how much stability can be expected in performance. This stability is likely to differ across jobs and career stages, and it is likely to be influenced by a wide range of contextual variables. What we can say is that there is sufficient stability to allow for substantial correlations between several conceptually and theoretically relevant predictors of performance and measures of job performance (see, for example, Schmidt & Hunter, 1981, 1998). This would not be possible if performance was constantly changing and if the rank-order of employees (in terms of their overall job performance) was not at least relatively stable.

THE DISTRIBUTION OF JOB PERFORMANCE

It is common to assume that performance is normally distributed, which means that there is a large group of individuals who fall near the average, and then small groups of truly good and of truly poor performers. Even if it is not exactly normal, most studies and most estimates of the value of performance[3] assume at least a roughly normal distribution.

O'Boyle and Aguinis (2012) challenged the assumption that job performance is normally distributed. They examined almost 200 samples of performance in a wide range of jobs (e.g., researchers, entertainers, politicians, athletes), and they found consistent evidence of important deviations from normality. In particular, in many fields, they found data indicating that there are often a small number of star performers whose performance level is far above what a normal distribution would imply, and that these star performers are often responsible for a large proportion of the total output of the group or organization in which they work. They also found that the substantial proportion of the individuals in most groups perform well below the mean. This may seem counterintuitive, but as the data in Table 3.2 show, if there really is a superstar in the group, most other members of the group *must* fall well below the mean.

Beck, Beatty, and Sackett (2014) questioned the generality of O'Boyle and Aguinis's (2012) findings, noting that these authors studied performance in jobs or situations that were unusual in many respects (e.g., the frequency with which actors are nominated for Emmys—which is zero for most actors and a large number for a few superstars), and that the distribution of performance in most jobs is likely to be more similar to a normal distribution than O'Boyle and Aguinis (2012) would suggest. We regard this issue as far from settled, but it is useful to think through the implications if O'Boyle and Aguinis (2012) are right.

Aguinis and Bradley (2015) claim that the "secret sauce for organizational success" involves producing and managing star performers. They suggest that organizations should concentrate many of their policies on making sure that they attract, develop, and retain star performers. They suggest a variety of interventions (e.g., removing situational constraints at work, having more transparent and fair policies, compensation based on performance and success), most of which would probably benefit all workers, not just star performers. Their core message, however, is that making sure a handful of star performers are found, retained, and kept happy is more important than interventions targeted at the majority of employees.

TABLE 3.2 ■ Work Groups With Normal Performance Distribution Versus Groups With a Star Performer			
Normal		**Group With Star Performer**	
Output	**Number**	**Output**	**Number**
5	2	5	1
20	3	20	3
35	5	35	5
50	8	50	8
65	5	65	5
80	3	80	3
95	2	95	1
		200	2
Mean = 50		Mean = 60.71	
# above = 10		# above = 11	
# below = 10		# below = 17	

Suppose on the other hand that Beck et al. (2014) are right, and that performance *is* normally distributed. This would imply a very different strategy. In particular, if performance is normally distributed, interventions that are aimed squarely at average performers have the most potential, simply because there are many more average performers than stars or stragglers. For example, if performance is normally distributed, training should be focused on improving the skills of average workers, who are likely to be competent but not outstanding at their jobs. If the success of an organization depends mainly on a handful of star performers, there is hardly any reason to offer training to most workers; rather, training should be highly advanced and restricted to the very best performers.

The controversy over whether performance is normally distributed or distributed according to a power law (in which there are many substandard and a handful of extremely good performers) is a complex and challenging one. In our view, the assumption that most workers can be effectively ignored and that resources, attention, and interventions should be restricted to a handful of stars is a risky strategy. Even if this approach yields a higher average level of individual performance, it runs the risk of creating a very negative organizational culture, in which the great majority of employees believe (with some justification) that they are not important and not valued by the organization.

Kim and Glomb (2014) make the important point that work groups often pressure high performers to limit their productivity, in part because this level of productivity makes other workers look bad.[4] Workers who make their colleagues look bad by substantially

SPOTLIGHT 3.1 HOW *SHOULD* PERFORMANCE BE DISTRIBUTED

The material in this section deals with the way job performance *is* distributed; depending on how job performance is defined, a case can be made for either normal distributions or power function distributions. Suppose, however, we ask a different question: what distribution would be optimal?

From the perspective of fields such as operations management (for an overview of this field, see Stevenson, 2015), the optimal distribution of job performance is likely to be a distribution with very little variance. The three authors of this text are psychologists, and from our perspective, individual differences in performance and in the attributes that allow individuals to perform their jobs well are of fundamental interest. From the perspective of operations management, individual differences can be a substantial nuisance, because they introduce unpredictability into production systems. If the success of production systems depends on individuals whose rate of production, production quality, or other indices of performance vary across individuals and across time, this variability will place some limits on the predictability of production systems, and in the long run are likely to contribute to inefficiency.

In one sense, many of the key activities of managers (including performance management) are ultimately aimed at producing performance that is uniformly high, hopefully creating a distribution of job performance in which the mean is as large as possible and in which the variance in performance is relatively low. It might not be realistic to bring the entire workforce to the same levels of performance and productivity shown by the all-stars studied by Aguinis and his colleagues, but a case can be made that in an organization that is effectively managed, many employees will perform at a consistently high level, which will have the effect of reducing the variability and increasing the predictability of performance and productivity.

out-performing them are likely to face criticism and ostracism, and this tendency might be especially strong when organizations attempt to strongly link performance and important rewards (e.g., promotions, salary). While in theory it might seem logical to encourage star performers, and to single them out for praise and reward, this practice might in the end lead these very stars to suppress their excellence and to fit in rather than to stand out. This tendency might be particularly strong in collectivist cultures (e.g., Korea, Japan; Hofstede, 1980); as an old Japanese proverb notes, "the nail that sticks out gets hammered down" ("deru kugi wa utarèru"). The social forces that limit productivity in groups may push the distribution of job performance toward a normal distribution rather than the sort of power distribution envisioned by Aguinis and his colleagues.

DIMENSIONS OF JOB PERFORMANCE

Most measures of job performance yield scores that represent the employee's overall performance level. While there is evidence that many aspects of job performance are intercorrelated, and that a general overall performance factor can sensibly be created (Ree, Carretta, & Teachout, 2015; Russell et al., 2017; Viswesvaran, Schmidt, & Ones, 2005), there is also clear evidence that job performance is multidimensional. Most generally, job performance typically involves some mix of at least four potentially separate types of performance: (1) task performance, (2) contextual/citizenship performance, (3) adaptive performance, and (4) counterproductive workplace behavior. Recent research has suggested a fifth general type of behavior in the workplace that fits under the broad umbrella of "job performance": ethical performance (Russell et al., 2017).

Task Performance

The first step in defining precisely what "job performance" is involves asking what tasks and duties different jobs require. Most jobs have tasks that are unique to them (e.g., a railroad engineer carries out different tasks than a neurosurgeon does), but there are some broad similarities in tasks that cut across many jobs. Borman, Grossman, Bryant, and Dorio 2017 reviewed several existing taxonomies of job performance (Borman, Ackerman, & Kubisiak, 1994; Borman & Brush 1993; Campbell, McCloy, Oppler, & Sager, 1993; Hunt, 1996; Peterson, Mumford, Borman, Jeanneret, & Fleishman, 1999; Viswesvaran, 1993), and they suggest that task performance in most jobs can be thought of in terms of the dimensions listed in Table 3.3. That is, virtually all jobs require their incumbents to communicate and interact with other workers or with clients, customers, or others outside of the organization. All jobs specify some tasks that must be performed, and proficiency in executing these tasks is a very important component of job performance.

The *ability* to execute job tasks is not the same thing as the likelihood that tasks *will* be carried out; successful job performance involves effort and persistence as well as ability. Finally, virtually all jobs require incumbents to solve problems (which might range from fairly simple and routine ones to quite complex problem solving; Neubert, Meinert, Kretzschmar, & Greiff, 2015) and to plan and organize their work and perhaps the work of others. Jobs differ greatly in terms of the specific content and the relative importance of the behaviors included in this list, but this list is an excellent starting point for defining the first component of job performance—that is, the behaviors that are part of your formal job

TABLE 3.3 ■ Dimensions of Task Performance
Communicating and interacting
Task proficiency
Persistence and effort
Problem solving
Organizing and planning

description and your formal role in the organization. An individual who fails to perform these adequately will almost certainly be evaluated as a poor performer. However, these behaviors are not a complete description of successful job performance. Rather, there are several other categories of behavior that go into determining successful job performance.

Contextual Performance/Organizational Citizenship

In addition to the specific tasks that are included on most job descriptions, the domain of job performance includes a wide range of behaviors such as interpersonal support, conscientiousness, and general support for the organization. These behaviors are not always necessary to accomplish the specific tasks in an individual's job, and they are not part of the formal reward structure of most organizations, but are absolutely necessary for the smooth functioning of teams and organizations (Borman & Motowidlo, 1993; Brief & Motowidlo, 1986; Edwards & Morrison, 1994; Hoffman, Blair, Meriac, & Woehr, 2007; McIntyre & Salas, 1995; Murphy, 1989b; Organ, 1988; Smith, Organ, & Near, 1983). These are not necessarily tasks or duties that show up in one's job description, but they are behaviors that must be carried out if work groups, departments, and organizations are going to succeed. This category of behaviors is often referred to as "organizational citizenship" or "contextual performance." Another term that is used to refer to this cluster of behaviors is "citizenship performance" (Borman & Penner, 2001).

Organ (1997) defined this type of organizational citizenship as "performance that supports the social and psychological environment in which task performance takes place" (p. 95). Organ (1988, 1990) proposed that several distinct behaviors comprise organizational citizenship, including altruism, courtesy, conscientiousness, civic virtue, sportsmanship, peacekeeping, and cheerleading. Van Scotter and Motowidlo (1996) suggest a somewhat simpler structure, grouping organizational citizenship behaviors (OCBs) into interpersonal facilitation behaviors (e.g., helping coworkers) and job dedication (e.g., taking initiative, working hard).

Perhaps the most comprehensive definition of organizational citizenship is the one offered by Borman and his colleagues, who suggest that citizenship can be thought of as consisting of three broad dimensions: (1) personal support, (2) organizational support, and (3) conscientious initiative (Borman et al., 2001). Personal support includes behaviors such as helping, cooperating, and showing courtesy. Organizational support includes behaviors such as loyalty to the organization and compliance with its rules and policies. Conscientious initiative includes behaviors such as self-development and showing initiative and persistence

(Dorsey, Cortina, & Luchman, 2010). There is not a complete separation between OCB and task performance; conscientious initiative includes behaviors that are clearly task-oriented (e.g., persistence) as well as others whose ultimate aim is often to improve task performance (e.g., self-development).

Williams and Anderson (1991) suggest a different perspective, organizing OCBs into categories on the basis of the target or direction of the behavior. More specifically, they call behaviors directed toward the benefit of other individuals OCB-I, whereas behaviors directed toward the benefit of the organization are called OCB-O. Williams and Anderson originally identified Organ's (1988, 1990) altruism dimension as an exemplar of OCB-I. However, based on the fact that courtesy, peacekeeping, and cheerleading behaviors are aimed at helping other individuals, it is also appropriate to include them in the OCB-I category.

Although there are different dimensions that can be used to characterize precisely what behaviors are or are not OCBs, there is evidence that different types of OCBs tend to be correlated, and that there is justification for treating OCBs in terms of a one-factor model. That is, it is reasonable to say that some people show higher levels of OCB than others, and while the specific behaviors they exhibit might not be identical, there is a strong enough general factor to treat OCBs as a single entity, much in the same way that it is possible to talk sensibly about overall job performance, even though this construct is known to be multidimensional (Viswesvaran, Schmidt, & Ones, 2005).

Supervisors pay attention to both task performance and contextual performance when completing performance appraisals (Werner, 1994; Whiting, Podsakoff, & Pierce, 2008) and when making decisions about rewards and promotions (Van Scotter, Motowidlo, & Cross, 2000).

Podsakoff, Whiting, Podsakoff, and Blume (2009) summarize evidence showing the OCBs/contextual performance are related to a variety of individual and organizational outcomes, and that they do indeed contribute to the successful functioning of organizations. In many cases, contextual importance seems every bit as important as task performance in driving a range of organizationally important outcomes (Podsakoff et al., 2009).

What is the relationship between task and contextual? A common finding is that they are highly correlated, suggesting that the same people who engage in OCBs also demonstrate higher levels of performance. If this is true, the distinction between these two aspects of performance might be essentially academic—interesting, but not very important in a practical sense. The true relationship between OCBs and task performance, however, can be difficult to discern because ratings of both are almost always obtained from the same rater. Podsakoff, Whiting, Welsh, and Mai (2013) demonstrated that the use of the same rater and often the same scale to measure task performance and OCBs substantially inflates these correlations, and that when independent sources of data are used to estimate task performance and OCBs, you are much more likely to conclude that they are quite distinct aspects of performance.

Comparing Dimensions: Influence, Antecedents, and Consequences of Task Versus Contextual Performance

All five categories of behavior described above might have different antecedents and consequences; the most extensive body of research on antecedents seeks to understand why people succeed or fail at task performance versus contextual performance. Task performance and contextual performance certainly appear to have different antecedents. In particular, task performance appears to be more strongly related to general cognitive abilities and job knowledge than to broad personality characteristics such as conscientiousness, whereas contextual performance appears strongly related to broad personality characteristics such as conscientiousness than to general cognitive abilities (Borman & Motowidlo, 1993; see Murphy & Shiarella, 1997 for a review of meta-analytic evidence relevant to these linkages between ability, personality and facets of job performance).

Murphy (1989a) developed a model of potential changes in the antecedents of task performance over time; this model suggests that as task demands change or as the environments in which tasks are carried out become more unstable or complex, many job tasks require new learning or complex judgments, which may increase the cognitive demands of the job. The proposition that jobs are getting more complex and unpredictable (e.g., National Research Council, 2012; Pulakos, Arad, Donovan, & Plamondon, 2000) suggests that cognitive ability will continue to be an important driver of task performance, even for experienced employees who, in the past, might have learned their jobs so well that they no longer needed to exert much cognitive effort to perform well.

There is clear evidence that supervisors consider both task performance and contextual performance when evaluating their subordinates and that they understand the distinction between the two (Allen & Rush, 1998; Conway, 1996; Johnson, 2001; Motowidlo & Van Scotter, 1994; Posthuma, 2000). There is also evidence that raters and ratees believe that it is appropriate and fair to consider contextual performance in evaluating job performance (Johnson, Holladay, & Quinones, 2009). This distinction between task performance and contextual performance is probably clearer in non-managerial jobs than in managerial ones (Conway, 1996), in part because so many of the core tasks managers perform involve interacting with others in organizations. Contextual performance is probably more important in jobs where workers interact and depend on one another; Bachrach, Powell, Bendoly, and Richey (2006) present evidence that contextual performance is seen as more important when there is extensive task interdependence than when workers perform their tasks independently.

Task and contextual performance can place competing demands on workers, and workers who devote an extensive amount of their time and energy to one domain may fall short in the other. For example, a worker who focuses exclusively on the tasks assigned to him or her, to the extent that he or she does not take steps to help out colleagues who require assistance, or who do not take the time or effort to represent their company well to customers might not be an effective employee. Similarly, an employee who is always volunteering to help might never get his or her own work done, and might be similarly ineffective.

Ellington, Dierdorff, and Rubin (2014) studied potential tradeoffs between task performance and contextual performance. Their results suggest that this tradeoff depends on the social context in which work is performed, and that when work is highly interdependent, there may not always be any such thing as too much contextual performance. On the whole, good contextual performance has more payoff (in terms of the overall evaluations and rewards ratees receive) when employees often show strong task performance; when task performance is weaker, good contextual performance may not be enough to compensate for the inability to get core job tasks done (Kiker & Motowidlo, 1999).

Adaptive Performance

Pulakos et al. (2000) note that as jobs become more complex and as organizations and their environments become more unpredictable, an increasingly important aspect of effective job performance involves adapting to new demands and new circumstances. At one time, it may have been enough to simply learn what tasks a job entails and carry these out, but the changing environment of the workplace has put more emphasis on dealing with novel demands and changing to meet the demands of the job (National Research Council, 2012). Pulakos et al. (2000) suggest that adaptive performance can best be understood in terms of the eight factors listed in Table 3.4.

Jundt, Shoss, and Huang (2015) reviewed 15 years of research on adaptive performance. They note that different researchers use the term "adaptive performance" to refer to a fairly wide range of phenomena, and that many definitions of adaptive performance differ in important ways from the Pulakos et al. (2000) model illustrated in Table 3.4. For example, most definitions of performance (e.g., Campbell et al., 1993; Campbell & Wiernik, 2015) describe performance in terms of behaviors, but many models of adaptive performance appear to include attitudes and beliefs (e.g., willingness to make changes). Jundt et al. (2015) suggest that a coherent definition of adaptive performance should include several components, including: (1) adaptive performance occurs in conjunction with some external change or event (e.g., adopting a new technology), (2) adaptation should be aimed at maintaining current performance levels in the face of change or minimizing the disruptions those changes produce, (3) adaptive performance can have both anticipatory and reactive components (i.e., learning new skills in anticipation of a change or as a result of a change would both constitute adaptive performance), and (4) adaptation will often have both cognitive (i.e., learning how to think differently about a familiar problem) and interpersonal (e.g., changes in the way you interact with others in the organization) components. They suggest a general, but simple definition of adaptive performance—that is, "task- performance-directed behaviors individuals enact in response to or anticipation of changes relevant to job-related tasks" (p. S55).

Rosen et al. (2011) note that adaptation is a different process for individuals versus teams, which suggests that adaptive performance might look quite different at individual versus

TABLE 3.4 ■ Dimensions of Adaptive Performance
Handling emergencies or crisis situations
Handling work stress
Solving problems creatively
Dealing with uncertain and unpredictable work situations
Learning work tasks, technologies, and procedures
Demonstrating interpersonal adaptability
Demonstrating cultural adaptability
Demonstrating physically oriented adaptability

team levels of analysis. Team adaptation often involves multiple, coordinated changes for multiple team members. In particular, teams need to self-assess (i.e., make a determination of who needs to make which changes to function well in a changing environment, then form a new set of plans for accomplishing the team's mission). It is unclear whether individual skills in adaptive performance translate into effective team adaptation.

Counterproductive Workplace Behavior

In the workplace, people not only engage in behaviors designed to accomplish important tasks and to further organizational goals, they also spend a significant portion of their time goofing off, surfing the web, gossiping, and generally wasting time (the taxonomy proposed by Murphy, 1989a includes this category of behavior, referred to as down-time behaviors). Worse yet, they may engage in behaviors that are willfully destructive or harmful. This entire range of behaviors falls under the heading of workplace deviance, or counterproductive workplace behavior (Rotundo & Spector, 2010).

Robinson and Bennett (1995) defined counterproductive workplace behavior as "voluntary behavior that violates significant organizational norms and in so doing threatens the well-being of the organization, its members, or both" (p. 556). It can include acts that inflict harm on individuals, such as verbal harassment, assault, and spreading rumors (interpersonal deviance), or acts directed against the company, such as sabotaging equipment, stealing, and wasting resources (organizational deviance). It is often believed that counterproductive workplace behaviors and organizational citizenship are opposite ends of a single continuum (see, for example, Berry, Ones, & Sackett, 2007), but the weight of evidence suggests that OCBs and counterproductive behaviors are essentially independent, and that at least some people who engage in some forms of interpersonal or organizational deviance also sometimes engage in helping behaviors or other forms of citizenship (Spector, Bauer, & Fox, 2010). That is, the same person might engage in some forms of organizational deviance and in some forms of organizational citizenship; categorizing organizational members as either saints or sinners (i.e., people who either are good organizational citizens or who act to harm others or the organization) it probably an unduly simplistic way of thinking about behavior in organizations.

Like OCBs, counterproductive behaviors are sometimes categorized into behaviors that are aimed at other individuals (e.g., bullying, sexual harassment, rumor mongering; this category is labeled CWB-I) and those that are aimed at the organization (e.g., production deviance, sabotage, employee theft; this category is labeled CWB-O). Although the base rates for these behaviors can be low (i.e., they are not frequent, and tend to be committed by a small proportion of the workplace), the costs associated with these behaviors can be quite substantial (Murphy, 1993). For example, the Society for Human Resource Management estimated that in 2014, businesses lost $15 billion to employee theft alone.[5]

Ethical Performance

Russell et al. (2017) note that ethical behavior falls within the broad domain of job performance, in the sense that it is behavior in the workplace that has a definite influence on the likelihood that the organization and units within the organization will accomplish their key strategic goals. There have been numerous examples in recent years of ethical misbehavior having dire consequences for organizations, ranging from Barings Bank and Enron to AIG and Volkswagen, and a case can clearly be made for the necessity of identifying and studying the components of ethical behavior in the workplace.

SPOTLIGHT 3.2 CYBERBULLYING IN THE WORKPLACE

In the last 10–15 years, there has been a great deal of attention in the media to the use of social media (e.g., cell phones, Facebook) to harass and bully individuals. The initial focus of much of this work was on the bullying of children and adolescents, often by other children and adolescents, but it has become increasingly clear that cyberbullying is also a serious issue in the workplace (Privitera & Campbell, 2009). Workplace bullying is often defined as a pattern of behavior that purposefully offends, intimidates, sabotages, or harms a coworker; this behavior often occurs in settings where there is an imbalance of power or where the perpetrator of this behavior is attempting to establish power over the target (Barron, 2003; Rayner & Cooper, 2006). Estimates of the prevalence of workplace bullying vary, depending on the research methods used and the precise definition of bullying used; some studies have estimated that over 2 million employees have been the target of systematic bullying in the workplace (Privitera & Campbell, 2009).

Cyberbullying involves the use of electronic media to send derogatory or threatening messages to a victim or others, or to make public confidential or embarrassing information or images, with the intent of harming, shaming, or gaining power over the target. There is an emerging body of evidence that cyberbullying is prevalent in the workplace (Privitera & Campbell, 2009), and it is likely that the increasing use of electronic media to carry out work (including working remotely) has led to an increase in cyberbullying (Vranjes, Baillien, Vandebosch, Erreygers, & De Witte, 2017). In environments where interactions are not conducted face-to-face, where some interactions are anonymous, and where the perpetrator may not witness of be fully aware of the effects of this type of bullying, barriers to engaging in bullying behaviors may be lowered.

Workplace bullying has substantial costs, both to individuals and organizations. Bullying can have serious consequences for the physical and emotional health of both the targets of bullying and those who witness or become aware of bullying (Manners & Cates, 2016; Vranjes et al., 2017), and it almost certainly has costs to the organization as well (Rayner & Cooper, 1997). Cyberbullying has been associated with higher levels of workplace stress, lower levels of productivity, and increased legal liability in organizations that tolerate this behavior (Manners & Cates, 2016).

The explanation for bullying in general and cyberbullying in particular has proved somewhat elusive. There is broad agreement in the research community that power is an important issue in bullying in the workplace, and that bullies often act when they feel their power, status, or standing may be threatened. There is also evidence that bullying of all sorts is more prevalent in male-dominated work environments, particularly those that are characterized by authoritarian or hostile work environments (Privitera & Campbell, 2009). There has even been some speculation that the apparently high incidence of workplace bullying in general and cyberbullying in particular may both be the cause of and caused by work-related stresses. A cyberbullying model developed by Vranjes et al. (2017) suggests that stressful workplace experiences lead to responses of anger and frustration, which in turn can lead to acting out against others in the workplace.

Cyberbullying can be thought of as a form of counterproductive behavior that is aimed at one or more individuals in the organization (i.e., CWB-I). This behavior almost certainly detracts from the ability of employees and work groups to work together and be productive. Organizations that do not have specific policies that define and forbid bullying and cyberbullying are ignoring this behavior at their own peril; organizations that can effectively discourage this behavior benefit by removing an unnecessary barrier to effectiveness.

On the basis of a wide-ranging review and several scale-development efforts, Russell et al. (2017) proposed a 10-dimension taxonomy of ethical behavior in the workplace, shown in Table 3.5. Because this taxonomy is new, we do not know the relationships between

TABLE 3.5 ■ Dimensions of Ethical Performance
Truthfulness—does not knowingly mislead clients, coworkers, supervisors, or others in the workplace
Full disclosure—acknowledges potential conflicts of interest
Intellectual property—respects intellectual property rights of others, does not take credit for or steal ideas, plans, etc.
Confidentiality—maintains appropriate confidentiality with clients, coworkers, supervisors, etc.
Unfair treatment—does not take unfair advantage for oneself or of others
Defamation of others—does not maliciously use information (true or untrue) to harm others
Workplace bullying—does not subject others to physical or psychological harassment
Whistleblowing—reports harmful or unlawful behaviors to appropriate authorities
Abuse of power—does not coerce others, using formal or informal power, to do unethical or unlawful things
Rule abiding—does not violate federal, state, or local laws, policies, or contractual arrangements

specific facets of ethical behavior and other aspects of job performance. It is clear that ethical performance overlaps with counterproductive behavior to some extent (e.g., ethical performance includes avoidance of misrepresentation, bullying, abuse of power), but there are aspects of ethical performance that are clearly quite distinct (e.g., whistleblowing). Whistleblowing is especially interesting and important because this is an aspect of job performance that is often not welcomed, and whistleblowers are routinely mistreated and harassed (Rehg, Micelli, Near, & Van Scotter, 2008).

Whistleblowers are often treated as traitors to their organization, but this reaction only makes sense if one believes that the misconduct whistleblowers reveal would have otherwise been kept hidden forever. Even in this case, one can argue that without whistleblowers, some organizations would be able to continue to commit crimes, engage in fraud, or carry out a pattern of misdeeds until they were caught by some external agency, in the meantime doing harm to their customers, to society, and to the employees engaged in this sorry pattern of unethical behavior.

UNITS OF ANALYSIS AND METHODS OF MEASUREMENT

The final two topics considered in this chapter involve questions of *who* should be evaluated and *how* they should be evaluated. First, should we evaluate the performance of individuals, or should we instead evaluate the groups and teams they belong to? This is, of course, not necessarily an either–or question; we could evaluate both individuals and groups. Nevertheless, there are likely to be different issues in defining and evaluating the performance of individuals versus teams. Second, should we attempt to develop objective measures of performance, or should we rely on the judgments of supervisors, managers, and other raters in evaluating job performance? The answer might seem obvious—that is, that objective measures of performance would be preferable to subject measures that reflect someone's opinion or judgment, but unfortunately, things are not that simple.

Performance of Individuals Versus Teams

It is increasingly common to rely on teams to carry out important tasks and projects in the workplace (Cannon-Bowers & Bowers, 2011; Harrison, Johns, & Martocchio, 2000). The defining features of teams—interdependence of action, shared responsibility, and meaningful goals—have a substantial impact on the definition and assessment of team performance. In particular, team performance is *not* simply the sum of individual performance; the interdependence of teams makes the definition and modeling of performance more complex (DeNisi, 2000). Bell and Kozlowski (2002) suggest there are four dimensions of the work environment that are important for determining the relationship between the performance of individual members and the performance of the team: temporal pacing, dynamism of the task environment, strength of member linkages, and workflow structure. For example, a team that is working in an environment that is unpredictable and demanding works in a quite different way than a team working in a stable and predictable environment.

There are many different types of teams; Scott and Einstein (2001) suggest that they can be categorized in terms of task complexity and in terms of the extent to which team membership is stable or dynamic. The simplest teams (work or service teams) perform relatively routine tasks that are carried out by a consistent set of team members (e.g., teams on an assembly line). Project teams are sometimes given more complex tasks, but their defining characteristic is that they are put together to carry out a specific project and are disbanded as soon as the projects or tasks have been completed. Finally, the most complex work and the most variable membership is seen in network teams, groups that might be geographically disbursed and assigned to tasks that require multiple types of expertise. All three types of teams require teamwork, but the specific teamwork behaviors might vary across team types.

Although there are some general similarities between teamwork and organizational citizenship, there are some broad components of teamwork (e.g., team leadership, communication, monitoring, backup behavior) that are specific to facilitating team performance, as opposed to facilitating the performance of others in the work group whose work might not be interdependent with yours. Harris and Barnes-Farrell (1997) showed that teamwork behaviors do indeed influence the performance appraisals of team members. It is well known that organizational citizenship behaviors influence evaluations of job performance (e.g., Allen & Rush, 1998), and it is likely that the influence of teamwork on the performance appraisals of team members follows a similar logic—that supervisors recognize the importance of this class of behaviors for the smooth functioning of the organization.

The Interagency Advisory Group Committee on Performance and Recognition (1993) articulated four broad principles for measuring team performance and for using those measures to make decisions about team members, noting:

- Team performance measures should only be used to evaluate individual performance under narrowly defined circumstances and are most likely to be useful for evaluating team members who all carry out similar functions.

- The use of objective indices of indirect performance measures is more sensible when evaluating groups versus individuals. Evaluations of teams might include measures of customer satisfaction, timeliness of products and services, or ratios of costs to income. Groups or teams are also more likely to be the targets of gainsharing rewards, a reward method that has been strongly suggested by the National Research Council (Milkovich & Wigdor, 1991). Outcome-oriented performance measures are probably more useful for teams than for individuals (Scott & Einstein, 2001).

- Even when individuals work in teams, they do not have to be evaluated in teams; multiple models ranging from completely individual assessments to assessments that include dimensions reflecting contributions to team effectiveness, to wholly team-based ratings are plausible.

- In general, purely team-based measures should *not* be used to make decisions such as reductions in force, dismissal, or placement (in part because of potential legal consequences if these decisions have adverse effects on the employment opportunities that vary as a function of age, gender, race, or other protected categories), and they should only be relied upon when individual measures are not feasible.

Team-based reward systems are becoming increasingly common in organizations (Aguinis, 2013). However, individual assessment is still the norm; most corporations still evaluate individual performance, even if some of their units are evaluated and rewarded as a group (Scott & Einstein, 2001). Folger, Konovsky, and Cropanzano (1992) note that team-oriented appraisals are more likely to raise questions of equity and fairness than individually oriented appraisals.

OBJECTIVE VERSUS SUBJECTIVE MEASURES OF PERFORMANCE

Performance measures are described as subjective if some judgment is required to assign a grade or a numeric value to the thing being measured. For example, in grading essays or papers, professors must apply judgment to determine the adequacy of the work. If a supervisor is asked to evaluate a subordinate's oral communication skills, this will require judgment and it may not be possible to resolve this assessment down to objective measures such as word counts or sentence complexity. Performance measures that require no judgment, such as production counts, are usually referred to as objective. In this book, we will focus almost exclusively on subjective measures, even though some performance appraisal systems include objective data, such as sales totals or output rates, and this deserves explanation, especially because objective and subjective measures are not always strongly aligned.

Objective performance indices including production output, scrap rates, and time to complete a task have been used as measures of performance for routine, manual jobs since the 1940s and 1950s (e.g., Rothe, 1946a, 1946b, 1947, 1951; Rothe & Nye, 1958, 1959, 1961) and these measures received renewed attention in the 1960s and 1970s (Bass & Turner, 1973; Bassett, 1979; Goldstein & Mobley, 1971; Hackman & Porter, 1968; Kidd & Christy, 1961; Yukl & Latham, 1975). Further, other nonjudgmental measures (i.e., personnel data) that do not directly measure performance but potentially provide information on the general "health" of the organization, including absenteeism, turnover, accidents, and grievances, have received considerable research attention (Chadwick-Jones, Nicholson, & Brown, 1982; Fitzgibbons & Moch, 1980; Mowday, Porter, & Steers, 1981; Muchinsky, 1977; Steers & Rhodes, 1978). However, objective measures are not without their unique problems. Although it is not possible here to exhaustively discuss each of these measures (see Landy & Farr, 1983, for a detailed discussion), each objective performance is likely to have specific limitations. For example, absence measures (a) do not apply to many jobs, (b) are frequently inaccurate, (c) have a variety of causes depending upon the definition of absence, (d) vary in the length of observation, and most important, (e) different measures of absence do not correlate with each other (Landy & Farr, 1983).

Similarly, there are problems using turnover as a sort of performance, in part because it is difficult to distinguish between voluntary and involuntary turnover. In the same way, grievances are limited in scope and generalizability when used as performance measures, because often they are not available for nonunion employees. The major problem with using accidents as performance measures is that there is confusion about whether they are the result of people or their environments (i.e., hazardous behaviors versus hazardous environments), which calls into question the validity of such measures. Finally, rate of advancement or salary increases are poor criteria; the rate may be controlled by a quota, or salary adjustments may reflect organizational health (economic) but not individual performance.

Landy and Farr (1983) have identified several problems that seem to cut across the domain of objective performance indices and possible reasons why psychologists have focused more strongly on judgmental measures, especially for evaluating managerial behavior. First, objective measures such as absence measures tend to have low reliability (i.e., there is considerable measurement error in most assessments of absenteeism). One reason for the low reliability in this class of measures is that the observation period may be not stable across measures. For example, assessing absence during a one-week period and then correlating it with another week may yield a low correlation because a longer period is required for a reliable measure (Chadwick-Jones, Brown, Nicholson, & Sheppard, 1971; Farr, O'Leary, & Bartlett, 1971; Ilgen & Hollenback, 1977; Latham & Pursell, 1975). Further, factors external to the individual such as the organization's sick-leave policies may influence the reliability of absence measures. Second, objective measures tend to be available for only a limited number of jobs. For example, it would not be sensible to collect tardiness or absence measures from sales representatives or from corporate managers who may not have a predetermined or fixed eight-hour workday. Finally, Landy and Farr (1983) cite the changing nature of skilled and semi-skilled work as an important limitation to objective performance measures. For example, because operators are being replaced by machine tenders, productivity measures such as output are more dependent upon machine functions than individual performance. The changing nature of work suggests that objective measures may be even less appropriate for evaluating worker performance and subjective measures may become even more important.

Both Heneman (1986) and Bommer, Johnson, Rich, Podsakoff, and MacKenzie (1995) have examined the relationship between objective and subjective measures of job performance, and in general, they found that objective measures (e.g., output counts) were not strongly related to subjective measures such as performance ratings (they reported correlations in the .20s to .30s). However, Bommer et al. (1995) suggested that these two classes of measures were sometimes quite highly correlated, in particular when both objective and subjective measures were designed to tap the same constructs. This suggests that the frequent disjunction between objective and subjective measures of performance may not be an indicator of the fallibility of raters' judgments but rather an indicator of a failure to adequately measure the entire range of behaviors that constitute job performance. Because objective measures often capture only a part of most jobs (e.g., they rarely provide information about contextual performance or counterproductive behavior) supervisory ratings or some other form of subjective measure often represent the only feasible choice for measuring job performance.

Why Objective Measurement Is Often Impossible

There are many ways a measure can fail. First, all measures include some random measurement error, and excessive measurement error (i.e., low reliability) can doom *any* measure. Second, measures might exhibit *criterion contamination* and/or *criterion deficiency*. Figure 3.1 illustrates these two concepts. A measure shows criterion deficiency if it fails to adequately tap or cover the construct it is designed to measure. For example, suppose we measured the job performance of police officers by the number of arrests that he or she made. This *is* part of the job, but it is only part of the job and officers who make few arrests might nevertheless be very effective in their jobs.

A measure shows criterion contamination if scores are influenced by irrelevant constructs or constructs outside of the range of what you are trying to measure. For example, if performance ratings are higher for ratees who are highly agreeable than for those who are not, even though there are no systematic differences in their performance, we would think of agreeableness as an irrelevant construct that biases performance ratings.

It is often the case that objective measures will be available to capture some aspects of job performance, but that they will fail to capture others (e.g., organizational citizenship, quality of performance). Indeed, the main reason so many organizations rely on ratings or other subjective measures is because the objective measures that are available are likely to be recognized as deficient. Even in jobs where objective metrics are extremely important (e.g., in sales), there are often important parts of the job (e.g., completing paperwork accurately, passing customer feedback to appropriate members of

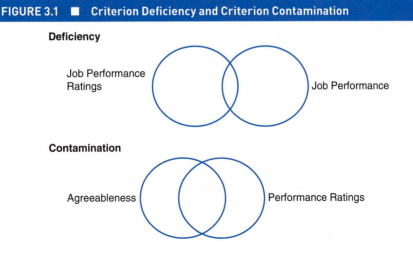

FIGURE 3.1 ■ Criterion Deficiency and Criterion Contamination

Deficiency

Job Performance Ratings   Job Performance

Contamination

Agreeableness   Performance Ratings

the organization, assisting coworkers) that will not be adequately covered by objective measures. Thus, the frequent reliance on subjective measures of performance in organizations is not necessarily an endorsement of subjectivity, but rather a recognition that objective measures are rarely sufficient for capturing the complex and wide-ranging construct of job performance.

SUMMARY

The first challenge in evaluating job performance is to determine what "performance" really means. Modern models of job performance include a number of distinct components, notably task performance, contextual performance, or organizational citizenship and counterproductive workplace behavior. As jobs are becoming more complex, the importance of adaptive and ethical performance is also becoming more obvious.

The multidimensional nature of performance implies that two employees in the same job whose work behavior is very dissimilar might nevertheless show similar levels of overall job performance, even if they get to that level in very different ways (e.g., by excelling in task performance, by showing consistently high levels of citizenship). It also means that different supervisors or managers who value one type of performance more than another might come to very different conclusions about the effectiveness of particular employees, even if they agree completely about the work behaviors they have observed.

Finally, it is useful to think about the similarities and differences in performance as you move across levels of analysis. That is, the things that make an individual worker a very good employee might not be the same as the things that make a work team highly effective. The effectiveness of departments, divisions, or even whole organizations might be defined in quite different terms. Regardless of the level of analysis chosen, some choices need to be made about whether to rely on objective or subjective measures of job performance. The long and unsuccessful history of attempts to develop objective performance measures in most jobs suggests that we will have no choice but to rely on the informed opinions of supervisors, managers, or other raters when evaluating job performance. As several of the following chapters will show, there are things we can do to improve the quality and fairness of these judgments, but at present there is no way to avoid relying on judgment when evaluating the performance of individuals in most jobs.

ANALYSIS: VALUES AND VALIDATION—HOW THE DEFINITION OF PERFORMANCE INFLUENCES CONCLUSIONS TEST VALIDITY

Suppose an organization is considering using a test to select among applicants, and there are 20 positions to be filled. How do we know whether or not the test is valid for that purpose? The usual strategy is to conduct a criterion-related validity study (i.e., a study that examines the relationship between test scores and some criterion). Most of the chapters in this book focus in one way or another on the most common criterion measure in a study

of this sort, performance ratings, but there are a wide range of criteria that might be considered. For example, Murphy (2009) outlined five different definitions of what might constitute a good hiring decision, by hiring the 20 applicants most likely to (1) perform the core technical tasks of their job well, (2) perform behaviors (e.g., organizational citizenship) that support the organization's overall ability to function as a unit, (3) support their coworkers and reduce unnecessary conflict and stress in the workplace, (4) minimize the likelihood that the organization will be drawn into controversy and litigation (e.g., over equal employment opportunity), or (5) maximize the likelihood that a stable workforce will be hired. Three of these five types of criteria involve focusing on different dimensions of performance (task performance, OCBs, CWBs), and any of these might represent plausible definitions of good performance. The same test might be viewed as highly valid in reference to some of these criteria and essentially useless in reference to others.

In the end, the definition of "good performance" represents a choice—a choice to emphasize some aspects of performance over others. That is, in some organizations, "job performance" might be essentially synonymous with "task performance," whereas in others OCBs, CWBs, adaptive behaviors, and so on might be important in defining performance. If the definition of "good performance" is a choice to emphasize some aspects of performance and deemphasize others, it is worth asking just who makes this choice and when. Cleveland, Murphy, and Colella (2017) note that choices about how to define performance are made by powerful members of the organization, and are often made in ways that benefit and reinforce these members. For example, given the disparity in family responsibilities, it is

likely that the choice to define good performance in terms of a high level of task proficiency and task involvement will benefit male employees and harm female employees, because this definition of good performance requires employees to put the interests of the organization first, something that can be hard for female employees with disproportionally demanding family roles to do. Cleveland et al. (2017) argue that one explanation for gender differences in career outcomes is that powerful members of organizations, who are almost always men, tend to gravitate toward definitions of performance that are male-friendly.

We suspect that in many organizations, the working definition of "good performance" is not so much a matter of a conscious choice to emphasize task performance more than OCBs or OCBS more than CWBs, but rather it is a manifestation of the more general climate and culture of the organization. In many ways, organizations might benefit if the choice of which performance dimensions to emphasize *was* a conscious, thoughtful decision. We think it is valuable to ask the question, "How does this organization define good performance?" but perhaps even more important to ask, "Is this the way we *want* to define good performance?" Asking careful questions about what the organization values and why can be a very good place to start the process of analyzing and improving the climate and culture of an organization.

NOTES

1. There are other models that attempt to accomplish the same goals as the Campbell models (e.g., Murphy, 1989b), but none have achieved the same level of empirical support as the models developed by Campbell and his colleagues.

2. Hofmann, Jacobs, and Baratta (1993) present additional evidence of dynamic performance in sales jobs.

3. See, for example, Schmidt, Hunter, McKenzie, and Muldrow (1979).

4. Similar points have been made by ethnographers for over 70 years (e.g., Whyte, 1943).

5. http://www.shrm.org/hrdisciplines/ safetysecurity/articles/pages/employee-theft-costs-retailers-billions.aspx

THE PERFORMANCE APPRAISAL PROCESS

4

THE FOUR KEY CHALLENGES TO PERFORMANCE APPRAISAL

Performance appraisals have a very high failure rate; up to 90% of appraisal systems in organizations are viewed as ineffective (Pulakos, Mueller-Hanson, Arad, & Moye, 2015; Smith, Hornsby, & Shirmeyer, 1996). Performance management systems do not seem to fare much better; the conclusion that performance management is broken is shared among many researchers (Pulakos & O'Leary, 2011; Pulakos et al., 2015). Given the very high rate of apparent failure of performance appraisal and performance management systems, it is unlikely that the shortcomings of these systems are simple or easy to fix. Rather, this sort of failure rate suggests that there are broad, systematic problems with the way we typically evaluate job performance, provide feedback, and act on that feedback. In this chapter, we describe in a general way the four most important reasons why performance appraisal systems fail in organizations. This chapter lays out broad conceptual arguments about why performance appraisal systems fail. In Chapters 5–12, we examine in more detail the research, theory, and insights from practical applications of performance appraisal that are relevant to understanding these four seeds of failure. In Chapters 13 and 14, we discuss ways of creating performance appraisal systems that might overcome at least some of these challenges, and that provide organizations an opportunity to obtain useful measures of the performance of their employees.

There are several obvious shortcomings in the performance appraisal systems in many organizations. First, they are often expensive and time-consuming. For example, Buckingham and Goodall (2015) tallied the amount of time spent at Deloitte on performance appraisal (e.g., meetings, time spent filling out forms) and concluded that over *2 million hours* per year were spent evaluating the performance of 65,000 employees. This investment of time and resources might be justified if managers and employees saw concrete benefits, but in many organizations very little actually happens as a result of performance appraisals. Thus, performance appraisal often looks like a lot of pain for very little gain. Employees do not feel that they receive useful feedback, and when they *are* given feedback, they do not often change. No matter how much time and effort is invested in performance appraisal, there is little clear evidence that performance appraisal is actually contributing to the success of individuals or organizations.

LEARNING OBJECTIVES

4.1 Learn about the challenges supervisors and managers face when trying to evaluate the performance of their subordinates

4.2 Understand the ways both proximal and distal context factors influence the way performance appraisal is conducted and used in organizations

4.3 Understand the range of uses of performance appraisal and the potential for these uses to come into conflict

4.4 Consider the factors that motivate supervisors and managers to inflate the performance ratings they provide

We see issues such as the cost of performance appraisals and the lack of clear benefits to individuals and organizations as symptoms or indicators of the failure of performance appraisal, not as root causes. That is, high costs and questionable benefits are *symptoms* of failure, but they do not explain *why* appraisal systems appear to fail in so many organizations. In our view, the problem is not with the surface features of appraisal systems, such as the types of scales used to evaluate performance, the way raters are trained, or the frequency of appraisal and feedback meetings. Rather, there are four structural causes that we believe are at the heart of the failure of performance appraisal systems.

THE STRUCTURAL CAUSES OF FAILURE

Our review of research, theory, and practice in the area of performance appraisal leads us to conclude that there are four core problems at the heart of most performance appraisal systems in organizations. First, the task of evaluating performance, even under the most favorable conditions, is a very difficult one. Second, there are numerous layers of contextual variables, ranging from broad national cultures to the climate and culture of the organization, to the nature of the relationships between individual raters and ratees that complicate the design, implementation, and interpretation of performance appraisals, and that allow nonperformance factors to systematically influence the evaluation of individual performance. Third, organizations often use the same performance appraisal system for multiple purposes, and these purposes are often in conflict. Finally, there are a number of social and political factors in organizations that motivate most raters to give high ratings, regardless of the rater's judgments about the performance and effectiveness of each rate. For example, 99.9% of the federal employees examined in a recent Government Accounting Office report were rated "Fully Effective" or higher (GAO, 2016). This pervasive rating inflation undermines many of the potential uses of performance appraisals, and efforts to overcome this inflation (e.g., by relying on ranking or forced distributions rather than on performance ratings) create their own problems in the measurement of job performance.

The Task of Measuring Performance Is Inherently Difficult

Suppose you supervise seven skilled production workers in a small electronics manufacturing facility. You are asked to evaluate the performance of these seven employees each year. Doing a good job of measuring performance entails several steps, each of which can be challenging. First, you must obtain information about each of your subordinates and have some level of assurance that this information is representative of their overall performance. It is common for supervisors to have limited opportunities to directly observe their subordinates as they perform their job, especially if workers are dispersed in ways that makes it impossible to observe all employees simultaneously. You might try to solve this problem by walking through the workplace on an irregular schedule (this is one component of what Peters and Waterman, 2004, describe as "management by walking around"), but it is likely that your subordinates will know (at least part of the time) when they are being watched, and that they will be on their best behavior when you are in sight. Thus, while you might obtain a lot of information by walking around and observing, you will always have to worry about the possibility that what you see is not representative of what happens on a regular basis in the workplace.

Having obtained information, you must do two things: (1) make sense of what you have seen (encoding information), and (2) recall at some later time what you observed. Performance appraisals are often an annual affair (often performed in conjunction with the determination of pay raises), so you might have to encode and recall a lot of information. We know a great deal about human memory (Chapter 5 reviews this research), and it is likely to be a significant challenge to correctly recall information over a much shorter time, much less recalling information about performance that occurs over the course of a year.

Suppose you clear the first several hurdles and are able to obtain, make sense of, and accurately recall representative information about each subordinate's performance. You will next be faced with the problem of integrating all of that information. Most employees will exhibit a mix of good and poor performance over time, perhaps showing distinct strengths and weaknesses, or perhaps simply showing some inconsistency in their behavior. Your task will be to integrate information about performance that may vary over time, and that may exemplify a mix of things an employee typically does very well and things he or she typically does less well.

The next challenge supervisors face is to apply consistent and correct evaluative standards. It will not do you much good if you correctly observe, encode, recall, and integrate information if your definition of what constitutes good versus poor performance is both idiosyncratic and inconsistent with the standards other members of the organization rely upon.

Of course, obtaining good measures of performance is only the start of what it would take to make performance appraisal effective. DeNisi and Pritchard (2006) presented a detailed model that relates features of performance appraisal and performance management systems with the motivation to improve performance. This model suggests that the links are far from simple. For example, they note the following:

- Performance appraisal and performance management systems that make the relationship between an employee's actions and the results of those actions clear will be associated with higher levels of performance improvement.

- Performance appraisal and performance management systems that increase the employee's capability to perform well (e.g., through a developmental focus) or that provide adequate resources and authority to employees to allow them to perform their jobs will be associated with higher levels of performance improvement.

- Performance appraisal and performance management systems that result in high levels of agreement across rating sources will be associated with higher levels of performance improvement.

- Performance appraisal and performance management systems that provide clear expectations and performance standards will be associated with higher levels of performance improvement.

- Performance appraisal and performance management systems viewed as fair and unbiased will be associated with higher levels of performance improvement.

- Performance appraisal and performance management systems that provide consistent evaluations over time will be associated with higher levels of performance improvement.

- Performance appraisal and performance management systems that consistently link performance with rewards and sanctions will be associated with higher levels of performance improvement.

- Performance appraisal and performance management systems that produce outcomes that are consistent with employees' needs and preferences will be associated with higher levels of performance improvement.

As Chapters 5–12 show, there are barriers to virtually all of the suggestions listed above, and it is difficult to develop a performance appraisal or performance management system that provides good measures of performance *and* makes appropriate use of those measures.

Thus, the first of the seeds of failure for performance appraisal systems is that they ask supervisors or other raters to successfully execute a very challenging task—to arrive at well-founded and consistent evaluations of the performance of each subordinate, and then turn these evaluations into useful performance feedback. Even under optimal conditions (e.g., where there are few stressors or distractions and where the task of observing and evaluation performance is a top priority), it is difficult to do this consistently and well. Under more normal conditions, where performance evaluation is only one of many tasks the supervisor is charged with and where there are multiple distractions and barriers to successful evaluation, this task is even more challenging. Most supervisors, managers, and executives do not work under conditions that are especially favorable for completing the task of performance appraisal, and it is no wonder that the measures that *are* obtained are somewhat suspect.

Finally, it is worth remembering that the task of performance appraisal is not only difficult in a technical sense, it is also a stressful and emotionally draining task (Pearce & Porter, 1986). In several later chapters, we will discuss in some detail research on the discomfort raters and ratees experience when they confront the task of performance appraisal, and especially the task of giving and receiving feedback. Performance appraisal is one of the least favorite activities for raters, and it is hardly a picnic for the employees they rate.

Contextual Factors Influence Appraisals

Performance appraisal does not occur in a vacuum, but rather in the context of many important and impactful variables, ranging from the values of the society in which the organization is located to the climate, culture, and norms of the organization, to the particular values, assumptions, and experiences of the supervisor and his or her subordinates. All of these can influence the way performance appraisal is carried out and used in organizations, as well as the reactions of managers, supervisors, and employees to the performance appraisal system. A number of authors have emphasized the importance of contextual variables (e.g., Judge & Ferris, 1993; Mitchell, 1983; Murphy & Cleveland, 1995), and research on contextual influences on performance appraisal and performance has emerged as an important area of study. This research is reviewed in detail in the next chapter.

The reason why contextual factors are important is that they influence the way people implement, use, and interpret performance appraisal. Thus, the performance appraisal systems in two different organizations might both yield equally accurate and relevant information about the performance of the people being rated, but the way that information is interpreted, used, or ignored might vary considerably because of differences in national cultures, organizational policies and practices, or even supervisor–subordinate relationships.

The term "context" can refer to variables at a number of different levels of analysis, as illustrated in Figure 4.1. Most generally, there are two categories of contextual influences: (1) distal context variables that have a generally indirect influence on performance appraisal, and (2) proximal variables that are more directly related to the performance appraisal practices and to the effects of performance appraisal. For example, both broad cultural variables (e.g., the extent to which a culture is collectivistic versus individualistic) and legal and economic variables (e.g., whether personnel practices are legally regulated, whether the job market is very tight or very loose) can indirectly influence performance appraisals by helping to set conditions that make different approaches to conducting and using performance appraisal more or less likely to succeed. More proximal variables, such as the organization's policies regarding how and why it conducts appraisals, or the nature of the relationship between supervisors and subordinates in a particular work group, have a more direct influence on the way performance appraisal is conducted and used and the reactions of users to the performance appraisal system. Thus, the same appraisal system, placed in different contexts, may end up looking, feeling, and working in quite different ways.

Two of the most widely studied facets of contexts or environments are turbulence and munificence (Katz & Kahn, 1978; March & Simon, 1958; Thompson, 1967). Turbulence refers to the extent to which the environment changes or remains stable. For example, Katz and Kahn (1978) note that the economic environment of Western nations was highly turbulent in the 1970s, with unpredictable swings between inflation and depression. Turbulent environments are thought to lead to uncertainty in organizations; this uncertainty could affect performance appraisal practices. For example, organizations

FIGURE 4.1 ■ Levels of Contextual Variables

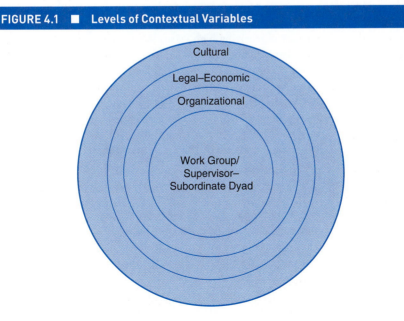

facing uncertainty may be less willing to commit resources to developing employees and may place less emphasis on developmental feedback in their performance appraisal systems. Munificence refers to the degree of scarcity versus abundance of critical resources in the environment. For example, when unemployment is high, the labor market is, from the organization's point of view, a munificent environment. When the organization is flush with money, the environment for creating performance-based rewards is munificent. Scarcity of critical resources is likely to lead to conflict within organizations (March & Simon, 1958). The implications of this conflict will depend largely on which environments are munificent, and which are plagued by scarcity.

For example, if the labor market is very tight, performance appraisals may be used quite differently than if the physical environment is characterized by abundance. If the labor market is very tight, organizations will have an incentive to reward and retain good performers, whereas a looser labor market might make organizations more open to terminating poor performers and attempting to replace them with better-qualified job applicants. Katz and Kahn (1978) noted five aspects of the environment that organizations must monitor and respond to in order to be effective: (a) societal values, (b) the political/legal environment, (c) the economic/labor environment, (d) the information/technological environment, and (e) the physical/geographical environment. Each of these aspects of the environment is likely to affect performance appraisal in some way, with some having a more direct impact on appraisal (i.e., legal environment may act like a proximal cue, that directly influences rater behavior), and others (e.g., societal values) having a very indirect, but nevertheless important, effect on performance appraisals.

How Does the Context Affect Appraisal?

Murphy and Cleveland (1995) identified six variables that appeared most likely to mediate the relationship between contextual variable (particularly distal context) and performance appraisal: (1) performance standards, (2) the choice of performance dimensions, (3) the frequency of appraisal, (4) the quality of supervisor–subordinate relations, (5) the consequences of receiving high versus low ratings, and (6) the perceived legitimacy of the appraisal system. These six variables do not exhaust the list of possible mediating variables, but they do give us a basis for describing the different ways in which various aspects of the environment might indirectly affect performance appraisal.

Environments are complex, and different aspects of the environment could have different effects on each of the intervening variables listed above. To help structure our discussion of environmental effects, we will restrict our attention to the effects of the munificence of the five aspects of the environment identified by Katz and Kahn (1978). Munificence can be defined in the following ways for each aspect of the environment: (a) societal—the extent to which socio-political norms and values support the concept of performance appraisal, as typically practiced in organizations; (b) legal—the extent to which the legal system facilitates and allows typical performance appraisal practices; (c) economic—extent to which general economic conditions are favorable for the organization; (d) technical—extent to which an organization possesses or controls the technology and work methods needed to carry out the organization's functions; and (e) physical—the extent to which necessary physical resources are available.

Murphy and Cleveland's (1995) review suggested that some contextual variables had stronger effects on particular mediators than on others; some of their more important conclusions are summarized in Table 4.1. For example, the question of whether we should expect all workers to perform well, or should we set standards that allow some workers to succeed and others to fail might depend on the values of society as a whole. A society that emphasizes competition and achievement might lead to different (probably higher) performance standards than one that emphasizes satisfaction with work. The legal system probably also affects performance standards, although to a lesser degree. That is, the legal system may not have a direct effect on standards (i.e., raising or lowering standards), but it is likely to affect the degree to which standards are made explicit, as well as the degree to which they are enforced. A legal system that is basically antagonistic to performance appraisal will probably lead to the formulation of explicit, concrete standards that are communicated directly to employees.

We would expect different (higher) performance standards during a business recession than during a period of economic growth or stability. We would also expect the technological position of a company to affect standards. A company that is behind the times technologically might try to compensate by setting high standards; a company that is technologically sophisticated might not see strong links between the performance standards enforced for individual workers and the output of the organization. Companies that employ assembly-line technologies might have different performance standards than companies that rely on semi-autonomous work teams to produce their product. Finally, the effects of physical munificence are likely to be very similar in strength to those of economic munificence, but perhaps in a different direction. When the physical resources needed for production are not available, it may be necessary to adjust performance standards downward (Peters, O'Connor, & Eulberg, 1985).

The definition of what constitutes performance and the relative importance of different parts of the performance domain are likely to be affected by the environment. A comparison of American versus Japanese management styles provides an example of societal influences. An American manager is likely to emphasize individual task performance, whereas a Japanese manager is likely to emphasize ability to work with the group when evaluating the performance of the same subordinate (Pascale & Athos, 1981). The legal system will probably also have a moderate influence. As the legal system becomes less munificent (i.e., less favorable to current appraisal practices), we predict that organizations will emphasize dimensions that involve clear, concrete, objective outcomes, and will de-emphasize interpersonally oriented performance dimensions.

The munificence of the economic environment will strongly affect the choice of performance dimensions. In an unfavorable economic environment, we expect that organizations will define performance in terms of short-term, bottom-line goals. Thus,

TABLE 4.1 ■ Effects of Environmental Munificence on Three Aspects of Appraisal Systems					
Aspects of Appraisal	**Aspects of Environment**				
	Societal	**Legal**	**Economic**	**Technical**	**Physical**
Standards	Strong	Moderate	Strong	Strong	Strong
Dimensions	Moderate	Moderate	Strong	Strong	Strong
Consequences	Moderate	Strong	Strong	Weak	Moderate

a supervisor who is not good at producing products but who is good at developing subordinates might receive different evaluations, depending on the economic environment. The technical environment will also have a strong impact on the choice of performance dimensions. The importance of technically oriented dimensions will probably vary across industries, and across companies with varying levels of technical sophistication.

The munificence of the physical environment will strongly affect the extent to which performance is defined in terms of efficiency versus output. When resources are scarce, the worker who produces less but conserves materials and resources might receive a more favorable evaluation than a worker who produces a great deal but is wasteful. The reverse might be the case when resources are cheap and plentiful.

One of the key determinants of whether the supervisor gives high or low ratings is the consequences that are attached to the ratings. Rating inflation is quite likely when ratings have a strong influence on salaries, promotions, and so on, and is least likely if ratings are not used to make administrative decisions (see Chapters 11 and 12). All five of aspects of the environment will have at least a moderate effect on the consequences of giving high versus low ratings; for two of the five aspects, this influence may be substantial.

SPOTLIGHT 4.1 FAILURE TO WARN
A UNIQUE PERFORMANCE APPRAISAL LAWSUIT

Gregory Anderson, a former employee of Yahoo, filed a suit alleging that Yahoo manipulated its performance appraisal system and that he received lower-than-deserved performance ratings, leading to his separation from the company. This lawsuit illustrates some of the unexpected legal conflicts that can arise as a result of the way organizations use performance appraisal.

In 2102, Yahoo adopted a performance appraisal system that required managers to evaluate the performance of each employee, comparing him or her to immediate peers.[1] Employees were placed in one of five categories (e.g., Greatly Exceeds, Occasionally Misses, Misses); the proportion placed in each category is (the lawsuit claims) fixed in advance by the organization. Employees in the lowest category are liable to be terminated.

While the facts of each case always differ, there is nothing unusual about a lawsuit alleging that a performance appraisal system has treated some employee or group of employees unfairly. What makes this case unique is that it claims that Yahoo used this appraisal system to sidestep the federal Work Adjustment and Retraining (WARN) Act. This law requires companies to give advance notice of reductions in force and to give the employees who will be laid off or released certain benefits and opportunities for alternative employment. The suit claims that Yahoo shed over 1,000 employees between late 2014 and early 2015, claiming that these employees were released due to poor performance, and that this policy resulted in a de facto layoff. In essence, by forcing a certain number of employees into the lowest performance category each year, Yahoo might be able to lay off as many employees as it wanted without triggering the WARN Act by pretending that employees were let go for performance reasons.

Employment litigation often focuses on claims of discrimination (this layoff also includes such claims), but the legal context of performance appraisal is more complex, sometimes including issues that are covered by a range of state and federal laws that have little to do with employment discrimination. Human resource managers need to be aware of the broader legal environment when designing performance appraisal systems.

[1] http://www.lexology.com/library/detail.aspx?g=024a6698-f4f7-4300-b195-363ad858a49a

Societal norms and values will have some influences on the consequences of high versus low ratings; the extent of this influence will be determined by the degree to which societal values support or discourage treating good versus poor workers differently. For example, the question of whether individuals should be rewarded in proportion to their level of performance would probably be answered differently in the United States than in Japan.

The legal system will strongly affect the degree to which performance appraisals are likely to be connected to administrative decisions. A legal system that is hostile to performance appraisal, as it is typically practiced, will also be hostile to the use of performance ratings as a primary basis for allocating organizational rewards. A legal system that strongly acknowledges management's rights to evaluate the performance of workers will probably also support linking rewards directly to performance ratings.

The lower the munificence of the economic environment (and, to a lesser extent, the physical environment), the greater the incentive to tie rewards to performance levels. We would predict that organizations will be more likely to use performance appraisals to make administrative decisions, ranging from salary and promotions to layoffs, when the economic environment is unfavorable than when it is favorable. In part this is because organizations have less slack (i.e., less ability to survive given substandard performance) in an unfavorable economic environment than in a favorable one.

In the next chapter, we will examine the influence of contextual variables, as well as the results of research on contextual influences on performance appraisal in some detail. For now, simply understanding that contextual variables influence the design, implementation, interpretation, and use of performance appraisal systems is enough to help you understand why these systems so often fail. The same performance appraisal system may work well in some contexts and poorly in others, making it hard to identify best practices that will actually work across the many contexts in which performance appraisal systems are found.

The Conflicting Purposes of Performance Appraisal in Organizations

Ratings are used for many purposes in organizations (e.g., to determine promotions and salary increases, to evaluate developmental needs, to serve as criteria for validating tests and assessments, to provide documentation for legal purposes), and these purposes often come into conflict (Cleveland, Murphy, & Williams, 1989; Murphy & Cleveland, 1995). Fifty years ago, Meyer, Kay, and French (1965) noted the incompatibility of using performance appraisal simultaneously to make decisions about rewards and to provide useful feedback, and suggested that the different uses of performance appraisal should be separated by creating different evaluative mechanisms for rewards versus feedback. The rewards versus feedback distinction continues to be an important one, but there are many uses of performance appraisal in organizations that have little to do with rewards or feedback.

Cleveland et al. (1989) reviewed studies published in several scientific and professional journals, and identified 20 different uses for performance appraisals in organizations; these uses are shown in Table 4.2. They surveyed organizations to determine the relative importance of these 20 uses for performance appraisal. Of the 20, the most important included using performance appraisals for salary administration, for identifying individual strengths and weaknesses, and for documenting personnel decisions. More to the point, every organization surveyed indicated that performance appraisals were used for multiple purposes.

TABLE 4.2 ■ Twenty Uses of Performance Appraisal
Salary administration
Promotion
Retention and termination
Recognition of individual performance
Layoffs
Identify poor performance
Identify individual performance
Performance feedback
Determine transfers and assignments
Identify individual strengths and weaknesses
Personnel planning
Determine organizational training needs
Evaluate goal achievement
Assist in goal attainment
Evaluate personnel systems
Reinforce authority structure
Identify organizational development needs
Criteria for validation research
Document personnel decisions
Meet legal requirements

Cleveland et al. (1989) noted that two of the critical uses of performance appraisal focus on using performance ratings to either identify differences *between* individuals (i.e., determining which ratees perform better than others, overall) or differences *within* individuals (i.e., determining individual strengths and weaknesses), and that many organizations use performance appraisals for both purposes. This is potentially problematic, because these two purposes can be in conflict. In particular, just about everything you do to enhance accuracy and discriminability when identifying differences between people will tend to detract for accuracy and discriminability when identifying individual strengths and weaknesses. To understand why, consider the two sets of performance profiles illustrated in Figure 4.2. The top set of profiles illustrates performance patterns that make it easy to distinguishing between employees; employee 1 is clearly the better performer. In this set of profiles, each employee is at a pretty similar level on all four performance dimensions, and if one employee is pretty good at most aspects of his or her job and another is not so good,

FIGURE 4.2 ■ Performance Profiles Illustrating Between- Versus Within-Person Differences

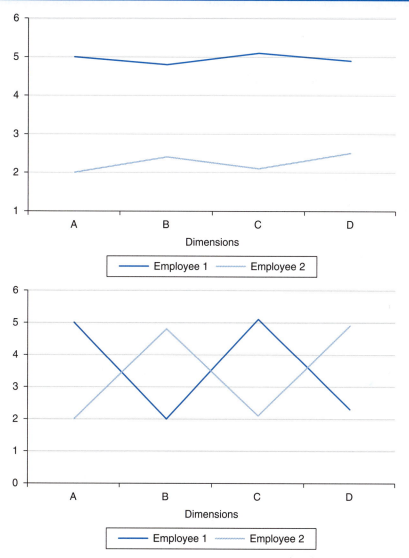

it will be relatively easy to distinguish between them. The bottom set of profiles shows performance patterns for employees who have strong strengths and weaknesses. Because of the peaks and valleys in the performance profiles, the overall performance levels of these two employees will end up being highly similar; they will both be "average" performers, even though their strengths and weaknesses are so different. A system that highlights relative strengths and weaknesses tends to produce a lot of overall ratings that are "average," making it hard to distinguish one employee from another in terms of their overall performance level.

The implications are clear. If you work hard to identify individual strengths and weaknesses, you will end up with performance profiles that classify many employees as pretty similar in terms of their overall performance level. If you work hard to identify who is the best and who is the worst performer, and where everyone else fits in that performance distribution, you will tend to end up with relatively flat profiles, which are great for distinguishing between people but almost useless for identifying individual strengths and weaknesses.

Cleveland et al.'s (1989) survey suggested that most organizations used performance appraisals for multiple conflicting purposes, and that this attempt to satisfy incompatible goals with performance appraisal is one source for the continuing evidence of dissatisfaction with performance appraisal in organizations. Some goals might be compatible. For example, use of performance appraisal for salary administration is not *necessarily* incompatible with using performance appraisal as a tool for validating selection instruments (both uses focus on differences between ratees). However, even when there is no underlying conflict among uses, the particular dynamics of one use of appraisals (e.g., for determining raises) might limit its value for other uses (e.g., the range restriction that is likely when most ratees receive high ratings might limit the value of appraisals as criteria for validating selection tests). One of the general conclusions of Cleveland et al. (1989) is that if an organization tries to do too many things with its performance appraisal system, it might end up doing *all* of them poorly.

There are many reasons why it is common for the same performance appraisal system to serve many purposes, but one is that it is hard to tell who "owns" performance appraisal. At one level, this is a system that is likely to be developed and maintained by the human resources department. At another level, it is an important part of the interaction between individual supervisors and their direct reports. At yet another level, it is a system that has potentially diagnostic value across the entire organization. For example, suppose you find that the average rating on a 5-point scale (where "4" indicates that the employee exceeds expectations and "5" indicates that the employee far exceeds expectations) is a 4.25 and that 80% of all employees receive an overall rating of 4 or 5 (this is not an unusual outcome). There are three possibilities. First, maybe the employees of this organization *are* that good. Second, it is possible that expectations are simply set too low. Third, and most likely, there is rampant rating inflation; inflation appears to be so common that you will need an organization-level explanation for this phenomenon (i.e., the explanation must involve forces that cross boundaries within the organization). This type of rating inflation is in fact quite common, and it forms the fourth explanation for the frequent failure of performance appraisal and performance management systems.

Raters Are Motivated to Distort Performance Appraisals

Imagine once again that you are the supervisor of seven employees, and it is your task to rate their performance. Based on your observations and the information you have collected, you conclude that one employee exceeds expectations for his or her job, five meet expectations, and one falls a bit short of expectations. Should you give these three groups ratings of 4, 3, and 2, respectively? The answer depends on two things. First, what goal or goals are you pursuing when you complete the performance appraisal form? If your goal is to provide accurate ratings, it is pretty clear what you should do (i.e., you should turn in one 4, five 3s, and one 2). On the other hand, suppose your goal is to motivate your employees to perform better next year. You might conclude that you are more likely to achieve this goal if you give high ratings than if you give low ones, *even when low ratings are deserved.*

Think about the possible consequences if you give a poor-performing employee the 2 he or she deserves, versus the likely consequences if he or she gets a higher rating, and perhaps a better raise or better protection from an upcoming layoff. If this employee gets a low rating, it is a good bet that he or she will resent this and see it as unfair; Chapters 9 and 11 review research that will show why this is such a common reaction. This employee will probably get a lower raise and may feel more vulnerable. It is unlikely *any* of these will motivate this employee to improve, and it is likely that these will all contribute to an antagonistic relationship between you and this employee. On the other hand, if you give this employee an inflated rating, a raise is more likely, there is less likelihood that the rating will be seen as biased or unfair, and the employee will be more secure and will possibly even feel some gratitude to you. It might be quite reasonable for a rater to purposefully give inflated ratings, because the consequences of inflated ratings might be much more positive (and perhaps even better for the organization) than the consequences of accurate ratings.

Performance appraisal is a tool for influencing the behavior of the individuals being evaluated, and a supervisor would be a fool to not at least *consider* the possibility that giving inflated ratings might be a more effective management strategy than giving accurate ratings. Put another way, if you are a manager, what would you choose: (1) a strategy that is likely to lead to resentment, lower motivation, and worse relations with your subordinate (accurate ratings), or (2) a strategy that is likely to improve your relationship with subordinates and to motivate them to perform better (rating inflation)? We do not see this as a difficult choice.

Of course, while giving inflated ratings might improve some outcomes that *you* care about as a manager, giving accurate ratings might improve some outcomes that are important to the organization, such as providing accurate criteria to be used when validating selection tests or assessments or when justifying decisions that are made on the basis of ratings. There are probably some uses of ratings where inflated ratings are better than accurate ones and others where the reverse is true, and there are likely to be some instances where top management will want raters to act against their self-interest to provide accurate rather than inflated ratings. Whether and under what conditions this expectation might be a reasonable one will be examined in Chapters 13 and 14.

SUMMARY

If performance appraisal failed in some organizations and was seen as a rousing success in others, we might try to identify specific aspects of the appraisal system that caused it to fail, such as bad rating scales or inadequate training. By all indications, the failure of performance appraisal and performance management systems is the norm rather than the exception, and where there is broad systematic failure, it is best to look for broad systematic causes. Our review of more than a century of performance appraisal research suggests that there are at least four broad causes for the failure of performance appraisal systems.

First, under even the most favorable circumstances, it is hard to accurately evaluate the performance of several individuals over time. Performance rating is rarely done under favorable circumstances; rather, the observation and evaluation of performance is just one of many duties most supervisors and managers take on. Second, context matters, so that an appraisal system that seems successful in one setting might fail dismally in another, and the same intervention (e.g., more rater training) might have quite different effects in different settings. Context is a complex construct that can be defined at many levels, and the effects of some context variables (e.g., national cultures) might work in the opposite direction of the effects of others (e.g., organizational culture).

Third, performance appraisal systems are used for many purposes in organizations, and these purposes may place conflicting demands on the system. In this chapter, we have highlighted the conflict between two uses of performance appraisal—that is, for distinguishing *between* individuals versus distinguishing *within* individuals, but as we will show in Chapter 8, there are many possible purposes and many possible sources of conflict surrounding performance appraisal.

Finally, the dynamics of performance appraisal in many organizations set up a number of incentives to inflate ratings, while at the same time creating disincentives for accuracy in performance appraisal. These incentives sometimes involve the rater's self-interest (e.g., a rater who claims that all of his subordinates are performing well also ends up looking like a successful manager), but organizations can benefit from rating inflating as well, at least if inflation is more likely than accuracy to help supervisors maintain positive relations with their subordinates and to motivate employees to perform better in the future. More than 30 years ago, Banks and Murphy (1985) noted that raters do not turn in inflated ratings because they *can't* accurately evaluate performance, but rather because they *do not want to*. In several of the chapters that follow, we will examine research on what motivates raters to provide accurate versus distorted ratings, and how this research can be used to help build better performance evaluation systems.

EXERCISE: MAINTAIN A BEHAVIOR DIARY

Performance appraisal researchers have tried a number of strategies for making the task of observing and evaluating the behavior of employees more manageable. One that has received consistent support is the use of behavior diaries. Several studies have shown that taking notes about the behaviors different employees show in the workplace can make evaluation more reliable and valid. However, the task of maintaining a behavior diary is not a simple one. The best way to get an appreciation of the costs and benefits of behavior diaries is to try this method out.

For a week, try and take reasonably frequent notes about the behaviors of four or five individuals who you regularly observe. The notes should be in behavioral form, describing *what* each person did. For example, if you are observing call center workers, something like "Jane presented several potential solutions to the caller she was working on" would be a behavioral note, whereas "Jane had a very good call" would not be behavioral information. At the end of a week, ask yourself several questions:

- What did you write down?—The best behavior diaries will include a mix of behaviors, some illustrating good, poor, or average performance incidents, but many behavior diaries are dominated by incidents of very good or very bad performance.

- How much did you write down?—You might find yourself starting out by taking notes on a regular basis, but also find out that the notes start to tail off quickly.

- Are your observations representative?—Do you record behaviors pretty much as they occur, or only the outstanding and unusual ones?

- Are your observations driven by prior impressions?—If Joe is generally a good performer and Sally is generally a poor performer, you might find that you only record good behaviors for Joe and poor performance instances for Sally.

- How intrusive is the task?—Time and energy you devote to maintaining a behavior diary might have been spent doing other things. What sorts of tasks are displaced by the need to record behaviors?

We think a short "test drive" will give you a concrete sense of the costs and benefits of maintaining behavior diaries. While the research on the potential contributions of this method is both solid and supportive, many of the studies of this method involve students whose only task is to take diaries, and who do this over a fairly short period. Before you commit yourself or your organization to this strategy, we think it is very valuable to try the method out and make an informed judgment about whether or not this strategy is likely to be helpful in your organization

5

OBTAINING INFORMATION AND EVALUATING PERFORMANCE

LEARNING OBJECTIVES

5.1 Understand the advantages and disadvantages of using peers, self-ratings, and subordinate ratings versus or as adjuncts to ratings from direct supervisors and managers

5.2 Learn how electronic performance monitoring is used in organizations and why it is not always a good substitute for judgmental measures of performance

5.3 Understand the roles of attention and memory in determining the performance judgments of supervisors and managers

5.4 Learn how liking and affect can influence performance ratings

5.5 Understand the processes used to set performance goals and standards

Performance appraisal requires people to make judgments about job performance based on observations they have made, knowledge they have obtained, and information they might receive. In this chapter, we consider two important facets of this process: (1) *who*—who should be charged with the task of evaluating job performance, and what are the advantages and disadvantages of different options an organization might consider? and (2) *how*—how does that person or set of persons acquire and make sense of the information needed to make these judgments? The *who* question is strongly related to a number of factors discussed in previous chapters. For instance, the question of who is given the responsibility of evaluating performance might depend on cultural factors (both national and organizational cultures) as well as the purpose of performance appraisal (different evaluators might make sense, depending on the purpose of performance appraisal in a particular organization).

Traditionally, the question of *who* completes your performance appraisal has rarely been an issue. In most organizations, appraisals are completed by one's immediate supervisor or manager, and each supervisor or manager in an organization has been solely responsible for evaluating his or her direct reports. Supervisory evaluations are still very important, and it is the norm in virtually all organizations that use performance appraisal to collect evaluations from supervisors, but there are many other options. It might be feasible to obtain evaluations of performance from self-ratings, from peers, from subordinates or customers, or some combination of any of these. Indeed, many organizations use some sort of multisource evaluation or feedback system, and it is not unusual to collect performance evaluations and feedback from many sources (Morgeson, Mumford, & Campion, 2005).

The *how* issue is to some extent distinct from many of the issues that have been discussed in previous chapters, although the structure of workplaces and organizations can have a bearing on precisely how information about performance is obtained. For example, both the content of what people observe or consider, and the standards they use to evaluate that information, are substantially influenced by the context in which performance appraisal occurs. Nevertheless, there are some cognitive processes involved in forming judgments about job performance that are likely to operate similarly in a wide range of different contexts.

WHO SHOULD EVALUATE PERFORMANCE

In discussing the different players who might be involved in evaluating a person's performance, we find it useful to arrange this discussion in terms of the distance between the target and the evaluator. Thus, we will start by considering self-ratings, then move on to the rating source that is most proximal and most similar to the target – i.e., peers. We then consider supervisors, and finally other sources (e.g., subordinates, customers, some combination of multiple sources).

Self-Ratings

Many performance rating systems include self-ratings, and there is evidence that these ratings influence the judgments of supervisors; employees who give themselves higher self-ratings tend to receive higher ratings from their supervisors (Shore, Adams, & Tashchian, 1998). There are several reasons why it might be useful to include self-ratings as a part of performance appraisal. First, asking for self-ratings at the same time as you are asking supervisors to evaluate performance may help supervisors and subordinates adopt a common frame of reference when discussing job performance, particularly if both self-ratings and supervisory ratings are obtained on the same set of performance dimensions. By focusing both raters and rates on specific aspects of performance over the past year (or over some other period for organizations that obtain performance ratings on a different schedule), including self-ratings in the process might help raters and ratees reach some common understandings of what the ratee did well and what he or she did poorly during the rating period. Self-ratings also give employees some voice in the appraisal process, which can enhance perceptions of the fairness and reasonableness of the appraisal system (Korsgaard & Roberson, 1995; Lizzio, Wilson, & MacKay, 2008; Whiting, Podsakoff, & Pierce, 2008). That is, asking ratees to evaluate their own performance implies that the organization values their perspective and takes their input seriously. Unfortunately, including self-ratings in a performance appraisal system can be a source of conflict, because self-ratings and supervisory ratings often disagree. In particular, it is common to find that self-ratings are higher than supervisory ratings of performance (Harris & Schaubroeck, 1988; Meyer, 1980; Thornton, 1980). In fact, one source of resistance to including self-ratings in performance appraisal is the belief that they are often unrealistically high.

Are Self-Ratings Inflated?

The finding that self-ratings of job performance tend to be higher than supervisory ratings has been so widely replicated that the question is not *whether* self-ratings are likely to be higher than ratings from others, but rather *why* self-ratings are so high. One possibility is that inflated self-ratings are a result of *fundamental attribution error* (Jones & Nisbett, 1971; Ross, 1977) that is, the tendency to explain one's successes in terms of stable personal factors (e.g., ability, effort) and explain failures in terms of unstable situational factors (e.g., bad luck, someone else cheating), whereas others' successes are attributed to these situational factors, while their failures are attributed to lack of ability or lack of effort.

This asymmetry in understanding why people succeed or fail will lead you to overestimate your own performance (because you see yourself as responsible for your success, but see situational explanations for your failures) and underestimate others' performance (e.g., believing others' success is due to luck or cheating). While this error is widely cited in social psychology, evidence for its effects is somewhat equivocal. On the whole, there is clearer evidence for biases in explanations for one's own success than for biases in explaining one's own failures (Miller & Ross, 1975). Nevertheless, there is a good deal of evidence that this bias in our perceptions of our own performance versus the performance of others will lead to systematic over-rating of one's own performance and systematic under-rating of others' performance (Campbell, Campbell, & Ho-Beng, 1998).

The fact that self-ratings are usually higher than supervisory ratings is not by itself necessarily evidence of the invalidity of self-ratings, since it is possible that self-ratings are accurate and supervisory ratings are unduly harsh. Similarly, evidence that self-ratings are not highly correlated with supervisory ratings (Landy & Farr, 1983; Steel & Ovalle, 1984; Thornton, 1980) is difficult to evaluate, because supervisory ratings are not the optimal criteria for evaluating self-assessments. However, there are two lines of evidence that would seem to point unambiguously to deficiencies in self-ratings. First, self-ratings tend to move closer to supervisory ratings if extensive performance feedback is given (Steel & Ovalle, 1984). Second, there is evidence that self-ratings are less lenient if raters know that the ratings will be checked against some objective criterion (Farh & Werbel, 1986). The finding that self-ratings tend to be higher than ratings from *any* other source supports the hypothesis that there are self-seeking biases in self-ratings of performance.

Heidemeier and Moser (2009) propose a different explanation for inflated self-ratings, noting that external observers have access to a different set of cues and they integrate them differently than individuals do when evaluating their own performance. That is, self-ratings might be based on a different set of information than ratings provided by others. This hypothesis is consistent with the findings of Williams and Johnson (2000), who report that self–supervisor agreement is higher in environments where there is more frequent feedback and more sharing of information between supervisors and subordinates, as well as the findings of Schrader and Steiner (1996), who found that self-ratings were more similar to supervisory ratings when common standards were used for evaluating behavior in the workplace. Finally, Brutus and Fleenor (1999) note that discrepancies between self-ratings and ratings provided by others vary by gender (female employees are less likely to inflate self-ratings), age (older employees are more likely to inflate), and organizational level (managers at higher levels in the organization are more likely to inflate self-ratings than lower-level managers).

Leniency bias in self-ratings is not necessarily universal. Farh, Dobbins, and Cheng (1991) suggested that the self-ratings may be *lower* than ratings from others in Asian cultures, and that in these cultures there might be a modesty bias. Subsequent studies have painted a more complicated picture. While there are some broad differences in the levels of individualism and collectivism (cultural dimensions assumed to be responsible for leniency and modesty biases) in Asian nations as compared to North American and European nations, there is significant nation-to-nation variability, and it is unwise to assume that there are distinct East–West differences in the structure or outcomes of performance appraisal (Barron & Sackett, 2008; Yu & Murphy, 1993). Thinking about self-ratings in particular, it appears that self-ratings are sometimes higher than and sometimes lower than ratings from others in Asian nations, and that nation-specific cultural factors may be as important as broad East–West cultural differences for understanding the conditions under which self-ratings will or will not be higher than ratings from others.

In addition to cultural factors, there are characteristics of the task and the rating environment that can lead to people to under-rate their own performance. In particular, when engaging in group tasks, there is evidence that self-ratings are a bit lower than they should be, while ratings of the group's performance as a whole tend to be slightly inflated (Jourden & Heath, 1996). This tendency may be an instance of group ethnocentrism, because people consistently rate their own group as performing better than other peoples' groups. Nevertheless, this finding does suggest that, even in Western cultures, inflation of self-ratings is not a uniquely self-serving process, and that this inflation extends to one's own group, perhaps even more strongly than to self-ratings.

Do Self-Ratings Contribute to the Accuracy or Acceptance of Appraisal?

In principle, including self-ratings as part of a performance appraisal system should increase ratees' satisfaction with the appraisal process because they have some voice in their appraisal and this increases the quality of the conversation between the rater and ratee. Unfortunately, it is not clear whether self-rating delivers these advantages. Roberson, Torkel, Korsgaard, Klein, Diddams, and Cayer (1993) conducted careful evaluation of the effects of including self-ratings, randomly assigning groups of ratees to rating conditions in which both the rater and ratee provided performance ratings or conditions in which there were no self-ratings. They found no evidence of systematic improvements, and in fact found that self-rating was associated with *lower* levels of perceived influence on the appraisal discussion and lower levels of rater–ratee agreement.

From the rater's perspective, self-ratings can be problematic, especially if the rater has access to the ratee's self-rating prior to completing the performance appraisal form. Shore et al. (1998) showed that raters who know that the self-rating is high are likely to inflate the ratings they give. This makes sense, because discrepancies between supervisory ratings and self-ratings are likely to lead to conflict and discomfort when giving performance feedback; by minimizing the spread between your own rating and your subordinate's self-rating, you can avoid this conflict.

Peer Ratings

Peer rating systems have long been used in the military (Landy & Farr, 1983), but until recently, they were more rarely used in other settings (Bernardin & Klatt, 1985; McEvoy & Buller, 1987). With the introduction of 360-degree feedback systems (Dierdorff & Surface, 2007; Levy & Williams, 2004; Morgeson et al., 2005; Seifert, Yukl, & McDonald, 2003), peer ratings of performance have become substantially more common.

Peiperi (1999) noted that the success or failure of peer rating systems probably depends on a number of factors, ranging from the organizational culture and the types of positions involved to the purpose of rating and the methods used to decide who rates who. He tested an elaborate model of the likely causes and indicators of the success or failure of peer rating systems, and found strong support for some predictions (e.g., the interdependence of work and the use of performance-based rewards is related to successful peer rating), with mixed support for others (e.g., he predicted that peer ratings would be successful in cohesive cultures, but found that cohesion actually *reduces* the success of peer rating, perhaps because cohesive groups resist rating systems that attempt to distinguish performance levels within groups).

Other researchers have examined more narrow hypotheses about the determinants of peer rating success. For example, Maurer & Tarulli, 1996) report that peer ratings are more likely to be accepted if it is believed that peers have the opportunity to observe relevant behaviors.

There are some clear advantages to obtaining performance ratings from peers. Because peers often work in close proximity, they have ample opportunity to observe each other's behavior. Peers' frequent opportunity to observe task behaviors, interpersonal behaviors, and results may make them a uniquely valuable source. Wherry's theory of rating cites rater–ratee proximity as one key to accuracy in rating (Wherry & Bartlett, 1982), and this theory suggests that the opinions of peers are especially reliable because they have more opportunity than supervisors to observe each other. However, Imada (1982) cautions that there is little data to support the assumption that peers' opportunity to observe behavior is related to the accuracy of their judgments. Considerations of the work roles of peers might even suggest that their observations will *not* be the best source of information about a particular individual's performance. Unlike supervisors, evaluation of the performance of other employees is not a core part of the job, and peers may be less systematic in their observation or in their evaluation of what they observe.

Despite the shortcomings of peer ratings noted above, there is evidence for the reliability and validity of peer ratings (Gregarus & Robie, 1998; Saavedra & Kwun, 1993), and there are many reasons to believe that incorporating information from peers could improve the quality of performance appraisal. Peers often see different aspects of performance than supervisors see (especially citizenship behaviors, many of which are directed at peers), and the perspective they apply in evaluating those behaviors may be more similar to that of the ratee than the evaluative framework applied by supervisors.

There is evidence that peers anchor their ratings in terms of their own performance levels. That is, higher-performing peers have more demanding standards when evaluating others' performance (Saavedra & Kwun, 1993). There is also evidence that, like other raters, peers' judgments about the performance of their colleagues are influenced by the degree to which they like each other or have similar personalities (Antonioni & Park, 2001).

The behavior observed by peers is both quantitatively and qualitatively different from that observed by supervisors and subordinates, in that peers see both more behaviors and different behaviors than do other sources. This is particularly true in the domain of interpersonal relations. An individual may be on his or her guard when interacting with superiors or subordinates, but is more likely to behave naturally (whatever the person's natural style of interaction) among peers. Peers are also likely to encounter secondhand information about interpersonal behaviors; colleagues tend to talk about colleagues, and interpersonal issues are likely to be a frequent topic of conversation.

Resistance to Peer Rating

Despite the advantages noted above, there are several sources of resistance to the use of peer ratings in evaluating performance. First, the use of peer ratings violates the traditional power hierarchy in organizations. Traditionally, evaluations have flowed in a top-down fashion, in which people at higher authority levels evaluate the performance of their subordinates. Peer rating violates this principle. Second, the use of peer ratings puts workers in an uncomfortable position that could interfere with their ability to work together effectively. By forcing people who work side by side and who may work together on joint projects to evaluate one another, appraisal systems that include peer ratings will require workers to make hard decisions about their colleagues, increasing the possibility that negative peer feedback will make it difficult for the work group to work together well in the future. Because peers are often directly competing for the same rewards (e.g., it is common for organizations to set aside a specific amount of money for raises), peer rating systems can also introduce unhealthy competition and self-seeking behavior. That is, a person who rates his or her peers as poor performers may increase the probability that *he or she* will receive rewards that peers are denied because of the low ratings they receive. Research on peer ratings suggests that these ratings are more readily accepted if they are used for developmental purposes than if they are used to help determine pay raises or promotions (McEvoy & Buller, 1987).

The resistance to peer ratings does not seem to be connected to concerns over their psychometric shortcomings. There is ample evidence that peer ratings show levels of reliability and validity comparable to supervisory ratings (Kane & Lawler, 1978, 1980; Landy & Farr, 1983; Wexley & Klimoski, 1984). An advantage of peer ratings is that they can be pooled, a procedure that can substantially increase reliability and partially remove idiosyncratic biases of any particular rater (Kenny & Berman, 1980; Murphy, 1982a). Despite these potential advantages to including peers in performance rating, there is often substantial resistance to this idea. It appears that the resistance to peer ratings can be traced to two causes: (a) concerns over role reversals, and (b) concerns over distortion. The first issue, role reversals, has been noted earlier. Incorporation of peer ratings changes the power structure of an organization in such a way that people who are at the same level in the formal power hierarchy nevertheless have power over one another.

There are two reasons that lead many managers to conclude that peer ratings will be unduly lenient. First, it is widely believed that the friendship between peers will lead to inflated ratings (Landy & Farr, 1983). In fact, there is little evidence that friendship bias is an important factor, although bias might be a problem if the ratee is aware of individual raters' scores. A second problem, and a potentially more serious one, is range restriction. It is plausible that peers will be unwilling to differentiate good from poor performers in the work group, for fear of "rocking the boat." While this problem is no doubt present in some settings, there is little evidence to suggest that peers are any more susceptible to range restriction than are supervisors.

Supervisors as Raters

Mayhew (1983) surveyed societies and organizations ranging in time from the sixth century B.C. to the present, and in scope from the Achaemenid Empire of ancient Mesopotamia and Persia to the modern police departments, and concluded that hierarchical differentiation with a unity of the flow of authority and power from the top down is essentially universal. That is, organizations are structured so that decisions, orders, and control flow from the top levels down, with very few instances of egalitarian or bottom-up rule. One of the many manifestations of hierarchical power relations in organizations is that evaluations usually flow from higher levels to lower ones. Scott (1975) noted, "evaluation is required if power is to be employed to control behavior" (p. 134). Thus, one argument for obtaining performance evaluations from supervisors or direct managers is that it is the normal thing to do in an organization that is hierarchically structured.

Evaluation is not just a social norm; it is tied directly to the nature and key requirements of the job of supervisor or manager. A supervisor has the responsibility of making sure that his or her subordinates complete assigned tasks within the constraints of resources and budgets, so it is critical that he or she is aware of how well each subordinate is performing. Indeed, because of this responsibility for ensuring that key production or performance goals are met, a person's supervisor or direct manager is often best informed about the demands and constraints of a job and of each subordinate's success in meeting the key objectives of that job. In addition, supervisors and direct managers often have considerable direct knowledge about the job. Supervisors, in particular, are often promoted from the ranks of workers in the job they now supervise, and are thus genuine subject matter experts. It is little surprise, therefore, that input from supervisors or direct managers is an almost universal component of performance appraisal systems in organizations.

Changes in the workplace are slowly disrupting the normal flow of evaluations from the direct supervisor to the ratee. As Thomas (1999) notes, it is increasingly common to find that workers have no immediate supervisor. Consider, for example, telecommuters who work from home. There may be supervisory or managerial employees who are familiar with the *results* of their work, but it is unlikely that there is any supervisor who is familiar with the work itself. This raises the question of who (if anyone) is sufficiently qualified and sufficiently familiar with the work being performed to complete performance appraisals. To the extent that work is performed with little meaningful supervision, it is possible that performance appraisal will simply not be possible in any meaningful sense. If there is no supervisor or direct manager with knowledge about the work behavior of a particular employee, it is unlikely that there will be others in the organization who have that knowledge. It will still be possible to measure the results of performance, but if the work is done remotely, it might not be possible to measure the behaviors that constitute job performance.

Using Ratings From Subordinates in Performance Appraisal

Upward appraisals, where subordinates evaluate their superiors, are rare (Hall, Leidecher, & DiMarco, 1996), except perhaps as part of a broader 360-degree evaluation system. In many ways this is a shame, because there is evidence that upward appraisals can improve both communication and employee satisfaction. Subordinates have a unique perspective and are likely to observe and experience aspects of their supervisor's performance that are not readily observed by other potential raters. Of course, these systems can be uncomfortable for raters, who may reasonably fear that giving poor performance feedback to their supervisor will negatively influence *their* evaluations. For this reason, Hall et al. (1996) suggest that upward feedback be anonymous (e.g., supervisors could receive information about the distribution of ratings they received, without necessarily being aware of who gave what ratings). Nevertheless, the potential value of these systems would seem to suggest that they should be more common.

First, each potential rating source sees different behaviors and different outcomes, and subordinates may be able to add unique information to the performance evaluation process. Second, the use of subordinates provides an opportunity (also present in peer ratings, though perhaps to a less extent) to increase the reliability of information about performance by aggregating information from several raters. Third, the use of subordinate input in a performance appraisal system conveys a potentially powerful message about the climate and culture of the organization (i.e., its willingness to buck traditional norms), and it might even be thought of as an intervention used to influence the culture of an organization. That is, if you wanted to install a more egalitarian culture, one place to start might be to solicit input from subordinates when evaluating the performance or their supervisors and managers.

In our view, the biggest obstacle to implementing upward feedback systems is similar to the main obstacle to the use of peer ratings—it involves considerations of power and influence. Involving subordinates in evaluation is an even more serious violation of the status hierarchy than involving peers (Dornbusch & Scott, 1975; Thompson, 1967).

The typical definition of a supervisor in an organization is as someone who has the right and responsibility to evaluate the performance of some number of employees who report to him or her. Upward feedback violates this fundamental dynamic, upending the power hierarchy in organizations. The rigid distinction between management and labor, or between supervisors and subordinates, is violated if subordinates evaluate their superiors *and* those evaluations are taken seriously. Some organizations might be happy to upend this hierarchy, but hierarchical organization is still certainly the norm, and upward feedback may often turn out to be uncomfortable to both raters and ratees.

SPOTLIGHT 5.1 ARE YOU A BIASED RATER?

One of the common concerns in traditional performance appraisal systems is that rater biases can influence performance ratings. Raters might be biased against members of particular groups (e.g., racial and ethnic minorities, older workers, women) or they might simply be biased in favor of or against particular individuals who they like or dislike. While many people think their manager or supervisor is a biased rater, few people think they themselves are biased. However, with the widespread availability of the Implicit Association Test (IAT), peoples' beliefs about their ability to give ratings that are unbiased or fair is increasingly being challenged.

The IAT is a computerized test that purports to reveal peoples' biases, even ones people are completely unaware of (Greenwald, McGhee, & Schwartz, 1998). There are many variations of the IAT (Harvard's Project Implicit offers tests assessing biases involving sexuality, race, skin tone, weight, age, religions, and many other categories), but in general, they involve computerized tasks that require you to associate pictures with concepts, as quickly as possible. For example, you might be presented with a picture of a face and classify it, as quickly as you can, with "Old" or "Young" categories. There are many different tasks that are used in IATs, but the general idea is that small but consistent differences in the speed of association and in the links people make between

pictures and categories reveal hidden biases. It is not unusual for people to take a test of this sort and come away saying, "I never realized I was biased against...."

There are significant questions about the meaning and validity of IAT scores (Greenwald, Banaji, & Nosek, 2015; Oswald, Mitchell, Blanton, Jaccard, & Tetlock, 2013). For example, suppose you found, using an IAT, that a particular rater was biased against people of different races. Does that mean that he or she would be likely to give lower ratings to minority group members he or she supervises? The best answer is that nobody knows. There are often significant problems using results from social psychology experiments to predict important outcomes in organizations (Copus, Uglow, & Sohn, 2005), and it is not clear whether differences of a few milliseconds in the speed of associating pictures to concepts will tell you much about how a supervisor will evaluate people who he observes and works with on a day-to-day basis.

It is a good bet that if you take the IAT, you will be shown to exhibit biases toward or against some groups, possibly toward or against many groups. Does this mean you cannot give people a fair shake when you evaluate their performance? In our view, it is a long and risky leap from current tests of implicit biases to drawing meaningful conclusions about rating behavior.

Electronic Performance Monitoring

Traditional discussions of performance appraisal have been built around a model where some rater or group of raters observes or obtains information about the performance of a set of employees and makes judgments about their performance. Electronic performance monitoring (EPM) systems represent application of electronic technology to observe, record, and monitor various aspects of employee performance (Bhave, 2014), and in principle it might be possible to bypass subjective measures such as ratings altogether if sufficient data about performance can be obtained electronically. For example, Neary (2002) describes the development of a computerized performance management system for nearly 100,000 employees at TRW Automotive.

Organizations frequently use a range of electronic monitoring methods to collect information about the performance and behaviors of employees (Wells, Moorman, & Werner, 2007). These range from monitoring web usage to keystroke monitoring; some organizations even use GPS data to monitor the whereabouts and movements of their employees. Reactions to this electronic monitoring are often negative, but this might depend on the perceived purpose of this monitoring. Wells et al. (2007) suggest that if the purpose of this monitoring is seen as developmental, reactions may be more positive than if the purpose of monitoring is seen as a technique for controlling employee behavior.

Electronic monitoring systems have some clear advantages over reliance on human observers. EPM systems allow continuous monitoring, and they provide unbiased information about employee behavior and performance. There is evidence that the use of EPM systems as one tool in performance appraisal (in particular, in appraisal systems where the supervisor receives EPM reports and considers them when evaluating subordinates) is associated with increases in task performance (Bhave, 2014; Goomas, 2007; Kolb & Aiello, 1997). These systems provide both supervisors and subordinates with detailed information about the performance of many aspects of the job, and provide an opportunity to obtain frequent, verifiable, and credible feedback (Goomas, 2007).

There are a number of potential limitations to EPM systems. First, they place a great premium on aspects of job performance that are easily measured. For example, Goomas (2007) describes an EPM system in an automotive parts warehouse that included measurement of travel time (seconds per foot) and time spent handling each case of material; to evaluate performance, these metrics were compared to standard metrics established through careful industrial engineering studies. The problem with focusing on behaviors and outcomes that are most easily countable is that you might end up missing critically important aspects of task performance, such as exercising judgment, planning, communication, as well as missing just about all aspects of citizenship and adaptive performance. An overemphasis on EPM is likely to lead to criterion deficiency, overemphasizing the easily countable aspects of performance and underemphasizing the rest.

Employees whose work is electronically monitored (for example, call center employees whose keystrokes and call times are often recorded and fed back to supervisors) often find such systems intrusive and stressful (Bates & Holton, 1995; Sewell, Barker, & Nyberg, 2011), particularly if these systems are seen as a tool for speeding up and intensifying work. There is empirical evidence that EPM systems can increase stress (see, for example, Aiello & Kolb, 1995), and it is possible that the productivity gains that can be achieved by speeding up work (a common outcome of EPM) will be offset by the increased costs due to stress-related health problems among workers. Even if the organization does not suffer ill effects resulting from the stresses it imposes on employees, the employees themselves are quite likely to suffer if these systems are put into place. The stressful nature of EPM can be mitigated somewhat if employees are given a role in the development and use of EPM.

Non-Electronic Alternatives

Stanton (2000) notes that performance monitoring existed well before electronic methods of monitoring were available, and that non-electronic monitoring continues to this day. Human judges can be used to collect and categorize detailed records about performance, and despite some clear differences between EPM and the use of human monitors (e.g., EPM is likely to be continuous, and is not hampered by the perceptual and cognitive limitations of human monitors), there are clear similarities. Both humans and electronic devices monitor performance for reasons that range from providing feedback to motivating employees to perform at a higher level. Both can be stressful and can contribute to negative perceptions of the job and the organization. Stanton (2000) suggests that trust in management and trust in supervisors is a critical factor in determining reactions to performance monitoring, and that when trust is low, monitoring is more likely to be seen as punitive and coercive.

Agreement Across Rating Sources

Self-ratings, peer ratings, supervisory ratings, ratings from subordinates, and other sources of information for evaluating performance often lead to somewhat different conclusions about the performance and about the strengths and weaknesses of the people being evaluated. You could think of this as either an advantage or as a disadvantage of using multiple sources in evaluating performance. This disagreement is a good thing in the sense that is suggests that each rating source might have something unique to contribute. If self-ratings, peer ratings, supervisory ratings, and others all agreed, there would hardly be any point in collecting information from multiple sources. On the other hand, disagreement can undercut the credibility of the appraisal system. We noted earlier that self-ratings tend to be high, and that people often rate their own performance higher than it would be rated by others. If ratings from multiple sources disagree, this implies that the rating a particular employee receives from some sources will be higher than the ratings he or she receives from other sources. For example, suppose your peers rate you a "4" on oral communication, but your supervisor and your subordinates give you ratings of "2" and "3," respectively. If, like most people, you over-rate your own performance, you are likely to accept the peer rating as most accurate, *and* to use the fact that some raters gave you a "4" to cast doubt on the accuracy of the "2" and "3" ratings you receive. Thus, disagreements between raters might both cast some general doubt on the accuracy of evaluations and provide evidence that the ratee can use to discredit whoever gives him or her a low rating.

There have been several reviews of research on agreement between ratings obtained from different sources, and in general they suggest that different ratings sources tend to show low to moderate levels of agreement. (Greguras & Robie, 1998; Harris & Schaubroeck, 1988). For example, correlations between supervisor ratings and peer ratings of performance tend to be in the .30–.40 range (Conway & Huffcutt, 1997; Viswesvaran, Schmidt, & Ones, 2002). Self-ratings and ratings from other sources do show even lower levels of agreement (Atwater, Ostroff, Yammarino, & Fleenor, 1998; Landy & Farr, 1983; Steel & Ovalle, 1984; Thornton, 1980). For example, the correlations between self-ratings and peer ratings and between self-ratings and supervisory ratings tend to be closer to .20 (Conway & Huffcutt, 1997; Heidemeir & Moser, 2009). Within-source agreement (e.g., the correlation between ratings given by two different peers) is typically higher than between-source agreement (Conway & Huffcutt, 1997), which suggests that the unique perspectives and the differences in what peers, supervisors, subordinates, and others tend to observe contributes to the relatively low level of agreement. Both demographic (e.g., gender, age) and personality factors (e.g., dominance, empathy) are related to cross-level agreement (Brutus, Fleenor, & McCauley, 1999).

How the Structure of Organizations and Workgroups Influences Observation of Work Behavior and Agreement Regarding Performance

The changing nature of the workplace means that supervisors are unlikely to have the opportunity to directly observe the performance of their subordinates all of the time. Approximately 20–25% of the U.S. workforce telecommutes at least some of the time, and approximately 50–60% of workers in Fortune 1000 companies work away from their desks at least some of the time (Latest Telecommuting Statistics, 2015). As a result, it is likely that at least some of the information supervisors receive about the performance of their subordinates will be indirect, either secondhand reports from other sources or inferences the supervisor might make from the work products he or she sees. We should note that even in traditional workplaces, supervisors often obtain information about the performance of their subordinates from sources other than direct observation (Raymark, Balzer, & DeLaTorre, 1999); however, with the growth of telecommuting and other methods of working away from the traditional workplace, the use of indirect information in evaluating performance is likely to become more common and more important.

The question naturally arises of how supervisors put together whatever direct information they receive by observing subordinates with indirect information to arrive at an overall evaluation of each subordinate's performance. There is evidence that supervisors pay considerably more information to performance they have observed than they do to indirect information about the performance of their subordinates (Golden, Barnes-Farrell, & Mascharka, 2009). Indirect information that is inconsistent with the rater's own observations receives little weight in evaluating performance (Uggerslev & Sulsky, 2002).

Although there are few empirical tests of this hypothesis, we believe that differences in what people at different levels of an organization observe are at least in part responsible for differences in performance ratings. These differences in observation are driven by a wide range of factors, from the physical arrangement of the workplace to the likelihood that particular individuals will either work together or work in settings where they can observe coworkers' performance. It is also likely that changes in the structure of workplaces will have a strong influence on across-source differences in opportunities to observe work behavior. Many organizations are moving in the direction of an "open office," where employees share work spaces (e.g., multiple employees might work at the same table and few employees might have their own office). This trend is not universally welcomed (Kaufman, 2014), and its implications for the structure of work are still unfolding, but it is likely to influence the dynamics of performance appraisal. In an open office, more individuals will have an opportunity to observe more of your work behavior, and it is likely that these observations will filter into appraisals.

COGNITIVE PROCESSES IN PERFORMANCE EVALUATION

Research on performance appraisal and the potential difficulties in forming sound judgments about performance can be traced back almost 100 years (Thorndike, 1920), and until the late 1970s much of this work proceeded on the assumption that supervisors and managers observed the behavior of those they are asked to rate with reasonable accuracy, and that at the time they were asked to make judgments about performance, could recall a good deal of this information and pull it together to make judgments about performance. Thus, the job of industrial and organizational psychologists working in this field was to give raters the tools (e.g., well-developed rating scales, rater training) to help them do the best possible job evaluating their subordinates' performance. By the 1970s and 1980s, the cognitive revolution in psychology had completely overturned the assumption that human cognition worked like a movie camera, faithfully recording what was seen and allowing you to replay it with reasonable accuracy at some later time. Rather, the set of processes involved in acquiring and making sense of information about the external world was understood to be a complex one that involved multiple systems for processing information (Kahneman, 2011; Shiffrin & Scheider, 1977), in which categories and prototypes often structure the storage and retrieval of information (Feldman, 1981) and in which even the most vivid and concrete memories might be false or misleading (Loftus, 2005).[1]

Landy and Farr's (1980) review of research on performance appraisal suggested that interventions such as improving rating scales had little impact on the quality of rating data, and this review was instrumental in turning the field toward a more careful examining of the cognitive processes involved in performance rating. Several subsequent authors (e.g., Murphy & Cleveland, 1991; DeNisi, 2006) noted that cognitive research is probably more relevant to understanding *performance judgment* than understand the ratings that are given in organizations, noting that ratings that are actually recorded on performance appraisal forms do not always correspond to the rater's judgments regarding the performance level or the strengths and weaknesses of the individuals being rated. Nevertheless, research that gives us a better understanding of how judgments about performance are formed has the potential to shed light on performance ratings, even when these ratings do not precisely mirror these performance judgments.

DeNisi, Cafferty, and Meglino (1984) developed an influential model of the cognitive processes underlying performance appraisal; the studies that led to this model and the development of the key concepts in this model are described in DeNisi (2006). This model and others developed at about the same time (e.g., Feldman, 1981) identified a set of activities a rater goes through when making judgments about a subordinate's performance. These are shown in Table 5.1. First, the rater must observe and form a mental representation of behaviors that are part of the domain of job performance. Next, these representations are stored in memory, and at some later time retrieved. Next, information about performance, both what the rater has observed and other information obtained by inference (e.g., if the results of behavior on the job are favorable, the rater might infer that the behaviors themselves are appropriate) or from other sources (e.g., feedback from customers) must be integrated to form a judgment about the ratee's effectiveness.

Table 5.1 suggests a relatively straightforward linear process in which information is acquired, stored, retrieved, and integrated to form judgments. Research in the 1980s and 1990s suggested that this process was neither linear nor straightforward, and that

TABLE 5.1 ■ Cognitive Processes That Underlie Judgments About Job Performance
1. Behavior is observed by the rater
2. Rater forms a cognitive representation of the behavior
3. This representation is stored in memory
4. Stored information is retrieved from memory when needed
5. Retrieved information is integrated, along with other relevant information, to form a judgment about the ratee

Source: From DeNisi (2006), p. 28.

this process could loop and bend in numerous ways, so that judgments made today might influence attention, encoding, and retrieval tomorrow, or that information that had been stored in memory in one way might be reprocessed and might, when retrieved, look quite different from what was originally stored. Although some of the most basic cognitive processes in forming judgments might be pretty much the same across a wide range of contexts, there were a number of contextual factors that have turned out to be very important for understanding how people obtain and process the information needed to make judgments about job performance.

Attention and Mental Representation

Earlier in this chapter we noted that in organizations, the task of observing job behavior or of acquiring information about the behavior of the people to be evaluated is likely to be one of the many things the evaluator is doing at any point in time. For example, your supervisor might decide to make a concerted effort to observe you doing your work, but he or she almost always has a number of other tasks to worry about, and it is unlikely that evaluators are able to devote their full attention to performance evaluation much of the time. Thus, the first question that might be considered in thinking about the cognitive processes that underlie judgments about performance is how evaluators sort the wheat from the chaff—what do they pay attention to and how do they mentally represent what behavior they have observed or what information they have acquired? Most generally, there appear to be two different cognitive processes for handling this task: automatic and controlled processes (Feldman, 1981; Kahneman, 2011). Familiar stimuli are usually processed automatically, with strong reliance on existing patterns and structures (e.g., categories and prototypes) while more novel or unexpected stimuli are often processed using a more controlled, conscious, and effortful process.

A category is a group of related objects that takes the form of a "fuzzy set" (Rosch, 1977; Rosch, Mervis, Gray, Johnson, & Boyes-Braem, 1976). That is, categories do not have rigid boundaries, but rather represent potentially unstable groups of objects that are held together by similarity or "family resemblance." A prototype is an exemplar of that category. It is an image that summarizes the typical and distinguishing features of a category. Thus, if the categories are "dependable economy car" and "American sports car," a Subaru and a Corvette might serve as prototypes of their respective categories. Finally, schema (or schemata) refers to higher-level memory structures that contain verbal or propositional information (Feldman, 1986; Ilgen & Feldman, 1983). Schema can be used to represent the self and/or others in familiar situations (Ilgen & Feldman, 1983). One type of schema, referred to as a script (Abelson, 1976) refers to a mentally stored representation of a familiar event (e.g., visiting a restaurant). All of these terms—categories, schemas, and scripts— are useful for understanding the way raters acquire and make sense of information about the performance of the individuals he or she is called upon to evaluate. In particular, the behaviors a rater has observed are not stored as simple mental movies that can be played back at some later time. Rather, the mental representation of what one has observed is strongly influenced by the categories and schema that are relevant or activated at the time of observation, and this initial representation will have a decisive effect on what is later retrieved from memory. For example, if your first impression of a new employee is that he or she is uncomfortable collaborating with peers, you will tend to pay more attention to and more easily remember behaviors that seem in line with this impression.

The most important theme of cognitive research on performance evaluation is that the process of information acquisition is active rather than passive. That is, the rater does not simply bring in all of the available information from whatever he or she has an opportunity to observe, but rather selectively attends to some features of the ratees and their behavior, and devotes little attention to others. If we focus for the moment on the perception of behaviors, cognitive research suggests that the attention we devote to any particular behavior is a function of three variables: (a) the behavior itself, (b) the context of observation, and (c) the purpose of observation. That is, some behaviors are likely to attract more attention, regardless of the context or purpose of observation. Organizational norms and standards (see Chapter 7) define some behaviors as important, desirable, unacceptable, or forbidden. It also seems likely that behaviors that carry strong evaluative implications will receive attention, almost regardless of the local context (Murphy, 1982b; Wegner & Vallecher, 1977). That is, categorization is very likely to involve placing each person along a good–bad, preferred–non-preferred continuum. Cognitive models have generally assumed that evaluation was the end product of the cognitive process, but there is evidence that evaluation is primitive and universal, and that evaluation may occur at the same time as, or even precede, other information-processing activities (Kim & Rosenberg, 1980; Osgood, 1962; Wegner & Vallecher, 1977; Zajonc, 1980). Research by Hastie and Park (1986) suggests that evaluations are stored at the time that behavior is observed, and that subsequent memory may be for evaluations rather than for behaviors.

Research on the effects of context on the cognitive processes involved in performance judgment suggests two conclusions. First, the salience of most behaviors (i.e., the likelihood that they will be the focus of attention) varies across situations (McArthur, 1980; Taylor & Fiske, 1978). In part, this is probably due to differences in the evaluative implications of specific behaviors in different situations. For example, a loud, verbally aggressive style of conversation may not attract any attention among a group of heavy equipment salesmen, but might be very noticeable in a receptionist; the behavior is appropriate in one situation, but not in others. Second, distinctive, novel features of the ratee or of his or her behavior will be highly salient (Langer, Taylor, Fiske, & Chantowitz, 1976). Behaviors that are infrequent might become salient through their novelty; behaviors that are important but commonplace may attract less attention.

Research on the purpose of observation, sometimes referred to under the heading of observational goals, is very relevant for understanding what behaviors will or will not be attended to by raters in organizations. Supervisors typically face multiple task demands and rarely have the luxury to devote all of their attention to behavior observation and evaluation (Balzer, 1986; Murphy, Philbin, & Adams, 1989). Thus, raters in organizations are likely to acquire information about ratees' performance while they are concentrating on tasks other than evaluation.

Even when raters do consciously seek out information about ratees, the purpose of observation will affect their information-acquisition activities. In general, raters will seek different information if they want to find out about people, tasks, or characteristics of the group (Murphy, Garcia, Kerkar, Martin, & Balzer, 1982; Williams, DeNisi, Blencoe, & Cafferty, 1985). The information they attend to will depend largely on what goals they have and on what else they are doing when they observe the behavior of the individuals they are asked to evaluate (DeNisi, Cafferty, & Meglino, 1984; DeNisi & Peters, 1996; DeNisi, Robbins, & Cafferty, 1989). For example, Kinicki, Hom, Trost, and Wade (1995) suggest that variations in the rating task and the rating environment might prime different categories (i.e., make them easier for the rater to access and use at the time when performance is being observed), and that the information that is most likely to be recalled at some later point is information that is related to and consistent with the categories that are most accessible to the rater while he or she is observing performance. Hauenstein (1992) suggests that subjects' expectations about the rating task (e.g., whether they will provide face-to-face feedback to ratees) affect encoding of performance information, and subsequently affect ratings.

Memory: Storage and Retrieval

A dominant theme of much of the research on memory in the last 30–40 years has been the fallibility of human memory. This should not blind us to the fact that people are capable of remembering a great deal of information and of retrieving detailed and accurate information that was stored in memory a long time ago. Unfortunately, people have a notoriously difficult time distinguishing between accurate memories and memories that *seem* accurate, in part because they can be so vivid and detailed. Peoples' belief that they can accurately recall what they have seen is an important explanation for the fact that so many managers and so many organizations continue to rely on subjective evaluations of job performance. That is, most of us believe we can accurately observe and recall behavior and that we can therefore form reasonably accurate evaluations of the performance of those we are asked to evaluate (Simons & Charbris, 2011), and therefore do not doubt our ability to fairly and accurately evaluate performance. Raters may lack confidence in *others'* ability to observe, recall, and evaluate the behavior of their subordinates, but they rarely doubt their own ability to execute this daunting task.

In Table 5.1, we noted that one of the steps in forming judgments about a ratee's performance is to retrieve information about his or her behavior from memory. One of the dominant themes of research on memory for the behavior of the people one is asked to evaluate is the decisive role of general evaluative impressions—that is, the global impression that a particular person is a good or a poor performer—in structuring what one recalls from memory. There is compelling evidence that memories of and evaluations of specific performance episodes are influenced by general evaluative impressions (Murphy, Balzer, Lockhart, & Eisenman, 1985; Murphy, Gannett, Herr, & Chen, 1986; Smither, Reilly, & Buda, 1988), and that we will more readily recall behaviors that are consistent with these general impressions than other behaviors. Indeed, there is evidence that raters may infer behavioral details from their evaluations, rather than (as is generally assumed) basing their evaluations on the total set of behaviors they have observed (Murphy, Martin, & Garcia, 1982). That is, if you believe that a particular subordinate is a generally good performer: (1) you will more readily recall instances of good performance than instances of poor performance, and (2) you may even believe that you remember positive behaviors, even if you never actually observed those behaviors. This reliance on general evaluative impressions in retrieving information from memory is one of the key reasons for the "halo effect"—that is, the tendency to rate specific aspects of job performance on the basis of overall judgments about whether the employee is a good or a poor performer rather than on the basis of information about the specific performance dimensions being rated. We will discuss halo errors in more detail in Chapter 11.

The ratings that are given to past performance are likely to influence ratings of future performance (Murphy, Balzer, Lockhart, & Eisenman, 1985; Reilly, Smither, Warech, & Reilly, 1998). First, previous performance influences the rater's general impressions about the ratee, and these impressions have a considerable effect on memory for behavior and on the evaluation of that behavior (Martell & Evans, 2005; Murphy & Balzer, 1986; Murphy, Martin, & Garcia, 1982; Woehr & Feldman, 1993). Slaughter and Greguras (2008) suggest that escalation of commitment might also represent a partial explanation for this finding. They note that once people are committed to a judgment or decision, they tend to increase their commitment over time, even in the face of clear evidence that the initial judgment or decision was wrong. So, if you start out thinking that Jennifer is a good performer, you might resist changing that evaluation, even in the face of behavioral evidence that suggests poorer performance. Over time, you will probably have a harder time recalling Jennifer's failures than her successes.

Similarly, the performance of other ratees can influence evaluations of the performance of a target ratee. There is evidence of both assimilation and contrast effects in performance ratings (Becker & Miller, 2002; Murphy, Gannett, Herr, & Chen, 1986; Sumer & Knight, 1996). Assimilation effects occur when your evaluation of a person is pulled in the direction of evaluation of others, whereas contrast effects occur when differences between the person to be rated and others are magnified. Assimilation is more likely when there are small differences between the people to be rated, whereas contrast effects are more likely when the differences are large enough to pay attention to.[2] On the whole, contrast effects appear more common and more difficult to eradicate (Jennings, Palmer, & Thomas, 2004; Maurer, Palmer, & Ashe, 1993; Palmer, Maurer, & Feldman, 2002; see, however, Becker & Villanova, 1995, who argue that many lab studies overestimate the strength of contrast effects).

As DeNisi (2006) notes, although general evaluations are critical determinants of what is or is not recalled, the situation is not always that simple. It is true that it is often easier to recall behavioral information that is consistent with general evaluative impressions, but sometimes the opposite can occur. That is, behavioral incidents that are *sharply* inconsistent with overall impressions might receive additional attention and might be more easily recalled. However, available research supports a general trend of memory biases in favor of behaviors that are consistent with your general impressions of a ratee's overall level of effectiveness.

A second major theme of research on memory for behaviors is that memory is dynamic rather than static. That is, memory is *not* like a bank vault, where items are stored for some period of time and later retrieved in their original form. Rather, memory can be influenced by task demands, and information that is stored in one way might be changed if information-processing objectives are changed. For example, Williams, DeNisi, Meglino, and Cafferty (1986) studied the way memory for behaviors changed if behavioral information was obtained for one purpose (e.g., identifying the best performer in a group) and subsequently used for another purpose (e.g., comparing the performance levels of all of the members in a group), and presented clear evidence that the new purpose could change the way behavioral information was stored in memory. .

Information Integration

At some point, a rater who is asked to evaluate a particular subordinate's performance over the course of a year (or over the life of a project) will have to integrate a large body of information, some of which is likely to be based on direct observations of performance and other based on indirect sources (e.g., input from other supervisors, inferences based on the results of behavior). The set of available information is likely to include both instances of effective performance and instances of less effective performance, and for all but the best workers, it is likely that a thorough review of performance will include both positive and negative information. The question of how this information is put together to arrive at a judgment about the ratee's performance is an important one that has been extensively studied.

There is a long history of research in judgment and decision making showing that negative information tends to get disproportionate weight when decisions are made; DeNisi, Cafferty, and Meglino (1984) review this research, with special attention to its implications for performance appraisal. Ganzach (1995) analyzed several data sets and presented consistent evidence that when performance profiles include both positive and negative elements, the negatives receive more weight. The one exception is for performance profiles of high performers. These individuals may have their relative strengths and weaknesses, but their weaknesses are not instances of poor performance (i.e., negative information), but rather information that is positive but not as stellar as information about strengths. When all of the information in a performance profile is generally positive, there does not appear to be any tendency to over-weight the least positive dimensions.

One of the challenges in forming judgments about overall performance levels is that performance is not constant; all workers have good days and bad ones (Zyphur, Chaturvedi, & Arvey, 2008). Raters who are asked to evaluate their subordinates are faced with the difficult task of pulling together information about performance that is sometimes better and sometimes worse, and the different patterns of performance people show can pose particular problems for raters (Reb & Gregarus, 2010). For example, workers whose performance is improving probably benefit from this upward trend, and will be evaluated more positively than other workers whose average level of performance is just as good (Lee & Dalal, 2011).

The way performance information is conveyed to supervisors can influence their evaluations. Consider the two reports shown in Table 5.2. In the success report, it is clear that both John and Sam performed well, and they might both be regarded as highly successful and pretty similar in their performance levels. In the failure reports, a supervisor might correctly infer that John is twice as likely to fail as Sam and (ignoring the high success rate each achieves) conclude that there are large differences in their performance. Drawing on Prospect Theory (Kahneman & Tversky, 1979), Wong and Kwong (2005) presented evidence

TABLE 5.2 ■ Performance Reports That Emphasize Successes Versus Failures	
Success	John was successful in 90% of the tasks he attempted. Sam was even more successful, achieving success in 95% of the tests he attempted.
Failure	John failed in 10% of the tasks he attempted, whereas Sam failed in only 5%.

that differences in the likelihood of failure get more attention than corresponding differences in the likelihood of success when evaluating performance (See also Lee & Dalal, 2011).[3]

LIKING AND EMOTION: AFFECTIVE INFLUENCES ON PERFORMANCE APPRAISAL

It is clear that there is a strong relationship between liking and performance ratings (Judge & Ferris, 1993); a meta-analysis by Sutton, Baldwin, Wood, and Hoffman (2013) suggests a very strong correlation between the rater's liking for particular ratees and the performance ratings they receive (liking accounts for over 60% of the variance in overall performance ratings). This correlation might be interpreted as evidence of bias, but only if liking has nothing to do with performance and effectiveness on the job. Sutton et al. (2013) review several studies that suggest that the correlation between liking and performance ratings is not simply due to bias. First, a supervisor's liking for particular subordinates is quite likely to be partially driven by their performance and effectiveness. High-performing employees are vitally important to the organization and they directly help supervisors accomplish the tasks and goals assigned to their work group. Second, raters who like and trust particular employees are likely to give them information, support, and assistance that allows them to perform well (Graen, 1976; Graen & Uhl-Bien, 1995; Kacmar, Witt, Zivnuska, & Gully, 2003).

In the previous section of this chapter, we discussed cognitive processes that influence the judgments raters make about the performance of the individuals they are called upon to rate. Interpersonal affect (liking versus disliking ratees) also influences judgments about job performance (Varma, DeNisi, & Peters, 1996), but the precise mechanism by which this occurs is not clear. One possibility is that there is a strong affective component to overall impressions of ratees (Zajonc, 1980), and that liking a particular ratee leads to the inference that he or she is a good performer, much in the same way he or she is seen as having a number of other positively valued traits. Lefkowitz (2000) reviewed research showing the affective regard is related to higher appraisals, but also to higher interdimensional correlations. The effect of liking on these correlations is consistent with the overall impression hypothesis.

Another possibility is that raters pay more attention to behaviors that are consistent with their general affective response, and therefore will pay attention to positive performance if they like one ratee, and attend to negative performance if they dislike another. Still another possibility is that raters rely on different prototypes and mental schema when thinking about ratees they like than when thinking about ratees they dislike, and that they are biased in favor of recalling behaviors that are consistent with these prototypes (Kinicki, Hom, & Trost, 1995; Robbins & DeNisi, 1993, 1994).

Robbins and DeNisi (1994) suggest that affect has a direct effect on performance evaluations, in addition to its effects on cognitive processes. Interpersonal affect is likely to be a performance cue, albeit an indirect one. The rationale here is that subordinates who are consistently ineffective, and therefore fail to make an adequate contribution to the success of a work group will, in the end, be disliked. Although interpersonal affect is not solely instrumental, and it is entirely possible that an ineffective worker will still be liked, it is reasonable to assume some link between effectiveness and liking. Interpersonal affect also influences both attention and memory, and it is likely that raters who like a particular ratee will find it easier to bring to mind instances of good performance.

Finally, affect is likely to play a role in bias in performance appraisal. In Chapter 11, we will review research suggesting that performance appraisals are not strongly influenced by the age, gender, or race of the ratee, but in cases where there is animosity or dislike of a ratee, the probability that demographic differences between raters and ratees will lead to lower ratings probably increases (Fiske, Harris, Lee, & Russell, 2016). It appears likely that affect can influence discrimination against members of various demographic groups, and liking an individual may reduce the effects of stereotypes, while disliking may make reliance on negative stereotypes more likely.

Finally, we should remember that "affect" is a fairly broad term. Performance appraisal research that has examined affect has generally concentrated on liking (Cardy & Dobbins, 1986; Dobbins & Russell, 1986). Liking can be thought of as directed affect—it represents an emotional reaction to a specific person. However, not all affect is directed toward a specific person. Rather, there are at least two categories of undirected affect: (a) mood—which represents transient undirected affect, and (b) temperament—which represents chronic undirected affect. It is likely that both mood and temperament influence evaluations. A rater who is in a good mood at the time of observation and/or evaluation may give more positive evaluations than one who is in a sour mood. Raters who have a very positive, upbeat disposition may evaluate performance differently than raters whose temperament is surly or mean.

There have been comparatively few studies on the way mood or temperament influence performance appraisals. Sinclair (1988) suggested that mood influenced the way behavioral information was encoded and stored in memory; his study suggested that the most accurate ratings are obtained from raters who are in less positive moods. This finding is hardly a fluke; there is evidence that negative moods improve problem solving (Barth & Funke, 2010), and that a range of emotions can enhance performance on tasks that require cognitive activity (Blanchette & Richards, 2010; Seo & Barrett, 2007).

STANDARDS FOR EVALUATING PERFORMANCE

Earlier in this chapter, we noted that different people often come to different conclusions about whether or not a particular employee has performed his or her job well. There are two possible explanations for this disagreement. First, they may have different information about the individual, either because they have observed different things or because they have received different inputs about that person's behavior and effectiveness. Second, they may interpret the same information differently because they apply different standards for defining good or poor performance.

We can think about the term "performance standards" in two ways. First, there are the *implicit* standards raters use to evaluate performance (i.e., their definition of good, average, poor performance). Second, there are *explicit* performance standards. The U.S. Office of Personnel Management (1998) defines a performance standard as "a management-approved expression of the performance threshold(s), requirement(s), or expectation(s) that must be met to be appraised at a particular level of performance."[4] Both types of standards are important; implicit standards play a critical role in the judgments raters make about performance whereas explicit standards play a critical role in the *organization's* evaluation of that same performance.

Personal values and beliefs are likely to influence implicit performance norms and standards. Most workers and supervisors have well-developed ideas of what constitutes a "fair day's work" (Zaleznik, Christensen, & Roethlisberger, 1958). These ideas reflect the individuals' opinions about the amount of effort and production that should be exchanged for the pay and benefits associated with the job. General beliefs about human nature are likely to affect both the standards themselves and their application (Wexley & Youtz, 1985). For example, popular theories of management describe two sets of assumptions about human behavior that are likely to affect the choice of a leadership style (McGregor, 1960). Managers who ascribe to Theory X believe that workers are inherently lazy and that they must be motivated by external rewards and should be closely supervised in order to achieve acceptable levels of performance. Managers who ascribe to Theory Y believe that workers are intrinsically motivated and that they will respond most readily to challenges and opportunities for growth at work. A Theory X manager is likely to have a detailed, strict set of standards and is likely to give very low evaluations to behaviors that deviate from those standards. A Theory Y manager is likely to have standards that allow for greater latitude in behavior and that are less punitive with regard to behaviors that deviate from those standards.

Several models of judgment and evaluation include the assumption that evaluative judgments are made with reference to standards that may vary from rater to rater (DeCotiis & Petit, 1978; Higgins & Stangor, 1988; Ilgen, 1983; Sherif & Sherif, 1969). West (1998) suggests that these standards are part of the rater's broader implicit theory of performance. Different supervisors and managers sometimes have very different ideas about what constitutes good or bad performacne or about *why* people perform well or poorly (Heslin, Latham & VandeWalle, 2005; Heslin & VandeWalle, 2011), and these implicit theories can lead to strong disagreements about performance even if there are few disagreements about the behaviors that were actually observed.

Explicit Standards

There are a variety of methods that might be used in setting explicit performance standards in a workplace. Work that involves relatively routine and repetitive activity (e.g., retrieving materials from a warehouse) is amenable to systematic work study, which can be used to develop *engineered labor standards*. Goomas and Ludwig (2009) describe the steps in creating this type of standard. First, "a task is subdivided into its elements, and each element (e.g., travel time) is given a discrete value (e.g., allocated number of minutes or seconds to travel from Point A to Point B). Values are arrived at based on activity sampling, group sampling, and time-series studies, as employees in these large industrial settings perform their job duties. The time needed for a qualified worker to carry out a task is then established" (p. 246). Performance is then assessed by comparing the standard time required to complete tasks with the actual time a worker takes to complete these tasks.

Kane and Freeman (1997) proposed a more general method for setting performance standards that is potentially applicable across a range of jobs. They note that for most job tasks, it might be possible to scale task performance from the lowest level that would be tolerated by an organization without taking administrative action (e.g., a level of performance where you would seriously consider firing the employee in question) to essentially perfect performance (or perhaps the highest level recorded), making it possible to scale performance (regardless of the task or job) on a 0–100 (i.e., worst to best possible) scale, and to express individual performance in terms of the percentage of maximum performance that was actually achieved. This, then, would allow organizations to create standards that were comparable across jobs, units, and the like.

The Kane and Freeman (1997) model is mainly concerned with setting standards for performance-based pay, but there can be a wider array of uses for performance appraisal than simply pay administration (see Chapter 8), and standards might be set for reasons that have very little to do with pay. For example, the performance standards that are created and enforced in an organization can say a good deal about the climate and culture of the organization. Some organizations exist in reward-rich environments (e.g., they have the resources and features necessary to attract a high-performing workforce) and might choose to set high standards as a way of defining their identity as a hard-charging firm. In other organizations, it might not be possible for workers to approach the maximum possible performance level, because of constraints (e.g., lack of materials, information, or support) or lack of a high-quality pool of applicants and incumbents, and they might be forced to set lower standards.

Bobko and Colella (1994) note that there are a number of aspects of performance standards (e.g., who sets standards, specificity, rationale, difficulty) that influence reactions to performance standards. Standards are an important part of the whole performance appraisal process; appraisal systems that include many desirable features (e.g., frequent feedback, good communication between raters and ratees) may still fail if performance standards are seen as unreasonable. Inappropriate standards can lead to work overload (Brown & Benson, 2005), which in turn can have negative impacts on the physical and mental health of employees, as well as long-term degradation in their performance.

Setting Explicit Standards

Standards are sometimes set through formal negotiation, particularly when unions or other bargaining units are involved. Saal and Knight (1988) note that union contracts often include clauses concerned with

- determining disciplinary procedures,

- scheduling of work and overtime,

- determining work methods, and

- determining production rates.

Each of these clauses defines a particular standard. For example, negotiations over disciplinary procedures in organization determine what types and levels of behavior can be a cause for official sanctions, what time frames apply in applying discipline (e.g., maximum time that can elapse between the infraction and the response), and what procedures will be followed to determine whether discipline is required or allowed for specific incidents. Negotiations regarding schedules and overtime might determine both actual working hours and the degree of latitude in determining whether schedules are met (e.g., how late an employee has to be to be classified as late). Negotiations over work methods might determine the standard procedures that are followed. Negotiations over production rates are likely to define standards for desired production levels, as well as standards for defining the amount of variance in production that will be acceptable.

It is more common for performance standards to either be imposed by managers and supervisors or to be negotiated between managers and their subordinates. Non-managerial employees are likely to have less of a role in setting performance standards, and supervsior–subordinate differences in the perceptions of reasonable standards can be a source of stress and conflict in organizations (Motowidlo & Peterson, 2008). One way to reduce the potential for conflict is to allow employees to have some input in defining performance standards, a common practice in performance appraisal methods that is based on assessing progress toward specific performance goals.

Setting Performance Goals

In earlier chapters, we mentioned management by objectives (MBO), which involves creating explicit standards through negotiation, albeit not in the formal, adversarial mode that is typical of negotiations between management and unions. MBO often involves a process in which the employee proposes a set of standards or goals that will define performance on his or her job, the supervisor reviews the goals and suggests revisions (if needed), and the two parties negotiate to reach a set of mutually agreeable goals (Szilagyi & Wallace, 1983). Although MBO is no longer a widespread method of management, the process of employees and their managers jointly setting performance goals and metrics for determining whether or not these goals are met has become quite common in perfomance appraisal.

Research on goal setting suggests that participating in determining goals is critical to success (Locke, Shaw, Saari, & Latham, 1981). That is, goals have a greater impact on performance when the employee helps to determine the goals than when goals are imposed from above. Because goals represent one type of external performance standard, the question of how goals are set might be a critical one for evaluating a goal-oriented performance appraisal system, at least with regard to the acceptability of the system to those who are being evaluated. Participation in the goal-setting process is likely to lead to stronger perceptions that the system is fair (Korsgaard & Roberson, 1995). However, the negotiation of goals, metrics, and standards opens the way for manipulation of the performance appraisal system.

The interests of the employees being evaluated versus the organization may not always be in sync when setting performance goals. It is to the employee's interest to make sure that performance goals are achievable and that whatever metrics are used to evaluate performance are under the employee's control. A more cynical, but probably realistic view is that it is in the employee's interest to make goals as simple to achieve as possible. The organization, on the other hand, has an interest in making performance goals more challenging. That does not mean that they benefit by making goals as difficult as possible; research on goal setting has clearly established that performance is maximized when goals are difficult but attainable, and are accepted as reasonable by employees (Erez & Kanfer, 1983; Locke & Latham, 1990). One of the challenges of management is to negotiate performance goals that serve the interests of both employees and the organization.

One of the key principles of effective performance management is that performance goals and objectives should be aligned with the goals, objectives, and strategy of the organization. As we have noted earlier, this alignment is probably easier for jobs and units that are closer to the core function of the organization and more challenging for jobs that are closer to the periphery. For example, if the primary strategy pursued by an organization involves cost containment, it makes sense for performance goals and objectives to emphasize efficiency in the use of organizational resources, minimization of waste, and the like. In an organization whose strategy emphasizes developing innovative products and services, there might be more emphasis on creative problem solving and on generating unique solutions.

SUMMARY

We started this chapter by describing two key questions in designing a performance appraisal system: who should be involved in appraisal and how will they obtain the information needed to form sound judgments about the performane of the people being evaluated. Supervisory ratings are still the norm, but many organizations include self-ratings or ratings from other sources (e.g., peers). There are unique advantages and disadvantages with each plausible rating source, and there is no clear concensus that one source is always best. This might suggest that we should simply obtain information from multiple sources, but the answer is not so simple.

It is clear that ratings obtained from different sources do not often agree. Self-ratings are usually higher than ratings from other sources. Peers, supervisors, and other potential rating sources show disappointing levels of agreement. One implication is that in a multisource performance rating system, it will be common to find that different raters have quite different opinions about the performance of the people they are asked to evaluate, and these differences can undermine the success of multi-rater systems.

The "how" question represented a dominant theme in research on performance appraisal in the 1980s and 1990s, when studies of cognitive and affective processes in performance judgment were common. Interest in these basic processes has waned somewhat, in large part because of the realization that performance ratings do not always correspond with judgments about performance, which implies that a better understanding of the cognitive processes involved in forming judgments about performance might not tell us much about performance appraisals in organizations. Nevertheless, these judgments are an important starting point for understanding performance appraisal, and research on cognitive and affective processes in evaluating performance has made a definite contribution. Most generally, this research tells us that the task of observing performance, retrieving relevant information from memory at the time performance ratings are needed, and pulling together the information from various sources and various points in time to arrive at an overall evaluation is a complex one in which global impressions are at least as important as specific observations of or recollections of behaviors.

Finally, the judgments about performance involve some sort of comparsion between what a person has done and a set of performance standards. These standards might be implicit, representing a rater's opinion about what represents a "fair day's work," or they might be explicit performance standards and goals that are defined by management, negotiated with the union, or jointly arrived at by the supervisor and the employee. In a well-designed performance management system, these goals and objectives will be aligned with and will contribute to the execution of the organization's key strategies for success in a competitive environment.

EXERCISE: WRITING PERFORMANCE STANDARDS

One way to get a sense of the range of issues you might need to consider when evaluating a subordinate's performance is to try out some of the tasks that are involved in performance appraisal. One common task is to develop and articulate standards that can be used to evaluate job performance.

Performance standards fulfill two functions. First, they tell employees what they are supposed to do or acomplish. Second, they tell employees how their performance will be evaluated. In Chapter 2, we described how the broad goals and strategies of organizations are used in performance management systems to drive the goals and standards used to direct and evaluate the performance of individual employees, and the goals and strategies of the organization and the work unit are an important source of information for establishing performance standards, but these higher-level goals do not always provide all of the information you will need. The checklist below is useful for writing performance standards; we suggest you use it to write standards for a job you are familiar with.

Performance standards should be measurable, realistic, and clear, and they should describe the behaviors or accomplishments that characterize sucessful performance, as well as providing clear guidance about performance levels that would fail to meet or that would substantially exceed expectations.[5] In describing steps for writing performance standards, we will assume that a job analysis has been carried out and that the appropriate performance dimensions have been identified. Performance standards describe what people need to do to perform adequately in each of the performance areas.

Performance Standards Checklist

1. What behaviors and outcomes does each performance dimension involve?

2. How many performance levels will these standards describe?

    a. Acceptable versus unacceptable performance—will performance be described solely in terms of whether or not specific expectations are met?

    b. Graded performance levels—will performance at several different levels be described?

3. Which metrics are relevant for evaluating these behaviors?

    a. Quality—do stakeholders care how well essential tasks were performed?

    b. Quantity—do stakeholders care how much work was performed?

    c. Timeliness—are deadlines or effectiveness in meeting schedules important to key stakeholders?

    d. Cost-effectiveness—is efficiency in using organizational resources to accomplish tasks important to stakeholders?

4. What specific measures should be applied?

    a. Objective indices—what should be counted, how, and how often?

    b. Judgments—if objective counts are not available or sufficient, who should make judgments about quality, quantity, timeliness, and so on?

To give an example of how such a checklist might be used to develop performance standards, consider the performance evaluation system that was used to evaluate faulty performance at one of the universities one of the authors worked at. Faculty performance was evaluated in terms of performance in teaching, research, and service. The performance standards for research required faculty to publish a certain amount each year. There were both quality and quantity standards, in the sense that publication in top-quality journals counted for more total points than publication in lower-tier journals, and there were formulas for establishing equivalence among a range of possibilities (e.g., books versus journals, first author versus second or third author). The metrics were mainly objective, but there was always some judgment applied in evaluating the quality of different outlets. This particular performance standard involved accomplishment rather than behavior, in the sense that it was the total number of publications and not the time or effort these involved that counted.

To apply the checklist yourself, think about a job that O*NET describes as having bright prospects for employment: bicycle repair. This job involves a mix of key tasks, including

- installing vehicle parts or accessories,

- adjusting vehicle components according to specifications,

- explaining technical product or service information to customers,

- assembling mechanical components or machine parts, and

- aligning equipment or machinery.

If you write performance standards for these tasks, you will find that some are likely to involve objective metrics and others to involve subjective measures. Depending on the nature of the bike shop there might be different levels of emphasis on quantity, quality, and timeliness metrics; a custom shop might emphasize high-quality work, whereas a shop that caters to a large drop-in customer base might emphasize timeliness and quantity. If you put yourself in the position of a manager in a bike shop and write some potential performance standards that might be used to evaluate bike repair specialists, this will give you a concrete understanding of the range of issues that need to be considered when creating standards of this type.

NOTES

1. The study of false memories can be traced back to Freud and his contemporaries.

2. Sumer and Knight (1996) note that when raters are asked to rate previous performance, contrast effects are more likely than assimilation.

3. Image theory (Beach, 1990) makes similar predictions, and these predictions have been confirmed (Pesta, Kass, & Dunegan, 2005).

4. https://www.opm.gov/policy-data-oversight/performance-management/performance-management-cycle/planning/developing-performance-standards/

5. https://www.opm.gov/policy-data-oversight/performance-management/performance-management-cycle/planning/developing-performance-standards/

RATING SCALES AND RATER TRAINING

In one of his most stirring orations during World War II, Winston Churchill once told Americans "Give us the tools and we will finish the job." Psychologists and human resource specialists have devoted nearly 100 years to giving organizations the tools to effectively evaluate job performance. One way to characterize research on performance appraisal prior to 1980 is as a continual search for better tools—better rating scales, better methods of rater training, and better rating aids. As this chapter will show, these efforts have helped to improve performance *appraisal* in a number of ways, but it is fair to say that modifications of rating scales do not do much to improve the quality of performance *ratings*.

A second strategy for improving performance ratings is to improve the rater's capability to accurately evaluate performance. For example, a wide range of methods of rater training have been proposed, and there is evidence that training can help. We might also make the rater's task easier by introducing memory aids, such as behavior diaries. Again, there is evidence that these tools can help.

In this chapter, we start by reviewing research on efforts to develop better rating scales, particularly scales that include specific behavioral information. We also consider tools designed to assist raters in remembering the behavior of the employees they are asked to rate. We finish this section by considering alternatives to rating scales, and by considering how the incorporation of goals into performance rating changes rating processes and outcomes.

The second half of this chapter examines the impact of training on performance appraisal. We consider two very different strategies for training raters, one that focuses on minimizing errors and the other that focuses on maximizing consistency and agreement.

LEARNING OBJECTIVES

6.1 Learn how behaviorally based rating scales are designed and used

6.2 Understand how memory aids such as behavioral diaries can help improve the accuracy of ratings, and why their effects are often limited

6.3 Learn a variety of ways of incorporating performance goals into performance appraisal

6.4 Understand the strengths and weaknesses of rater error training programs

6.5 Examine methods used to train raters to provide high-quality feedback

RATING SCALES

Most of the rating scales used by organizations are variations of the type of graphic rating scale shown in Figure 6.1. The graphic rating scale is simple, and it provides a relatively straightforward way of obtaining a quantitative measure of job performance. Supervisors

FIGURE 6.1 ■ Three Examples of Graphic Rating Scales

Example 1

Planning and Organization

1	2	3	4	5
Poor		Average		Good

Example 2

Dimension	Performance Level			
	Unacceptable	Below Expectations	Meets Expectations	Exceeds Expectations
Planning	_____	_____	_____	_____
Oral Communication	_____	_____	_____	_____
Written Communication	_____	_____	_____	_____
Leadership	_____	_____	_____	_____
Efficient Use of Resources	_____	_____	_____	_____

Example 3

How effective was the team leader in assigning and describing the roles of team members?

_____ 1 – Completely ineffective

_____ 2 – Somewhat effective

_____ 3 – Average effectiveness

_____ 4 – Better than average effectiveness

_____ 5 – Highly effective

and managers in organizations routinely use this type of scale to record their evaluations of the performance of their subordinates.

The big advantage of a graphic scale is its simplicity, but this type of scale has many disadvantages. First, these scales do little to define the performance dimensions being rated. If different raters have different ideas about what "leadership" or "planning" mean, they are likely to disagree in their evaluations. Second, these scales do little to define what the performance levels being rated mean. Different raters might have very different ideas about what "average," "good," "meets expectations," and others mean, and this could lead them to disagree in their evaluations. The ambiguity of both the performance dimensions and the performance levels included in these scales often make performance appraisals seem subjective and capricious. A substantial portion of performance appraisal research published during the 1970s and 1980s was concerned with attempts to develop better rating scales.

Before we discuss the different types of performance rating scales that were developed during this period, it is useful to think a bit about *why* scale development became such an important area of research. In our view, studies of rating scale formats were popular for a number of reasons. First, this is a topic that plays to the strengths of psychologists. That is, psychologists have a long history of involvement in scale development and measurement, and the development of rating scales for measuring job performance fit squarely within that tradition. Second, the development and refinement of rating scales provided what appeared to be a successful marriage of science and practice. It was easy for psychologists to develop, and for organizations to adopt new types of rating scales, and compared to many of the other interventions psychologists have developed, new rating scales seemed to be a simple application of scientific advances. Finally, the development of new and better rating scales seemed for a very long time to be a way psychologists could contribute to making the process of performance appraisal more fair and accurate and less fraught with conflict. Unfortunately, things did not turn out this way.

Behaviorally Anchored Rating Scales

In a highly influential article, Smith and Kendall (1963) described a procedure for developing clear, behavioral anchors for rating scales that could help reduce error and subjectivity in performance ratings, an approach they described as "retranslation of expectations." This process involves input from several groups of potential raters. First, a group of supervisors, managers, or other subject matter experts is given a list of performance dimensions and asked to generate critical incidents—that is, examples of behaviors that indicate good or poor (or perhaps even average) performance on each dimension. Next, this list of behaviors is given to an independent group of supervisors, managers, or other subject matter experts who are asked to make judgments about which performance dimension each behavior example corresponds to. Next, this group, or perhaps another independent group of supervisors, managers, or other subject matter experts, is asked to indicate the performance level each behavioral example corresponds to. If these raters do not agree about which performance dimension or which performance level a behavior example corresponds to, that example is discarded. What is left is a list of behavioral examples that: (1) are written in language that makes sense to the supervisors or managers who will be using the scale, (2) provide clear examples of the dimension being rated, and (3) provide clear examples of specific performance levels. These behavioral examples are used as scale anchors; Figure 6.2 provides examples of behaviorally anchored scales developed by Murphy and Constans (1987) for evaluating the performance of lecturers.

In theory, behaviorally anchored rating scales (BARS) accomplish two distinct goals. First, they provide rating scales that help to define both what the performance dimensions mean and what the performance levels mean in clear behavioral terms. Second, they provide increases buy-in by involving a number of the potential users of the scales in the process of scale development. Even those raters and ratees who do not participate in scale development may view the scales favorably because of the heavy reliance of their colleagues' feedback in developing scales.

The literature on BARS is voluminous (for a sampling of studies, see Bernardin, 1977; Bernardin, Alvares, & Cranny, 1976; Borman & Vallon, 1974; Hauenstein, Brown, & Sinclair, 2010; Jacobs, Kafry, & Zedeck, 1980; Schneider, 1977; Shapira & Shirom, 1980). However, this line of research eventually died out, for two reasons. First, as we discuss later in this section, by 1980 there was growing skepticism that adjustments to rating scale formats really made much of a difference in the quality of performance ratings. Second, there was evidence that BARS could introduce new biases in performance evaluation (Murphy & Constans, 1987; Piotrowski, Barnes-Farrell, & Esrig, 1989). Suppose, for example, that a store asks sales managers to rate their sales staff in terms of their success in maintaining good customer contact, and the rating scale uses the behavior "Calls customers to follow up, even after the end of the shift." The sales manager observes one of her salespeople, who is usually

FIGURE 6.2 ■ Behaviorally Anchored Rating Scales

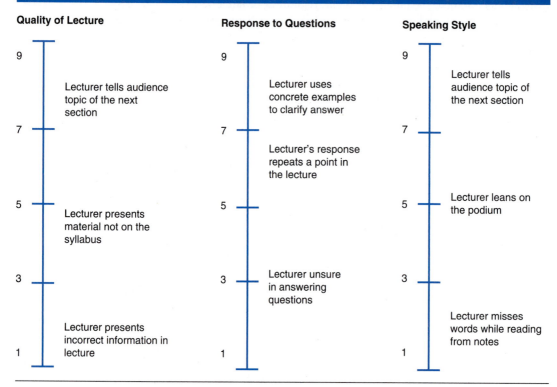

Source: Adapted from Murphy & Constans (1987).

lackadaisical in contacting customers, doing just this. There is evidence that observing this one behavior, because is corresponds with the behavior described on the rating scale, will bias ratings of customer contact.

Behavior Observation Scales

A variation on the use of behavioral examples in evaluating performance is the behavior observation scale (BOS). A BOS presents a rater with a list of behaviors and asks how frequently he or she has observed each. Latham and Wexley (1977) present an example of a BOS item that might be used to evaluate the performance of a salesman—that is, "Knows the price of competitive products." The rater would be asked to indicate how frequently this behavior has been observed, on the following scale: (1) Never (0–19% of the time), (2) Seldom (20–39% of the time), (3) Sometimes (40–59% of the time), (4) Usually (60–79% of the time), or (5) Always (80–100% of the time). They describe the development of BOS for logging supervisors that contained 78 behaviors measuring performance dimensions such as interactions with associates and crew, safety, and manpower and equipment management.

Proponents of BOS suggested that this method removes much of the subjectivity that is usually present in evaluative judgments. First, the scale was entirely made up of behaviors that are a normal part of the job. Second, the rater's task was simplified, in the sense that rather than making an evaluative judgment about each behavior (e.g., Meets Expectations,

Good, Bad), all the rater had to do was indicate the frequency with which each behavior was observed. Unfortunately, research into the cognitive processes involved in responding to BOS (Murphy & Constans, 1987; Murphy, Martin, & Garcia, 1982) suggests that the process of judging behavior frequency is every bit as subjective as the process of forming evaluative judgments. In fact, behavior frequency ratings may be more subjective than trait ratings or overall judgments; overall evaluations of the ratee's performance appear to serve as a critical cue for estimating behavior frequencies. Thus, the use of BOS probably does not allow you to avoid the subjectivity of overall impressions or judgments.

Memory Aids

Behavior diaries have been suggested as a method of making performance appraisals more accurate and less susceptible to the effects of memory distortions (Balzer, 1986; Bernardin & Buckley, 1981). On the surface, the suggestion that raters should write down the behaviors they observe makes a good deal of sense, and there is evidence that these diaries can sometimes contribute to the accuracy of ratings (DeNisi & Peters, 1996). After all, it is difficult to remember behavior in any detail over long periods of time, and some of the inaccuracies that are introduced by relying on raters' memories might be reduced if good behavior diaries were available. Unfortunately, there are two problems with the suggestion that supervisors or managers should keep behavior diaries. First, the task of keeping detailed behavior diaries is time-consuming and burdensome. Suppose you supervised a dozen line workers and tried to write a diary entry every time one of them did something that was either effective or ineffective. You might not have time to do much else. Second, there is considerable evidence that the behaviors that *are* recorded in behavior diaries are not a representative sample of what the rater has observed. Even when simple checklists are used, there is evidence that overall impressions of ratees influence what is recorded or noted (Maurer, Palmer, & Ashe, 1993).

The suggestion that supervisors of managers should keep behavior diaries ultimately involves tradeoffs. These diaries take both time and effort, and the decision to collect this information can only be justified if the likely benefits outweigh this time and effort. There are two sorts of benefits that might reasonably be expected if raters kept behavior diaries. First, their memory for rate behavior *might* improve, which presumably would lead to better more accurate ratings. We are skeptical that the quality of ratings actually *will* improve. As we mentioned earlier, it appears that the same factors that bias memory for behaviors (i.e., a strong reliance on general impressions) are likely to bias behavior diaries, and if we encourage raters to keep these diaries, what we are likely to observe is a collection of behavioral incidents that are consistent with pre-existing opinions rather than an objective record of what the rater actually saw. A second benefit is perhaps more plausible. Suppose you maintain a detailed behavior diary. If, at the end of the year, an employee was not happy with his or her ratings (something that happens quite often), you could bring out the diary of behavioral records that support the ratings you gave. Of course, this feature of behavior diaries might only give the *appearance* of fairness if the record of behaviors you are able to produce is in fact a biased sampling of the real behavior of the employee. Nevertheless, the appearance of fairness is an important thing, and good behavior diaries could certainly enhance this appearance.

Evaluating Behavior-Based Rating Methods

Both BARS and BOS were designed to improve the quality of performance appraisals by making them more closely linked to the behavior of the individuals being rated and less subjective. Assessments of the effects of improvements in rating scales in general, and of the effects of using behavioral anchors in particular, suggest that these goals were not accomplished. There is compelling evidence that ratings are influenced by general impressions and global evaluations, and that by the time supervisors or managers get to the point that they have to evaluate performance over some period of time (e.g., an annual appraisal), the detailed behavioral information that might have once existed in the rater's memory is largely gone, and using behaviorally oriented rating scales is not enough to restore access to that behavioral information (Murphy & Cleveland, 1995).

More generally, the belief that improving rating scales would improve the quality of performance ratings simply did not pan out. DeNisi and Murphy (2017) reviewed nearly 100 years of research on performance appraisal and performance management. They noted that between 1917 and 1980, the most widely studied questions had to do with the hypothesis that some rating scale formats might be substantially superior to others as a means of collecting and recording evaluations of job performance. This hypothesis never received substantial support, and research on different types of rating scales eventually tailed off.

Landy and Farr's (1980) review was the first to reach the conclusion that adjustments to rating scale formats had few effects on the performance ratings individual employees received or on the quality of performance judgments. On the basis of the ongoing failure to demonstrate that changes to rating scale formats had much effect on the validity or usefulness of performance ratings they suggested a moratorium on rating scale research. This suggestion was highly influential (DeNisi & Murphy, 2017), and while there have been sporadic efforts over the years since 1980 to improve rating scales, this set of tools has received less attention in recent years.

It is useful to speculate on *why* over 60 years of scale format research failed to make a meaningful difference. It is likely that the answer is partly due to the way the cognitive processes involved in forming judgments about performance work. As we noted in Chapter 5, the processes involved in perceiving, categorizing, recalling, and integrating behavioral information are complex, and they are substantially influenced by overall impressions of whether a particular employee is a good worker or a poor worker. Behavior-based rating scales would make a lot more sense if performance judgments were built from the ground up—that is, if raters perceived and recalled behaviors pretty much as they happened and based their evaluation on the specific behaviors that were observed and recalled. It appears, however, that performance judgments are *not* simply an evaluation of the particular behaviors an employee has exhibited during the last year, but rather are influenced by conclusions you have already reached about that employee; the extent to which you like, trust, or depend on that employee; and the context within which evaluations occur.

More generally, the failure of rating scales to influence performance judgments is likely a symptom of a faulty diagnosis. That is, much of the research published between 1917 and 1990 was based on the assumption that performance ratings were not sufficiently reliable, valid, or fair because raters lacked the *ability* to form accurate judgments. Thus, it made lots of sense to try and develop tools to help the rater do his or her job. Since 1990, more emphasis has been placed on an alternative explanation, that raters lack the *motivation* to rate accurately (Banks & Murphy, 1985). Chapter 12 will examine this theme in more detail.

Scale formats might not have a large effect on reliability or validity of ratings, but behavior-based methods can have other effects, ranging from acceptance of ratings and satisfaction with performance appraisal to clarity regarding rating dimensions and levels (Tziner, Joanis, & Murphy, 2000; Tziner, Kopelman, & Livneh, 1993). There are three ways in which behavior-based rating scales might contribute to the success and acceptance of performance appraisal systems. First, as noted earlier, the process of developing these scales involves a good deal of input from many of the same people who will be using these scales in the future, something that is likely to enhance the perceived relevance and credibility of these scales. Second, they provide a common language for users to rely on when describing what performance dimensions and performance levels mean in a concrete sense. Finally, they *appear* to be more objective and fair than scales that provide no behavioral information at all.

Performance Distribution Assessment

Job performance is rarely constant; any employee's performance is likely to vary over time, and if the variability is extensive, a rating that captures the average level of performance may not be enough. A single number (the overall performance rating) can at best capture some aspect of performance (the average), while necessarily ignoring the rest. For example, suppose Sam shows average performance just about every day, whereas Frank shows excellent performance half of the time and terrible performance the other half. If they both received a single overall rating, they would receive the same score, but their performance is clearly not the same. To deal with this shortcoming, Kane (1983, 1986) proposed *performance distribution assessment* (PDA), in which raters are asked to describe the distribution of ratee performance rather than simply its average. In a more recent paper, Kane (1996) proposed a variety of metrics that might be used to characterize the distribution of job performance.

Distributional rating scales ask raters to indicate how frequently the individual being evaluated has demonstrated good, average, or poor performance. For example, Jako and Murphy (1990) describe performance distribution scales that might be used to measure teacher performance, and illustrate how this technique could be applied at several different levels of analysis, ranging from overall assessments to assessments of quite specific behaviors. These scales are illustrated in Figure 6.3.

PDA represents a more sophisticated version of the basic approach exemplified by BOS. In PDA, raters must indicate the frequency of different outcomes (e.g., behaviors, results) that indicate specific levels of performance on a given dimension. For example, the scale might describe the most effective outcome and the least effective outcome that could reasonably be expected in a particular job function, as well as several intermediate outcomes. The rater is asked to estimate the frequency of each outcome level for each ratee. One of the potential advantages of this format is that it allows you to consider the distribution or the variability of performance as well as the average level of performance in forming an evaluation. PDA involves some fairly complex scoring rules (a concise description of PDA is presented in Bernardin & Beatty, 1984; software now exists for PDA scoring), and results in measures of the relative effectiveness of performance, the consistency of performance, and the frequency with which especially positive or negative outcomes are observed.

Although the link is rarely made explicit, the use of distributional metrics rather than (or in addition to) the mean performance level to characterize job performance makes sense only if performance is dynamic. If most people perform at the same level most of the time, there would be no meaningful distribution of performance, and the mean would adequately capture the entire distribution. If performance is highly variable, the mean will capture only one aspect of the performance distribution.

FIGURE 6.3 ■ **Performance Distribution Scales at Three Levels of Specificity**

General

Of all the lecturer's behaviors indicating his/her overall performance level, please list

_____% poor _____% below _____% average _____% above _____% excellent
                            average   average

More Specific

Of all the lecturer's behaviors involving nonverbal mannerisms, please list

_____% poor _____% below _____% average _____% above _____% excellent
                            average   average

Highly Specific

Of all the lecturer's behaviors involving effective use of facial expressions, please list

_____% poor _____% below _____% average _____% above _____% excellent
                            average   average

Second, the type of distributional metrics that might be used depends substantially on the shape of the performance distribution. Suppose each person's performance varies from day to day or from week to week. If the distribution of performance is essentially normal, only two statistics, the mean and the standard deviation, will be needed to fully characterize the distribution of performance. If the distribution is skewed or irregular, more statistics might be needed, and if the distribution is sufficiently irregular, nothing short of a graph of performance levels might suffice.

The question of what might be accomplished using distributional performance assessments or what might be missed if organizations rely solely on the average level of performance probably depends substantially on the purpose of appraisal. If performance appraisals are used to set annual salary, the mean might be quite sufficient, but if they are used to provide feedback, it probably makes sense to give different performance feedback to Sam (who is always average) than to Fred (who is sometimes brilliant and sometimes awful).

Evaluating PDA

Evaluations of distributional rating methods have been somewhat mixed. Deadrick and Gardner (1997); Steiner, Rain, and Smalley (1993); and Woehr and Miller (1997) presented evidence supporting the validity and value of these methods, whereas Jako and Murphy (1990) found little evidence that these methods yield useful information. It is possible, as noted earlier, that the value of these methods depends substantially on the distribution of performance, and that the performance of specific individuals is more variable (or distributed differently) in some situations than in others. Woehr and Miller (1997) showed that distributional ratings often lead to similar conclusions to those reached using other rating methods about the average level of performance, but the additional information obtained by asking about rating distributions may help reduce the amount of measurement error in ratings.

Multi-Attribute Rating Systems

Manoharan, Muralidharan, and Deshmukh (2011) proposed an appraisal system based on multi-attribute decision making (MAUT).[1] They note that performance measures and judgments about performance are not always exact (e.g., a rater may conclude that Jeff is usually better at verbal communication than Dan), and they propose a complex application of fuzzy analytic tools to cope with this uncertainty. While their approach has the advantage of making the key issues in performance evaluation (e.g., identifying key performance dimensions, taking into account the intercorrelation among these dimensions, determining the weight to apply to each dimensions) explicit and mathematically rigorous, their approach would make performance appraisal more complex and less transparent. In particular, this approach requires complex calculations to translate the judgments of raters to actual performance scores, making it difficult for raters or ratees to understand precisely why an individual receives a good or a poor performance rating at any point in time.

The approach proposed by Manoharan et al. (2011) has not, to our knowledge, been implemented. While sophisticated in many ways, this approach is likely to cause more problems than it solves. In particular, this sort of system, in which the relationships between the evaluations of supervisors and the performance scores ratees actually receive are at best indirect is likely to make performance appraisal more confusing and less credible. We believe it is important to move in the opposite direction—to make performance appraisal transparent and easy to understand. Appraisal systems that involve setting and monitoring concrete performance goals are an example of this trend.

Using Performance Goals in Performance Appraisal

In Chapter 5, we noted that self-ratings are widely used in performance appraisal systems. The formats for these ratings vary from company to company, but these self-ratings often include two components: (1) articulation of performance goals and the metrics that will be used to assess the accomplishment of those goals, and (2) evaluations of the extent to which these goals have been accomplished. Performance goals are sometimes the result of discussions and negotiations between supervisors and subordinates. For example, an employee might be asked to propose performance goals and metrics for evaluating whether or not these goals are accomplished. These goals might be modified on the basis of input from his or her supervisor, or they might be accepted. This type of goal setting has some clear advantages. First, it directly involves the employee in determining what he or she will try to accomplish and how that accomplishment will be evaluated. Second, it provides a clear and objective basis for performance reviews. On the other hand, this goal-setting process provides a golden opportunity for the employee to "game the system." There is a clear motivation to try and set goals that are easy to meet, and even if your supervisor is well aware that you are trying to set easy goals, he or she may decide to play along; in Chapters 9 and 12 we will explore reasons why supervisors may choose to avoid conflict, even if it means lower performance levels from some employees.

In Chapter 2, we noted that the philosophy of performance management implies that goals will be imposed from above rather than being generated by the employees themselves. The reality is probably a bit more complex. That is, regardless of the performance management systems a company puts in place, it is probably common (and certainly smart) to get input from the employees and to take that input seriously. To be honest, despite the large literature on performance management, too little is known about how these systems actually operate. Nevertheless, a company that wants employees to actually accept performance goals will almost certainly want to give employees some genuine role in setting those goals.

It is widely recommended that performance goals and objectives should be written to be S.M.A.R.T.[2] That is, goals and performance objectives should be:

- Specific
- Measurable
- Agreed Upon and Achievable
- Realistic
- Time-Bound

Table 6.1 provides some examples of S.M.A.R.T. (and Not-So S.M.A.R.T.) performance objectives for a high school teacher. For example, the objective "All student exams will be graded and returned to the student within 5 days next semester" is specific (exams will be graded and returned), measurable (All … within 5 days), achievable and realistic (assuming that other demands of the job make this objective possible to reach and time-bound (next semester). In contrast, "Parents will become more engaged in their children's education" is vague. It is not clear how engagement will be evaluated, or what the time frame is for its evaluation. It is not clear it is even a realistic goal; teachers do not typically have much control over parents' level of engagement. Similarly, student scores on the state's standardized graduation examination will increase by 10% next year may not be a S.M.A.R.T. objective. It is specific, measurable, and time-bound, but is it realistic and achievable? Depending on the test, it may or may not be possible to boost student achievement by this much.

There is clear evidence that setting and monitoring performance goals can lead to increases in performance and effectiveness (Cunningham & Austin, 2007; Ivancevich, 1982; Locke & Latham, 1990; Locke, Shaw, Saari, & Latham, 1981), particularly when goals are accepted as legitimate and reasonable by employees (Erez & Kanfer, 1983). In addition to increasing performance, the process of setting and monitoring performance goals has the potential to increase the perceived fairness and accuracy of appraisals. These goals and objectives provide a clear idea about two things: (1) what is important to

TABLE 6.1 ■ Examples of Performance Objectives for a High School Teacher	
S.M.A.R.T. Objectives	All student exams will be graded and returned to the student within 5 days next semester
	Lesson plans will be drafted and submitted to senior teachers for comment at least one week before each class this year
Not-So S.M.A.R.T. Objectives	Parents will become more engaged in their children's education
	Student scores on the state's standardized graduation examination will increase by 10% next year

achieve, and (2) performance standards. If you receive a rating of "Meets Expectations" on "Oral Communication" from your supervisor, it may be hard to know precisely what this really means. On the other hand, a S.M.A.R.T. objective not only tells you what it is you need to accomplish, it also provides a metric for evaluating whether you did in fact meet the goal.

One problem with goal-oriented appraisal systems is that they sometimes involve multiple, conflicting goals. For example, Cheng, Luckett, and Mahama (2007) examined the use of performance goals in measuring the effectiveness of call center employees. Performance measures included call time, net sales, adherence to schedule, accuracy in entering customer data into computer system, and call quality (e.g., is the caller polite and friendly?). They noted that these goals could come into conflict, especially when challenging goals were set. For example, if a goal of keeping call time as short as possible is set, this is likely to have an adverse effect on call quality. Another challenge of appraisal systems that incorporate specific performance goals is that they make failures more visible and less ambiguous. That is, if your performance plan includes a goal of increasing customer sales by 10%, and you do not reach that goal, it is clear to you and to your supervisor that you have failed. Unfortunately, failure to meet goals this year can have a negative influence on your performance next year. There is evidence that personality characteristics such as learning orientation can influence the way we react to failure and negative feedback, and that for some people, failure to meet a performance goal can lead to an avoidance of feedback and a propensity to minimize risk in the future (Cron, Slocum, VandeWalle, & Fu, 2005).

Another problem with appraisal systems built around the articulation and measurement of performance goals is one we have already encountered in our discussion of objective performance measures (Chapter 3)—that is, criterion deficiency. Appraisal systems built around objectives and metrics place a great deal of emphasis on those aspects of job performance that are most easily measurable, and place less emphasis on aspects of performance that are not so easily measured. In Chapter 3, we noted that job performance includes a good deal beyond simply accomplishing the tasks that are listed in your job description, and that important aspects of performance such as organizational citizenship or organizational deviance are not easy to translate into concrete, measurable performance objectives. Table 6.2 illustrates two S.M.A.R.T objectives that might be written to reflect important aspects of organizational citizenship and organizational deviance. While these objectives might be specific, measurable, achievable, realistic, and time bound, we doubt that anyone's performance objectives will include examples like these.

Finally, performance appraisal systems that incorporate S.M.A.R.T. objectives have the potential to change the power dynamics of performance appraisal, particularly if the goals and objectives are set by the individual employee. In particular, other than perhaps approving or editing goals proposed by the employee, a system built around S.M.A.R.T. objectives pretty much takes the supervisor or manager out of the picture in terms of performance evaluation and feedback. Suppose you have 10 S.M.A.R.T. objectives for the year. The whole point of S.M.A.R.T. objectives is to remove subjectivity about what it is people are supposed to do and whether or not they have successfully done it. Who needs a supervisor or manager to evaluate performance or to provide feedback? If the objectives are sufficiently wide-ranging to cover the full range of job tasks, the need for supervisory evaluations might be greatly diminished.

TABLE 6.2 ■ Examples of Why It Is Hard to Write S.M.A.R.T. Objectives for Organizational Citizenship or Organizational Deviance	
Citizenship	Will not complain or irritate coworkers during the next six months
	Will go above and beyond what is called for in job description at least four times during the next six months
Deviance	Will not steal materials or supplies worth more than $20 over the next six months
	Will not engage in bullying or sexual harassment during working hours for the next six months

Performance Appraisals Are Not Simply Numbers: Narrative Comments

Brutus (2010) notes that while most performance appraisals include both words (comments about performance) and numbers (numerical ratings of ranking), the narrative comments that are part of most appraisal rarely receive attention from researchers. She notes that narrative comments can add detail to numerical ratings (citing an example of an employee whose performance is below average, and who receives specific comments about performance deficiencies—in this case, an unwillingness to pay attention and act on input from coworkers), and that the recipients of feedback often pay more attention to the narrative comments than to the numerical ratings. She also notes that advances in research methods have made it increasingly practical to rigorously analyze the content of narrating comments and to use these analyses to help advance our understanding of performance evaluations. For example, she suggests that the amount and the specificity of commentary makes a difference (specific and detailed comments have potential value for identifying specific issues that represent strengths or weaknesses). Comments that provide suggestions are more useful than those that simply note problems, and comments that span the performance domain are more useful than comments that focus on a narrow slice of performance.

In their review of the performance appraisal system used by U.S. Navy officers, Bjerke, Cleveland, Morrison, and Wilson (1987) noted that raters sometimes use the narrative section to overcome the limitations of the numerical rating system. They noted that, like most organizations, performance ratings in the Navy tend to be inflated. If many officers receive high ratings, it can be difficult for raters to convey to their superiors that a particular officer really *is* excellent. Bjerke et al. (1987) noted that raters use narrative comments, offering faint praise to some officers ("looks good in his uniform") and strong and specific comments about salient performance dimensions for others ("his men will follow him anywhere"). Despite the clear importance of narrative comments, there has been little research on training raters to provide better or more useful narratives.

Research in performance evaluation has paid a great deal of attention, but there have been only a handful of empirical studies of the narrative comments that often accompany ratings (David, 2013; Gorman, Meriac, Roch, Ray, & Gamble, 2017; Wilson, 2010). This is a shame, because it is likely that employees pay more attention to the narrative comments they receive than to their numerical ratings (David, 2013). In some performance appraisal systems, narrative comments may be brief pro forma summaries of information already conveyed by ratings (e.g., a narrative comment of "Meets Expectations" for an employee who receives a rating in the middle of the rating scale), but in systems where comments are more extensive and individualized, narratives might provide critically important information to employees.

We see narrative comments as an untapped gold mine for advancing our understanding of performance appraisal. We suspect that numerical ratings have been more extensively studied precisely because they are numbers, which makes ratings relatively easy to study using a range of familiar statistical tools. Narrative comments are more difficult to analyze, but with the explosion of computerized text mining methods (Aggarwal & Zhai, 2012; Kuckartz, 2014), empirical research on narrative comments in performance appraisal is becoming increasingly feasible. So little is known about narrative comments, that it is difficult to do more than speculate about what an analysis of these comments might reveal, but we will offer two predictions. First, narrative comments might tell us a good deal about the rater. Some raters are probably more likely than others to give detailed, individualized comments. Second, they might tell us even more about the relationship between the rater and the ratee. We expect that high-quality narratives are most likely when the relationship between an individual rater and an individual ratee is either very good or (perhaps) very bad. High-quality supervisor–subordinate relationships should generate both more opportunities and a higher willingness to comment on the subordinate's performance. When the relationship is bad, raters might end up providing more detailed narrative feedback in an effort to either improve the relationship or to protect themselves by justifying poor ratings.

RANKING AS AN ALTERNATIVE TO RATING

In Chapters 1 and 3 we noted that one of the serious problems with performance ratings is inflation. It is not unusual for 80% of employees to be rated "above average," and the resulting tendency for most employees to receive pretty similar ratings severely undercuts many of the possible uses of performance ratings. One alternate is to do away with ratings altogether and ask supervisors or managers to rank their subordinates instead.

Ranking has been used in the performance appraisal systems in the military, usually as an adjunct to rather than a replacement for rating. Although ranking is generally regarded as a solution to rating inflation, even performance evaluation scales that rely on ranking rather than on rating are subject to manipulation. For example, during the 1980s, the performance appraisal form used by the U.S. Navy to evaluate the performance of its officers (Fitness Report) asked raters to provide performance ratings and also asked them to rank each ratee relative to his or her peers. So, if there were four lieutenants who reported to me, one of my jobs when completing the annual Fitness Report would to be rank-order these four.

On the surface, ranking should solve the problem of rating inflation. There is evidence, however, that raters "inflated" the rankings in the Fitness Reports they completed by using an unrealistic comparison standard, magnifying the number in the comparison group to make each actual subordinate look good (Kozlowski, Chao, & Morrison, 1998). For example, a ranking of third out of 15 looks a lot better than a ranking of third out of four, and by creating an inflated comparison group, a supervisor can avoid giving a low ranking to any of his or her actual subordinates.

The Fitness Report used by the Navy in the 1980s called for a full ranking of all subordinates. A more common application of ranking in performance appraisal is some sort of partial ranking, such as the forced distribution ranking systems that are used in many organizations (Grote, 2005; Guralnik, Rozmarin, & So, 2004; Pfeffer & Sutton, 2006; Stewart, Gruys, & Storm, 2010). Forced distribution ranking systems require supervisors to sort their subordinates into ordered categories, based on their overall performance or effectiveness. For example, a manager who has 10 direct reports might be asked to sort them into three categories, such as top 20%, middle 60%, and bottom 20%. That is, the supervisor might be asked to identify the top two performers and the bottom two performers; everyone else will end up in the middle category.

These systems provide a potential solution to some of the problems caused by rating inflation, by forcing raters to make distinctions between ratees when evaluating their performance. However, these systems are often disliked by raters (because they may not want to make these distinctions, especially if they believe that the differences between subordinates are small; Schleicher, Bull, & Green, 2009) and ratees alike. Blume, Baldwin, and Rubin (2009) studied reactions to forced distribution systems, and concluded that reactions are most likely to be negative when there are harsh consequences for ratees and when the group size is small. On the whole, rating systems (e.g., those that do not call for comparisons between employees) are seen as more fair than relative rating (ranking) systems, and forced distribution systems are seen as the least fair (Roch, Sternburgh, & Caputo, 2007).

Rank and Yank

General Electric, during the tenure of Jack Welch as its CEO (Welch & Byrne, 2001), instituted a forced distribution system in which a set proportion of employees (usually 10%) was forced into the lowest-performance category, and in which this lowest-performing group could be subject to a number of negative consequences, including dismissal. The "rank-and-yank" philosophy is based on the assumption that replacing the poorest-performing employees with new hires is an important part of maintaining and improving the effectiveness of organizations. While this system can seem cruel to the employees who are dismissed, proponents of rank and yank argue that keeping ineffective employees is ultimately harmful to the entire organization, and could even put everyone's job at risk.

There is evidence that forced distribution rank-and-yank systems *can* help increase performance, especially if the identification of the best and worst performers is reliable and accurate (Scullen, Bergey, & Aiman-Smith, 2005). The effects of this method are especially dramatic in the first few years it is applied, but the payoff associated with these systems declines over time. Giumetti, Schroeder, and Switzer (2015) note that a rank-and-yank policy can have potentially negative consequences for members of minority groups. Even though the average performance ratings for white versus minority employees tend to be similar (Chapter 11 examines demographic effects on performance ratings), it is often the case the members of minority groups will be slightly more likely to receive lower rankings, and even small differences can have a large effect on who is fired and who is retained (Giumetti et al., 2015).

To understand why rank-and-yank systems have a short shelf life, consider the scenario illustrated in Table 6.3. Suppose there are 100 employees in an organization, and their absolute performance level can be scored on a scale from 1–5, with an average score of "3."

TABLE 6.3 ■ How the Effects of Rank-and-Yank Systems Diminish Over Time				
Performance Level	**Year 1**	**Year 2**	**Year 3**	**Year 4**
5	10	10	10	10
4	20	20	20	20
3	50	60	70	80
2	20	20	10	0
1	10	0	0	0
Average	3.0	3.2	3.3	3.4

Note: Each year, dismiss the 10 lowest-performing incumbents and replace them with new recruits whose performance level is "3."

Suppose also that new employees this organization recruits will have performance scores of "3." In the first year of the rank-and-yank system, you dismiss 10 employees whose performance ranked lowest and replace them with new recruits. This will produce a boost in performance (the average performance score will go from 3.0 to 3.2), but this strategy will not work for long. The first year, you replace 10 people whose absolute performance levels is "1" with 10 new recruits whose performance level is "3." The next year, there are no longer any "1s," but you still benefit by replacing 10 of the "2" performers with 10 recruits whose performance level is "3." The year after that, you do the same thing, replacing 10 of the "2" performers with 10 recruits whose performance level is "3."

By the time you get to Year 4 in this system, there are no longer any people in the organization who are truly poor performers (absolute performance scores of 1 or 2), and if you continue to rank and yank, you will get rid of 10 people who are "3" performers and replace them with 10 new "3" performers. You will not be any better off, and because you will need to spend time and money training new employees, you are probably even worse off.

Unsurprisingly, rank-and-yank systems are often unpopular with employees. After using variations on the rank-and-yank system for many years, even GE has decided to replace this system with one that emphasizes performance feedback rather than one that emphasizes identifying poor performers.[3] Blume, Baldwin, and Rubin (2009) note that reactions to forced distribution systems depend on a number of characteristics of these systems, including consequences for employees who are rated in the top and bottom categories and the size of the comparison group. Perspective also matters; managers are much more likely to be favorably inclined to forced distribution systems than are employees (Blume et al., 2009).

What Problems Does Ranking Solve and What Problems Does It Create?

Replacing performance rating with ranking has the potential to solve the problem of rating inflation, although as Kozlowski et al. (1998) note, the solution is far from foolproof. On the whole, however, we believe ranking creates more problems than it solves. First, ranking only makes sense if there are sharp and meaningful differences between individual employees (full ranking) or if there really are distinct classes of employees (e.g., top, middle, and bottom performers). Otherwise, ranking systems force supervisors or managers to make distinctions where there might be little meaningful difference between people. Suppose your three best subordinates are very similar, but the ranking system only allows you to designate two as top performers. Forced distribution systems often force supervisors or managers to group employees in ways that do not truly reflect their performance. Finally, forced distribution evaluation systems only make sense if you assume that all work groups have the same average level and the same distribution of performance. Suppose one manager really is better at his or her job and really succeeds in creating conditions that lead to high performance levels. That manager will be forced to give performance ratings that are indistinguishable from another manager who supervises a group of truly poor performers.

Ranking systems might be quite appropriate for some purposes. In Chapter 8, we differentiate between using appraisal to distinguish between employees (e.g., to determine who should get raises or promotions) versus distinguishing within employees (identifying individual strengths and weaknesses). Ranking is potentially compatible with between-employee uses of appraisal, but is likely to be of little value for providing feedback or for guiding development. Suppose you find out that, in your manager's opinion, you are a better employee than Fred but not as good as Susan. This sort of information might not tell you much about how you might develop into a better performer.

We believe that framing this question in terms of rating versus ranking is the wrong way to look at things. A case can be made that if ranking is used at all, it should be used in conjunction with rating rather than as a replacement for performance ratings. Both rating and ranking methods have their strengths and weaknesses, and it is probably better to incorporate both techniques in performance appraisal than to rely on either rating or ranking alone.

RATER TRAINING

All of the different approaches to improving rating scales, or to developing alternatives to rating described in the first half of this chapter, share the same general goal: making performance evaluation easier, fairer, more consistent, and more accurate. Behaviorally anchored rating scales were designed with the idea that the scale itself could make it easier for supervisors and managers to understand what different performance dimensions and performance levels meant. Rating systems that asked employees to articulate performance goals were designed in part to remove ambiguity in evaluation. Once goals and metrics were defined, there would be little doubt about whether or not they were accomplished. On the whole, these efforts to perfect rating scales and evaluation methods did make a contribution by increasing the transparency and apparent fairness of performance ratings, but it is clear that the effects of variations in rating scale formats on the consistency, accuracy, and validity of performance ratings is small at best (Landy & Farr, 1980).

A second strategy for making performance evaluation easier, fairer, more consistent, and more accurate involves rater training. This strategy is based on the assumption that raters may lack the knowledge or the skills to consistently and accurately evaluate their subordinates. A wide range of strategies for training raters has been developed, including new methods that use virtual environments as a tool for training managers about performance appraisal (Morse, 2010). Two particular strategies have been extensively researched, one aimed at training raters to avoid particular errors (such as giving high ratings to all of their subordinates), the other aimed at training raters to develop a common frame of reference when evaluating their subordinates.

Rater Error Training

It has long been known that a large majority of employees receive performance ratings well above the scale midpoint (this midpoint if often used to represent average performance), suggesting that raters are unduly lenient in evaluating their subordinates. It has also long been known that ratings of separate aspects of performance (e.g., planning, oral communication) tend to be highly correlated even though these are in theory quite different behaviors, suggesting that raters rely on general impressions (leading to what Bingham, 1939, first labeled halo errors).[4] One of the most widely studied methods of rater training is referred to as rater error training (RET).

In general, RET involves: (1) giving raters information about errors such as leniency or halo, (2) giving them feedback regarding the possible presence of these errors in the performance ratings they give, (3) helping raters diagnose these errors, and (4) encouraging raters to avoid these errors when evaluating their subordinates. Latham, Wexley, and Pursell (1975) and Pulakos (1984) describe RET programs that go beyond simply encouraging raters to avoid giving high ratings to everyone, or giving the same ratings on all aspects of performance; a careful RET program might involve multiple rounds of information sharing, practice, and feedback. Nevertheless, the goal of most RET programs is a negative one—that is, encouraging raters to avoid certain common pitfalls.

RET training is potentially vulnerable to what Wegner and Schneider (2003) describe as the "white bear problem." Suppose I tell you to try, for the next 10 minutes, to *not* think about a white bear. The harder you try, the more the white bear will dominate your thinking. Similarly, if I train you *not* to give high ratings to everyone or *not* to give ratings that are too highly intercorrelated, you may end up focusing more on what you are trying to avoid than on what you are trying to accomplish:, fairer, more consistent, and more accurate performance ratings.

There is evidence that if you train people to avoid giving high ratings or to avoid giving ratings that are too highly correlated, they will comply (Latham et al., 1975: Pulakos, 1984). That is, if I train supervisors not to give too many ratings of "4" or "5" and to give more ratings of "3," they will do pretty much what they are told (although this sort of training, like most other sorts of training, is likely to have effects that fade over time). However, many studies have shown that while RET can help reduce leniency or halo, it probably does not make performance ratings more accurate (Bernardin & Beatty, 1984; Bernardin & Pence, 1980; Borman, 1979; Hedge & Kavanagh, 1988; Landy & Farr, 1983; Pulakos, 1984; see, however, Stamoulis & Hauenstein, 1993).

Woehr and Huffcutt (1994) conducted a meta-analysis to explore the effects of different types of rater training on performance ratings. They found RET had no clear effect on the accuracy of performance ratings. However, they were able to distinguish between studies that conducted rater error training as it was originally intended (i.e., increasing awareness of common errors) and those that conducted inappropriate response training (i.e., identifying an alternative "correct" rating distribution). Training that focused on increasing awareness of rater errors had a large positive effect on rating accuracy ($d = .76$) whereas training that referenced alternative rating distributions led to a decrease in rating accuracy ($d = -.20$).

These findings emphasize the importance of avoiding inappropriate response training and focusing instead on educating raters about common rating errors (Woehr & Huffcutt, 1994). This study also showed that raters who have received this training that was aimed at effectively distinguishing between various categories of performance (performance dimension training) were less susceptible to providing common ratings across all dimensions. Performance dimension training, however, was not significantly related to rating accuracy or leniency errors (Woehr & Huffcutt, 1994).

By the mid-1990s, RET was falling out of favor, in part because of the lack of evidence that it improved the accuracy of performance ratings. However, the larger concern was a philosophical one. RET is essentially aimed at convincing raters not to do things that seem to undercut the value of performance rating, such as giving everyone high ratings or giving essentially the same rating on every aspect of performance. Consensus has grown that a better approach is a positive one—a training approach that tells raters what they *should* do rather than warning them about what they *shouldn't* do. Frame of reference training has emerged as a positive and effective alternative to RET.

Frame of Reference Training

The goal of frame of reference (FOR) training is to ensure that all raters use a consistent set of ideas about work performance to assess employees (Athey & McIntyre, 1987).

The process begins with providing raters with common standards for evaluating performance, and training programs teach raters how to match specific behaviors to performance dimensions using these standards. These evaluations are then connected to numerical ratings on a rating scale (Bernardin & Buckley, 1981). During frame of reference training sessions, raters are often given the opportunity to discuss examples of behaviors that fit into each performance dimension and to practice using the common standards to make

SPOTLIGHT 6.1 JUSTIFY YOUR RATINGS

One approach to dealing with rating inflation has been to require raters to provide explicit justification for very high or very low ratings. For example, some rating systems require raters to provide a concrete rationale for extreme ratings (e.g., ratings of "1" or "5" on a 5-point scale). What happens if you impose this sort of requirement?

It appears that raters react in one of several ways when faced with this sort of requirement. Some do precisely what the system asks them to do—give concrete explanations for extreme ratings. Others appear to react with boilerplate—by giving explanations that are pro forma statements, such as justifying a rating of "5" (where "5" = far exceeds expectations) by using the statement, "This employee far exceeds expectations" when giving ratings of "5." The most common reaction appears to be to simply avoid extreme ratings altogether, thus avoiding the need to give detailed justifications.

Convincing raters to avoid extreme ratings strikes us as a poor solution to a very real problem. One problem that many performance ratings face is rating inflation. Convincing raters to avoid giving the highest-possible rating *appears* to solve some problems (if raters avoid the top of the rating scale, the mean rating will indeed come down), but in fact it does very little good. If raters decide to avoid ratings of "1" or "5," all they accomplish is to transform a 5-point rating scale into a 3-point scale, and it is a good bet that the mean rating will be very close to "4," rather than to "5." This "solution" merely kicks the can down the road, and it does little, if anything, to improve the ratings

ratings for these behaviors. Trainers typically also provide feedback regarding how well the ratings reflect the intended frame of reference for performance (Woehr & Huffcutt, 1994). The goal of this method is similar to the goal of behaviorally anchored ratings scales—that is, to encourage raters to adopt a consistent understanding of performance dimensions and performance levels. That is, FOR attempts to put all raters "on the same page," by making sure that they all have a consistent understanding of the work behaviors they are asked to evaluate. The assumption here is that if raters adopt a consistent and appropriate set of categories for organizing and communicating information about the performance of their subordinates, this should enhance accuracy in recalling, making sense of, and evaluating the performance of their subordinates (Athey & McIntyre, 1987; Day & Sulsky, 1995; Woehr, 1994).

As Gorman and Rentsch (2009) note, "the ultimate goal of frame of reference training is to train raters to share and use common conceptualizations of performance when providing their ratings" (p. 1336). Although there is considerable evidence that this method of training improves the accuracy in recognizing, recalling, and evaluating rate behavior (Arvey & Murphy, 1998; Roch, Woehr, Mishra, & Kieszczynska, 2012; Stamoulis & Hauenstein, 1993; Woehr & Huffcutt, 1994), the assumption that this method actually changes performance schema (i.e., conceptualizations of what represents good versus poor performance and what performance includes) has rarely been tested. Gorman and Rentsch (2009) presented the first direct evidence that the effects of FOR can indeed be explained, at least in part, by the fact that this method helps raters adopt a consistent view of what they are looking for and what represents good versus poor performance. Their study showed that: (1) FOR training leads raters to have more similar and more accurate schema regarding performance dimensions and levels, and (2) the increased accuracy of performance schema is directly related to increasing levels of rating accuracy.

FOR is designed to help raters develop a consistent mental model of the performance domain and of what good versus poor performance looks like. Uggerslev and Sulsky (2008) note that the effectiveness of this training depends in part on what the rater's mental model looked like prior to training. On the whole, FOR is most effective when raters' initial conceptualization is similar to the one taught by FOR. Raters who have a substantially different view of what good versus poor performance entails, or of what is included in the performance domain, gain less from FOR training.

One of the key components of FOR (i.e., helping raters develop common standards for evaluating performance) might also be relevant for reducing disagreements between supervisors and subordinates. Schrader and Steiner (1996) note that disagreements between supervisors and subordinates are not always driven by different perceptions of subordinate behavior; supervisors and subordinates often agree on *what* was done in the workplace. Rather, they might apply different standards when evaluating that behavior, and training programs that help them adopt common evaluative standards might lead to higher agreement between raters and ratees.

FOR training is a well-liked tool in organizations. Uggerslev, Sulsky, and Day (2003) suggested that positive reactions to this type of training might help to mitigate some of the negative connotations associated with performance appraisals that many employees and managers endorse. Further, Sulsky and Kline (2007) found that participants generally had favorable reactions after receiving frame of reference training. The results of their study also pointed to the idea that more positive reactions were associated with higher learning as a result of the training. This research is consistent with the emerging trend of widening the scope of rater training research to focus on contextual factors including ratee reactions.

Alternatives to RET and FOR

Sometimes raters have the skills and the information needed to accurately evaluate their employees, but they do not believe that they have these essentials. As a result, training programs have been developed to help increase raters' confidence that they *can* provide accurate evaluations. Hauenstein (1998) suggested that rater training programs should include content to increase raters' self-efficacy—that is, their ability to accurately evaluate and rate performance. This idea was originally proposed by Bernardin and Buckley (1981), but it was largely ignored in most training programs, which focused instead on the type of frame of reference training that was included in the same article. Neck, Stewart, and Manz (1995) discuss the concept of increasing rater self-confidence using what they described as self-leadership training. The idea behind this emerging theme is that raters often experience uncertainty about their ratings, leading them to be more susceptible to biases and other rating errors. Training to enhance confidence in ratings might therefore increase the accuracy of performance appraisal ratings (Hauenstein, 1998). Whether this training actually *does* increase the consistency or accuracy of ratings is difficult to determine, in part because of the difficulty in measuring the accuracy of ratings. (Chapter 11 examines measures of the consistency and accuracy of performance ratings.)

Martell and Evans (2005) introduced a new form of rater training referred to as source-monitoring training. The goal of source-monitoring training is to address biases that stem from rater expectations of employee behavior. In these training programs, participants are instructed during the rating process to only report on behaviors that induce vivid and detailed memories rather than focusing on behaviors that just seem familiar to the rater. The results of Martell and Evans's (2005) study suggested that raters are able to separate memories of behaviors that actually occurred from memories of behaviors that seem to be familiar but may not have actually occurred. Thus, source-monitoring training can be effective for separating accurate judgments from those influenced by raters' expectations of ratees' performance behaviors. Martell and Evans (2005) called for additional research to further explore the value of source-monitoring training, but the idea has received limited attention in the literature since then.

Coaching the Coaches: Training Raters to Provide Feedback

Performance appraisal involves two distinct steps. First, managers or supervisors much evaluate the performance of their subordinates and assign ratings, rankings, and/or narrative statements to each of the important performance dimensions. Second, they must give feedback to employees, often in the form of a face-to-face performance appraisal interview. There is a large and detailed research literature dealing with the first step (i.e., performance rating), which we have reviewed in some detail. There is much less empirical research on how to train raters to give useful feedback.

To be sure, there are excellent books and reports discussing both the process of giving and the process of receiving feedback (e.g., Gregory & Levy, 2015; London, 2003; Society for Human Resource Management, 2017; Stone & Heen, 2014), and practically every publication aimed at human resource professionals is filled with advice about giving feedback, but it is striking how little we know about *how* supervisors and managers are trained to give performance feedback to their employees. We know even less about whether this training works or what sort of training works best in different circumstances.

Much of the discussion of performance feedback in the practitioner literature falls under the heading of *coaching*—that is, giving employees information and help designed to allow them to grow and improve their performance. Coaching is recognized as a critically important management competency by the U.S. Office of Personnel Management (2017), which provides practical advice on the essentials of coaching. What is missing from most of the literature on coaching is a clear understanding of *how* supervisors and managers learn this essential skills or what steps organizations undertake to develop this skill.

It appears that many organizations treat skill in coaching and providing feedback as a form of tacit knowledge—a skill that is picked up and developed without any clear and explicit program of training. This strikes us as a mistake, and also as a void in the current literature. It would be wonderful to provide organizations with concrete, data-driven guidance on how to best develop skills in providing feedback, but the current literature just does not support any particular program of development. What we do know from the broader literature on skill development is that both practice and feedback are required to develop most skills. This does lead to one practical suggestion that we believe is amply supported by research: it is important to evaluate the quality of feedback given by supervisors and to give *them* feedback on the quantity and quality of the performance feedback they provide. Beyond this, the field is wide open, and we eagerly await the development of empirical studies of the methods organizations use (or fail to use) to train supervisors and managers in giving performance feedback.

SUMMARY

Recognizing the shortcomings of many performance appraisals, researchers have attempted to increase the consistency, validity, and accuracy of performance ratings by giving raters better tools for evaluating their subordinates. Much of the performance appraisal research published prior to 1980 was devoted to one strategy for improving performance ratings that involved improvements to rating scales. Scales that included specific behavioral anchors (behaviorally anchored rating scales) or that asked questions about the frequency of particular behaviors (behavior observation scales) received a great deal of attention, but other variations in scale formats, ranging from performance distribution assessments to assessments that abandoned ratings in favor of full or partial ranking (i.e., forced distribution scales) methods also exist. Landy and Farr's (1980) review of the literature suggested that the effects of improving rating scale formats were very

small, and they called for a moratorium on future rating scale research. With some limited exceptions, this moratorium has held. It is recognized that adjustments to rating scales can sometimes have benefits (adding behavior anchors makes scales appear less subjective and increases their acceptance), but that improving the scale often does little to improve the quality of ratings.

Rater training provides a more successful avenue for improving performance ratings. Early attempts at reducing rater errors by instructing raters to avoid particular errors were at best partially successful. If you train raters not to give so many high ratings, they will play along, but there is little evidence that decreasing the number of high performance scores does much to increase the consistency or accuracy of performance ratings. Frame of reference training, which is designed to ensure that all raters share common conceptions of the meaning of the performance dimensions they are asked to rate and of the different levels included on rating scales, has been more successful. There is evidence that this method of training can increase accuracy in recalling ratee behaviors and evaluating that behavior.

EXERCISE: DEVELOPING BEHAVIOR-BASED RATING SCALES

One of the recurring problems in performance rating is that different managers, supervisors, or raters sometimes disagree about what particular performance dimensions (e.g., planning, communication with external customers) actually refer to, or about what constitutes good, average, or poor performance on these dimensions. Performance appraisal researchers have used several different strategies to attack this problem, notably training (e.g., frame of reference training) and scale development. On the whole, it does not seem that refinements in performance rating scales have had much impact of inter-rater agreement (Landy & Farr, 1980), but nevertheless, there are a number of reasons why it makes sense to develop behavior-based scales. Rating scales that include concrete behavioral examples may contribute to the perceived fairness and acceptability of performance ratings, and the fact that rating scale development often involves getting a number of users of the appraisal system to participate in scale development may contribute further to users' willingness to participate actively in performance appraisal.

There is no set system for developing performance rating scales that include behavioral examples, but there are three general steps that are likely to be common to just about any process of behavior-based scale development. First, generate behavioral examples by asking participants in the appraisal process to provide examples of things that people do that illustrate different levels of performance or success in each of the performance areas that are rated. Next, use a "retranslation" process to identify the behaviors that are the clearest exemplars of particular performance dimensions and levels. For example, a group of users can engage in a linkage exercise, where they are asked to identify which performance dimension each behavioral example is linked to. If you have a reasonably large group of raters available, you can use a simple grid like the one below to record linkages.

Which dimension should each behavior be linked to? (check one)

Behavior	Planning	Customer Communication	Time Management
Sends e-mails that include incorrect information	_____	_____	_____
Orders supplies before they run out	_____	_____	_____
Is often late with reports	_____	_____	_____

For example, if there are 10 people who complete this grid, and 7 or 8 link "Is often late with reports" to Time Management, that would constitute evidence that this is a good illustration of this particular aspect of performance. A second group of users can work with the list of behaviors that is most clearly linked to each performance dimension to determine what level of performance each example best illustrates. Here, you could use of similar grid, or you could ask each rater to place the behavioral examples somewhere on a 5-point rating scale, and then identify those ratings that can be most consistently scaled (e.g., items where the standard deviation of the performance level ratings is small). The result of these two steps will be a list of examples that clearly illustrate particular levels of performance on specific dimensions.

Murphy and Constans (1987) followed a similar process to create the scale shown in Appendix A, and illustrated below:

Speaking Style

9

_____ *Very High*

Lecturer varies pitch and tone to emphasize points

_____ 8

Lecturer uses hand and body movement to emphasize points

_____ 7

_____ 6

Lecturer leans on the podium

_____ 5

_____ 4

_____ 3

Lecturer misses words while reading from notes

_____ 2

Lecturer reads directly from notes without looking at audience

_____ *Very Low*

1

NOTES

1. Murphy and Cleveland (1995) suggest MAUT as a framework for analyzing the outcomes of performance appraisal, but the Manoharad et al. (2011) paper suggests a broader embrace of the MAUT framework, using it as the basis for collecting performance evaluations.

2. Some practitioners have moved in the direction of advocating S.M.A.R.T.E.R goals, where E = Evaluate and R = Revise.

3. http://blog.impraise.com/360-feedback/how-ge-renews-performance-management-from-stack-ranking-to-continuous-feedback-360-feedback.

4. Halo and leniency errors are discussed in detail in Chapter 11.

7 HOW CONTEXT INFLUENCES PERFORMANCE APPRAISAL

The way performance appraisal is designed, implemented, used, and interpreted is strongly influenced by the social and organizational context in which performance appraisal occurs. Imaging two organizations, one that is seen as highly successful, that has lots of resources and that operates in a nation whose culture strongly values individual excellence, and the other that is in an authoritarian country with a failing economy and that provides poor pay and worse opportunities. Even if all of their performance appraisal practices (e.g., rating scales, rater training, frequency of appraisal, individual feedback meetings with the supervisor) are the same, it is safe to assume that these two appraisal systems will function quite differently, will be used for different purposes, and will be interpreted by organizational members very differently. In this chapter, we explore the different levels of context and the contextual influences that are most likely to have an impact on performance appraisal in organizations.

We start by defining contexts, noting that there are both aspects of the broad society in which performance appraisal operates (distal context) and aspects of the organization itself (proximal context) that influence the design, implementation, and use of performance appraisal systems. We examine two distal factors in some detail, national cultures and the legal environment within which organizations operate. We next examine a number of proximal factors, ranging from the climate and culture of the organization to the structure and nature of work groups to the structure of performance appraisal systems (e.g., who provides input, how often is performance evaluated). One broad theme of this chapter is that the success or failure of performance appraisal systems often depends as much upon these contextual factors as it does on the design and implementation of the appraisal system itself.

LEARNING OBJECTIVES

7.1 Learn how national cultures and legal and political environments influence the way performance appraisal is conducted and used

7.2 Understand how the work environment influences the supervisors' ability to observe and evaluate the performance of their subordinates

7.3 Learn how organizational climates influence performance appraisals

7.4 Understand the way supervisor–subordinate relationships influence and are influenced by performance appraisals

7.5 Understand why performance appraisal policies and practices that work in one organization may not work as well in another

THE EMERGENCE OF CONTEXT-ORIENTED RESEARCH

Landy and Farr's (1980) review of performance appraisal research published between 1920 and 1980 helped ignite a steady stream of research on cognitive processes in performance appraisal. This work proved to be extremely useful for understanding how judgments about performance are made and how difficult it could be to accurately perceive, remember, and make sense of performance over the long periods of time typical for performance appraisals (usually done yearly). By the early 1990s, the weaknesses of this cognitive research were becoming apparent. First, this work had little relevance to the problems faced by organizations that were trying to improve their appraisals (Banks & Murphy, 1995; Murphy & Cleveland, 1991). More important, this research paid scant attention to the organizational context within which appraisals are conducted in organizations (Bretz, Milkovich, & Read, 1992; Ilgen, Barnes-Farrell, & McKellin, 1993), but rather focused on some basic principles of judgment that might cut across organizations or even across nations. In the last 30–40 years, considerably more attention has been paid to the influence of contextual variables on performance appraisal (Arvey & Murphy, 1998; Bernardin & Beatty, 1984; DeCotiis & Petit, 1978; Ferris, Munyon, Basik, & Buckley, 2008; Landy & Farr, 1980; Levy & Williams, 2004; Murphy & Cleveland, 1991, 1995).

Aycan (2005) points out paying attention to the context is by no means unique to performance appraisal research; a wide variety of theories of organization and management outside of the domain of performance appraisal have long been concerned with the way context shapes the behavior of organizations. For example, *general systems theory* (Katz & Kahn, 1978) was developed to help explain the way the effects of organizational policies and practices are influenced by the social, legal, and political contexts in which organizations operate. *Strategic fit* models (e.g., Schuler & Jackson, 1987) help to explain how human resource policies and practices interact with the broader strategy of the firm. *Agency theory* (Jensen & Meckling, 1976) examines the way the titles and descriptions of jobs and occupations (e.g., managerial versus non-managerial job titles) influence HR policies and practices. Kanungo's *model of culture fit* (Kanungo & Jaeger, 1990) was developed explicitly to examine the interplay between societal cultures and internal work cultures in determining HR policies and practices and their effectiveness. Thus, the trend in performance appraisal research to emphasize context can be thought of as a specific instance of a much broader trend in the organizational sciences over the last 50 years of paying careful attention to the way the context in which organizational policies are carried out influence the implementation, interpretation, and effects of those policies.

What Is Context?

One of the definitions of the term "context" that we find most useful is that the context is the "setting within which something exists or happens, and that can help explain it."[1] This definition has two appealing features. First, as applied to performance appraisal, context is the setting or the set of circumstances that surrounds the practice of performance appraisal in organizations. Thus, context is "bigger" than the thing it surrounds, but that thing (here, performance appraisal) cannot be fully separated from all that surrounds it. That is, performance appraisal cannot be taken out of its normal context without changing important aspects of the appraisal process, and research that ignores this context may not tell us much about how performance appraisal actually works in organizations. Second, context has explanatory power. That is, performance appraisal is designed, implemented, used, and interpreted in particular ways in part because of the context in which it occurs. The more we know about important aspects of this context, the better we are likely to understand performance appraisal.

TABLE 7.1 ■ Multiple Levels of Context	
Distal	National culture
	Legal and economic system
	Economic environment
	Technical environment
	Physical environment
Proximal	Organizational climate and culture
	Organizational strategy
	Work group characteristics
	Supervisor–subordinate relationships

The context in which performance appraisal exists can be defined at many different levels of analysis. It is common in performance appraisal research (see, for example, Murphy & Cleveland, 1995; Murphy & DeNisi, 2008) to distinguish between distal and proximal contexts, where the proximal context refers to variables within the organization while the distal context refers to variables that exist outside of the organization. Distal context usually does not directly affect the practice or the use of performance appraisal, but it sets conditions that will strongly influence this process (Murphy & Cleveland, 1995). Proximal context, on the other hand, has a more direct effect and may play a direct role in forming or influencing the use and interpretation of performance appraisal in organizations. Table 7.1 lists distal and proximal influences on performance appraisal that have been studied most extensively in the last 30 years. Each of these is examined in the sections that follow.

DISTAL CONTEXT

The first of the contextual variables listed in Table 7.1, national culture, has been the focus of a considerable amount of research, some of which deals with performance appraisal and some of which deals with the more general question of how cultures should be defined and measured. Considerable progress has been made in measuring national cultures and in developing and testing theories of the fit between human resource practices and national culture.

National Culture

The most useful model for studying national cultures is based on the widely cited work of Geert Hofstede (See Hofstede, 1980; Hofstede, Hofstede, & Minkov, 2010; See House et al., 2004 and Schwartz, 1999 for similar models). On the basis of his analysis of over 100,000 questionnaires completed by employees of IBM in 72 countries, Hofstede (1980) argued that national differences in work-related values and preferences could be understood in terms of a small number of dimensions: (1) Power Distance—social inequality, or the degree of separation between people at different levels in organizations or groups; (2) Individualism–Collectivism—orientation toward individuals versus groups;

FIGURE 7.1 ■ Exemplars of Hofstede Dimensions

Power Distance[a]	
100	
80	Arab Countries
	France
60	
40	USA, Netherlands
20	

Uncertainty Avoidance	
100	
	Japan
80	
60	Germany
40	USA
	Great Britain
20	

Individualism	
100	
	USA
80	
	France
60	
40	Brazil
20	Hong Kong
	Indonesia

Masculinity	
100	
	Japan
80	
60	USA
40	France
20	
	Netherlands

Long-Term Orientation	
100	Hong Kong
80	Japan
60	Brazil
40	Netherlands
20	
	West Africa

Indulgence	
100	
80	New Zealand
	USA
60	Belgium
40	
20	China

[a] Approximate values on all dimensions from Hofstede (1994), Hofstede, Hofstede, & Minkov (2010).

(3) Masculinity–Femininity—preference for achievement and assertiveness versus cooperation and caring; and (4) Uncertainty Avoidance—tolerance for versus avoidance of ambiguity and lack of control. His later work added the dimensions of: (5) Long-Term versus Short-Term Normative Orientation—focus on immediate versus more distant outcomes, and (6) Indulgence versus Restraint—orientation toward free expression and satisfaction of desires versus suppression of these desires (Hofstede, 2001; Hofstede, Neuijen, Ohayv, & Sanders, 1990), but the relevance of the first four dimensions for performance appraisal has been studied more extensively.

Hofstede and his colleagues have measured these factors in several large-scale studies and have collected an extensive database that allows them to describe national cultures for over 75 nations. Figure 7.1 gives some examples of countries that exhibit high, medium, and low levels of the six Hofstede factors.

The potential relevance of the Hofstede culture dimensions to performance appraisal is clear. Consider, for example, some of the decisions that might be involved in designing a performance appraisal system, such as who should evaluate performance, how often, with what tools, and for what purpose. Each of these is likely to be influenced by one or more of the dimensions of national culture Hofstede identified. Table 7.2 identifies dimensions of national culture that might be most relevant to particular aspects of performance appraisal.

For example, in a culture that is high on Power Distance, there is considerable respect for hierarchy and for understanding one's place in the scheme of things. Most crucially, in societies where Power Distance is high, the low-power members of that society accept the existing hierarchy as natural and reasonable. In these societies, power relationships are paternalistic, autocratic, and centralized, and bosses are expected to make unilateral decisions that will be accepted and respected by all members of the organization. In a nation

TABLE 7.2 ■ Dimensions of National Culture Potentially Relevant to Design of a Performance Appraisal System		
Design Feature	**Relevant Dimension**	**Rationale**
Who Provides Ratings	Power Distance	Self-ratings and upward feedback are unlikely to be acceptable if there is a large distance between supervisors and subordinates
How Often	Uncertainty Avoidance	Systems with more structure and predictability (e.g., annual appraisals are likely to be preferable to more informal systems)
What Type of Rating Scales	Power Distance	Methods that involve goal setting may be inconsistent with strict hierarchies because they place responsibility for defining performance on the ratee
	Uncertainty Avoidance	Discomfort with ambiguity may make detailed behavioral scales more acceptable
Purpose of Rating	Individualism	Preference for individual versus group evaluations and for using performance appraisal as a basis for promotion and salary may vary as a function of individualism–collectivism

where Power Distance is high, top-down appraisals will seem sensible and natural, whereas appraisals that are participative will simply not fit, and will not be accepted by supervisors or subordinates.

A culture that is high on Collectivism emphasizes identification with the group (e.g., the family, work groups) as well as a high degree of loyalty to that group and a strong aversion to things that separate the individual from the group. Team-based performance appraisals are much more likely to be accepted in a Collectivistic culture than in an Individualistic culture (which places more emphasis on the individual), whereas programs to recognize individual achievements may not be accepted as sensible in a Collectivist society.

A culture that scores high on Uncertainty Avoidance is likely to value strict laws, policies that are uniformly applied, and predictability, and performance appraisal practices that are regular and well-defined (e.g., annual appraisals and feedback meetings) are likely to feel more comfortable and sensible to members of this culture than evaluation practices that are unstructured and unpredictable (e.g., the practice of giving organizational members frequent but irregular feedback as part of a performance management program). Rating scales that spell out what performance dimensions and performance levels mean (e.g., behaviorally anchored rating scales) are likely to be more acceptable than more abstract scales that leave much to the judgment of the individual rater.

Cross-National Performance Appraisal Research

There have been numerous studies reporting the characteristics of performance appraisal systems in different countries (see, for example, Amba-Rao, Petrick, Gupta, & Von Der Embse, 2000; Arthur, Woehr, Akande, & Strong, 1995; Grund & Sliwka, 2009). While some of the specific features of performance appraisal systems (and other human resource systems) common in particular countries are a function of differences in economic and legal systems, cross-national differences in performance appraisal practices and outcomes appear to be largely a function of differences in national cultures (Aycan, 2005). For example, Maley (2013) notes that the purpose of performance appraisal is likely to vary across nationalities and cultures; several studies discussed below provide support for this prediction.

Human resource management practices of 35 countries in the Organization for Economic Development and Cooperation (OECD) are summarized at http://www.oecd.org/gov/pem/hrpractices.htm. OECD data confirm there are differences in the extent to which performance appraisals are done and in the ways in which these appraisals are used. For example, performance appraisals are used frequently in the United States, but even more frequently in Japan and Denmark. Performance appraisals are used to make promotion and salary increase decisions in the United States, but the use of appraisal as a tool for making decisions about salary is less common in Brazil, and is quite rare in Russia. These cross-national differences are likely to be influenced by differences in the economic and legal systems of the countries involved, but cross-national cultural differences appear to be most important.

As noted earlier, the purpose of appraisal varies across countries (Maley, 2013). A study examining 10 different countries regarding their performance appraisal purposes revealed that, for example Canada, Latin America, Taiwan, and the United States emphasize performance appraisal for pay decisions more than Australia, Indonesia, and Japan (Milliman, Nason, Zhu, & De Cieri, 2002). Chiang and Birtch (2010) found that communication-development purposes were most frequent in Finland and Sweden, and formal feedback was more prevalent in low collectivist countries, such as the United Kingdom, the United States, and Canada.

Aycan's (2005) review of research of human resource practices led to some specific propositions regarding performance appraisal, some of which have received considerable support in subsequent research. For example, Aycan (2005) proposed the following:

- In collectivist, high Power Distance cultures, interpersonal competencies (e.g., teamwork facilitation, respect for others) and process (e.g., intentions, motivation) will be more important than task related competencies and processes.

- In low Power Distance cultures, performance will be regular and formalized and involve multiple sources, but high Power Distance cultures will be less structured and will depend more on the opinions and perceptions of supervisors and superiors.

- In collectivist cultures, group feedback will be preferred over individual feedback, and feedback will be indirect and non-confrontational.

Tests of National Culture Hypothesis

Discussions of and theories about the roles of national cultures in shaping human resource practices are common, but rigorous empirical examinations of these effects are less common. Peretz and Fried's (2012) study is a noteworthy exception. These authors examined the effects of national culture on performance appraisal, absenteeism, and turnover in 21 countries. In particular, they examined the relationships between power distance, individualism–collectivism, uncertainty avoidance, and future orientation (Hofstede, 1980) on appraisal system features and on some of the potential outcomes of performance appraisal. Table 7.3 summarizes some of their key findings. For example, both Individualism and Power Distance are related to a preference for a single rating source as opposed to multi-rater systems, such as those frequently used to provide 360-degree feedback.[2]

A related study by Adsit, London, Crom, and Jones (1997) suggested that the acceptability of upward feedback varies across countries, and that this variance can be accounted for (at least in part) by national differences in power distance, individualism–collectivism,

TABLE 7.3 ■ Empirically Supported Relationships Between Cultural Variables and Performance Appraisal System Features	
Higher Power Distance	Lower likelihood of using multiple sources (e.g., peers, supervisors)
Higher Individualism	Lower likelihood of using multiple sources
Higher Uncertainty Avoidance	Higher likelihood of having a formal PA system
Higher Future Orientation	Higher likelihood of using multiple sources
	Larger proportion of workforce is evaluated
	Higher likelihood of having a formal PA system

uncertainty avoidance, and masculinity. Similarly, Chiang and Birtch (2010) presented data suggesting that the purpose of appraisal (e.g., salary, promotion, identify strengths and weaknesses) and the formality of appraisal systems varies across nations, and that some of this variability can be accounted for by the cultural values identified by Hofstede (1980). There is evidence that the acceptability of appraisal systems that involve upward feedback or even lateral feedback (e.g., peer ratings) varies as a function of culture (Entrekin & Chung, 2001).

A number of papers have examined the effects of presumed East–West cultural differences on performance appraisal practices and outcomes. This research highlights the danger in making broad assumptions about East–West differences, for example that members of Asian cultures are collectivist, whereas members of American and European cultures are individualistic. For example, Snape, Thompson, Yan, and Redman (1998) compared performance appraisal practices and attitudes in Britain and Hong Kong. Their results suggest that British performance appraisals tended to be more participative and more focused on development, whereas Hong Kong appraisals tend to be more authoritarian, with a stronger focus on evaluation and performance-based rewards. They also found that employees in Hong Kong support this reward-oriented application of performance appraisal, an attitude that seems inconsistent with the assumption that collectivism reigns across all of Asia. Similarly, Yu and Murphy (1993) showed that the assumption that Asian employees will be modest in their self-ratings of performance (as opposed to the usual pattern of inflated self-appraisals in U.S. organizations) is not always a sound one, and that collectivism-inspired modesty may be unique to specific countries or cultures within Asia.

Claus and Briscoe's (2009) review suggests that despite the assumption that broad cultural differences will lead to large differences in the way human resource systems such as appraisal are implemented and used, the data tend to indicate more convergence than differentiation. For example, Shadur, Rodwell, and Bamber (1995) compared HR practices in Japanese versus non-Japanese corporations operating in Australia. In the 1990s, it was widely believed that the unique cultural features of Japanese organizations gave them a genuine competitive advantage. While this might be true (or might have been true at the time; Japan is no longer seen as the type of cultural and economic juggernaut it once seemed to be), whatever cultural differences existed, they did not translate into large differences in human resource practices. While cultural values are likely to matter, they may have a great impact on attitudes toward human resource practices than on the practices themselves.

Culture and Multisource Rating Systems

Evaluation plays a critical role in defining power and hierarchy in organizations; the defining characteristic of a supervisor is that he or she has the right and responsibility to evaluate the performance of subordinates. Multisource rating systems, which collect information about and evaluations of performance from supervisors, peers, customers, and even sometimes subordinates, violate this hierarchical principle, allowing people who do not have formal authority over a ratee to participate in his or her evaluation. It is likely that this sort of inversion of traditional hierarchy is more acceptable in some cultures than in others, especially cultures that differ in terms of power distance or collectivism–individualism. Furthermore, it is likely that the characteristics of ratings from different sources, in particular the mean and the intercorrelations among ratings, are influenced by broad cultural variables. For example, in high Power Distance and in high Collectivism cultures, subordinate ratings tend to be both higher and more intercorrelated than peer or supervisor ratings (Ng, Koh, Ang, Kennedy, & Chan, 2011).

Power Distance and Collectivism can sometimes have opposite effects on the use of and reactions to multisource rating systems. For example, there are countries that are high on both Power Distance and Collectivism (e.g., Indonesia[3]); the use of peer ratings would be discouraged if Power Distance is high but encouraged if Collectivism is high. Because these two facets of culture lead to different conclusions about the acceptability of multisource systems, it is difficult to make confident predictions about how such systems might be received in this country.

Cross-Cultural Differences in Multinational Organizations

Multinational organizations are becoming an increasingly important part of the world economy, and these organizations face a number of challenges in designing human resource systems (Maley, 2013). The challenge in designing sustainable and effective performance appraisal systems is especially complex for multinational organizations whose various divisions are characterized by different cultures (DeNisi & Smith, 2014; Kostova, 1999; Murphy & DeNisi, 2008). Cross-cultural differences in individualism and collectivism appear to be particularly important in determining whether specific human resource management practices will work across borders (Erez, 2011).

Multinational organizations face competing pressures in deciding whether to adopt consistent human resource management practices across their various divisions or to develop unique systems for each. On the one hand, there is considerable efficiency and potentially better control of the costs and outcomes of different human resource systems if similar systems can be used across national boundaries (Schmid & Kretschmer, 2010). On the other hand, human resource systems that work well in some nations might be culturally inappropriate in others. To add another layer of complexity, multinational organizations differ in the extent to which they tend to impose uniform human resource practices across their divisions in different countries versus adapting their human resource systems to local cultures and norms. Comparisons of European-owned versus American-owned multinational corporations suggest that American-owned multinationals are more likely than European-owned multinationals to tolerate diversity in the human resource systems used in their international affiliates (Cleveland, Gunnigle, Hearty, Morley, & Murphy, 2000; Gunnigle, Murphy, Cleveland, Hearty, & Morley, 2002). However, the use of human resource practices that are based on the expectations of the home country are likely to be employed in evaluating top managers (Janssens, 1994).

The finding that cultural variables can influence performance appraisal system design and use should not be taken to indicate that every country will follow its own unique practices. For example, Claus and Briscoe (2009) note broad across-nation similarities (e.g., performance appraisal systems in Ghana and Nigeria are more similar than dissimilar to those in the United States; see also Arthur et al., 1995) and within-nation heterogeneity (they note differences within India; see also Amba-Rao et al., 2000). On the other hand, similarities or differences in cultural factors do not always predict differences in human resource management practices. Even within regions of the world that are broadly similar in terms of general culture factors such as individualism–collectivism, there can be significant variation in the way human resource practices such as performance appraisal are carried out and used (Paik, Vance, & Stage, 2000).

The increase in multinational organizations and the increasing frequency of expatriate assignments implies that there will be an increasing number of rater–ratee pairs where raters and ratees are of different nationalities (Caliguiri & Day, 2000). First, raters and ratees may have different expectations regarding the nature of performance (e.g., the relative importance of task and contextual performance) and in the specific behaviors that are expected under each of the major dimensions of performance. Caliguiri and Day (2000) suggest that ratees who are higher on self-monitoring are more likely to make appropriate adjustments as they move into cultures where expectations regarding performance may vary as a function of nationality.

As multinational corporations become more dominant, the need to develop performance appraisal systems that serve the needs of the organization and its members and that make sense in the cultures where they are applied is becoming increasingly apparent. One particularly difficult issue is developing appraisal systems for expatriates. As more and more managers undertake international assignments, the question of how to evaluate their performance has become more pressing. Martin and Bartol (2003) suggest that appraisal systems for expatriates are most likely to be successful if the clarify expectations, if appraisals are frequent, if they are seen as fair, and if they have a developmental focus.

Limits on the Effects of Broad Cultural Variables

Mishra and Roch (2013) note that while there is important variability in cultural values across nations and regions of the world, there is also often considerable variability within nations, which implies that even in the same nation, some raters are likely to be higher or lower on particular dimensions of culture (e.g., power distance) than others. In particular, they argue that within national cultures, there are often differences in the extent to which raters adopt an independent versus an interdependent self-construal, and that this difference might influence performance appraisals. Raters who view themselves as independent tend to view their own behavior, and by extension the behavior of others, as being caused by individual differences in abilities, skills, motivation, and the like. Raters who view themselves and others as interdependent tend to emphasize the role of situational factors and constraints in explaining behavior. These differences translate into predictable differences in rating behavior and in feedback; raters who take an interdependent view tend to give higher ratings and tend to avoid giving feedback that focuses on differences in performance.

Although there is clear evidence that cultural variables have an impact on the way performance appraisals are designed, conducted, and used, it is not so clear that culture has a strong effect on performance ratings themselves. Ployhart, Weichmann, Schmitt, Sacco, and Rogg (2003) studied the measurement equivalence of performance rating from three countries with substantially different cultures, Canada, South Korea, and Spain. They found similar factor structures and general evidence of measurement equivalence, although there was more error variance in ratings of several performance dimensions in some countries than in others. Nevertheless, these data suggest more communality than distinctness, and that performance ratings might be more comparable across cultures than has sometimes been thought.

Even in cases where there are broad cultural effects on performance ratings, these effects are often not as simple and straightforward as they seem. For example, collectivism is typically associated with leniency in performance ratings, but Barron and Sackett (2008) note that it is important to distinguish between in-group and institutional collectivism.

Institutional collectivism focuses on societal and organizational practices that encourage and reward collective action and the collective distribution of rewards, and institutional collectivism is correlated with leniency in rating. In-group collectivism, on the other hand, focuses on pride, loyalty, and cohesiveness in organizations and families, and this type of collectivism does not have clear implications for leniency in rating.

Legal and Political Environment

Passage of the Civil Rights Act of 1964 dramatically changed the legal environment of performance appraisals in the United States. Prior to 1964, it was difficult for any employee to legally contest his or her performance evaluation, no matter how subjective, capricious, or inaccurate the appraisal. The reason for this is that there was no legal requirement that private organizations accurately evaluate workers' performance. The same is true today, except in the case where a performance measure has adverse impact on some protected group (typically minorities or women). Adverse impact occurs when a test, measurement device, or procedure has systematically different outcomes for different groups. For example, if most

SPOTLIGHT 7.1 PERFORMANCE APPRAISAL IN JAPAN

In this chapter, we have discussed the role of broad cultural and legal systems in shaping the way performance appraisal is conducted and used. To illustrate this phenomenon more concretely, it is useful to examine some similarities and differences in the performance appraisal systems used by firms in the United States and Japan. Shibata (2000, 2002) describes some of the distinctive features of Japanese performance appraisal systems.

Like many American organizations, Japanese organizations often conduct annual appraisals of their employees. However, because pay in blue-collar positions is determined by a combination of skill levels and age[4], ratings tend to focus on broad abilities, skills, and attitudes (e.g., diligence, cooperation). Work attitudes of white-collar employees are not assessed in a comparable way, perhaps on the assumption that most white-collar employees exhibit uniformly high levels of the required work attitudes.

Endo (1998) notes an interesting difference between American and Japanese performance appraisal systems—that is, that Japanese employees are not always informed about the ratings they receive. In American organizations, employees almost always know the performance ratings they receive, a design feature that may lead to higher levels of rating leniency (Shibata, 2002). It is possible that the relatively high levels of Power Distance in Japan makes it easier

to conduct evaluations without informing employees of the results of those evaluations, but other cultural factors may push performance appraisal systems in more egalitarian directions. For example, Shibata (2002) notes that the appraisal systems used for blue-collar and white-collar workers tend to be more similar in Japanese than in American organizations. Furthermore, it is unlikely that blue-collar employees in Japanese firms who receive the lowest ratings will be laid off (as oppose to the "rank-and-yank" systems championed by Welch and Byrne, 2001) or that high-rated employees will be put on a fast track for promotion.

In the 1930s, many Japanese firms incorporated American performance appraisal practices (Endo, 1998), but the appraisal systems in these two countries have evolved in different directions. Shibata (2002) notes that the very difficult economic situation confronting Japan from the 1990s has probably accelerated changes in Japanese performance appraisal systems, perhaps making them less distinctively Japanese and more closely targeted toward market forces than toward the national culture. Nevertheless, it seems clear that differences in economic systems (e.g., different levels of unionization) and cultural values can have a strong and lasting impact on the way performance appraisal is administered and used.

men passed a strength test, but most women failed, the test would have adverse impact on women if it was used to make hiring, firing, promotional decisions, and so on. Similarly, if you found that across many jobs men received systematically different performance ratings than women, it would constitute evidence of adverse impact. Any measure that has, or that might have, adverse impact is potentially vulnerable to legal scrutiny, and if adverse impact is demonstrated, the employer must establish the validity or business necessity of that measures, or in the case of performance appraisal, of the performance appraisal system. That is, the law allows companies to use tests, assessments, or appraisal systems that result in systematically different scores for member of different demographic groups (e.g., old versus young workers, men versus women, members of different racial and ethnic groups), only if they demonstrate that the scores on these measures are related to differences in performance or effectiveness on the job. For example, if you use a cognitive ability test in selecting among job applicants, it is possible that the test might lead to different selection rates for different racial and ethnic groups, but if this test can be shown to be job related, the law allows you to use this test.

Legal issues connected with performance appraisal are reviewed by Bernardin and Beatty (1984), Cascio (1987), Cascio and Bernardin (1981), and Latham (1986).[5] Some general guidelines for complying with federal anti-discrimination laws in carrying out performance appraisals are listed in Table 7.4. All of these guidelines can be thought of as safeguards designed to protect employees from arbitrary or subjective evaluations that may more closely reflect the rater's biases than they reflect the ratee's performance.

There is clear evidence that the legal environment affects the way in which performance appraisals are done. For example, Cleveland, Murphy, and Williams (1989) surveyed over 100 corporations to determine the degree to which performance appraisal was used for various purposes in organizations. In their confirmatory factor analysis of 20 potential uses, one of the four factors is labeled "Documentation," and refers to the uses of performance appraisals to meet federal, state, and local requirements, in particular to justify adverse

---

TABLE 7.4 ■ General Guidelines for Legal Compliance in Performance Appraisal

1. Performance appraisals should be based on specific dimensions whose relevance has been established through job analysis.

2. Raters should receive training or instruction.

3. Performance dimensions should be defined in terms of behaviors.

4. There should be feedback to the ratee, and an appeal process for ratings the individual feels are inaccurate.

5. Raters should have adequate opportunities to observe the performance they will be asked to evaluate.

6. Extreme ratings should be documented.

7. If possible, there should be multiple raters.

8. Appraisals should be frequent—at least annually.

9. Employees should have meaningful input into their evaluations (e.g., self-ratings).

Sources: From Bernardin & Beatty (1984); Feild & Holley (1982); Werner & Bolino (1997).

personnel actions (e.g. firing a worker for poor performance). Their surveys showed that documentation represented one of the most frequent uses of performance appraisal. Although Cleveland et al. (1989) did not investigate the issue, we suspect that the use of performance appraisal to document personnel decisions is highest in organizations that are willing to fire poor performers, and is lowest in situations where it is not possible to take action in the face of performance that is at least marginally acceptable (e.g., where a strong union prevails, or where contractual provisions make for-cause firing difficult). Only the most foolish employer will now dismiss a worker for poor performance without first collecting clear and convincing documentation of poor performance, as well as documentation of efforts on the part of the organization to provide opportunities for and encouragement of improvements in performance.

There have been numerous court cases in which performance appraisal figured meaningfully either as a personnel practice that was being challenged or as a criterion used to evaluate other personnel practices. In general, the same features that are thought to influence the perceived fairness of performance appraisals (e.g., giving employees a voice in appraisal, giving raters clear instructions and training, review of results with ratees, triangulation among multiple raters) appear to influence the outcomes of litigation (Werner & Bolino, 1997). The bottom line for organizations is that it is in their best interests to make sure that the performance appraisal systems they employ are clearly job related (in the sense that there is evidence that they are designed to carefully measure performance on the job, as opposed to yielding global judgments about individuals that cannot be reliably linked to the job itself) and fair.

Most discussion of legal issues in performance appraisal focus on the United States, which makes sense given the size and importance of the U.S. market and the uniquely American reliance on litigation as a method of law enforcement. However, many nations and groups of nations have their own laws and policies dealing with human resource practices such as performance appraisal. For example, the directives of the European Union provide some guidance to individual members establishing minimum standards for labor law (e.g., equal pay for men and women is mandated by EU directives), but at the same time European organizations operate under a number of different legal and regulatory regimes.[6] Sisson and Storey (2000) note that a number of countries follow the "Roman-Germanic system," which prioritizes statutory regulation, whereas other members follow a "Nordic system," based on the emphasis of collaborative agreements characteristic of Denmark and Sweden. There has been movement within the EU to develop a more uniform pattern that draws from both systems. However, the different political and legal systems in Nordic nations versus most other European nations may tend to encourage more participatory systems in countries like Denmark or Sweden than in, for example, France or Italy.

Countries that follow different political and legal systems often differ in other ways that makes it difficult to isolate the effects of political and legal considerations. In particular, political and legal differences are often confounded with cultural differences. For example, several papers describe performance appraisal in China (e.g., Cheng & Cascio, 2009; McEvoy & Cascio, 1990), and these often make the point that different aspects of Chinese culture lead to specific effects on the use and interpretation of performance appraisal in Chinese companies. For example, Chinese companies appear to be less likely than their non-Chinese counterparts to have traditional top-down performance appraisal systems and to be more likely to use multiple sources of input and to include both on-the-job and off-the-job behavior as components of performance appraisal. These features of performance appraisal in Chinese companies tend to be attributed to broad cultural factors such as Collectivism and Power Distance, but it is possible that these features are also influenced by the political and legal systems of China. Unfortunately, cross-cultural studies of performance appraisal tend to ignore political differences between nations that share common cultural backgrounds (Yu & Murphy, 1993).

Performance Appraisal in Unionized Workforces

There are political, legal, and economic forces involved in the relationship between management and labor, and these can have an impact on the way performance appraisal systems are designed, implemented, and used. Union membership is shrinking, particularly in the private section. The U.S. Bureau of Labor Statistics reported that in 2014, approximately 11% of wage and salary workers were members of unions, and of these a large number were in the public sector (e.g., police, fire, teachers, or administrative workers' unions; approximately 35% of these workers are unionized).[7] Nevertheless, there are still a large number of workplaces in which employees are members of unions, and this membership can substantially influence performance appraisal policies and practices.

In workplaces that are not unionized, employees may have little effective chance of influencing human resource policies, although their input is sought and considered in some organizations. Unions give employees a tool to potentially affect a number of characteristics of their work conditions. We typically think of unions as being primarily concerned with salary and with preserving the jobs of their members, but they can have an important role in shaping other human resource policies, including those that govern performance appraisal.

Although unionized firms are less likely to have a performance appraisal system than comparable nonunionized firms (Ng & Maki, 2008), unions are not in principle opposed to performance appraisal. Rather, they are likely to be opposed to performance appraisal systems that are informal or that appear to be unduly subjective. For example, there is evidence that in unionized settings, performance appraisal processes tend to be more regular and formalized than in comparable settings that are not unionized (Ng & Maki, 2008; Verma, 2005). Unions are more likely to be concerned with the uses of performance appraisal than with appraisal per se. In a union environment, performance appraisal is less likely to be used for salary, promotion, or layoffs (Bennett & Kaufman, 2007).

Finally, unions may take a role (at least a consultative role) in the development of performance appraisal systems. Later in this book, we will review evidence that employees have more positive attitudes toward performance appraisal if they have some input or voice in the development of these systems and in the evaluations they receive, and a union can be an effective method of giving employees this voice. In addition to giving employees a voice, union involvement may help safeguard organizations from making poorly considered changes to performance appraisal systems to reflect the latest management fad or craze.

Economic Environment

Changes in economic conditions can lead to substantial changes in the way performance appraisals are conducted and used. For example, there is evidence that during economic downturns, organizations tend to favor human resource systems that maximize managerial control and predictability (Maley, 2013). For example, this might mean more emphasis of top-down evaluation and less on participative appraisal systems.

Although research on the growth and decline of organizations is not concerned solely with the economic environment, this literature is nevertheless the source for several hypotheses about the relationship between the state of the economy and the methods used to evaluate workers' performance. Early in their life cycles, organizations are often characterized by liberal goals and flexible structures. However, as organizations prosper and grow, they tend to become inflexible and autocratic (Whetten, 1987). As organizations decline, relationships within the organization become increasingly politicized (Pfeffer & Salancik, 1978). Decline leads to higher levels of conflict, secrecy, and scapegoating, and to lower levels of morale, innovation, and participation (Whetten, 1987). We might expect similar phenomena to occur during either highly prosperous (growth) or economically unfavorable (decline) times.

As organizations grow and prosper, we would expect that performance appraisal will become increasingly formalized. In part, this is a product of the size of the organization; as the organization gets larger, informal relations between workers at different levels become less likely. As organizations decline, you might find more emphasis on documentation of poor performance, especially if the organization is forced to lay off a significant portion of its workforce. We might also expect less emphasis on feedback and development (as a result of the increasing emphasis on secrecy), and more interest in using performance appraisal as an instrument to increase production.

Negative economic trends probably have a greater impact on behavior in organizations than do positive ones. In particular, personnel practices that are adopted during hard times are likely to be retained when the economy rebounds. This is precisely the pattern with union–management relations in the early and mid-1980s. The recession in the early 1980s created conditions where unions were forced to make substantial concessions to management, often in the form of decreases in pay. When the recession ended, few organizations restored their earlier contracts; requests for pay cuts and other major concessions are still common in union–management negotiations.

Similarly, broad economic trends can have effects on labor markets that indirectly influence virtually every HR practice including performance appraisal. For example, during the period 2007–2014, the global financial collapse led to high unemployment in many countries. This, in turn, substantially changed the balance of power between employers and employees, making employees reluctant to change jobs or to raise complaints that might lead them to losing their current jobs. There is evidence of substantial growth in the part-time and contingent workforce, although the role of the financial crisis in this growth is uncertain.[8] What is beyond dispute is that organizations must frequently change their HR systems to adjust to both the different balance of power between management and labor and to the changing nature of the workforce. For example, an increased reliance on temporary and contingent workers is likely to decrease the role of performance appraisal in determining salary raises and promotions, since large sectors of the workforce might not qualify for these. The changing balance of power and influence might encourage more top-down appraisal and less participative systems, on the theory that some workers might have less strong and stable connections to the organization than others.

The Work Environment

Many personnel programs and interventions are built around the assumption that individuals are largely responsible for their high or low performance levels, and that interventions aimed at improving ability and/or motivation should increase performance (Dobbins, Cardy, Facteau, & Miller, 1993). However, poor performance is often the result of situational constraints rather than individual effort or skill (Kane, 1993). Situational constraints include lack of information needed to complete tasks; lack of adequate tools, equipment, material, and supplies; insufficient budgetary support; inability to obtain necessary help from others; lack of adequate preparation; lack of time; and environmental hazards and obstacles (Peters & O'Connor, 1980; Peters, O'Connor, & Eulberg, 1985). Of the 11 categories of situational constraints reviewed by Peters, O'Connor, and colleagues, three represent aspects of the physical environment that might constrain an individual's ability to perform well: (a) shortages of tools and equipment, (b) lack of materials and supplies, and (c) an unfavorable work environment (e.g., poor lighting).

Unfortunately, raters and ratees do not always have consistent perceptions of these constraints, and a ratee who is unable to perform well because of such constraints might receive a negative evaluation from a rater who is unaware of them. On the other hand, situational factors can enhance performance (Cardy, Dobbins, & Carson, 1995). Workers who have an abundance of resources, help from others, limited time pressures, and the like probably perform better than other workers whose ability and effort is similar but whose situations are less bountiful.

Jawahar (2005) suggests that raters do in fact take situational factors into account when evaluating their subordinates, but that some raters are better than others at making appropriate adjustments in their evaluations. In particular, raters who are higher on self-monitoring ability appear to do a better job taking situational constraints into account.

Effects of Situational Constraints on Performance Appraisal

Research has identified a number of consequences of situational constraints. First, there is evidence that situational constraints lead to lower levels of performance (Peters & O'Connor, 1980). This should not be surprising, since situational constraints are defined as variables that constrain one's ability to perform well. Second, it has been hypothesized that the presence of situational constraints will lead to decreased variability in performance, in part because of a ceiling effect. Empirical research, however, has not consistently supported this hypothesis (Peters et al., 1985; Peters, O'Connor, & Rudolph, 1980). As we will note below, the failure to find range restriction effects may say more about the extent to which situational constraints exist than about their effects. Third, situational constraints appear to lead to negative affective reactions and to lower motivation, although research results here are somewhat mixed (Peters et al., 1985; Phillips & Freedman, 1984).

In their review, Peters et al. (1985) note that serious situational constraints are rare. It may be that the small effect sizes found in situational constraint research reflect the fact that work environments are generally munificent, and that the situational constraints that do exist are too minor to have much of an impact. This is another area in which cross-cultural and historical research methods may be worthwhile. We may be underestimating the effects of situational constraints as a result of doing research in a time and place where these constraints are rare. We predict that there would be stronger effects in settings where the seriousness of situational constraints was variable, rather than being uniformly low.

In situations where we cannot remove situational constraints, it will be necessary to develop methods of measuring performance that take these constraints into account. It is hardly fair to compare the performance of someone who has all of the tools, equipment, and supplies necessary to complete the task to someone else who does not. Peters et al. (1985) review the results of several studies that have attempted to develop performance appraisal methods that take situational constraints into account. Unfortunately, the results of these studies have not been encouraging. To date, no methods have been developed that leads raters to appropriately adjust for the presence or absence of situational constraints.

As you may have noted earlier, some of the effects of the physical environment tend to mirror those of the economic environment. In both cases, we expect that shortages and scarcity will lead to increased levels of conflict, and to increasing politicization of the organization. Scarcity also leads to an emphasis on conservation and efficiency, which may lead to a change in the performance dimensions that are viewed as most important by an organization. The physical environment may, however, have a more immediate and vivid impact. If the tools, resources, and information necessary to do the job are not available, the consequences are felt immediately, whereas poor economic conditions may take a significant period to lead to changes on the shop floor.

Technological Changes and Performance Measurement

The world of work is becoming increasingly complex, and more jobs than ever require both the ability to deal with complex problems and skill in working with technology (National Research Council, 2012; Organization for Economic Cooperation and Development [OECD], 2012). One result is that an increasing number of workers perform in jobs or in settings that make it possible to automatically measure some aspects of their performance through technologies that range from cameras to keystroke monitoring software. We reviewed the topic of electronic performance measurement in more detail in Chapter 5, but it is useful to note here that the mere availability of such methods can change both performance and performance measurement. For example, employees who work using computers belonging to or networked with their organization have good reason to be concerned that their patterns of computer use might be monitored by their employer, and that there could be adverse employment outcomes if their behavior does not match the preferences and regulations of their employer. Even if employers do not engage in monitoring their employees' computer use, the very fact that they can and they might could have an impact on employees. As our discussion Chapter 5 suggested, these effects can be positive or negative, and employers should not assume that electronic performance monitoring is necessarily a good idea.

PROXIMAL CONTEXT

There are a number of variables within organizations that can directly influence the way performance appraisal systems are designed, implemented, and used. Levy and Williams (2004) distinguished between proximal variables that influence how performance ratings are carried out (*process proximal variables*) and those that deal with the configuration of the appraisal system itself (*structural proximal variables*). We believe it is useful to expand the definition of process proximal variables to those that influence both how ratings are carried out and how they are interpreted, since many of the proximal context variables that have been studied influence the interpretation of performance appraisal as well as its implementation. Table 7.5 lists examples of process and structural proximal context variables that have been

TABLE 7.5 ■ Proximal Context: Process and Structural Variables	
Process	Organizational climate and culture
	Organizational strategies
	Work groups
	Supervisor–subordinate relationships
Structural	Who—the targets of appraisal
	When—the timing of appraisal
	By whom—source of ratings/evaluations

most extensively studied. We will discuss process variables here; structural proximal context variables are discussed in several of the chapters that follow.

Organizational Climate and Culture

Schneider, Ehrhart, and Macey (2013) note that

> organizational climate may be defined as the shared perceptions of and the meaning attached to the policies, practices, and procedures employees experience and the behaviors they observe getting rewarded and that are supported and expected. . . . On the other hand, organizational culture may be defined as the shared basic assumptions, values, and beliefs that characterize a setting and are taught to newcomers as the proper way to think and feel, communicated by the myths and stories people tell about how the organization came to be the way it is as it solved problems associated with external adaptation and internal integration. (p. 361)

DeNisi and Smith (2014) suggest that understanding the climate and culture of an organization can help us understand why performance appraisal succeeds or fails. In particular, shared perceptions (to the extent which they actually are shared) regarding the behaviors that are valued, the policies that are important, and the norms of the organization can help support performance appraisal systems. However, if the shared perception is that performance appraisal is unimportant, or that it is unduly political, these perceptions can undermine even the most carefully constructed system (see, for example, Tziner, 1999). DeNisi and Smith (2014) propose that both national cultures and corporate cultures represent critically important contextual factors that define what types of performance appraisal systems are more or less likely to work.

Defining and Measuring Organizational Culture and Climate

There are many different measures that purport to shed light on the climates and cultures of organizations (Schneider, Ehrhart, & Macey, 2011, 2013), and there is no single dominant model to define precisely what defines the climate or culture of any particular organization. Rather, the literature on organizational climates and cultures has focused on a wide array of quite specific climates (e.g., climates related to safety, service, procedural justice, ethical behavior, or diversity) and on the relationships between specific organizational cultures and dependent variables such as leadership or firm economic performance (Schneider et al., 2013). There have not been many successful taxonomies of organizational cultures; perhaps the most useful way to describe organizational cultures in a general way is through Quinn and Rohrbaugh's (1983) competing values framework.

Quinn and Rohrbaugh (1983) propose that organizational cultures can be characterized in terms of the 2 x 2 framework illustrated in Figure 7.2. This model has received considerable support; its relevance to performance appraisal can be most easily illustrated by considering the types of performance appraisal systems that would be most likely to succeed or fail in organizations that exhibit the four different types of cultures this framework describes.

Organizations whose culture is flexible and internally focused exhibit what this model describes as a Clan Structure, in which the underlying assumption is that people will behave appropriately if they have trust in and loyalty to the organization, and in which the primary values reflect attachment and support. A performance appraisal that attempts to separate employees into different classes (e.g., the "rank-and-yank" system developed at General Electric, in which a set proportion of lowest-ranked employees was designated to be terminated each year and replaced by new hires) will probably fail here, while developmentally oriented appraisal systems (e.g., those that focus on identifying developmental needs) are more likely to succeed.

Organizations whose culture is stable and internally focused exhibit what this model describes as a Hierarchy Structure, in which the underlying assumption is that people will behave appropriately if they have clear, well-defined roles and formally defined policies and procedures to follow, and in which the primary values reflect communication and formalization. Performance appraisal systems that violate these structures (e.g., 360-degree feedback systems in which peers and subordinates give performance feedback that may be as influential as the feedback given by superiors) will probably fail, whereas appraisal systems that respect these structures (e.g., traditional top-down appraisals) may be more likely to succeed.

Organizations whose culture is flexible and externally focused exhibit what this model describes as an Adhocracy Structure, in which the underlying assumption is that people will behave appropriately if they understand the importance and the impact of the tasks they are asked to perform, and in which the primary values reflect growth and autonomy. Performance appraisal systems that are consistent with these values (e.g., developmentally

FIGURE 7.2 ■ The Competing Values Framework of Organizational Cultures

	Internal Focus	External Focus
Flexibility	Focus on attachment, trust, support —*Clan Structure*	Focus on rapid and flexible responses to the environment —*Adhocracy Structure*
Stability	Focus on achievement and goal setting —*Hierarchy Structure*	Focus on risk taking, creativity, adaptability —*Market Structure*

oriented appraisal systems) will be more likely to succeed than appraisal systems that contradict them (e.g., highly formalized systems that restrict evaluation to a predetermined set of dimensions, with little room for employee voice or for individual goal setting).

Organizations whose culture is stable and externally focused exhibit what this model describes as a Market Structure, in which the underlying assumption is that people will behave appropriately if they have clear objectives and are rewarded for their individual accomplishments, and in which the primary values reflect achievement and competence. Appraisal systems that recognize and reward individual differences in accomplishments will be more likely to succeed than systems that treat all employees pretty much the same, such as appraisal systems that are tied to merit pay systems with pay pools so small that there is no room to effectively distinguish truly good from average performers.

There are, of course, alternatives to the competing values framework. In addition to studying national cultures, Hofstede developed an influential model of organizational culture (Hofstede, 2001). He described organizational cultures in terms of: (1) means oriented versus goal oriented—emphasis on how work is carried out versus what outcomes are achieved, (2) internally versus externally driven—extent to which concern for doing what organizations believe is best versus doing what customers prefer, (3) easygoing versus strong work discipline—relative emphasis on control and discipline, (4) local versus professional—extent to which employees identify with the local organization versus their discipline and profession, (5) open versus closed system—accessibility and ease of entry into an organization, (6) employee-oriented versus work-oriented—emphasis on pressure to perform versus the welfare of employees, (7) degree of acceptance of leadership style—extent to which the leadership styles of direct supervisors are consistent with subordinates' preferences, and (8) degree of identification with your organization—extent to which employees feel a direct link with the organization as a whole. Table 7.6 lays out some ways in which organizational differences in these characteristics might influence performance appraisal.

TABLE 7.6 ■ How the Hofstede Dimension of Organizational Culture Might Influence Performance Appraisal	
If the organization is:	**Performance appraisal systems might:**
Goal oriented	Include detailed measures of whether appropriate procedures were followed
Externally driven	Include input from customers or clients
Easygoing	Be highly informal
Professional in orientation	Focus on development of high-level skills
An open system	Include input from customers or clients
Work-oriented	Focus on objective productivity metrics
High on acceptance of leadership style	Be more likely to be characterized by a higher level of trust
High on degree of identification with your organization	Be more likely to be accepted and trusted

Do All Organizations Have Discernable Climates or Cultures?

The most difficult issue is understanding whether organizations actually have climates or cultures in any meaningful sense. As Schneider et al. (2013) note, the constructs of organizational climate and culture assume some level of shared agreement, and this is not likely to be true in all organizations. Even if an organization has a well-defined climate and culture, the relevance of that climate and culture to performance appraisal might be limited. For example, many organizations whose employees engage in dangerous activities might develop a strong safety culture, which might be largely irrelevant to performance appraisal.

Organizational climates and cultures are most likely to influence appraisal systems when they focus on one or more of the issues described in Table 7.7. For example, if an organization's culture emphasizes equity and transparency and its climate is one in which trust predominates, this will probably have a strong influence on how performance appraisal is conducted and on the success or failure of appraisal systems. Another organization in which competition and building and exercising influence predominates might develop a quite different type of appraisal system.

In Chapter 10, we will review research on reactions to performance appraisal systems in more detail, but it is useful to make the point here that climates that inspire trust (these climates often put an emphasis on transparency and fairness) are much more favorable environments for the development of a successful performance appraisal system than climates that inspire cynicism and political manipulation. In the final two chapters of this book, we will note how successful performance appraisal cannot be achieved in a vacuum, and that there are specific organizational characteristics that make it easier or harder to develop effective performance appraisal systems.

Organizational Strategy

Businesses can pursue a wide range of strategies in their pursuit of success. Consider, for example, the four different strategies that are shown in Table 7.8 for distinguishing your organization from its competitors. An organization that pursues a growth strategy will place a premium on innovation and development, whereas an organization that follows a cost-containment strategy will place more emphasis on efficiency and reduction of errors. Many businesses follow some mixture of the four strategies listed below, but in general, organizations that pursue different strategies are likely to prefer different methods

TABLE 7.7 ■ Aspects of Climate and Culture Most Likely to Influence Appraisal Systems

Equity versus Efficiency—climates and cultures are most likely to influence appraisal systems when they take a strong stance on the question of whether people should be treated the same versus treated in accordance with their individual accomplishments

Trust versus Cynicism—climates and cultures are most likely to influence appraisal systems when they are driven by strong norms of mutual trust or by strong levels of cynicism

Transparency versus Political Intrigue—climates and cultures are most likely to influence appraisal systems when they are driven by strong norms of either making decisions and decision processes as transparent as possible or by reliance on political skill and influence to accomplish desired ends

TABLE 7.8 ■ Four Strategies for Gaining a Competitive Advantage	
Growth	Add new products or add new features to existing products
Product Differentiation	Distinguish yourself from competitors through superior products or service
Cost Control	Provide goods and services at a lower price than your competitors
Acquisition	Purchase or take control of potential competitors

for evaluating the performance of individuals, work groups, and organizations (Dekker, Groot, & Schoute, 2013). Dekker et al. (2013) review research linking performance measurement methods with business strategy. One of their principal conclusions is that organizations that pursue mixed or hybrid strategies (e.g., using both growth and cost control to maximize their competitive advantage) are likely to need more complex methods of defining and measuring performance than organizations that pursue only one type of strategy. This makes a good deal of sense, because each strategy emphasizes potentially different aspects of performance.

Dekker et al. (2013) also note that strategies can have a bearing on the ways performance information is used. As we note in Chapter 8, there are many different uses for performance appraisal in organizations, including administrative uses (e.g., using appraisals in determining pay or promotion) and developmental uses (e.g., giving feedback about strengths and weaknesses). They suggest that mixed or hybrid strategies are often linked to a wider range of uses of performance appraisal than is common among organizations that pursue a single strategy for gaining competitive advantage. They also tested the hypothesis that organizations that pursue mixed or hybrid strategies might employ a wider range of incentive schemes than organizations that pursue a single business strategy, but found only mixed support for this hypothesis.

Work Group and Team Characteristics

Most jobs involve working in groups or teams, at least part of the time, and these groups can influence both the job performance and the supervisor's rating of each group member (Hackman, 1976). First, groups can influence the knowledge and skills of individuals, the level of psychological arousal while working, and the member's effort and performance strategies. A work group can be a source of help and assistance, providing each member with resources he or she might not otherwise have, but it can also be a drag on the performance of group members. Norms or expectations develop within groups regarding acceptable levels of performance, and these norms become stronger as the group increases in cohesiveness. In a classic ethnographic study, Whyte (1943) showed how work group members enforce these norms, shunning or otherwise punishing group members who out-performed the group norm (thus making everyone else look bad).

Not only do norms develop concerning productivity, they also develop to define what are acceptable or unacceptable performance ratings. For some groups, a norm develops that leads raters to believe that high or inflated ratings are the only acceptable ratings. For example, Cleveland, Morrison, and Bjerke (1986) found that when there were high entrance or educational standards for admission into a group or job community, raters were reluctant to evaluate employees as average or below. The rater's rationale was that these individuals passed through numerous performance hurdles in order to gain access to the group, and therefore were all "superior."

The characteristics of a group such as the performance variability of its members (Ilgen & Feldman, 1983; Liden & Mitchell, 1983) and the salience of specific group members (Brewer, 1979; Linville & Jones, 1980; Quattrone & Jones, 1980) also influence performance ratings. Raters do not evaluate one person on a single occasion; rather, evaluation occurs for many people over an extended time, or covering many tasks. As a result, each group member becomes a point of reference for evaluating other members (Ilgen & Feldman, 1983). For example, Mitchell and Liden (1982) found that in a work group with one poor performer and two good ones, the evaluation of the poor performer was higher than it should have been, and the evaluations of good performers were lower. This was especially true when the poor performer was portrayed as high in popularity and leadership skills.

There is a useful distinction between work groups and work teams. Teams have two defining characteristics, interdependence and shared responsibility for outcomes (Guzzo & Dickinson, 1996; Hollenbeck, Beersma, & Schouten, 2012), whereas a work group might not exhibit interdependence if each member works pretty much on his or her own. In teams, however, the ability of team members to perform their tasks sometime depends on other team members performing *their* tasks well, and the team as a whole is responsible for particular products or outcomes.

Various types of teams exist in organizations, including: (1) project teams/task forces— teams put together to carry out a particular task or project, which are dissolved when the project is done; (2) cross-functional teams—teams whose members have different skills or specialties; (3) virtual teams—teams whose members are scattered geographically, and who work together via electronic communication or some other method of sharing tasks without meeting in the same physical location; and (4) self-managed teams—teams with a flat authority structure, where formal leadership is less important than emergent leadership (i.e., the emergence of some member or members who take on a leadership role even though their formal titles do not give them authority over others). Hollenbeck et al. (2012) suggest that rather than thinking about different *types* of teams, it is more useful to think of teams as varying on three core dimensions: (1) skill differentiation—the extent to which members possess similar or different skills, (2) authority differentiation—the extent to which different team members have formal authority over others, and (3) temporal stability—the extent to which team members have a history of working together and an expectation of continuing to work together in the future.

The existence of teams has clear implications for performance appraisal. First, teams provide an obvious opportunity to use peer ratings in evaluating performance. Team members are likely to be knowledgeable about each other's performance and contribution to the team effort, and they have a vested interest in improving each other's performance. There is evidence, however, that team members are sometimes reluctant to evaluate each other, and when forced to do so, may resist differentiating between members in terms of their performance. This tendency is far from universal, but in teams that decline to differentiate, team members report higher satisfaction and stronger perceptions of procedural justice (Drexler, Beehr, & Stetz, 2001). Whether these attitudes are the cause or the effect of an unwillingness to differentiate among team members when rating their performance is unclear, and arguments can be made for either causal flow.

Second, the existence of teams probably changes the content of appraisals. For example, when switching from evaluations of individuals working alone to evaluations of team members, the relative importance of task performance versus organizational citizenship is likely to change. Harris and Barnes-Farrell (1997) identified several core components of teamwork (e.g., team leadership monitoring, communication, feedback, backup behavior, coordination) and showed that all of these were related to evaluations of the effectiveness of team members. This makes perfect sense, because all of these behaviors are likely to make the team as a whole effective. In teams where the level of interdependence is high, team members who exhibit high levels of behaviors that support the team as a whole might be viewed as good performers even if their individual task performance might not be not so good.

Finally, the three characteristics of teams identified by Hollenbeck et al. (2012) have clear implications for performance appraisal. For example, when a team is high on skill differentiation, one implication is that the content of appraisals (i.e., the performance dimensions that are evaluated) will vary from member to member, making it hard to directly compare the performance of different team members. Consider, for example, a type of team that has been extensively studied: a flight crew (Guzzo & Dickinson, 1996). The iconic U.S. bomber aircraft, the B-52, has a crew that typically includes a pilot, co-pilot, navigator, radar navigator/bombardier, and electronic warfare officer. Because these team members have distinctly different roles and responsibilities it can be hard to determine whether the co-pilot performs better at his job than the navigator does in his particular role.[9]

A team that is high on authority differentiation will probably require different strategies for performance appraisal than a team where there are few differences in formal authority; peer evaluations are more likely to be acceptable in teams with a flat authority structure. Finally, teams that are long-lived will probably be evaluated in different ways than teams that are put together for a specific purpose and disbanded soon afterward. Teamwork is probably a more critical performance dimension for members of teams that are going to be together for extended periods than for short-lived task forces. In a short-lived team, people can probably get along for a limited period even if they do not possess well-developed teamwork skills.

Supervisor–Subordinate Relationships

The nature of your relationship with your supervisor has a strong influence on the performance ratings you receive. For example, Duarte, Goodson, and Klich (1994) showed that regardless of objective measures of performance, ratees who experience high-quality leader–member relationships receive higher performance ratings. Of course, ratee characteristics such as competence and dependability affect the nature of the leader–member relationship, and someone who is a perennially poor performer is unlikely to attain or remain in a high-quality relationship with his or her supervisor. Nevertheless, employees who have established a pattern of good performance and who maintain a strong relationship with their supervisor may receive high ratings even if their performance during the period the ratings covered is in fact not so good.

Supervisor–subordinate relationships not only influence ratings, they also influence the type of feedback ratees receive. Among the contextual factors thought to influence the likelihood of seeking and receiving feedback, the relationship between supervisors and subordinates has received the most attention (Lam, Peng, Wong, & Lau, 2015). Leader–member exchange (LMX) theory proposes that leaders have qualitatively different relationships with employees who are members of in-groups versus out-groups (Dansereau & Graen, 1975; Graen, 1976; Graen & Uhl-Bien, 1995). In-group employees are those employees who are trusted and valued by the leader and who often have a stronger connection with the leader, whereas out-group employees are those employees whose performance, motivation, or ability are not highly regarded by the leader and who have more formal and perhaps even adversarial relationships with their leaders. The defining feature of the in-group is trust, which makes it easier to give and receive feedback. On the other hand, leaders often value and depend on members of the in-group, and may be reluctant to give them negative feedback, even when it is deserved.

There is considerable evidence that a high-quality relationship between leaders and followers encourages feedback seeking and that a low-quality relationship encourages feedback avoidance. Moss, Sanchez, Brumbaugh, and Borkowski (2009) showed that the likelihood of feedback avoidance can explain the relationship between relationship quality and subordinate performance. That is, it is often the case that employees who have a low-quality relationship with their supervisor avoid and ignore performance feedback, which in turn makes them less effective at their job. This is not to say that feedback avoidance is the only mechanism by which LMX quality influences subordinate performance, but it does indicate that the relationship between LMX quality and feedback avoidance is sufficiently strong to make this sort of mediation possible (see also Chen, Lam, & Zhong, 2007).

Finally, the physical arrangement of the workplace itself can affect the nature of the supervisor–subordinate relationship in a way that influences performance appraisal. The physical distance between raters and ratees and between ratees is important in supervisor–subordinate interactions and evaluations because it can affect the opportunity to observe behavior and performance (Wexley & Klimoski, 1984). The less your supervisor sees of your performance, the less likely it is that you will be a member of his or her in-group, and this could influence both the performance ratings and the feedback you receive.

The Implications of Context Dependence on Transferring Policies or Practices Across Contexts

The ways performance appraisal systems are designed, implemented, interpreted, and experienced are all influenced by the organizational and social context in which these systems exist (Judge & Ferris, 1993; Mitchell, 1983; Murphy & Cleveland, 1995). Both proximal contexts, such as the climate and culture of the organization and the composition of work teams and departments and distal contexts, such as the state of the economy or the nature of the legal system influence performance appraisals. For example, performance appraisal is probably used and interpreted differently during good economic times (when organizations might have the ability to reward good performance) than during economic downturns (where there are few rewards available). Performance appraisal is conducted and used differently if organizations are worried about the potential for legal scrutiny (e.g., because of a pending discrimination charge or the possibility of being investigated) than when they are not. Performance appraisals are conducted and used differently in organizations with supportive and open climates than in organizations where suspicion and cynicism abounds (Bernardin, Cooke, & Villanova, 2000; Tziner, Murphy, & Cleveland, 2005; Tziner, Murphy, Cleveland, Beaudin, & Marchand, 1998).

The practical impact of this context dependence is that it can be very difficult to predict whether or not a particular performance appraisal system will work when it is transferred to a new context. A system that seems to works well in one culture, organization, or setting might fail absolutely in another. A system that seemed to work well one year might fail terribly the next year. The lack of transferability of performance appraisal systems across organizations or across contexts is a serious problem, especially because of the well-known strategy of organizations to attempt to copy human resource management systems and innovations that seem to be successful in prestigious companies (DiMaggio & Powell, 1983). For example, during the highly praised tenure of Jack Welch as CEO, General Electric introduced a "rank and yank" system of evaluation in which employees were sorted into a small number of categories, and in which employees in the lowest category (typically the lowest 10%) were liable to be dismissed or laid off. Because of the prestige of Welch and General Electric, this type of system spread into a number of other companies, regardless of whether it fit the missions, climates, cultures, or circumstances of those companies. At least in the field of performance appraisal, this tendency to try and copy the policies and practices of prestigious companies is unlikely to work, in part because the new context in which those policies are applied is unlikely to be identical to the context in which these systems or policies were developed.

SUMMARY

Performance appraisal occurs in a specific context that influences virtually all aspects of the appraisal process. First, there is the broad culture in which appraisals are done. These cultures vary on a number of characteristics, including Collectivism–Individualism and Power Distance, which can have a strong influence on the type of appraisal system that is developed, the way it is applied in organizations, and the way appraisal information is used. Next, appraisal occurs in a specific legal and political context. For example, laws designed to encourage equal employment opportunities strongly influence the way appraisals are conducted in the United States, pushing American performance appraisal systems in the direction of careful documentation of the job-relatedness of appraisals and of the fairness and freedom from bias of performance evaluations.

Appraisals are influenced by the economic climate. For example, during tough economic times organizations may need to focus on minimizing costs and errors and on maximizing short-term profitability. In a more relaxed economic environment, this same organization might be able to invest more time and energy in employee development. Appraisals are also influenced by the physical and technological environment. When workers lack the resources, information, tools and equipment, or materials needed to perform their jobs, performance appraisal might be pointless; unless employees have at least a *chance* of success, there is little to be learned by measuring their individual performance.

Much like national cultures, organizational climates and cultures influence appraisal. The extent to which the climate and culture of an organization encourages trust and involvement versus cynicism and political manipulation is likely to be highly important. Organizational strategies also make a difference. An organization that focuses on cost control will probably develop a quite different appraisal system than one that attempts to produce the highest-quality products.

If we drill down to contextual variables within organizations, two stand out as most critical. First, the nature of the work group or team can have a substantial impact on the way appraisals are conducted and the way they are interpreted. Similarly, the relationship between the supervisor and subordinate will be an important driver of performance ratings and performance feedback.

The most general message of this chapter is that performance appraisal can only be properly understood within its particular context. The same exact performance appraisal system might work quite differently in organizations in different countries, or during different sorts of economic times or in organizations that pursue different strategies. For most of the history of scientific research on performance appraisal, context has been largely ignored, but in the last 20 years there has been a substantial surge of interest in understanding how the contexts in which performance appraisals are carried out influence the appraisal process and outcomes.

CASE STUDY: WHY RANK AND YANK FAILED AT MICROSOFT

Many major corporations have adopted some variation of the GE "rank and yank" system in which employees are ranked or sorted into groups based on their performance, and in which the employees who are in the lowest group are under some real pressure to improve or to face meaningful consequences. Technology companies, notably Microsoft, have tried this system, with generally unsatisfactory results, and many are abandoning the idea (Olson, 2013). Why?

Different explanations might be needed to fully capture the reasons why appraisal systems that rely on ranking or stacking employees do not work well in technology firms, but in the case of Microsoft, Olson (2013) argues that it is culture that is to blame. In particular, she notes that Microsoft relies heavily on an information-sharing culture, in which people are willing to take risks and willing to help others succeed. A rank-and-yank system pits employees against one another, and helping a coworker accomplish his or her tasks can directly can make you look worse. Conversely, if other workers fail, you will look relatively good even if your performance is mediocre. Microsoft determined that cooperation and information sharing was more important than the benefits they might expect from a rank-and-yank system.

Even GE, the originator of this system, is abandoning rank and yank, and once again, culture seems to be the culprit. As Nisen (2015) notes, the norms, values, and expectations of workers are different now than they were when Jack Welch first installed the rank-and-yank system, and millennial employees, who prefer frequent and immediate feedback and who value information more than evaluation, are simply not willing to work under a system that pits employees against one another. As a result, GE has moved to a system with a much stronger developmental orientation.

In both cases, the failure of a system that appeared to be highly successful at GE in the 1980s appears to be the result of a mismatch between the demands of the system and the culture of the organization and the society in which the organization is embedded. At Microsoft, the decision to abandon rank and yank was driven by the differences in the culture of Microsoft and GE. At GE, the decision to abandon rank and yank was driven by the differences in the GE workforce of the 1980s and 1990s and the current GE workforce.

NOTES

1. http://dictionary.cambridge.org/dictionary/english/context (British usage).

2. 360-degree feedback systems are discussed in Chapter 9.

3. http://geert-hofstede.com/indonesia.html

4. Over time, the use of age as a criterion for setting wages and evaluating contributions to the organization in Japanese firms has declined.

5. See also Werner and Bolino, 1997.

6. There are some rules and regulations that are common across nations within the European Union, but national legal and regulatory systems are still more important than EU-wide regulations in determining human resource policies.

7. http://www.bls.gov/news.release/union2.nr0.htm; to illustrate the decline in union membership, this same report noted that in 1983 over 20% of workers were members of unions.

8. http://www.cbsnews.com/news/temp-work-raises-long-term-questions-for-economy/

9. We use the masculine pronoun here because, at present, B-52 crews are exclusively male.

8

HOW ORGANIZATIONS USE PERFORMANCE APPRAISAL

Performance appraisal can be described as the Swiss Army knife of human resource management—it is a tool with many purposes. Cleveland, Murphy, and Williams's (1989) survey showed that performance appraisals were used in organizations for up to 20 separate purposes, ranging from salary administration and promotion to assessing training and development needs, to meeting legal requirements. In this chapter, we will discuss the major purposes of performance appraisal in organizations and the potential conflicts between different uses of the same performance appraisal system. We will argue that organizations often attempt to use the same performance appraisals for conflicting purposes, effectively undermining the usefulness of performance appraisals for *any* of these purposes.

Performance appraisal is not only a tool for human resource management, it is also a tool for influencing the behavior of individuals and the outcomes of those behaviors. That is, performance appraisal is not simply something the organization does to collect information, but it is also part of the ongoing process by which individuals manage their relationships with superiors and subordinates. As such, performance appraisal is

an integral part of the way individuals in organizations influence each other's behavior. In this chapter, will consider both the formal uses of performance appraisal on the part of the organization and the informal uses of performance appraisal (i.e., the uses of appraisal as a tool for influencing the opinions and behaviors of both your subordinates and your superiors).

We start this chapter by reviewing how the purpose of performance appraisal has evolved over time. We note that there are many potential uses of performance appraisal, but that these can be grouped into four major categories that involve using performance appraisal to: (1) make distinctions between people—using appraisal as a tool for determining raises or promotions; (2) make distinctions within people—using appraisal to identify individual strengths and weaknesses in order to prioritize training and development; (3) to support other human resource systems—using appraisal to identify organization-wide training needs, or as criteria to validate selection tests; and (4) documentation—using appraisal to document and justify personnel decisions. We also note that these uses can pose conflicting demands, and that organizations routinely use appraisals for multiple conflicting purposes, undermining the effectiveness of appraisal systems.

Finally, we note that performance appraisal systems are not only a part of the formal decision-making process in organizations, but they are also used informally to influence the behavior of participants. We usually focus on downward influence, where supervisors or managers use appraisals to influence and shape the behavior of their subordinates, but performance appraisal also involves upward influence. The individuals being evaluated are not merely passive recipients of their supervisor's ratings and feedback, but rather are actively engaged in attempting to influence and shape those evaluations and that feedback.

THE PURPOSE OF PERFORMANCE APPRAISAL

Before launching into a discussion of the purpose or purposes of performance appraisal in organizations, it is useful to make a distinction between the *declared* purpose, the *effective* purpose, and the *perceived* purpose of performance appraisal. Most organizations maintain handbooks or other documents describing their human resource management systems, and these may include a description of the different potential uses of information from performance appraisal. However, the fact that some set of documents claims that performance appraisals are used for some purpose (e.g., in determining merit pay) does not mean that performance appraisal has any real or meaningful effect on those processes or outcomes. Suppose, for example, an organization claims to use performance appraisal as a key driver of its merit pay plan. On close examination, you discover that everyone gets raises that are pretty small, but also pretty comparable most years. You might conclude that the organization is either unable or unwilling to pay high performers more than it pays low performers, regardless of what the personnel handbook says, and that in this organization, performance appraisal is not *actually* used to make meaningful decisions about pay.

Finally, and perhaps most important, members of organizations have a series of perceptions and beliefs regarding the purpose of performance appraisal in their organization, and even if these beliefs are incorrect, they are likely to act on those beliefs. Different members of an organization are likely to have different information about how the performance appraisal system actually works and how information from performance appraisal is actually used,[1] and organizational policies sometimes have the effect of limiting that information. For example, pay secrecy is common in many organizations, and in the absence of information about how performance appraisal outcomes actually link with pay, the members of organizations are likely to develop a wide range of attitudes and beliefs about these links. As we will note in this chapter, much of the dissatisfaction organization members express about performance appraisal systems may be the result of discrepancies between what is *actually* done with performance appraisals and what people *believe* is done (Bretz, Milkovich, & Read, 1992).

Historical and Cross-Cultural Perspectives

Historically, the main use of performance appraisals in organizations has been to provide input for administrative decisions such as salary increases, promotions, or layoffs (Whisler & Harper, 1962). In the late 1950s, McGregor proposed that performance appraisal be used for feedback and developing employees (DeVries, Morrison, Shullman, & Gerlach, 1986), and the use of appraisal for this purpose has become common. Proponents of management by objectives (MBO) suggested using appraisals for organizational planning (Drucker, 1954; Odiorne, 1965), and there is evidence that they are in fact sometimes used for those purposes. By the 1980s, there were calls for increasing the use of performance appraisal as a tool for human resource planning, such as proactively identifying personnel replacement needs (Bernardin & Beatty, 1984; DeVries et al., 1986), extending the range of applications of performance appraisal.

Since the passage of the 1964 Civil Rights Act, the Age Discrimination in Employment Act (1967), and related equal employment opportunity legislation, performance appraisal has also been viewed increasingly as a tool that might help safeguard organizations against discrimination lawsuits. If performance appraisals are well-designed, carefully done, and thoughtfully used, this may help shield organizations from the charge that they are making arbitrary or biased decisions. On the other hand, if appraisals are badly done, performance appraisal might become a basis for successful lawsuits rather than a safeguard. Surveys in the 1970s (e.g., Bureau of National Affairs, 1974; Lacho, Stearns, & Villere, 1979; Lazer & Wikstrom, 1977) suggested that by that time, the majority of the organizations surveyed used performance appraisals for at least one of the following purposes: (1) individual performance planning; (2) salary administration; (3) promotion, training, and development; and (4) retention and discharge.

Performance appraisal is not only an American phenomenon; it is also widespread in many parts of the world. Approximately 82% of organizations in England have some type of formal appraisal system, with a substantial increase in appraisals for non-management employees since the 1970s (DeVries et al., 1986). The most frequently cited uses of performance appraisal in England are to: (a) improve current performance, (b) set objectives, and (c) identify training and development needs. Further, there is a recognition and trend toward the separation of performance review from potential review.

Milliman, Nason, Zhu, and De Cieri (2002) examined the differing uses of performance appraisal in 10 countries in Asia, North America, and Latin America. In particular, they evaluated the extent to which performance appraisals are used for pay administration, documentation, employee development, promotion, and as a vehicle for employees to express their opinions. On the whole, the use of performance appraisal for pay and promotion was moderately common in all countries, but it was most likely to be viewed as valuable in some Asian and Latin American countries. The use of performance appraisal for developmental purposes was common in virtually all countries, while the use of appraisal for documentation and subordinate expression was viewed as most acceptable in North American and Australian settings.

Ratings, Narratives, and the Appraisal Interview Can Serve Different Purposes

Before we get too far into a discussion of the purpose of performance appraisal, it is useful to remember that performance appraisal has many components, and the purpose of different components may not always be identical. For example, the numeric ratings that are part of most performance appraisals might be better tailored to administrative purposes (e.g., for determining who gets a raise or a promotion), while narrative comments that often accompany these ratings probably straddle the developmental versus administrative divide that is so often seen when considering the purpose of performance appraisal (Meyer, Kay, & French, 1965).

Numeric ratings and narrative comments represent only one part of the overall appraisal process. They are often followed by what is the most stressful part of the appraisal process: the appraisal interview (Gordon & Stewart, 2009). This interview is usually a face-to-face discussion between raters and ratees about the rater's evaluation, the bases for that evaluation, and the action steps that need to be taken to improve future performance.

One reason appraisal interviews are approached with a mix of dislike and dread by raters and ratees alike is that both sides are likely to expect some conflict (Cleveland, Lim, & Murphy, 2007). Bad news (here, low performance ratings) is hard to give and hard to receive, but even when ratings are relatively high, conflict may still occur. As we note elsewhere (see, for example, Chapters 9–11), ratees often expect higher ratings than they are likely to receive, and they are likely to resent ratings that are lower than what they think they deserve. Even if there are no explicit complaints in an appraisal interview, raters are likely to be quite uncomfortable if they are aware that their evaluations are less favorable than the individual's self-rating. The frequent practice of including self-ratings in appraisal systems can thus be a real source of conflict and stress for raters.

Gordon and Stewart (2009) note that the framing of performance discussions can have a substantial impact on their content and processes. For example, the same discussion might feel quite different if it is labelled a "performance review" than if it is labelled an "appraisal"—the latter framing has a stronger connotation of conveying what was good and what was bad about performance, whereas the former has a stronger connotation of summarizing the totality rather than hitting the highs and lows of the performance distribution. Similarly, "appraisal interview" has a different meaning than "conference"—the former implies that the ratee will be told what was good or bad, whereas the latter implies a discussion.

Gordon and Stewart (2009) analyzed the appraisal interview from the perspective of communication theory, and they make the important point that the most critical criterion for evaluating these interviews—efficiency in communicating key information—is rarely measured when evaluating appraisal interviews. They note, for example, that ratees who are dissatisfied with their appraisal interview might nevertheless learn important things about their performance, particularly if they can get over the disappointment that bad news usually brings. They also note that a common suggestion from communication research, that the appraisal interview should be conducted as a structured interaction rather than an unplanned discussion, is rarely followed.

THE USES OF PERFORMANCE APPRAISAL

Performance appraisal is almost always thought of as a difficult and unrewarding task, one that requires the investment of a great deal of time and energy (including emotional energy, since performance appraisal is often a source of interpersonal conflict between raters and ratees) and one that promises uncertain rewards. It is fair to ask why organizations put up with all the hassle. What do they *do* with performance appraisals? Different researchers have suggested different answers.

Most generally, researchers going back as far as Meyer, Kay, and French (1965) have suggested there are two main uses of performance appraisals: for administrative purposes (e.g., raises, promotions, layoffs) and developmental purposes (e.g., identifying training needs). Other researchers have discussed a somewhat wider range of purposes for performance appraisal. For example, Behn (2003) studied the use of performance measurement in the

TABLE 8.1 ■ Eight Potential Uses of Performance Appraisal	
Evaluate	To determine how well individuals or units are performing
Control	To change or direct the behavior of those being evaluated
Budget	To help make decisions about which people, units, or tasks deserve resources and investment
Motivate	To increase the willingness of individuals and units to exert effort
Promote	To convince stakeholders that individuals or units are doing good and achieving worthwhile ends
Celebrate	To recognize success
Learn	To understand what is or is not working and why
Improve	To give direction to ongoing efforts to improve performance

public sector. He was more concerned with the performance and success of units than individuals, but the purposes he identified have clear relevance at several levels of analysis. He suggested eight different purposes for performance appraisal, which are shown in Table 8.1.

Behn (2010) describes what organizations *might* or *could* do with performance appraisals. Cleveland, Murphy, and Williams (1989) studied different ways organizations *actually use* performance appraisals. They identified 20 separate uses for performance appraisal that have been discussed in the research literature and surveyed human resource management experts to determine the frequency with which appraisal was used for each of these purposes in their organizations. On the basis of an analysis of survey responses, Cleveland et al. (1989) suggested that appraisals are used by organizations for four general purposes: (1) to distinguish between people—to identify candidates for salary increases, promotions, and so on and to identify both very good and very poor performers; (2) to distinguish individual strengths and weaknesses—by identifying variability within people, using this information to identify training needs and to shape feedback; (3) to support other organizational systems—by identifying organizational training needs, by serving as criteria for evaluating the validity of personnel selection systems, and by reinforcing organizational authority structures; and (4) as a method of documenting the bases for important actions and decisions. These uses are discussed in detail in the sections that follow.

It is sometimes assumed that different appraisal systems, tools, or methods might be best for different purposes, and that one system might not be able to serve all of the purposes performance appraisal systems are sometimes used to address (Behn, 2003; Murphy & Cleveland, 1995; Sridharan & Bui, 2015). However, it is unusual to find organizations that actually maintain multiple appraisal systems, each tied to a specific set of purposes.[2] Even though some organizations develop complex, multipart systems whose different components *might* provide inputs relevant to different purposes, this is not what usually happens in organizations. For example, Toegel and Conger (2003) note that while 360-degree feedback systems were originally created as tools for development, they increasingly were viewed as yet another method of performance appraisal, and that the outcomes of these measures might be used for the same wide range of uses as other types of performance appraisals.

They even suggest that this might be beneficial, claiming, "There are clear advantages to addressing multiple objectives such as developmental feedback and performance appraisals using a single 360-degree assessment tool" (p. 298). We are not sure this is a good idea; in a later section of this chapter, we review the potentially detrimental effects of designing performance appraisal systems to serve multiple purposes.

Identifying Differences Between People: Administrative Uses of Appraisal

Most organizations use performance appraisal as a basis (and perhaps as the sole basis) for making decisions about rewards and sanctions. To do this, they need an appraisal system that will reliably identify good versus poor performers. Probably the most common use for performance appraisal is in making decisions about salary increases, often with the intention of motivating future performance by linking good performance with concrete rewards. Appraisals can also play an important role in promotion decisions, in part on the basis of the theory that people who have performed well in their current job are more deserving of promotions than people who have performed poorly. Of course, if the job people are being promoted into requires different abilities and skills than the current job, it is entirely possible that the best candidate for the *next* job might not be the person who performed best in the *last* job.

Appraisals are also sometimes used to make decisions that have negative consequences. For example, a person who is performing poorly might end up being dismissed, especially under appraisal systems that resemble the rank-and-yank system that was used for several years at General Electric (in this system, employees were sorted into ordered categories, and employees who were in the lowest category were in serious jeopardy of being dismissed; for a description of the rationale for this system, see Welch and Byrne [2001]). More commonly, employees who receive poor performance appraisals are likely to be put on some sort of performance improvement plan, where they are given help and opportunities to improve their performance, and dismissal will occur only if repeated attempts to improve performance fail. Thus, in most organizations, a single poor performance rating is unlikely to lead to dismissal. Nevertheless, performance appraisals can play a major role in the decision to dismiss some employees.

Performance appraisals are also used when making decisions about layoffs. When organizations decide to shrink their workforce, a variety of approaches might be implemented, ranging from getting rid of entire departments or functions to trimming staff across the board, and when departments must trim staff, it is not unusual to consider the performance ratings various staff members receive when making this decision. It is therefore important that performance appraisals do a good job at distinguishing people whose performance is consistently poor from those who are performing better.

The decision to use performance ratings as input to administrative decisions influences both the ratings themselves and peoples' attitudes toward and reactions to performance appraisal. First, when performance ratings are used to make decisions about salary, promotions, layoffs, and the like, performance ratings tend to go up. That is, when performance ratings are tied to important rewards, raters tend to assign higher ratings. Several studies, starting in the 1950s, documented the impact of purpose of rating on leniency, or the level of ratings. Field research, in particular, has consistently documented that when ratings are used to make high-stakes decisions, people tend to receive higher ratings. For example,

Taylor and Wherry (1951), using ratings from Army personnel, found that average ratings of officers were significantly higher for administrative purposes than when ratings were collected for research purposes. Using ratings of 400 job applicants, Heron (1956) obtained results similar to Taylor and Wherry, with a negatively skewed distribution of ratings for administrative purposes. Sharon and Bartlett (1969) found that ratings used in making real administrative decisions were more lenient than ratings obtained for research purposes. The majority of the studies that have compared ratings obtained for different purposes suggest that ratings that are collected for administrative purposes (e.g., salary administration) show strong correlations with ratings collected for research purposes only, but higher means (Harris, Smith, & Champagne, 1995). Meta-analyses of the effect of purpose on ratings suggests that the difference in mean ratings for administrative versus research is about one-third of a standard deviation (Jawahar & Williams, 1997). Some studies have found no mean difference in ratings when comparing administrative and research purpose conditions (Berkshire & Highland, 1953; Sharon, 1970) or comparing administrative and feedback purposes (McIntyre, Smith, & Hassett, 1984; Meier & Feldhusen, 1979), but the general trend is for higher ratings when information from performance appraisal will be used to make administrative decisions that have important stakes.

In Chapter 12, we will examine in detail why the use of performance ratings to make administrative decisions tends to drive ratings higher, but a moment's reflection will make the underlying dynamics clear. Suppose you are a supervisor, and your decision to give a subordinate a high rating or a low one is the only thing that stands in the way of a raise or a promotion. It is a good bet that a low rating will lead to disappointment and resentment on the part of the ratee, making your future relationship more difficult. It is unlikely that the ratee will be *more* motivated by the failure to receive a reward than he or she would be if a raise or promotion was forthcoming. Raters who give high ratings will probably end up with happier, more cooperative, and more motivated subordinates than raters who give low ratings.

Youngcourt, Leiva, and Jones (2007) note that perceptions of the purpose of performance appraisal are linked to a number of job attitudes. In particular, their data suggest that the stronger the belief that performance appraisals are used for administrative purposes, the higher the level of satisfaction with performance appraisal.[3] This implies that employees share a common commitment to a core assumption of performance appraisal, that information about job performance *should* be used in making decisions about salary, promotion, and the like.

Merit Pay

One widespread use of performance appraisals is in merit pay systems, where rated performance is one factor (and often the dominant factor) in determining salary increases. Schaubroeck, Shaw, Duffy, and Mitra (2008) note that this is probably the most popular method of implementing pay plans designed to create financial incentives to perform well. These systems are, on the surface, tightly linked to the concept of distributive justice—that is, people who perform better should be rewarded for their work (Campbell, Campbell, & Ho-Beng, 1998). However, there are several potential barriers to effective merit pay systems.

First, these systems assume that available performance measures are good indicators of the performance levels of the people being rated, an assumption that is questionable at best (Landy & Farr, 1980; Milkovich & Wigdor, 1991; Murphy & Cleveland, 1995).

Even if performance appraisal systems are carefully designed to provide the best-possible measurement of performance, the widespread tendency of raters to provide high ratings to virtually all of their subordinates often makes it impossible to link pay to performance in any consistent way (Kane, Bernardin, Villanova, & Peyrefitte, 1995). Second, these systems imply the belief that performance ratings will be accepted by ratees as reasonable indications of their performance level, again a questionable assumption. (See Chapter 9, which deals with performance feedback.) If ratees believe that they are being unfairly rated, they are also likely to believe that basing pay increases in performance ratings will lead to unfair outcomes. Even if they do not believe that ratings are *systematically* unfair, employees who question the accuracy of performance ratings are likely to be skeptical about merit pay plans that rely on these ratings (Li, Alam, & Meonske, 2013).

Third, instrumentality beliefs—the belief that pay is in fact tied to rated performance levels—are important. Even if ratings are accepted as accurate, if ratings do not seem to translate into pay increases, merit pay systems are likely to fail (Schaubroeck et al., 2008; Vest, Scott, Vest, & Markham, 2000). That is, regardless of the actual link between pay and performance, employees must *believe* that pay is linked to performance if merit pay plans are to succeed. Employees who do not trust their supervisors or managers are unlikely to believe that performance ratings are fair and accurate, and are likely to doubt that genuine performance–pay relationships exist in their organization (St-Onge, 2000; Vest et al., 2000).

Fourth, the managers and supervisors whose input is critical to the success of these systems must believe in and support linking pay to performance (Harris, 2001). If managers and supervisors do not support the goals or the structure of the merit pay system, the system is likely to fail. For example, Lawler and Jenkins (1992) note that despite the fact that merit pay systems are designed to give different rewards to people whose performance differs, supervisors are often unwilling to differentiate among their subordinates when rating performance. Rather, when ratings are linked to important rewards, it is common for virtually everyone to receive high ratings. We will examine the reasons for this reluctance to distinguish among rates in Chapters 9 and 12.

Fifth, if the pay differentials for good versus poor performers are small (Campbell et al., 1998, note that they typically are), attempts to reward good performance with pay increases may fail, because ratees are likely to believe that the rewards they receive are not in proportion to their value and contribution to the organization. As Mitra, Gupta, and Jenkins (1997) note, merit pay raises are often so small that they are hardly regarded as a genuine reward.

On the whole, a review by the National Academy of Sciences (Milkovich & Wigdor, 1991) concluded that merit pay systems that are based on traditional performance appraisal systems are unlikely to work well. They did note that other methods of linking performance and effectiveness with financial rewards (e.g., profit sharing) have a better track record, but that the lack of trust in and acceptance of performance rating systems was a barrier to the success of merit pay.

Using Appraisals to Recognize Good Performers

Many organizations, even those that do not implement merit pay programs, use a variety of other mechanisms to recognize individual performance. The most familiar example is an "Employee of the Month" program in which an exemplary employee receives public recognition, and perhaps some sort of tangible reward (e.g., a designated parking space). You could think of this as "merit pay lite," a performance-driven rewards program with rewards that are at best ephemeral. In our view, this sort of recognition program could end up a double-edged sword. Employees usually appreciate being recognized, but someone who is recognized as exemplary but who receives no meaningful reward might end up feeling cheated rather than appreciated. Recognition programs that are accompanied by some sort of genuine reward might be more effective than those that do not include rewards, although linking rewards with evaluations of performance will always be potentially problematic. The higher the stakes that are tied to performance appraisals, the higher the likelihood that performance ratings will be distorted.

Identifying Within-Person Differences: Developmental Uses of Appraisal

Suppose that you receive ratings of your overall job performance, and find that (at least in the opinion of your supervisor), you are a better performer than two of the people in your work group, but that your performance is worse than the other six people in your work group. Suppose further that you want to do something about this. If all you learn from your performance rating is whether you are a relatively good or a relatively poor performer, this information will not be much help in telling you what to do, or where to devote your time and energy to improve your performance.

Performance appraisal systems that help workers identify their strengths and weaknesses have the potential to also help guide their development. That is, they can give you and your organization specific ideas about areas where development is needed. They allow individuals and organizations to make informed decisions about which training and development programs and resources are most necessary. Of course, knowing what skills or knowledge needs to be developed does not necessarily mean that development will occur. Successful employee development requires both the motivation to improve and the resources to support that improvement (Feldman & Ng, 2008).

Developmental opportunities can be motivating. When individuals believe that their organization is invested in developing their skills and abilities, they are more likely to be motivated to exert effort and are more likely to be committed, especially if they are interested in further developing their skills and knowledge (Cropanzano & Mitchell, 2005; Kuvaas & Dysvik, 2009). A performance appraisal system that accurately identifies developmental needs can be very valuable in this case.

Although appraisal systems *can* be useful for developing employees, they do not always turn out to help all that much. In fact, instead of being a valuable source of information about training needs, performance appraisal can be a serious obstacle to effective training and development. Wilson and Western (2000) note that the training and development plans that result from performance appraisals are often the same year after year and are often unrelated to the needs of organizations. As Meyer, Kay, and French (1965) noted more than 50 years ago, performance appraisal often involves split roles, in which the supervisor is both a judge who can influence rewards and sanctions (e.g., promotions, raises) and a helper who can aid employees in developing the knowledge and skills needed to perform well. Unfortunately, these roles are often in conflict and performance appraisal is often an ineffective tool for either purpose (see also Murphy & Cleveland, 1995).

The use of performance appraisal for administrative versus developmental purposes can be thought of as implementations of two different theories of behavior change. The use of performance appraisal as a tool for administering raises or giving promotions suggests that what is needed to change behavior is motivation. That is, this use of performance appraisal can be thought of as a way to motivate employees to devote more effort or to devote more attention by linking rewards with performance. Appraisal programs that focus on development suggest that employees need information rather than motivation, and that their performance will improve if they have a better understanding of what they are doing well, what they are doing poorly, and what they might do to improve future job performance. Surprisingly, there have been few direct comparisons of the relative effectiveness of these two strategies for changing behavior. Jhun, Bae, and Rhee (2012) used longitudinal data collected as part of an upward feedback program over seven years to evaluate the effectiveness of appraisal programs based on these two competing theories, and concluded that appraisal programs that focus on rewards may be more effective in motivating future performance.

Earlier, we noted that performance appraisal systems designed to support administrative decisions can influence employee attitudes, and that they can be a source of positive attitudes toward organizations if they are designed and used appropriately. The same is true for appraisal systems that are designed to support employee development. The use of performance appraisal for developmental purposes is associated with higher levels of satisfaction (Boswell & Boudreau, 2000). There is also evidence that using performance appraisal for developmental purposes is related to higher levels of affective commitment (Si & Li, 2012). This result suggests some level of reciprocity—that employees who believe that the organization is committed to their development feel a stronger level of commitment to the organization.

SPOTLIGHT 8.1 PERFORMANCE APPRAISAL IN A TEAM ENVIRONMENT

One of the common criticisms of performance appraisal is that it undermines teamwork by forcing employees to compete with one another (Culbert & Rout, 2010). The evidence regarding the effects of performance appraisal on teams is mixed, but it is important to give careful thought to the way performance appraisal will be used in a team-based work environment.

The U.S. Office of Personnel Management (1998) offered helpful guidance for evaluating performance when work is performed by teams. First, it noted that even when work is team based, there is a clear place for individual performance evaluation. In particular, it is useful and important to evaluate each individual's contribution to the team. It provided examples of

evaluation standards for relevant interpersonal skills and for team participation. Second, it noted that the team itself can and should be evaluated both in terms of processes (how it gets its work done) and outcomes (what gets accomplished). It offered examples of performance standards relevant to communication, to the definition and accomplishment of team roles, and decision-making processes. It also described a number of possible metrics for evaluating team outputs.

Performance appraisal can be a source of friction in teams if the focus of evaluation is solely on individual performance. This threat to teamwork can be substantially mitigated by including teamwork itself as one of the important dimensions along which performance will be evaluated.

On the whole, research suggests that employees react most positively when performance appraisal is used for developmental purposes and when the appraisal procedure appears to be fair (Boswell & Boudreau, 2000). Opportunities to discuss goals and career issues are related to positive reactions to performance appraisal, although these discussions do not always have clear links to subsequent performance (Lee & Son, 1998).

Using Performance Appraisal to Support and Maintain Other Organizational Systems

Cleveland et al. (1989) noted that organizations use performance appraisal for a wide range of purposes other than identifying differences within or between people. These include personnel planning, identifying organizational training needs, evaluating personnel systems, reinforcing authority structures, identifying organizational development needs, and validating other personnel systems. They described this cluster of uses as systems maintenance.

A performance appraisal system that is used primarily for administrative purposes needs to be very good at rank-ordering people in terms of their overall performance levels. Most performance appraisal systems include ratings on specific areas or dimensions of performance as well as an overall performance rating (which is not necessarily the average of the dimension ratings since some dimensions might be more important than others). For all intents and purposes, ratings of specific performance dimensions are not very important when appraisals are used to determine raises, promotions, or layoffs; the overall rating is what counts. When performance appraisal systems are used for developmental purposes the opposite is true. It is the dimension ratings that are critical; the overall rating might not have much value in making decisions about training and development. When performance appraisal systems are used for systems maintenance purposes, the attributes of the appraisal system that are most critical might depend on the specific use.

For example, suppose performance ratings are used for validating personnel selection systems. Since the goal of personnel selection is to rank-order job candidates and select candidates who are most likely to perform well, it is critical that you must have confidence in the overall performance rating. On the other hand, if performance appraisals are used to identify organizational training needs, it will be important to determine what the people in a particular unit of the organization currently do well and where their developmental needs lie, meaning that you must have faith in the dimension ratings.

One of the systems maintenance uses identified by Cleveland et al. (1989) is using performance appraisal to clarify and strengthen authority structures. This is an especially interesting and important use because of its relationship with performance appraisal as part of the system of political relationships within organizations. For example, consider two organizations, one of which relies entirely on supervisory evaluations and the other of which incorporates self-ratings and peer ratings into performance appraisal. One way to interpret this difference is as an indication of the power structure in the two organizations, the first showing a strictly hierarchical structure and the second showing a flatter, more democratic structure. The question of who determines whether you are viewed as a good or a poor performer in organizations, and whether you have any meaningful input into this process, may speak volumes about the Power Distance in this organization. In Chapter 7, we discussed cultural values that could be used to distinguish nations, but they can also be used to distinguish one organization from another, and performance appraisal can be a powerful tool for communicating who is in charge and whose opinions count.

Appraisal as a Source of Documentation

There are several reasons why it is important to carefully document decisions made on the basis of performance appraisal. First, there is the simple issue of fairness. If you are indeed using the best information you have about an employee's performance to make high-stakes decisions about him or her, you owe it to that employee to be able to document the bases for decisions. Organizations that are unable or unwilling to document why they made important decisions are likely to be suspected of acting in an arbitrary fashion. If you are going to use performance information to make important decisions about people, a respect for that person's basic worth and dignity implies that you should be able to convincingly explain your actions if questioned. Second, if basic decency does not move you, the threat of a lawsuit should.

Malos (2005) notes that performance appraisal has been involved in hundreds of legal challenges and that appraisal sometimes takes center stage (see also Martin, Bartol, & Kehoe, 2000). Formally, performance appraisal takes the same role, and should be held to the same standards as any other test or assessment that is used in making high-stakes decisions, although it is unusual to find litigation where they are actually judged by strict standards that involve detailed job analysis and credible evidence of validity. Unlike selection tests, where most employment litigation is carried out under an adverse impact theory (i.e., tests or assessments that lead to systematically different outcomes as a function of age, gender, race, and so on are subject to legal scrutiny), performance appraisal cases often involve allegations of differential treatment—for example, that performance appraisals are conducted differently for minority employees than for white employees. Careful documentation of each employee's performance, of the information that was used to assess each employee, and of the way the appraisal system was administered and interpreted is essential when decisions that are based on performance appraisal are challenged in a court of law.

Martin et al. (2000) note that there are numerous technical factors that can come into play when evaluating performance appraisal in litigation, such as evidence that the dimensions that are rated on an organization's appraisal form are indeed important parts of the job, or evidence that raters have been adequately trained to provide accurate ratings. However, the courts also pay careful attention to factors such as the employee's opportunity to provide his or her own perspective, of the availability of formal procedures for challenging what appears to be an unfair rating. Martin et al. (2000) conclude that performance appraisal systems that do not *seem* fair are probably at more legal risk.

Competing Purposes for Performance Appraisal

Both performance appraisal researchers (Cleveland et al., 1989; Curtis, Harvey, & Ravden, 2005; DeCotiis & Petit, 1978; Jacobs, Kafry, & Zedeck, 1978; Mohrman & Lawler, 1983; Prowse & Prowse, 2009; Rees & Porter, 2003; Starbuck, 2004; Wexley & Klimoski, 1984) and practitioners (Burchett & DeMeuse, 1985; Cocheu, 1986; DeVries et al., 1986; Haynes, 1986; Massey, 1975) have recognized that there are many uses or goals to which a performance appraisal system can contribute. Unfortunately, these uses often come into conflict.

First, different units in an organization may have different interests and needs, and these can lead to differences in the way appraisal systems are designed, implemented, and used (Starbuck, 2004). Whereas employees in the marketing department may be rated on whether they were able to tend to customers' needs by developing new products, production personnel are more likely to be rated on saving costs by producing large quantities of products in ways that minimize wasted resources and machine downtime. More generally, the major uses of performance appraisal that cut across departments or units often come into conflict, because different applications of performance appraisal may involve or require different types of data and different levels of emphasis on specific aspects of those data. This is most obvious when we compare the two most important uses of appraisal in most organizations: for identifying differences between people versus for identifying relative strengths and weaknesses, or differences within people.

Fifty years ago, Meyer et al. (1965) noted the incompatibility of using performance appraisal simultaneously to make decisions about rewards and to provide useful feedback, and suggested that the different uses of performance appraisal should be separated, by creating different evaluative mechanisms for rewards versus feedback. Murphy and Cleveland (1995) suggested that the conflict between these two uses involves both incompatible roles and incompatible measures. When giving developmental feedback, the rater's role is that of a counselor and advisor, helping ratees to identify developmental needs and to find and take advantages of resources in the organization to assist in their development. When making ratings that determine salary increases or promotions, the rater takes the role of a judge or evaluator, charged with making decisions about who is a better performer overall (regardless of what they are better *at*). Perhaps even more important is the conflicting data requirements of systems that attempt to identify differences between versus differences within individuals.

In Chapter 4, we presented a figure very much like Figure 8.1. In Figure 8.1, we have added the sort of data that you might obtain from performance ratings to illustrate the way different patterns of findings tend to support administrative versus developmental uses of performance appraisal. The top pattern illustrates the type of data that allow organizations to make the sharpest distinctions between employees. Here, where there are few peaks and valleys, Employee 1 has an average rating of 3.9 and Employee 2 has an average rating of 2.97. Even if you decided that some performance dimensions were more important than others or should be given more weight than others, you would almost always conclude that there is a difference in the performance and effectiveness of these two employees, and that you can say with some confidence that Employee 1 is the better performer.

Performance profiles that are relatively flat make it easier to sort out employees in terms of their overall performance. If performance ratings have distinct peaks and valleys (i.e., areas of strength and weakness), it will usually be hard to tell one employee from another in terms of their overall performance. For example, in the bottom panel (ratings that allow you to sort strengths from weaknesses) Employee 1 has an average rating of 2.95 and Employee 2 has an average rating of 3.1. The conclusions you might reach about the overall performance of these two employees might differ substantially if you put more emphasis on one aspect of performance (e.g., communication) and less on another (e.g., planning). Different decisions about how much emphasis or weight to give to different aspects of job performance might lead to completely different conclusions about which employee is the better performer.

The data used to produce Figure 8.1 are hypothetical, but they are not unrealistic. When there are rewards or sanctions (e.g., raises, layoffs) associated with performance

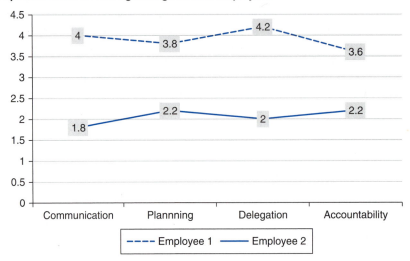

FIGURE 8.1 ■ Data Patterns Consistent With Between- Versus Within-Person Uses

Optimal Pattern for Distinguishing Between Employees

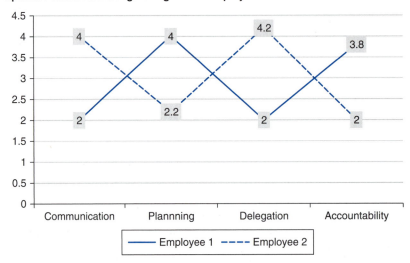

Optimal Pattern for Distinguishing Within Employees

ratings, raters will and should concentrate on who should get what reward, and that will tend to produce flat profiles like those in the top panel of Figure 8.1. If the purpose of appraisal is to identify strengths and weaknesses, even small differences in performance across performance dimensions will be magnified, and profiles with distinct peaks and valleys, such as those in the bottom panel of Figure 8.1, will result.

There are many organizations that use appraisals for both administrative and developmental purposes; Cleveland et al. (1989) found that over 71% of HR experts they surveyed indicated that in their organization, information from appraisals was used "moderately to extensively" for both between-person decision (i.e. pay, promotion) and within-person decisions (i.e., feedback). We believe this is a mistake, and that ratings used for both administrative and developmental purposes run the risk of not being truly useful for either purpose.

Of course, not all of the uses of performance appraisal are mutually incompatible. For example, use of performance appraisal for salary administration is not necessarily incompatible with using performance appraisal as a tool for validating selection instruments, because both uses focus on differences between ratees. However, even when there is no underlying conflict among uses, the particular dynamics of one use of appraisals (e.g., for determining raises) might limit its value for other uses (e.g., the range restriction that is likely when most ratees receive high ratings might limit the value of appraisals as criteria for validating selection tests).

Separating Multiple Uses

Although there is a strong conceptual argument for separating administrative and developmental uses of performance appraisals (Cleveland et al., 1989; Meyer et al., 1965), the actual consequences of this policy are not so clear. Prince and Lawler (1986) performed one of the first empirical studies of the consequences of separating these two uses of performance appraisal, and their data suggested that separating administrative and developmental uses of performance appraisal had little real impact, with small effects at best on the content or the process of appraisals. Boswell and Boudreau (2002) showed that separating these two functions had some impact on employees' attitudes regarding future developmental activities, but on the whole employees did not seem to have different attitudes toward systems that combined administrative and developmental uses of appraisal than to systems that separated them. An important caveat in both studies is that rewards seem more important to ratees than development (for example, there may be less motivation to use feedback to develop new skills or strengths if these new skills and strengths do not lead to rewards), and regardless of the intended purpose of appraisals, ratees may always be mindful of the potential effects of appraisals on rewards.

We are skeptical of the value of creating two appraisal systems, one for administrative and the other for developmental purposes. There is hardly any point in doing so unless the two systems provide different information, and if you receive two appraisals that disagree, for example, an administrative one that identifies you as an excellent performer and a developmental one that identifies several important weaknesses, it is possible that the credibility of *both* systems may be undermined. In Chapters 13 and 14 of this book, we will discuss some strategies for minimizing conflict in the uses and discrepancies in the information provided by performance appraisal systems in organizations.

INFORMAL USES OF PERFORMANCE APPRAISAL: DOWNWARD AND UPWARD INFLUENCE

Performance appraisal is an important human resource management tool, but it is much more than that. The appraisal interview is an important and often stressful interaction between employees and their supervisors or managers. The process of rating is one that encourages supervisors to pay careful attention to each of their subordinates' behavior and effectiveness on the job. Performance feedback can be both a source of information and a source of motivation for employees. Performance appraisal is also a method of influencing others. That is, the participants in performance appraisal use this process to influence others in the organization—both their subordinates and their superiors. Supervisors and managers try to influence the behavior of their subordinates through the performance ratings and the performance feedback they give, hoping to motivate and direct them to perform better. However, influence can be a two-way street; employees are likely to try to influence their supervisors to give them high ratings. For example, in performance appraisal interviews, employees are often given an opportunity to explain their performance and behavior. This provides an opportunity for the ratee to influence the supervisor's judgments, by providing additional information that the rater may not have access to or may not have fully considered (Backburn, 1981; Mechanic, 1962; Potter, Allen, & Angle, 1981). Finally, supervisors and managers use the performance ratings they give to influence the perceptions and opinions of *their own* superiors. That is, a manager whose ratings convey the impression that all of his or her subordinates are star performers is also conducting a message that he or she is a good manager. In Chapter 12 we will explore a number of ways in which raters might benefit from distorting the ratings they give.

Performance appraisals are also an exercise of power. In most performance appraisals, raters evaluate workers who are at a lower level in the organization, and this evaluation is both a manifestation and an application of power. We often talk about performance *evaluation* or performance *appraisal* without thinking concretely about the meaning of these terms, but evaluation and appraisal are both the act of assigning value to something, and whoever has the right to assign value (i.e., to decide what is good and what is not, to decide if one employee is better than another) by definition, has power over the person being evaluated. Performance appraisal systems help to clarify and reinforce power hierarchies in organizations; in most organizations, employees with more power and influence are the ones who are called upon to evaluate the performance of employees occupying lower and less powerful positions (Pfeffer, 1981).

Finally, the use of performance appraisal to influence others' behavior can be thought of as an exercise in politics, in the sense that politics can be defined as a set of self-interested behaviors—that is, behaviors designed to advance the interests of the sender (Treadway et al., 2005). The term "politics" often has the implication that it involves manipulation or dishonesty, but it need not involve any sort of disreputable behaviors. Rather, it is better to think of politics as a set of behaviors that are characterized by an awareness of consequences and an effort to mold the consequences of behavior in the sender's favor. Although political behavior need not be disreputable or ill intentioned, it is often interpreted in this way by others, in part because the advantages one person accrues through political behavior may come at someone else's expense (Treadway et al., 2005). For example, a supervisor who manipulates performance ratings to make sure his or her subordinates get the largest salary increase possible may achieve this goal by costing more deserving employees *their* raises. Nevertheless, performance appraisals have an important role in the informal influence processes that occur in organizations, and we should not dismiss the political aspects of performance appraisal as uniformly negative. A good deal can be accomplished in organizations by raters and ratees who use performance appraisal as a tool to influence the perceptions and behaviors or others in the organization. We will consider the political aspects of performance appraisal in more detail in Chapter 10.

Downward Influence

First and foremost, performance appraisal gives managers and supervisors an opportunity to influence the behavior of their subordinates. They can use appraisal as a method of targeting rewards (e.g., raises, promotions) toward deserving employees. They can also use appraisal as a way of communicating performance expectations, and as a way of communicating about the strengths and weaknesses of employees.

In addition to these uses, which are tied in one way or another to the formal HR systems for rewarding and developing employees, managers and supervisors can use performance appraisal as a tool for building relationships and for creating networks of reciprocal obligations with the employees they rate. We will take up this topic in detail in Chapters 12 and 13, but it is useful to comment in a general way on this informal use of appraisal as a tool for influencing employees here. As we have already noted (and will explore in more detail in Chapter 11), performance ratings often seem quite lenient; it is not unusual to find that 80% of the employees in an organization are rated as "above average," and up to 70% of managers admit to distorting ratings (Longenecker & Ludwig, 1990). One of the many possible explanations for this leniency is that raters are making a conscious effort to influence the perceptions and behaviors of their subordinates by deliberately giving high ratings, even when lower ratings might be deserved (Kane, 1994; Murphy & Cleveland, 1991, 1995; Spence & Keeping, 2011).

Ratees who receive favorable performance ratings are more likely to receive rewards (e.g., pay increases) from the organization, and as a result, may be more satisfied with both their ratings and their supervisor or manager. Thus, a rater who distorts his or her ratings, giving higher performance ratings than his or her subordinates deserve, may end up building a better relationship with those subordinates *and* motivating them to perform better in the future. If the subordinates understand that the rater is doing them a favor, this could even build a sense of obligation. In the movie *The Godfather*, a Mafia don who does a favor for you today will expect you to reciprocate at some later time. In a similar way, a manager or supervisor who makes sure that you receive a raise by giving you a higher rating than you deserve might put you under some obligation to return the favor in the future, perhaps by exerting extra effort or by going above and beyond what the job formally requires when there is a deadline or emergency in your work group. It is very much in the supervisor or manager's interest to build a sense of loyalty and mutual obligations in the work group, and giving people high ratings is certainly one tool for accomplishing this end.

A high overall rating is not the only tool that might be useful for influencing the attitudes and behavior of subordinates. Performance appraisal often includes detailed feedback, and a supervisor may choose to get a subordinate's attention by giving faint praise, or may choose to build up an employee's confidence and perception that his or her work is valued by giving strongly supportive feedback that deals with important aspects of the job. A supervisor might even use the content of the narrative that accompanies ratings to send clear signals to the ratee and the organization. Bjerke, Cleveland, Morrison, and Wilson (1987) studied the performance rating system used for officers in the U.S. Navy (the Fitness Report). Like many organizations, the Navy is plagued by rating inflation; almost everyone receives high ratings. This created a dilemma for raters who wanted to communicate to ratees and to the Navy that a particular officer really *was* a superior performer. If almost everyone received high ratings, the numerical ratings were not much help here, so raters learned to use the narrative that accompanied the rating to communicate their true judgments. Thus, an officer who received a high rating, but whose narrative said "This officer looks good in his uniform" would understand and would be perceived by superiors as a less successful officer than another who received the same numerical rating but whose narrative said "This officer is a natural leader."

Upward Influence: Impression Management

There is considerable evidence that ratees engage in a variety of strategies designed to influence the evaluations they receive, and this can be thought of as political behavior on the part of ratees. Much of the research examining this process has centered on activities that are designed to influence the opinion of one's supervisor, or of some other power person— that is, impression management.

Impression management occurs at all levels of the organization. For example, Drymiotes (2008) discusses the ways senior managers attempt to influence their board of directors to receive more favorable evaluations and larger raises and bonuses. Interestingly, he makes the case that behaviors on the part of top managers aimed at maximizing their performance evaluations and their raises and bonuses can in fact be good for the organization and its shareholders. In particular, when top managers *are* performing well, their efforts to make sure the board of directors is aware of their performance and success can help to remove noise and uncertainty from the performance evaluation system, and more efficiently match compensation with performance. On the other hand, if managers attempt to make the board of directors *think* they are performing well when they are not, the organization can be hurt by this type of impression management behavior. Although he does not make this case explicitly, the same distinction could be applied to impression management behaviors at all levels of the organization. That is, impression management can take at least two forms: (1) actions on the part of the ratee to increase the likelihood that superiors are aware of and appropriately reward good performance, and (2) actions on the part of the ratee to increase the likelihood that superiors *believe* their performance is good, when in fact it is not. The first type of impression management is arguably beneficial to both the ratee and the organization (because it appropriately links rewards with good performance), whereas the latter is potentially good for the ratee (at least in the short term) but harmful to the organization.

Impression management might amount to little more than making sure your supervisor is aware of your successes, but it can also take several other forms. First, it might involve efforts to take more credit for successes in the organization or in the work group than is deserved. It might involve efforts to hide or to deflect failures (perhaps blaming them on others). It might involve efforts to ingratiate oneself with one's supervisor, or to cast competitors in a negative light. It might even involve efforts to intimidate one's supervisor.

Bolino and Turnley (2003) discuss the use of intimidation tactics by professional employees in a large law enforcement agency.[4] The intimidation behaviors they measured included letting others know that they can make things difficult if pushed too far and by dealing forcefully with others, even their supervisors, who interfere with their ability to accomplish their goals. As is the case with so many other behaviors (Fiske, Bersoff, Borgida, Deaux, & Heilman, 1991), engaging in the same intimidation behaviors had different consequences for men than for women. Women who engage in these behaviors are viewed very negatively in organizations, whereas men who engage in the same behaviors sometimes end up getting higher performance evaluations.

There is evidence that ratees' social skills influence their choice of impression management tactics. Brouer, Badaway, Gallagher, and Haber (2015) suggested that individuals who were well-networked in their organization and who were socially astute would be more likely to use positive impression management tactics (e.g., ingratiation, self-promotion) than negative ones (e.g., intimidation, supplication). They suggested that social skills and connections within organizations are combined with skill in conveying sincerity and in influencing others, impression management behaviors would be likely to lead to improvements in performance ratings, but this hypothesis received only partial support. Nevertheless, their study presented evidence that there are meaningful differences in political skill, and that political skills influence the likelihood that impression management will succeed (See also Harris, Kacmar, Zivnuska, & Shaw, 2007; Kolodinsky, Treadway, & Ferris, 2007). Treadway, Duke, Ferris, Adams, and Thatcher (2007) suggest that one of the ways political skill contributes to the effectiveness of impression management is that employees with high levels of political skill do not *seem* to be engaging in impression management. Without some level of political skill, impression management behavior can come off as a type of "brown nosing," which will be resented. The most skilled political actors are probably the ones who do not seem to be acting at all.

Wayne, Liden, Graf, and Ferris (1997) suggest that impression management influences human resource decisions through three different channels: (1) raters' perceptions of ratees' skills and accomplishments, (2) raters' liking of ratees, and (3) raters' perceptions of similarity to ratees (see also Wayne & Liden, 1995). They suggested that different impression management tactics might be linked to each of particular channels. For example, they found that reasoning, bargaining, and assertiveness on the part of ratees was related to raters' perceptions of their skills; self-promotion was related to both skill perception and liking; and rendering favors to supervisors was related to both liking and perceptions of similarity.

Impression management is more likely to occur in some contexts than in others. Ratees are especially likely to engage in behaviors designed to impress or influence their supervisors when they are feeling insecure about their jobs or about their prospects for advancement and rewards (Huang, Zhao, Niu, Ashford, & Lee, 2013). Impression management is also more likely if ratees believe that others are engaged in similar behaviors. Earlier, we noted that there are two forms of politics in performance appraisal, manipulation on the part of the rater and manipulation on the part of the ratee. Zivunska, Kacmar, Witt, Carlson, and Bratton (2004) examined the interaction between these two forms of political behavior. They note that there is research suggesting that ratees who perceive their performance appraisal systems as political might be more likely to engage in impression management behaviors than other ratees who believe their appraisal systems are fair and accurate. The belief that an organization's performance appraisal system is influenced by political factors probably encourages some degree of cynicism toward the process, and this could in turn increase the temptation to engage in political behavior as a ratee. If nothing else, ratees who believe their performance appraisals are determined in part by political considerations might consider it necessary to engage in impression management to help protect themselves from being unfairly evaluated by raters who are pursuing their own political ends.

SUMMARY

Performance appraisals have the potential to provide information that is relevant to a wide range of activities and decisions in organizations, ranging from selecting employees for raises, promotions, or layoffs to fostering the development of individual employees to providing documentation to support decisions. In addition to the formal uses of performance appraisal on the part of the organization, appraisal is an important part of the informal efforts of superiors to influence the behavior and attitudes of their subordinates and subordinates to influence the behavior and attitudes of their supervisors. This interpersonal influence represents one of the ways in which performance appraisal is a uniquely political activity. For many years, performance appraisal researchers treated performance appraisal as a measurement problem, on the assumption that the participants in this system were all trying to obtain accurate assessments of performance. It is clear that performance appraisal is not simply an exercise in performance

measurement, but rather an important part of the process by which the behavior of individuals in the workplace is molded and in which perceptions, attitudes, and beliefs are shaped.

The idea that administrative versus developmental uses of performance appraisal are distinct and potentially a source of conflict has been with us for more than 50 years. Over 30 years ago, Cleveland et al. (1989) proposed two additional categories of uses of performance appraisal: for maintaining and supporting other systems in organizations and for documentation. Our review of the literature suggests that this taxonomy is still a useful one.

Organizations that attempt to use performance appraisal for multiple conflicting purposes run the risk that *none* of these purposes will be achieved. In Chapters 13 and 14, we will examine the possibility that using performance appraisals to support a narrower range of HR functions may be beneficial.

CASE STUDY: EVEN TERRORISTS GET PERFORMANCE APPRAISALS—AND ACT ON THEM!

Performance appraisal is ubiquitous. In a 10-page letter discovered in Timbuktu, Moktar Belmoktar, an aspiring leader in the North African branch of Al Qaeda received a detailed and highly critical performance review (Knowles, 2013). The complaints about his performance included issues familiar to any manager: poor work attitude, failure to file expense reports, failure to work through the usual bureaucratic channels, lack of initiative. Stung by the sharp tone of this review, Belmoktar quit Al Qaeda and founded his own terror group, The Masked Brigade.

Unfortunately, this represents a case where performance feedback led to action. The Masked Brigade pulled off several operations, including one of the largest hostage takings in history. There seems to be a clear link between the criticisms

Belmoktar received from Al Qaeda leadership and his subsequent waves of action.

It should not come as a surprise that terrorist organizations rely on performance reviews. Like any other organization, Al Qaeda has a number of objectives it wants to accomplish, uses a range of systems for distributing resources and for managing and directing the activities of its branches, and faces the problem of evaluating and giving feedback to its members. The Belmoktar documents are unusual mainly in the fact that they became public, but even a loosely structured organization like Al Qaeda is likely to provide feedback to its members that functions very much like performance appraisals in regular work organizations—that is, as a tool for motivating and directing the activities of its members.

NOTES

1. Maley (2013) noted substantial numbers of employees do not know why performance appraisals are conducted or how they are used.

2. In a later section of this chapter and in the final two chapters of this book, we will consider whether organizations *should* attempt to develop and use multiple performance appraisal systems.

3. However, this relationship might hold only when performance ratings are high. If you believe that ratings are used to make high-stakes decisions and you receive low ratings, your satisfaction might go down.

4. These employees were not law enforcement officers, but rather professional support personnel, such as forensic scientists or computer support personnel.

SECTION III

CHALLENGES IN IMPLEMENTING AND EVALUATING PERFORMANCE APPRAISAL SYSTEMS

GIVING AND RECEIVING FEEDBACK

Everyone wants feedback—unless, of course, the feedback is negative. There is a substantial body of research on feedback and its effects, and the only consistent conclusion we can see from this research is that the effects of feedback are inconsistent. Sometimes feedback helps and leads to improvements in performance, sometimes it hurts (leading to decrements in performance), and sometimes it has very little effect one way or the other (Kluger & DeNisi, 1996). In this chapter, we examine research on performance feedback in depth, with the goal of understanding why it sometimes succeeds and sometimes fails.

THE DEFINITION AND PURPOSE OF FEEDBACK

What do we mean by "feedback"? Kluger and DeNisi (1996) define feedback interventions as "actions taken by (an) external agent(s) to provide information regarding some aspect(s) of performance" (p. 255). Three aspects of this definition are important. First, feedback comes from some external source or agent. It does not have to be a person; any of a variety of automated monitoring systems might be a source of feedback.[1]

LEARNING OBJECTIVES

9.1 Learn how feedback is defined and how feedback is assumed to work

9.2 Understand the strengths and weaknesses of multisource feedback programs

9.3 Understand why feedback is difficult to give and difficult to receive

9.4 Examine the role of organizational climate and culture in the feedback process

9.5 Learn why feedback sometimes fails

9.6 Understand the role of feedback acceptance in the feedback process

Second, feedback is performance related. Of course, performance information might be interpreted as personal; if your supervisor tells you that you have not met an important goal, you might interpret this as a personal attack. Third, although many performance feedback interventions are intended to improve performance, intentions do not form a part of the formal definition of a feedback intervention. Although intentions might not be part of what defines a feedback intervention, the recipient's *beliefs* about the intentions behind feedback are likely to be an important determinant of the effects of feedback.

Feedback is likely to be most useful when the recipient is new to the task, or is a newcomer in the organization. At that point, the recipient may not have the knowledge or information needed to identify successful or less successful behaviors or to evaluate his or her own performance. Li, Harris, Boswell, and Xie (2011) note that feedback can be an important part of the process of socializing organizational newcomers. Developmental feedback (i.e., feedback about future actions that might increase skills and effectiveness) is particularly critical, although feedback about past performance can also be useful in helping newcomers adapt to their roles in organizations. Even for newcomers, some types of feedback are likely to be more valuable than others. For example, Nurse (2005) noted that developmental feedback was most likely to be viewed as useful and followed if it was perceived as fair.

Feedback is used systematically in many aspects of our lives. For instance, we receive feedback from visual stimuli to interpret information about depth and distance. If we make a mistake, such as running into the corner of a desk, our body sends us immediate feedback about the error (i.e., pain). This can work similarly in the workplace. Cues from the work environment, such as an unhappy customer or an incorrectly developed product, provide feedback for an employee. Although this direct, environmental-based form of immediate feedback exists every day, other types of performance-related feedback (such as comments from a manager) have proven to be complex. As it will be discussed in this chapter, many variables interact to make feedback both hard to give and receive.

How Does Feedback Work?

It is useful to consider *how* feedback works (or should work), and there are three main competing models: (1) control models—feedback provides information about potential discrepancies, performance, and some accepted standard, which in turn motivates behavior to reduce that discrepancy (Carver & Scheier, 1981; Klein, 1989); (2) push models—feedback motivates and energizes future behavior; and (3) pull models—feedback influences goals for future behavior. For example, someone who receives feedback that he or she is not reaching a particular goal might revise that goal (Tolli & Schmidt, 2008).

Pull models appear to be the most influential in guiding feedback research, and a number of studies have examined variables that influence the relationships between feedback and goals.

For example, VandeWalle (2003) proposed that individual differences in goal orientation influence both the likelihood of seeking feedback and the type of feedback that is sought. Applying Dweck's (1986) goal taxonomy, he suggests that individuals whose dominant goal orientation is in the direction of learning goals (which focus on the development of new skills and competencies) will pursue and accept different types of feedback than individuals whose dominant goal orientation is in the direction of performance goals (which focus on demonstrating competence and avoiding negative feedback).[2] Consistent with this theory, Cianci, Schaubroeck, and McGill (2010) present evidence that individuals who are pursuing learning goals perform better after negative feedback and worse after positive feedback, whereas the opposite pattern holds for individuals pursuing performance goals.

Janssen and Prins (2007) note that differences in goal orientation can also influence the way the same feedback is interpreted (e.g., as a threat versus an opportunity to improve). Ilies and Judge (2005) note the importance of affective reactions to feedback and propose that these reactions help determine whether changes in goals following performance feedback will result in upward or downward revisions of goals and expectations (see also Cron, Slocum, VandeWalle, & Fu, 2005).

The Performance Appraisal Narrative

Most performance appraisal research focuses on the numerical scores that are used to characterize performance levels; it is common to refer to the process of formally recording the results of a performance evaluation as "performance rating." Many rating systems also ask supervisors or those doing the evaluation to record comments about the ratee, and these narratives do not get the attention they deserve (Brutus, 2010; David, 2013; Wilson, 2010). A notable early exception was Bjerke, Cleveland, Morrison, and Wilson, 1987, who noted that performance evaluations among officers in the U.S. Navy were so uniformly lenient that the only way of distinguishing among ratees was often in terms of the tone and content of the narrative comments that were given. Systematic examination of narrative comments as a source of information above and beyond numerical ratings is a recent phenomenon.

The written comments that accompany many performance appraisals inhabit a space halfway between performance rating and performance feedback. They *might* serve as feedback to the employee, or they might be little more than a rationale for the rating that was given. Like feedback, narrative comments are probably most useful when they are specific and directive, giving the ratee clear direction for improving performance. David (2013) presents evidence that high-quality comments (i.e., comments that are directive, specific, favorable, and fair) are indeed related to improvements in performance.

Returning to Bjerke et al. (1987), comments on performance appraisals might be especially useful if there is a widely shared framework for understanding them. For example, suppose two Navy officers received the same high numeric rating, but the comments they received were "Accomplishes the tasks assigned to him or her" versus "is a natural leader." In the Navy, there is sufficient consensus about the importance of leadership to make it clear that the first comment is an instance of damning with faint praise, whereas the second is one that deserves a lot of attention.

Performance Management and Feedback

Feedback is an experience that can happen either separate from performance appraisal or as a part of the performance appraisal process. It is possible for an employee to be rated without receiving any feedback, but it is more common that the primary use of the performance appraisal process is to provide feedback. Even when there is no feedback session per se, feedback could be provided to the employee through narrative comments that are included on the performance evaluation form. There is evidence that feedback quality and favorability have the potential to influence perceptions of the performance appraisal system (Dipboye & de Pontbriand, 1981). It has also been shown that perceptions of performance appraisal helpfulness are related to work performance, and this relationship is moderated by regular feedback (however, this relationship holds only for employees reporting high levels of feedback; Kuvaas, 2011).

Whereas performance appraisal might be carried out without providing feedback, performance management, by definition, *requires* feedback. Most models of performance management assume that subordinate reactions to the feedback they receive is an important component of the process. Performance management also starts with the assumption that performance feedback that is not accepted and acted upon will not improve performance (DeNisi & Smith, 2014). In fact, performance-based feedback is a focal part of performance management, as discussed in Chapter 2.

Finally, the use of performance feedback in performance management is most consistent with *pull* theories of feedback. That is, in performance management, the primary purpose of feedback is to give employees a clear idea of what they should be doing in the future.

SPOTLIGHT 9.1 COACHING AND PERFORMANCE FEEDBACK

Coaching has become a popular approach to employee development, and while coaching often involves performance feedback, the idea of coaching is considerably broader than simply providing employees with information about their performance. The Society for Industrial and Organizational Psychology (2017) describes coaching in terms of a two-way relationship between a coach (usually a supervisor or manager) and an employee, where the employee is motivated to improve his or her performance, learn new skills, or adapt to new situations and where the coach provides information, support, suggestions for activities to achieve the employee's goals, insight into the situation, and feedback.

There is a growing body of evidence that employee coaching can be effective (Carr, 2016; Gregory & Levy, 2010, 2011), but it is also clear that there are significant challenges to effective coaching. First, the success of coaching depends substantially on the organizational environment (Steelman, Levy, & Snell, 2004). Coaching is more to succeed in organizations where feedback is trusted and where there is an emphasis of high performance. Second, coaching demands a good deal of both the coach and the employee. Coaches are most likely to succeed if they are willing to and skilled at giving feedback, are willing to work with employees and to believe that employees can improve, and are willing to try a range of approaches to helping their subordinates (Gregory & Levy, 2011; Heslin, VandeWalle, & Latham, 2006). Coaching also requires a substantial commitment on the part of the employee, who must be motivated to improve and receptive to help, guidance, and feedback. On the whole, coaching is probably more likely to succeed if there is a good relationship between the supervisor and the employee; coaching an ineffective employee (the employee who probably needs it most) may be especially difficult.

Coaching has certainly become a popular topic in human resource management, but we are skeptical about its broad relevance to employee development. There is no doubt that coaching *can* be an effective strategy for developing employees but there is a good deal of doubt about how often effective coaching relationships are actually developed and carried through in organizations. First, as we noted above, effective coaching requires an organizational environment characterized by flexibility and trust, and this is not necessarily the norm in most organizations. Second, it requires a good deal of motivation and commitment on the part of the employee, and while there are definitely some employees who show this level of commitment, they may be the employees who are least in need of coaching. Third, coaching requires a set of skills on the part of the manager or supervisor that are definitely important (U.S. Office of Personnel Management, 2017), but that are probably not universally shared. Because effective coaching requires the confluence of a conducive environment, willing employees, skilled supervisors and managers, and a high-quality relationship between the coach and the employee, we believe it is reasonable to conclude that effective coaching relationships are relatively rare, and that many supervisors struggle to provide useful performance feedback, much less to act as effective coaches for their employees.

MULTISOURCE FEEDBACK

Systematic programs to obtain feedback from multiple sources, often referred to as multisource feedback (MSF) or 360-degree feedback, are widely used in organizations (Atwater, Brett, & Charles, 2007; Bracken, Rose, & Church, 2016; Bracken, Timmreck, & Church, 2001; Levy & Williams, 2004; Morgeson, Mumford, & Campion, 2005; Taylor & Bright, 2011). Although initially developed in North American organizations, these systems are increasingly popular across the globe (Bailey & Fletcher, 2002; Brutus et al., 2006; McCarthy & Garavan, 2001). The typical MSF program collects information from supervisors, peers, and subordinates (and sometimes customers) and provides aggregated feedback from each source (e.g., average ratings on particular dimensions, anonymous comments). It is typically meant to be an ongoing process.

MSF programs are most commonly developed and used for developmental purposes; however, Bracken et al. (2016) note that these are also often used to made administrative decisions and assist efforts to change and develop organizations. It is possible to use MSF for more than one purpose, and debate exists regarding whether or not MSF should be used outside of within-employee development. Nonetheless, it is commonly used for other purposes in organizations, and credible arguments both for and against this practice exist (see London, 2001; Bracken, Dalton, Jako, McCauley, & Pollman, 1997). Using MSF administratively can look like a variety of functions that fall on a continuum, but this must be done systematically in order to be successful. Most importantly, the goal of the system (i.e., developmental or for personnel decisions) must be considered when the process is designed, before data is collected (Bracken et al., 2016). This must be communicated with those using the program on both ends (raters and ratees), and if the organization wants multiple uses from the MSF, this can complicate the design and evaluation of MSF systems, because each use of performance information might require different criteria. For example, MSF used for within-employee development could emphasize collecting data for fostering growth for the employee and improvement through future planning, whereas information collected for between-employee decisions should closely align with performance appraisal dimensions.

There can be unintended consequences when using MSF for decision-making processes, and it has been suggested that there are certain decision areas where MSF should not be used, such as compensation and succession planning (Fleenor & Brutus, 2001). Again, MSF has been used successfully for some personnel decisions, yet there is potential for problems. For example, when information used from MSF is used to make important decisions, legal concerns may arise due to the potential lack of job relatedness, based on the assumption that raters at different levels have very different opportunities to observe a range of job-relevant behavior and it is possible that peers, subordinates, and clients have access to and consider different information than the direct supervisor. Instead, Bernardin and Tyler (2001) suggest that personnel decisions should be made upon formal procedures that are rooted in an objective performance appraisal system that was created through standardizing means such as job analysis, something that is not always the case when designing MSF systems. They make recommendations for how to best make MSF the most legally defensible. These recommendations include: (1) formally communicating the expectations, criteria, and indented outcomes or goals for the MSF system; (2) providing employees the opportunity to read and appeal their MSF results; (3) avoiding using character traits; (4) keeping written records and all documentation; and (5) training raters and make sure they are qualified for the task.

Bracken and Rose (2011) note that the features of actual MSF programs often vary considerably from organization to organization, and they propose that four characteristics of MSF programs are likely to be particularly important to their success. These characteristics are shown in Table 9.1.

Of the four criteria listed in Table 9.1, participation is probably the most critical. Church, Rogelberg, and Waclawski (2000) note that MSF instruments are very much like surveys, with each survey targeted toward a specific individual recipient, and like

TABLE 9.1 ■ Characteristics of MSF Programs Thought to Be Important for Success[a]	
Relevant Content	Do the scales or instruments used to collect feedback focus on meaningful and important behaviors?
Credible Data	Are the data reliable, reasonable, and acceptable to users?
Accountability	Are there mechanisms that hold raters accountable for the feedback they provide?
Participation	Is there consistent participation across organizational levels?

[a] As proposed by Bracken & Rose (2011).

most other surveys, response rates for MSF instruments can be low. They investigated the hypothesis that nonresponse might be linked to the performance level of the recipient, on the assumption that some raters might not want to respond and give their coworkers low ratings. On the whole, response rates do not seem to depend on performance levels, but they may be a useful indicator of attitudes toward and acceptance of the feedback system.

Bracken et al. (2016) note that technological developments have made it easier to implement MSF systems. Computerized systems not only make it easier to collect and collate information from multiple sources, but they also make it easier to respond to (and sometimes harder to ignore) requests for feedback.

Effects of MSF

While multisource feedback systems have several advantages, they suffer from the same shortcoming as all other feedback systems: negative feedback is not easily accepted or acted upon. Murphy, Cleveland, and Mohler (2001) and Cleveland, Lim, and Murphy (2007) note another drawback to these systems. A worker who receives a negative evaluation from some sources will almost always receive more positive evaluations from *some* source or sources, and this discrepancy might make it actually *easier* to ignore unwanted negative feedback. A review of multisource feedback research by Seifert, Yukl, and McDonald (2003) confirms that these systems have at best inconsistent effects on performance and development.

Like other feedback programs, the effects of MSF on subsequent behavior and performance appear to be mixed, at best (Atwater, Brett, & Charles, 2007; Atwater, Waldman, & Brett, 2002; Smither, London, & Reilly, 2005; Seifert, Yukl, & McDonald, 2003). This may be in part due to the diversity of MSF programs. Smither et al. (2005) suggest that the question of whether MSF works is likely to be impossible to answer, given the diversity of these programs and that the better question is probably under what conditions do they work.

Like other systems for evaluating performance and providing feedback, MSF systems are influenced by a wide array of contextual variables (e.g., the overall health of the organization, whether organizations are growing or downsizing). In particular, cynicism and distrust on the part of raters and ratees are often barriers to effective appraisal and feedback systems, and MSF systems can be undermined by these factors in the same way as traditional PA systems (Atwater et al., 2002). It might be possible to enhance trust in these systems by allowing the recipients of feedback to have some say in determining who provides feedback (Becton & Schraeder, 2004).

The effectiveness of MSF systems also depends on a number of characteristics of the recipients of feedback, in particular core self-evaluations, defensiveness, and beliefs about the extent to which change is possible (Atwater et al., 2007; Bono & Colbert, 2005; Taylor & Bright, 2011). Finally, MSF systems may be a better fit for some types of organizations than others. For example, Brutus, Fleenor, and London (1998) found some differences in MSF outcomes as a function of organization type (e.g., private versus public sector).

Organizations often invest significant amounts of time and money in developing and administering MSF programs, but they fail to invest in a serious way in supporting changes in behavior following feedback (Atwater et al., 2007). For instance, the phenomenon referred to as "desk drop" happens when MSF data is collected, organized into a report, and then "dropped" on the supervisor's desk without direction or support (Church & Waclawski, 2001). This lack of supporting changes in behavior following feedback is by no means unique to MSF systems; the same complaint can often be raised for more traditional PA systems. Nevertheless, if organizations are serious about using MSF as a tool for behavior change, they are well advised to invest in training and development programs to provide strong follow-up to ensure that feedback leads to systematic activities to change behavior.

Reactions to MSF

It should be no surprise that reactions to MSF, like reactions to more traditional appraisal and feedback programs, are strongly driven by the favorability of ratings (Brett & Atwater, 2001; Bono & Colbert, 2005). More favorable ratings are typically seen as more accurate and more credible. As Murphy, Cleveland, and Mohler (2001) note, the very design of MSF systems makes it likely that some ratings will be more positive than others, and that ratees will tend to place more emphasis on and credence in the most favorable feedback they receive.

Reactions also depend in part on who provides ratings. There is evidence that raters pay more attention to feedback from supervisors than from peers or subordinates (which is consistent with the traditional structure of PA programs), and it is plausible that they react more strongly to negative feedback from this source than to equivalent feedback from other sources (Greguras, Ford, & Brutus, 2003).

Waldman and Bowen (1998) developed a model for studying the acceptability of MSF systems that is based on relationships typical between customers and suppliers. They note that different stakeholders in the MSF process face different challenges, and that many of these challenges parallel those in customer–supplier relationships. For example, members of work groups are both customers and suppliers, in the sense that they both give and receive peer ratings, whereas external customers (a frequent source of MSF ratings) may have only partial knowledge about the individuals (suppliers) they are asked to evaluate, and may fall back on general impressions rather than particularized information.

Disagreement in Evaluations of Performance

Because ratings are obtained from sources that differ in perspectives, and often in the specific behaviors and outcomes they observe, it is natural to expect that different sources will disagree in some of their evaluations, and there is considerable evidence that this is exactly what happens (Hoffman & Woehr, 2009). Disagreement in MSF can be both helpful and harmful. The expectation that feedback for a given employee will be obtained from multiple perspectives that perhaps observe different performance information can be a useful resource to a manager. If different sources disagree, it can be helpful to explore *why* they arrive at different conclusions regarding an employee's performance. One of the purposes of MSF is to compare rater perceptions within employees, between employees, and over time (Bracken et al., 2016). Because raters at each level only see the employee in one aspect of their performance in certain circumstances, acknowledging feedback from other employees, leaders, subordinates, or customers can be a comparative exercise to develop the individual.

However, it is clear that rater disagreement can be problematic. This disagreement can undercut the credibility of MSF systems, and the fact that some groups of raters will typically be more positive in their evaluation of particular aspects of performance than others may make it easier for ratees to ignore negative feedback (Murphy, Cleveland, & Mohler, 2001). In addition, if employees receive conflicting information they might not know who to trust or what to make of the knowledge. The topic of disagreement is crucial, particularly because it is known that the effectiveness of the MSF system depends largely on ratee perceptions of the system (including perceptions of consistency; Murphy, Cleveland, & Mohler, 2001).

It is important to note that most often the largest disagreements exist between the employee (self-ratings) and the supervisor ratings (van der Heijden & Nijhof, 2004). Peer ratings and supervisor ratings are typically more highly related to each other than with self-ratings, though agreement still has the potential to be low (Conway & Huffcutt, 1997). There are many reasons for this (fundamental attribution error, protecting self-esteem, leniency effect) but the most fundamental issue in understanding relationships between self-assessments and assessments from others is that there is a strong and systematic tendency to portray one's self more positively than others would. While disagreement between self-ratings and manager ratings can be an important point of developmental conversation for the manager to utilize, this can be discouraging and overwhelming for an employee if not discussed effectively.

WHY IS FEEDBACK HARD TO GIVE AND RECEIVE?

People do not like feedback, especially when it is negative. Unfortunately, people often associate feedback with negativity, and this can lead to unpleasant feelings. We have seen some practitioners moving away from the label "feedback," trending toward fresh terms such as "insight" in order to shed the adverse connotation. There are several reasons as to why the feedback process is difficult on both ends (for the manager and subordinate), and these are discussed in the present section.

Training, Time, and Accountability

The most obvious explanations for why feedback is hard for mangers to give appear to involve three issues: (1) lack of training, (2) time, and (3) accountability. It is common to find that managers are not given instruction on how to give feedback or how to handle difficult situations surrounding the feedback relationship. Training can not only help managers understand the procedural aspects of how to deliver effective performance feedback, but it can also be used to relieve anxiety associated with communicating uncomfortable or negative information. It has been shown that managers who feel adequately prepared to give feedback are more likely to provide useful feedback to their employees, and training managers to develop their feedback skills has shown to be effective. For instance, training has been used to effectively reduce attribution biases about subordinates' behavior (e.g., the tendency to ignore situational factors when employees fail to perform well; Wiswell & Lawrence, 1994). Training has also been shown to improve perceptions of trust and quality interactions through an increase in effective feedback, and to improve usefulness of the feedback delivered by managers (Lawrence, 1992).

Feedback can also be difficult to receive, and training subordinates on how to receive feedback can be an important element for them to understand what to do with the information and assist in developing a mutual understanding of the process, forms, and expectations (Bernardin & Tyler, 2001). Unfortunately, not enough training exists for guiding managers or subordinates in the feedback process, and this is a need for future research and practice (Steelman, Levy, & Snell, 2004). Training is discussed in more depth later in the chapter as an explanation for why feedback can sometimes succeed.

It is also worthwhile to briefly mention the notion of time and accountability as obstacles to why feedback is difficult. For one, managers are busy individuals, and taking the time to give feedback to each employee can take valuable space in their schedules. In addition, a lack of accountability of both the rater and the ratee can be detrimental to the feedback process. To begin with the ratee perspective, if a subordinate is not held accountable for the feedback they are receiving, that feedback is less likely to make an impact. In order to increase accountability for performance areas in which they received poor feedback, employees and supervisors together can enhance learning and performance by setting goals and action plans. Raters or managers should also be held accountable by giving accurate and helpful feedback. This objective can be achieved by requiring them to document the process, work with employees to develop goals and improvement plans, and identify other accountability mechanisms that might work for the particular job (London, Smither, & Adsit, 1997). The organization must also be held accountable for feedback by providing the resources that are needed for raters and ratees to be successful in the process.

Anticipation of Uncomfortable Reactions

Managers can feel reluctant to give feedback when they are anticipating an uncomfortable conversation. People do not like to convey bad news because they might be anticipating the discomfort of the receiver (Tesser & Rosen, 1975) and people typically want to avoid interpersonal conflict. In fact, people will deliver feedback more positively during a face-to-face meeting than they will during an indirect meeting (e.g., recording) in order to reduce interpersonal conflict (Waung & Highhouse, 1997). It has also been shown that one will be less likely to give bad news to a ratee when they are expected to act more emotionally than a calm ratee (Tesser & Conlee, 1973).

It is also important to note that the emotionality of the manager can also influence these relationships. For instance, it has been shown that managers who have higher levels of empathy are more likely to give honest, realistic feedback (even if it is negative, thus uncomfortable) to subordinates (Waung & Highhouse, 1997).

Negative Feedback

Negative feedback is difficult for managers to give, and also hard for people to receive. Generally, people do not like to deliver negative messages. It has been shown that when managers need to give negative feedback, they often want to avoid the process, delay the process, or distort the feedback to be more positive than it should be (Waung & Highhouse, 1997). This reluctance to deliver negative feedback can eventually disadvantage someone who needs the information to improve. In fact, Larson (1986) showed that managers were less likely to give negative feedback over positive feedback, and often gave positive feedback when it was not deserved (when the subordinate performed poorly).

Unfortunately, when a manager actually does deliver the negative message, even if this is delivered well, it can lead to problems. For instance, Geddes and Baron (1997) found that the majority of managers experienced adverse reactions from employees after they gave them negative feedback (most commonly in the form of indirect verbal aggression, such as speaking negatively about the manager). Fortunately, there are ways to train managers to give feedback effectively, including methods for reducing negative reactions from employees. Managers can also be trained to best prepare for negative reactions from employees. It has also been shown that organizational justice and trust can buffer this relationship (Chory & Hubbell, 2008).

Brown, Kulik, and Lim (2016) investigated the process a manager uses when strategizing their feedback delivery. More specifically, they identified the main strategies that managers use when communicating negative feedback, and measured how managers use these to address performance issues (sometimes they are bundled with one another). The three managerial feedback tactics identified were emotive tactics (appealing to the employee's feelings about the poor performance; expressing empathy), evidence (use of examples and concrete expectations), and communication tactics (encouraging conversation about the poor performance and striking a balance between positive and negative feedback). These tactics can also be bundled for further combinations of tactics. They found that there is not a single best practice of a method (or combination of methods) for delivering negative feedback, but that it changed based on the characteristics of the ratee and their appraisal of the situation. Thus, this supported the "best fit hypothesis" (that the best practice for delivering negative feedback changes with the relationship and situation) and did not support the "best practices" hypothesis (that there is a most effective strategy for giving performance feedback regardless of the circumstances surrounding it).

Feedback sign (whether it is viewed as positive or negative) can influence reactions, effectiveness, and eventually satisfaction with the overall performance appraisal system (Brett & Atwater, 2001). Positive feedback is often positively related to performance appraisal satisfaction, whereas negative feedback is often negatively related to performance appraisal satisfaction (Culbertson, Henning, & Payne, 2013). Whether the feedback is ultimately interpreted as being negative is highly subjective and up to the interpretation of the receiver. Culbertson et al. (2013) showed that the relationship between feedback sign and performance appraisal satisfaction was moderated by the recipient's goal orientation. Goal orientations are the types of motivation a person has during an achievement situation (e.g., Dweck, 1986), and these can be learning achievement goal orientation (LAGO; person wants to pursue challenges for growth despite setbacks), performance-avoid (PAGO; want to avoid their efforts looking bad, avoid difficult tasks), or performance-prove (PPGO; want to demonstrate their performance and get positive judgments about their performance). It was found that the relationship between negative feedback and lower levels of performance appraisal satisfaction became stronger for those with higher LAGO, PAGO, and PPGO.

Negative feedback is usually unwelcome and stressful, but the *way* negative feedback is delivered may make a difference. In particular, *destructive criticism*, defined as negative feedback that is negative in style and/or content and that attributes poor performance to personal shortcomings, is likely to elicit negative reactions, ranging from anger and conflict to setting lower goals or to avoidance. These effects are moderated somewhat by personality; competitive individuals are more tolerant of negative criticism (perhaps even of destructive criticism), as long as they see it as information that might allow them to outperform their peers (Raver, Jensen, Lee, & O'Reilly, 2012). Criticism that focuses on things the recipient cannot control is likely to be especially destructive, whereas feedback that focuses on things under the recipient's control can be helpful if it is delivered in a constructive way (Martocchio & Dulebohn, 1994).

Even when it is not delivered in a destructive way, negative feedback takes an emotional toll (Belschak & Den Hartog, 2009). The effects of negative feedback can be softened in a number of ways. For example, if negative feedback is accompanied by a legitimizing statement (i.e., one that explains why the negative feedback is deserved), its effects can be softened (Waung & Jones, 2005). More generally, it might be possible to mitigate some of the potential problems with negative feedback if the feedback is constructive in nature.

Constructive feedback is specific, timely, problem-focused (rather than person-focused), respectful, and courteous (Sommer & Kulkarni, 2012). It reflects respect for the recipient, clear standards for evaluating performance and is oriented toward improvement rather than toward punishment. Sommer and Kulkarni (2012) suggest that constructive feedback can increase job satisfaction and organizational citizenship behaviors, especially when there are opportunities for appropriate rewards for improved performance. Giving the recipients of feedback an opportunity to express their opinions and perspectives (voice) can further mitigate the effects of receiving negative feedback (Lizzio, Wilson, & MacKay, 2008).

Feedback Avoidance Behavior

When an employee is engaging in behavior to actively avoid the feedback process, this is feedback avoidance behavior (FAB), and this can make feedback hard to give and receive. This can occur in many forms. An individual might physically prevent running into the manager, conversationally avoid bringing up the topic of their performance or feedback, divert conversation, evade eye contact, stop coming to work, or other similar strategies (Moss, Valenzi. & Taggart, 2003) with the goal of hiding his or her supposed negative performance to protect their image.

FAB has shown to fully mediate the relationship between leader–member relationship quality and subsequent member performance. In other words, employees with a low-quality relationship with their leader (e.g., lack trust, mutual respect) are more likely to engage in FAB than those with a high-quality relationship with their leader (who are more likely to engage in feedback seeking), thus the performance gap between the groups are perpetuated (Moss, Sanchez, Brumbaugh, & Borkowski, 2009). In more severe circumstances, feedback avoidance behavior can be considered a coping mechanism in response to an abusive supervisor, and often results in emotional exhaustion of the subordinate (Whitman, Halbesleben & Holmes, 2014).

Contrastingly, feedback mitigating behaviors (FMB) are those in which an employee engages in order to *reduce* what they believe will be negative feedback from their supervisor (Moss, Valenzi, & Taggart, 2003). Unlike FAB, those engaging in FMB are actually engaging with the manager with the attempt to reduce the severity of negative feedback, not avoid it (Moss et al., 2003).

Similar to employees engaging in FAB, managers or raters can also participate in behaviors to avoid giving feedback for different reasons. A large reason as to why managers might want to avoid giving feedback is due to the discomfort of delivering negative messages.

How Attributional Biases Influence Reactions to Feedback

There is a well-known psychological phenomenon in which raters attribute biases to different behaviors that are not always correct. This is attribution bias, and it comes in many forms. For instance, there is a recency effect in which a manager might give a typically poor-performing employee slightly better feedback if they were performing well in the last week. There is also a stability component in which causes of performance might be seen as fixed and consistent or likely to change over time. For the purposes of this section, we will be discussing the internality component: whether performance is attributed to internal or external influences.

The fundamental attribution error occurs in a feedback setting when a manager overestimates the role of internal causes (such as low effort) rather than external causes (such as a lack of training or resources; Korn, Rosenblau, Rodriguez Buritica, & Heekeren, 2016) in explaining an employee's poor performance. Conversely, managers are more likely to make the opposite attributions when explaining their own behavior, attributing the poor performance to external rather than internal variables. In a similar way, most raters (including managers) are likely to attribute other peoples' success to external factors (e.g., unfair advantages, luck), while attributing their own success to internal factors such as ability, skill, and motivation. Fortunately, it has been shown that managers are less likely to form judgments based on attribution biases when they are trained in effective feedback skills (Wiswell & Lawrence, 1994).

The fundamental attribution error has the potential to make it difficult for managers to give feedback accurately and give realistic suggestions, notably when external factors are contributing to the low performance of an employee. Because managers are biased in their interpretations of the causes of both good and poor performance, they might set goals for the employee that are unrealistic, such as telling them to put in more effort instead of sending them to developmental training or providing other accommodations. In addition, delivering negative feedback that is based on a presumed lack of ability or skill is more difficult to give and difficult to receive. People would rather give negative feedback when it is related to low effort than low ability, because effort is something subordinates can actually change (Ilgen & Davis, 2000). However, if the diagnosis of performance problems is fundamentally wrong (attributing performance shortfalls to internal causes when external ones are in fact more relevant), performance feedback is unlikely to be accepted or helpful.

Discrepancies Between Self-Assessments and Others' Assessments of Performance

The term *rating discrepancy* refers to a disagreement between the feedback or ratings the employee was expecting or hoping for and the feedback they actually receive. Disagreements of this sort are common and can have negative consequences. For example, Kwak and Choi (2015) reported that the magnitude of discrepancies is related to turnover; the larger the gap between the ratings an employee believes he or she should get and the ratings managers actually provide, the higher the likelihood of turnover. Perhaps the most interesting aspect of their findings was that turnover intentions increased when the ratings were lower than expected, but they also increased when ratings were *higher* than expected. This suggests that it is not merely getting a low rating that is upsetting, but rather finding out that your beliefs about the rating you deserve are quite different from the rating you receive that may contribute to disillusionment with the organization.

If a manager is giving feedback to an employee and there are discrepancies between self-assessments and this performance feedback, this can make the conversation difficult. This ultimately means that the manager and subordinate do not agree on the criteria and/or the performance interpretation of the rater. Discrepancies between self-ratings and manager ratings can lead to negative appraisal reactions and eventually put a strain on the feedback relationship (Kwak & Choi, 2015).

At this point it should be clear that feedback is hard for both parties. This is a complex relationship involving psychological phenomenon (e.g., fundamental attribution error was discussed) and a number of other structural and political variables (e.g., lack of time and training, distorted information). To conclude this section, we will emphasize the importance of the context as it relates to the organizational culture and the larger, national culture surrounding the feedback system.

SPOTLIGHT 9.2 GIVING BAD NEWS WITHOUT GIVING OFFENSE

Sometimes, performance feedback is likely to be negative, or at least less positive than the recipient believes he or she deserves. It is important to reduce the likelihood that negative feedback will be seen as unfair or as an attack. In particular, it is critical that negative feedback be seen as constructive, not as punitive.

One frequent piece of advice when delivering negative feedback is to place it in the context of other feedback that is positive. There is a great deal of research showing that negative information is perceived differently from positive information, with negative events of comments likely to receive more attention and to be seen as more extreme (Ilgen & Davis, 2000; Kahneman & Tversky, 1979). One implication of this research is that positive comments should substantially outnumber negative ones when giving feedback. Because negative information can be so difficult to receive, it is especially important to not let negative comments and feedback build up. That is, if someone is performing poorly now, it is better to give them real-time feedback than to build up a long list of failures to review at the annual appraisal.

More generally, negative feedback should not be the only feedback people receive. Rather, employees should receive regular positive feedback, recognizing their strengths and the things they do well. Your goal should be to make negative feedback unusual, not to make feedback equal criticism.

Negative feedback is likely to be more effective if it is accompanied with targeted coaching. That is, rather than simply telling a person what he or she has done wrong, give them help, advice, and information that will help them do better; do not simply tell people what they should not do, but give them clear information and help so that they can more effectively do what they should do.

It will never be easy to give disappointing feedback, and doing this poorly can make a bad situation worse. Criticism that is general and personal (you are lazy) does little more than make employees angry, disengaged, and distrustful. Supervisors, managers, and others in positions of authority will certainly find themselves giving negative feedback to at least some employees, and there are likely to be real advantages to doing it well.

CULTURE, CLIMATE, AND FEEDBACK

Organizations differ in terms of their feedback culture (London 2003; London & Smither, 2002). In some organizations, managers and employees are more comfortable giving and receiving feedback than in others. In organizations with a learning culture, employees are more likely to seek feedback (van der Rijt, van de Wiel, Van den Bossche, Segers, & Gijselaers, 2012), implying that it may be possible to increase feedback-seeking behavior by changing the organizational culture. Organizations with cultures that facilitate and promote learning are also more likely to provide more consistent and useful feedback to employees (van der Rijt, Van den Bossche, van de Wiel, Segers, & Gijselaers, 2012). Another important organizational contextual variable is social support, which can increase the likelihood that employees will engage in on-the-job development (e.g., practicing skills on the job) and off-the-job development (e.g., reading a career-related book) following feedback (Maurer, Mitchell, & Barbeite, 2002).

The feedback process never occurs in a vacuum, and it is important to understand the context to fully gain an appreciation for why it might succeed or fail. As Murphy and Cleveland (1995) note, sometimes an employee receives feedback from a supervisor who is not fully aware of the contextual constraints existing that limit performance. If employees are working in a context where the tools, information, or resources necessary to do the job are not available, there is little point in giving them feedback that they are not performing up to a standard. Rather than focusing on the individual alone, managers should consider the resources available to the employee and what control they actually have over the outcomes.

The term *feedback environment* refers to the extent to which the contextual aspects of the workplace encourage feedback (Steelman, Levy, & Snell, 2004). Feedback environment can be measured in relationship to two factors: coworker feedback environment and supervisor feedback environment. In organizations that have a positive or strong feedback environment, it is likely that there will be more feedback-seeking behaviors on the part of employees and higher levels of role clarity, job satisfaction, and personal control over information and decisions (Sparr & Sonnentag, 2008; Whitaker, Dahling, & Levy, 2007). When the feedback environment is weak, there is an increased likelihood of negative outcomes such as helplessness, job depression, and higher intentions to turn over (Sparr & Sonnentag, 2008). There is also evidence that the feedback environment contributes directly to the culture of the organization. In particular, organizations that develop a culture that is receptive to feedback are likely to be seen as less political than organization in which feedback is not provided or not welcome (Rosen, Levy, & Hall, 2006).

We usually think of the context as an external influence on processes like feedback-seeking. However, type of feedback that is available can help to define the feedback environment. In particular, when timely and specific feedback is available for some tasks, the likelihood that individuals will invest time and effort and that they will seek feedback increases (Northcraft, Schmidt, & Ashford, 2011). The underlying message is a simple one: if you want to create an environment that is more conducive to feedback, provide better feedback.

National Culture and Feedback

Similar to the way in which organizational culture and the feedback environment of a workplace can influence the nature of feedback relationships, the larger the natural culture surrounding the organization has been shown to influence the way feedback is given and received in organizations. Sully de Luque and Sommer (2000) developed a model that attempts to explain the role of culture in understanding employees' willingness to seek, receive, and act upon feedback. They examined the potential role of four cultural variables: (1) specific-holistic orientation, (2) tolerance for ambiguity, (3) individualism–collectivism, and (4) status identity. Specific-holistic orientation refers to the extent to which context is important for understanding performance information and the extent to which performance is viewed as a distinct attribute versus as a part of a holistic pattern of how one behaves. The remaining cultural variables closely parallel Hofstede's (1980) risk aversion, individualism, and power distance dimensions. Specific-holistic orientation is assumed to influence *how* feedback is conveyed (directly versus implicitly) and how it is requested. Tolerance for ambiguity is assumed to influence the use of formal versus informal methods and channels for feedback, as well as the overall willingness to seek feedback. Individualism is assumed to influence the target of feedback (individuals versus groups) as well as the method of feedback seeking (e.g., in individualistic cultures, direct inquires for feedback will be more common). Status identity is assumed to influence *who* provides feedback, with more top-down feedback in cultures where power distance is high.

MacDonald, Sulsky, Spence, and Brown (2013) investigated the effects of national culture on feedback-seeking, comparing the responses of Chinese and Canadian subjects in a policy-capturing task. On the whole, Chinese feedback-seeking behavior was more strongly driven by image management, while Canadian feedback-seeking behavior was more strongly influenced by ego defense. That is, Chinese respondents appeared to be more concerned with how others viewed them, while Canadian respondents appeared to be more interested in maintaining a positive self-image.

Within a culture, demographic changes can have implications for the way feedback is given and received. Kikoski (1999) proposed that the increasing amount of cultural diversity in the United States will have effects on interpersonal communication. For instance, understanding someone's cultural historical background could be helpful when communicating, because not everyone is familiar with the same nonverbal understandings (body language, how close to stand, how much eye contact should be made), behavioral patterns (such as Western cultures are more likely to engage in self-promoting language and behavior than Eastern cultures), and verbal styles (word choice, colloquialisms, and so on). The type of feedback that is appropriate in one culture may not be as appropriate or effective in another, and as the United States becomes more culturally diverse, managers may need to adapt their feedback to these changes if they hope to be effective.

THE EFFECTS OF FEEDBACK AND REACTIONS TO FEEDBACK

Feedback can have several different effects. For the purposes of this section we will focus on the effects of feedback on job performance, though it is important to note that performance is not the only variable likely to be affected by feedback. Reactions to feedback are a potentially important determinant of the effects of feedback, and these are discussed in this section.

Several reviews have questioned the assumption that feedback is likely to lead to improvements in performance (e.g., Seifert, Yukl, & McDonald, 2003; Smither, London, & Reilly, 2005). In one of the most thorough reviews of this literature, Kluger and DeNisi (1996) reviewed over 3,000 papers and technical reports dealing with feedback interventions. Only a subset of these provided sufficient information to provide a consistent measure of the size of the effect of feedback (e.g., means and standard deviations or statistics that would make it possible to compute standard effect size measures), but they were about to obtain over 600 effect size estimates, and on the basis of this analysis, make several important statements about the effects of feedback interventions. First, on average, feedback interventions have a small to moderate positive effect (the standardized mean difference between feedback and no feedback conditions is d = .41). Second, and perhaps more important, the effects of feedback interventions are highly variable; over one-third of the feedback interventions studied had a *negative* effect on performance. Third, large positive effects from feedback are quite rare; over 90% of the effect size studied were small (d of .20 or smaller). Even in cases where reactions to feedback and the feedback process are positive, the effects of feedback on subsequent behavior are often small (Lee & Son, 1998).

This being said, there are still those instances in which feedback interventions *do* produce desirable effects on performance, and it is useful to determine what is contributing to this success. Kluger and DeNisi (1996) proposed several ways in which performance feedback influence future performance and suggested specific strategies for increasing the effectiveness of feedback, including goal setting or evaluating against agreed-upon standards. They also identified specific variables that might help to determine whether or not feedback succeeds, including locus of attention (does feedback direct the employee's attention toward more effective behaviors) and task properties.

First, it is beneficial to pair feedback with goal setting. It has been shown that goal setting increases the likelihood that feedback will lead to improvements in performance (Kluger & DeNisi, 1996). Second, attention is limited, and feedback interventions will have a greater likelihood of changing performance in a desirable way when attention is directed to the task at hand instead of toward the self (i.e., meta processes). That is, giving employees feedback about specific things they are doing that are effective or ineffective can be more useful than giving them broad person-oriented feedback (e.g., you are not trying hard enough). When attention or cues are focused on the self instead of the task (i.e., task-motivation or task-learning processes), this sort of feedback can be debilitating rather than helpful, in part because broad feedback about you as a person is likely to produce affective reactions, and if the feedback is negative the affective reactions will also be negative. In addition, it is typically harmful to compare the employees to others; these comparisons do not typically lead to improvements in performance.

Finally, task properties are important to consider. For example, Kluger and DeNisi (1996) found that effectiveness of the feedback intervention varied across tasks. Task-relevant variables that appear to be important include task mastery (how subjectively hard is the task?) and task complexity (how objectively hard is the task?). They concluded that tasks with high mastery (those that are more familiar to the participant) and low task complexity (that are easier) were ones in which performance feedback was particularly likely to be helpful. The authors note the irony: that those employees who probably need feedback most (i.e., those who are performing more complex tasks that are not familiar) are likely to benefit the least from feedback (Kluger & DeNisi, 1996).

Additional research is needed before the suggestions outlined by Kluger and DeNisi (1996) can be considered a "golden standard" of feedback intervention theory, but for now it seems reasonable to accept their practical conclusions for increasing effectiveness of feedback, including setting suitable goals, refraining from feedback about the person (deconstructive criticism), delivering content more about the task than about the person, and addressing tasks that are more familiar and less complex to the participant. Finally, it is always important to evaluate the feedback program using meaningful tests (effect size measures) to really understand the magnitude and significance of the change, if the change occurs at all.

Other researchers have offered additional advice for improving feedback effectiveness. For instance, Larson, Patel, Evans, and Saiman (2013) propose that feedback is most effective when it includes four key features: (1) individualization, (2) timeliness, (3) lack of punitiveness, and (4) customization. They reviewed over 100 studies of feedback effectiveness and concluded that none of the programs they examined included all four features. Johnson (2013) proposed a somewhat simpler set of requirements, suggesting that feedback is likely to be most effective when it includes both objective and evaluative components, especially in cases where the objective feedback provides a plausible justification for supervisors' judgments about the employee's effectiveness. As we noted in Chapter 1, objective indicators of performance are readily available in some jobs, and either unavailable or only tangentially relevant in others, but in cases where they can be collected, consistency between objective indicators and evaluative comments is likely to be an important determinant of the credibility and acceptability of feedback.

Reactions to Feedback

There is a substantial literature dealing with the way people evaluate, perceive, and react to the performance feedback they receive. One of the most influential models of this process was proposed by Ilgen, Fisher, and Taylor (1979); the essential features of their model are shown in Figure 9.1 below.

According to Ilgen et al. (1979), characteristics of the environment (e.g., the availability of information needed to provide accurate feedback) and the source (e.g., source credibility) influence perceptions of the accuracy of feedback. Perceptions of accuracy in turn influence both the desire and the intention to engage in behavior change, which in turn leads to changes in behavior. This model has received substantial support (see, for example, Kinicki, Prussia, Wu, & McKee-Ryan, 2004).

It is clear that perceptions of and reactions to feedback are important. First, employees who feel that the feedback they receive is biased, inaccurate, or irrelevant are unlikely to take feedback seriously and use it to modify their behavior. This model suggests that reactions to feedback moderate the effects of feedback on behavior. Jawahar (2010) suggests

FIGURE 9.1 ■ Model of Feedback Effects

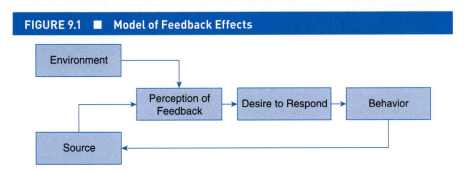

a simpler alternative—that it is the reactions to feedback themselves that drive behavior. His study suggests that characteristics of the rater (e.g., job knowledge) and characteristics of the feedback itself (e.g., whether it includes suggestions for improvement) determine perceptions of the accuracy, utility, and fairness of the feedback, and that it is the reactions themselves (positive or negative) that motivate and influence behavior.

Team Reactions to Feedback

Unger-Aviram, Zwikael, and Restubog (2013) note that teams may deal with feedback differently than individuals; project teams, which are put together for specific tasks and which do not have a long life cycle, might have quite unique reactions to feedback. When individuals receive negative feedback, that can be seen as a threat to one's ego, but if a temporary team receives similar feedback, it is likely to be less threatening because it is not necessarily directed toward any individual or toward any group that is important to the individual. These temporary teams are more likely to engage in task-focused than in person-focused activities, and the impersonal nature of their attachment to the group might insulate them from the effects of negative feedback.

In more permanent teams (e.g., long-standing work groups), the role of feedback may be more complex. Young and Steelman (2014) suggest that when environments are conducive to feedback, workers who seek and incorporate feedback from their supervisors and peers are more likely to develop a strong identification with the team. While individual feedback might help build links to the team, negative feedback to the team as a whole might have the same unfortunate consequences as negative feedback to individuals. That is, if individuals strongly identify with the team (a state that is more likely if they seek individual feedback from team leaders and team members), feedback that reflects negatively on the team might be interpreted and reflected just as negatively on members who identify strongly with the team.

Finally, van der Vegt, de Jong, Bunderson, and Molleman (2010) note that feedback to individuals within a team versus feedback to the team as a whole might have quite different effects. On the whole, feedback to individuals within teams often reinforces differences in skills, knowledge, and other sources of expert power, undermining team cohesion. Feedback to the team as a whole, on the other hand, builds cohesion and may make it easier for team members to work together on shared tasks, even though some members of the team are not able to contribute as much as others to the team's success.

Individual Differences in Reactions to Feedback

Individuals differ in their feedback orientation—that is, their general receptivity to feedback, their belief that feedback is valuable, and their tendency to carefully consider feedback and act on it (London & Smither, 2002). Employees who are generally receptive to feedback are more likely than less receptive employees to deal constructively with negative feedback and to use feedback to shape their plans and their approach to their jobs, and they are more likely to seek feedback (Dahling, Chau, & O'Malley, 2012). Dahling et al. (2012) suggest that the combined effects of feedback orientation, the feedback environment (i.e., the extent to which the environment is conducive to and supportive of feedback), and the emotional intelligence of the recipient strongly influence feedback-seeking behavior.

More generally, individuals differ in their goal orientation. Dweck (1986) suggests that individuals differ in their orientation toward situations that provide opportunities for achievement, with some people showing a *learning* goal orientation (i.e., a preference to develop their skills and competence by taking on challenging tasks) while others show a *performance* goal orientation (i.e., a preference for demonstrating competence and for receiving favorable feedback and avoiding negative feedback). VandeWalle, Cron, and Slocum (2001) showed that these differences have an impact on how people respond to feedback. In particular, a learning goal orientation makes it easier for people to receive and respond constructively to feedback, even when this feedback is negative. A performance orientation is probably no problem when feedback is positive, but this goal orientation can make it difficult to respond constructively to negative feedback.

Age makes a difference in how feedback is received and responded to. Older workers show higher levels of social awareness, often showing a better understanding of how to use feedback to gauge others' views of them and to weigh their social quality (e.g., their standing in relation to others in the work group). On the other hand, older workers are less likely to use performance feedback information to attain personal performance/career goals in comparison to younger workers (Wang, Burlacu, Truxillo, James, & Yao, 2015). Older workers also demonstrate different reaction patterns to feedback. Older workers are more likely to have positive reactions to feedback when they perceive the feedback as favorable and are more likely to care about the method by which it is delivered (e.g., is the source of feedback being considerate, supportive, empathetic?) than younger workers. Younger workers appear to respond more strongly to perceived feedback quality (e.g., is the feedback content specific, relevant, detailed), and their feedback reactions are likely to have stronger effects on feedback effectiveness than the reactions of older workers.

Gender can also be relevant when examining feedback reactions. There are many similarities between genders, such as similarities in feedback orientation (Dahling, Chau, & O'Malley, 2012), but there are also some important differences. Generally, men are more likely to disregard negative feedback than women (Roberts & Nolen-Hoeksema, 1989). Women are equally influenced by positive and negative feedback, whereas men are more selective (i.e., are more influenced by positive feedback than negative).

The gender of the supervisor has also been shown to be influential. For instance, it has been shown that those with male supervisors typically show less favorable reactions to feedback than those with female supervisors (Wang et al., 2015). When taking the composition of the feedback relationship into account (i.e., the gender combinations of the supervisor and employee), same-gender pairs reported less positive feedback reactions than those with opposite-gender pairs (Wang et al., 2015). This pattern also was true for satisfaction with the feedback. However, it is important to note that men typically rate their female leaders lower than their male leaders, while females rate their leaders similarly (Atwater & Roush, 1994). Men react more unfavorably to feedback (and performance appraisal information) when it comes from an opposite-gender supervisor than women (Geddes & Konrad, 2003).

Finally, personality influences responses to feedback. For example, individuals who are low on the personality trait of emotional stability are especially likely to react with anger following negative feedback (Niemann, Wisse, Rus, Yperen, & Sassenberg, 2014). However, individuals who are highly competitive may be better equipped to take advantage of the information that is present in negative feedback to improve their performance, especially if it is framed in terms of performance relative to their peers (Raver et al., 2012).

Why Does Feedback Succeed or Fail?

The effects of feedback are highly variable, and feedback effectiveness can be difficult to predict and determine. However, researchers have identified circumstances in which feedback is more likely to be successful, and in this section we further explore variables that are related to feedback success or failure.

Perceived Fairness and Accuracy

When feedback is perceived to be fair, it is more likely to be successful. Even the most psychometrically sound system can lead to perceptions of ineffectiveness if it is not seen as being fair and accurate (e.g., Keeping & Levy, 2000). When the feedback process is perceived to be fair by the employees, there is a greater likelihood for acceptance and desired change in behavior (Leung, Su, & Morris, 2001).

Whether or not the feedback is accurate (or perceived to be accurate by the recipients) is also an influential variable. Typically, when feedback is perceived to be inaccurate by the employees, this leads to negative reactions and intentions to respond to feedback (e.g., Kinicki et al., 2004). In addition, inaccurate feedback or performance appraisal could potentially stimulate legal concerns, especially if performance appraisals are used to make high-stakes decisions, including salary, promotions, and layoffs (see Chapter 8).

Palmer, Johnson, and Johnson (2015) investigated whether or not the accuracy of the feedback information had an influence on performance. In lab studies, they generally found that accurate feedback leads to better performance, but additional research is still needed to examine if these relationships generalize to the workplace. Nonetheless, it is clear that *perceptions* of accuracy are related to the success or failure of feedback.

Feedback can be inaccurate for a host of reasons, including political biases (these will be explored in detail in Chapters 7 and 12), cognitive biases (conscious or unconscious), rater discomfort with giving accurate feedback, or reliance on limited or incorrect information when providing feedback. Different explanations for low-quality feedback might suggest different strategies for improving feedback, but regardless of the reasons for inaccurate feedback, it is clear that this feedback can be harmful. For instance, employees can develop unrealistic ideas about their performance and be dissatisfied if rewards do not match their expectations. What was *not* said can also be important and contribute to inaccuracy. That is, the failure to give feedback about particular aspects of performance, because of discomfort, lack of information, or a wish to avoid conflict, can be a problem. However, it is wrong to assume that inaccurate performance feedback will always have negative consequences. There are times when managers are rewarded from when they give inaccurate feedback (e.g., by avoiding an emotional meeting with a subordinate), and there are a range of situations in which the subordinate's performance is more likely to improve if they receive inflated ratings and overly positive feedback. We explore the factors that drive rating inflation and the likelihood that inflated ratings can actually be beneficial in Chapters 10 and 12.

Similar to the way in which the relationship between the accuracy and the effectiveness feedback is complex, the specificity of the feedback content can have complex and sometimes counterintuitive effects. In principle, it might seem that more specific feedback should generally be preferred to less specific feedback, but the data suggest that the effects of feedback specificity are not so simple. In particular, Goodman and Wood's (2004) data suggest that specific feedback might be beneficial for learning from good performance, but could be detrimental for learning from poor performance. This may be because the appropriate responses to feedback about good versus poor performance are quite different. If you receive feedback about good performance, the appropriate response is to keep on doing what worked. If you receive feedback about poor performance the appropriate response is to make changes, and detailed feedback about poor performance may require more changes than less detailed feedback.

Participant Involvement and Voice

Feedback is more likely to succeed when the participant feels that they are involved and able to participate. Allowing the participant to have a voice in the evaluation of their performance increases perceptions of fairness and intentions to adopt changes based on the feedback (motivation to improve). In a meta-analysis, Cawley, Keeping, and Levy (1998) examined the influence of different types of participation on employee reactions. Allowing the subordinate to have a voice and also instrumental participation in the appraisal process (i.e., factoring self-evaluations into the overall evaluation of performance) was found to be positively related to acceptance of the performance feedback system. Cawley et al. (1998) found that value-expressive participation (where the subordinate's voice is being heard) was more strongly related to reactions than instrumental participation (participation for influencing end results). This is an interesting result, because giving participants the ability to voice their viewpoints and concerns, without the expectation of this will necessarily influence the outcome of appraisal, appears to be more important than giving employees the chance to directly increase their ratings.

There are several types of feedback strategies that combine components such as positive versus negative messages, an opportunity for a subordinate to reply or not, and an opportunity for a subordinate to participate with a self-appraisal or not. Lizzio et al. (2008) examined a large number of potential feedback strategies (e.g., each strategy alone and in combination with all others). They found that *all* of the most successful combinations or patterns of feedback included the voice component.

What Is the Right Amount of Feedback?

One common recommendation for improving performance appraisal systems is that they should provide more frequent feedback (e.g., Anseel, Beatty, Shen, Lievens, & Sackett, 2015; Northcraft et al., 2011). Indeed, one of the key ideas in many performance management systems is that instead of providing annual feedback in a formal appraisal meeting, it might be better to provide more frequent informal feedback (Aguinis, 2013). This recommendation is consistent with the common finding that there are reasonably linear relationships between many of the relationships we study in the organizational sciences. For example, the relationship between cognitive ability and job performance is generally linear; higher levels of ability usually translate into higher levels of performance (Coward & Sackett, 1990). It is worth asking whether the same is likely to be true for performance feedback. There are a number of reasons to believe that the answer is no.

Suppose we took the proposition that more frequent feedback is good to its logical extreme, and provided daily performance feedback to each employee. Would this be a good thing? Suppose I tell you today that you need to be more timely when submitting invoices and reports. Tomorrow, I tell you the same thing. For the next 10 days, I repeat this observation. It is unlikely that frequent repetition of essentially the same feedback would have beneficial effects; from the ratee's perspective, it would begin to feel more like harassment than feedback. There is probably a point where more feedback is not better.

Pierce and Aguinis (2013) have argued that virtually *all* relationships in the organizational sciences have an inflection point, in which more of X no longer leads to more of Y. They cite a number of compelling examples (e.g., high levels of conscientiousness are often beneficial, but individuals who are at the extreme upper end of this distribution are inflexible and rule-bound to the point where they cannot perform effectively in many organizations), and while their assertion that most relationships are nonlinear is hard to prove or disprove, their argument that more is not always better probably applies to performance feedback.

There are several dimensions of performance feedback that are likely to matter in determining the optimal frequency for delivering feedback. First, performance feedback that addresses things that are very difficult to change should probably be infrequent. For example, suppose your personality does not fit the requirements of your job (e.g., an introverted, disagreeable individual might not do well in face-to-face sales). Adult personality is highly stable and very difficult to change (Costa & McCrae, 1997), and frequent feedback about this lack of fit is unlikely to lead to changes (although some feedback along these lines might encourage the individual to seek another career). If a particular behavior is amenable to change and improvement, frequent feedback might be beneficial.

Second, the optimal frequency for feedback is related to the performance cycle of the task in question. If tasks take a long time to reach fruition (e.g. writing a journal article), over-frequent feedback might be pointless, and even perhaps harmful (because it is unlikely to incorporate knowledge of the effectiveness of the behaviors that are the target of feedback). Optimal frequency is also related to the purpose of the feedback. For instance, if the purpose of the feedback is developmental rather than administrative reasons, in many circumstances it could make sense to give this type of feedback more often than just on an annual basis.

Third, frequent feedback might make more sense for people who are learning how to perform a task, or who are performing tasks that require frequent adjustments or updating. Murphy (1989a) noted that the determinants of task performance are likely to be different when performing familiar, well-learned tasks than when performing tasks that are new or that require changing or adapting familiar routines. Feedback that involves giving people information and support might be more beneficial during these transition phases, where people are learning new skills or trying new tasks than during maintenance phases, where they are carrying out familiar tasks that do not require much learning or thought. In longitudinal studies of feedback systems, there is evidence that the largest performance improvements come early in the process, and that subsequent feedback might have less influence on the behavior of recipients (Reilly, Smither, & Vasilopoulos, 1996).

Who Should Give Feedback?

In addition to *what* feedback is delivered, *who* delivers it might be important. Feedback can be more likely to succeed when it comes from the right people and when it is given to the right recipients. For instance, feedback will generally elicit more positive reactions when the source is perceived to be credible (e.g., Albright & Levy, 1995) and employees are more likely to perceive that the feedback is accurate when the source is credible (Kinicki et al., 2004).

Like credibility, whether or not the employee trusts the feedback source can influence how the employees perceive the feedback process. In fact, trust in the supervisor and quality of feedback moderates the relationship between feedback and performance (Nae, Moon, & Choi, 2015). In order to gain the benefits that the process offers, and to minimize the adverse consequences, organizations need to create an atmosphere of trust, openness, and sharing (McNabb & Whitfield, 2001). Feedback is most meaningful when there is a genuine desire on both sides for a meaningful and authentic exchange of perceptions.

Clearly, there is an important relationship between leadership and feedback. Tuytens and Devos (2012) note that charismatic leaders are seen as delivering feedback that is both accurate and useful. Whether the content of the feedback that is provided by charismatic leaders is different from that delivered by other leaders is not certain, but it is plausible that the personal characteristics that make some leaders charismatic has an effect similar to halo, making their feedback seem more accurate and useful.

The person delivering feedback (the source) is important, and so is the person receiving the feedback. For example, we discussed that newcomers in organizations typically benefit highly from feedback. Unfortunately, people who need feedback are not always the ones who are seeking it. Feedback-seeking behaviors will be discussed in depth later in this chapter, but there is a general trend showing that poor performers, individuals who are simply unsure about their performance, and individuals who have poor relationships with their supervisors are less likely to seek feedback than good performers. Conversely, individuals who are confident that the feedback will be positive or individuals whose leaders trust and depend on them are more likely to seek it.

Upward Feedback

Upward feedback is the process of subordinates providing feedback to their superiors. It shares some of the same dynamics as other sorts of feedback (Johnson & Ferstl, 1999). That is, the effect of upward feedback on subsequent behavior is influenced by a number of factors that influence the credibility and acceptability of that feedback. For example, the effects of upward feedback on subsequent performance is probably smaller when there is disagreement between self-assessments and assessments from others (particularly when ratings from others are lower than self-ratings) and when there is disagreement among the different external raters who provide evaluations. Like downward feedback, the forces that motivate raters to provide honest upward feedback represent a complex mix of personal and organizational variables. For example, the intention to provide honest upward feedback is influenced by one's general attitudes toward management and toward appraisal; employees who are cynical toward management or toward performance appraisal are less likely to provide honest upward feedback (Smith & Fortunato 2008). Motivation to provide honest upward feedback is also influenced by the rater's belief that there are positive benefits to providing honest ratings and that the recipients of feedback (particularly negative feedback) will not retaliate. Beliefs that raters have an adequate opportunity to observe the performance of the individuals they are asked to evaluate influences acceptance of upward feedback much in the same way that it influences acceptance of other types of feedback (Maurer & Tarulli, 1996; Smith & Fortunato, 2008). If it appears that raters lack the information needed to accurately evaluate performance, their feedback is less likely to be accepted.

Empirical findings on upward feedback are mixed. For instance, it has been shown that managers who receive upward feedback generally improve after the intervention, and also that managers who initially receive lower ratings improve the most from the upward feedback (Walker & Smither, 1999). However, it has also been shown that like the effects of general feedback interventions at work, the effects are often small and sometimes nonexistent (Antonioni, 1995).

An Alternative to Feedback: The Feedforward Interview

Feedback is in many ways a no-win situation. To begin with, it is retrospective. The thing you are giving feedback about cannot be changed, so the rationale for giving people information about that past event must depend on an assumption that it might change some future events. However, it is well established that the providers of feedback and the recipients of feedback have different perceptions of and evaluations of past performance (See Chapter 5). As a result, feedback often starts off in a hole, in the sense that provider–recipient differences in the perception and interpretation of the events and performances that are the focus of feedback undercut the credibility and usefulness of feedback. Second, even where there is general agreement about what happened in the past, negative feedback leads to negative reactions, such as anger, which can interfere with subsequent performance.[3] It is no surprise that performance feedback rarely has substantial positive effects on future performance (Kluger & DeNisi, 1996).

Rather than giving feedback about something that has already happened Kluger and Nir (2010) suggest using *feedforward*. The feedforward interview focuses on (1) articulating what has gone well, by eliciting description of positive experiences from the target; (2) understanding how the strengths of the target and the context in which the event or experience contributed to that positive experience; and (3) helping the target to apply those strengths and/or situational resources to increase the likelihood of success and positive experiences in the future. Feedback is often focused on mistakes or what went wrong, and even when it focuses on what went well, there is rarely any systematic exploration of *why* it went well. Feedforward fits solidly within the tradition of positive psychology (for reviews of positive psychology, see Lopez & Snyder, 2009; Snyder & Lopez, 2007), with its strong focus on identifying strengths, and it has the potential to overcome much of the defensiveness inherent in receiving feedback about past performance, especially past failures.

There is empirical evidence that feedforward interventions can lead to long-lasting improvements in performance (Budworth, Latham, & Manroop, 2015). Budworth et al. (2015) suggest that there are two mechanisms that might help to explain the success of this intervention. First, a system that focuses on strengths and success is likely to lead the recipients of this information to set higher and more challenging goals. Feedback, particularly feedback about past failures or mistakes, is likely, in the best of circumstances, to elicit goals that include or center on avoiding future errors. Feedforward of the type described here is likely to lead to the development of goals that focus on future success. Second, because the feedforward interview focuses on helping the recipient to articulate past successes and positive experiences, this method guarantees that the recipients of feedforward will have a chance to express voice, a key determinant of perceptions of the fairness and accuracy of information about performance.

Additional methods have been inspired by the feedforward interview. Bouskila-Yam and Kluger (2011) proposed a fundamental re-orientation of performance appraisal and feedback. Rather than attempting to measure performance levels or to give feedback about performance deficiencies, they proposed a *strength-based* performance appraisal (SBPA) system. Borrowing key ideas from positive psychology (Seligman & Csikszentmihalyi,

2000), they proposed that performance reviews should focus on what people do well, and should work toward establishing goals that are based on strengths rather than weaknesses. There are six main steps involved in SBPA: (1) a supervisor–subordinate meeting where the feedforward interview protocol is used to reflect on the best-self of the employee, and the manager is instructed to communicate with the employee a time when they performed well; (2) the subordinate fills out a web-based questionnaire; (3) a second supervisor–subordinate meeting is held, informed by the questionnaire results to assess strengths and set goals; (3) using the composite scores from the web-based questionnaire across the entire organization, many strengths and one weakness are identified on an organizational level; (5) a "feedforward party" is held to communicate results; and then (6) six months later a follow-up discussion occurs to reflect on goals and so on. (See Bouskila-Yam & Kluger, 2011, for full detail.)

DO EMPLOYEES WANT FEEDBACK AND DEVELOPMENT?

Ashford and Cummings (1983) proposed that individuals in organizations are not merely passive recipients of feedback, but that they often actively engage in an active search for feedback. In the years since this influential paper, a large and robust literature dealing with feedback-seeking behavior (FSB) has developed. A large number of hypotheses regarding individual and situational factors that influence FSB have been tested, and a number of models of FSB have been put forth (for reviews, see Anseel et al., 2015; Ashford, Blatt, & VandeWalle, 2003). For example, Ashford et al. (2003) proposed that there are several distinct motives for seeking feedback (e.g., feedback might be instrumental, in the sense that it helps you achieve goals, or it might be sought to protect your self-image or image in the organization), and that different motivations might lead to very different patterns of FSB and reactions to feedback (See also Dahling, O'Malley, & Chau, 2015; Hays & Williams, 2011).

Cost-benefit frameworks provide a useful way of understanding FSB. For example, Park, Schmidt, Scheu, and DeShon (2007) propose that feedback has: (1) expectancy value, (2) appraisal value, (3) ego cost, and (4) self-presentation cost. Cost-benefit frameworks state that employees determine whether or not to engage in FSB by assessing the costs and benefits. Expectancy value refers to the perceived value of feedback as a tool for increasing performance or effectiveness; Park et al. (2007) suggest that strong perceptions of expectancy value will lead to a preference for diagnostic feedback (feedback on what went well or poorly and why). Appraisal value refers to the perceived value of feedback for evaluating your performance level, in particular, in comparison to others. Individuals who value this information are likely to prefer normative feedback (feedback regarding performance levels) over diagnostic feedback. Ego costs are those evaluative losses that an employee determines might occur as a result of seeking feedback. For instance, they might receive negative feedback. Another type of costs that could be associated with feedback are self-presentation costs, and this is when employees believe that seeking feedback might make them look weak or incompetent and expose them to criticism. These costs would make it less likely for an employee to engage in FSB.

In principle, feedback should lead to improved performance, which should in turn enhance the likelihood of career success, but again there is little evidence to support this supposed cycle. For example, FBS is not consistently related to performance levels. Some studies have reported a positive correlation between performance levels and the likelihood of seeking feedback (Nae et al., 2015), but this relationship is not always found (Anseel et al., 2015). In fact, there are several studies and models that suggest that poor-performing employees actively *avoid* feedback (e.g., Moss et al., 2009; Moss et al., 2003). Similarly, FSB does not appear to be related to career success (Cheramie, 2013), although there is some evidence of increased FSB following changes in jobs or careers (Callister, Kramer, & Turban, 1999).

There are two general classes of reasons for seeking feedback: (1) to improve performance, or (2) to enhance self-image (Jordan & Audia, 2012). The decision about which objective to pursue is likely to be influenced by individual differences, particularly differences in mindset (Dweck, 2006). For instance, people with lower self-esteem are less likely to seek feedback, particularly if there is a risk that this feedback will be negative (Bernichon, Cook, & Brown, 2003). Individuals who seek feedback as a means of improving performance might actually find negative feedback useful, whereas individuals who seek assurance that they have performed well are likely to avoid negative feedback. The use of feedback for improvement versus assurance is likely to be influenced by individual differences, particularly differences in mindset (i.e., belief that skills and abilities are fixed or changeable; Dweck, 2006). However, some situations (e.g., those in which seriously negative feedback is expected) might push individuals in the direction of feedback avoidance, even if they are normally interested in improvement. Similarly, variation in performance standards might push individuals in the direction of performance improvement or in the direction of self-enhancement. In particular, when performance standards are unclear (making it harder for individuals to predict whether the feedback they are likely to receive will be positive or negative), individuals may be more likely to avoid feedback and to focus on self-enhancement.

There are additional individual differences that have the potential to influence FSB. Wu, Parker, and de Jong (2014) note that there are a number of personality variables that might influence an employee's probability of engaging in FSB. In particular, social anxiety is likely to influence both the likelihood of seeking feedback and the source from which feedback can be sought. For example, individuals who are high on attachment anxiety (i.e., a strong concern with having and maintaining relationships) appear to be more likely to seek feedback from peers (Wu et al., 2014).

It has been shown that FSB has more value to younger employees, but this is typically related to tenure, because newer employees are more likely to engage in FSB (Anseel et al., 2015). However, the topic of age differences in the frequency of FSB is still being debated. It has been suggested that age had a negative impact on FSB, thus as a person becomes older they are less likely to engage in FSB (Gupta, Govindarajan, & Malhotra, 1999), whereas other studies have indicated there is no relationship (e.g., van der Rijt et al., 2012).

Whether or not gender influences the likelihood that employees will seek feedback is also unclear. Some researchers have found significant relationships between gender and FSB, while others have not (e.g., London, Larsen & Thisted, 1999). Miller and Karakowsky (2005) studied groups that differed in their gender composition and in the extent to which the task they performed was stereotypically masculine (e.g., negotiating the purchase of a used car) or feminine (e.g., negotiating the resolution of an interpersonal conflict with sexual overtones). In general, they found that feedback was most likely to be sought when the gender composition of the team was consistent with the gender stereotype of the task (e.g., a male-dominated team negotiating the purchase of a used car). Women were more receptive than men to seeking feedback in tasks and groups that were male-dominated but the reverse did not hold for men. In female-dominated groups performing female-stereotypes tasks, men were not likely to seek feedback.

The characteristics of jobs themselves can influence the likelihood that incumbents will seek feedback. Krasman (2013) examined the influence of several key dimensions of Hackman and Oldham's (1980) job characteristics model on feedback seeking. His results suggest that individuals who hold jobs that are *low* on autonomy and task identify are most likely to seek feedback. That is, in jobs where incumbents have a good deal of freedom to decide how to complete tasks, and where they engage in tasks that are personally meaningful, they are less likely to seek feedback than are incumbents in more routine jobs. One possibility is that these incumbents might have the expertise to evaluate their own work, and that feedback from others would provide little additional information. Another possibility is that surrendering control of their performance to some outside entity is less appealing for employees with jobs that provide strong autonomy and task identity.

Feedback Acceptance

In order for feedback to have its full effect, it must be accepted as reasonable, credible, and fair. Anseel and Lievens (2009) adapted models of perceptions of fairness in employment selection to identify characteristics of feedback and feedback programs that might influence its acceptance. In particular, they suggest that both distributive and procedural justice perceptions influence feedback acceptance. First, feedback about performance levels should seem fair and reasonable. As we have noted elsewhere, because people tend to have overly favorable views about their own performance, perceptions of distributive feedback in performance feedback are closely tied to the favorability of the feedback. In a nutshell, favorable feedback strikes most recipients as more fair and reasonable than unfavorable feedback.

However, the *way* feedback is phrased and delivered might also matter. For example, it is possible that the effects of negative feedback might be buffered if it is clear that the process used to obtain performance information was thorough and unbiased (Anseel & Lievens, 2009). Voice is an important component of procedural justice perceptions, and giving feedback recipients a chance to have some input may make it easier for them to accept unwelcome feedback.

People who receive unfavorable feedback appear to react differently, depending on the inferences they make about *why* feedback is unfavorable. In particular, feedback that appears to be the result of interpersonal animus on the part of the deliverer is unlikely to be accepted. Studies of constructive versus destructive criticism (e.g., Leung et al., 2001) suggest that negative feedback that is delivered in a manner that is respectful and constructive (e.g., that avoids undue blame, that avoids public criticism, and that is caring and future-oriented in tone) is more likely to be accepted than criticism that is destructive or vindictive. Similarly, negative feedback that appears to be the result of a thorough and fair attempt to evaluate performance is more likely to be accepted than negative feedback that appears to result from a cursory review.

The likelihood of accepting feedback also depends on cultural variables. For example, Lee and Akhtar (1996) studied reactions to feedback in a Chinese sample, and suggested that cultural values such as paternalism and personalism (an emphasis on strong personal relationships) made it easier for recipients to accept feedback from respected supervisors. MacDonald et al. (2013) reported that Chinese and Canadian subjects differed in the motives and methods of seeking feedback, and since it is likely that feedback that is inconsistent with the motives for seeking feedback is unlikely to be accepted (e.g., if feedback is sought to enhance or protect one's ego, negative feedback is particularly unwelcome), it is likely that these cultural factors also influence feedback reactions.

SUMMARY

... of the most frequently cited purposes of performance appraisal is to give employees feedback. As this chapter shows, there are important questions about the definition, effects, and effectiveness of feedback, and it is naïve to assume that simply giving people performance feedback will lead to improvements in their job performance. A number of studies have examined the question of who should give feedback, how it should be given, and the likelihood that it will be accepted, and it is clear that there is no simple solution to the problem of building an effective performance feedback system. Because of fundamental differences in the way people view their own performance and the way managers, peers, and others view that same performance, it can be very hard to deliver feedback that will be accepted as fair and useful. It is no surprise, therefore, that managers dislike giving and employees dislike receiving performance feedback or that the effects of feedback on job performance is weak and inconsistent. Feedback can be improved by giving employees a meaningful role in evaluations and by tailoring feedback toward specific task-related behaviors that are relatively easy to change. However, even feedback systems that incorporate these suggestions produce effects that are difficult to predict. Feedback can be useful and valuable, but it is wise to approach claims about the benefits of providing performance feedback with some degree of skepticism and caution.

EXERCISE: EVALUATE YOUR COMPANY'S FEEDBACK PROGRAM

Is your company's feedback program effective? This is not always an easy question to answer. First, organizations rarely conduct systematic evaluations of human resource programs. Even if they are willing to attempt an evaluation, there are often a number of difficult questions that need to be dealt with, in particular, determining what metrics will be used to evaluate the success or failure of the feedback that is given.

Evaluating the success or failure of various programs and policies in an organization involves a sequence of steps that are fairly consistent regardless of the specific details of the programs to be evaluated. They include:

- **Identify the goals of the program**—What are you trying to accomplish by giving employees feedback? Are you trying to correct performance errors, assist poor performers to improve, or maintain the performance levels of adequate and superior performers? Different goals imply different evaluation protocols.

- **Determine the right methods and metrics**— Once goals are defined, it is important to identify appropriate measures that can be used to track success in accomplishing these goals. Will performance ratings be sufficient for this purpose (probably not), or will you need to combine traditional performance ratings with other measures? You will probably want to measure both the feedback itself (how much feedback was given, who did or did not receive feedback, and the effects of that feedback (e.g., did behavior change, what did people perform better after receiving feedback). Developing credible metrics is probably the biggest single challenge in evaluating a performance feedback program, and evaluation efforts that do not pay careful attention to this step will almost certainly fail.

- **Design an evaluation study**—Once you know what you want to measure, you need to give careful thought to how measurements can be designed to allow you to draw firm conclusions about the effectiveness of feedback. At a minimum, it is best to have information collected *before* feedback is given as a comparison point. Otherwise, it might be very hard to determine whether feedback is having its desired effect. Consider, for example, the conclusions you can draw if all you know is that people performed pretty well after they received feedback. This might mean that feedback was effective, but it is also possible that they were performing well before they received feedback, and that feedback has little effect. It is even possible that they were performing *better* before they received feedback, and that feedback made things worse. There are a wide range of choices that can be made in designing an evaluation study (Shadish, Cook, & Campbell, 2001), and different research designs might allow you to extract a great deal of information about how feedback influenced subsequent behavior and effectiveness.

- **Collect and interpret data**—If you have made a good choice of metrics that provide information about the success or failure of your feedback program in meeting its stated goals, the final step—collecting and interpreting data—should be a relatively straightforward

one. However, it is important to recognize that data collection can be both expensive (in terms of time, effort, and even in terms of data handling and storage) and sensitive. The very fact that you are collecting data might have an impact on the types of feedback that are given and on the outcomes of that feedback, and it can be challenging to develop data collection methods that are both effective and unobtrusive. Interpreting program evaluation data in organizations can be especially challenging because stakeholders may have vested interests that could be challenged by the data you collect. For example, suppose your manager is the head of human resources and she is the one who designed the performance feedback program. It may not be easy to tell her if your conclusion is that the program is not working. Unfortunately, a genuine program evaluation effort has to include the possibility that it will convey a message that key decision makers do not want to hear, and this may be one reason why genuine program evaluation is relatively uncommon in many organizations.

NOTES

1. Note, however, that the source of the feedback might make a substantial difference in the way the feedback is interpreted and acted upon.

2. See also VandeWalle, Cron, and Slocum (2001), who present evidence of differences in performance following feedback as a function of goal orientation.

3. Anger following negative feedback is especially likely for individuals who are low on the personality trait of emotional stability (Niemann, Wisse, Rus, Van Yperen, & Sassenberg, 2014).

10 DEALING WITH REACTIONS AND ATTITUDES

LEARNING OBJECTIVES

10.1 Learn about the range of reactions that can influence the success or failure of an appraisal system

10.2 Understand how aspects of the appraisal system, individual factors, and organizational factors influence reactions to appraisal systems

10.3 Learn about how reactions to appraisal systems influence the process of giving and receiving performance feedback

10.4 Understand the concept of a "death spiral," and learn how negative reactions to appraisal systems can initiate such a spiral

In an influential paper, Kirkpatrick (1967) argued that four criteria should be considered in evaluating training programs: reactions, learning, behavior, and results. That is, in evaluating the effectiveness of training programs, we should consider how people reacted to the training (e.g., did they find it credible, did they find it worthwhile?), what they learned, how their behavior changed following training, and the results of those changes in behavior. His suggestion that reactions should be given a prominent place in understanding how and why training interventions succeed or fail has turned out to be useful for evaluating and making sense of a wide range of human resource programs, including performance appraisal.

The study of reactions to performance appraisals and feedback has blossomed in the recent decades (Levy & Williams, 2004). A wide range of reactions to performance appraisal systems have been studied, including satisfaction with performance appraisal (Russell & Goode, 1988), attitudes toward various components of appraisal systems (Korsgaard & Roberson, 1995), perceptions of justice (Greenberg, 1991) and fairness (Holbrook, 1999), perceived accuracy of appraisals (Taylor, Tracy, Renard, Harrison, & Carroll, 1995), acceptance of appraisal systems (Reinke, 2003), perceived utility of appraisal systems (Levy & Williams, 2004), and even anxiety about giving or receiving performance feedback (Ivancevich, 1982).

Acceptability has emerged as an especially important criterion for evaluating performance appraisal systems (Bernardin & Beatty, 1984; Hedge & Teachout, 2000). That is, differences in the extent to which appraisal systems are seen as reasonable and fair appear to be particularly important; appraisal systems that are not accepted by participants as providing relevant and useful information are very likely to fail. The attitudes of participants toward performance appraisal systems are related to a number of systems features including the frequency of appraisals, the type of performance standards used, and the use of appraisal to develop in areas where performance is relatively low, as well as the supervisor's knowledge of the job duties and the subordinate's performance (Hedge & Teachout, 2000; Landy, Barnes, & Murphy, 1978). Before examining reactions research in detail, it is worth thinking about what we mean by "reactions" and precisely how reactions to performance appraisal systems can influence the success or failure of these systems.

REACTIONS TO APPRAISAL SYSTEMS

We find it useful to group the types of reactions to performance appraisal systems that have been studied in recent years into three broad categories: (1) evaluative and affective reactions, (2) perceptions of utility, and (3) perceptions of legitimacy. These three classes of reactions are certainly not independent; appraisal systems that are seen as useless and illegitimate will probably be disliked. Nevertheless, it is useful to think about the determinants and implications of these three classes of reactions separately.

Evaluative and Affective Reactions

First, we can ask whether participants in performance appraisal like or dislike the system and whether they see it as a generally good thing or a generally bad thing. Evaluative and affective reactions are likely to be driven in part by specific aspects of components of the system, such as the time and energy required to complete appraisals, provide feedback, or deal with the feedback you have received, but reactions of liking versus disgust or perceptions that the appraisal system is either a good or a bad part of being a member of the organization are unlikely to be driven solely by a cold appraisal of the appraisal system. Rather, they are also likely to be driven by the belief that the system is or is not fair and just.

There is a large literature dealing with perceptions of fairness and justice in organizations, and a substantial portion of this literature deals with or is applicable to performance appraisal (for reviews of this literature, see Cropanzano & Kacmar, 1995; Erdogan, 2002; Flint, 1999; Folger & Cropanzano, 1998; Holbrook, 2002). This literature distinguishes between three different types of justice: (1) procedural—whether or not procedures and processes appear to be fair and balanced, (2) distributive—whether or not the outcomes of actions (e.g., promotions, salary increases) appear to be equitable, and (3) interpersonal—whether or not the individuals involved are treated with due respect and consideration. Table 10.1 lists some of the more frequently studied aspects of fairness and justice in performance appraisal.

Ratees are likely to experience feelings of distributive injustice when the ratings they receive are not as high as the ratings they feel they deserve. When a discrepancy arises between the rewards employees expect to receive for their contributions and those they actually receive from their employer, employees are likely to feel cheated, or at least badly treated, and this is likely to lead to negative feelings about the entire appraisal system. Given the extensive evidence discussed in several chapters that ratings from others are typically lower than self-ratings, it is likely that many employees feel that they have not received the rewards they deserve.

Justice researchers have often suggested that concerns about distributive justice might be at least partially reduced if employees believe that fair procedures have been used and that they have been treated with respect. For example, Giles, Findley, and Feild (1997) identify features of the appraisal system (e.g., rules, policies, organizational support for appraisal), features of the appraisal system itself (e.g., opportunities for participation, feedback, pleasant interactions), and behavior of the supervisor outside of the context of the appraisal and feedback session (e.g., observation of performance, providing assistance and support

TABLE 10.1 ■ Elements of Perceived Justice in Performance Appraisal[a]	
Procedural Justice	Voice
	Accuracy and completeness
	Due process (e.g., adequate notice, judgments based on evidence)
	Apparent freedom from bias
	Agreement on standards
Distributive Justice	The rating that is received
	Outcomes associated with appraisal (e.g., pay, promotion)
Interactional Justice	Respect
	Communication
	Sensitivity
	Truthfulness
	Explanations for ratings or decisions

[a] Research on aspects of appraisal that influence perceptions of justice is summarized in Erdogan, 2002; Heslin & VandeWalle, 2011; Nurse, 2005; Palaiologos, Papazekos, & Panayotopoulou, 2011.

needed to perform well) that contribute to the perception that appraisal procedures are fair. Other researchers have noted that the opportunity to have some impact on the process and the outcomes of appraisal (i.e., voice) is an important determinant of perceptions of procedural justice (Korsgaard & Roberson, 1995). Thus, affective and evaluative responses to performance appraisal systems are likely to be determined by a combination of the way appraisals are conducted and the outcomes of appraisal. On the whole, performance appraisal systems that treat employees with some level of consideration and respect (e.g., systems that are not overly burdensome, that give employees some voice, that follow transparent and consistent procedures) and that lead to desired rewards are more likely to be evaluated positively.

Although most studies have examined the impact of perceptions of justice on attitudes toward performance appraisal, there is longitudinal research suggesting that it is one's experience with performance appraisal that shapes perceptions of justice (Linna et al., 2012). That is, employees who find their first experience with a performance appraisal system to be helpful to their career development are more likely to view that system as just than employees whose early experiences are less helpful. In the final section of this chapter, we return to examine the potentially decisive role of early experiences with performance appraisal systems in determining reactions to those systems.

Perceptions of Utility: Are Appraisals Seen as Useful?

Second, we might ask whether performance appraisal systems are seen as useful. From managers' or supervisors' perspective, performance appraisal systems that help them accomplish important goals (e.g., motivating their subordinates, ensuring that deserving employees receive rewards) are likely to be seen as useful. Chapter 12 examines the way raters use performance appraisal to accomplish desired outcomes or to avoid negative ones in some depth, but it is useful here to recognize that performance appraisal can be viewed as a tool managers and supervisors use to carry out their jobs, and appraisal systems that help them be more effective in their roles might be viewed as highly useful.

From the perspective of the individuals being evaluated, performance appraisal systems are probably seen as most useful when they receive performance feedback that (1) helps them improve their performance or to avoid performance problems, (2) delivers new information (i.e., tells them something they do not already know), and (3) delivers information that is credible. Thus, performance appraisal systems that deliver only vague and general feedback (e.g., last year, you performed very well) or that tells an employee something he or she already knows (e.g., your annual sales fell below targets) or that delivers information that is not seen as credible (e.g., one that gives negative feedback to employees who strongly expect more positive feedback) may be seen as less useful than a system that delivers credible information not readily available to the individuals being rated that helps them perform their jobs well.

From the perspective of managers and supervisors, performance appraisal systems are useful if they help them do their jobs well, and are not useful if they get in the way of accomplishing the key objectives of their jobs. In general, the overall goal of most supervisory and managerial jobs is similar, in the sense that their role in organizations is to create conditions that make it possible for the work to get done and to ensure that the employees they supervise or manage are performing up to their capabilities. Performance appraisal can be a very useful tool for accomplishing these goals, but it can also be a hindrance. Performance appraisal systems that help motivate employees and that give them clear direction and support for improving their performance or for maintaining currently high performance levels are likely to be viewed as useful. Performance appraisal systems that lead to cynicism and distrust, or that drain employees' motivation and willingness to work hard, or that give them useless or confusing feedback, are likely to be viewed as harmful.

Perceptions of Legitimacy

Finally, appraisal systems might differ in terms of their apparent legitimacy. For example, appraisal systems that focus on trivial parts of the job, or that appear to be based on favoritism or political considerations, might not be accepted as legitimate by its users. Ratees, in particular, are likely to view appraisal systems that deliver results that do not seem to depend on how well the people being evaluated have performed major job functions as something worse than ineffective—that is, as illegitimate systems that are robbing truly good performers of opportunities for advancement or rewards. One of the major determinants of perceptions of legitimacy is the belief that performance appraisal systems are overly political, in the sense that the likelihood of a favorable appraisal does not depend so much on what you as an employee do as on the biases or the self-serving goals of raters.

Longenecker, Sims, and Gioia (1987) refer to politics of appraisal as the "deliberate attempts by individuals to enhance or protect their self-interests when conflicting courses of action are possible" (p. 184; see also Kacmar & Baron, 1999). Other researchers define organizational politics in terms of the ability to understand the work environment and to use that knowledge to influence others (Ferris, Davidson, & Perrewé, 2005; Ferris & Treadway, 2012; Ferris et al., 2007). Organizations are most certainly political arenas, in which members of the organization are constantly engaged in behaviors that are intended to influence other members of the organization (Mintzberg, 1983), and it is naïve to think that appraisal systems will be completely devoid of politics. The question is whether appraisal systems will be seen as *too* political—that is, the extent to which they are seen as cynical attempts to manipulate employees or other members of the organization.

The extent to which performance appraisal is seen as a political process rather than a straightforward process for evaluating performance in organizations is likely to depend on a number of factors, starting with whether the performance appraisal is taken seriously in the organization. Virtually every human resource handbook we have ever read *claims* that performance appraisal is an important function, but if the norm in an organization is to put a minimum amount of time and effort into appraisal, and to largely ignore the results of appraisals, that could substantially influence the perception of performance appraisal as a political process. There are a number of influences on the culture of organizations, including the economic health and growth potential of the organization, the extent to which top management supports or does not practice political tactics when appraising their own subordinates, the extent to which executives believe appraisal is necessary, the extent to which executives believe they would be scrutinized by superiors on their appraisal of subordinates, the extent to which organizations will train managers on performance appraisal, the degree of open discussion of appraisal process among executive and subordinates (i.e., trust), and the extent to which executives believe that the appraisal becomes more political at higher levels of the organizational hierarchy. In general, when top management believes strongly in the necessity of performance appraisal, the influence of political factors on ratings is not likely to be substantial (Longenecker et al., 1987). When appraisal is not strongly and visibly supported by top management, political factors are more likely to emerge. In the context of performance appraisal, politics is usually thought of as the conscious use of distortion in performance ratings or performance feedback to help raters accomplish important ends, such as avoiding conflict or maximizing rewards (Murphy & Cleveland, 1995). If performance appraisal is *perceived* to be political—that is, a system in which ratings have more to do with the objectives of the rater than the performance of the people being evaluated, distortion is more likely to occur (Curtis, Harvey, & Ravden, 2005; Tziner, 1999).

Although "politics" need not be thought of as an exercise in cynical manipulation, it often is exactly that. That is, the perception of organizations or of interactions between supervisors and subordinates as too political seems to be associated with a variety of negative outcomes. For example, Hochwarter, Witt, and Kacmar (2000) reported that when organizations are perceived as political, that could lead to lower job performance, at least among employees who are not high on conscientiousness. On the other hand, highly conscientious employees may perform a bit better in settings that are perceived as political. Hochwarter, Ferris, Zinko, Arnell, and James (2007) reported that political behavior could lead to either increased or decreased job performance, depending on the reputation of the individual (employees with positive reputations benefit from political behavior). Rosen, Levy, and Hall (2006) linked perceptions of politics with the type and amount of feedback employees receive, noting that when employees receive high-quality feedback, performance appraisal is perceived as less political and performance is enhanced. This study suggests at least one mechanism by which perceptions of a politicized environment might influence performance. That is, if politicized environments (particularly politicized performance appraisal systems) are likely to be ones in which the evaluations employees receive depend on the goals or the strategies of the rater rather than on their own performance, and as performance feedback becomes more clear and detailed, there is less room for uncertainty about the relationship between the employee's behavior and performance and the performance feedback he or she receives. Tziner (1999) notes that raters often distort their ratings to accomplish political goals. Tziner, Latham, Price, and Haccoun (1996) describe the development and validation of a measure of the extent to which specific political considerations are taken into account when completing performance appraisals; this instrument can be useful in diagnosing problems in appraisal systems.

Efforts to decrease the use of politics in performance rating and performance feedback often take the form of interventions to increase rater accountability (Curtis et al., 2005). Tetlock (1985) argued that when raters are held accountable for the accuracy of their ratings, they are more likely to be thorough in forming their judgments. In a later section, we will examine the effects of accountability interventions in some detail.

The term *politics* often has a somewhat negative connotation, suggesting some sort of corrupt and sleazy manipulation, but we prefer to think of this term more in the line of Winston Churchill's definition. He liked to refer to politics as the "art of the possible." That is, political behavior involves attempts to influence the behavior of others, and while this influence can be harmful or corrupt, it does not have to be. Performance appraisal is inherently political; there is substantial evidence that raters do *and should* consider how the ratings they give will affect them and the work groups they supervise. That is, the essence of the job of supervisors and managers is to influence others (e.g., through leadership, through the use of rewards and sanctions, through efforts to create conditions where key goals can be accomplished), and a supervisor or manager who forgoes politics is probably not doing his or her job. Tetlock (1985) proposed that raters are motivated to understand and conform to the preferences of others in the organization that will be evaluating them. In the accountability literature, this generally boils down to either ratees or superiors (Harris, 1994; Levy & Williams, 2004). It is presumed that ratees prefer higher ratings, but it can be more difficult to determine precisely what superiors prefer or expect. The manager who is politically astute is more likely to understand what his or her superiors want and expect than a manager who attempts to ignore politics.

Politics is not the only factor that influences perceptions of legitimacy; the content of performance appraisals might have an influence. One of the distinctions between core task performance and organizational citizenship is that the former is explicitly required by organizations and are usually formally rewarded, whereas the latter are important but optional. That is, an electrician who refused to run wire, work with tools, and install electrical switches and devices would not be doing his or her job, and might be dismissed. An electrician who does not go out of his way help others when they need it, or who complains and makes life miserable for others might be regarded as a selfish jerk, but will probably not face sanctions. It is worth asking whether including organization citizenship behaviors (OCBs) in performance appraisal is likely to make appraisal systems seem fairer or less fair.

There is considerable evidence that raters *do* consider organizational citizenship behaviors when evaluating their subordinates (Borman, White, & Dorsey, 1995; Motowidlo & Van Scotter, 1994; Van Scotter, Motowidlo, & Cross, 2000). If these behaviors are not explicitly required, and not an official part of the job, it is likely that at least some employees (particularly ones who do not engage in OCBs) will see the inclusion of these behaviors in performance appraisal as unfair, but on the whole, most employees seem to accept the idea that citizenship should be part of appraisal.

On the whole, employees appear to view appraisal systems in which organizational citizenship behaviors receive some weight as fairer than systems in which these behaviors are ignored altogether, but only to a point. That is, an appraisal system that gives organizational citizenship behaviors more weight than core task performance is probably not seen as quite fair (Johnson, Holladay, & Quinones, 2009). Women seem to be more receptive to placing substantial weight on organizational citizenship than men.

HOW REACTIONS AFFECT PERFORMANCE APPRAISAL PROCESSES AND OUTCOMES

There are three ways reactions to performance appraisal systems might influence the behavior and perceptions of raters and ratees. First, there are direct effects. That is, reactions to and perceptions of performance appraisal systems will affect the way people use those systems. Raters who view the entire exercise as a waste of time will almost certainly approach performance appraisal differently than raters who are strongly invested in making the system work. Ratees who believe the appraisal system is neither credible nor useful will almost certainly approach performance feedback differently than ratees who believe that feedback might include information that is credible and useful. There are, however, also indirect effects. Performance appraisal systems can be seen as beneficial in and of themselves, or they might be seen as harmful. The extent to which performance appraisal is viewed as a positive versus a negative part of working in an organization may influence a range of outcomes. In addition, the performance appraisal system can be thought of as a signal of the way management thinks about its employees. Employees who view their performance appraisal system as a time-consuming nuisance may also think differently about other human resource systems and about the competence and the motives of upper management than employees who see their appraisal system as a good-faith effort to improve the organization.

Direct Effects

Reactions can be the result of the success or failure of a performance appraisal system, but they can also be a cause. If employees do not see the appraisal system as reliable or relevant, they may be less willing to put in the time and effort needed to do a good job evaluating performance and to provide useful feedback. If employees fail to see the value of appraisal, they may end up putting less time and effort into performance appraisal, in effect causing the system to live up to their low expectations. On the other hand, employees who see appraisal systems as fair, useful, and legitimate will probably take appraisal more seriously. For example, raters who support their company's performance appraisal system are likely to give better, more detailed feedback, and employees who see the system as credible and fair are more likely to take that feedback seriously.

Perceptions of and attitudes toward performance appraisal systems are likely to be self-reinforcing, in the sense that they are likely to trigger behaviors that are consistent with those perceptions and beliefs. Thus, supervisors, managers and employees who believe in and support their company's performance appraisal system are likely to engage in behaviors that make those systems more successful, ranging from devoting the time and effort needed to do good appraisals to talking about their appraisal systems in positive terms. On the other hand, if participants believe that their company's performance appraisal system is a joke, they will probably behave accordingly, making the system increasingly unreliable and useless. We examine the way negative perceptions can doom performance appraisal systems in a later section of this chapter.

Signaling

Perceptions of and beliefs about performance appraisal systems are likely to have indirect as well as direct effects on how well these systems work. Recent research has focused on the key role of employees' perceptions of human resource programs and practices in understanding the likely success or failure of these programs (Aryee, Walumba, Seidu, & Otaye, 2012), and it suggests that beliefs about human resource systems including performance appraisal may generalize to the organization as a whole, and that employees' experiences with human resource systems may serve as a signal about the way organizations view and treat their employees.

There is evidence that employees draw inferences about management's intentions based on their interpretation and understanding of a firm's human resource practices (Ehrnrooth & Björkman, 2012; Nishii, Lepak, & Schneider, 2008; Wayne, Shore, & Liden, 1997; Whitener, 2001). For example, if employees view their performance appraisal system as credible and helpful, this is likely to lead to the conclusion that top management is sincerely interested in their development. On the other hand, if performance appraisal is seen as a pointless waste of time, employees are likely to draw the inference that top management does not truly care about them and does not object to subjecting them to pointless and annoying appraisals.

Their experience with a company's human resource systems might tell employees something about the competence or incompetence of their management. That is, employees who believe that key human resource systems, including performance appraisal, are poorly designed or poorly executed may come to the conclusion that the management of their organization is not highly competent, or at least that they do not care enough to hire competent staff to design and implement their human resource systems. One of the important bases of power for an organization's leaders is its perceived expertise and competence (French & Raven, 1959), and top managers who are seen as unable or unwilling to put together a workable system for evaluating performance and for rewarding people who do their jobs well may lose the respect that is an important part of accepting their power and influence.

Social Exchange

Piening, Baluch, and Salge (2013) suggest social exchange theory is a useful perspective for understanding how and why reactions to human resource systems are important. In particular, they note that when organizations provide things (e.g., training, opportunities for salary increase and advancement) that are of potential value to employees, employees are likely to respond with favorable perceptions and behaviors.

In theory, if implemented effectively, well-constructed human resource programs and practices are likely to cause employees to view themselves in a social exchange relationship characterized by mutual trust, respect, and support (Evans & Davis, 2005; Kehoe & Wright, 2013). This positive relationship, in turn, is likely to motivate employees to perform well and to increase their commitment to the organization. On the other hand, a performance appraisal system that is viewed as unreliable, irrelevant, or tainted by politics is not only a nuisance in and of itself, it is also a signal about human resource systems more generally and even about the organization itself. That is, a performance appraisal system that does not appear to work well or to deliver rewards employees believe they deserve might be viewed as a symptom of a larger concern—that is, the organization's lack of concern for and commitment to its employees.

The questions of whether an organization's performance appraisal system is seen as a benefit or as a cost of working in an organization probably depends substantially on attitudes and perceptions we have discussed in preceding sections of this chapter. In particular, performance appraisal systems are likely to lead to a positive social exchange (i.e., one in which the employee believes he or she has received a benefit and is therefore more willing to invest in and commit to the organization) when the appraisal system is seen as fair and useful, and are likely to become a drag on the employee's willingness to exert effort for, to be loyal and attached to, and to work to advance the interests of the organization when these systems are seen as arbitrary, illegitimate, and untrustworthy.

DETERMINANTS AND EFFECTS OF REACTIONS TO APPRAISAL SYSTEMS

The preceding sections laid out the logic and theory that might be used to understand why people react in different ways to performance appraisal systems and how those reactions might influence both the appraisal system itself and other systems in the organization. This section examines the empirical evidence regarding the determinants and the effects of reactions to performance appraisal systems.

Determinants of Reactions to Appraisal Systems

There are several features of performance appraisal system that are likely to influence reactions to those systems. Dipboye and de Pontbriand (1981) identify three system components that can increase satisfaction with performance appraisal: (1) allowing system participants to have a voice, (2) rating employees on job-relevant factors, and (3) discussing plans and objectives with employees. Their recommendations are echoed by Bobko and Colella (1994), who emphasize the importance of clear performance standards.

Burke and colleagues (Burke & Wilcox, 1969; Burke, Weitzel, & Weir, 1978) focused on identifying characteristics of effective performance reviews interviews. They considered a number of criteria in defining what constituted an effective review, including subordinates' satisfaction with the appraisal, satisfaction with their supervisor, perceived fairness and utility of the appraisal, subordinates' motivation to improve performance, and actual performance improvement. Higher levels of participation (i.e., the degree to which subordinates' felt they had the opportunity to present their own ideas and feelings during the performance interview), goal setting, and identifying and "clearing up" job problems all were found to be significantly related to satisfaction with the appraisal, perceived fairness and utility of the performance review, more positive attitude toward future reviews, motivation to improve performance, and actual improvement in performance (Burke et al., 1978). Subsequent research has provided additional support for several of these findings, particularly regarding the role of participation in driving reactions to performance appraisal

SPOTLIGHT 10.1 DOES ANYONE LOVE PERFORMANCE APPRAISAL?

There is no shortage of articles criticizing performance appraisal (Adler et al., 2016; Ford, 2004; Gordon & Stewart, 2009; Pettijohn, Parker, Pettijohn, & Kent, 2001; Taylor, 1985). Does anyone love performance appraisal? One way to answer this question is to conduct a Google Search using a range of relevant search terms. We did just that using the following set of search terms: (1) loving performance appraisal, (2) liking performance appraisal, and (3) positive views of performance appraisal.[1] We found a large number of stories about why people hate performance appraisal, or about the impending demise of performance appraisal, with a sprinkling of stories of performance appraisal and performance management systems that produced some positive effects, but it is clear that performance appraisal is tolerated,

not loved. It is also clear that performance appraisal is not going away any time soon (Cleveland & Murphy, 2016). It fulfils a number of important functions in organizations, and there is no viable replacement on the horizon.

We believe it is best to think about performance appraisal much in the same way you think about your visits to the dental hygienist. It is not fun, but it is something that must be done frequently, and must be done well. Failure to attend to performance appraisals will lead to some of the same consequences as failure to get your teeth professionally cleaned—an increased chance of decay and eventual rot. We may never learn to love performance appraisal, but we should learn to put up with it and to do the best job possible when performance appraisal time rolls around.

systems. Cawley, Keeping, and Levy's (1998) meta-analysis found a strong relationship ($r = .61$) between participation and positive reactions. In particular, these authors identified participation to be most related to satisfaction. Echoing the findings of Korsgaard and Roberson (1995), Cawley and colleagues also show that reactions are more related to value-expressive participation (voice) than instrumental participation (influencing the end result).

Several studies have showed that perceptions of fairness and accuracy can be influenced by other system design features, including existence of a formal evaluation program, the frequency of performance evaluations, supervisor's knowledge of subordinate's job duties and performance levels, the relevance of performance dimensions, opportunities for subordinates to express their opinion, and the development of performance improvement plans (Landy, Barnes-Farrell, & Cleveland, 1980; Dipboye & de Pontbriand, 1981). In addition, there is evidence that when raters are seen as credible, this can lead to positive reactions to both the source and the evaluation (Albright & Levy, 1995). However, if ratees perceive a large discrepancy between their perception of performance and the evaluations they receive, the positive effect is reduced (Albright & Levy, 1995).

Low evaluations often lead to negative reactions and beliefs that the feedback is inaccurate, which reduced the likelihood ratees will actually use the feedback they receive (Brett & Atwater, 2001; Williams & Lueke, 1999). Flint (1999) found that when ratings are low, ratees rely on perceptions of procedural justice in determining fairness. If the ratee perceives the system to be just, they are more likely to be motivated to accept low ratings and make efforts to improve performance. Further research in procedural justice yielded the possibility of two unique dimensions within the construct. Erdogan, Kraimer, and Liden (2001) differentiate between system procedural justice, made up of perceived validity and knowledge of performance criteria, and rater procedural justice, made up of perceived performance feedback and fairness of voice. Research also examines the implementation of new systems. When previous systems were perceived as unfair, a new procedurally just system is likely to lead to more favorable reactions (Taylor, Masterson, Renard, & Tracy, 1998).

Trust in the appraisal process also influences supervisor and subordinate acceptance (Hedge & Teachout, 2000). Mayer and Davis (1999) sought to clarify the construct of trust as applied to the subordinate–supervisor relationship in the context of performance appraisals. They found three major components: (1) ability to appraise, (2) benevolence toward employees, and (3) integrity. All three components lead to predict favorable employee attitudes. Trust might also influence the relationship between attitudes toward human resource systems and attitudes toward the organization on the whole. For example, there is evidence that attitudes toward performance appraisal help shape, and are themselves shaped by, attitudes toward the organization. In particular, there is evidence that perceptions of the procedural, distributive, and interactional fairness of performance appraisals is higher in units where there is stronger trust in senior management, and that perceptions of justice in performance appraisal enhance the link between trust in senior management and organizational commitment (Farndale & Kelliher, 2013). Reactions to performance appraisal are systematically affected by the quality of the rater–ratee relationship, trust in the supervisor, and perceptions of social support (Levy & Williams, 2004). Favorable performance ratings and participation in the appraisal process are also related to reactions to performance appraisal systems (Cawley et al., 1998; Dulebohn & Ferris, 1999).

Attitudes toward appraisal systems are not determined solely by the features of those systems, but are also influenced by demographic variables. The literature shows that in general, men react less positively to feedback from female supervisors (Geddes & Konrad, 2003). There has also been recent research on the effects of age on reactions to feedback. Wang, Burlacu, Truxillo, James, and Yao (2015) found a stronger association between favorability and delivery of feedback and reactions for older workers, whereas feedback quality was more strongly related with reactions for younger workers.

Attitudes toward appraisal may depend substantially on whether you are the rater or the ratee. For example, Bernardin, Dahmus, and Redmon (1993) studied the attitudes of raters and ratees toward appraisal in a government agency. Across a range of appraisal systems, supervisors generally showed more positive attitudes than their subordinates. Supervisors and managers often have more knowledge about the design, operations, and goals of performance appraisal systems, and this knowledge can influence their perception of the fairness of appraisals and their satisfaction with the performance appraisal system (Williams & Levy, 2000). In general, higher levels of knowledge about performance appraisal systems are associated with higher levels of satisfaction and a stronger likelihood that the system will be perceived as fair.

There are both individual differences and system-level variables that have been shown to influence raters' perceptions of and beliefs about performance appraisal systems. For example, studies have found that perceived ability to evaluate employees' performance is dependent on a rater's level of confidence (Tziner & Murphy, 1999) and self-efficacy in the performance appraisal process (Bernardin & Villanova, 2005; Tziner, Murphy, & Cleveland, 2005). Tziner, Murphy, and Cleveland (2005) attest that the proximal factor of self-efficacy is linked to a rater's tendency to provide inflated ratings.

Raters often express some degree of discomfort with performance appraisal (Bernardin, Cooke, & Villanova, 2000; Tziner & Murphy, 1999; Villanova, Bernardin, Dahmus, & Sims, 1993); this discomfort can be especially acute when there is a strong level of interdependence in the work group (Saffie-Robertson & Brutus, 2014). For example, in collectivistic cultures, there is often a strong resistance to activities or processes that distinguish some members of the work group from others. In highly interdependent work groups, raters are likely to feel uncomfortable when they are put in the role of identifying good versus poor performers.

Effects of Reactions to Appraisal Systems

Positive perceptions of and reactions to an organization's performance appraisal systems are thought to be essential to the effectiveness and long-term viability of that system (Levy & Williams, 2004; Cawley et al., 1998; Keeping & Levy, 2000). Reactions alone do not guarantee the appraisal system will be a success or a failure, however negative reactions will most certainly undermine even the most carefully developed system (Murphy & Cleveland, 1995). For example, subordinates' negative reactions to performance feedback are thought to be a key cause of the failure of many performance appraisal systems (Burke & Wilcox, 1969; Burke et al., 1978).

Perceptions of and reactions to performance appraisal systems are thought to influence a wide range of criteria. There is evidence that perceptions of human resource systems as fair or unfair influence many aspects of employee behavior and work attitudes, including job performance, job satisfaction, organizational commitment, evaluation of authority, organizational citizenship behaviors, counterproductive work behaviors, and work withdrawal (Cohen-Charash & Spector, 2001; Colquitt, Conlon, Wesson, Porter, & Ng, 2001). Implementation of a more acceptable performance appraisal system can enhance trust for management (Mayer & Davis, 1999). Finally, Jawahar (2006) found that satisfaction with performance appraisal feedback predicted future performance, and satisfaction with performance feedback was positively related to organizational commitment, job satisfaction, commitment to and satisfaction with the supervisor, and negatively related to turnover intentions (Jawahar, 2006).

Reactions appear to be an important determinant of the effectiveness of performance feedback. Jawahar (2010) argues that it is not the feedback itself that changes performance, but an employee's reaction to the feedback. If ratees view the performance appraisal system with dislike and distrust, it is unlikely that performance feedback will be accepted or acted upon (Cardy & Dobbins, 1994; Keeping & Levy, 2000). Research shows that reactions to performance feedback can influence counterproductive behavior, turnover intentions, citizenship behaviors, and affective commitment (Belschak & Den Hartog, 2009).

Satisfaction with performance appraisal processes and outcomes is not only an important determinant of the success of performance appraisal systems, it is also an important determinant of attitudes toward the organization, including trust for management, organizational commitment, and turnover intentions (Kuvaas, 2006; Mayer & Davis, 1999). The use of performance appraisal for developmental purposes, in particular, is related to job satisfaction and affective commitment to the job (Youngcourt, Leiva, & Jones, 2007). Lee and Son (1998) note that discussing the ratees' career development in the appraisal process led to higher satisfaction scores with the process as a whole. Even when appraisals are not used solely for developmental purposes, Pettijohn, Pettijohn, Taylor, and Keillor (2001) showed that a fair performance appraisal process with the option of discussing results between the rater and ratee has a positive effect on job satisfaction.

Raters' beliefs regarding performance appraisal systems not only affect attitudes toward the organization, but they also affect the quality of rating data. Tziner et al. (1998) showed that trust in performance appraisal systems, perceptions of a positive organizational climate, perceptions of strong links between performance appraisals and important outcomes (e.g., promotion, salary increase), and high-quality relationships with supervisors were related to both the mean ratings assigned and the extent to which ratings discriminated among ratees and dimensions. Tziner et al. (2005) note that attitudes toward the organization, in particular commitment to the organization, can also influence the quality of rating data.

Raters who show more trust in the performance appraisal system are more likely to discriminate among ratees when completing their performance appraisals. Commitment to the organization and perceptions of organizational climate have even stronger effects on ratings. Raters who were committed to the organization or who perceived a positive climate in the organization are *less* likely to discriminate among ratees. It is possible that raters believe that distinguishing among their subordinates will have negative impact on the climate of the workplace, but the results of Tziner et al. (1998) are at best preliminary, and this hypothesis has not been directly tested.

Finally, reactions to performance appraisal systems can lead directly to rating inflation. Raters who are uncomfortable with performance appraisal or who wish to avoid the conflict that goes with negative appraisals often respond by inflating their ratings (Bernardin et al., 2000; Villanova et al., 1993).

The Death Spiral of Appraisal Systems

Reactions to performance appraisal systems can be positive, but they are more often negative in nature. We have rarely met people who say, "The best thing about working here is the performance appraisal system." We started this book with a series of quotes illustrating the generally negative stereotype of performance appraisal systems in organizations (job managers love to hate, nobody wants to get one, nobody wants to give one . . . more of an organizational curse than a panacea . . . the performance review is dreaded). These are not simply isolated complaints; up to 90% of appraisal systems in organizations are viewed by users as ineffective (Pulakos, Mueller-Hanson, Arad, & Moye, 2015; Smith, Hornsby, & Shirmeyer, 1996). We have also described some deep-seated problems that hamstring performance appraisal systems, most notably the consistent difference between self-ratings of performance and ratings obtained from supervisors. The joint effect of a negative reputation and built-in conflicts between those who provide feedback and those who receive it creates a set of conditions we like to describe as a "death spiral," in which initially negative perceptions of performance appraisal feed on themselves and lead to appraisal behaviors that further undermine the potential effectiveness of performance appraisal systems in many organizations.

In describing the process by which beliefs about performance appraisal systems lead to behaviors, which in turn either strengthen or reverse initial beliefs, we borrow two concepts from Bayesian approaches to opinion change (Box & Tiao, 1973). First, prior opinions and beliefs are important. That is, before individuals have any concrete experience with their organization's performance appraisal system, they are likely to have some opinions or some beliefs about that system, and if prior opinions are strong, these beliefs might be quite resistant to change. Thus, a new manager who studies human resource management in college and reads paper after paper detailing the shortcomings of performance appraisal systems may come into an organization predisposed to believe that the performance appraisal system in that organization is probably not very effective. If this belief is strongly held, it may be very difficult to change this manager's mind, regardless of the actual characteristics or the actual effectiveness of the system. However, if prior opinions are not too firmly entrenched, experience with the system can lead to some revision of those opinions. That is, experiences can lead to meaningful modifications of initial impressions and beliefs, but these changes are often limited because of the ways beliefs influence the behaviors of participants in the performance appraisal process.

Figure 10.1 illustrates a sequence of events we believe is common in most performance appraisal systems. Both raters and ratees start with some general beliefs about their company's performance appraisal system, and those initial beliefs, together with their early experiences with the system, lead to potential revisions in those beliefs. Their beliefs also lead to particular sets of behaviors. In particular, raters and ratees whose initial evaluation of the performance appraisal system are positive will be more likely to respond with behaviors

FIGURE 10.1 ■ The Death Spiral of Performance Appraisal (PA) Systems

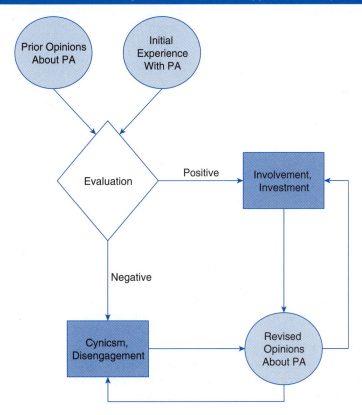

that tend to make performance appraisal successful (i.e., involvement and investment in the appraisal process). Thus, raters whose evaluations are positive may put more time and effort into delivering detailed feedback or into cross-checking their impressions of the individuals they rate. Ratees whose evaluations of the performance appraisal system are positive may be more willing to pay attention to feedback and to use it to improve their performance and effectiveness. On the other hand, raters and ratees whose evaluations are negative are more likely to react with cynicism and disengagement, putting minimal effort into appraisal and disregarding or arguing with performance feedback.

Most important, Figure 10.1 includes feedback loops. That is, your evaluation of the performance appraisal system at time 1 is likely to influence your behavior at time 2, which in turn can influence your beliefs about and reaction to the performance appraisal system. For example, a belief that your company's appraisal system is a waste of time could lead to behaviors (e.g., devoting minimal effort, disregarding feedback) that *make* the system a genuine waste of time. Thus, beliefs about performance appraisal systems may have a self-reinforcing quality, in which the way you act toward the appraisal system influences future beliefs about the system, which in turn influence future actions, influencing subsequent beliefs, and so on.

The cycle illustrated in Figure 10.1 *can* make performance appraisal systems more effective, but there are strong reasons to believe that it will generally have a negative effect, creating what we describe as a death spiral. First, there are good reasons to believe that many users start out with generally negative opinions about performance appraisal in general. Surveys of opinions regarding performance appraisal consistently show that this practice is held in low regard in many organizations (Pulakos et al., 2015; Smith et al., 1996). Second, because of persistent differences in the way people view their own performance versus the performance of others, it is almost axiomatic that many employees will end up disappointed with the evaluations and the feedback they receive, making performance appraisal a negative experience for both raters and ratees (Cleveland, Lim, & Murphy, 2007). That is, it is reasonable to expect that many people start off with somewhat negative opinions about performance appraisal in general *and* have experiences with the system that are less than positive. If this combination of initially negative opinions and beliefs and initially negative experiences with appraisal leads to behaviors that undercut the potential success of performance appraisal systems, it is likely that this set of behaviors will reinforce and strengthen negative beliefs. If this feedback system, where negative beliefs lead to negative behaviors, which in turn lead to even more negative beliefs, is allowed to go on unchecked, it is very unlikely that a successful performance appraisal system will emerge.

What should an organization do to avoid this death spiral? We will consider this question in more depth in Chapters 13 and 14, but we will note here that early intervention is probably critical. Even if raters and ratees have generally negative opinions about performance appraisal in general, they may not have strong opinions about *their particular* appraisal system until they actually use it, and an initially positive evaluation of the appraisal system could lead to a virtuous cycle rather than a death spiral, in which good impressions lead to good appraisal behaviors, which in turn lead to increasingly positive impressions of the system. Whether this can be realistically accomplished is an open question, but it is clear that intervention before employees have formed a strong negative impression (which may be highly resistant to change) is crucial.

SUMMARY

Reactions to performance appraisal systems appear to be an important determinant of the success or failure of those systems. In addition to the direct effects of reactions on performance appraisal itself, these reactions can also have wide-ranging consequences, influencing the way people think about the organization and their role in that organization. A wide range of reactions has been studied, including evaluative and affective reactions (approval and liking), beliefs about the usefulness of performance appraisal, and even beliefs about the legitimacy of performance appraisal. On the whole, the research literature suggests that several components of performance appraisal systems, especially opportunities for participation and voice, are important determinants of reactions to appraisal, but that factors such as the likelihood of receiving high ratings and rewards are also quite important.

It is likely that reactions to performance appraisal systems influence the behaviors of raters and ratees, setting up the possibility of feedback loops. In particular, negative reactions to performance appraisal may lead raters and ratees to take the system less seriously and to engage in a range of behaviors that undermine the appraisal system. It is possible that positive reactions will dominate, but in many organizations, the combination of widespread cynicism about performance appraisal and the built-in conflict between the high ratings many employees think they deserve and the less favorable opinions supervisors, peers, and other raters are likely to hold can create a "death spiral." This happens when negative reactions lead to lower engagement and involvement in appraisal, which in turn leads to even more negative reactions, and so on. Chapters 13 and 14 take up potential responses to these negative cycles in organizations.

CASE STUDY: UNDERSTANDING RESISTANCE TO PERFORMANCE APPRAISAL

Ancorr Construction employs 650 construction workers, building small to medium-size commercial properties. There are 23 managers, whose work is overseen by four senior managers. Last year, they introduced a performance appraisal system that included peer ratings and ratings from the senior managers, but they are facing increasing resistance. The managers do not like rating their peers, do not believe that the system provides useful feedback, and do not believe they are being fairly evaluated. They cooperate, grudgingly, with performance reviews, but the grumbling and dissatisfaction are visibly increasing.

Your task as a consultant is to devise a strategy to improve this system and make it more palatable and useful to the managers whose performance is being evaluated. You start by asking for more information about how the appraisal system was designed and implemented, and you find that it was adopted on the recommendation of a credible consulting firm and that the decisions about adopting and implementing this system were made by the four senior managers, in consultation with the owners of Ancorr Construction.

Research on perceptions of fairness and justice suggests one important step that can be taken to improve reactions to this appraisal system. Several studies suggest that participation and voice are important determinants of reactions to performance appraisal systems, and it appears that the managers who are being evaluated did not participate in the initial design of the performance appraisal system. You might consider several activities to get them involved in the redesign of the current system, including participation in scale development, surveys of their attitudes and perceptions, and participation in focus groups tasked with improving the system design.

Increased participation will contribute to more favorable perceptions of the system, but it probably will not fully resolve the perception that performance ratings are unfairly low. You might consider one of two approaches to reducing concerns over the fairness of ratings. First, you might increase the amount and range of information that is used in rating, incorporating more sources, ratings from multiple superiors, and more detailed, specific ratings. Alternatively, you might reduce the perceived consequences of low ratings, perhaps by de-coupling performance ratings and rewards. (We consider this strategy in more detail in Chapters 13 and 14.)

11 EVALUATING PERFORMANCE RATINGS

Performance appraisal systems ask supervisors, peers, customers, and others to make judgments about the performance of the individuals or teams being evaluated; one question that immediately comes to mind is whether these judgments are correct, or at least, whether they are close enough to being correct that we should pay attention to them. This chapter examines the different methods that are used to determine whether performance ratings provide reliable, valid, and accurate information about the performance of the ratees who are being evaluated. Furthermore, we consider a question that is important but often overlooked in performance appraisal: whether performance ratings are useful to organizations and their members.

A simple example helps to illustrate the types of information that might be used to evaluate ratings and rating systems, as well as the range of questions that might be asked when evaluating the validity, accuracy, or usefulness of ratings. Suppose that there are two supervisors (Sam and Jose) who are asked to evaluate the performance of five new nurses on a hospital ward. Each nurse is evaluated on four performance dimensions: (1) quality of patient interactions, (2) timeliness in responding to calls and emergencies, (3) accuracy in recording patient information, and (4) making good decisions about treatments and medications. Each of these performance dimensions is rated on a 7-point scale (1 = falls far short of expectations, 4 = meets expectations, 7 = far exceeds expectations), and the overall performance score is a simple sum of these four scores. Table 11.1 shows the ratings Sam and Jose give. A quick look at the ratings in Table 11.1 tells you several things:

- Sam and Jose do not agree—Sam thinks Juanita is the best nurse and Pria is second worst, but Jose thinks Pria is the best and Juanita is second from the bottom.[1]

- Jose is a more lenient rater than Sam, usually giving higher scores.[2]

- Sam does not distinguish much among performance dimensions, giving pretty similar ratings to all four performance dimensions, but Jose is more likely to distinguish relative strengths from weaknesses.[3]

LEARNING OBJECTIVES

11.1 Learn how inter-rater agreement measures are used to evaluate rating data

11.2 Understand why rater error measures were first proposed and why they turned out to be deficient measures of the quality of rating data

11.3 Learn how rating accuracy is defined and measured

11.4 Examine evidence regarding bias in performance ratings

TABLE 11.1 ■ Performance Ratings for Five Nurses		
	Rater	
Nurse	**Sam**	**Jose**
April		
Quality	5	3
Timeliness	5	5
Accuracy	4	2
Judgment	4	4
Total	18	14
Pria		
Quality	4	7
Timeliness	4	6
Accuracy	5	6
Judgment	4	7
Total	17	26
Anne		
Quality	7	7
Timeliness	5	7
Accuracy	7	4
Judgment	5	6
Total	24	24
Jasmine		
Quality	3	6
Timeliness	4	5
Accuracy	5	7
Judgment	3	5
Total	15	23
Juanita		
Quality	6	5
Timeliness	5	7
Accuracy	7	4
Judgment	7	6
Total	25	22

All three of these observations (low agreement, differences in average ratings, differences in the variability of ratings) *might* be taken as evidence that the performance ratings in Table 11.1 are not good measures of job performance. After all, Sam and Jose are evaluating the same people, but they come to very different conclusions about their performance. These data do not necessarily tell us, however, whether to believe Sam or to believe Jose (they disagree substantially), or even whether to believe either of them. The evaluation of performance appraisal systems, particularly of performance ratings or other measures of performance, is a complex undertaking, and there are a wide range of methods, indices, and metrics that have been used to evaluate ratings.

In this chapter, we will review four classes of measures that are used to evaluate rating data:

1. Measures of agreement and reliability

2. Rater error measures

3. Rating accuracy measures

4. Assessments of the validity and the usefulness of performance ratings

We will note that each of these classes of measures provides a partial answer to the questions of whether you should believe ratings like those shown in Table 11.1, and if so, whose judgment should you trust (Sam or Jose), but that in some cases, none of them fully answers these questions.

DO RATERS AGREE? THE RELIABILITY OF PERFORMANCE RATINGS

Tests, measurements, and assessments of all types are known to be imperfect, and a substantial literature has developed describing ways of assessing and improving the quality of our measures. One of the most basic requirements of a measure is that it should produce consistent scores. So, if I evaluate your overall job performance today and next week, I should expect to obtain similar scores. If two different raters evaluate the same employee's performance, they should provide similar ratings. That is, tests, assessments, and measures such as performance ratings should be consistent, or *reliable*. Tests and measures that do not demonstrate this sort of consistency might be strongly tainted by measurement error, and measures that are mostly error will have little value to the individual or to organizations.

Measurement error is an important consideration in evaluating virtually all measures, including performance ratings. Viswesvaran, Ones, and Schmidt (1996) reviewed several methods of estimating the reliability (or the freedom from random measurement error) of job performance ratings and argued that *inter-rater correlations* provided the best estimate of the reliability of performance ratings. The basic idea here is that disagreements in the ratings that two separate raters give to the same employee are an indication of measurement error, and that inter-rater correlations therefore provide a means of estimating how much measurement error is present in ratings. In several subsequent papers, they elaborated upon the rationale for using inter-rater correlations as the best estimate of the reliability of performance ratings (e.g., Schmidt, Viswesvaran, & Ones, 2000; Ones, Viswesvaran, & Schmidt, 2008).

The correlations between ratings given to the same employees by two separate raters are typically somewhat low. Viswesvaran et al. (1996) suggest that the best estimate of the average inter-rater correlation for performance ratings is approximately .52. If these inter-rater correlations are used to estimate the reliability of performance ratings, one conclusion you would reach is that approximately half (48%) of the variability in performance ratings represents random measurement error, while the other half (52%) is related to job performance.[4] A number of authors have argued that Viswesvaran et al. (1996) have greatly overestimated the role of random measurement error in performance rating, in large part because they have relied on an outdated approach to analyzing the quality of measurement (LeBreton, Scherer, & James, 2014; Murphy & DeShon, 2000). In particular, this approach to estimating the reliability of performance ratings is based on a theory of measurement that separates all of the variability in performance ratings into two categories: (1) true differences in performance, and (2) random measurement error. This approach is no longer accepted as reasonable by specialists in psychological measurement.

The methods proposed by Viswesvaran and colleagues for estimating the reliability of performance ratings are based on classical test theory (CTT), a theory that was once central to psychological measurement. The core idea of CTT is that observed scores (X) can be broken down into two independent components, true scores (T) and random measurement error (e), or $X = T + e$. This simple equation provided a starting point for a sophisticated theory of measurement and for many methods of estimating reliability (Lord & Novick, 1968). If we apply this framework to performance rating, this theory suggests that rater agreement can be explained in terms of true scores and that rater disagreement can be explained in terms of random measurement error.

By the 1970s, doubts about the usefulness of CTT were being raised (Cronbach, Gleser, Nanda, & Rajaratnam, 1972). The main problem with this framework is that it ignores sources of variability in ratings that are not either a function of the thing you are trying to measure (true scores) or random measurement errors. For example, Murphy and DeShon (2000) noted that there are many reasons why raters agree that have nothing to do with job performance. For example, there is a well-known attractiveness bias (see, for example, Drogosz & Levy, 1996); attractive ratees tend to receive more favorable ratings, and this bias can lead to systematic agreement between raters, even if the raters know nothing about the performance of the people being evaluated. Similarly, there are many reasons that raters disagree, and some of these are systematic rather than being sources of random measurement error. Murphy and DeShon (2000) suggested that generalizability theory offers a more sensible model than CTT for analyzing the reliability of performance ratings.

Generalizability theory starts with an analysis of the different sources of variability in rating. For example, suppose two raters evaluated the performance of 10 subordinates (ratees) on four performance dimensions (e.g., Production Quality, Timeliness, Efficient Use of Resources, Communication). Table 11.2 lists the potential sources of variability in ratings.

Most important, generalizability theory does not require you to assume that the only reason raters agree is because of the true performance of the people being evaluated or that the only reason they disagree is because of random error. For instance, some raters give higher ratings than others. This might be evidence of disagreement if, as in the example

TABLE 11.2 ■ Sources of Variability in Performance Ratings With Multiple Raters and Rating Contexts	
Source	**Meaning**
Ratees	Some employees perform at a higher overall level than others.
Dimensions	The group of ratees might perform better on some aspects of the job (e.g., timeliness) than others.
Raters	Some raters are more lenient than others and give higher average ratings.
Rater X Dimension	Some raters will give high ratings on some dimensions and lower ratings on others.
Ratee X Dimension	Some ratees differ from others in terms of their relative strengths and weaknesses.
Rater X Ratee	Some raters will give high ratings to some ratees and lower ratings to others.
Unexplained Variability	Some of the variability in ratings has nothing to do with raters, ratees, or contexts, and probably represents random measurement that, taken together, resemble random measurement error.

illustrated in Table 11.1, they both evaluated the same ratees (in this example, Sam gave slightly higher ratings than Jose), or it might be evidence of systematic differences in the performance of the people being rated by different supervisors. The assessment of what represents true scores and what represents errors of measurement might depend on the way rating systems are designed (e.g., do multiple raters evaluate each ratee?) and used.

In most organizations, the point of performance appraisal is to help evaluate who is doing well or poorly, and to evaluate peoples' strengths and weaknesses. If the purpose of rating is to help make between-person decisions (e.g., promotion, salary), variability due to ratees represents true score. In generalizability theory, variability due to other possible sources, such as differences between raters, differences between dimensions, or interactions (e.g., rater X ratee, and rater X dimension) are all potential sources of *systematic* measurement error. For example, in a multisource rating system, where each rater has a different perspective (e.g., supervisor, peer, subordinate), variability due to raters is expected and is not considered measurement error. If you expected supervisors, peers, subordinates, and others to all give similar ratings, there would be no real point in obtaining ratings from multiple sources (Ock, 2016).

Generalizability theory encourages you to carefully consider various explanations for the variability in performance ratings and to collect data that will allow you to estimate exactly how each of these effects will influence the generalizability of ratings. Generalizability depends substantially on exactly what you are trying to measure (e.g., between versus within-person differences), and you cannot simply assume that these effects are small or even that they are independent from one another or from true scores. Thus, generalizability theory requires a detailed and sophisticated understanding of how ratings will actually be used and interpreted before numerical estimates of reliability can be obtained.

A number of studies have examined the roles of systematic and random error in performance ratings, as well as methods of estimating systematic and random error (Fleenor, Fleenor, & Grossnickle, 1996; Greguras & Robie, 1998; Hoffman, Lance, Bynum, & Gentry, 2010; Hoffman & Woehr, 2009; Kasten & Nevo, 2008; Lance, 1994; Lance, Baranik, Lau, & Scharlau, 2009; Lance, Teachout, & Donnelly, 1992; Mount, Judge, Scullen, Sytsma, & Hezlett, 1998; Murphy, 2008a; O'Neill, McLarnon, & Carswell, 2015; Putka, Le, McCloy, & Diaz, 2008; Saal, Downey, & Lahey, 1980; Scullen, Mount, & Goff, 2000; Woehr, Sheehan, & Bennett, 2005). In general, these studies suggest: (1) that there are indeed systematic sources of measurement error that CTT overlooks, and (2) there is considerably less random measurement error in performance ratings than studies of inter-rater correlation would suggest. For example, Scullen et al. (2000) and Greguras and Robie (1998) examined sources of variability in ratings obtained from multiple raters. They found that about one-third of the variance in performance ratings obtained from multiple raters is likely due to ratee performance. There is both systematic and idiosyncratic rater variance present in ratings; about 15% of the variance is likely due to differences in ratings due to perspective (i.e., differences in the ratings from raters at different levels in the organization). The largest source of variance in ratings is due to raters, some of which is likely due to biases or general rater tendencies (e.g., leniency).

Greguras, Robie, Schleicher, and Goff (2003) applied generalizability theory to the analysis of ratings collected from multisource rating systems that were used for either administrative or developmental purposes. Their analysis showed that a substantial portion of the variability in performance ratings in these systems is due to Rater and Rater x Ratee effects, and that variability due to performance differences across Ratees was smaller than variability due to Raters and Rater x Ratee interactions of unexplained variability in ratings (measurement error).

Dierdorff and Surface (2007) analyzed peer ratings collected in a variety of contexts, and while they did not apply generalizability theory in their analysis, their findings converge with those cited above, showing that there are strong and systematic context effects in peer ratings, and that these are distinct from both ratee performance and random error. Similarly, in their analyses of multirater systems, both Hoffman et al. (2010) and Woehr et al. (2005) report substantial source effects, indicating systematic differences in what ratings obtained from different sources (e.g., supervisors versus peers) measure.

In general, studies of the sources of variability in performance ratings lead to a few important conclusions:

- Differences between ratees are usually to be larger than differences within ratees. That is, performance ratings appear to more reliably tell us who is a better or worse performer than what strengths and weaknesses individual employees show.

- Differences between raters are, on the whole, at least as big as differences between ratees. This may be an effect of rating inflation; if most ratees receive high ratings, differences between ratees must be small.

- Ratings are not as unreliable as inter-rater correlations would suggest, but they often include multiple sources of variability that is probably not linked to the performance of the individuals being rated.

Rather than attaching a single reliability coefficient to ratings, O'Neill et al. (2015) suggest that we consider the inferences we are attempting to draw from ratings. Consider the following possibilities:

- Based on their overall average, can I conclude that Juanita is a better performer than Pria?

- Based on the overall averages, can I conclude that the overall performance of the four people who report to one supervisor is higher than the overall performance of the six people who report to another supervisor?

- Based on their scores on individual performance dimensions, can I conclude that Pria has different strengths and weaknesses than Juanita?

Different reliability coefficients would be used in answering each of the questions above, and generalizability theory provides a useful framework for calculating these coefficients.

Reliability of Multisource Ratings

Performance appraisal systems that use multiple raters, including but not limited to 360-degree rating systems, provide unique opportunities to isolate and reduce several potential sources of systematic and random measurement error in ratings. For example, in a traditional performance appraisal system, in which each employee is rated by his or her direct supervisor, it is hard to tell what ratings tell us about the rater versus the performance of the person being rated. If there are multiple raters, it might be possible to separate variability that is due to the rater from variability that is due to the person being rated, and in a multilevel system, it might be possible to go further, separating systematic differences in what is observed or the perspectives taken by peers, supervisors, subordinates, or customers from variability in ratings that is due to simple disagreements between similarly situated raters. Conway (1998) proposed and demonstrated methods for analyzing multi-rater or multilevel data and showed how these methods could be used to test specific hypotheses about biases in rating. Lance (1994) described a related model that could be used to identify rater and rating source biases in performance ratings.

There are two questions that are important to ask when comparing ratings from different sources: (1) are there systematic differences? and (2) do they agree? The answer is yes and no. There are systematic differences; self-ratings are generally higher than ratings from others (Valle & Bozeman, 2002). Agreement between subordinates, peers, and supervisors is typically modest, with uncorrected correlations in the .20s and .30s (Conway & Huffcutt, 1997; Valle & Bozeman, 2002). However, given the low levels of reliability for each source, it is likely that the level of agreement among sources is actually somewhat higher. Harris and Schaubroeck (1988) report corrected correlations between sources in the mid .30s to low .60s. Viswesvaran, Schmidt, and Ones (2002) apply a more aggressive set of corrections and suggest that in ratings of overall performance and some specific performance dimensions, peers and supervisors show quite high levels of agreement.

This disagreement between rating sources is not necessarily a bad thing. Different sources have very different information and perhaps different standards when evaluating performance; the rationale of multisource systems is that different sources *should* disagree and that by obtaining information from many sources, you will get the fullest possible picture of each ratee's performance (Borman, 1974; Bozeman, 1997; Gorman, Cunningham, Bergman, & Meriac, 2016; Hoffman et al., 2010). Nevertheless, these data do suggest that the common practice of relying on only one source (the direct supervisor) is unlikely to provide high-quality assessments of performance.[5] Hoffman et al. (2012) suggest that the quality of multisource ratings could be improved by adopting rating scales that more clearly define performance dimensions, but it is not clear that this will fully resolve the potential problems caused by differences in the perspectives of subordinates, supervisors, and peers.

Classical test theory suggests that adding more raters should increase both the reliability and validity of performance ratings, but as Howard (2016) has shown, adding more raters has limited effects on reliability and validity, in part because raters often show a mix of random and systematic disagreements. When you are developing an ability test, or a test of knowledge, it is sometimes possible to make the test more reliable by adding items that are essentially parallel measures (i.e., items that all measure pretty much the same thing). The same strategy is not feasible in performance rating—raters are simply not parallel measures. Rather, each rater brings different information, perspectives, biases, and rating tendencies to the task, and these do not simply cancel out as you add more raters to the appraisal process.

Tornow (1993) asked the provocative question of whether multisource ratings should be thought of as a means or an end. That is, we could think of multisource rating systems as a means to get the most accurate assessment of a ratee's performance, in which case disagreements among raters could be a real problem. Alternately, we could think of multisource systems as a tool for development and discovery, in which disagreement among sources becomes just another data point that might prove useful. That is, it might be more useful to find out that your peers regard you as a poor communicator while your customers think you are quite good in communicating information and advice than to find out the average across all raters. Unfortunately, the data presented by Greguras, Robie et al. (2003) suggests that multisource ratings do not provide reliable measures of ratees' overall performance level. What should be a strength of a multisource system (obtaining data from multiple perspectives) is likely a weakness if these ratings are used to make distinctions between ratees.

It is commonly assumed that raters are more likely to agree on specific, observable aspects of behavior than on more abstract dimensions (Borman, 1979). Roch, Paquin, and Littlejohn (2009) conducted two studies to test this proposition, and their results suggest that the opposite is true. Inter-rater agreement is actually higher for dimensions that are less observable or that are judged to be more difficult to rate. Roch et al. (2009) speculate that this seemingly paradoxical finding may reflect the fact that when there is less concrete behavioral information available, raters might fall back on their general impressions of ratees when rating specific performance dimensions.

Other studies (e.g., Sanchez & De La Torre, 1996) have reported that accuracy in observing behavior is positively correlated with accuracy in evaluating performance. That is, raters who have an accurate recall of what they have observed do appear to be more accurate in evaluating ratees. Unfortunately, accuracy in behavioral observation does not appear to be related in any simple way to the degree to which the behavior in question is observable or easy to rate.

RATER ERROR MEASURES

There are several well-known patterns in performance ratings that suggest that these ratings are flawed measures. First, it is not unusual to find that 80–90% of all employees are rated as "Above Average." Second, differences in the ratings received by different employees often seem small, given obvious differences in their performance. Third, ratings on conceptually distinct aspects of performance are often highly correlated. One explanation for these phenomena is that raters make systematic errors in their evaluations of performance.

Discussion of the three most common rater errors—leniency, range restriction, and halo error—can be traced back over 60 years (Bingham, 1939; Kingsbury, 1922, 1933). These concepts still influence the ways in which rating data are analyzed (Saal et al., 1980; Sulsky & Balzer, 1988) and have provided the foundation for a large body of research. We find it useful to deal separately with two classes of so-called "rater errors": (a) distributional errors, and (b) correlational errors.

Distributional Errors

Examining the distribution of the performance ratings a particular rater assigns has long been thought to provide important clues to particular rating tendencies that might create problems in organizations and that might indicate symptomatic errors on the rater's part. Suppose, for example, that there are three supervisors (Frank, Janice, and Al) in different parts of a manufacturing plant who each rate 10 employees, and the distributions of their ratings take the form shown in Figure 11.1.

Frank gave low ratings to just about everyone. Janice gave ratings near the middle of the scale to everyone. Al gave high ratings to just about everyone. It is, of course, possible that all of Al's subordinates are great workers, all of Frank's are terrible, and all of Janice's are truly average employees, but it is more likely that the ratings tell us more about the raters than about the employees being rated. Figure 11.1 suggests that Al is a lenient rater, while

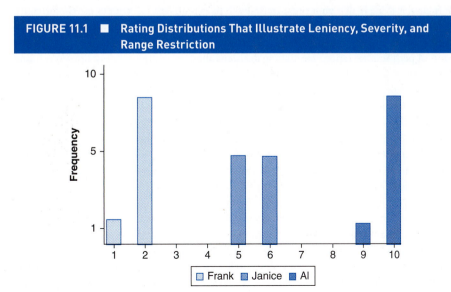

FIGURE 11.1 ■ Rating Distributions That Illustrate Leniency, Severity, and Range Restriction

Frank is a severe one. It also suggests that Janice is unwilling to identify either high or low performance, and that none of the three raters makes distinctions among the 10 employees he or she supervises. That is, the three raters appear to be committing common rater errors. We say these raters *appear to* commit rater errors because we assume that there are usually some meaningful differences in the level of performance individual employees exhibit and that not everyone is either a wonderful or a terrible employee, but we do not necessarily *know* this.

The assumptions that underlie most measures of leniency, range restriction, and central tendency have been criticized. First, the true distribution of the performance of the group of employees who report to a single supervisor is almost always unknown, and there is typically no empirical justification for the assumption that it is normal and centered around the scale midpoint (Bernardin & Beatty, 1984). Rather, organizations exert considerable effort to assure that the distribution of performance is not normal. Saal et al. (1980) point out that a variety of activities, ranging from personnel selection to training, are designed to produce a skewed distribution of performance. Any rational personnel manager would be pleased if all of the employees in a company were exceptional workers. Second, these assumptions imply that there is no variation, from work group to work group, in terms of their actual performance (Murphy & Balzer, 1989). Thus, if I give ratings whose mean is 5.0 (7-point scale), and you give ratings whose mean is 4.1, I am likely to be labeled as the more lenient rater. However, it is entirely possible that my subordinates *are* better performers than yours. There is a substantial literature on leadership that assumes that work groups will differ in their performance, depending in part on the effectiveness of the leader (Landy, 1985). It seems illogical to assume that all groups perform at the same level, regardless of their resources, their leadership, their task, and so on.

The distribution of performance ratings is probably more informative when analyzing the performance rating system of an organization or of some large unit in that organization than when it is used to analyze the ratings given by an individual supervisor. If you find (as is often reported in organizations) that 90% of employees receive ratings of "Well Above Average" or higher, it is likely that your organization will have problems if it tries to use performance ratings to make promotions or to assign merit raises. The tendency of raters to give all of their subordinates high ratings, or even similar ratings, could greatly diminish the potential value of performance ratings for making decisions about promotions, raises, or even training needs (Barrett, 1966; Bretz, Milkovich, & Read, 1992). On the other hand, when we look at the ratings given by individual raters, it sometimes is plausible that the distributions of performance ratings *do* reflect the true performance of employees. Going back to Figure 11.1, it is possible (but perhaps not likely) that Al's subordinates really *are* very good performers. Despite the fact that distributional measures have been used in many studies to indicate the presence and severity of rater errors (DeNisi & Murphy, 2017), our inability to sort out the roles of raters, ratees, and the rating environment in explaining why performance ratings show particular distributions severely limits the value of measures of leniency, severity, central tendency, or range restriction as criteria for evaluating performance ratings.

On the other hand, it is likely that some raters are more lenient in their performance evaluations than others. It has long been believed that some raters are consistently more likely to give high ratings than others (Guilford, 1954), and there is evidence to support this belief (Kane, Bernardin, Villanova, & Peyrefitte, 1995). On the whole, leniency appears to be related to the rater's personality, particularly his or her level of agreeableness and conscientiousness (Bernardin, Cooke, & Villanova, 2000; Roch, Ayman, Newhouse, & Harris, 2005). However, there is also considerable evidence that leniency is influenced by contextual variables such as the purpose of rating. Ratings are consistently highest when they are used for administrative purposes (Bernardin & Orban, 1990; Dobbins, Cardy, & Truxillo, 1986; Harris, Smith, & Champagne, 1995; Murphy & Cleveland, 1995; Taylor & Wherry, 1951). Jawahar and Williams' (1997) meta-analysis suggests that ratings for administrative purposes are one-third of a standard deviation higher than ratings used for research or developmental purposes.

Correlational Errors

Raters tend to give similar evaluations to separate aspects of a person's performance, even when performance dimensions are clearly distinct (Bingham, 1939; Newcomb, 1931; Thorndike, 1920). The result is an inflation of the intercorrelations among dimensions, which is referred to as halo error. Cooper (1981b) suggests that halo is likely to be present in virtually every type of rating instrument.

There is an extensive body of research examining halo errors in rating, and a number of different measures, definitions, and models of halo error have been proposed (Balzer & Sulsky, 1992; Cooper, 1981a, 1981b; Lance et al., 1994; Murphy & Anhalt, 1992; Murphy, Jako, & Anhalt, 1993; Nathan & Tippins,1989; Solomonson & Lance, 1997). While there is disagreement regarding some minor points, there is clear agreement regarding several propositions:

1. The correlation between ratings of separate performance dimensions reflects both actual consistencies in performance (true halo, or the actual level of correlation between two conceptually distinct performance dimensions) and errors in processing information about ratees or in translating that information into performance ratings (illusory halo).[6]

2. Illusory halo is driven in large part by raters' tendency to rely on general impressions and global evaluations (e.g., Sam is a generally good worker) when rating specific aspects of performance (see, for example, Balzer & Sulsky, 1992; Jennings, Palmer, & Thomas, 2004; Lance et al., 1994; Murphy & Anhalt, 1992).

3. Halo is likely to limit the accuracy of ratings as tools for identifying individual strengths and weaknesses, but it may *enhance* the accuracy of ratings as tools for distinguishing between ratees in terms of their overall performance levels.

This last point might seem counterintuitive, because it implies that rater errors can make performance ratings more accurate. As we will describe in more detail in the section that follows, "accuracy" can mean many different things, and it is in fact true that if ratings on different aspects of performance are highly correlated, this will tend to increase the reliability of overall performance evaluations, in effect maximizing the differences *between* rates by minimizing the differences in ratings *within* rates.

Like distributional measures, measures of halo error are very difficult to interpret because it is difficult, if not impossible, to separate true halo from illusory halo. For example, suppose ratings of Oral Communication are correlated .60 with ratings of Planning and Organization. Does this indicate that halo error is present? This conclusion can only be drawn if there is a good reason to believe that accurate ratings of this set of ratees would result in a different (almost certainly lower) correlation between Oral Communication and Planning and Organization. Even if the expected correlation between two rating dimensions is known in general (for example, in the population as a whole several of the Big Five personality dimensions are believed to be essentially uncorrelated), that does not mean that the performance of a small group of ratees on these dimensions will show the same pattern of true independence.

SPOTLIGHT 11.1 IS HALO ERROR REALLY AN ERROR?

Bingham (1939) introduced the idea that raters might make an error in evaluating different aspects of the performance of the people they supervised by relying too heavily on general impressions or overall evaluations—that is, they might make halo errors. For the next 50 years, measures of halo represented one of the most common criteria for evaluating performance ratings. Different researchers suggested different indices, but in general, the higher the correlation among ratings of supposedly separate performance dimensions, the more likely ratings would be regarded as exhibiting halo.

Measures of halo error have always been problematic. As Bingham (1939) recognized, it is very difficult to determine whether ratings of separate aspects of performance are correlated because of halo errors, or whether they are correlated because the dimensions themselves are correlated (Murphy & Anhalt, 1992). Suppose, for example, that when you analyze performance ratings in your organization, you find that ratings of Planning are correlated .50 with ratings of Oral Communication. This might be evidence of halo error, but it also might be evidence that people who are good at planning are also good at oral communication. It is even possible that the correlation between ratings of these two performance dimensions are too low, and that the correlation between the behaviors that constitute Planning and Oral Communication is higher than .50. Murphy, Jako, and Anhalt (1993) argue that there were so many ambiguities associated with the most common measures of halo that they should not be used as criteria for evaluating ratings.

It is worth asking the more basic question of whether we should think of halo as an error at all. First, there is evidence that the validity of common

predictors of job performance is *higher* when ratings of separate aspects of performance are highly intercorrelated than when they are uncorrelated (Nathan & Tippins, 1989). Second, the argument that evaluations of separate aspects of performance should be independent of your evaluation of each ratee's overall performance is in many respects illogical (Murphy, 1982b). Would it be possible, for example, for someone to be a poor performer on each performance dimension that is rated, but still be regarded as a generally effective employee? Overall performance is almost certainly based on an employee's success in carrying out the major aspects of his or her job, and in a performance appraisal system that has any level of job-relatedness, the performance dimensions that are rated should cover most of the essential functions of the job. From this perspective, finding that ratings of each of the major aspects of job performance were independent of evaluations of the employee's overall performance would be a signal that there was something wrong with the performance appraisal system.

You might argue that raters commit halo errors if they rely too heavily on their overall impressions when rating separate performance dimensions, but nobody has been able to articulate sensible criteria for determining when raters are paying too much attention, too little attention, or just the right amount of attention to employees' overall effectiveness when rating their performance on specific aspects or dimensions of performance. There is no doubt that raters sometimes make halo errors, but attempts to control or eliminate halo in performance ratings have rarely made things better, and have often had a negative impact on the quality of rating data (Murphy, 1982b; Murphy et al., 1993).

Evaluating Rater Error Measures

As we have noted in several chapters, it is common for the great majority of employees to receive ratings near the top end of the rating scale. It is also common for ratings on conceptually independent aspects of job performance to be highly correlated. Unfortunately, rater error measures that are based on the distributions and the intercorrelations among the ratings given by an individual rater have proved essentially useless for evaluating performance ratings (DeNisi & Murphy, 2017; Murphy & Balzer, 1989). First, we cannot say with any confidence that a particular supervisor's ratings are too high or too highly intercorrelated unless we know a good deal about the true level of performance, and if we knew this, we would not need supervisory performance ratings. Second, the label "rater error" is misleading. It is far from clear that supervisors who give their subordinates high ratings are making a mistake. Chapters 9 and 12 examine in detail the reasons for rating inflation and related phenomena, and they make the case that raters who give high performance ratings are sometimes making a smart decision about the best way to use performance appraisal systems to motivate their subordinates.

Rater error measures represent one of the first concerted efforts to evaluate performance ratings. Research on so-called rater errors may not have told us much about the quality of rating data, but it has substantially advanced our understanding of topics ranging from cognition to motivation. Chapters 13–14 will discuss some of the insights this research has produced.

RATING ACCURACY

Rater error measures and measures of the reliability of ratings can be thought of as indirect assessments of the accuracy of performance ratings. That is, performance ratings that are not reliable cannot be very accurate measures of performance. If ratings reflect little more than random measurement error, they cannot tell you much about the performance of the people being evaluated. Similarly, ratings that are unduly lenient, or that fail to provide distinct information about distinct aspects of performance, are probably not very accurate. Both reliability and rater error measures are essentially negative indicators, in the sense that the absence of measurement error or of distributional or correlational errors makes it possible that ratings are accurate. However, there is no guarantee that error measures that do not suffer from excessive measurement error, leniency, or halo *will* provide accurate assessments of performance. It is possible that raters whose ratings are normally distributed and not highly intercorrelated are nevertheless inaccurate in their assessments of ratee performance.

For many decades, the lack of direct measures of the accuracy of performance ratings was a serious impediment to determining whether or not the conditions under which performance ratings were sufficiently accurate to provide credible assessments of job performance. Starting in the late 1970s, laboratory studies of performance rating provided opportunities for directly measuring rating accuracy. Two distinct types of accuracy measures were developed: behavior-based measures and judgmental measures. Behavior-based measures are considerably simpler, and are based on the rater's accuracy in recognizing specific behavioral incidents (Lord, 1985). For example, Murphy, Philbin, and Adams (1989) studied the effects of purpose of observation on behavior-recognition accuracy. They asked raters to indicate whether each of 36 behavioral incidents had or had not occurred in the videotapes of performance they had observed. Since the true status of each behavior can be determined (here, 18 behaviors actually occurred and 18 did not), it was possible to measure observational accuracy in terms of true positives and true negatives (hits), false positives (false alarms), and false negatives (misses). When responses are coded in this way (e.g., true positives, true negatives) signal detection theory can be employed to derive measures of response bias and sensitivity (Lord, 1985).

Even more useful were the measures developed by Borman (1977, 1978, 1979). Borman's key insight was that in laboratory studies, where it is common for subjects to make judgments about videotapes of people performing various jobs, it would be possible to develop a credible standard for evaluating whether or not a particular rater's judgments were accurate. In particular, if multiple well-trained raters were given opportunities to view performance under optimal rating conditions (e.g., no distractions of competing task demands), the average of their ratings could be considered a type of "true-score" measure of performance. The true-score measures represent assessments that remove the biases that might characterize individual judgments (by pooling over multiple raters) as well as the errors in observation, encoding, and memory that are typical of performance judgments in the field, and a rater whose judgments are close to those true scores can reasonably be labeled as an accurate rater. Measures of accuracy in judgment have been widely used, especially in cognitively oriented research on performance judgments (Becker & Cardy, 1986; Borman, 1977, 1978, 1979; Cardy & Dobbins, 1986; McIntyre, Smith, & Hassett, 1984; Murphy & Balzer, 1986; Murphy, Balzer, Kellam, & Armstrong, 1984; Murphy, Garcia, Kerkar, Martin, & Balzer, 1982; Pulakos, 1986; see Sulsky & Balzer, 1988 for a review of accuracy measures).

Operational Definitions

Suppose a panel of experts evaluates the performance of 10 individuals, rating each individual on five different performance dimensions. The average rating from this panel could be used as true-score measures, and a comparison between an individual rater and this true-score average could be used to evaluate that rater's accuracy. As Cronbach (1955) noted, there are several ways we could define and assess the agreement between an individual rater who evaluates the same 10 individuals and these true scores. He identified four separate components of accuracy: (1) Elevation, (2) Differential Elevation, (3) Stereotype Accuracy, and (4) Differential Accuracy.

Elevation refers to the accuracy of the average rating, over all ratees and dimensions. So, if the average true score for these 10 individuals is 3.5, and the average rating a particular rater assigns is also 3.5, you could think about this rater as showing perfect accuracy, at least with regard to the overall rating level. Measures of Elevation are conceptually related to leniency measures, with the advantage of providing a direct standard for judging whether a particular rater is giving ratings that are too high (lenient), too low (severe), or in the right ballpark.

Differential Elevation refers to accuracy in discriminating among ratees. If the pooled judgment of experts indicates, for example, that Joe is a better performer than Adam, and that Adam is a better performer than Scott, a rater who also gives higher ratings to Joe and lower ratings to Scott will be accurate in making these between-ratee distinctions. As we noted in Chapter 8, many of the most important uses of ratings (e.g., for making decisions about promotion of salary) depend on making accurate distinctions between people, which suggests that Differential Elevation is a critically important aspect of rating accuracy.

Stereotype Accuracy refers to accuracy in discriminating among performance dimensions. For example, if dimensions being rated include "Planning" and "Oral Communication," Stereotype Accuracy involves accuracy in determining whether a group of workers is in fact better at planning or at oral communication. If the purpose of rating includes diagnosing training and development needs in a work group or an organization, Stereotype Accuracy might be the most important aspect of performance.

Finally, Differential Accuracy refers to accuracy in detecting ratee differences in patterns of performance (i.e., accuracy in diagnosing individual strengths and weakness). For example, in evaluating individual training needs, it might be important to figure out each employee's distinct strengths and weaknesses, and Differential Accuracy might be very important for this purpose.

Cronbach's (1955) found components are not the only measures of the accuracy of performance judgments. Measures of distance accuracy and correlational accuracy have also been proposed (Becker & Cardy, 1986; Borman, 1977; Wiggins, 1973). Research suggests that the different accuracy measures are not highly correlated (Sulsky & Balzer, 1988). For example, Murphy and Balzer (1989) noted that the average correlation among Cronbach's (1955) four measures is essentially zero. One implication is that the conclusions you draw about a rater's accuracy results may depend more on the choice of accuracy measures than on the rater's ability to evaluate his or her subordinates (Becker & Cardy, 1986).

Rater Errors and Rating Accuracy

Research on the relationship between rater errors and rating accuracy confirmed many of the concerns of researchers and practitioners who had questioned the value of using measures of leniency, halo, or other rater errors to evaluate performance ratings. The general trend in this literature is clear: rater error measures are largely unrelated to direct measures of the accuracy of ratings (Becker & Cardy, 1986; Bernardin & Pence, 1980; Borman, 1977; Murphy & Balzer, 1989).

One additional indication of the dubious relationship between rater errors and rating accuracy comes from the rater training literature. A favorite method of training has been to inform raters of the existence and nature of rater errors, and exhort them to avoid those errors. This method does indeed reduce rater errors, but it also reduces the accuracy of ratings (Bernardin & Beatty, 1984; Bernardin & Pence, 1980; Borman, 1979; Landy & Farr, 1983). It appears that rater error training leads raters to substitute an invalid rating bias (avoid rater errors) for whatever strategy they were using before rating. Avoiding errors simply doesn't address the question of accuracy.

Is Accuracy a Useful Criterion?

One of the challenges in evaluating the quality of rating data is that direct measures of rating accuracy are notoriously difficult to obtain in the field (Murphy & Cleveland, 1995). Proxies, such as rater error measures, are not good indicators of accuracy (Murphy, Jako, & Anhalt, 1993). Furthermore, raters appear to have a hard time evaluating the accuracy of the ratings they provide (Roch, McNall, & Caputo, 2011), although they do have some ability to determine their accuracy in observing and recording behavioral information.

There is evidence that we can increase rating accuracy by encouraging raters to take careful behavioral notes and to attend carefully to ratee performance (Mero, Motowidlo, & Anna, 2003; Sanchez & De La Torre, 1996). There is also evidence that increasing accountability (e.g., by asking raters to justify their evaluations) may increase rating accuracy (Mero & Motowidlo, 1995). However, as with many other suggestions for improving the quality of rating data, it is always worth asking whether the probable payoff offsets the probable costs.

Mero et al. (2003) based their conclusions on simulations and laboratory studies, where raters have little to do other than observing and evaluating ratee behavior. In work settings, supervisors and managers have a number of tasks they must perform, and time they spend on taking behavioral notes and careful observation is arguably time they could have spent doing their other tasks. That is, if raters increase the time and energy they devote to getting the most accurate ratings, they will tend to devote less time and energy to their other duties, and this will have a payoff to organizations if and only if getting more accurate ratings is more valuable and useful than whatever else supervisors and managers were doing.

On the whole, research on rating accuracy has been useful, but it has also been limited in terms of the types of questions it can answer. Accuracy measures are only feasible in artificial laboratory environments, where expert ratings obtained under ideal rating conditions can be pooled to create credible "true score" measures. This means that rating accuracy cannot be measured or studied in real-world settings, where there may be barriers to accuracy in rating due to the pressure of competing job responsibilities (unlike laboratory experiments, raters in organizations have a number of jobs to do in addition to observing and evaluating ratee performance) or to a wide range of motivational factors that will be discussed in Chapter 12. While accurate ratings might be desirable in many situations, there are simply no good methods for evaluating the accuracy of ratings in most organizational settings. Instead of directly evaluating accuracy, we are often forced to rely on indirect criteria. Some of these, such as measures of agreement and reliability, are broadly useful, while others, such as measures of halo or leniency, are of dubious value. An alternative to relying on measures of agreement and rater error measures to evaluate the quality of rating data is to apply a strategy that is widely used in psychological testing—that is, using multiple types of data to evaluate the construct validity of performance ratings (Astin, 1964; James, 1973; Smith, 1976).

CONSTRUCT VALIDITY OF PERFORMANCE RATINGS

Many tests and assessments are designed to measure *constructs*, such as Intelligence or Agreeableness. A construct is a label we use to describe a set of related behaviors or phenomena. Constructs do not exist in a literal sense (you cannot put a pound of Agreeableness on the table in front of you), but they are an extremely useful tool for describing and understanding human behavior. Most assessments of the validity of tests, rating scales, and the like can be thought of as assessments of the construct validity of those instruments (Cronbach, 1990; Murphy & Davidshofer, 2005).

There is no single method that is used to evaluate the construct validity of a test or a measure. Rather, construct validation involves the collection of evidence from a range of sources about whether a test measures what it is intended to measure. In this sense, the assessment of the construct validity of performance ratings involves collecting evidence that can help you determine whether or not, and how well, performance ratings measure actual job performance.

Several classes of evidence might be used in evaluating the construct validity of job performance ratings. First, we might look at the content of the scales used to rate performance. Rating scales that are based on a careful analysis of the job and that provide clear, unambiguous definitions of the performance dimensions to be rated are more likely to provide a valid measure of job performance than ambiguous scales that are not clearly job related. In Chapter 6, we noted that one advantage of using behaviorally anchored rating scales was that these scales provided clear and concrete definitions of the performance dimensions to be rated. This clarity could almost certainly contribute to the construct validity of performance ratings.

Second, we might look at evidence of convergent validity—that is, the extent to which performance ratings and other measures of job performance provide consistent information. For example, there is evidence that performance ratings are positively correlated with a number of objective measures of job performance. Several reviews have suggested that performance ratings and objective performance measures are related (with corrected correlations in the .30s and .40s), but they are not substitutable (Bommer, Johnson, Rich, Podsakoff, & MacKenzie, 1995; Conway, Lombardo, & Sanders, 2001; Heneman, 1986; Mabe & West, 1982).

Third, we might look at criterion-related validity evidence. Performance ratings are one of the most common criteria for validating personnel selection tests, and there is a massive body of research showing that tests designed to measure job-related abilities and skills are consistently correlated with ratings of job performance (Schmidt & Hunter, 1998, review 85 years of research on the validity of selection tests, and document consistent correlations between many predictors and job performance ratings; see also Woehr & Roch, 2016). Usually, we think of these correlations as evidence for the validity of selection tests, but we can just as well use them as evidence for the construct validity of performance ratings. That is, there is a substantial body of evidence showing that measures (e.g., ability tests) that *should be* related to job performance *are*, in fact, related to ratings of job performance. This suggests that performance ratings are capturing at least something about the performance of those individuals being evaluated.

Another way of gathering evidence about the construct validity of performance ratings is to determine whether ratings have consistent meanings across contexts or cultures. Performance appraisals are used in numerous countries and cultures; multinational corporations might use similar appraisal systems in many nations. The question of whether performance appraisal provides measures that can reasonably be compared across borders is therefore an important one. Ployhart, Wiechmann, Schmitt, Sacco, and Rogg (2003) examined ratings of technical proficiency, customer service, and teamwork given to fast-food workers in Canada, South Korea, and Spain and concluded that ratings show evidence of rating invariance. In particular, raters appear to interpret the three dimensions in similar ways and to apply comparable performance standards when evaluating their subordinates. However, there was also evidence of some subtle differences in perceptions that could make direct comparisons across countries complex. In particular, raters in Canada perceived smaller relationships between Customer Service and Teamwork than did raters in South

Korea and Spain. On the whole, however, Ployhart et al. (2003) concluded that ratings from these countries reflected similar ideas about the dimensions and about the performance levels expected, and could therefore be used to make cross-cultural comparisons.

Similarly, there is evidence of measurement equivalence when performance ratings of more experienced and less experienced raters are compared (Greguras, 2005). Even though experience as a supervisor is likely to influence the strategies different supervisors apply to maximize the success of their subordinates, it appears that supervisors using a well-developed performance appraisal system are likely to agree regarding the meaning of performance dimensions and performance levels.

Finally, we might use evidence regarding bias in performance ratings to evaluate the construct validity of these ratings. The rationale here is that if performance ratings can be shown to be strongly influenced by factors other than job performance, that would tend to argue *against* the proposition that performance ratings provide valid measures of job performance (Colella, DeNisi, & Varma, 1998). There is a substantial literature dealing with the question of whether or not performance ratings are biased by factors that are presumably unrelated to actual job performance, such as the demographic characteristics of ratees or the characteristics of work groups.

Are Performance Ratings Biased?

There are a number of reasons to believe that performance ratings might be biased. Several theories and models in social and cognitive psychology, such as role congruity theory (Nieva & Gutek, 1980), the lack of fit model (Heilman, 1983), relational demography theory (Tsui & Gutek, 1999), and stereotype fit models (Dipboye, 1985), predict that attributes such as race, gender, or age *should* influence supervisors' perceptions of the competence and performance of their subordinates, particularly subordinates who are members of minority groups. Roberson, Galvin, and Charles (2007) note that despite some progress in workplace equity, there are still large differences in the likelihood that women or members of racial and ethnic minority groups will advance to the top of their organizations, and they suggest that bias in performance appraisal might be a factor in these differences.

There are some studies showing what appears to be bias in performance ratings. For example, laboratory studies suggest that women may receive lower evaluations when they occupy jobs that are stereotypically held by men (Lyness & Heilman, 2006). Other studies suggest that older raters tend to rate older employees a bit more favorably, while younger raters tend to favor other younger employees (e.g., Gibson, Zerbe, & Franken, 1993). It is also likely that some attributes are viewed unfavorably by most of the population (e.g., obesity, low levels of physical attractiveness), and these broadly negative characteristics could lead to lower ratings (Bento, White, & Zacur, 2012; Nieminen et al., 2013).

Studies of demographic biases in performance rating sometimes appear to yield mixed results. Table 11.3 summarizes the results of 19 studies of the relationship between age, gender, race, and disability and performance ratings. This table glosses over numerous important features of many of these studies (e.g., different conditions under which ratings were obtained), including variability in what is being rated (e.g., overall performance, trainability), and it is far from comprehensive (no studies prior to 1993 are included). Nevertheless, this table does suggest that the literature on potential biasing factors in performance appraisal might yield mixed results.

TABLE 11.3 ■ Results of 19 Studies of Demographic Differences in Performance Ratings	
Little or No Effect	**Meaningful Difference in Ratings**
Age	
Cox & Beier (2014)	Finkelstein, Burke, & Raju (1995)
Lefkowitz & Battista (1995)	Rupp, Vodanovich, & Credé (2006)
Ng & Feldman (2008)	
Siegel (1993)	
Treadway, Ferris, Hochwater, Perrewé, Witt, & Goodman (2005)	
Gender	
Bowen, Swim, & Jacobs (2000)	Lefkowitz & Battista (1995)
Lyness & Heilman (2006)	Heilman, Block, & Stathatos (1997)
Robbins & DeNisi (1993)	Heilman & Chen (2005)
Race/ethnicity	
Baltes, Bauer, & Frensch (2007)	Ho, Thomsen, & Sidanius (2009)
McKay & McDaniel (2006)	
Roth, Huffcutt, & Bobko (2003)	
Disability	
Colella, DeNisi, & Varma (1998)	
Miller & Werner (2005)	
Ren, Paetzold, & Colella (2008)	

A much clearer picture of the influence of demographic variables on performance rating emerges from the numerous meta-analyses that have been conducted in this field. Table 11.4 summarizes the key findings of these analyses. The values shown in Table 11.4 are based on the combined results of many individual studies, and they are remarkably consistent. On the whole, they suggest that age, gender, race, and disability tend to have small effects on performance ratings (Landy, 2010). There are no doubt specific conditions where these variables might have larger effects (e.g., Heilman & Chen [2005] report larger differences when men and women perform helping behaviors), but the hypothesis that performance ratings are substantially biased against women, members of minority groups, older workers, or disabled workers does not seem credible.

TABLE 11.4 ■ Meta-Analytic Estimates of Biasing Factors on Performance Appraisal	
Potential Biasing Factor	**Percentage of Variance in Overall Performance Ratings Explained**
Age	Less than 1%[a]
Gender	Less than 1%[b]
Race & Ethnicity	1.7%[c,d]
Disability	1.5%[e]

[a] Ng & Feldman (2008); [b] Bowen, Swim, & Jacobs (2000); [c] McKay & McDaniel (2006); [d] values presented in Roth, Huffcutt, & Bobko (2003) are corrected for attenuation, but the value shown here is uncorrected. Both McKay & McDaniel (2006) and Roth, Huffcutt, & Bobko (2003) reported average uncorrected *d* values of .27, which translated into r^2 = .017; [e] Ren, Paetzold, & Colella (2008).

Several other authors (e.g., Arvey & Murphy, 1998; Bass & Turner, 1973; Baxter, 2012; Bowen et al., 2000; DeNisi & Murphy, 2017; Kraiger & Ford, 1985; Landy, Shankster, & Kohler, 1994; Pulakos, White, Oppler, & Borman, 1989; Waldman & Avolio, 1991) have reached similar conclusions regarding the lack of bias in performance ratings, as have studies of more specific biases (e.g., pregnancy bias; Gueutal, Luciano, & Michaels, 1995, suggest that pregnancy has a small effect on ratings, and that pregnant workers receive higher ratings) but this conclusion is not universally accepted. Stauffer and Buckley (2005) note that while studies of racial and ethnic differences in performance ratings do show relatively small mean differences, there are some important caveats. In particular, they present data showing that there are nontrivial differences in the ratings received by white and black ratees when the rater is white (when the rater is white, white ratees receive higher ratings). However, even in these carefully selected rater–ratee pairs, the proportion of variance in performance ratings explained by race is fairly small (approximately 2.5% of the variance in ratings performed by white raters is explained by rate race).

Studies using laboratory methods (e.g., Hamner, Kim, Baird, & Bigoness, 1974; Rosen & Jerdee, 1976; Schmitt & Lappin, 1980) sometimes suggest that there are larger demographic differences in performance ratings. However, there are reasons to believe that the findings of these laboratory studies (particularly those involving vignettes rather than observations of actual performance) overestimate the effects of the demographic characteristics of both raters and ratees (Landy, 2010). Wendelken and Inn (1981) noted that demographic differences are made especially salient in laboratory studies where other ratee characteristics (including performance levels) are tightly controlled and where raters are untrained and have no prior knowledge of and no relationship with ratees. Murphy, Herr, Lockhart, and Maguire's (1986) meta-analysis confirmed that vignette studies do indeed tend to produce larger effects.

Most assessments of bias in performance appraisals focus on the numerical ratings that are provided. Wilson (2010) went further, examining potential differences in the narrative comments that are included in most performance appraisals. He hypothesized that members of minority groups might receive more negative comments, but he found small differences in the opposite direction. On the whole, supervisors made positive comments, even when ratees received lower ratings. Asian employees were slightly more likely to receive positive comments than white employees, while black employees were slightly more likely to receive negative comments than their white counterparts. The operative term here is "slightly"; on the whole, there are few differences in the narrative comments received by ratees from different racial/ethnic groups.

Finally, it is often argued that performance appraisal systems that rely on general rather than specific performance criteria (e.g., graphic scales versus behavioral scales) are more prone to bias and unfair discrimination; expert witnesses in employment discrimination litigation often testify to this effect. In fact, there is little evidence to support this belief (Bernardin, Hennessey, & Peyrefitte, 1995; Hennessey & Bernardin, 2003). As noted above, demographic differences in ratings are generally small, and what differences there are do not seem to be affected by the rating scales used.

CONCLUSIONS ABOUT THE RELIABILITY, VALIDITY, AND ACCURACY OF PERFORMANCE RATINGS

Performance appraisal researchers have spent decades developing methods and indices that can be used to evaluate the quality of rating data. Some methods have proved more useful than others and some problems have turned out to be easier to solve than others. Our review of this research leads to four broad conclusions, shown in Table 11.5.

First, it seems clear that performance ratings tell you *something* about the performance of the individuals being rated, but that performance ratings are influenced by things that have little to do with job performance (Landy & Farr, 1980; Milkovich & Wigdor, 1991). By the 1970s, it was pretty well established that performance ratings showed evidence of reliability and validity, but it was also well understood that many factors other than performance were important in determining the ratings an individual rater received. Research in the 1980s examined the role of cognitive processes in determining the strengths and weaknesses of performance ratings; this research showed how the way we attend to, mentally represent, and recall behavior could influence ratings. By the 1990s, researchers were starting to turn their attention to the role of contextual factors, ranging from broad national and organizational contexts to the immediate environment in which performance is observed and evaluated influenced ratings, and this contextual orientation is still a dominant theme in research on

TABLE 11.5 ■ Four Conclusions About the Reliability, Validity, and Accuracy of Performance Ratings
Ratings of performance are determined in part by the behavior and effectiveness of the employees being rated and in part by factors that seem to have little to do with performance.
Performance ratings are influenced by both random and systematic measurement errors, and the reliability of performance ratings is neither as high as the reliability of well-constructed tests and assessments nor as low as most researchers and practitioners assume.
The measures most frequently used to evaluate the quality of rating data (i.e., rater error measures) are probably the least useful for this purpose.
It is easier to evaluate the quality of rating data in the aggregate (e.g., at the organizational level) than it is to evaluate the quality of rating data provided by a single rater.

performance ratings. On the whole, all of these streams of research have shown that it is unrealistic to expect performance ratings to be a perfect representation of the performance of the individuals being rated, but that these ratings can and do provide useful information about performance.

Second, measurement error is a serious problem in performance rating, and it is important to devise practical strategies for reducing the influence of measurement error. On the other hand, the widely circulated claim that supervisory ratings represent an almost equal mix of valid information about ratee performance and random measurement error (Viswesvaran, Ones, & Schmidt, 1996) is clearly wrong. Researchers who have applied classic test theory to the analysis of performance ratings have reached two conclusions— that ratings are highly unreliable and that it is easy to correct for the effects of this unreliability, which do not hold up when more comprehensive models of measurement (e.g., generalizability theory) are applied to the same data. It now seems clear that there are both systematic and random sources of measurement error in performance ratings, and that the influences of both of these depends very much on what one is trying to capture with ratings. Thus, the reliability of information about between-person differences might be quite different from the reliability of information about within-person differences. Performance ratings can be highly reliable for some purposes and less reliable for others.

Third, the most widely used criteria for evaluating ratings—rater error measures—are sometimes the least useful. As we noted in our discussion of rater error measures, it is often hard to tell whether ratings are so high that you can conclude that a particular rater is lenient or so intercorrelated that you can conclude that halo error is present. When you use measures of this sort to evaluate the ratings provided by an individual rater, it is hard to tell whether or to what extent the distributions or intercorrelations those ratings exhibit is a reflection of the performance being evaluated or the actual behavior of the employees you are evaluating.

Fourth, the task of evaluating ratings is more challenging when trying to draw conclusions about the ratings obtained from a particular rater than when trying to draw conclusions at some higher level of analysis. For example, if the average rating I give to subordinates is 4.25 on a 5-point scale, this *might* indicate that I am lenient, but it could also reflect the truly above-average performance of my subordinates. On the other hand, if the average rating in an entire organization is 4.25 on a 5-point scale, it is hard to accept the possibility that *everyone* is above average, and it is more likely that the ratings in this organization are unrealistically high. This is exactly what many assessments of organizational-level leniency have found; Chapters 9 and 12 explore the reasons why performance ratings are so often unrealistically high. Traditional measures of leniency and halo were developed with the individual rater in mind, but they might prove more valuable when evaluating ratings in the aggregate than when trying to draw conclusions about individual raters.

Are Ratings Useful?

Performance appraisal researchers have spent a long time asking whether performance ratings are reliable, valid, and accurate, and devising methods of measuring these attributes. A case can be made that we have spent a lot of time asking the wrong question, and that it is more important to ask whether ratings are *useful*. In the best of all possible worlds, organizations would use performance ratings for a range of important purposes, starting with using ratings to help make decisions about important rewards and sanctions (e.g., raises, promotions, identifying candidates for layoffs), to help direct employee training and development, to evaluate and validate HR policies (e.g., to determine whether selection tests are likely to lead to better hiring decisions), and to draw conclusions about the health of the organization. In some organizations, it is not clear that *any* of these purposes are actually achieved, and we would argue that if organizations are not going to use performance ratings for purposes of this sort they should not collect them.

Validity and accuracy might be a precondition for the optimal use of ratings. That is, if an organization truly wants to distribute rewards on the basis of job performance, or to tailor training to the strengths and weaknesses of individual employees, reliable, valid, and credible information about performance is a starting point. However, accurate performance ratings are no guarantee that they will be used effectively, and as we will see in Chapters 9 and 12, accurate performance ratings can cause more problems than they solve. For example, we noted in Chapter 5 that people tend to evaluate their own performance more positively than other people evaluate it. One implication is that truly accurate performance feedback is likely to *feel* to the recipient like it is unfair and unduly negative; we examined the implications of this in Chapters 9 and 10. We believe it is absolutely critical to understand how organizations actually use performance ratings (if they use them at all in any meaningful way) in order to determine whether they are useful. As we noted in Chapter 8, organizations often shoot themselves in the foot by trying to use the same performance appraisal system for multiple conflicting purposes. The most comprehensive evaluation of the usefulness of ratings must go beyond looking at the ratings themselves, to consider what the organization is trying to accomplish with performance appraisal and to identify (and if possible remove) the barriers to accomplishing these goals.

SUMMARY

A number of approaches have been identified for evaluating the quality and potential usefulness of performance ratings. First, we might consider whether different raters who are evaluating the same employees reach similar conclusions. If they do not, we may need to make hard decisions about whose ratings to believe and whose to give the most weight to. Second, we might examine the distributions and the intercorrelations among ratings. If performance ratings are seriously skewed (e.g., if most employees are rated well above average) or if ratings on conceptually distinct areas of performance are redundant, that might limit the potential value or uses of rating data. Measures of so-called rater errors are probably more useful for evaluating ratings across organizations or across many raters, and are harder to interpret when used to evaluate

an individual rater. Similarly, assessments of the validity of ratings appear more useful for aggregated ratings than for drawing conclusions about the ratings given by an individual supervisor or manager.

In laboratory settings, it is possible to develop measures of the accuracy of performance ratings, and while these have some value for performance appraisal research, they have only limited applicability in the field. These measures have proved useful for exploring the factors that contribute to or detract from accuracy, but they are not practical for use in organizations.

The ultimate criterion for evaluating rating data is the usefulness of ratings, and usefulness depends as much on what the organization does or attempts to do with performance ratings as on the ratings themselves. To be sure, criteria such as reliability, validity, and accuracy have implications for evaluating usefulness—ratings that have little to do with the actual performance of the individuals being evaluated are unlikely to be useful. However, the extent to which performance ratings are useful will necessarily depend on answering the question *"useful for what?"* and the answer to this question is not always clear. Too often performance appraisal seems like an exercise in futility, in the sense that a lot of information is collected (at the cost of large investments of time and other resources) with little apparent purpose. If you cannot convincingly answer the question of why your organization collects performance ratings, you should seriously consider shutting down your performance appraisal program.

EXERCISE: ANALYZE RATING DATA

Near the beginning of this chapter, we presented some data in Table 11.1 to illustrate some of the questions that might be asked when evaluating performance ratings. In that table, two raters evaluated the performance of five nurses, rating them on four separate performance dimensions (Quality, Timeliness, Accuracy, Judgment). One way to get a concrete sense of how performance ratings are evaluated is to analyze these data and see what conclusions you might draw.

First, create a spreadsheet with 20 rows and 4 columns, where the first two columns identify the target (who is rated) and the performance dimension being rated and the third and fourth columns include the performance ratings the two raters assigned. If you copy this dataset into a data analysis program (e.g., SPSS, R), you will be able to ask several questions about inter-rater agreement. For example, do raters agree more in their evaluations of some dimensions than others?

If you select one performance dimension at a time and correlate the ratings of the five nurses on each dimension, you should find:

	Inter-Rater Correlation
Quality	.00
Timeliness	.45
Accuracy	.01
Judgment	.31

That is, there is virtually no agreement at all in ratings of Quality or Accuracy, with much higher levels of agreement for ratings of Timeliness and Judgment.

Suppose you wanted to ask whether raters agreed, in general, in terms of their rank-ordering of the nurses' performance. This would require a new data set, with five rows and two columns, with the average rating (across the four performance dimensions) assigned by each rater to each of the five nurses. If you correlate these two ratings, you should find $r = .149$, which indicates a low level of agreement. On the whole, these two raters do not agree in their evaluation of these five nurses.

Finally, suppose you wanted to apply the concepts associated with generalizability theory to get a better sense of which factors explain variations in rating and what conclusions might be drawn about the reliability of these performance ratings. This analysis is most easily done by creating a data set with 40 rows and four columns indicating the target (which nurse is rated), the performance dimension, the rater, and the performance rating that is assigned. This allows you to do a simple Target × Dimension × Rater analysis of variance, which yields:

Source	Sum of	Eta Squared[7]
Target	22.15	.297
Dimension	.40	.005

Rater	2.50	.033
T × D	12.85	.172
T × R	18.75	.252
D × R	8.30	.111
Residual (T × D × R)	9.45	.127
Total	74.39	

Eta Squared indicates the percentage of the total variability in scores due to each of the sources. This analysis suggests that there are two important sources of variability in performance ratings, differences between nurses (Targets) and Target by Rater interactions (i.e., the two raters have different ideas about which nurses perform best and worst). You could use the results of this analysis of variance to calculate generalizability coefficients, and while these can be informative and useful, the descriptive information provided by the Eta Squares is probably even more useful, because it allows you to understand both strengths (there are substantial differences in ratings across the people being rated) and weaknesses (the raters do not agree about which nurses perform best and worst) of the performance ratings shown in Table 11.1.

The data analyzed here would not give you much confidence in these performance ratings. What you hope to find is stronger and more consistent agreement, and also to find that sources of systematic disagreement (e.g., T x R interactions) have only a small effect on ratings. That is not what this particular set of data shows.

1. Their overall ratings are almost completely uncorrelated, with an inter-rater agreement level of $r = .14$.

2. Sam's mean rating is 4.95, Jose's is 5.45.

3. If you calculate the standard deviation in the ratings given to each nurse, then average these, the variability of Jose's ratings of each nurse is 34% larger than the variability of Sam's (1.10 vs .82).

4. If we symbolize the reliability of a measure as r_{xx}, then $1 - r_{xx}$ = the proportion of the variance in ratings due to random measurement error.

5. Some studies, however (e.g., Facteau & Craig, 2001; Maurer, Raju, & Collins, 1998) suggests that ratings from different sources provide reasonably equivalent measures.

6. Bingham (1939) was the first to distinguish between true and illusory halo.

7. Eta squared for targets = Sum of Squares for Targets/Sum of Squares Total = 22.15/74.39.

12 RATER GOALS AND RATING DISTORTION

In Chapter 1, we noted that performance ratings appear inflated in most organizations; a very large percentage of the workers who receive performance appraisals receive ratings that are well above "average," and it is not unusual to find 80% of all performance appraisal ratings to be at or near the top end of the rating scale. This is not a recent phenomenon; Bjerke, Cleveland, Morrison, and Wilson (1987) report that evaluations of naval officers, going back as far as the 1860s, show evidence of inflation, with most officers receiving ratings of above average or excellent. Similarly, this is not a phenomenon that is unique to North American organizations, but rather it is seen in many countries (e.g., several recent papers describe rating inflation in Asian organizations, including Barron & Sackett, 2008; Ng, Koh, Ang, Kennedy, & Chan, 2011).

The fact that ratings are high does not automatically mean that they are inaccurate. It is always possible that a rater who assigns high ratings to his or her subordinates is simply recognizing that these employees *are* good performers. There is evidence, however, that raters do indeed distort performance ratings, consciously choosing to give their subordinates higher evaluations than they deserve. For example, more than 70% of managers in Longenecker and Ludwig's (1990) study admitted giving their subordinates ratings that did not reflect their actual level of performance. Usually, this involves inflating ratings, but in some cases raters deliberately gave their subordinates unduly low ratings, often to send a message to poor performers that improvements were needed.

There are multiple lines of evidence suggesting that deliberate distortion is more prevalent than unintentional bias (Bernardin & Villanova, 1986). First as noted above, when supervisors and managers are interviewed about the ratings they assign, they readily admit giving their subordinates inflated ratings. There is also indirect evidence of conscious distortion. For example, making raters more accountable has been shown to lead to lower performance ratings (Bamberger, 2007; Mero & Motowidlo, 1995). The usual interpretation of this finding is that when raters are held accountable, they realize that they will not get away with distortion, and therefore give more accurate ratings.

Most of the research on distortion in performance ratings focuses on supervisory ratings of performance, but there are reasons to believe that distortion also occurs when giving upward feedback (e.g., rating the performance of your superiors). This sort of upward feedback is a popular component of 360-degree rating systems, but the process of giving performance feedback to one's superiors is a potentially risky one. Much like supervisory rating of their subordinates, employees who are asked to provide upward feedback may be motivated to give inflated ratings. This motivation depends in large part on the employees' perceptions of the benefits of giving honest feedback versus the risk of retaliation if they give low ratings or critical feedback (Smith & Fortunato, 2008). The motivation to provide honest versus inflated feedback is also likely to be influenced by the employee's degree of trust versus cynicism regarding the motives of top management and the reasons for seeking upward feedback, as well as their belief that they have the information, knowledge, and skills needed to accurately evaluate the performance of their superiors.

WHY ARE RATINGS INFLATED?

For many years, the shortcomings of performance appraisal systems were assumed to reflect problems with the rating scales or with rater training, and it was believed that the difficulty in providing accurate and useful performance ratings could be reduced if we gave raters better tools and skills. The flaw in this line of thinking is that it treated raters as passive measurement instruments, and assumed that raters were always trying their best to provide accurate measures of each ratee's performance. Starting in the 1980s, several authors (e.g., Banks & Murphy, 1985; Cleveland & Murphy, 1992; Longenecker, Sims, & Gioia, 1987; Murphy & Cleveland, 1991, 1995; Spence & Keeping, 2011) suggested that some of the apparent failures of performance appraisal could be better explained in terms of motivation than in terms of ability and skill. That is, it is wrong to assume that the reason that managers and supervisors fail to provide accurate and useful performance evaluations is that they *cannot* accurately evaluate performance. Rather, it appears that raters often appear to give ratings that are inflated, or ratings that fail to discriminate among their subordinates, because they prefer giving inflated or distorted ratings to giving accurate performance ratings.

The critical breakthrough in research and theory came as a result of something researchers too often forget to do. Starting in the 1980s, several researchers (e.g., Bjerke et al., 1987; Longenecker et al., 1987) spent time systematically sitting down with supervisors, managers, and others involved in performance appraisal, talking with them about what they were thinking and about what they were trying to accomplish when completing performance appraisal forms, and paying attention to what they said. Two themes emerged from these conversations. First, very few people said, "I am trying my best to provide accurate appraisals, but just cannot seem to manage it." Second, the raters these researchers talked with almost always had sensible rationales for giving ratings that appeared to be inflated or that failed to distinguish between employees, even when the differences in their performance levels seemed fairly obvious. These explanations usually involved using performance appraisal as a tool for accomplishing some important goals (e.g., motivating employees) rather than using performance appraisal as a simple measurement instrument.

It is important to keep in mind that the fact that people *say* that they are pursuing some goals and not pursuing others does not necessarily mean that these goals actually drive their behavior. However, their consistent claim that they had good reasons for giving performance ratings that were not accurate did stimulate the development of models of the appraisal process that gave prominent attention to the goals and intentions of raters (e.g., Cleveland & Murphy, 1992), and these models have received considerable empirical support (Murphy, Cleveland, Skattebo, & Kinney, 2004; Murphy, Deckert, & Hunter, 2013; Wang, Wong, & Kwong, 2010; Wong & Kwong, 2007).

In our opinion, a consistent pattern of rating inflation, which is seen across many organizations and across many cultures, can only be adequately understood in terms of the goals and strategies raters adopt when completing performance appraisal forms. After all, it is unlikely that raters do not *know* that some of their subordinates actually perform better than others. One of our professors, Frank Landy, enjoyed telling a story about an interview with the fire chief of a major city, who claimed that there were no differences in the performance of his firefighters, and that they were all equally excellent. Frank then asked him if he would care who responded if his own house was on fire, and of course he had no difficulty telling Frank which engine and which firefighters he would want to come to try and save *his* house. If managers *know* that some of their subordinates are in fact average or poor performers, why do they consistently give them high performance ratings? Goal-directed models propose that ratings are inflated because raters believe that a number of important ends are more likely to be achieved if ratings are inflated than if they are accurate (Cleveland & Murphy, 1992; Murphy & Cleveland, 1991, 1995).

In this chapter, we discuss the nature and content of the goals that might direct the rater's behavior. Early work on rater goals was largely anecdotal (Bjerke et al., 1987; Longenecker et al., 1987); a number of more recent studies have helped in identifying the goals raters pursue and have confirmed that raters who pursue different goals often end up assigning different performance ratings. For example, Spence and Keeping (2011) reviewed several studies of the goals raters pursue when completing performance ratings, and suggested that the factors that influence a rater's likelihood of providing inflated ratings included: (1) avoiding confrontations with subordinates, (2) the reluctance to take time away from other valued tasks to provide accurate ratings, (3) a desire to be in compliance with organizational norms, (4) the need to promote problem employees out of a department, (5) the desire to look like a successful and competent manager, and (6) to motivate and act in the best interest of the employee. This list is far from exhaustive, but it does give an indication of the range of considerations that may weigh on raters when they complete performance appraisal forms.

Whose Goals?

It is useful to distinguish between the purpose of performance, as articulated by the organization, and the rater's goals when completing a performance appraisal. Cleveland, Murphy, and Williams (1989) note that the organization often imposes, or attempts to impose, a number of goals on the rater that are linked to the way they use performance appraisal. In particular, they suggested that appraisals that are designed for developmental purposes should differ in important ways from appraisals designed to be used to determine pay or promotions. (This idea is far from original; it dates back to at least Meyer, Kay, & French, 1965.) If appraisals are used primarily for developmental purposes, raters should be focusing on the individual strengths and weaknesses of individual employees, and should pay less attention to their overall performance levels. On the other hand, if appraisals are used to make administrative decisions (e.g., merit pay, promotion, layoffs), raters should be focusing on rank-ordering employees in terms of their overall effectiveness, and should pay less attention to within-ratee variability in performance. You might notice that we use the term *should* here. The question of whether raters actually *will* use the appraisal from the way the organization wants them to will depend largely on whether or not they accept and internalize the goals set out by the organization. That is, if the organization proposes using appraisal to identify strengths and weaknesses, the likelihood of obtaining the sort of developmental information that is desired (e.g., identification of strengths and weaknesses) is higher if raters accept this goal as legitimate and important.

Similarly, organizations impose performance goals on individuals, work groups, and larger organizational units (Cheng, Luckett, & Mahama, 2007). While these goals are important for determining how organizations evaluate the effectiveness of these individuals or groups, such externally imposed goals and metrics are distinct from the sort of rater goals this chapter describes. When we use the term *goals*, we refer to the objectives both raters and ratees seek when they participate in the performance appraisal process. Thus, the organization's policies, their statements about the purpose of appraisal, and the goals or targets organizations set are likely to have quite different impacts on the behavior of raters and ratees when they are consistent with the rater's own objectives than when they are not (Erez & Kanfer, 1983). Consider the following example.

The personnel policies of an organization might indicate that performance appraisal is used to make decisions about pay—rewarding merit with salary increases. This claim may or may not be credible; an organization that claims to pay for performance but that allocates only a small amount of money for merit raises may be doing no more than giving lip service to actually rewarding performance (we consider this issue more fully in Chapter 13). However, even if the organization does make a good faith effort to reward good performance, there is no guarantee that individual supervisors and managers will adopt the goal of differentiating good from poor performance and allocating the largest rewards to the best performers. They may conclude, for a number of reasons, that it is more sensible to give everyone high ratings than it is to give high ratings to the best performers and low ratings to other employees who are not performing so well. In this chapter, we explore the reasons or rationale for this type of rating inflation.

Of course, rater goals are not the only factor that might lead to rating inflation. For example, Fried, Levi, Ben-David, and Tiegs (1999) showed that negative affectivity, the tendency to experience negative mood states over time and across situations, is related to rating inflation. They argue that raters who are high on negative affectivity will tend to pay attention to and recall more negative information, and as a result will arrive at more negative judgments about their subordinates. Given the strong situational pressure to give high ratings, raters whose initial judgments are more negative will be more likely to provide distorted ratings. Raters who are lower on negative affectivity might have more positive judgments in the first place, and have less need to inflate ratings.

RATER GOALS

The specific goals pursued by raters will depend on a wide range of factors, including the values and experiences of the rater, the climate and culture of the organization, the performance level of subordinates, and so on.

A Taxonomy of Rater Goals

Murphy and Cleveland (1995) proposed that the most frequently pursued goals can be identified with one of four general categories: (a) task performance goals, (b) interpersonal goals, (c) self-serving goals,[1] and (d) internalized goals.

Task Performance Goals

If you ask raters why they give unrealistically high ratings, they frequently claim that they are using performance appraisal to increase ratees' performance levels or to maintain present performance levels. For example, giving an employee a favorable evaluation this year may lead to more rewards, more recognition, and perhaps a higher level of motivation to perform well in the future. Specific performance goals will necessarily depend on whether the ratee being evaluated is in fact (or in the rater's opinion) performing well. If the individual is performing well, the rater's goal might be to maintain that performance level. If the ratee is performing poorly, the rater's goal might be to increase motivation, or to identify and correct weaknesses.

A manager or supervisor who gives inflated ratings and overly positive feedback creates a variety of positive conditions that might contribute to improving performance in the future (or to maintaining current high levels of performance) in a number of ways. First, these ratings are likely to increase the probability that ratees will receive rewards and that they will view their supervisor and the performance appraisal system (and by extension, other HRM systems) favorably. This might make them more motivated and more receptive to feedback. On the other hand, ratings that are lower than ratees believe they deserve may lead to resentment, fewer rewards, and cynicism, and it is hard to see how any of these will contribute to future performance.

Interpersonal Goals

There is evidence that supervisors and managers use appraisal to maintain or improve interpersonal relations between the supervisor and subordinates. The interpersonal goal that has been discussed most frequently in the literature (e.g., Mohrman & Lawler, 1983; Napier & Latham, 1986) involves maintaining a positive climate in the work group. Because low ratings can lead to resentment and perceptions of inequity, the maintenance of a positive work group climate often involves rating inflation. We should note that some studies (e.g., Napier & Latham, 1986) have questioned the extent to which raters are concerned with interpersonal relations. If the rater doesn't care what others think of him or her, or of each other, this goal may not influence the rater's behavior. However, most raters do seem to care about their relationships with the people they evaluate, and if they don't they probably should. Positive relationships between supervisors and managers and employees can have a substantial effect on the ability and willingness of individuals and work groups to function well and perform effectively (Elangovan & Xie, 1999; Michael, 2014).

Sometimes, interpersonal goals may involve efforts to achieve or restore equity. If a supervisor believes that a specific subordinate deserved some reward that he or she did not receive (e.g., a promotion or raise), subsequent ratings may be distorted to achieve those outcomes. If work group members believe that rewards have not been distributed equitably, the supervisor might have a strong incentive to restore perceptions of equity. Yet another class of interpersonal goals are those that involve attempts to establish or maintain interpersonal influence. For example, a rater who demonstrates that he or she can have a substantial influence on administrative decisions (e.g., salary) may have a great deal of power and influence over subordinates.

Finally, and perhaps most significantly, supervisors and managers may be strongly motivated to avoid the sorts of interpersonal conflicts that can arise if employees receive lower ratings than they think they deserve. It is well known that supervisors dislike giving feedback (Cleveland, Lim, & Murphy, 2007), in part because they often expect that anything other than very positive feedback is going to be disregarded or is going to lead to arguments with or bad feelings on the part of subordinates. The motivation to avoid negative consequences can be substantially stronger than the motivation to pursue positive ones.

Self-Serving Goals

It seems clear that supervisors and managers can and do use performance appraisal to increase their standing and/or the work group's standing in the organization. There are several ways to accomplish this. First, uniformly high ratings might reflect positively on both the rater and the work group, especially if the rater is viewed as a credible source. Second, the standing of both the rater and the work group may be enhanced if work group members are given widely sought promotions and assignments; raters may distort their ratings to increase the likelihood of these valued outcomes. Third, the rater and the work group might both look better if the supervisor succeeds in transferring poor performers to someone else's workgroup. Again, performance ratings may influence this type of decision.

The ratings a supervisor or manager gives are also a reflection of his or her effectiveness. Consider two managers. Janice tells her superiors that all of her subordinates performed well last year. Frank tells his superiors that there were a few good performers, a few average ones, and a few real failures in his work group. One of the most important duties and roles of a manager is to create conditions that get the best performance out of the people he or she supervises, and by giving inflated ratings, Janice has just told her bosses that she was successful, whereas Frank (who might have given much more accurate ratings) has told his bosses that he failed. A rater who gives inflated ratings not only makes his or her subordinates look good, but also is engaging in self-promotion.

Although there are reasons to believe that many raters routinely give inflated ratings, this can become a self-defeating strategy. In particular, if too many raters use performance appraisal in blatantly self-serving ways, this is likely to lead to increased cynicism toward performance appraisal, perhaps even convincing organizations to curtail or abandon performance appraisal (Curtis, Harvey, & Ravden, 2005). If, as is true in most organizations, most raters turn in ratings that are moderately high, but perhaps not ridiculously so, rating inflation will end up being a matter of self-preservation rather than a way to make yourself look good. That is, the more extensive inflation is in an organization, the less benefit any individual rater is likely to get from giving inflated ratings and the more a rater who gives accurate ratings is likely to stand out from the pack. Unfortunately, in this instance, standing out means that a rater who gives accurate appraisals when virtually all of his or her colleagues give inflated ratings will probably ensure that his or her subordinates will look particularly bad in comparison with almost everyone else who is rated higher, will receive smaller raises and fewer promotions, and will probably resent the low ratings they receive.

Internalized Goals

Finally, it is worth considering goals that are the product of the rater's own values and beliefs. For example, a rater who believes that he or she should be honest in completing performance appraisals may turn in very different appraisals than a rater who believes that he or she should try to obtain valued rewards for subordinates. The rater's self-image may also affect rating behavior. Raters who believe that they are or should be participative leaders will probably devote more time and attention to feedback than will raters whose self-image is more authoritarian. Finally, raters might want to make sure that their subordinates do well in the organization, and might give high ratings because they know that good performance scores will be needed to qualify their subordinates for promotions or rewards (Smither, 2015).

The distinction between internalized goals and the other goals discussed in this section is that task performance, interpersonal, and self-serving goals are all instrumental in nature. That is, they involve giving high ratings in order to accomplish some particular end (i.e., increased performance, decreased conflict, self-promotion). Internalized goals are not directly instrumental, but rather represent rating strategies that reflect the rater's belief about the right thing to do. For example, a manager who is committed to giving his or her employees accurate feedback may do so even though he or she understands that accurate performance appraisals are likely to lead to negative outcomes, such as interpersonal conflict.

Alternative Goal Taxonomies

Wang et al. (2010) propose an alternate taxonomy of rater goals. First, they suggest that raters might pursue *harmony* goals, minimizing the distinctions between ratees. This might involve inflating the ratings of poorer performers, and perhaps forgoing inflation for better performers. Second, raters might pursue *fairness* goals, giving ratees the evaluations they deserve. Third, raters might pursue *identification* goals, with a focus on identifying strengths and weaknesses, and a relative de-emphasis on distinguishing between ratees. This might lead to smaller distinctions between ratees, but here the minimization of between-ratee differences would be a side-effect rather than the main goal of the rater. Finally, raters might pursue *motivational* goals, assigning the ratings they believe most likely to lead to increases in future performance. Wang et al. (2010) suggest that pursuit of these goals might lead to rating inflation for poor performers and rating *deflation* for good performers, but this is not the only pattern of rating that might be motivating. Depending on the rater's underlying assumptions about why subordinates perform well or poorly, ratings that are inflated, deflated, or accurate might be seen as motivating.

Development of Goals

When they first start their jobs, it is unlikely that supervisors or managers have well-articulated goals that direct their behavior in performance appraisal. Indeed, this group might be unique in that they function in a way that some appraisal researchers assume *all* raters function—their principal goal might be to do the best job they can to provide accurate and honest evaluations of their subordinates' performance. With more experience, raters are likely to develop a more complex, sophisticated set of goals that reflect the realities of their organization, department, or work group. In part, these goals will be shaped by their own experiences on the job. That is, they will learn what outcomes to expect as the result of giving good or poor ratings, and will also learn which of these outcomes is of concern to the organization. However, this type of trial-and-error process is not the only one involved in acquiring goals and beliefs regarding performance appraisal. Organizations make formal and informal efforts to socialize their members (for a wide-ranging review of research on organizational socialization, see Wanberg, 2012), and one aspect of being socialized into the role of "supervisor" or "manager" is to learn the appropriate behaviors and strategies for evaluating your subordinates.

Socialization Processes

Organizations are composed of a number of individuals who perform interlocking roles. Thus, it is important for newcomers to quickly learn the roles they are expected to carry out. Until they learn their roles, coworkers whose jobs are in some way linked to theirs will find it more difficult to perform their jobs. The precise content of what is learned in role socialization will vary from job to job, but there are some broad categories of learning that are likely to be present in most jobs (Fisher, 1986). First, and most obvious, you must learn how to do the job. Thus, training activities (both formal and informal) are one component of socialization. Second, you must learn the values and norms of the immediate work group. Third, you must learn the values, culture, goals, and norms of the organization; these are not always the same as those of the work group. Finally, you must incorporate your new role into your identity or self-image. One implication of this final category of learning is that a fully socialized individual will not only learn the role, but he or she will also internalize at least some aspects of the role.

The socialization process refers to the transition from the status of a naïve newcomer, who knows little about the role, to that of a knowledgeable insider, who understands the nuances of his or her role, as well as the relationship between that role and the roles of others in the organization (Chao, 1988). Much of this socialization occurs via the "role episode process," in which other members of the role set (i.e., other persons with a vested interest in how well you perform your role) send information evaluating the focal person's role performance (Graen, 1976). Behaviors that are consistent with the role are met with approval, while behaviors inconsistent with the role are sanctioned.

Schein (1967) suggests that organizational socialization is concerned with five general themes, summarized in Table 12.1. The second and fourth items in Table 12.1 are particularly relevant to performance appraisal. First, managers must learn the means by

TABLE 12.1 ■ **Key Themes in Organizational Socialization**

Socialization into an organization involves learning

- the basic *goals* of the organization;

- the preferred *means* by which these goals should be attained;

- the basic *responsibilities* of the member in the role, which is being granted to him by the organization;

- the *behavior patterns* that are required for effective performance in the role; and

- a *set of rules or principles* that pertain to the maintenance of the identity and integrity of the organization.

which key organizational goals are accomplished. Some of this learning takes the form of simple declarative and procedural knowledge—that is, learning who does what, how supplies and resources are obtained, who to go to for particular pieces of information, what forms to complete, how to submit reports, and so on. Some of this learning takes the form of *tacit knowledge* (Polanyi, 1966; Wagner, 1986)—that is, informally obtained knowledge that is rarely written down and is often informally obtained through experience. For example, you might learn through experience that the best way to get a task expedited is to demonstrate interest in or do small favors for the staff member who can best get that task moving.

Second, managers must learn what behavior patterns are most effective for performing their roles. One part of being socialized as a manager is to learn how people in your organization use performance appraisal, and how you should complete performance appraisals in ways that will maximize the likelihood of desirable outcomes and minimize the likelihood of undesirable ones. We will examine this hypothesis more fully in Chapters 13 and 14, but it is reasonable to believe that managers or supervisors with very little organizational experience (e.g., new hires, fresh from completing their BA or MBA) may approach performance appraisal in a relatively straightforward way, trying to do a diligent job observing the performance of their subordinates and giving them accurate ratings and feedback. Over time, they are likely to learn whether or not this strategy is an effective one, and also to learn how their rating strategy compares with the rating strategies of their peers. As they become more experienced as managers, they are likely to learn how to make the most effective use of performance appraisal as a tool for motivating employees, for building a positive work group climate, and even for self-promotion.

It is clear that some aspects of role socialization are easier than others. For example, expectations about the content of work are easily changed through experience (Wanous, 1980). Values and general work orientation are much less easily changed. In part this is because values are more firmly entrenched and more central than specific expectations about the content of work. However, there is another factor that influences the degree to which a person can be changed through socialization: the method of training. It might be difficult to impart values and norms directly; these may require somewhat indirect methods of socialization. However, individuals who share common experiences early in their tenure with the organization (e.g., while going through training and learning how to perform their jobs together) may also come to share perceptions and values that influence their subsequent behavior as raters. Weiss (1978), for example, suggests that organizational values are learned through modeling the behavior (and apparent values) of others. The ease with which modeling affects probably depends on the number of opportunities the focal person has to make relevant observations of others' behavior, as well as the power and status of the role sender (Fisher, 1986).

Organizational Culture and Rater Goals

Modeling of the behaviors of specific role senders is only one way in which newcomers acquire the values of the work group and the organization. These values and expectations that define the climate and culture of the organization influence many of the interactions between the focal person and other members of the organization (Rousseau, 1988; Schneider, Ehrhart, & Macey, 2011, 2013; Schneider & Reichers, 1983); these values will probably therefore influence the development of specific goals for performance appraisal.

Martin and Siehl (1983) note that the culture of an organization offers "an interpretation of an institution's history that members can use to decipher how they will be expected to behave in the future" (p. 52). Thus, the culture defines the behaviors that are either accepted or sanctioned, and the process of transmitting that culture (e.g., through stories or rituals) may serve as a powerful socializing force. In the context of performance appraisal, the culture might determine what approach to appraisal and what behaviors are evaluated positively or negatively in the organization.

It is reasonable to expect that beliefs, values, and norms regarding performance appraisal will often be a part of the organization's culture. In some organizations, appraisal is treated as important, and in others it is treated as a joke. Feedback is readily given and readily received in some organizations, and avoided in others (Sully, De Luque, & Sommer, 2000). Ratings are a critical determinant of decisions in some organizations but are ignored in others. It is possible that all of these aspects of appraisal are influenced by the culture of the organization, and the newcomers must learn that culture before they can use the appraisal system effectively to achieve their goals.

Organizational cultures can be described in terms of both the content and intensity of the values and beliefs that are part of that culture (Rousseau, 1988). The culture of an organization is most likely to affect the behavior of raters when: (a) it includes beliefs, values, and so on that are directly relevant to appraisal, and (b) those values, beliefs, and so on are strongly held. For example, Bjerke et al. (1987) studied the performance appraisal system used to evaluate officers in the U.S. Navy (the Fitness Report). They observed that there appears to be a strong norm in that organization that appraisals should be used to secure promotion for deserving subordinates (and for those who show promise of performing well in more responsible jobs). Most raters appeared to accept this norm, and filled out their appraisals with promotion in mind (Bjerke et al., 1987). These same conditions (i.e., strongly held beliefs about how appraisal should be done) may make it difficult to change the appraisal system in an organization without first changing the culture of the organization. However, it is possible that the relationship between performance appraisal norms and organizational culture is bidirectional. That is, changing the culture of an organization may make it easier to change performance appraisal systems, but it is also possible that making a substantial change in appraisal systems could change an organization's culture. In particular, an appraisal system that includes extensive opportunities for voice and for participation may help to make the entire organization more egalitarian and less rigidly hierarchical.

Goals as a Function of Subordinate Performance

To some extent, the rater's goals will be driven by the climate and culture that pervades the organization, as well as by the formal demands of the performance appraisal system. However, it is unlikely that a given rater pursues the same set of goals when evaluating each of his or her subordinates. Rather, there are likely to be very different goals when evaluating a chronically poor performer than when evaluating someone whose work is usually excellent. In the case of poor performers, the rater's goals might be to improve the performance, or to improve the chances that the worker will be transferred to some other work unit, or to justify a decision to discipline or dismiss the worker; the choice among goals such as these may depend in part on the extent to which the work group accepts your evaluation and supports your acting on it. In the case of good performers, the rater's goals will probably center on maintaining current performance; giving ratings that lead to raises, bonuses, or awards might be one mechanism for accomplishing this goal.

Although goals will be tailored, to some extent, to the subordinate, it is important to note that some goals are probably relevant to all subordinates (e.g., the goal of maintaining a positive work group climate), and probably do not vary as a function of the subordinate's performance level. The goals that are most likely to vary as a function of the ratee's performance are those in the categories we have labeled "task performance" and "self-seeking" goals.

Before discussing the specific goals that are pursued for good versus poor performers, it is useful to discuss a related, but somewhat more complex distinction among the individuals who report to a given supervisor. That is, the members of the work group can often be divided into two categories: (a) those in the in-group, and (b) those in the out-group. Raters probably pursue different goals when evaluating members of these two groups.

In-Group Versus Out-Group

Supervisors do not treat all subordinates the same way, nor should they. A widely researched theory of leadership, leader–member exchange (LMX) theory (Dansereau, Graen, & Haga, 1975; Erdogan & Liden, 2002; Gerstner & Day, 1997) suggests that different supervisor–subordinate dyads may involve distinctly different styles of interaction. In particular, the theory also suggests that dyads can be classified into those involving members of the in-group and those involving members of the out-group. Members of the in-group are chosen on the basis of (a) competence and skill, (b) the degree to which they can be trusted by the supervisor, and (c) their motivation to assume responsibility at work (Liden & Graen, 1980). In-group members perform the tasks that are most critical and challenging, whereas out-group members perform more mundane tasks. Furthermore, members of the in-group receive more information, as well as more confidence and concern from supervisors than do those in the out-group (Graen & Uhl-Bien, 1995).

One way to characterize the difference between the in-group and the out-group is that in-group members are treated by supervisors as trusted assistants, whereas out-group members are treated as hired hands (Vecchio & Gobdel, 1984). That is, in-group members are treated as valued colleagues; out-group members are treated as if they are temporary employees who are not really the concern of the supervisor. Supervisors typically devote more attention, resources, and the like to in-group members, even though out-group members might have a greater need for assistance, information, and other resources to perform their jobs.

Research on the LMX model suggests that supervisors adopt very different leadership styles when dealing with members of the in- versus the out-group (Graen & Uhl-Bien, 1995). In general, supervisors are more participative when dealing with in-group members, and more directive or authoritarian when dealing with out-group members. In the context of performance appraisal, this suggests that supervisors will more readily incorporate information from in-group members in their evaluations, and will usually devote more time and effort to feedback for in-group as opposed to out-group members.

Research on in- versus out-groups has dealt with several issues that are directly relevant to performance appraisal. First, and most fascinating, there is evidence that in-group status is related to subjective ratings of performance, but not to objective indices of performance (Vecchio & Gobdel, 1984). This implies that the perceived competence of in-group members may be an effect rather than the cause of their assignment to the in-group. It is possible that supervisors who feel that they can trust certain subordinates will perceive their performance as better than it actually is. A second relevant finding is that out-group members typically receive more extreme evaluations than do in-group members (Linville & Jones, 1980). These evaluations are usually negative, but the out-group member who actually does perform well may receive highly inflated ratings. One possible explanation for this effect is the fact that out-group members are expected to perform poorly. Performance that violates those expectations may attract more attention than performance that conforms to expectations (Hastie, 1980; Murphy, Balzer, Lockhart, & Eisenman, 1985).

Another finding in this research is that out-groups are seen as relatively homogeneous, whereas differences between in-group members are readily noticed by supervisors (Park & Rothbart, 1982). As a result, out-group members may all receive similar evaluations; stereotypes of the group as a whole may generalize to all group members. One implication of this finding is that performance evaluations may not provide feedback that is useful to out-group members. This feedback may reflect the group, and may not be tailored to specific individuals in the group. Another implication is that there will often be range restriction in ratings of out-group members. Thus, raters who have small in-groups and large out-groups may be especially likely to provide ratings that do not discriminate among most subordinates.

The terms in-group and out-group are not synonymous with "good performer" and "poor performer." Nevertheless, research on in- versus out-group status may be useful in forming hypotheses about the goals that raters are likely to have when rating subordinates who have performed well or poorly. In particular, this literature suggests that good and poor performers may differ not only in the ratings they receive, but also in terms of how they are treated by supervisors in the appraisal process (e.g., the degree to which developmental feedback is given). In particular, there might be substantial differences in the goals being pursued by the rater when the ratee is a good, average, or poor performer.

Goals for Superior Performers

As we note in the next chapter, rating inflation is the norm in most organizations rather than the exception. One implication is that raters might find it difficult to give ratings to truly good performers that adequately reflect their actual performance level. If nearly everyone receives ratings at or near the top end of the scale, numerical ratings cannot be used to communicate to the ratee that he or she has really performed well. Thus, one goal that will often be relevant to the rater when evaluating a truly good performer will be to communicate to the ratee and the organization the fact that this individual's performance is in fact better than that of others who have received high ratings.

As we noted earlier, raters may address this problem by developing a special vocabulary (Bjerke et al., 1987) or communication rules (Schall, 1983) that allow them to give ratings that are acceptable to all subordinates (in practice, this usually means giving inflated ratings to most ratees) and still communicate their evaluations of their subordinates. For example, a subordinate might receive a rating of "6" on a 7-point scale, and may be described as "somewhat above average" in the narrative or comment section of the appraisal. However, a phrase such as "somewhat above average" might connote poor performance; phrases such as "excellent in all respects of the job" might be used to signal performance that is actually above average. This process of developing special communication rules is especially likely to occur in organizations that have a strong and uniform culture. In such organizations, supervisors are probably well aware of what aspects of the job are treated as important, and are probably also aware of the special meanings that are given to specific evaluative terms in that organization.

A second goal that is highly relevant when evaluating good performers is to guide their development in such a way that they will be prepared for promotion, or for more complex assignments. The supervisor might accomplish this, for example, by giving feedback on aspects of performance that are not especially relevant for the subordinate's current job, but that are highly relevant for the next higher job in the organization. The popular literature contains many descriptions of mentoring and coaching: this approach to performance appraisal may correspond closely to one of the roles of a mentor or a coach.

One self-serving goal that might be pursued is to bring higher management's attention to the accomplishments of superior performers. Exceptional performance by your subordinates is likely to enhance your own standing as a supervisor; this is particularly true in organizations where the evaluation of the supervisor depends in part on the performance of the subordinates. We expect that the probability that this goal will affect rater behavior will be positively correlated with the subordinate's performance level. The better the subordinate's performance, the more the supervisor has to gain by bringing that performance to the attention of others in the organization.

Goals for Average Performers

It is reasonable to assume that in a large work group, the true distribution of job performance is reasonably normal (see, however, O'Boyle & Aguinis, 2012). One implication is that the number of truly good or truly poor performers will be small relative to the number of individuals whose performance can best be described as "average." Although average performers are the most numerous, we believe that raters do not pay a great deal of attention to their goals for evaluating average performers. There are several reasons for this. First, good performers are probably in the in-group and will therefore naturally receive much of the rater's attention and concern. Second, poor performers require attention; their low level of performance can directly affect the overall output of the work group, particularly if the work performed requires a high level of interdependence. Third, average performance is probably not as salient (or interesting) as either outstandingly good or outstandingly poor performance. As a result, average performers may not receive the attention they deserve.

There are a few goals that might become relevant for average performers, depending on the characteristics of both the person and the situation. First, there might be some individuals who because of their trustworthiness and responsibility, would be good candidates for the in-group. The rater's goal when evaluating these individuals might be to improve their performance, and bring it up to the level of other in-group members. Second, the rater might have a strong incentive to help improve the performance of individuals who are members of specific groups. For example, the supervisor whose values encourage affirmative action efforts might devote considerable time and attention to the development of members of protected groups whose performance is at or below the work group's average. On the other hand, the supervisor who is prejudiced against members of specific groups might be inclined to give them harsh ratings; the underlying goal may be to remove these individuals from the work group.

Goals for Poor Performers

The research literature dealing with supervisors' reactions to poor performance is extensive. Although relatively few studies deal directly with performance appraisal, several conclusions can be drawn about the appraisal goals that might be pursued when evaluating poor performers.

It is clear that managers prefer to avoid dealing with the problem of poor performance (Mitchell & O'Reilly, 1983). In the context of appraisal, raters might avoid the problem by giving relatively high ratings, accompanied by vague and noncommittal comments. In this case, feedback is likely to be perfunctory, and little effort will be expended to improve the subordinate's performance. In many cases, however, it may be impossible to ignore poor performance, either because it is extremely bad or because there are situational factors (e.g., coworkers' resentment) that force the rater to attend to the problem of poor performance.

The rater's reaction to a poor-performing subordinate probably depends on the attributions he or she makes when deciding about the cause of that performance (Jones & Nisbett, 1971; Mitchell & O'Reilly, 1983; Ross, 1977). Mitchell, Green, and Wood (1981) described several different categories of attribution, including those that explain poor performance in terms of a lack of ability, a lack of values and standards, an unfavorable environment, or a variety of temporary barriers to performance (e.g., family crises). These specific categories of attributions can in turn be classified in terms of two dimensions that are frequently encountered in attributional research: (a) attributions to internal versus external causes, and (b) attributions to stable versus temporary causes. The supervisor's response may be very different, depending on the type of attribution.

Attributions depend on a number of factors, including the behavior itself, and the values, standards, and inclinations of the supervisor (e.g., some supervisors make more internal attributions than others). Another factor that appears to influence the supervisor's attributions is the outcome of the behavior. The same behavior might be evaluated differently, and different causes might be cited for that behavior, depending on the seriousness of the outcomes of that behavior. For example, if two subordinates follow the exact same unsafe work practices, and one of them causes or experiences an accident, they will probably be evaluated differently, with harsher evaluations for the person involved in the accident.

Research on attributions suggests systematic differences in the supervisors' versus subordinates' explanations for poor performance. In general, supervisors make more internal attributions (e.g., the person did not perform well because of poor work values), whereas subordinates are biased in favor of external attributions (e.g., constraints in the situation made it impossible to perform well; Gioia & Sims, 1985; Ilgen, Mitchell, & Frederickson, 1981). The tendency of supervisors to make internal attributions increases the likelihood that their responses will involve discipline or punishment for the poor-performing subordinate.

Arvey and Jones (1985) note that the topic of discipline or punishment in organizational settings has been largely ignored by behavioral scientists. Studies that have examined punishment suggest that performance appraisal is sometimes used as a vehicle for administering discipline. For example, Jones, Tait, and Butler (1983) studied the degree to which different supervisory behaviors were perceived by subordinates as punishing. Behaviors that were cited as being very punishing included: (a) telling a superior about your mistakes, (b) documenting the negative things you do, and (c) publicly praising everyone in the group but you. These and other punishing behaviors may be used differently in in-groups versus out-groups (Arvey & Jones, 1985); in general, the frequency and severity of punishment will be lower in the in-group.

If the attribution is external, the supervisor may avoid punishing the subordinate. Task performance goals for poor-performing subordinates (assuming that the attributions are external) will probably involve efforts to develop the subordinate, to maintain or increase motivation, and to move the subordinate to circumstances that are more favorable (e.g., a less difficult assignment or a different, more supportive work group). The rater who intends to develop a poor-performing subordinate will probably (a) give higher ratings than deserved, in an effort to avoid organizational sanctions and maintain motivation, (b) devote more attention to feedback, and (c) identify weaknesses in feedback sessions, but not in the performance evaluation forms that are turned in to the organization.

When attributions are internal, strategic goals that involve getting rid of the poor-performing subordinate may strongly influence rating behavior. This will depend in part on how bad the performance really is. The worse the performance, the stronger the incentive will be to get rid of the subordinate. The strength of this goal may also depend on what specific aspects of performance are below standard. For example, supervisors might be more strongly inclined to get rid of subordinates whose poor performance reflects an inability to get along with coworkers than those whose performance reflects sincere effort but low ability. In general, performance deficiencies that may affect other coworkers may present a stronger incentive to get rid of the subordinate than will deficiencies that involve the individual only.

Raters' responses to poor performance may depend in part on their level of power in comparison to the person they are rating. Raters who have substantial power are more likely to make a proactive response, either engaging the ratee in activities designed to develop better performer or confronting the ratee over his or her shortcomings. Ratees who have less power may be somewhat more likely to avoid interacting with poor performers or to compensate for their poor performance in some way (Ferguson, Ormiston, & Moon, 2010; see, however, Liden et al., 1999).

The exact rating strategy for accomplishing the goals described above will depend in part on the policies of the organization. For example, if the organization is very reluctant to fire poor performers, it may not be a good idea to give low ratings. If the subordinate consistently receives low ratings, it may be very difficult to persuade the organization to transfer him or her to another work group. The attractiveness of "dumping" a poor-performing subordinate on another work group will vary as a function of the nature and size of the organization. In a small organization, supervisors are more likely to know one another, and to be friends. It may be very difficult, in this case, to transfer a poor-performing subordinate to someone else's work group without negatively affecting your relationship with that supervisor.

ANALYZING PERFORMANCE RATING STRATEGIES AS A CHOICE BETWEEN ALTERNATIVES

A series of influential articles in the 1980s (e.g., Feldman, 1981; Landy & Farr, 1980) encouraged performance appraisal researchers and practitioners to think about performance appraisal as an information processing exercise. That is, topics such as attention, memory, and the integration of information were held out as important for making progress in understanding performance rating and performance evaluation. This type of research did make many contributions, but by the 1990s the field was shifting its attention from cognition to understanding how the context in which performance appraisal occurs drives rating behavior and toward examining the factors that motivate raters to give high or low ratings (Banks & Murphy, 1985; Longenecker et al., 1987; Levy & Williams, 2004; Murphy & Cleveland, 1991, 1995; Murphy & DeNisi, 2008).

As we have noted in several places, it is important to distinguish between the judgments raters form when completing performance appraisal forms and the actual ratings they assign (Landy & Farr, 1980; Murphy & Cleveland, 1995; Murphy & DeNisi, 2008). Judgments about performance are not something that occur only when it is time to complete performance appraisal forms, but rather they represent an ongoing process that involves a number of separate cognitive and affective processes (e.g., what did you observe, how did you interpret it, how do you feel about the person being evaluated?).

Regardless of the judgments they may have formed about the performance and effectiveness of their subordinates, raters need to make two choices when it comes time to complete performance appraisal forms. First, should the rater record the number that best represents his or her judgment about the performance of the ratee? There may be a number of good reasons to record a number that is not identical to the rater's judgments about the ratee. If the rater does choose to distort (i.e., put a number on the appraisal form that is different from his or her private judgment), he or she will have to choose whether to give higher ratings or lower ratings than the ratee appears to deserve. Schematically, the choice raters face when completing a performance appraisal form is portrayed in Figure 12.1.

If performance appraisal is approached from the perspective of a cost-benefit analysis, it is clear that supervisors have few good reasons to give accurate ratings and even fewer to give harsh ratings (i.e., ratings that are lower than the ratee's performance would warrant), but that they have many good reasons to give inflated ones (Longenecker et al., 1987; Murphy & Cleveland, 1995). Mohrman and Lawler (1983) note that there are typically few rewards and many penalties for doing accurate appraisals. Various studies have shown that raters manipulate performance ratings to avoid negative consequences (e.g., Bernardin & Beatty,

FIGURE 12.1 ■ From Judgments to Ratings

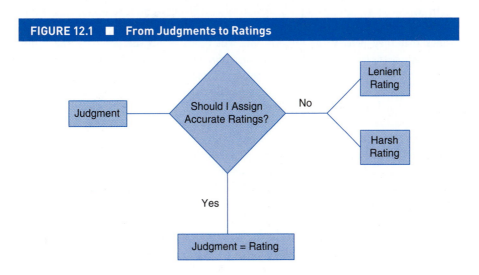

1984; Cleveland & Murphy, 1992; Longenecker et al., 1987; Spence & Keeping, 2010; Tziner, Murphy, & Cleveland, 2005), to comply with organizational norms (Bernardin & Beatty, 1984; DeCotiis & Petit, 1978; Spence & Keeping 2010; Tziner et al., 2005) and to further their own interests (Spence & Keeping, 2010; Villanova & Bernardin, 1989).

A number of authors (e.g., Kane, 1994; Murphy & Cleveland, 1991, 1995) have proposed models of raters' decisions to distort ratings. These models start by considering the likely outcomes if raters give performance ratings that are either accurate or inflated.[2] Because most employees overestimate their own level of performance, performance ratings that are reasonably accurate will often seem unfair and harsh, whereas ratings that are inflated will seem reasonable and fair. The models used to describe and explain distortion in performance ratings can give you important insights into why performance ratings often seem to fail in organizations.

Outcomes of Accurate Versus Distorted Ratings

Suppose you are a typical employee and you think your performance is above average. You would be in good company—most people rate themselves above average on a wide range of indices. For example, about 80% of all drivers think they are above average in driving skills (McCormick, Walkey, & Green, 1986). Accurate ratings of your job performance will probably be lower than what you expect and believe you deserve, and this is likely to have several consequences. First, if you expect positive feedback but receive feedback that your performance is not as good as you thought, you will probably feel disappointed and may even feel you have been treated unfairly. Your relationship with your supervisor may deteriorate. You might not receive as big a raise as you think you deserve, and you may end up concluding that the whole performance rating system is unreliable. On the other hand, if your supervisor gives you ratings that are higher than you actually deserve, you will probably be more satisfied and will probably have a more positive feeling about performance appraisal. It is perhaps ironic, but there is evidence that distorting ratings may actually *contribute* to the perception that they are accurate and fair, and giving fair and accurate ratings can contribute to the perception that ratings are rigged.

In general, we can group the probable outcomes of giving accurate versus inflated ratings into four categories. First, there are interpersonal consequences. Giving your subordinates ratings that they perceive as unfairly low will probably not be good for the future relationship between you and that subordinate. Second, there are systemic consequences. As we noted in Chapters 9 and 10, the ratings people receive influence their reactions to and their beliefs about the performance appraisal system in their organization. Receiving ratings that you believe are unfairly low could shake your confidence in this system. Third, there are practical consequences. Ratees who receive accurate ratings may miss out on chances for raises and promotions if their peers are receiving inflated ratings. Finally, there are self-serving consequences. A manager who tells the organization that all of his or her subordinates are performing well is also indirectly telling the organization that he or she must be an effective manager (Bowman, 1999; Murphy & Cleveland, 1995), whereas a rater who gives accurate (i.e., lower) ratings is telling his or her superiors that he or she is not doing the thing managers are most responsible for—that is, helping their subordinates to perform their jobs at peak efficiency. Table 12.2 lists a number of the likely consequences of giving accurate versus inflated ratings.

TABLE 12.2 ■ Probable Consequences of Giving Accurate Versus Inflated Ratings

Accurate

Interpersonal Consequences

    Disappointment and resentment on the part of the ratee

    Deterioration in relationships with raters

Systemic Consequences

    Reduced confidence in the rater

    Reduced confidence in performance appraisal

Practical Consequences

    Fewer rewards

    Decreased motivation

Self-Serving Consequence

    Negative impressions on the part of your own superiors

Inflated

Interpersonal Consequence

    Positive relations with subordinates are maintained and reinforced

Systemic Consequences

    Ratees will perceive performance evaluations as fair and accurate

    More trust in and commitment to the organization

Practical Consequences

    Ratees receive valued rewards

    Motivation increases

Self-Serving Consequence

    Positive impressions are conveyed to your own superiors

Contingencies

In addition to thinking about the possible consequences of giving accurate versus inflated ratings, raters may need to consider the strength of the link between ratings and consequences. For example, if a supervisor gives inflated ratings, this increases the likelihood of subordinates getting raises and promotions, but there is no guarantee that they *will* receive these raises or promotion. If other raters also give inflated ratings, simply inflating your own ratings may not be enough to guarantee that your subordinates get raises. On the other hand, if other raters are lenient and you choose to give accurate ratings, this might have a strong and immediate effect on outcomes that are important to your subordinates. Similarly, giving high ratings *may* lead to good feelings on the part of your employees (however, they are likely to believe that they fully deserve good ratings, so it is not a good idea to expect gratitude), but you can be pretty sure that if you give accurate ratings, which appear to be unduly harsh to your subordinates, they will resent what appears to be shabby treatment.

On the whole, the links between ratings, behaviors, and negative outcomes are likely to be stronger than the links between ratings and more positive outcomes. That is, giving inflated ratings will often help, but since most other raters are also giving inflated ratings, they may not have a strong effect. On the other hand, if most other raters give inflated ratings and you give accurate ones, these low scores will really stand out, and they will be likely to trigger some unfortunate consequences.

Numerous models of decision making and choice start with the two variables described here—the likely outcomes of different choices and the perceived links between the choices a rater makes and those outcomes—and combine these two factors to make predictions about what choices raters will make (Beach, 1990; Busemeyer & Townsend, 1993; Edwards, 1980; Edwards & Newman, 1982; Hammond, McClelland, & Mumpower, 1980; Kahneman, 2011; Kahneman & Tversky, 1979; Keeney & Raiffa, 1976; Roe, Busemeyer, & Townsend, 2001; Vancouver, Weinhardt, & Schmidt, 2010). These models differ in a number of important ways, but they all agree that people are likely to choose a particular course of action if: (1) this action is linked to valued outcomes, and (2) the links between that choice and those outcomes are strong and dependable. Thus, a choice that might lead to highly valued outcomes might not look so attractive if the links between that choice and those outcomes are uncertain or weak. For example, a person might believe that the chance to go into space would be a wonderful accomplishment, but also understand that the likelihood of being selected for and succeeding in astronaut school is extremely low. Virtually all models of decision making and choice suggest that even though the outcome might be a very desirable one, if the perceived likelihood of accomplishing that outcome is low, there will not be much motivation to pursue that choice of action.

Integrating Multiple Perspectives on Motivation to Distort Ratings

Murphy and Cleveland's (1995) discussion of rater motivation focuses largely on the rater's decision of what rating to record, and is based on the assumption that this rating might not always correspond to the rater's judgments about ratee performance. Like many

SPOTLIGHT 12.1 A MULTIPLE GOAL PURSUIT MODEL

Ballard, Yeo, Loft, Vancouver, and Neal (2016) have developed and tested an integrative model of motivation and decision making, referred to as the MGPM* model. This model is an extension of an earlier model developed by Vancouver, Weinhardt, and Schmidt (2010), and it is a very useful framework for understanding how raters might make choices among various rating strategies when evaluating the performance of their subordinates.

Ballard et al. (2016) start by noting, "people often pursue multiple, competing goals, striving to achieve desired outcomes while avoiding undesirable outcomes. Because individuals have limited time and resources, they often have to choose which goal to prioritize at the expense of progress toward others" (p. 1240). They developed a model to help them study and predict the choice among different courses of action. Some of the key concepts of this model are summarized in Table 12.3.

One of the key insights in the MGPM* model is that the choice to pursue particular goals is not a "one-and-done" event. That is, it is wrong to assume that

TABLE 12.3 ■ Key Concepts in the MGPM* Model
• Discrepancy—difference between the current state of a variable and the reference state, or the goal
• Expected utility—multiplicative function of the value of a goal and the perceived likelihood of reaching that goal
• Goal types—approach goals involve a desirable state people want to pursue, whereas avoidance goals involve undesirable states people want to avoid
• Dynamism—the value of a goal can change as a function of the size of the discrepancy; the motivational value of approach goals decreases the closer you are to accomplishing the goal, whereas the motivational value of avoidance goals increases the closer you are to the undesirable state
• Attention weight—likelihood that people will attend to each possible consequence of attaining a goal

individuals choose one goal, then continue to pursue it to the exclusion of other goals over time. Rather, this model assumes that the attractiveness of different goals can change over time, especially as people make progress toward accomplishing a goal, and people might switch goals in a predictable way. The other key insight of this model is that framing matters. The value that is attached to a goal might change depending on whether it is framed and understood by the decision maker to be an approach goal (e.g., maintain good relationships with your subordinates) or an avoidance goal (e.g., avoid interpersonal conflicts over performance evaluation). This theory helps to explain why people often shift priority from approach goals to avoidance goals over time.

According to the MGPM* model, raters who have the option to pursue a number of different goals when completing performance appraisals make this choice by considering the possible consequences of achieving different goals, the likelihood that they *can* accomplish these goals, and the value of the different consequences. Their assessments of several of these factors might change as the discrepancy between the current state and the desired goal state grows or shrinks. Thus, we might assume that the goals pursued by raters when they complete performance appraisals might differ both across raters (Murphy et al., 2004) and within raters across time.

Finally, this model suggests that the motivational power of particular goals change as you approach accomplishing each goal. On the whole, the power of positive goals (e.g., goal of seeking a reward) to motivate behavior *decreases* as you approach accomplishing the goal, which implies that the anticipation of good outcomes might be more motivating than the outcomes themselves. On the other hand, the motivating power of negative goals (e.g., goal of avoiding punishments) *increases* the closer you get to reaching them. Thus, raters might not worry much about negative outcomes that might occur in the distant future, but might be strongly motivated to avoid imminent threats. If we apply this to performance appraisal, the MGPM* model suggests that raters might be influenced by potential positive outcomes as they are thinking about how they want to approach performance appraisal in the future, but as they approach the time when they will actually have to prepare and submit performance ratings, they become more and more focused on avoiding negative consequences.

Ballard et al. (2016) suggest that one practical application of their theory is to illustrate the potential benefits of reframing goals in ways that allow people to appropriately balance competing objectives over time. For example, using performance feedback with the goal of building and maintaining good relationships with subordinates might entail different choices over time than using performance with the goal of minimizing conflict with employees. An approach goal might encourage more frequent positive feedback (consistent with the philosophy of performance management), whereas an avoidance goal might encourage raters to give inflated ratings when they complete performance appraisals in an effort to avoid conflict in the annual appraisal meeting.

other models (e.g., Ballard et al., 2016; Spence & Keeping, 2011), their focus is largely on conscious distortion in rating—that is, the decision at the time performance ratings are required to give employees ratings that are higher than they truly deserve. Other authors suggest that the processes that lead to widespread rating inflation occur at a very different point in time and unfold in ways that models of conscious distortion fail to capture.

Harris (1994) notes that the same factors that motivate raters to distort the ratings they provide (e.g., rewards, avoidance of negative consequences, impression management) might also influence rater behaviors throughout the process of acquiring information about ratee performance, recalling and integrating this information to form a judgment, deciding what rating to assign, then deciding what feedback to provide. Although Harris recognizes the potential role of rating distortion, he makes the important point that during the time in which raters complete performance appraisal forms, this is probably not the only circumstance in the appraisal process in which rater motivation matters. Rather, raters who are motivated to provide accurate ratings are likely to be more careful in their observations, to take steps to accurately recall ratee behavior (e.g., keeping behavior diaries), and might be more mindful when pulling this information together to reach judgments about ratee performance. Raters who know that at the end of the day they are going to give high ratings to everyone will probably put less time and effort into evaluating their subordinates.

So far, we have focused on understanding what motivates raters to distort their ratings but Spence and Keeping (2011) note that the same forces that often lead to distorted ratings can in some circumstances provide motivation to rate accurately, especially if accurate rating serves at least one of three goals: (1) enhancing relationships with subordinates, (2) improving the rater's image within the organization, or (3) increasing the likelihood of achieving the goals of the organization. They argue that some employees want accurate feedback, and that they may value accurate ratings because these ratings can help them improve their future performance. Similarly, in an appraisal system where just about everyone gives inflated ratings, that small group of raters whose evaluations are more accurate and honest might be recognized as people who are doing their best to make the appraisal system work as intended. Finally, one of the cornerstones of performance management is the idea that feedback about performance can be used to direct employee behavior in ways that will maximize the likelihood of accomplishing important organizational goals, and accurate feedback (even if that feedback is painful) may be more useful than distorted feedback.

Spencer and Keeping's (2011) point that there can be strong motives to provide accurate rather than distorted ratings is well taken. Other models (e.g., Murphy & Cleveland, 1995) have focused on raters' motivation to distort ratings, but have not given much consideration to raters' motivation to provide accurate ratings. What both Spencer and Keeping (2011) and Murphy and Cleveland (1995) failed to explicitly consider is the possibility that accuracy in rating might help in achieving some goals (e.g., advancing the interests of the organization) while decreasing the likelihood of other goals (e.g., enhancing relationships with subordinates). The question then is how raters will balance the potential gains and losses associated with accuracy in rating.

There is little empirical research on how these tradeoffs might be resolved, but we can suggest some possibilities. Distortion in rating (usually leniency) is likely to help with two things. First, it helps in maintaining a positive relationship with subordinates. Second, it helps with maintaining the image of success as a supervisor or manager (because all of your subordinates are "successful"). On the other hand, accuracy is more likely to help the organization achieve its goals. It seems likely that raters will pick that which is good for the organization over that which is good for themselves and their subordinates if (1) there is a strong identification with the goals of the organization, (2) the rater is sufficiently confident of his or her image in the organization that the incentive to enhance that reputation via rating distortion is minimal, and/or (3) relationships with subordinates are either so good that lower ratings will not hurt them, so negative that lenient ratings will not help, or so unimportant that they do not really matter to the rater. We believe that raters who either (a) depend very much on the cooperation and good will of their subordinates or (b) have not established a strong and lasting image in the organization will be most likely to distort their ratings.

Avoiding Negative Outcomes

One of the themes of numerous models of choice and decision making is that negative outcomes often have stronger influence on decisions and choices than positive ones. For example, according to prospect theory (Kahneman & Tversky, 1979), losses are often seen as more substantial than equivalent gains. That is, gaining $200 feels good but losing $200 feels *very* bad, and people will work harder to avoid a $200 loss than they will to pursue a $200 gain.

The effect of negative outcomes is likely to be especially important in performance appraisal because of the certainty of positive and negative outcomes if inflated versus accurate ratings are given. That is, in a context where most raters give and most ratees expect highly positive ratings, the likelihood of resentment, reduced rewards, conflict, and the like may be pretty high if you give accurate ratings, whereas giving inflated ratings does not really do anything to make you stand out from the crowd. That is, raters have a number of reasons to give inflated ratings, but they have even stronger reasons to avoid giving accurate ratings. Thus, in an organization where accurate performance feedback really is desired, it might be more important to find ways to shield raters from negative consequences than it is to give them positive reasons to provide accurate ratings. We take up this suggestion in more detail in Chapters 13 and 14.

Explaining Rating Distortion

So far, we have focused on motivational models that use some combination of beliefs about the outcomes of different choices when completing performance ratings and about the strength of the links between ratings and those outcomes to make predictions about whether raters will give accurate or distorted ratings. These models have considerable explanatory power, but they probably put too much emphasis on cold, rational choice. It is misleading to assume that raters simply weigh the consequences of different choices they might make when rating and blindly pursue the course of action with the highest expected utility (that is, value of outcomes multiplied by the perceived link between particular choices and these outcomes). There are attributes of individuals and of the context in which ratings occur that may lead raters to choose evaluation strategies that may not be optimal from a strictly rational point of view.

Individual Differences

Our discussion of leniency in rating has focused mainly on motivational factors (e.g., a desire to avoid negative relationships with subordinates), but there are also individual differences that influence the likelihood that raters will be lenient in their ratings. For example, Markus and Kitayama (1991) proposed that some supervisors have an *independent* view of human behavior, with an emphasis on the role of the individual and his or her own characteristics in determining behavior, whereas others have an *interdependent* view of human behavior, with a stronger emphasis on the role of society and the context in shaping behavior. There is evidence that raters whose worldview emphasizes interdependence tend to give higher performance ratings than raters who emphasize independence (Mishra & Roch, 2013).

The independent–interdependent dichotomy suggested by Markus and Kitayama (1991) is clearly related to the broader cultural dimensions of collectivism–individualism (Hofstede, 2001). There is evidence that raters from more collectivistic cultures tend to be more lenient (Ng et al., 2011). This same study also presented evidence that the cultural dimension of Power Distance may help to explain the tendency of some rating sources (e.g., peers) to be more lenient than others.

In addition to broad worldviews and cultural factors, there are aspects of raters' personalities that can influence performance ratings, although the effects of personality on leniency are not always clear. For example, the weight raters place on different performance dimensions when forming their overall evaluations can differ, depending on rater personality. Ogunfowora, Bourdage, and Lee (2010) reported that raters who are high on Openness to Experience tend to place more emphasis on success in dealing with complex and unpredictable environments, whereas raters who are high on Modesty tend to place more weight on maintaining control and abiding by rules. Although there have not been direct empirical tests of the links between these personality dimensions and rating inflation, it is reasonable to expect that raters who are high on Agreeableness will be more likely to be lenient than less Agreeable raters.

Finally, there are a range of beliefs about the task of performance appraisal and about the organization that can influence distortion in rating. Rater's beliefs that they have the tools, information, and skills to evaluate their subordinates' behavior are an important component of the motivation to rate accurately (Bernardin & Villanova, 2005; Brutus, Fletcher, & Baldry, 2009); there is even evidence that perceptions of self-efficacy as a rater are related to the quality of rating data (Bernardin & Villanova, 2005; Tziner & Murphy, 1999). Tziner (1999) and Tziner and Murphy (1999) present evidence that beliefs about the organization (e.g., perceptions of the climate of the organization, commitment to the organization), relationships between supervisors and subordinates, and perceptions of self-efficacy as a rater (i.e., beliefs that you have the necessary information and skills to accurately evaluate rate performance) all influence the likelihood that raters will inflate their evaluations of subordinates.

Contextual Factors

In several previous chapters, we have discussed the effects of contextual factors on performance appraisal processes and outcomes. The term *contextual factors* can include a wide range of variables, but there is one particular aspect of the rating context that appears to be particularly important in influencing rating distortion: the way organizations react when raters submit performance ratings that appear to be distorted. One way of determining whether organizations *actually* care about performance appraisal is to ask whether they attempt to reward raters for accuracy or to sanction raters for providing ratings that are clearly inaccurate. If there are genuine rewards for providing accurate ratings and useful feedback, or genuine sanctions for providing inaccurate evaluations, this might decrease the likelihood of rating distortion.

Bjerke et al.'s (1987) study of the U.S. Navy's Fitness Report (the form used to evaluate the performance of Naval officers) suggested that there were usually few negative consequences for raters who give inaccurate, inflated ratings (i.e., raters are not penalized for inaccuracy). However, they also found that there were limits to the amount of rating inflation that was viewed as acceptable, and that in some cases, raters were criticized for overdoing it—that is, providing ratings that were so blatantly unrealistic as to violate organizational norms. On the whole, we suspect it is easier to sanction rating distortion when it is so blatant that it offends the sensibilities of other managers and executives who are also providing inflated ratings than it is to reward accurate ratings. In virtually any organization, norms develop regarding the extent to which employees and managers are allowed to bend rules and skate around the edges of personnel policies versus doing things strictly by the book.[3] Raters who go beyond these implicit bounds when they rate their subordinates may be sanctioned.

Rewarding accuracy is arguably more difficult because it may be more difficult to tell if a particular rater is being accurate than it is to tell if he or she is distorting. A rater who consistently tells you that all of his or her subordinates are excellent in all aspects of performance all of the time is almost certainly pulling your leg. Ratings like this might serve a number of goals that are important to the rater, but it should be obvious that they are likely to be distorted and untrustworthy. On the other hand, a rater who tells you that some subordinates are performing well, some are performing poorly, and some are near average *might* be giving you accurate information, but it is also possible that the distribution is realistic but that the particulars are all wrong. That is, the rater might be giving you inaccurate information about *who* is a good performer, a poor performer, or an average performer, and if you do not have other information that can be used to cross-check these ratings, it might not be possible to tell if that rater really is providing accurate evaluations.

SUMMARY

The best explanation for rating inflation, which is rampant in most organizations, is that raters believe that giving high ratings (even unrealistically high ratings) will lead to valued outcomes and that giving accurate ratings will lead to undesirable outcomes. An analysis of the goals that appear to influence raters' choice to distort ratings suggests that distortion can influence task performance, interpersonal relationships, and the rater's own standing in the organization. Raters appear to develop their goals and strategies for using appraisal to accomplish these goals over time, and organizations often employ a mix of formal and informal socialization processes that are likely to help shape these goals and strategies.

Models of decision making and choice provide useful insights for understanding decisions to provide either accurate or distorted ratings. In particular, these models suggest that we need to consider both the range of outcomes that are likely to be tied to accurate versus inaccurate ratings and to the strength of the link between the ratings and these outcomes, and that the choice to distort ratings is often driven by an understanding that accurate ratings are very likely to lead to negative outcomes and that distorted ratings increase the probability of several positive outcomes. However, goals are not the only factor influencing rating distortion. There are both individual differences and a number of features of the context in which rating occurs that often push raters to give high ratings to virtually all of the people they rate.

EXERCISE: BUILD A GOAL ASSESSMENT TOOL

In this chapter, we have argued that raters are often motivated to inflate performance ratings in order to avoid conflict, to increase the motivation of their subordinates, to make themselves look good, and so on. You might get insight into rating dynamics if you knew what goals individual raters were pursuing, and the relative emphasis they placed on different goals. However, we suspect that if you ask supervisors "are you giving your subordinated high performance ratings in order to make yourself look good?", you may not get an honest answer. A better approach might be to assess whether: (a) ratings are likely to be inflated in your organization, and (b) conditions in your organization are likely to create pressures to inflate performance ratings.

First, take a careful look at both the distribution of performance ratings and the relationships between performance ratings and other likely indicators of performance or success. Suppose, for example, that you find that performance ratings are very strongly concentrated in the top few rating categories. This would be *potential* evidence of rating inflation, but suppose you also find that the people who receive the highest ratings are consistently more productive, or achieve better outcomes than the people who receive lower ratings. High average ratings, by themselves, do not allow you to draw strong conclusions about rating distortion, and if other evidence supports the usefulness of ratings (albeit with restricted range), you might conclude that whatever inflation is present is not necessarily something to be concerned about.

Suppose you determine that ratings do appear to be seriously distorted. The taxonomies of rater goals presented earlier in this chapter suggest that there are several likely explanations for ratings inflation. First, raters might inflate ratings to improve their relationships with subordinates. Second, raters may inflate ratings to help their subordinates obtain valued outcomes (e.g., raises). Third, raters might inflate ratings to make themselves look good. Organizational surveys might allow you to assess the likely strength of each of these motives.

First, you might survey employees to evaluate their perceptions of the fairness and accuracy of the ratings they receive, with a particular focus on the extent to which employees believe *their supervisor* is giving them fair evaluations. The more sensitivity to the fairness and accuracy or ratings from direct supervisors, the more pressure there is likely to be on raters to inflate ratings. Second, you can survey higher-level managers to determine how they evaluate the ratings supervisors provide. In organizations where raters are viewed unfavorably when their subordinates receive less positive evaluations, and viewed favorably when their subordinates are rated as effective performers, supervisors are more likely to pursue self-serving goals. Third, you can assess both the actual and the perceived links between performance ratings and valued rewards in your organization. If supervisors and employees believe that high performance ratings are a key to getting raises and promotions, this is likely to lead to motivation to inflate ratings— even if these beliefs are incorrect. As we will note in Chapters 13 and 14, many organizations claim that pay is linked to performance, but put in place policies (e.g., small merit pay pools) that make these links weak and inconsistent. Employees and supervisors, however, sometimes do not have the information to make informed judgments about the actual strength of these links, and they are more likely to act on their perceptions and beliefs.

Suppose you find that the conditions in your organization are ripe for rating inflation (e.g., employees believe that there are strong links between ratings and rewards and are strongly concerned that they are being unfairly evaluated, ratees are evaluated more positively if they hand in high ratings for their subordinates). It is not always clear that these conditions can, or even should be changed in organizations—the pursuit of more accurate performance ratings is valuable only if organizations actually use this information to make better decisions and to improve their workforce. The sort of assessment envisioned here will at least give you better insight into why ratings might be inflated and what might be done to counter that inflation, but the decision about whether or not these changes *should* be made will not always be a simple one.

NOTES

1. Murphy and Cleveland (1995) labeled these "strategic goals," but the label "self-serving goals" is more precise, because the strategic objective here is to make the rater look good.

2. Raters who distort their ratings typically give their subordinates more positive evaluations than they deserve, but there are instances where purposely harsh ratings are assigned to send a message to or to punish an ineffective employee.

3. If the norms of an organization, or a work group, are highly tolerant of bending and perhaps even breaking rules, the likelihood of counterproductive behaviors will probably increase (Murphy, 1993).

SECTION IV

IMPROVING PERFORMANCE APPRAISAL SYSTEMS

13

THE PERFORMANCE APPRAISAL DEBATE

Performance appraisal requires supervisors, managers, and employees to invest a lot of time and energy into a system that is widely disliked and distrusted, and whose benefits can seem limited (Buckingham & Goodall, 2015). Both performance appraisal and performance management systems appear to fail in many organizations (Pulakos, Mueller-Hanson, Arad, & Moye, 2015; Smith, Hornsby, & Shirmeyer, 1996), and it is no surprise. Chapters 3–12 have documented a number of reasons why it is so difficult to create a successful performance appraisal or performance management system, and some of the problems that lead these systems to fail (e.g., reluctance to accept feedback, raters' motivation to distort performance ratings) may be very difficult to address. Some large organizations have abandoned performance appraisal altogether or have significantly reduced their reliance on appraisals (Buckingham & Goodall, 2015; Culbert & Rout, 2010; Cunningham, 2015), and it is worth asking whether it is time to pull the plug on performance appraisal. We believe the answer is no, but we also think it is worth taking a careful look at arguments for and against getting rid of performance appraisal.

In this chapter, we make two arguments. First, performance appraisal *must* be saved. It serves many important functions in organizations, and there is no plausible replacement. Second, it *can* be saved, but this will require a series of hard choices by organizations. Before laying out these two arguments, it is worth taking a detailed look at the current wave of enthusiasm for getting rid of performance appraisal.

LEARNING OBJECTIVES

13.1 Learn how increasing transparency benefits both the rater and the organization

13.2 Understand the features of performance appraisal that make the systems seem more or less fair

13.3 Learn how to make performance appraisal more forward-looking

13.4 Understand why it is helpful to focus on a small number of uses for performance appraisal

13.5 Learn how to enhance the credibility and legitimacy of a performance appraisal system

GETTING RID OF PERFORMANCE APPRAISAL?

The idea that performance appraisal systems are not working well and that major changes are needed is not a recent one. More than 60 years ago, Meyer, Kay, and French (1965) pointed out the potential failure of appraisal systems, particularly in organizations that attempt to use performance appraisal for both administrative and developmental purposes. By the 1980s, performance appraisal was being labeled as more of an organizational curse than a panacea (Taylor, 1985). By the early 2000s, there were an increasing number of reports of organizations rejecting performance appraisal systems, replacing them with less structured evaluations (DeNisi & Pritchard, 2006). However, the belief that performance appraisal is about to disappear seemed to take hold in a serious way only in recent years. Since 2015, the business press has featured a number of high-profile stories about the demise of performance appraisal (see, for example, Buckingham & Goodall, 2015; Cunningham, 2015). In a similar fashion, the scientific literature has featured spirited debates about the desirability of getting rid of performance appraisal (Adler et al., 2016).

As we noted in Chapters 1 and 2, claims that performance appraisal are on their way out are often made, but they appear to be greatly exaggerated. Surveys of human resource management practices in organizations have consistently shown that the great majority of organizations still use some type of formal performance appraisal system (Lawler, Benson, & McDermott, 2012; Mercer, 2013). Even organizations that have embraced performance management still often rely on traditional performance appraisal as one component of a broader system for managing performance (Pulakos, 2009). There are, however, serious arguments that can be made for abandoning performance appraisal because it is: (1) unduly burdensome and (2) unproductive.

The Costs of Performance Appraisal

There is no doubt that performance appraisal is costly, and that it consumes a lot of time and energy. Consider Buckingham and Goodall's (2015) description of the performance appraisal system used for many years by the professional services firm Deloitte. They note that "objectives are set for each of our 65,000-plus people at the beginning of the year; after a project is finished, each person's manager rates him or her on how well those objectives were met. The manager also comments on where the person did or didn't excel. These evaluations are factored into a single year-end rating, arrived at in lengthy 'consensus meetings' at which groups of 'counsellors' discuss hundreds of people in light of their peers" (Buckingham & Goodall, 2015, pp. 40–41). They estimated that this system required Deloitte to invest over *2 million* hours per year on completing forms, holding meetings, and rating performance. It is little wonder that Deloitte found the idea of simplifying this system so attractive.

Performance appraisal systems incur at least two types of costs, setup costs and administration costs. Setup costs might involve something as simple as creating forms or purchasing performance management software, but it is likely to also entail costs such as training (which will also be an ongoing cost as new managers or supervisors come on board) and legal review. The creation of a new performance appraisal system is likely to involve job analyses or systematic studies on the duties and responsibilities of each of the jobs being evaluated; these reviews are essential to defend the job-relatedness of these systems (Werner & Bolino, 1997).

Administration costs are likely to be even more important than setup costs, because these represent recurring expenses. For example, suppose your appraisal system requires 100 managers to generate and record ratings for 1,000 employees, to have feedback meetings with their employees, and to write recommendations to senior management on the basis of their evaluations and their discussions with employees. You must first spend some time training supervisors to use the system, and then devote a good deal of each supervisor's time to observing performance, completing ratings, holding feedback meetings, and communicating the results of his or her evaluation and of the feedback meeting to others in the organization (e.g., superiors, HR department). At a minimum, this would probably require 2–3 hours per employee, and it might involve a good deal more, but even with this level of investment, costs add up quickly. Assume, for example, that managers receive an average pay of $50 per hour.[1] The costs for the managers' time alone would add up to $100,000 to $150,000, and the total costs for managers, employees, and staff to administer this system could quite easily add up to several hundred thousand dollars per year. Even this figure might represent an underestimate of the dollar costs of an appraisal system because performance appraisal also involves opportunity costs. That is, the time managers, employees, and staff spend on performance appraisal is time that might be spent on activities that are more productive or more central to the mission of the organization.

The costs of performance appraisal are not limited to the financial burden of creating and administering this system. There are also psychological costs. As we have noted in several of the preceding chapters, performance appraisal is often an unwelcome and stressful process. Supervisors do not like to give and employees do not like to receive performance feedback (Cleveland, Lim, & Murphy, 2007). Negative reactions to performance appraisal are common (Adler et al., 2016; Keeping & Levy, 2000; Waite & Stites-Doe, 2000; Williams & Levy, 2000), and these can contribute to negative perceptions of the organization or of management (Mayer & Davis, 1999). These psychological costs are far from trivial, and if they could be avoided by abandoning or greatly simplifying performance appraisal, this reduction in the psychological costs of performance appraisal might represent a serious argument for making substantial changes in appraisal systems.

The Limited Benefits to Organizations

The belief that performance appraisal and performance management systems are not delivering substantial benefits is widespread (Pulakos et al., 2015). In many organizations, there is a lingering suspicion that performance appraisal is pointless, and that supervisors and employees are merely going through the motions when they complete performance appraisals. A performance appraisal system that is not worth the time and effort is not merely an annoyance; as noted above, negative experiences with performance appraisal systems can reduce overall trust in the organization and in management.

To some extent, the benefits of performance appraisal may be limited by the built-in conflicts in so many performance appraisal systems. It is common for organizations to use the same performance appraisal systems for both administrative and developmental purposes (e.g., for setting pay raises and for identifying developmental needs), but these two purposes require different sorts of data and they require different mindsets on the part of the rater (Murphy & Cleveland, 1995). Organizations that attempt to use the same appraisal system for both pay administration and for identifying training and development needs may find that they do not do either well. In other cases, appraisal systems may fail to yield anticipated benefits because of half-hearted applications of potentially sound ideas. For example, it is common in many organizations to claim to have a merit pay system in place, but to devote inadequate resources to allow such a system to work. We will explore in more detail the problems encountered in many merit pay systems in a later section.

The second factor that often places limits on the benefits obtained from performance appraisal systems is the type of range restriction that results from the widespread tendency to give high ratings. As we have noted in Chapters 11 and 12, it is common for the great majority of employees in an organization to be rated as "well above average," and given all of the forces pushing raters to give high ratings and to avoid low ones, the only surprise is that things are not even worse. Nevertheless, if just about everyone receives ratings of 4 or 5 on a 5-point scale, it will be hard to use ratings to reward good performers or to identify people whose performance needs improvement. In this chapter and in the one that follows, we will suggest some ways of building performance appraisal systems that reduce pressures to give high ratings to most employees, but these require some difficult and potentially painful decisions, and the path to overcoming rating inflation and range restriction is likely to be a long and difficult one.

Finally, some of the benefits that *should* arise from both performance appraisal and performance management do not in fact materialize because of a failure to take participants' perceptions, beliefs, and reactions into account when designing and administering these systems. For example, it is widely assumed that it is useful to provide employees with frequent and timely feedback (Aguinis, 2013). This assumption flies in the face of the fact that we know that many employees dislike receiving feedback, do not accept the feedback they receive, and work to actively avoid receiving feedback if possible (Cleveland et al., 2007; Moss, Sanchez, Brumbaugh, & Borkowski, 2009; Whitman, Halbesleben, & Holmes, 2014). If employees find feedback stressful and they do not trust the feedback they receive, giving them even more feedback may not be a good idea. Some of the supposed benefits of performance appraisal might be seen as useless or even noxious by raters and ratees.

WE CAN'T GET RID OF PERFORMANCE APPRAISAL

We are well aware of the shortcomings of traditional performance appraisal systems in organizations, and indeed have written extensively about these difficulties inherent in trying to evaluate employees' job performance, provide them with useful feedback, and take sensible actions on the basis of those performance evaluations (Adler et al., 2016; Cleveland & Murphy, 1992; Murphy & Cleveland, 1991, 1995). Nevertheless, getting rid of or sharply curtailing performance appraisal in organizations is potentially risky, and quite possibly foolish. Researchers, practitioners, or managers who want to get rid of or drastically reduce the use of performance appraisal in their organizations will have to consider three key points.

First, formal, structured evaluations of job performance continue to serve a number of important functions in organizations. Second, there is a long history of efforts to develop alternatives to traditional performance evaluations, but to date, no better method has been developed to accomplish the important task of evaluating the performance of employees. Third, when high-stakes decisions are made on the basis of measures of job performance, it is essential that these measures be demonstrably job related. If these measures are challenged as potentially discriminatory, none of the alternatives to performance appraisal or structured performance management systems is likely to survive legal scrutiny in the way that a well-designed performance appraisal or performance management system might.

The Uses of Performance Appraisal in Organizations

The first question you should ask before deciding whether to retain or abandon performance appraisal in an organization is why organizations conduct formal performance appraisals, or more generally, what do they *do* with the information coming out of performance appraisals. In Chapter 8, we detailed the many uses of performance appraisal, highlighting four main functions: (1) to distinguish between people (e.g., as input for decisions regarding pay or promotions), (2) to distinguish individual strengths and weaknesses (e.g., as input for making choices regarding training and development), (3) to support other human resource systems in organizations (e.g., for validating selection tests, evaluating training programs), and (4) documentation. Numerous surveys have confirmed that appraisal is an important component in many decisions in organizations (Cleveland, Murphy, & Williams, 1989; Mercer, 2013). Furthermore, the use of performance appraisal to serve a number of important purposes in organizations is not limited to American organizations. Milliman, Nason, Zhu, and De Cieri (2002) examined the differing uses of performance appraisal in 10 countries in Asia, North America, and Latin America. In particular, they evaluated the extent to which performance appraisals are used for pay administration, documentation, employee development, promotion, and as a vehicle for employees to express their opinions. On the whole, the use of performance appraisal for pay and promotion was moderately common in all countries, but it was most likely to be viewed as valuable in some Asian and Latin American countries. The use of performance appraisal for developmental purposes was common in virtually all countries, while the use of appraisal for documentation and subordinate expression was viewed as most acceptable in North American and Australian settings.

As we noted in Chapter 8, the use of the same performance appraisal system for multiple purposes can be a problem, especially when the purposes require different information or when they involve conflicting emphases. Unfortunately, the two most common uses of performance appraisal—pay administration and training and development—are also the most likely to come into conflict, and a case can be made that performance appraisals should not be used for so many purposes. However, the reality is that it *is* used for a number of important purposes, and if we get rid of performance appraisal, it is far from clear what will replace it.

Are There Useful Alternatives to Traditional Performance Ratings?

Recent publications have suggested several different approaches to replacing traditional performance appraisals. The first comes from research on performance management, where it has been suggested that annual performance appraisals might be replaced by more frequent, informal, and immediate feedback from supervisors or managers (Aguinis, 2013). The rationale here is that by providing feedback immediately at the point where good or poor performance occurs, the likelihood of improvements in the future is increased. Traditional performance appraisals are summative and retrospective, providing an evaluation of what has happened over the past year. It is *possible* that feedback you receive about something you might have done many months ago will turn out to be useful in changing your future behavior, but it seems more likely that immediate feedback will be more useful than feedback about events that may have occurred quite some time ago. Unlike traditional performance appraisal, which focuses on successes and failures in the past, performance management often has a prospective focus, using performance feedback as a tool for changing present and future behavior. Rather than evaluating what you did last year, a manager might give feedback about what you are doing right now and use that feedback to try and improve future behavior.

While we appreciate the potential value of giving feedback sooner rather than later, we are not convinced that frequent feedback is an adequate replacement for traditional performance appraisal. First, as noted earlier, feedback is not always accepted, even if it is completely accurate, and it is hard to see how increasing the frequency of feedback will help if feedback is regarded as biased and not credible. Second, even if feedback is accepted as credible and accurate, it might not provide a firm basis for evaluating individuals or even a good basis for an individual to understand how he or she is evaluated by others. Suppose you receive frequent feedback about how to improve your performance on an important part of your job. This could mean that you have a very proactive supervisor. It could also mean that you are not very good at your job (feedback about failures seems to be more common than feedback about successes). It might not be easy to sort these two possibilities out. More to the point, organizations may need to make decisions about raises, promotions, protecting the best workers from layoffs, and the like, and the feedback systems proposed by proponents of performance management are not well suited for these important purposes.

A second approach to replacing performance appraisal comes from proposals to address problems in human resource management with "big data" (e.g., Wax, Ascencio, & Carter, 2015). Developments in computer software and information processing systems make it increasingly easy to collect large amounts of information, and this information might be synthesized to produce good measures of job performance. While this approach may show some promise, we view it as a computationally intense variation on a method that has been tried, without much success, for decades—the development of objective measures of job performance.

As we have noted in several preceding chapters, there is a substantial body of research on objective measures of job performance, ranging from indices such as production output, scrap rates, and time to complete (e.g., Rothe, 1946a, 1946b, 1947) to data obtained from personnel files, such as absenteeism, turnover, or grievance measures (Chadwick-Jones, Nicholson, & Brown, 1982; Fitzgibbons & Moch, 1980; Mowday, Porter, & Steers, 1981; Muchinsky, 1977; Steers & Rhodes, 1978). While these measures might have some value, it is clear that they rarely provide adequate measures of job performance. For example, absence measures were once proposed as good objective indices of at least some aspects of job performance, but measures of absenteeism (a) do not apply to many jobs, (b) are frequently inaccurate, (c) have a variety of causes depending upon the definition of absence, (d) vary in the length of observation, and most importantly (e) different measures of absence do not correlate with each other (Landy & Farr, 1983).

Landy and Farr (1983) have identified several problems that seem to cut across the domain of objective performance indices and possible reasons why both researchers and practitioners have to rely more heavily on judgmental measures (e.g., supervisory ratings) than objective indices in evaluating job performance. First, objective measures of job performance often have low reliability (i.e., there is considerable measurement error in most assessments of absenteeism (see Chadwick-Jones, Brown, Nicholson, & Sheppard, 1971; Farr, O'Leary, & Bartlett, 1971; Ilgen & Hollenback, 1977; Latham & Pursell, 1975). Second, objective measures tend to be available for only a limited number of jobs, and in these jobs they cover only a limited range of functions. For example, it would not be sensible to collect tardiness or absence measures from sales representatives or from corporate managers who may not have a predetermined or fixed eight-hour work day. Finally, Landy and Farr (1983) cite the changing nature of skilled and semi-skilled work as an important limitation to objective performance measures. For example, since operators are being replaced by machine tenders, productivity measures such as output are more dependent upon machine functions than individual performance. The changing nature of work suggests that objective measures may be increasingly inappropriate for evaluating worker performance and subjective measures may continue to dominate.

Performance ratings are far from perfect, but there simply does not appear to be any viable replacement. Objective indices capture only part, and often a small part of the domain of job performance. Informal feedback can be timely, but it is also inconsistently given (e.g., feedback is more likely when something has gone wrong than when it has gone well) and it is not always accepted. The domain of job performance is broad and complex (see Chapter 3), and we have not seen any alternative to fairly traditional performance ratings that is likely to capture the range of behaviors that represent effective or ineffective performance. In particular, it is hard to imagine any of the alternatives to formal performance appraisal that have been proposed surviving a legal challenge.

Legal Considerations

In Chapter 2, we described the appraisal system developed by Deloitte (Buckingham & Goodall, 2015). The centerpiece of this system is a simple set of four questions supervisors use to evaluate their subordinates: (1) given what you know of this person's performance,

SPOTLIGHT 13.1 IS MORE AND BETTER FEEDBACK THE ANSWER?

One of the dominant themes of research on performance appraisal, in particular on performance management, is that there is a need for feedback. Indeed, one of the distinctions between more traditional performance appraisal systems and performance management systems is that performance management is often built around the idea that frequent feedback is both necessary and beneficial. Unfortunately, there is a good deal of evidence that feedback often fails (Kluger & DeNisi, 1996).

There are many reasons why feedback interventions might fail, but one possible explanation for the frequent failure may be that feedback is a tool that is appropriate for only some purposes. In particular, feedback is a great solution when the problem is lack of knowledge. Employees who do know what to do, do not know what is expected of them, or are not sure what constitutes acceptable performance might benefit substantially from feedback. Employees whose problem is a lack of ability or a lack of motivation probably do not benefit as much from feedback, and you can even make a case that performance feedback is harmful in this circumstance because it offers the wrong sort of solution. Giving performance feedback to someone who is not willing or able to perform well is a bit like giving a sandwich to someone who is dying of thirst. It is meant to be helpful, but it is the wrong kind of help.

It can be difficult to diagnose precisely why an employee is performing poorly, but we suspect that the value of performance feedback diminishes over time. As employees gather more experience, they are probably well aware of what you would tell them if you gave performance feedback. As work conditions change or as tasks evolve, the need for feedback may increase (Murphy, 1989a), and the general value of feedback might be higher in complex and ever-changing work environments. On the other hand, if tasks, task demands, and the like stay pretty much the same over time, the value of feedback is likely to go down. The key idea to keep in mind is that performance feedback is not an all-purpose tool, but rather it is an approach to solving a very specific set of problems; if these are not the problems that are relevant in a particular situation, performance feedback is probably not the right approach.

and if it were your money, would you award this person the highest-possible compensation increase and bonus; (2) given what you know of this person's performance, would you always want him or her on your team; (3) is this person at risk for low performance; and (4) is this person ready for promotion today?[2]

Suppose your organization uses an appraisal system similar to the one developed by Deloitte and you are a team member who receives low ratings from your team leader, and therefore does not receive a raise or are denied a promotion. The four questions listed in the preceding paragraph would not tell you anything about *what* you are doing well or poorly, only that your team leader is not impressed. Suppose further that ratings like these are used to make a number of decisions about raises or promotions, and at the end of a year you find out that men receive more raises than women, or that older workers do not get promoted, or that white employees receive raises and promotions at a much higher rate than black employees. In our opinion, this organization would be in a very difficult position.

Federal laws, ranging from the Civil Rights Acts of 1964 and 1991 to the Age Discrimination in Employment Act, the Americans with Disabilities Act, and other similar laws, all embody a similar set of principles. Businesses are generally free to make decisions about hiring, firing, pay, promotions, and conditions of work *except* when it can be shown that these decisions have a systematically adverse effect on groups of people defined in terms of race and ethnicity, gender, age, religion, national origin, disability, and the like. Organizations are forbidden by law from relying on assessments of decision processes that have a systematically adverse impact on workers from different demographic groups *unless* the organization can show that their assessments and decisions are job related. For example, if a performance appraisal system leads an organization to give higher raises to men than to women, or to promote younger workers but not older ones or the like, it is up to the organization to demonstrate that this appraisal system does in fact reliably and fairly measure job performance. We do not see how a system like the one described by Buckingham and Goodall (2015) could possibly meet this test. How, for example would Deloitte be able to demonstrate that it is job performance and not simple dislike for particular types of people that is driving these ratings?

The usual tools for defending performance appraisal systems that are challenged as discriminatory rely heavily on a demonstration that the appraisal system is tightly linked to the job. For example, if you can show that the job a person occupies requires them to engage in planning, in managing the resources of their work group, and in communicating the results of work to group members and to the organization, an appraisal system that includes well-documented evaluations of Planning, Resource Management, and Communication is more likely to survive legal scrutiny than a system that relies entirely on general impressions.

Werner and Bolino (1997) note that in evaluating performance appraisal systems that are challenged in equal employment litigation, the courts have relied heavily upon whether or not (1) performance appraisals are clearly related to the content of the job being performed and (2) there were due process considerations in appraisals and the decisions based on appraisals. A critical question being ignored by organizations that are abandoning performance appraisal is how they will defend against charges of discrimination if their appraisal systems are not demonstrably job related. Our review of research and practice in this area suggests that organizations that abandon formal appraisal systems that are based on a careful analysis of the jobs people perform in favor of informal feedback or a few vague questions are practically *begging* for trouble if their appraisal systems lead to adverse decisions for members of legally protected groups.[3]

Toegel and Conger (2003) note that in addition to the potential for violations of equal opportunity laws, there are other legal pitfalls that might arise in performance appraisal. For example, an organization that claims to use job performance as a basis for important awards but that does such a slipshod job of evaluating ratee performance that the claim is palpably false might in theory be sued for negligence, especially if there is a ratee or set of ratees who can convincingly show that they are superior performers but who failed to receive the performance ratings (and therefore the rewards) they deserved. An employee who received an unfairly negative evaluation and whose evaluation was communicated to some third party (perhaps this employee is applying for a job elsewhere) might even sue for defamation.

CAN APPRAISAL SYSTEMS BE SAVED?

It is one thing to conclude that performance appraisal systems *must* be saved. It is quite another thing to actually save them. In Chapters 4–12, we documented what we believe are the four key challenges to performance appraisal: (1) the task of accurately evaluating performance over some period of time is a very difficult one; (2) performance ratings usually tell you something about the person being rated and something about the context, and it can be hard to sort these two factors out; (3) organizations use performance appraisals for multiple, conflicting purposes; and (4) raters are strongly motivated to give high ratings and to avoid giving low ratings. None of these challenges will be easy to overcome, and the sorts of changes organizations frequently embrace in an attempt to improve their appraisal systems (e.g., developing new forms, giving raters better training) are not going to work. What is needed is a radical re-orientation of performance appraisal in organizations.

We believe performance appraisal systems can be saved, and that doing so will require organizations and their members to embrace three key principles:

- Performance appraisal is not the same thing as performance measurement.

- Hard decisions need to be made about the purpose of performance appraisal, and they need to be carried through.

- The benefits of appraisal to managers, supervisors, and employees must exceed, and must be seen as exceeding the costs.

A realistic approach to using performance appraisal effectively in organizations must start with a clear recognition of what a good performance appraisal system can and cannot do. Performance appraisal can be a very valuable part of a human resource system, but it is not an adequate replacement for things like a qualified workforce or competent management. An organization that has an excellent performance appraisal system but that is unable to attract and retain workers who are competent to perform their tasks or that is led by abusive, incompetent, or dishonest managers and executives is likely to fail. A high-quality performance appraisal system can make a definite contribution to the success of an organization, but it will never be a panacea.

Performance Appraisal Is Not Performance Measurement

It has long been acknowledged that performance ratings do not do a particularly good job reflecting the performance of the people being evaluated (Greguras & Robie, 1998; Landy & Farr, 1980; Murphy, 2008a; Scullen, Mount, & Goff, 2000; Viswesvaran, Ones, & Schmidt, 1996). There have been vibrant debates over *why* there is a gap between how well people perform their jobs and the ratings they receive (Murphy, 2008a, 2008b), with some authors emphasizing the idiosyncratic nature of performance judgments (e.g., Viswesvaran et al., 1996), while others emphasize the cognitive limitations of raters (Landy & Farr, 1980) or the influence of contextual variables on ratings (e.g., Murphy & Cleveland, 1995). There is little disagreement, however, that performance ratings are not particularly good measures of performance. They may be better than the alternatives, but this is probably more of a function of the weaknesses of the alternatives than of the strengths of ratings.

For at least 40 years (roughly 1960–2000), researchers and practitioners tried a variety of strategies to improve the measurement quality of performance ratings, such as improving rating scales or developing better methods of training (DeNisi & Murphy, 2017), with generally disappointing results. As we noted in Chapter 6, some types of training (e.g., frame of reference training) can help, and some scales are probably better than others, but even with the best scales and the best training, performance rating provides measurements that cannot be fully trusted to accurately reflect the performance of the individuals being evaluated.

We think that the most compelling explanation for the shortcomings of supervisory ratings as measures of the performance of the individuals being rated is motivational (Banks & Murphy, 1985; Cleveland & Murphy, 1992; Murphy & Cleveland, 1995). Raters do not consistently provide accurate information about the performance of the people they are rating because they are not *trying* to provide accurate measures. The arguments implicit in cognitive approaches to performance appraisal, or in approaches built around improving the tools used by raters (e.g., scales, training), has always been that raters do not know who is a good or a poor ratee or that they need help to elicit and structure accurate judgments about the performance of their subordinates, and this argument has always struck us as unconvincing. The research reviewed in several preceding chapters (especially Chapter 12) convinces us that raters are not trying to simply convey accurate information about performance when they complete rating forms and hold performance review meetings. Rather, they are trying to do their real job—that is, to act as a manager and facilitator of performance rather than acting as a passive measurement instrument.

The first step toward saving performance appraisal is to recognize and accept what performance rating is and what it is not. Performance appraisal is certainly not a simple process of measurement. Raters are not simply trying (but failing) to provide accurate assessments of performance. Rather, performance appraisal is used by managers and supervisors as a tool for influencing the behavior of employees. That is, performance appraisal should be thought of as a *management tool*, not as a *measurement* tool. For example, in Chapter 12, we laid out a number of reasons why a rater might give high ratings to an employee who *is* performing poorly, and argued that these ratings might be evidence of sound management rather than being evidence of rater errors. A supervisor or manager who gives inflated ratings on the assumption and belief that these ratings will motivate the employee to perform better in the future is not making an error, but rather is making a potentially sound decision about how to improve that employee's performance.

In the end, like so many other things in organizations, performance rating is an exercise in politics. That is, a smart manager will use performance ratings as a tool to influence the behavior of his or her subordinates. Hand wringing about the accuracy of performance appraisals probably misses the point. The real question is not whether ratings are accurate but rather whether they are useful as a means of influencing the behavior of employees. If you are seriously interested in saving performance appraisal, we think the first thing you need to do is to accept and embrace performance ratings for what they are—a tool for influencing the behavior of employees.

Does this mean accuracy is irrelevant? Probably not, at least in part because some manifest connection between the ratings individuals receive and their behavior in the job is likely to be necessary if the users of an appraisal system are going to accept the appraisal system as fair and reasonable. Completely arbitrary performance ratings, even if they turn out to be an effective management tool, will probably undermine the long-term acceptability of a performance appraisal system. However, it is important to think carefully about the relative importance of different criteria that might be used to evaluate a performance appraisal system, and "is it useful?" is likely to be much more important than "is it accurate?"

Finally, it is important to remember that accuracy is a complex, multidimensional concept (see Chapter 11), and that some types of accuracy are more important or relevant than others. For example, it is unlikely that the great majority of employees in most organizations are above average in their performance, but rating inflation (i.e., rating just about everyone as above average) might not directly influence the key uses of performance appraisals (e.g., for making salary adjustments). If the *absolute* values of ratings are uniformly inflated, it is still possible that most of the useful and important information about the *relative* standing of employees might be retained. Of course, if rating inflation is too severe, you might lose important information about relative standing of different employees; if everyone receives ratings of 4 or 5 on a 5-point scale, it will be hard to identify top performers, whose contributions can be disproportionally important to an organization (Aguinis & Bradley, 2015; O'Boyle & Aguinis, 2012). Nevertheless, it is clear that some types of accuracy will be more important than others. The type of accuracy that should be of greatest concern might depend on how organizations use performance appraisal.

Decide What You Are Truly Willing to *Do* With Performance Appraisal

Performance appraisal is a multipurpose tool, but the range of potential uses for performance appraisals may be more of a curse than a blessing. As we have noted in several preceding chapters (especially Chapter 8), the two most common uses of performance appraisal, for administrative and for developmental purposes, are also the two most likely to come into conflict. The information needed to make smart decisions about raises, promotions, layoffs, and the like revolves around comparisons between persons, while the information needed to make smart decisions about training and development revolves around individual strengths and weaknesses, or within-person comparisons. Performance appraisal systems often appear to collect both types of information, by providing both overall performance estimates and ratings on several dimensions of performance, but appearances are deceiving. In most cases, raters and ratees emphasize between-person comparisons, recognizing that these can be tied to high-stakes consequences (e.g., raises).

A rater who tries to provide information about within-person variation will almost inevitably end up harming employees when it comes to between-person comparisons, because a rating profile that has peaks and valleys (i.e., high scores on some performance dimensions and low scores on others) will almost always also have a mean score that is pulled toward the middle of the rating scale. Thus, if *your* supervisor ignores strengths and weaknesses and gives everyone high scores on all dimensions and *my* supervisor tries to give useful developmental information by noting both strengths and weaknesses, you will do well and I will do poorly when raises are given out.

The first question an organization must face is to decide what it *really* wants to do with performance appraisal, and if the list of potential uses includes conflicting purposes, which use is most critical? This choice really involves two separate questions. First, which uses are most important to the effectiveness and the future of this organization? Second, which uses are the organization truly willing to embrace? It is in dealing with this second question where organizations most frequently fall short. An examination of merit pay systems in many organization provides an example of the way half-hearted implementation of a key human resource management practice can undermine the effectiveness of performance appraisal systems.

Merit Pay

Most North American organizations claim to provide some sort of performance-based pay, in which good performance is rewarded and encouraged by higher levels of pay (Gerhart, Rynes, & Fulmer, 2009; Schaubroeck, Shaw, Duffy, & Mitra, 2008). Despite the widespread acceptance of the idea that better performance should lead to better pay, serious questions have been raised about the effectiveness of merit pay in most organizations. There is surprisingly little evidence that merit pay systems are effective (Heneman, 1992; Milkovich & Wigdor, 1991).[4] Rather than being viewed as an effective tool for influencing employee performance, merit pay systems are often viewed with suspicion, and negative attitudes toward merit pay systems appear to be an important factor in their frequent failure (Heneman, 1992; Shaw, Duffy, Mitra, Lockhart, & Bowler, 2003).

There appear to be three reasons why many merit pay systems fail: (1) distrust, (2) rating inflation, and (3) underinvestment. First, trust in merit pay systems requires participants to accept two separate conclusions: (1) that performance ratings are reasonably accurate and (2) that there are strong links between performance ratings and raises. Both of these inferences are likely to be problematic. Performance ratings are often seen as being more strongly influenced by liking and politics than by actual performance (Longenecker, Sims, & Gioia, 1987; Tziner, 1999; Vest, Scott, & Tarnoff, 1995), and this sort of distrust of performance appraisal systems can generalize to more widespread distrust of other systems that rely on performance appraisal (Mayer & Davis, 1999). Even if ratings are accepted as generally accurate, the users of performance appraisal systems may find it hard to accept the belief that high performance ratings will automatically lead to large salary increases. A merit pay system that *did* create this strong instrumentality link (i.e., one in which pay directly reflected performance ratings) would almost certainly spiral out of control because of the strong tendency of most raters to provide high ratings.

As we have noted in several preceding chapters, rating inflation is widespread and it is not unusual that most employees will receive high ratings. If ratings automatically lead to raises, personnel budgets will become impossible to manage, because so many employees will be designated as eligible for large salary increases. In practice, many organizations find it necessary to calibrate across raters or departments so that those raters or departments who most shamelessly inflate their ratings do not soak up a disproportionate portion of the merit pay pool. Even in organizations that do not engage in widespread recalibration, there may be appeals or higher-level review that lead some ratings (and therefore some salary recommendations) to change. Either of these could disrupt the perceived relationship between ratings and pay decisions.

In practice, even when the link between performance ratings and salary increases is usually probabilistic rather than absolute (i.e., higher ratings increase the probability of, but do not guarantee larger raises) a system in which most employees receive high ratings can quickly overwhelm merit pay budgets and reduce the organization's ability to differentiate between high, average, and low performers (Miceli, Jung, Near, & Greenberger, 1991). If very few people receive low ratings, an organization that claims to pay for performance may find itself in a position where virtually everyone receives similar merit raises, regardless of their actual level of performance or effectiveness.

Suppose that the problem of rating inflation could somehow be solved. Even under these conditions, most merit pay systems are likely to fail because the portion of pay that is actually linked to performance is too small to allow organizations to adequately distinguish good from poor performers. In recent years, salary increases have been quite small; between 2010 and 2015, salary increases of 2–3% were common, and with the exception of top-level executives, salary increases for most employees have been modest for much of the preceding decade.[5] In most organizations, merit pay is only a portion of the total salary increase budget, and if the total pool of funds available for salary increases starts out small, the portion of pay actually available for differential rewards for good versus poor performers is likely to be modest indeed.

One of the authors of this book served as a department head for several years, and during that time, the budget allocation for salary increases was typically in the neighborhood of 3%, with a stipulation that all people who were performing at least at an adequate level should receive a cost of living increase of approximately 2%. The amount of money available to give performance-dependent salary increases was often so small that truly excellent performers received an increase that was barely different from the increases received by the majority of employees in this department. This appears to be a common occurrence in many organizations that claim to pay for performance, and there are reasons to believe that the typical merit increase in most organizations is much too small to produce meaningful changes in employee attitudes or behaviors.

How large does a pay raise need to be to have some discernible effect? There is a growing body of evidence suggesting that the smallest meaningful pay increase in many settings is in the ballpark of 7% (Mitra, Gupta, & Jenkins, 1997; Mitra, Tenihälä, & Shaw, 2016) and that the raises most employees receive are perceived as a drop in the bucket rather than as meaningful rewards. This research suggests that even those employees who receive the top rewards in a merit pay system are unlikely to see their increases as meaningful, much less as strong recognition of their worth relative to their peers.

In analyzing merit pay systems, it is important to pay attention to both the mean and the standard deviation of the distribution of merit pay awards. The mean of the merit increase distribution tells you whether recipients in general are likely to view their raises as meaningful, but it is the standard deviation that really tells you whether the system provides different rewards for good versus poor performance. If virtually everyone receives the same (or essentially the same) merit increase, the claim that organizations reward good performance with merit pay is likely to ring hollow.

In merit pay plans that put only a small proportion of pay at risk, it may be impossible to give raises to good performers that differ in any meaningful way from raises given to poor performers. Even if a large part of the salary pool is theoretically dependent on merit, the tendency of raters to give high ratings to virtually all employees will result is so much range restriction that there may be very little room for true differentiation in the rewards received by good versus poor performers. In practice, most merit pay systems appear to give raises to even the best performers that are too small to have a measurable effect and to give similar raises to employees whose performance clearly differ.

We view merit pay systems as a good example of a sound concept that is usually implemented in a half-hearted and inconsistent fashion. (See Gerhart & Fang, 2015, for a review of current developments in motivation theory that are relevant to merit pay systems.) An organization that claims to pay for performance but in fact gives virtually identical raises to everyone is almost certainly doing itself more harm than good, because the contrast between the claim to pay for performance and the reality of its merit pay system will be noticed by employees and this may contribute to cynicism toward management and toward the organization itself (Vest et al., 1995).

If performance appraisal is going to be saved, organizations need to be clear and realistic about two key decisions. First, they must decide what they *want* to do with performance appraisal. Second, they must decide what they are *willing* to do with performance appraisal. There is an old joke that was told in Russia and many Eastern European countries to portray frustration with their system for managing work organizations: "they pretend to pay us and we pretend to work."[6] This is precisely the type of cynicism a half-hearted stab at merit pay might encourage. Unless an organization is willing to fully embrace something like merit pay and provide meaningful increases to people who are performing well, while providing noticeably smaller increases (if any) to people whose performance is not as good, they are better off abandoning merit pay altogether.

In Chapter 14 we will return to the problems caused when performance appraisal is used for multiple conflicting purposes. The point we want to make here is that the widely cited conflict between administrative and developmental uses of performance appraisal (Meyer et al., 1965; Murphy & Cleveland, 1995) may be more apparent than real. If organizations are using performance appraisal for developmental purposes, but only claiming or pretending to use it for the purpose of setting salaries, they are probably better off dropping the pretense altogether, simply doing away with a half-hearted system for awarding merit pay.

Make It Worthwhile

Put yourself in the place of a supervisor or manager who is faced with the task of conducting performance appraisals. You have good reasons to approach this task with trepidation. You can be reasonably sure that the employees whose performance you rate will resent and reject any feedback that is not positive and that the experience of giving performance feedback will be uncomfortable for both you and the employee. You can be reasonably sure that truly good performers will not receive rewards that are comparable to their contribution and their value. You can be reasonably sure that if you give employees the ratings they truly deserve, *you* will end up looking bad, and that if you give ratings that are plainly and obviously inflated, there will be few sanctions from the organization. Why should you invest time and energy in this noxious and seemingly pointless activity? Your own manager and higher executives in the organization almost certainly know all of the pitfalls of performance appraisal, and they also know that at least some of the alleged purposes of appraisal (e.g., merit pay) are so meaningless that they are virtually a sham. Why, then, are they putting you and your employees through all of this pointless pain and suffering? In theory, the answer should be that the benefits of this activity exceed the costs, although we suspect that the true answer to "why are we doing this?" is either "we have always done this" or, more likely, "we don't know what else to do."

In thinking about whether performance appraisal is worthwhile, we find it useful to try and identify the costs and benefits of performance appraisal. We also find it useful to think about this question from the perspective of different units of analysis. That is, the question of whether performance appraisal is worthwhile to the organization may involve quite different sets of costs and benefit calculations than the question of whether it is worthwhile

SPOTLIGHT 13.2 GIVING MERIT RAISES WHEN THERE IS SIGNIFICANT VARIABILITY IN MERIT

Jane is a manager who supervises 12 clerical employees, each of whose current salary is just under $30,000 per year. She is given a budget of $14,400 for salary increases (about 4%). One of her employees, Suzanne, is truly excellent and the rest are generally competent employees. Employees can expect a 2% cost of living increase, leaving about $7,000 for merit increases. Jane has a number of options, ranging from giving all $7,000 to Suzanne to distributing merit raises to everyone. How would you recommend she proceed?

Analysis

A starting point for analysis is that everyone will receive about $600 as a cost of living adjustment. Giving everything else to Suzanne will give her a raise of $7,600, or 25%, which clearly exceeds the 7% barely noticeable threshold suggested by Mitra and colleagues. However, this will mean that everyone else gets no merit raise at all, and implicitly (unless they raise their performance level to Suzanne's) that they should not expect one in the future. This suggestion is somewhat in line with suggestions by Aguinis and colleagues (Aguinis & Bradley, 2015; O'Boyle & Aguinis, 2012) about the importance of identifying and catering to star performers, but it could lead her 11 coworkers to become demoralized and cynical. An alternative

might be to work backwards from the 7% threshold, giving Suzanne a raise of $2,100 (7% of $30,000), which would allow you to distribute a bit over $1,000 to each of Suzanne's colleagues ($600 in cost of living plus about $400 for merit).

In making choices about how to distribute merit raises, it is important to keep in mind that employees tend to have a positive view of their own performance, giving themselves higher ratings than they are likely to receive from others. One implication of this is that Suzanne's coworkers, even if they recognize her superior performance, are likely to think that the difference between their own performance and Suzanne's is smaller than it appears to you. If Suzanne receives a raise that is twice as large as the raise that anyone else receives (and whose merit component is more than twice as large as anyone else's) it is likely that they will believe that they are being treated unfairly. These beliefs could be especially problematic if the work requires other employees to cooperate with Suzanne. There is a good deal of evidence that people do not like it when their coworkers make them look bad (by performing at a much higher level than they are performing; Murphy, 1993), and this dislike may be intensified if Suzanne is perceived to be getting rewards that are larger than she deserves.

to the supervisors and managers who are responsible for actually doing the appraisals. We believe that saving performance appraisal must ultimately involve making it worthwhile for raters and ratees to take the system seriously. Without this sort of buy-in, nominal changes, such as developing new rating forms or new training programs, are certain to fail.

There are two different approaches you might take to make performance appraisal worthwhile to raters and ratees: increasing the benefits or reducing the costs. We recommend starting with costs, in part because it might be easier to reduce some of the costs raters and ratees experience when negotiating the performance appraisal system. In addition, there is also a good deal of evidence (see Chapter 5) that people think about costs and benefits differently, and that costs have a greater impact on decisions than corresponding benefits.

Protect the Rater

Raters face two costs when carrying out performance appraisals. First, appraisals require a lot of time and effort, and while this is one of the core functions supervisors and managers are paid to carry out, appraisal nevertheless is often perceived to be unduly labor intensive (Buckingham & Goodall, 2015). Second, as we noted earlier, raters face psychological costs, in the sense that performance appraisal is a stressful experience. Both of these costs might be mitigated by making performance appraisal less personal.

The typical performance appraisal places a lot of responsibility in the hands of each employee's direct supervisor or manager. An employee who does not get a raise or promotion is likely to hold his or her direct supervisor responsible for this outcome. Even if there are no financial consequences associated with low ratings or negative feedback, performance appraisal still involves a supervisor or manager giving his or her personal opinion about an employee's performance, and as we have noted in several preceding chapters, it is likely that this opinion will be less positive than employees' evaluation of their own performance. One of the reasons supervisors and managers dislike performance appraisal is that it puts them on the line, especially if the outcome of performance appraisal is less positive than the outcomes employees think they deserve. We think a good deal could be done to diffuse this situation by using multisource rating systems to help protect the rater.

In Chapter 11 we noted that multisource rating systems can create many problems because ratings from different perspectives (e.g., peers, subordinates) often disagree. Our suggestion is that information about performance should be *collected* from many sources, but *reported* as a single aggregate. That is, instead of telling your subordinate that *you* think he or she is a bad performer, it might be less stressful (and received less as a personal slight) if you could give feedback that information has been collected from many different sources, and the average of all of the pieces of information collected places him or her on the lower end of the scale. The key here is to give raters some protection and to make performance feedback less painful to give and less painful to receive.

Decoupling Pay From Performance Ratings

In the previous section, we argued that organizations often only pretend to pay for performance, when in fact they underfund merit pay pools and end up giving similar raises to just about everyone. We believe it is time for organizations to bite the bullet and either decouple performance ratings and pay or make the substantial investments needed to create a credible and trustworthy link. These investments would be twofold. First, organizations will need to develop performance measurement systems that are not susceptible to the biases that cause most raters to give inflated ratings. In a few of the preceding paragraphs, we suggested using multisource data to reduce pressure on the individual supervisor or manager, and this same suggestion might contribute to the credibility and trustworthiness of appraisal systems. However, even a change of this magnitude (which would magnify the current costs of performance appraisal systems) would not be enough to make merit pay systems effective. Organizations would also have to be willing to put a lot more at risk in order to make merit pay effective. The chance to earn a 3% raise if you are excellent, as opposed to a 2% raise if you are average, is not the sort of thing needed to make merit pay work. If a raise of 7% or more is the minimum needed to catch an employee's attention, raises that are substantially larger will be needed to signal that an employee is truly exceptional, and giving raises this large to some employees must also imply giving raises that are quite small (possibly smaller than the increase in cost of living) to others. On the whole, we think it will be difficult to make this work.

If they are going to give everyone comparable raises in the end, organizations could make life much easier for raters and ratees by decoupling performance ratings from salary. This would also resolve the conflict between administrative and developmental uses for performance appraisal (Meyer et al., 1965), making it easier to give truly developmental feedback without worrying that information about strengths and weaknesses will have an adverse effect on one's salary. More to the point, it would greatly reduce the costs to raters and ratees alike for giving honest evaluations when the ratee's performance is not up to standards.

Increase the Value of Feedback by Decreasing the Threat of Reduced Raises

We believe that in the end, decoupling pay from performance is likely to make developmental feedback more honest, accurate, and helpful. Employees who receive inflated ratings (this inflation is mainly done to protect employees from negative consequences when salary decisions are made) typically do not receive feedback that is particularly useful. Performance appraisals that *did* provide accurate performance feedback might be seen as beneficial by employees, particularly if that feedback can be given in a way that does not create negative reactions. For example, rather that providing absolute ratings on several dimensions (i.e., you were a "4" on Communication and a "3" on Planning), it might be better to provide comparative ratings (i.e., your communication skills are stronger than your planning skills). We base this recommendation on the recognition that ratees overestimate their standing in the organization compared to estimates obtained from other sources (see Chapters 9 and 10), and they may focus more on the level of the ratings than on the patterns that identify relative strengths and weaknesses.

Finally, we should not think about feedback as the sole benefit ratees get from performance appraisal. The appraisal interview provides an important and valuable opportunity for employees and their supervisor or manager to sit down and talk about what is going well and what might be improved. If we can reduce the aspects of this discussion that trigger anxiety and defensiveness (e.g., links to pay and emphasis on relative standing), it might be possible to change this conversation from the "job managers love to hate" into a positive and valuable experience for raters and ratees alike. In Chapter 14, we explore ways of using research on performance appraisal to improve the practice and the experience of appraisal in organizations.

SUMMARY

The idea that we should, or even that we could, get rid of performance appraisal has received a good deal of attention in recent years. We recognize the challenges to doing appraisal well in organizations, as well as the forces that tend to distort performance appraisals in organizations, but we believe that performance appraisal can and must be saved (Cleveland & Murphy, 2016). First, performance appraisal serves a number of important purposes in organizations. A case can be made that it serves *too many* purposes, and one of our key recommendations is for organizations to make and live with decisions about which uses are the most critical. Nevertheless, performance appraisal is an important tool in human resource management, and there are no clear replacements in sight.

It is tempting to replace performance appraisal with something much simpler, such as continuous informal feedback (Aguinis, 2013) or a simplified set of questions about the perceived value of each employee (Buckingham & Goodall, 2015), but this approach involves a number of risks. In particular, organizations that use information from a performance appraisal system to make high-stakes decisions about employees (e.g., salary, promotion, protection from layoffs) may find it necessary to defend these decisions in court if there is evidence that the outcomes of these decisions differ for employees who differ in age, gender, race, or other protected categorizations. Like other tests and assessments that are used to make important decisions about applicants or employees, performance appraisal systems that are challenged will be very difficult to defend unless they can be shown to be clearly job related. Traditional performance appraisal systems include many features that enhance their job relatedness, including the use of job analysis to make decisions about which performance dimensions to

measure, rater training, and multiple sources of input. A more informal system might be very hard to defend.

Organizations that decide to keep performance appraisal need to face up to many challenges. Appraisals in many organizations are used for conflicting purposes (e.g., salary administration versus identification of training needs), and some of these purposes (particularly those related to pay or advancement) are sources of anxiety and of motivation to distort appraisals. We believe there are two key decisions an organization that is attempting to save its performance appraisal system needs to make. First, they need to decide what it is they want to *do* with appraisals, and if some of these uses are in conflict, which one should be kept and which should be abandoned. Our review of research on merit pay leads us to believe that organizations that *claim* to use performance appraisal as part of a merit pay system are not really willing or able to reward merit, and if this is the case, they would be better off dropping the pretense that better performance leads to better pay.

Second, organizations need to think carefully about what they are willing and able to do to reduce the conflict, stress, and anxiety that is inherent in so many performance appraisal systems. Anything an organization can do to reduce the costs and increase the benefits of appraisal for both raters and ratees will help to improve the appraisal process. One possibility for reducing costs is to decouple pay from performance, but this is not necessarily the only way of reducing costs and increasing benefits. What organizations need to do is to take the costs and benefits of performance appraisal seriously and to put their effort into making the appraisal process at least palatable (and hopefully useful) to raters and ratees alike.

CASE STUDY: CAN THIS PERFORMANCE APPRAISAL SYSTEM BE SAVED?

Background: You are an industrial and organizational psychologist working for a consulting firm that specializes in performance appraisal

and management. An organization calls your firm because they are concerned that their current performance appraisal system is not effectively meeting their needs. Your organizational contact also describes to you that a new committee has been formed to make an action plan regarding this concern; however, this committee is having difficulty in reaching a conclusion.

You decide to take on this project and meet with the committee. Quickly you learn that there are two camps: half of the committee thinks it is wise to get rid of the performance appraisal system altogether and the other half thinks it can be salvaged. You pose many questions to the committee, notably including those surrounding the current system (e.g., "Does the current performance appraisal system advance the goals of the organization?") and those surrounding their ideal, "best-case scenario" performance appraisal system (e.g., "What needs to improve?" and "What would your organization actually embrace?").

It becomes apparent to you why a number of committee members want to abandon the system. First, the employees and managers alike are not prioritizing performance appraisal as important. Second, the approach is disorganized and managers seem to all have their own interpretation of what the rating process should entail. Third, there is a recent occurrence of high turnover in the organization over the past several years, and new employees will often not even engage in the performance appraisal interview until after they psychologically have a foot out the door already (so it seems "too little, too late"). Finally, the committee explained how, as a nonprofit organization, the budget is extremely tight. You realize that this has implications on the performance appraisal system such that there is no room for a raise or bonus that exceeds the standard rate of 2%, regardless of excellent performance. You hold focus groups to hear from managers and employees. These same concerns are echoed.

Recommendation: After speaking with the committee and focus groups, your professional recommendation is that the current performance appraisal system is indeed not working, and major revisions should be considered. You explain how a new system can be created that better meets the goals of the organization and also helps to address the fundamental concern of turnover. During your

presentation to the committee, you highlight the pitfalls of the current system: (1) it is inappropriately linked to pay, (2) it lacks opportunity for learning and development, (3) the frequency is not working, and (4) better organization is needed.

The current performance appraisal system was linked to pay, and the trivial amount of money (i.e., distinctions between 1.8% and 1.7%) tied to performance was causing more emotional distress for the managers and employees than it was worth. Rewards needed to be removed from the equation—because that was not the true goal here. (And even if it was, it would not be powerful enough to matter!) In the focus groups, you learned that employees were overwhelmed and felt a large amount of job stress. Employees voiced a need for more performance feedback and ongoing development. Thus, the emphasis needed to shift away from linking pay to performance toward a more forward-looking, developmental approach to sustain continual growth. This would require a change in the system's current emphasis as well as refreshing the outdated competency content. The original system was an annual meeting, whereas a more beneficial frequency would be three times a year for new employees (in their first year of employment) and twice a year for employees in their second year of tenure. This would provide employees with structured feedback, goal setting, and developmental targets where necessary much sooner after starting their jobs, potentially reducing the overwhelming feeling that was reported as a large reason for turnover. Annual appraisal seemed to be adequate for employees with longer tenure, thus that would remain consistent for those who have been with the organization three years or longer.

Finally, you explain to the committee that better organization surrounding the performance appraisal process is needed. This was not a secret to the committee. For instance, there was a paper rating form that was used each year during the performance appraisal meeting. Most managers had their own idea of how to use the current performance appraisal process, and this resulted in different practices within similar departments (e.g., some managers did not use the paper rating form, some managers used the form and kept it on file, some managers used the form and gave it to the employee to keep, and so on). This inconsistency in documentation raises red flags (e.g., in regard to legal issues, perceived trust from the employees), thus you propose a streamlined, paperless solution. The new system would be documented within the previously existing, online communications portal that is used on site. You spoke with the IT department with the organization and they assured you that both the manager and employee (rater and ratee) could have confidential access to the rating form and supplemental information discussed in the meeting.

Development: The committee votes in agreement with your proposal to repair the current performance appraisal system, and they want the development phase to start right away. You explain what constitutes successful performance appraisal might be different across organizations; therefore, sufficient data collection is necessary to accurately meet their needs. In your proposal you outline the steps needed to complete the development phase.

Conduct a job analysis. In order to ensure the new system includes relevant criteria, a job analysis should be conducted to identify the knowledge, skills, abilities, and other characteristics (KSAOs) needed to perform in the work setting. This is a comprehensive process that involves examining the people, the environment (e.g., the surrounding organizational context), reviewing source documents, leading interviews and focus groups, and collecting survey data. It is important to note it would include the input of managers and employees. They are subject matter experts (SMEs) in this circumstance, and when they are treated that way it helps to increase buy-in and ensure their voices are heard.

Identify the core competencies. This is what the organization wants to measure on the performance appraisal form. Using the information from the job analysis phase, the core competencies (i.e., performance dimensions, performance standards) should be identified. These should be measurable, under the employees' control to change, behaviorally based, and verifiable. There should also be a clear

link between these competencies and the organization's values or the strategic goals of the organization where applicable.

Develop the documentation procedure and the rating form, and integrate goal setting within this. In the present example, the organization chose to move in the direction of online documentation for performance appraisal. The rating form will also be electronic within this procedure. Constructing an appropriate rating form is foundational to an effective performance appraisal meeting. It should help organize and facilitate a productive discussion, guide the conversation to be forward-looking, and include areas for action plans, time lines, and goal setting (track goal progress to discuss at each subsequent meeting).

Work out the logistics. When developing the performance appraisal system, a number of details deserve attention. For instance, who will rate the employees, will there be one rater or multiple raters, what type of rating scales should be used, what frequency should be used, how long should the performance appraisal interview last, how will it be documented, who should coordinate or initiate the performance appraisal meeting, how much flexibility is allowed in the meeting, how will feedback be delivered, what will follow-up look like, how will employees who work remotely receive performance appraisal, and other questions should be deliberated. These answers can be different for each organization.

Build a resources bank. In the present example, the new performance appraisal has a large developmental focus; thus once employees' strengths and weaknesses are identified, it is crucial that the proper training and developmental systems are in place to support any decisions about further guidance. In order to improve performance in the future, relevant resources and training should be prepared to support each core competency.

You explain to the organization that this thorough process of grounding the appraisal instrument in job analysis, providing clear behaviorally based competencies, communicating in a transparent way with employees about the process, and documenting the information helps to avoid legal issues down the road. See Chapter 14 for a continuation of this case example: Executing a New Performance Appraisal System.

NOTES

1. According to O*NET, the 2015 median hourly wage for general and operating managers (code 11-1021.00) was $46.99.

2. The precise questions used by Deloitte are shown in Chapter 2, Table 2.2. These questions are paraphrased here.

3. The law protects employees from discrimination on the basis of race, nationality, religion, gender, disability, and age. The term *protected group* is not restricted to groups that have traditionally been the target of employment discrimination, but rather refers to the fact that the law protects all groups under these broad demographic headings equally.

4. In contrast, a review by the National Academy of Sciences (Milkovich & Wigdor, 1991) provides clear evidence that gain-sharing schemes that are tied to the overall performance of an organization or a unit in that organization can be effective.

5. The U.S. Bureau of Labor Statistics releases quarterly reports tracking national trends in salaries and labor costs. See also http://work.chron.com/average-salary-raise-percentage-17983.html, http://fortune.com/2015/02/12/salaries-raises-promotions/.

6. http://www.barrypopik.com/index.php/new_york_city/entry/they_pretend_to_pay_us_and_we_pretend_to_work

14 BUILDING BETTER PERFORMANCE APPRAISAL SYSTEMS

Performance appraisal is hard work, and some organizations seem inclined to simply abandon or severely curtail their appraisal systems (Buckingham & Goodall, 2015; Capelli & Tavis, 2016; Tziner & Roch, 2016). A number of high-profile organizations have made major changes to their appraisal systems (e.g., Buckingham & Goodall, 2015), and the business press has suggested that traditional performance appraisal is dying. The evidence suggests otherwise; performance appraisal is still with us, and there is no sign it is going to go away any time soon.

The great majority of organizations continue to rely on performance appraisal as an important tool for managing human resources (Lawler, Benson, & McDermott, 2012; Mercer, 2013). The question is not whether we can or even should get rid of performance appraisal, but rather whether performance appraisal can be improved. In Chapters 1–12 we outlined many of the challenges to evaluating performance in the workplace, and some of the problems that haunt performance appraisal (e.g., the strong motivation to give inflated appraisals) may be very difficult ones to solve. Nevertheless, we remain optimistic that performance appraisal can be substantially improved, and that the research that has been reviewed in this book points to some clear directions for improving performance appraisals.

It has long been argued performance appraisal research has not contributed very much to the quality of performance appraisals in organizations (Banks & Murphy, 1985; Ilgen, Barnes-Farrell, & McKellin, 1993; Murphy & DeNisi, 2008). There has been almost a century of research on performance appraisal, but this research has not led to notable improvements in the way performance is evaluated in organizations (DeNisi & Murphy, 2017). As a consequence, many consultants and practitioners seem to ignore this research and to advocate innovations that are not empirically supported, such as focusing on feedback or carrying out radical simplifications of appraisal systems. We think this is a mistake. Despite the somewhat mixed track record of using performance appraisal research to guide practice, we believe research on performance appraisal and performance management provides some eminently practical suggestions for improving performance appraisal in organizations. In this chapter, we lay out several ways of applying appraisal research to improve the practice of performance appraisal.

IMPROVING PERFORMANCE APPRAISALS

In Chapter 4, we laid out what we see as the four most serious challenges to evaluating performance in organizations. First, the task is difficult. Raters who want to accurately evaluate the performance of their subordinates must observe, recall, and integrate a lot of information, while at the same time attending to all of their other job duties. Second, the process and outcomes of performance appraisal are substantially influenced by a number of contextual factors, making it difficult to tell whether they represent assessments of performance or simple adjustments to the demands of the context in which they are carried out. Third, performance appraisals have many purposes in organizations, and these purposes can come into conflict. Finally, all of the participants in performance appraisal are motivated to distort the process in such a way that most employees receive high ratings. It is not easy to overcome all of these challenges, but we believe that performance appraisal research leads to some important and highly practical ideas for making progress on all four fronts. We group our suggestions for improving and reforming performance appraisal under four headings: (1) make appraisal easier and less risky for raters and ratees, (2) focus on the essential purpose of appraisals and sort out the conflicts among uses, (3) enhance the credibility and legitimacy of the system, and (4) do not waste time and effort on less essential features of your performance appraisal system.

Make Appraisal Easier and Less Risky

There are two reasons why performance appraisal research often has limited impact on the practice of performance appraisal in organizations. First, performance appraisal researchers have spent a lot of time studying topics that are of limited interest to practitioners (e.g., cognitive processes in rating; Banks & Murphy, 1985). It is also the case, however, that practitioners often fail to take advantage of findings that appear to have clear practical implications. Performance appraisal research *has* identified (and validated) a number of ways of making the task of evaluating performance easier and more reliable, and appraisals could be improved substantially if there was more consistent uptake of these suggestions by performance appraisal practitioners.

Two methods that could help make the task of evaluating performance in organizations easier have been extensively studied and validated. First, as we noted in Chapter 5, behavior diaries can be used to help reduce the demands on raters' memory when evaluating performance. There is evidence that the use of behavior diaries contributes to both the accuracy and the fairness of performance evaluations. These diaries require the investment of time and effort on the part of raters, and it would be naïve to expect that the contents of a behavior diary will be a completely accurate record of what raters have observed. The choice of what to record and what to omit from behavior diaries is influenced by a number of factors, and the contents of behavior diaries are probably biased by raters' overall impressions (i.e., raters who believe a particular employee is a generally good worker will probably attend to and record different entries in a behavior diary than would be recorded if the rater's overall impression was more negative; Maurer, Palmer, & Ashe, 1993; Murphy & Cleveland, 1995). Nevertheless, this method has some real potential, and we are struck by the lack of interest among practitioners in developing methods to make behavioral diaries simpler to use and more accurate.

Second, one of the real success stories in performance appraisal research has been the development of methods of rater training that are both successful in improving the consistency of performance ratings (Gorman & Rentsch, 2009; Woehr & Huffcutt, 1994) and viewed as reasonable by organizations and by raters (Sulsky & Kline, 2007; Uggerslev, Sulsky, & Day, 2003)—that is, frame of reference training. Some organizations provide this sort of training (Uggerslev et al., 2003), but we believe this method of training is not used in enough organizations, and that both the accuracy and fairness of performance appraisals could be improved if more performance appraisal practitioners took this method to heart.

The use of interventions such as behavior diaries and frame of reference training can make performance appraisal easier. The bigger challenge, in our view, is to make performance appraisal less risky for raters. In most performance appraisal systems, a rater who tries to give accurate performance feedback risks (1) harming his or her relationships with the employees who receive this feedback, (2) looking bad as a supervisor (i.e., the main job of a manager is to help his or her employees perform as well as possible, which means that low performance ratings are an admission of failure), and (3) getting no rewards from the organization for being accurate. As we have discussed in Chapters 9 and 12, the performance appraisal systems in most organizations create strong incentive to simply give everyone high ratings, and create strong disincentives to raters who attempt to give accurate performance feedback. Because raters and ratees are quite likely to have different views about the ratee's performance (see Chapters 5 and 9), it may not be possible to totally remove conflicts and differences in perspectives from performance rating, but we believe it is possible for organizations to take a number of steps that insulate or protect raters from some of the negative consequences of giving accurate performance feedback, by (1) making performance appraisal systems more transparent, (2) making them more fair, (3) making them forward-looking, and (4) reducing the visibility and impact of the direct supervisor's judgments.

Make the System More Transparent

Performance appraisal systems are more likely to be successful if the various participants have a clear and common understanding of the purpose of the system. Transparency is likely to pose especially daunting challenges in multinational corporations, where it is likely that both the actual purpose and the perceived purpose of performance appraisal will vary across units that are located in countries with different cultures and different political and legal systems (Maley, 2013). Nevertheless, increasing the transparency of appraisal systems is probably one of the first and easiest steps an organization can take to make the job of the rater easier and less risky.

Transparency has two components. First, the appraisal system must operate in a consistent and predictable fashion. Thus, one of the first tasks in making a performance appraisal system transparent is to remove or at least reduce the arbitrary and unpredictable parts of the system. This will reduce the flexibility and discretion of supervisors, managers, and executives, and transparency can potentially make performance appraisal systems bureaucratic and rule-bound, but this is arguably a price organizations must be willing to pay if they want to develop a system in which participants trust that it is their performance, and not the whim or self-interest of their superiors, that determines their evaluations. Second, communication is critical. If supervisors, managers, and employees do not *know* how the system works or how changes in employee performance are likely to affect things like rewards and sanctions, it hardly matters whether the system has achieved a high degree of consistency and predictability. Participants in the performance appraisal process act on their beliefs, not on the basis of objective characteristics of their environment, and the biggest challenge in achieving transparency is to get participants to *believe* that the system *truly* functions the way it is designed to function.

In the end, the communication problem organizations face is to convince the participants in the performance appraisal process that they will be treated consistently and reasonably. One way to accomplish this is to match actions to words—to actually and visibly treat employees in a consistent and reasonable fashion. For example, the U.S. Armed Forces represent one of the largest users of drug tests, and there was some initial concern that this type of testing could prove divisive and controversial. One of the decisions that led to a much higher level of acceptance of this type of testing was to make it uniform. *Every* active member of the U.S. Armed Forces, regardless of rank, is required to undergo a urinalysis drug test at least once a year (Smith, 2016). There are elaborate safeguards built into the system, but one key to its success is that it treats every member of the Armed Forces equally.

Transparency is a challenge to organizations for two reasons. First, transparency requires organizational decision makers to surrender power. In a truly transparent system, supervisors, managers, and executives cannot bend the rules or apply new criteria to shape the appraisal system to suit their purposes. Second, transparency requires careful and thoughtful design. A truly transparent system will probably make performance appraisal even more bureaucratic (it is not possible for everyone to follow consistent procedures and rules unless there *are* consistent procedures and rules), in part because a transparent system will require users to think through a wide range of contingencies. Suppose, for example, that you make a public commitment that anyone who receives ratings of "Exceeds Expectations" for all key performance areas will receive a raise. What are you going to do if all of the supervisors and managers in a department submit inflated ratings, giving the highest-possible ratings, even to employees who are visibly failing? A transparent system is going to require safeguards that protect both the users of the system and the organization.

Make Them Fair

We know a good deal about the factors that can make human resource systems seem to be either fair or unfair. Transparency can certainly contribute to perceptions of fairness, but transparency is often not enough to create the perception that an organization's performance appraisal system is fair.

There is a large body of research examining fairness and justice in organizations (Cohen-Charash & Spector, 2001; Colquitt, Conlon, Wesson, Porter, & Ng, 2001; Folger & Cropanzano, 1998; studies dealing specifically with performance appraisal include Erdogan, 2002; Flint, 1999; Holbrook, 2002; Korsgaard & Roberson, 1995). Most generally, this research suggests that three factors influence perceptions that a set of organizational practices is fair or just: (1) procedural justice, (2) distributive justice, and (3) interactional justice. First, the procedures used to evaluate performance and to use these evaluations to drive high-stakes decisions (e.g., raises, promotions) should be consistent, reasonable, and transparent (i.e., procedural justice). As we noted in the previous section, consistency and transparency are not easy to achieve; building an appraisal system that is viewed as procedurally just requires a good deal of thought and work. Second, the consequences of receiving positive or negative appraisals should be reasonable and consistent (i.e., distributive justice). That is, an employee who performs well should receive equitable, or at least consistent, rewards. Finally, the individuals who participate in performance appraisal should be treated with dignity and respect (i.e., interactional justice).

If you want your employees to believe that your performance appraisal system is fair, you must first give them some genuine reason to believe this, by making sure that the appraisal system *is* in fact fair, consistent, and reasonable. Beyond this, performance appraisal research has identified two additional courses of action that can contribute to the perception that your organization's performance appraisal system is fair: participation and voice.

Participation in performance appraisal is strongly related to satisfaction with and trust in appraisals (Cawley, Keeping, & Levy, 1998). Participation can mean many things, ranging from involving employees in the design and development of performance appraisal systems to two-way information sharing. In practice, many organizations involve employees in the development of their appraisal systems, and this involvement probably leads to increased acceptance of the system (Roberts, 2003). Giving employees voice—giving them opportunities to have input into their evaluations, voice their concerns, and have some expectation that their input will be taken into account—is a specific form of participation that appears to be particularly useful (Korsgaard & Roberson, 1995; Lizzio, Wilson, & MacKay, 2008; Whiting, Podsakoff, & Pierce, 2008).

Most generally, "voice" refers to behavior that changes the status quo with the intent of improving things rather than simply complaining or criticizing (LePine & Van Dyne, 1998). For example, employees who speak up about organizational issues or suggest ways of improving organizational processes are exercising voice (Van Dyne & LePine, 1998). In the context of performance appraisal, "voice" refers to giving the individuals who are affected by appraisals an opportunity to present information relevant to those appraisals. For example, many performance appraisal systems ask employees to rate their own performance or to comment on and sign off on appraisals, and these could both be thought of as forms of voice. Folger and Konovsky (1989) identified two distinct roles for voice in performance appraisal, feedback (i.e., providing information or input into the rating) and recourse (i.e., the ability to challenge or modify the evaluations you receive), and both appear to be useful. Voice appears to have both instrumental and non-instrumental effects (Korsgaard & Roberson, 1995). That is, voice can increase satisfaction with and trust in performance appraisals because the employee input often makes appraisals more accurate and more favorable to the employee (instrumental voice), but it can also contribute simply by virtue of the fact that an opportunity to provide input and to voice one's concerns makes the process seem fairer (non-instrumental voice).

One suggestion for increasing the effectiveness of voice is to build interventions to help make sure that the employee's voice is heard, taken seriously, and acknowledged. For example, many organizations ask employees to rate their own performance, but it is often unclear to the employee whether these ratings make any real difference. Suppose, for example, I rate myself as a "4" (out of 5) on Oral Communication, but my supervisor rates me as a "3." We think it is a very good idea for supervisors to (1) acknowledge this difference, and (2) provide some explanation for this difference. For example, a statement along the lines of "I see you rated yourself a '4' on Oral Communication and I rated you a '3.' Here are my reasons for assigning the '3' . . ." does several things. First, it acknowledges that employee's input. Second, it provides a rationale in cases where there is a difference in perspective. Of course, this sort of statement may open up a can of worms, in the sense that the employee might counter the reasons you offer for the rating of "3," but on the whole, we think this approach is worth the effort and risk. Voice is a good thing in performance appraisal, but if employees are asked to give input and come away believing that their input is ignored, the organization's efforts to provide opportunities for input could end up looking like a sham, and might lead to even *more* cynicism and distrust. If you are going to give employees voice, make sure that they know you are taking their input seriously.

Make Appraisals Forward-Looking

As we have noted in several preceding chapters, performance appraisal has many purposes, but two are usually cited as most important: (1) to support administrative decision such as raises and promotions, and (2) to provide information about strengths and weaknesses, which can be used to guide decisions about training. Unfortunately, many organizations devote meager resources to rewarding performance (Chapter 13 described the shortcomings of typical merit pay plans) and lack the resources to tailor training to the individual strengths and weaknesses of employees. One might argue that even in organizations that do not offer much in the way of merit pay or individually tailored training, there might still be some reasons for collecting information about job performance (e.g., for legal purposes, to use for validating tests), but it is hard to resist the conclusion that in traditional performance appraisal systems, too much attention is focused on evaluating past performance, and not enough is devoted to thinking about how to improve performance in the future.

A typical performance appraisal gives the individual and the organization fairly detailed information about how well each employee has performed over the last year. If the organization is unwilling or unable to do much in response to this information (e.g., because its merit pay budget is just too small to differentially reward good and poor performers), perhaps we should not concentrate so much on evaluating past performance. It might be better to devote more time and energy to the present and the future.

Many versions of performance management (e.g., Aguinis, 2013) involve giving employees frequent real-time performance feedback. This approach has two very attractive features. First, it focuses on the here and now—that is, giving feedback about what the employee is doing, and where necessary, helping him or her make changes that will improve subsequent performance. Second, because feedback is given in real time, it is likely to have the sort of immediacy and relevance that feedback about last year's performance may not possess.

Traditional performance deals largely with past performance. Performance management often focuses on the present. What about appraisal systems that are focused on the future? van Woerkom and de Bruijn (2016) suggest that instead of using retrospective appraisal systems, which focus on what you did (sometimes, focusing on what you did wrong) over the last year, it might be better to develop strength-based, forward-looking performance appraisal systems. They advocate developing appraisal systems that focus on identifying the unique abilities, skills, and other qualities each employee brings to the table and using those qualities to improve the organization. This sort of appraisal would shift the discussion from what was done well and poorly toward discussions of ways the employee might be able to contribute in the future toward accomplishing the mission of his or her work unit.

The feedforward interview represents an example of a future-oriented approach to performance appraisal (Bouskila-Yam & Kluger, 2011). In a feedforward interview (Kluger & Nir, 2010), employees are invited to tell about an experience at work during which they felt energized before knowing the results of their actions. This type of interview follows a three-step protocol, illustrated in Table 14.1.

TABLE 14.1 ■ Feedforward Interview Protocol
Elicit a success story—Have the employee tell you about a positive work experience, particularly one in which the positive feelings are generated by the work itself, not the rewards.
Describe a success code—Identify the conditions and events that made this experience possible.
The feedforward question—Ask the employee to consider ways they can accomplish similar conditions and experiences in the future.

The feedforward interview has two outstanding characteristics. First, it attempts to identify experiences at work that are intrinsically satisfying for employees. Second, it focuses on practical steps the individual and the organization can take to increase the likelihood that their experiences will be repeated. This method also has the interesting characteristic that it focuses on positive events.

Neville and Roulin (2016) note that in most feedback situations, negative feedback can swamp positive feedback, an observation that is consistent with a wide range of research in cognition and decision making that deals with the way we process negative events (e.g., Baumeister, Bratslavsky, Finkenauer, & Vohs, 2001; Kahneman & Tversky, 1979). They suggest that one strategy for reducing defensiveness in reaction to negative feedback is to maintain a substantial ratio (3 to 1 or more) of positive to negative feedback. The feedforward interview, with its singular focus on positive events and experiences, might represent one way of accomplishing this sort of ratio.

Assist and Protect Raters

A supervisor or manager who decides to be honest and accurate in his or her performance feedback faces a number of risks. If you give low ratings to subordinates who are hoping for and even expecting to receive higher ratings, it is likely that this feedback will hurt your future relationship with those employees, perhaps *decreasing* their motivation to work hard and perform well in the future. As we described in Chapter 12, supervisors and managers have many reasons to inflate ratings, and surprisingly few to provide honest and accurate appraisals. In Chapter 13, we noted that one way to get more accurate feedback to employees is to reduce the isolation and risk of the individual rater. If your supervisor is the only person who evaluates your performance, your disappointment over lower-than-expected performance ratings will be focused on him or her. This disappointment might be reduced if evaluations were seen as the product of the judgments of a group rather than a single individual.

In the past, we have expressed doubts about the value of 360-degree feedback (Cleveland, Lim, & Murphy, 2007), in part because a system that provides employees with feedback from supervisors, peers, subordinates, customers, and others is likely to sometimes give employees conflicting information. It is almost certain that peers or customers will rate a particular employee differently on at least *some* aspects of performance than supervisors rate that same employee. After all, different ratings sources are likely to observe different behaviors and may apply different standards when evaluating the behaviors they observe. Suppose, however, you modified the typical 360-degree protocol. One possibility, as described in Chapter 13, is that you might collect information from many sources, but feed it back in the form of a single aggregated report. We are attracted to this idea because it helps to solve multiple problems with performance appraisal, but it is important to understand the costs and benefits of this idea.

Suppose an organization solicited performance ratings and feedback statements from peers, supervisors, and subordinates, then fed them back to employees in a single report that did not differentiate among data sources. You could, for example, provide employees with a weighted average of all of the ratings you have collected rather than providing them with separate reports reflecting feedback from peer, subordinates, and others. You might even consolidate all of the comments about each performance area (e.g., Oral Communication) into a single report that does not treat comments from supervisors differently than comments from other sources. This sort of system would not be the most efficient, because it would require even more data collection than typical performance appraisal systems, but it could present several advantages. First, an employee who received disappointing feedback would know that this feedback is not simply the opinion of his or her supervisor, but rather represents the consensus of a large and diverse group. This might make disappointing feedback easier to accept, or at least harder to dismiss. Second, a system like this would increase participation and voice, since it would almost certainly include the opinions of coworkers, in effect involving each employee in the evaluation of each of the members of his or her own work group. Third, this sort of appraisal system would reduce the exposure of the individual supervisor, because disappointing ratings can no longer be blamed on the presumed biases or shortcomings of the supervisor.

The biggest impediment to adopting a system of this sort is probably not inefficiency, but rather the implications of this of "crowdsourcing" for the power, discretion, and influence of supervisors and managers. As we have noted throughout this book, performance appraisal is, in the end, an exercise of power. People who are at a higher level in a traditionally structured organization have the power and authority to evaluate the behavior and performance of their subordinates. We purposely use the term *evaluate* here, because traditional performance appraisal is not simply an act of reporting what subordinates have or have not done but also an act of assigning value to their performance. The appraisal system described here would substantially diminish the power and discretion of the individual supervisor, by shifting some of the responsibility for evaluation from the supervisor to the group of peers, subordinates, customers, and others who are asked to provide input. Suppose, for example, the supervisor is convinced that a particular worker deserves an overall rating of 2 (out of 5), but others in the organization think that a rating of 4 is more appropriate. The logic of the system described here is that the supervisor will just have to accept that his or her judgment is being overruled. Even if supervisory ratings are given more weight than ratings from other sources, this sort of system will inevitably say that in cases where the rater and others disagree, the rater will not fully get his or her own way.

We recognize that surrendering the power to unilaterally evaluate one's subordinates[1] can complicate the role of supervisors, but it could also liberate them. Rather than functioning mainly as a judge of their subordinates, taking the task of judgment and evaluation out of supervisors' hands could free them up to serve as coaches rather than judges. Instead of being seen as a problem by subordinates who receive disappointing evaluations, the direct supervisor might be seen as the solution—that is, as a person who can help employees who receive negative evaluations to improve.

Focus on the Most Critical Purpose of Appraisal

Performance appraisal systems in many organizations seem almost built to fail, because they are simultaneously used for multiple conflicting purposes (Cleveland, Murphy, & Williams, 1989; Murphy & Cleveland, 1995). For example, human resource researchers have understood for over 50 years that using the same performance appraisal system for both administrative purposes (particularly pay administration) and developmental purposes creates a set of conflicting demands and expectations that can make appraisal less useful for *either* purpose (Meyer, Kay, & French, 1965), but most organizations continue to use the same appraisal system for both purposes. As we have discussed in Chapters 8 and 12, we think there is compelling evidence that organizations shouldn't try to use the same performance appraisal system for both administrative and developmental purposes.

We think it is time for organizations to choose which of these purposes—administration of rewards or employee development—is more important, and to live with that choice. If you want to use performance appraisal as a tool for deciding who gets a raise or a promotion, you should not use it to assess training needs. If you want to use performance appraisal as a system for employee development, you should not use it for salary administration. It might be feasible to develop two separate appraisal systems, one designed for each purpose, but we think this would be a mistake. These separate systems will almost certainly lead to conflicting assessments, because they focus on two very different aspects of performance. A system designed for developmental purposes must reliably measure individual difference in overall performance levels, and rating profiles that have lots of peaks and valleys (i.e., clear patterns of strengths and weaknesses) will

SPOTLIGHT 14.1 IF AT FIRST YOU DON'T SUCCEED, STOP GIVING THE SAME FEEDBACK

As we have noted in several preceding chapters, performance feedback does not always lead to improvements in performance. Performance appraisal researchers often treat the failure to see meaningful improvements in performance after giving feedback as a failure of the performance appraisal system, but this might not be the right diagnosis.

Feedback is most valuable when employees are new to their job and do not know whether or not they are performing their tasks right. At that point, performance feedback is often new and useful information. As employees gain experience, it is reasonable to expect that many of them know how to do their jobs, and also know whether they are performing adequately. For experienced employees, poor performance is not likely to be due to a lack of knowledge; performance problems among experienced employees are more likely to reflect a lack of motivation or willingness to perform.

Probably the least effective feedback strategy is to tell an employee the same thing year after year; if this approach does not work the first or second time, the odds that it will work the third of fourth time strike us as low. This suggests one practical step raters can take before giving performance feedback: to review feedback that has been given in the past and to consider the changes (if any) in performance following that feedback. Poor performers are already biased in the direction of rejecting much of the performance feedback they receive (see Chapter 9). If the feedback is simply a rerun of last year or of the last few years, it is probably that much easier to tune out this year's feedback. Knowing what you have told an employee in the past and how well or poorly that feedback worked might turn out to be very helpful in shaping this year's performance feedback.

tend to produce average ratings that cluster toward the middle, making it difficult to rank-order individuals in terms of their overall performance. Ratings with few inter-dimensional differences make it easier to sort individuals on the basis of their overall performance levels, but ratings of this sort will not provide much information about strengths and weaknesses.[2] A choice needs to be made.

In making a choice between these two important uses of performance appraisal, we think it is necessary to consider at least two separate questions: (1) how important are decisions about rewards versus about development in this organization, and (2) to what degree is the organization willing and able to take action in relation to these two uses of performance appraisal. The second question strikes us as more important, because many organizations claim that things like merit pay or rewarding good performance are very important, but in fact put too few resources toward rewarding performance to make the system work.

On the whole, questions about the capability and will to reward good performance are probably easier to address than questions about the capability and will to engage in employee development. An organization is not truly serious about merit pay if it (1) puts very little money at risk in a merit pay pool, or (2) routinely puts up with performance ratings that do not meaningfully distinguish good from poor performers. Thus, in theory, all it takes to make a genuine commitment to merit pay is to actually put a significant portion of each employee's pay at risk (as we noted in Chapter 13, the amount needed to make merit pay work is often a lot more than organizations or employees are willing to put truly at risk) and the development of an evaluation system that forces raters to distinguish among ratees. Training can be a bit trickier to evaluate, because the desire to provide training and developmental opportunities may not be enough. First, the structure of the organization, the nature of the labor market, and/or the legal system might constrain the organization's ability to offer a range of developmental experiences. For example, many large organizations offer expatriate assignments or assignments to different divisions or offices as part of their process for developing managers and executives. The effectiveness of these strategies is not always clear (Bolino, 2007), but the very availability of this method of training and development depends on factors such as the size and complexity of the organizations, and some organizations may not be in a position to offer this type of developmental experience regardless of their wish to develop employees. Second, a thorough assessment of training and development is likely to identify some weaknesses that are easy to address and others that are very hard to address through the types of training and development programs available to organizations. If a needs assessment reveals that the principal shortcomings of the workforce are in terms of highly stable attributes like general cognitive ability or broad personality traits, training and development is probably not the right strategy; improving recruitment and selection is more likely to help in these cases.

Suppose an organization determines that it is not truly willing or able to do anything meaningful to reward good performance or is not in a position to offer meaningful training and development. We suspect that many workplaces fall into one or both categories. As we described in Chapter 13, many organizations that claim to offer merit pay in fact do little more than go through the motions, giving very similar pay to the best and the worst performers. In a similar vein, there are several reasons to believe that many organizations that claim to be committed to employee development are in fact unable to do much to develop their employees. First, about half of all employed adults work in firms of organizations that are classified as large (500 or more employees), but more than one-third work in firms that are small (fewer of 100 employees) or very small (fewer than 20 employees; Caruso, 2015).

Opportunities for growth assignments may be quite limited in small firms, and even larger firms may find it challenging to offer this sort of developmental assignment to some of their employees. Second, organizational training budgets are often constrained, especially during economically challenging times. If you want to evaluate an organization's real commitment to training and development, it is more useful to look at the resources the organization actually devotes to training than to consult the HR handbook. An organization that says that it is committed to developing its employees but devotes scant resources to doing so is making a misleading claim.

Organizations that are unable or unwilling to do something meaningful with the information they collect in performance appraisal should seriously consider dropping performance appraisal altogether. The fact that an organization devotes time and effort to performance appraisal is likely to suggest to employees that it will do something with the information they collect, and we suspect that much of the dissatisfaction with performance appraisal is a result of the failure of appraisals to have meaningful consequences. Sometimes, the things that constrain organizations from acting on performance appraisals are temporary (e.g., short-term economic trends) and employees will probably put up with the situation if they know that you will act on performance appraisals once the current crisis or constraint is resolved. In too many organizations, performance appraisals appear to be little more than a waste of time, and the belief that your organization collects but ultimately ignores performance appraisals can undermine even the best appraisal system.

Perhaps the most common criticism of traditional performance appraisal systems is that they are a form of paper punching that does not lead to any meaningful outcomes. In theory, performance management systems should be less vulnerable to this criticism. The underlying philosophy of performance management is essentially active, with a focus on identifying opportunities to improve performance and supporting that improvement through feedback, training, and the marshalling of the organizational resources needed to perform well (Aguinis, 2013; Pulakos, 2009). In practice, many performance management systems seem to fall short of this ideal (Pulakos, Mueller-Hanson, Arad, & Moye, 2015; Pulakos & O'Leary, 2011), but nevertheless, a key distinction between performance appraisal and performance management is that performance management systems are designed to *do* something with performance assessments and feedback, whereas performance appraisal systems sometimes collect a lot of information but ignore that information when making decisions about how to reward or develop employees. In an organization that fails to link performance appraisals to meaningful outcomes, performance appraisal does little more than set up false hopes (e.g., that good performance will lead to valued rewards) and force employees to participate in a time-consuming and tiresome charade.

It is always useful for organizations to give serious thought to the question of *why* they are conducting performance appraisals. If they cannot come up with a convincing answer, this is a clear indication that the organization needs to carefully evaluate its priorities and to engage in a systematic redesign of its human resource strategy. While it might be tempting for organizations like this to simply give up on performance appraisal, we think a much better strategy is to give serious thought to *why* they are not making better use of a human resource tool that can serve important purposes in organizations, and to find ways to improve and effectively use performance appraisal as a tool for improving individual and organizational effectiveness.

Enhance the Credibility and Legitimacy of the System

You might have noticed that most of the suggestions for improving performance appraisals discussed so far have little to do with the topics that have dominated performance appraisal research for most of the last century, such as scale development, criteria for evaluating ratings, ratings versus rankings, or subjective versus objective measures of performance (DeNisi & Murphy, 2017). In fact, with the exception of a brief mention of behavior diaries and frame of reference training, the suggestions for improving performance appraisal discussed so far have very little to do with improving performance *measurement.*

We do not want to create the impression that good measurement is unimportant, but it is essential to understand that performance appraisal is not the same thing as performance measurement (see Chapter 13). Performance appraisal involves evaluative judgments (e.g., someone has to decide whether an employee's performance is good enough), social influence (e.g., performance appraisal is always to some extent political; Longenecker, Sims, & Gioia, 1987; Murphy & Cleveland, 1995), contextual influences, and the application of a range of human resource strategies, and good measurement does not guarantee good performance appraisal. Nevertheless, organizations can benefit from applying many of the strategies that have been put forth to increase the measurement qualities of performance appraisals. Despite our emphasis on topics other than the accuracy of performance measures, we would argue that many of the strategies developed over the years for improving the reliability and accuracy of performance ratings and other measures used in appraisal *are* important, but often for a very different reason than you might think.

Consider some of the things you might do if your goal was to develop reliable and valid measures of job performance. You would probably start with a careful analysis of the job, to ensure that the performance dimensions measured by your rating instruments were in fact important to that job. You would probably develop scales that make it as clear as possible what each performance dimension actually refers to and what the organization means by "very good performance," "average performance," "bad performance," and so forth on each dimension (a number of the behaviorally based scales discussed in Chapter 5 would help here). You would train the raters to make sure they were applying consistent standards in evaluating their subordinates (e.g., by implementing frame of reference training). You might collect data from multiple raters, to minimize the effects of idiosyncratic rater biases. All of these strike us as good ideas that might increase the precision of your performance assessments. More important, all of these steps are likely to contribute to the perception, on the part of several stakeholders, that the appraisal system is carefully developed, relevant, and administered in a thoughtful way. In other words, all of the interventions described in this paragraph are likely to contribute to perceptions of legitimacy.

Consider, for example, the standards the law relies on in evaluating performance appraisal systems that are challenged on the basis of discrimination against members of some protected group. Courts seem to focus on two general themes in evaluating performance appraisal systems: (1) is there evidence that the system is designed in such a way that it is likely to provide reliable and job-related assessments? and (2) are there mechanisms in place to provide employees a chance to have input and to challenge evaluations they regard as unfair? (Werner & Bolino, 1997). All of the steps described above for improving the measurement quality of performance assessments will help in establishing the system's legitimacy in the eyes of the law.

Similarly, visible efforts to increase the reliability and job-relatedness of performance appraisal systems, *regardless of their actual effects on measurement accuracy*, are likely to contribute to the perception that these systems are at least designed and intended to provide good measures. We are not sure whether following "best practices" will have a real effect on the quality of measurement provided by performance ratings, but we are convinced that visible efforts to do a careful and thorough job in evaluating performance will pay off in terms of perceptions of legitimacy. If raters and ratees believe that their appraisal system is poorly designed and hastily put together, they are unlikely to invest much time or effort in evaluating performance, and equally unlikely to take performance ratings and performance feedback seriously. Organizations that make concerted and visible efforts to ensure the job-relatedness, reliability, and accuracy of evaluations are sending a signal that they take appraisal seriously and that they are willing to invest resources to make it work well. The ultimate payoff from interventions designed to improve the measurement quality of performance ratings may be in terms of enhancing the credibility and legitimacy of the appraisal system.

Do Not Waste Time and Effort on the Less Essential Features of Your Appraisal System

Finally, in designing or retooling a performance appraisal system, it is important to devote your time and effort to the essential features of your system, such as the credibility and legitimacy of the system, the way the system protects the rater, its transparency, and so on. Unfortunately, organizations often devote time and effort to aspects of performance appraisal systems that are much less important, in particular, rating scales and technology. Neither of these is necessarily trivial, but in the grand scheme of things, time and effort you devote to these peripheral concerns is time and effort you probably will not devote to the more essential features of performance appraisal.

Our advice regarding rating scales is simple: Define the performance dimensions as clearly as you can and include some behavioral examples in your rating scales. Beyond that, it is doubtful that fiddling with the rating scale will have much of an impact. A rating scale is simply a tool, and developing the perfect rating scale will probably do little to improve your performance appraisal system beyond what you can accomplish with reasonably clear rating dimensions and a few behavioral examples.

Making large investments in technology designed to simplify the performance appraisal process strikes us as a risky bet. Many organizations are investing in databases, apps, computerized systems for organizing performance appraisal information, and the like.[3] There is nothing wrong with using technology to simplify a task like performance appraisal, but technology is often used in an attempt to solve the wrong set of problems. Many of the technological solutions to performance appraisal appear to be aimed at solving the same problems that rater training and rating scale development tried to solve in the 1950s through 1980s—that is, the rater's *ability* to accurately assess performance. We have come to believe that supervisors and managers usually have a reasonably good idea of who is performing well and who is performing poorly in their organization. The real shortcoming in many performance appraisal systems is that raters and not *willing* to provide accurate performance ratings and feedback (see Chapters 9 and 12), and technology rarely provides a solution to this problem.

TRUST: THE ESSENTIAL CURRENCY OF PERFORMANCE APPRAISAL

Trust is absolutely essential to the success or failure of performance appraisal systems (Farr & Jacobs, 2006). Trust that supervisors and managers will evaluate performance accurately and fairly, that they can give feedback (even negative feedback) without suffering negative consequences, and that rewards will be given when people perform their jobs well and withheld when they perform their jobs poorly are each important determinants of the success of performance appraisal. There is a good deal of evidence that the level of trust users show toward their appraisal system is related to both the psychometric characteristics of ratings (e.g., reliability) and to satisfaction with the system and motivation to devote time and effort to appraisal (Bernardin, Orban, & Carlyle, 1981; Bernardin & Villanova, 1986; Kay, Meyer, & French, 1965; Longenecker & Gioia, 1988). Organizational climates characterized by low levels of trust present a serious challenge to the effectiveness of appraisal systems (Lawler, 1971).

Better Performance Appraisal Requires Better Organizations

One of the key themes of contemporary performance appraisal research is that the context within which performance appraisal occurs is critical for understanding the success or failure of performance appraisal (DeNisi & Murphy, 2017; Murphy & Cleveland, 1995). This is one reason why "one-size-fits-all" recommendations (simplify, give more feedback) are likely to fail in the long run. The success or failure of performance appraisal and appraisal systems depends to a large part on what else is happening in the organization and even in society. For example, a well-developed performance appraisal system might fail if the organization does not have the resources to reward good performers. A system that is technically sophisticated but that does not fit the culture (e.g., a system that rewards individual accomplishment in an organization or in a culture that emphasizes cooperation and teamwork) will probably not succeed.

The suggestions laid out above for improving performance appraisal systems also say a good bit about the types of organizations in which performance appraisal is likely to succeed or fail. In particular, we believe a climate of trust and respect is absolutely essential if you want performance appraisal to succeed. You can design an appraisal system to be transparent, equitable, accurate, and impactful, but if the people who use this system do not *believe* that they are going to get fair and accurate evaluations, or that the evaluations they receive will result in rewards they care about, the system will fail. We often think about performance appraisal as a means for improving the way an organization functions, but perhaps we have it backwards. If you want to build better performance appraisal systems, it is probably best to start by building better organizations.

We believe that dysfunctional performance appraisal systems are more likely to be a symptom of a larger dysfunction in organizations than to be a problem that can be solved by adjusting the surface features of the appraisal system. In an organization that treats its employees with suspicion and contempt, or one in which performance appraisal is seen as an exercise in office politics (Longenecker et al., 1987), minor adjustments, such as changing the items on an appraisal scale or with the frequency of feedback, strike us as virtually pointless. In our experience, performance appraisal is rarely a big deal, and even more rarely a problem in well-run organizations that are characterized by a climate of mutual trust and respect. Instead of getting rid of performance appraisal, we should focus on getting rid of organizational climates in which mistreatment and abuse run rampant, and in which employees are treated as disposable cogs in a profit-making machine. Improve organizations, and you will almost certainly improve performance appraisal.

Can organizations develop a culture of mutual respect, decency, and fairness? They probably can accomplish some of these things, but it is clear that building a culture of mutual trust and respect is a long and difficult process (Galford & Drapeau, 2003;

SPOTLIGHT 14.2 PERFORMANCE APPRAISAL IN DYSFUNCTIONAL ORGANIZATIONS

There is little doubt that many organizations are deeply dysfunctional, and it is hard to image performance appraisal working well in these organizations. For example, a number of technology-focused or information-based firms in Silicon Valley have been criticized in recent years for their "bro culture," an organizational culture that combines the worst aspects of fraternity life with the arrogance of sudden wealth (Chrisler, Bacher, Bangali, Campagna, & McKeigue, 2012). A bro culture is characterized by immature, misogynistic, male-oriented behavior in which the only rule is "boys will be boys," and in which misbehavior is not only tolerated but often encouraged. There have been numerous reports of the difficulties this type of culture has caused companies such as Uber (Minter, 2017), but this culture is not limited to high-tech startups; similar cultures have been reported in major banks and investment firms (Lewis, 1989) and the military (Sorcher, 2013). Media organizations, notably Fox News, have been described as having a culture that tolerates the harassment of female employees by powerful males (Carterucci, 2017), and it is easy to see how such a culture could undermine even the best performance appraisal system.

The "bro culture" is not the only manifestation of dysfunction in organizations. There is a substantial research literature dealing with the "dark triad" of personality traits, a combination of narcissism, Machiavellianism, and psychopathy (Paulhus & Williams, 2002). Individuals who exhibit these traits tend to be manipulative, dishonest, unpredictable, and power-hungry, and this pattern of behavior can cause a number of problems in the workplace. There

is evidence that this pattern of personality traits tends to draw people toward (and sometimes to succeed in) managerial and executive roles (Boddy, 2006, 2010; Jonason, Slomski, & Partyka, 2012), and even in organizations whose culture is generally tolerant and humane, the presence of a small number of dark triad managers or executives can create a climate of fear and mistrust.

Perhaps we don't even need a dysfunctional climate or darkly motivated managers to create a lack of trust in organizations. In many organizations where the culture does not seem particularly vicious and where managers and executives seem to have fairly normal personalities, there are still good reasons why employees might distrust managers. In too many organizations, employees are treated like commodities and are shown little respect or consideration. At the same time that employees are being laid off and pensions are being decimated (Jones, 2017; Miller, 2017), executives seem to be treating themselves very well, often receiving hefty bonuses at the same time that employees are being cut. Interestingly, there is evidence that the highest paid CEOs are among the worst performers (Cooper, Gulen, & Rau, 2016), and it is possible that the decision to give outsized rewards to top executives is a sign of organizational dysfunction, not a sign of success. Regardless of how top executives are paid, organizational culture almost certainly matters in determining the success or failure of performance appraisal. An organization that treats employees like cogs in a machine should not be surprised if those employees respond with cynicism, detachment, and distrust.

Lewicki & Bunker, 1996; Sims, 2000). Unfortunately, it seems much easier to lose a culture of respect and trust than to build one. For example, Galford and Drapeau (2003) describe how even benevolent behaviors, such as tolerating an employee who is incompetent, can be corrosive to trust because these behaviors frequently lead to inconsistent standards and the appearance of favoritism. We suspect that it is easier to build trust in organizations that are relatively egalitarian, and harder to build trust when there is a great deal of separation between employees and management, but there have not been compelling empirical tests of this proposition.

Six and Sorge (2008) outline six methods that are believed to be useful in building a culture of mutual trust in organizations; these methods are outlined in Table 14.2 and are described below.

Promote a Relationship-Oriented Culture

In organizations, we often interact with others in terms of roles, such as supervisor–subordinate, coworker, and staff member. Roles cannot and should not be done away with, but one of the keys to building organizational trust is to encourage a culture in which we interact with others as individuals, not solely as people defined by their role (e.g., manager, team leader, production employee). Six and Sorge (2008) suggest that one step in building trust is to establish a norm that says relationships between people are important and that showing care and concern for others' needs is valued.

Most organizations have handbooks that trumpet their support for a relationship-oriented culture, filled with phrases like "We Bring Out the Best in People," but it takes more than verbiage to build a relationship-oriented culture.[4] First, in a culture of this sort, roles will be important for some purposes (e.g., determining who is responsible for what when performing a task), but they will not sort people into distinct classes that differ in their value or worth. Organizations that maintain a strong and rigid separation among levels (e.g., having different areas, amenities, and so on for executives versus employees) or in which roles strongly define the behaviors people are expected to engage in may find it difficult to put interpersonal relationships front and center.

One indicator of a relationship-oriented culture is a set of values and norms that discourages the aggressive pursuit of self-interest in favor of pursuing the interests of the community or group. However, we should not confuse relationship orientation with collective values. In highly collective cultures (e.g., Japan), one might strive for the benefit of the group without showing similar attention to or regard for individuals. In a truly relationship-oriented culture, the group is less than the sum of its parts, and it is critical to

TABLE 14.2 ■ Strategies for Building a Trusting Organization
Promote a relationship-oriented culture
Facilitate unambiguous signaling
Socialize newcomers into the desired culture
Develop and manage the competencies required to sustain trust

interact with individuals rather than with people who are defined in terms of their role, even when the role is group member.

Signal Your Intentions

One of the more important insights of Six and Sorge (2008) is that a culture of trust depends substantially on the ability of individuals to signal that they can and should be trusted. In practice, this involves providing the people you interact with frequent, clear, and credible signals that you intend to act in a way that enhances their well-being. The authors suggest two strategies that can help individuals appropriately signal, and accurately recognize when others are signaling, the intent to act in ways that advance well-being. First, signaling is a skill, and skills often require both instruction (training) and practice to master. Six and Sorge (2008) describe some of the methods companies they studied use to train individuals to sharpen their skills in signaling their own intentions and in recognizing others' signals. For example, one of the organizations they studied provided structured coaching for employees to help them communicate their intentions more clearly. They also suggested that organizations should encourage informal, face-to-face meetings, in part because these give people an opportunity to practice signaling skills in a less threatening environment than in more formal settings.

This focus on signaling helps to bring home an essential point about the development of trust in organizations. It is not enough for individuals to *have* benign intentions, they must also communicate their intentions to others. Trust involves taking a risk—in particular, a risk that your effort to look out for the well-being of the person you are dealing with will not be reciprocated. Effective communication of intentions in a relationship can mitigate this risk.

Socialize New Members

Six and Sorge (2008) suggest that organizations need to devote time and resources to socializing new employees, with a particular emphasis on helping newcomers understand the norms and policies of an organization that support a relationship-oriented culture and helping them understanding the importance of developing the sort of signaling skills that make this culture possible. These authors emphasize the importance of being detailed and explicit in describing not only the values, but also the behaviors the organization prefers and expects. This type of socialization is especially valuable because statements of corporate values (especially mission statements or other similar documents) can be bland and abstract. Many organizations say things like "people are our most important resource," but unless you know what (if anything) this actually means in terms of day-to-day behavior, this value statement may not provide a sufficiently concrete indication of what you should actually do to put this value into practice.

In their paper, Six and Sorge (2008) describe two different organizations, one of which had a long and detailed socialization process, where new organization members were expected to learn and understand the norms and values of the organization before they were "released" into the organization. The other organization followed a culture of "throwing new members into the deep end," putting new members of the organization directly into their new job with little instruction on the precise demands of the job, much less the norms and values of the organization. Their conclusion was that the failure to socialize new members of the organization left many opportunities for miscommunication and misunderstanding and for behaviors that (unknown to the new member) were not received favorably by their coworkers. At least in the case of these two organizations, difference in socialization practice seemed to be manifest in differences in the level of trust shown within the organization.

Monitor and Develop Competency

Six and Sorge (2008) note that "trustworthiness consists of two dimensions, ability and intentions" (p. 877). Part of trust is a belief that the people you interact with intend to behave in ways that advance well-being, but ultimately, exhibiting these intentions in a work setting involves behaving in ways that allow and assist others in carrying out their job tasks and functions. From this perspective, competence is an important component of trust. That is, if you have the knowledge and skills required to do your job and others have the knowledge and skills required to do theirs, it is considerably easier to develop trust based on mutually supporting behavior than if both you and the person you are interacting with lack the competencies to perform well.

This emphasis on competence is one of the key differences in developing and maintaining trust in a work organization as opposed, for example, to an informal social group. In a relationship-oriented work organization, you are expected to behave genuinely and benevolently toward other individuals, all of whom are trying to perform tasks, complete projects, manage processes, and the like. In this sense, competence is an integral part of this benevolence and respect. Individuals who are not competent to perform their jobs well are not likely to be in a position to actively aid others in carrying out the core missions of the organization.

THE ETHICAL PRACTICE OF PERFORMANCE APPRAISAL

A long series of major frauds, crimes, and dishonest practices by organizations, ranging from Enron and WorldCom to Volkswagen, have reinforced the importance of ethical behavior in organizations. While much of the research literature in this area focuses on identifying and preventing major ethical lapses (e.g., white-collar crime, financial manipulation), ethical considerations are important in evaluating a wide range of organizational policies, including the human resource practices of organizations (Buckley et al., 2001). For job applicants and employees, HR represents one of their primary points of contact within larger organizations, and virtually every HR policy an organization might adopt has potential ethical implications. For example, in 2015, California adopted a Fair Pay Act aimed at eliminating pay gaps between men and women performing comparable work or work of equal value. This act is considerably more stringent that the Federal Equal Pay Act of 1963, which mandates equal pay for men and women who perform jobs that are essentially identical, but that does not require equal pay for similar work. The California law is arguably an outgrowth of an ethical judgment that the failure of many organizations to pay men and women on a comparable basis when the work they perform is essentially similar (but not necessarily identical) was fundamentally unfair.

Ethical judgments are required when implementing many human resource policies. For example, it is well known that cognitive ability tests are valid predictors of performance in many jobs, but that these tests are also most likely to systematically screen out members of many minority groups from employment opportunities (Murphy, 2002). This conflict between efficiency and equity is not one that is easily resolved; an ethical judgment is required to resolve the conflict between wanting to use the most efficient and valid tests versus providing fair opportunities for members of minority groups to compete for jobs.

Performance appraisal involves a number of ethical judgments (Buckley et al., 2001). For example, should employees have a right to provide meaningful input in the evaluation of their performance? Note that this is a different question than asking whether giving employees voice in performance appraisal is beneficial (to them or to the organization). It involves considering whether a fundamental respect for human dignity implies that failure to give employees voice is wrong, regardless of the effects of voice for them or for the organization.

Raters face a particularly challenging set of ethical judgments when they decide whether to give performance ratings that benefit the ratee, the rater, or the organization. (See Chapters 7, 8, and 13 for discussions of the way the interests of raters, ratees, and organizations can clash in performance appraisal.) For example, a rater who gives inflated ratings might benefit the ratee, by increasing the likelihood that the ratee receives a raise or a promotion, while at the same time giving the organization misleading information about the ratee's performance. It is useful to think through the ethical issues that might confront raters, ratees, and organizations as a result of their conflicting needs and interests when conducting performance appraisals.

Buckley et al. (2001) note that performance appraisal is one of the processes that frequently tests the norms and values of the participants in the appraisal process. Raters, who probably have a very good idea of who is performing well and who is performing poorly, have a number of reasons to give their subordinates high ratings rather than ratings that reflect their real performance levels (Murphy & Cleveland, 1991, 1995). Employees are strongly tempted to engage in impression management behaviors that might help them get a favorable rating, even if the impressions they strive to create are not a realistic reflection of their actual effectiveness. Human resource managers often find themselves claiming that performance appraisal is important, when they know full well that ratings are often collected then ignored.

In theory, people ought to be held accountable for their behavior (Tetlock, 1985), but performance appraisal represents a situation in which the deck is stacked against honest and accurate evaluations, or against honest ways of talking about human resource policies. We think this creates an ethical dilemma for raters, who are very likely to feel incentives and pressure to inflate the ratings they give. Earlier in this chapter, we suggested some practical methods for reducing the direct supervisor's visibility and responsibility in performance appraisal (e.g., by collecting information from a wide range of sources but feeding it back as a single average). We advanced this suggestion as a way to solve some practical problems, but this approach may also help solve some ethical problems. Performance appraisal, as it is usually implemented, puts managers and supervisors in a position where they will both be tempted and pressured to bend the truth, by giving high ratings even when low ones are deserved. Our first concrete suggestion for the ethical practice of performance appraisal is that organizations should try to avoid placing supervisors, managers, and employees in situations that consistently and predictably pressure them to provide dishonest ratings and feedback.[5]

Second, performance appraisal systems place raters in situations where they have competing moral demands, in particular, doing what is best for the organization versus doing what is best for the individual being evaluated. Suppose that it would be beneficial to the organization to give Sam a low rating, but beneficial to Sam (both because it will get him a raise and because it will help motivate him to improve in the future) to give him a high rating. Which choice should the rater make here? In one sense, the rater is acting as an agent of the organization and is obligated to uphold their interests, but this rater is also an individual with a moral duty to treat others with respect and consideration. We are not sure that there is a clear and simple ethical principle that can be used to resolve these conflicts. The best suggestion we have is for organizations to work to reduce these conflicts. For example, organizations that use performance appraisals mainly to help them identify developmental needs and opportunities probably put raters in fewer conflicts of this sort than organizations that use appraisals to make decisions about promotions, raises, or layoffs.

Finally, managers and supervisors are faced with self-serving motivations to inflate performance ratings. As we have noted in several previous chapters, the key job of a manager is to create conditions that increase the likelihood that his or her subordinates will perform well. A manager who gives low ratings—that is, reporting that his or her subordinates are *not* performing well—is taking a big risk. Our final suggestion is that organizations should take proactive steps to reduce the temptation to make yourself look good by providing inflated ratings. To our knowledge, few organizations reward raters who submit performance ratings that appear to be reliable and valid measures of performance, and even fewer sanction raters whose ratings are obviously inflated. This is another case where the collection of rating information from multiple sources might help. If a supervisor gives ratings of "Greatly Exceeds Expectations" on just about all aspects of performance, but peers, subordinates, and others who do not have self-serving interests give lower evaluations, organizations need to at least consider the possibility that the supervisor is giving biased evaluations. It may turn out that he or she is doing so for good reasons (e.g., on the expectation that high ratings will be more motivating than low ones), but if there are substantial reasons to believe that a supervisor is distorting his or her evaluations, it is at least worth discussing this trend. You can make a case that it is unethical for organizations to ignore evidence that ratings are either accurate or distorted. If an organization wants honest evaluations, it is surely better to structure its HR system in such a way that honesty is recognized and appropriately rewarded.

SUMMARY

Performance appraisal researchers spent much of the period between the 1930s and the 1990s trying to develop ways of improving the reliability and accuracy of performance measures. We believe these efforts led to some useful interventions, but that the more pressing problem is to find ways to make performance appraisals better by making the task easier and less risky for raters. The ultimate goal of performance appraisal is not simply to develop a system that accurately measures performance, but rather to build a system that helps to improve the efficiency and effectiveness of the organization.

Ultimately, the only type of appraisal system that is likely to accomplish this goal is one the users trust and believe in.

In our view, trust is the single most important factor in determining the success or failure of performance appraisal systems. If supervisors, managers, and employees do not trust that evaluations will be reasonably accurate and fair, and that the organization will use information from performance appraisals in a consistent and reasonable fashion, it hardly matters what scales you use or what your rater training program looks like. Ultimately, the key to building better performance appraisal is to build better organizations. In particular, if you want performance appraisal to succeed, we believe it is critical that the culture and climate of the organization supports mutual respect and trust among the users of this appraisal system.

Traditional performance appraisal systems often have a set of built-in moral challenges. In that abstract, most people believe that it is important to be honest, but performance appraisal systems predictably put raters, ratees, and human resource managers in positions where there is strong pressure to bend the truth (by inflating ratings, by working to build positive but misleading impressions, by pretending that performance appraisal is important when in fact it is largely ignored). We believe that organizations can and should take a number of steps to reduce the pressure and temptation to distort and misrepresent and that reducing these predictable moral hazards is likely to have real benefits.

In this book, we have devoted a great deal of attention to the challenges and shortcomings performance appraisal systems face. There is no

doubt that performance appraisal is hard work, and that many organizations fail to get as much out of their performance appraisal system as they should. We continue to believe, however, that it is possible to develop performance appraisal systems that contribute to the success of organizations, and that organizations that take effective steps to build a climate of mutual trust and respect have a real chance to succeed in the task of evaluating the performance of its members and using that information to make sound decisions. Performance appraisal can work, and the process of making performance appraisal systems effective is one that may provide lasting benefits to organizations. An organization that successfully develops and maintains the climate of mutual trust and respect that allows performance appraisal to succeed will become a better place to work, making it easier to attract and retain talented and dedicated employees. Performance appraisal is a real challenge, but we are more optimistic than ever that organizations can rise to this challenge, and that organizations that succeed in developing a good performance appraisal system will find themselves on the road to broader and more general success.

CASE STUDY: IMPLEMENTING A PERFORMANCE APPRAISAL SYSTEM

The case study in Chapter 13 describes the development or designing phase of restoring an old, ineffective performance appraisal system (for the nonprofit organization illustrated in the Chapter 13 example). This scenario is a continuation of that example, illustrating how the consultant might implement or deliver the new system.

Now that you have worked with the committee to develop a performance appraisal system that better addresses the organization's needs and aligns with its values, the committee is eager for your guidance in how to execute the new system.

Communication. As it was discussed in Chapter 13 and this chapter, trust is crucial. Involving the employees and managers in the development phase is essential, and it is also necessary to include them

in the execution phase to let them know their voices were heard. Communicating thoroughly with the raters and ratees about the changes that will be implemented contributes to the success and transparency of the program (e.g., What are the goals of the new program? What will change for you? Why is it needed? What will happen? What are the benefits and improvements?). This is also a time to set clear expectations so everyone is clear on the goals and objectives from the start. There should be no surprises by the time the new performance appraisal launches.

Training and preparation. Along the same lines as communication, training should occur to build understanding and set expectations for the new system. Raters could benefit from role-play scenarios, calibrate examples with other managers, a tutorial of the new paperless system, specific instruction on goal setting, long-term vision of the performance appraisal, and in many circumstances frame of reference training might be helpful. Further, training on how to lead a face-to-face meeting could help raters feel more comfortable with the process (e.g., discuss active listening, nonverbal body language, what to discuss, how to convey the right tone, how to handle difficult reactions from employees). This could also include protocol for disciplinary action, developmental action, and delivering criticism where necessary. As always, a discussion about legal concerns should be included in the training (e.g., do not use discriminatory language, do not make promises where not completely verified, avoid discussing personality traits or other attitudes/behaviors that are not in the employee's scope to change or develop).

Ongoing feedback and corrective guidance. The rater's job is not always finished after the performance appraisal meeting. When goals are not met or people need help achieving their goals, follow-up should include ongoing feedback, support, and resources.

Program evaluation. Performance appraisal should not be a static exercise. The program should be evaluated, updated, refined, and developed over time to ensure relevancy and validity. This is a complex process because the effectiveness of the program must be evaluated by measuring appropriate criteria (i.e., what was the performance appraisal supposed to achieve?). Further, valuable metrics can be collected afterward, such as data to determine if performance is improving, and establish satisfaction (employees and managers alike) with the new system.

NOTES

1. We recognize that even in systems where the direct supervisor is the only one to rate an employee's performance, the judgments of this supervisor are not likely to be absolute, in the sense that there may be some check-off by higher-level management, especially if ratings drive high-stakes decisions.

2. In Chapter 8, Figure 8.1 illustrates this pattern.

3. For example, General Electric has invested in mobile apps to aid supervisors and managers in conducting performance evaluations. See https://qz.com/428813.

4. Six and Sorge (2008) distinguish between espoused values and values that are lived or experienced.

5. There are a number of analogs in the law (doctrine of attractive nuisance, which states that landowners can be held liable if children are injured on their property that contains an object that is known to attract children to trespass and engage in unsafe behaviors, such as a trampoline or an unfenced swimming pool) and in theology (doctrine of occasion of sin—individuals have an obligation to avoid circumstances that they know are likely to incite or entice them to commit immoral acts).

APPENDIX A:
RATING SCALE FORMATS

Between 1950 and the 1980s, performance appraisal researchers devoted a good deal of time and energy to developing, refining, and evaluating alternative rating scale formats (DeNisi & Murphy, 2017). This research was motivated by a belief that we could improve performance appraisal in organizations by giving raters better tools. This line of research declined substantially after Landy and Farr's (1980) review concluded that formats had only a minimal effect on the quality of ratings, and that no one format was consistently better than the others. Their call for a moratorium on rating scale format research was heeded by most researchers, and as a result attempts to develop or refine new types of rating scales have been sporadic ever since. Nevertheless, it is useful to examine some of the features of widely used scale formats.

In this appendix, we discuss several scale formats, including graphic scales, behaviorally anchored rating scales, and behavior observation scales, as well as methods of defining performance criteria (e.g., management by objectives). We will not go into the question of which format or method is best overall (we agree with Landy and Farr, that formats probably do not have a large impact on the quality of rating data), but we will comment on factors that might lead you to adopt one format rather than another. In addition, we will briefly discuss several methods for comparing or ranking employees. While these are not rating scales per se, they are frequently included in performance appraisals and form the basis for some personnel decisions.

Graphic Rating Scales

The simplest scale format asks the rater to record his or her judgment about some specific aspect of the ratee's performance on a scale that can be used to obtain numeric values that correspond with the rater's evaluation of the ratee. Several examples of a graphic scale that might be used to record ratings of a performance dimension such as "Time Management" are presented below:

#1 Rate your subordinate's skill in Time Management

Very Poor	Very Good

#2 Rate your subordinate's skill in Time Management

Well Below Average	Below Average	Average	Above Average	Well Above Average

#3 Rate your subordinate's skill in Time Management

Fails to Meet Expectations	Sometimes Meets Expectations	Meets Expectations	Exceeds Expectations	Greatly Exceeds Expectations

This type of scale format provides little structure for the rater in recording his or her judgment. Graphic scales can range from those like our #1, which contain no definitions of what is meant by very poor, very good, or intermediate levels of performance, to those that define each level in terms of some label (e.g., #3), or even in terms of a brief description of what is meant by each level of performance.

The principal advantage of this scale type is simplicity. The disadvantage of this format, which led to efforts to develop alternative formats, is the lack of clarity and definition. First, the scale does not define what is meant by "Time Management." Different supervisors might include very different behaviors under this general heading. Second, the scale does not define what is meant by "Poor," "Average," and so on. Supervisors might apply very different standards in evaluating the same behaviors. Both behaviorally anchored rating scales and mixed standard scales attempt to solve these problems by defining performance dimensions and performance levels in behavioral terms.

Behaviorally Anchored Rating Scales

The development and use of behaviorally anchored rating scales (BARS) accounted for much of the research on performance appraisal in the late 1960s and the 1970s. These scales use behavioral examples of different levels of performance to define both the dimension being rated and the performance levels on the scale in clear, behavioral terms. The process of scale development can be long and complex, but it will usually result in scales that are clearly defined and well accepted by both raters and ratees.

An example of a BARS used by Murphy and Constans (1987) in one of their studies of teacher rating is presented below:

Speaking Style

9

_____ Very High

|

| Lecturer varies pitch and tone to emphasize points

|

_____ 8

| Lecturer uses hand and body movement to emphasize points

|

|

_____ 7

|

|

|

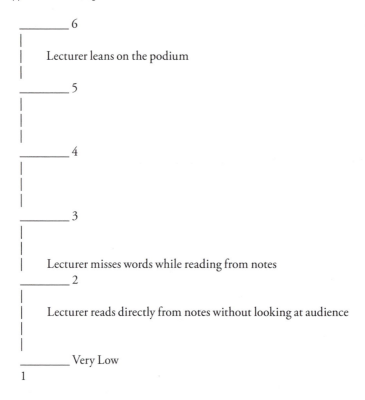

Much of the rating format research of the 1970s seemed to reflect the assumption that BARS were more objective than graphic scales, and that defining performance in behavioral terms would result in more accurate ratings. This assumption was not supported in subsequent research, which has led many researchers and practitioners to question the utility of BARS. This question is especially relevant because the process of developing BARS can be time-consuming and expensive. However, BARS appear to have one advantage that was not fully anticipated by early BARS researchers: they are accepted by the users. The reason for this is that most BARS development procedures incorporate feedback from large numbers of raters (and sometimes, ratees) in the process of constructing scales. As a result, many of the raters and ratees are likely to feel that they have some personal investment in the scales. Even those raters and ratees who do not participate in scale development may view the scales favorably because of the heavy reliance of their colleagues' feedback.

Mixed Standard Scales

Mixed standard scales (MSS) also incorporate behavioral examples, but they employ a different response format than that used in BARS. An example of an MSS helps to illustrate the similarities and differences. An MSS designed to measure two performance dimensions (Response to Questions and Speaking Style), again taken from Murphy and Constans's (1987) research, is given below:

Rate Your Lecturer—Is the lecturer's performance better than, worse than, or about the same as each example?

1. _____ Lecturer's response repeats a point in the lecture

2. _____ Lecturer stands behind the podium

3. _____ Lecturer misses words when reading from notes

4. _____ Lecturer insults or verbally attacks questioner

5. _____ Lecturer uses concrete examples to clarify answers

6. _____ Lecturer varies pitch and tone of voice to emphasize points

Here, items 1, 4, and 5 refer to behaviors that represent "Response to Questions." Items 2, 3, and 6 refer to behaviors that represent "Speaking Style." If you carefully examine the examples, you will note that for each dimension, there is one item describing good performance, one item describing average performance, and one item describing poor performance. The rater responds to an MSS by noting, for each item, whether the ratee's performance is better than, about equal to, or worse than the behavior described in each item. Several algorithms exist for translating these ratings into an overall numeric score for each dimension.

One apparent advantage of MSS is that it may simplify the rater's task. Rather than evaluating each lecturer's performance using vague, undefined terms (e.g., good), raters have only to compare the ratee with the example. However, it is important to note that research on MSS does not strongly support this claim. The complexity of the MSS scoring system is the source of one of its greatest disadvantages. Raters typically do not know which items measure which dimensions (they may not know what dimensions are measured), or how their ratings are translated into numeric scores. As a result, the rater using MSS will find it very difficult to give meaningful feedback. If a subordinate asks why he or she received a low rating on "Speaking Style," the rater may not be able to answer.

Behavior Observation Scales

A final variation on the use of behavioral examples in evaluating performance is the behavior observation scale (BOS). This type of scale uses the same class of items as does the MSS, but it asks for a different sort of judgment. Rather than asking for evaluations of each ratee, the BOS asks the rater to describe how frequently each behavior occurred over the period covered by the appraisal. Proponents of BOS suggested that this method removes much of the subjectivity that is usually present in evaluative judgments. Unfortunately, research into the cognitive processes involved in responding to BOS (Murphy & Constans, 1987; Murphy, Martin & Garcia, 1982) suggests that the process of judging behavior frequency is every bit as subjective as the process of forming evaluative judgments. In fact, behavior frequency ratings may be more subjective than trait ratings or overall judgments; overall evaluations of the ratee's performance appear to serve as a critical cue for estimating behavior frequencies. Thus, the use of BOS probably does not allow you to avoid the subjectivity of overall impressions or judgments.

We cited potential advantages for graphic scales, BARS, and even MSS. We are not as enthusiastic about BOS. The behavioral orientation of these scales appears, on the surface, to be a decided advantage, but there are several reasons to believe that raters do not respond to these scales in terms of behaviors. Rather, they use their overall, subjective evaluations to guide their behavior ratings. This type of scale might actually disguise the inherent subjectivity of evaluative judgment by phrasing judgments in an apparently objective behavioral language.

Performance Distribution Assessment

Performance distribution assessment (PDA) represents a more sophisticated version of the basic approach exemplified by BOS. In PDA, raters must indicate the frequency of different outcomes (e.g., behaviors, results) that indicate specific levels of performance on a given dimension. For example, the scale might describe the most effective outcome and the least effective outcome that could reasonably be expected in a particular job function, as well as several intermediate outcomes. The rater is asked to estimate the frequency of each outcome level for each ratee. One of the potential advantages of this format is that it allows you to consider the distribution or the variability of performance as well as the average level of performance in forming an evaluation. PDA involves some fairly complex scoring rules (a concise description of PDA is presented in Bernardin & Beatty, 1984) and results in measures of the relative effectiveness of performance, the consistency of performance, and the frequency with which especially positive or negative outcomes are observed.

For example, Jako and Murphy (1990) used the scale below to assess teacher performance.

Of all the lecturer's behavior involving using facial expressions to highlight the meaning of the lecture, please list:

% poor _____ % below average _____ % average _____ % above average _____ % excellent

Our evaluation of PDA is similar to our evaluation of BOS. Both depend on the rater's ability to accurately indicate the frequency of specific behaviors or outcomes. In our view, cognitive research suggests that raters are simply incapable of performing this task in an objective way. It is very likely that raters infer the frequency of different behaviors or outcomes from their global evaluations of individuals, and that when you ask for data on the frequency of effective or ineffective behaviors, what you actually get is a re-statement of the rater's overall evaluation. Thus, we do not believe that assessments obtained using PDA or BOS will be more specific, objective, or behavior based than assessments obtained with much simpler scales.

Management by Objectives

Management by objectives (MBO) is not a performance appraisal system per se, but rather it represents a method for defining goals, objectives, and priorities. However, MBO includes an appraisal component in the sense that a person working under an MBO system is evaluated in terms of the goals and objectives he or she (together with the supervisor) has previously defined. Thus, the MBO process defines objectives for a given period of time, and also defines the relevant dimensions and criteria for evaluating performance at the end of that period.

One danger in MBO is that goals and objectives will be set that are (a) easily quantified, (b) easily achieved, and (c) not really central to the job.

This simplifies the process of performance appraisal, but it also implies that appraisals will be virtually worthless. However, it is important to note that goals do not always have these characteristics, and that MBO can work. The effectiveness of MBO depends on the skills of both the supervisor and subordinate in defining appropriate goals and objectives. For this reason, it is somewhat difficult to evaluate MBO as a system. The same MBO program might work very well for some supervisor–subordinate dyads, and poorly for others.

Employee Comparison Methods

There is a useful distinction between rating and ranking (i.e., employee comparison). Rating involves comparing a person to a standard. This standard might be undefined or subjective (e.g., a scale in which the anchors of "good," "average," and "poor" are undefined), or it might be defined in exact behavioral terms. Ranking involves comparing a person to another person. We believe that the psychological processes involved in rating versus ranking may be different (Murphy & Constans, 1987). Even if this is true, however, ratings and rankings often lead to similar conclusions about the performance of a group of ratees.

To illustrate ranking procedures, consider the example of a supervisor who evaluates eight subordinates. One possibility is to simply rank-order these eight individuals, from the best performer to the worst. With small numbers of ratees, this should not be difficult. However, as the supervisor's span of control increases, ranking of all subordinates can become tedious, and sometimes arbitrary. While it might be easy to pick out the best and the worst performers out of a group of 30 workers, it can be very difficult to distinguish the 15th best from the 16th, 17th, or 18th. The forced-distribution ranking procedure provides a partial solution to this problem.

A forced-distribution scale requires supervisors to sort subordinates into ordered categories. An example of such a scale is given below:

Rate each of your subordinates using the scale below

3 – one of the best two performers in your work group
2 – neither one of the best or one of the worst
1 – one of the worst two performers in your work group

A supervisor using this scale to evaluate eight subordinates would have to decide who his or her two best and two worst performers are; the remaining subordinates will fall in the middle category. This procedure is particularly useful if administrative rewards correspond to the categories. For example, the supervisor who must designate two subordinates out of eight for promotion does not need to rank all eight subordinates. The forced-distribution scale illustrated above will be sufficient.

The principal distinction between a forced-distribution scale and a scale that requires you to rank all subordinates is that in a full ranking, the number of categories is equal to the number of persons being evaluated. In a forced-distribution scale, the number of categories is less than the number of persons. The choice between these two methods depends in part on the specificity of the information required. If there are different outcomes for each individual (e.g. the sixth best performer will get a larger raise than the seventh best receives), full ranking is worthwhile. Otherwise, a forced-distribution scale might be easier to use.

There is one more procedure that should be considered, especially if the rater or the organization requires precise information about the rank order of employees, as well as the size of the differences in performance among employees. The pair-comparison method allows you to scale subordinates with some precision on a ratio-level scale of overall performance. An example of a pair-comparison scale for a supervisor with four subordinates (A, B, C, and D) is given below:

Circle the better performer in each pair

A or B
A or C
A or D
B or C
B or D
C or D

If the number of comparisons is sufficiently large, scaling procedures can be applied that transform these comparisons into a ratio scale that establishes both the ranking and the extent to which subordinates differ in their performance. The principal drawback of this method is that the number of comparisons expands geometrically as the number of subordinates increases. In the example above, six comparisons were needed to evaluate four subordinates. If there were 10 subordinates, 45 comparisons are needed. With 20 subordinates, 190 comparisons are needed.

There is a real dilemma for users of a pair-comparison scale. The accuracy of the scaling is a direct function of the number of comparisons that are made. Thus, if the number of comparisons is sufficiently small to be easily carried out, the scaling may not be precise. If the number of comparisons is sufficiently large to yield accurate measurement, the pair-comparison procedure may be extremely time-consuming. For this reason, pair-comparison procedures seem to have attracted more attention in the basic research literature than in the field.

REFERENCES

Abelson, R. P. (1976). Script processing in attitude formation and decision making. In J. Carroll & J. Payne (Eds.), *Cognition and social behavior*. Hillsdale, NJ: Erlbaum.

Adler, S., Campion, M., Colquitt, A., Grubb. A., Murphy, K. R., Ollander-Krane, R., & Pulakos, E. D. (2016). Getting rid of performance ratings: Genius or folly. *Industrial and Organizational Psychology: Perspectives on Science and Practice, 9*, 219–252.

Adsit, D. J., London, M., Crom, S., & Jones, D. (1997). Cross-cultural differences in upward ratings in a multinational company. *International Journal of Human Resource Management, 8*, 385–401.

Aggarwal, C. C., & Zhai, C. (2012). *Mining text data*. New York, NY: Springer-Verlag.

Aguinis, H. (2009). An expanded view of performance management. In J. W. Smither & M. London (Eds.), *Performance management: Putting research into practice* (pp. 1–43). San Francisco, CA: Wiley.

Aguinis, H. (2013). *Performance management* (3rd ed.). Upper Saddle River, NJ: Pearson/Prentice Hall.

Aguinis, H., & Bradley, K. J. (2015). The secret sauce for organizational success: Managing and producing star performers. *Organizational Dynamics, 44*, 161–168.

Aguinis, H., Joo, H., & Gottfredson, R. K. (2011). Why we hate performance management—And why we should love it. *Business Horizons, 54*, 503–507.

Aiello, J. R., & Kolb, K. J. (1995). Electronic performance monitoring and social context: Impact on productivity and stress. *Journal of Applied Psychology, 80*, 339–353.

Albright, M. D., & Levy, P. E. (1995). The effects of source credibility and performance rating discrepancy on reactions to multiple raters. *Journal of Applied Social Psychology, 25*, 577–600.

Alder, G. S., & Ambrose, M. L. (2005). An examination of the effect of computerized performance monitoring feedback on monitoring fairness, performance, and satisfaction. *Organizational Behavior and Human Decision Processes, 97*, 161–177.

Allen, T. D., & Rush, M. C. (1998). The effects of organizational citizenship behavior on performance judgments: a field study and a laboratory experiment. *Journal of Applied Psychology, 83*, 247–260.

Amba-Rao, S. C., Petrick, J. A., Gupta, J. N. D., & Von Der Embse, T. (2000). Comparative performance appraisal practices and management values among foreign and domestic firms in India. *International Journal of Human Resource Management, 11*, 60–89.

Anseel, F., Beatty, A. S., Shen, W., Lievens, F., & Sackett, P. R. (2015). How are we doing after 30 years? A meta-analytic review of the antecedents and outcomes of feedback-seeking behavior. *Journal of Management, 41*, 318–348.

Anseel, F., & Lievens, F. (2009). The mediating role of feedback acceptance in the relationship between feedback and attitudinal and performance outcomes. *International Journal of Selection and Assessment, 17*, 362–376.

Antonioni, D. (1995). Problems associated with implementation of an effective upward appraisal feedback process: An experimental field study. *Human Resource Development Quarterly, 6*, 157–171.

Antonioni, D., & Park, H. (2001). The effects of personality similarity on peer ratings of contextual work behaviors. *Personnel Psychology, 54*, 331–360.

Arthur, J. B. (1994). Effects of human resource systems on manufacturing performance and turnover. *Academy of Management Journal, 37*, 670–687.

Arthur, W., Woehr, D. J., & Akande, A., & Strong, M. H. (1995). Human resource management in West Africa: Practices and perceptions. *International Journal of Human Resource Management, 6*, 347–367.

Arvey, R. D., & Jones, A. P. (1985). The use of discipline in organizations: A framework for future research. In L. Cummings & B. Staw (Eds.), *Research in organizational behavior*, Vol. 7. Greenwich, CT: JAI Press.

Arvey, R., & Murphy, K. (1998). Personnel evaluation in work settings. *Annual Review of Psychology, 49*, 141–168.

Aryee, S., Walumba, F. O., Seidu, E. Y. M., & Otaye, L. E. (2012). Impact of high performance work systems on individual- and branch-level performance: Test of a multilevel model of intermediate linkages. *Journal of Applied Psychology, 97*, 287–300.

Ashford, S. J., Blatt, R., & VandeWalle, D. (2003). Reflections on the looking glass: A review of research on feedback-seeking behavior in organizations. *Journal of Management, 29*, 773–799.

Ashford, S. J., & Cummings, L. L. (1983). Feedback as an individual resource: Personal strategies of creating information. *Organizational Behavior and Human Performance, 32*, 370–398.

Astin, A. (1964). Criterion-centered research. *Educational and Psychological Measurement, 24*, 807–822.

Athey, T. R., & McIntyre, R. M. (1987). Effect of rater training on rater accuracy: Levels-of-processing theory and social facilitation theory perspectives. *Journal of Applied Psychology, 72*, 567–572.

Atwater, L. E., Brett, J. F., & Charles, A. C. (2007). Multisource feedback: Lessons learned and implications for practice. *Human Resource Management, 46*, 285–307.

Atwater, L. E., Ostroff, C., Yammarino, F. J., & Fleenor, J. W. (1998). Self-other agreement: Does it really matter? *Personnel Psychology, 51*, 577–598.

Atwater, L., & Roush, P. (1994). An investigation of gender effects on followers' ratings of leaders, leaders' self-ratings and reactions to feedback. *Journal of Leadership Studies, 1*, 37–52.

Atwater, L. E., Waldman, D. A., & Brett, J. F. (2002). Understanding and optimizing multisource feedback. *Human Resource Management, 41*, 193–208.

Austin, J. T., & Villanova, P. (1992). The criterion problem: 1917–1922. *Journal of Applied Psychology, 77*, 836–874.

Aycan, Z. (2005). The interplay between cultural and institutional/structural contingencies in human resource management practices. *International Journal of Human Resource Management, 16*, 1083–1119.

Bachrach, D. G., Powell, B. C., Bendoly, E., & Richey, R. G. (2006). Organizational citizenship behavior and performance evaluations: Exploring the impact of task interdependence. *Journal of Applied Psychology, 91*, 193–201.

Backburn, R. (1981). Lower participant power: Toward a conceptual integration. *Academy of Management Review, 6*, 127–131.

Bailey, C., & Fletcher, C. (2002). The impact of multiple source feedback on management development: Findings from a longitudinal study. *Journal of Organizational Behavior, 23*, 853–867.

Ballard, T., Yeo, G., Loft, S., Vancouver, J. B., & Neal, A. (2016). An integrative formal model of motivation and decision making: The MGPM*. *Journal of Applied Psychology, 101*, 1240–1265.

Baltes, B. B., Bauer, C. B., & Frensch, P. A. (2007). Does a structured free recall intervention reduce the effect of stereotypes on performance ratings and by what cognitive mechanism? *Journal of Applied Psychology, 92*, 151–164.

Balzer, W. K. (1986). Biases in the recording of performance-related information: The effects of initial impressions and centrality of the appraisal task. *Organizational Behavior and Human Decision Processes, 37*, 329–347.

Balzer, W. K., & Sulsky, L. M. (1992). Halo and performance appraisal research: A critical examination. *Journal of Applied Psychology, 77*, 975–985.

Bamberger, P. A. (2007). Competitive appraising: A social dilemma perspective on the conditions in which multi-round peer evaluation may result in counter-productive team dynamics. *Human Resource Management Review, 17*, 1–18.

Banks, C., & Murphy, K. (1985). Toward narrowing the research-practice gap in performance appraisal. *Personnel Psychology, 38*, 335–345.

Barrett, R. S. (1966). *Performance rating.* Chicago, IL: Chicago Science Research Association.

Barron, L. G., & Sackett, P. R. (2008). Asian variability in performance rating modesty and leniency bias. *Human Performance, 21*, 277–290.

Barron, O. (2003). *Workplace violence and bullying: Your rights, what to do and where to go for help.* Melbourne, Australia: Jobwatch and WorkSafe Victoria.

Barth, C. M., & Funke, J. (2010). Negative affective environments improve complex solving performance. *Cognition and Emotion, 24*, 1259–1268.

Bass, A. R., & Turner, J. N. (1973). Ethnic group differences in relationships among criteria of job performance. *Journal of Applied Psychology, 57*, 101–109.

Bassett, C. A. (1979). PAIR records and information systems. In D. Yoder & H. C. Heneman (Eds.), *ASPA handbook of personnel and industrial relations.* Washington, DC: Bureau of National Affairs.

Bates, R. A., & Holton, E. F. (1995). Computerized performance monitoring: A review of human resource issues. *Human Resource Management Review, 5,* 267–288.

Baxter, G. W. (2012). Reconsidering the black-white disparity in federal performance ratings. *Public Personnel Management, 41,* 199–218.

Baumeister, R. F., Bratslavsky, E., Finkenauer, C., & Vohs, K. D. (2001). Bad is stronger than good. *Review of General Psychology, 5,* 323–370.

Beach, L. R. (1990). *Image theory: Decision making in personnel and organizational contexts.* Chichester, UK: Wiley.

Beck, J. W., Beatty, A. S., & Sackett, P. R. (2014). On the distribution of job performance: The role of measurement characteristics in observed departures from normality. *Personnel Psychology, 67,* 531–566.

Becker, B. E., & Cardy, R. L. (1986). Influence of halo error on appraisal effectiveness: A conceptual and empirical reconsideration. *Journal of Applied Psychology, 71,* 662–671.

Becker, B. E., & Huselid, M. A. (2006). Strategic human resource management: Where do we go from here? *Journal of Management, 32,* 898–925.

Becker, G. A., & Miller, C. E. (2002). Examining contrast effects in performance appraisals: Using appropriate controls and assessing accuracy. *Journal of Psychology: Interdisciplinary and Applied, 136,* 667–683.

Becker, G. A., & Villanova, P. (1995). Effects of rating procedure and temporal delay on the magnitude of contrast effects in performance ratings. *Journal of Psychology: Interdisciplinary and Applied, 129,* 157–166.

Becton, J. B., & Schraeder, M. (2004). Participant input into rater selection: Potential effects on the quality and acceptance of ratings in the context of 360-degree feedback. *Public Personnel Management, 33,* 23–32.

Behn, R. D. (2003). Why measure performance? Different purposes require different measures. *Public Administration Review, 63,* 586–606.

Bell, B. S., & Kozlowski, S. W. (2002). A typology of virtual teams implications for effective leadership. *Group and Organization Management, 27,* 14–49.

Bellows, R. M., & Estep, M. F. (1954). *Employment psychology: The interview.* New York, NY: Rinehart.

Belschak, F. D., & Den Hartog, D. N. (2009). Consequences of positive and negative feedback: The impact on emotions and extra-role behaviors. *Applied Psychology: An International Review, 58,* 274–303.

Bento, R. F., White, L. F., & Zacur, S. R. (2012). The stigma of obesity and discrimination in performance appraisal: A theoretical model. *International Journal of Human Resource Management, 23,* 3196–3224.

Bennett, J. T., & Kaufman, B. E. (2007). *What do unions do? A twenty-year perspective.* London: Transaction Publishers.

Berkshire, H., & Highland, R. (1953). Forced-choice performance rating: A methodological study. *Personnel Psychology, 6,* 355–378.

Bernardin, H. J. (1977). Behavioral expectation scales versus summated rating scales: A fairer comparison. *Journal of Applied Psychology, 62,* 422–427.

Bernardin, H. J., Alvares, K. M., & Cranny, C. J. (1976). A recomparison of behavioral expectation scales to summated scales. *Journal of Applied Psychology, 61,* 564–570.

Bernardin, H. J., & Beatty, R. W. (1984). *Performance appraisal: Assessing human behavior at work.* Boston, MA: Kent.

Bernardin, H. J., & Buckley, M. R. (1981). Strategies in rater training. *Academy of Management Review, 6,* 205–212.

Bernardin, H. J., Cooke, D. K., & Villanova, P. (2000). Conscientiousness and agreeableness as predictors of rating leniency. *Journal of Applied Psychology, 85,* 232–236.

Bernardin, H. J., Dahmus, S. A., & Redmon, G. (1993). Attitudes of first-line supervisors toward subordinate appraisals. *Human Resource Management, 32,* 315–324.

Bernardin, H. J., Hennessey, H. W., & Peyrefitte, J. (1995). Age, racial, and gender bias as a function criterion specificity: A test of expert testimony. *Human Resource Management Review, 5,* 63–77.

Bernardin, H. J., & Klatt, L. A. (1985). Managerial appraisal systems: Has practice caught up with the state of the art? *Public Personnel Administrator,* November, 79–86.

Bernardin, H. J., & Orban, J. A. (1990). Leniency effect as a function of rating format, purpose for appraisal, and rater individual differences. *Journal of Business and Psychology, 5*, 197–211.

Bernardin, H. J., Orban, J. A., & Carlyle, J. H. (1981). Performance ratings as a function of trust in appraisal and rater individual differences. *Proceedings of the Academy of Management,* 311–315.

Bernardin, H. J., & Pence, E. C. (1980). Effects of rater training: Creating new response sets and decreasing accuracy. *Journal of Applied Psychology, 65*, 60–66.

Bernardin, H. J., & Tyler, C. L. (2001). Legal and ethical issues in multisource feedback. In D. W. Bracken, C. W. Timmreck & A. H. Church (Eds.), *The handbook of multisource feedback* (pp. 447–462). San Francisco, CA: Jossey-Boss.

Bernardin, H. J., & Villanova, P. J. (1986). Performance appraisal. In E. A. Locke (Ed.), *Generalizing from laboratory to field settings* (pp. 43–62). San Francisco, CA: New Lexington Press.

Bernardin, H. J., & Villanova, P. (2005). Research streams in rater self-efficacy. *Group and Organization Management, 30*, 61–88.

Bernichon T., Cook, K. E., & Brown, J. D. (2003). Seeking self-evaluative feedback: The interactive role of global self-esteem and specific self-views. *Journal of Personality and Social Psychology, 84*, 194–204.

Berry, C. M., Ones, D. S., & Sackett, P. R. (2007). Interpersonal deviance, organizational deviance, and their common correlates: A review and meta-analysis. *Journal of Applied Psychology, 92*, 410–424.

Bhave, D. P. (2014). The invisible eye? Electronic performance monitoring and employee job performance. *Personnel Psychology, 67*, 605–635.

Bingham, W. V. (1939). Halo, invalid and valid. *Journal of Applied Psychology, 23*, 221–228.

Bititci, U., Garengo, P., Dörfler, V., & Nudurupati, S. (2012). Performance measurement: Challenges for tomorrow. *International Journal of Human Resource Management, 23*, 305–327.

Bjerke, D. C., Cleveland, J. N., Morrison, R. F., & Wilson, W. C. (1987). Navy Personnel Research and Development Center Report, TR 88-4.

Blanchard, K., Carlos, J. P., & Randolph, A. (2001). *Empowerment takes more than a minute.* San Francisco, CA: Berrett-Koehler.

Blanchette, I., & Richards, A. (2010). The influence of affect on higher level cognition: A review of research on interpretation, judgement, decision making and reasoning. In J. De Houwer, D. Hermans, (Eds.), *Cognition and emotion: Reviews of current research and theories* (pp. 276–324). New York, NY: Psychology Press.

Blume, B. D., Baldwin, T. T., & Rubin, R. S. (2009). Reactions to different types of forced distribution performance evaluation systems. *Journal of Business and Psychology, 24*, 77–91.

Bobko, P., & Colella, A. (1994). Employee reactions to performance standards: A review and research propositions. *Personnel Psychology, 47*, 1–29.

Boddy, C. R. (2006). The dark side of management decisions: Organizational psychopaths. *Management Decision, 44*(10), 1461–1475.

Boddy, C. R. (2010). Corporate psychopaths and organizational type. *Journal of Public Affairs, 10*, 300–312.

Bolino, M. C. (2007). Expatriate assignments and inter-organizational career success: Implications for individuals and organizations. *Journal of International Business Studies, 38*, 819–835

Bolino, M. C., & Turnley, W. H. (2003). Counternormative impression management, likeability, and performance ratings: The use of intimidation in an organizational setting. *Journal of Organizational Behavior, 24*, 237–250.

Bommer, W. H., Johnson, J. L., Rich, G. A., Podsakoff, P. M., & MacKenzie, S. B. (1995). On the interchangeability of objective and subjective measures of employee performance: A meta-analysis. *Personnel Psychology, 48*, 587–605.

Bono, J. E., & Colbert, A. E. (2005). Understanding responses to multi-source feedback: The role of core self-evaluations. *Personnel Psychology, 58*, 171–203.

Borman, W. C. (1974). The rating of individuals in organizations: An alternative approach. *Organizational Behavior and Human Performance, 12*, 105–124.

Borman, W. C. (1977). Consistency of rating accuracy and rating errors in the judgment of human performance. *Organizational Behavior and Human Performance, 20*, 238–252.

Borman, W. C. (1978). Exploring the upper limits of reliability and validity in job performance ratings. *Journal of Applied Psychology, 63*, 135–144.

Borman, W. C. (1979). Format and training effects on rating accuracy and rater errors. *Journal of Applied Psychology, 64*, 410–421.

Borman, W. C., Ackerman, L. D., & Kubisiak, U. C. (1994). *Development of a performance rating program in support of Department of Labor test validation research* (Unpublished manuscript).

Borman, W. C., & Brush, D. H. (1993). More progress toward a taxonomy of managerial performance requirements. *Human Performance, 6*, 1–21.

Borman, W. C., Buck, D. E., Hanson, M. A., Motowidlo, S. J., Stark, S., & Drasgow, F. (2001). An examination of the comparative reliability, validity, and accuracy of performance ratings made using computerized adaptive rating scales. *Journal of Applied Psychology, 86*, 965–973.

Borman, W. C., Grossman, M. R., Bryant, R. H., & Dorio, J. 2017. The measurement of task performance as criteria in selection research. In J. L. Farr & N. Tippins (Eds.), *Handbook of employee selection* (rev. ed.). New York, NY: Psychology Press.

Borman, W. C., & Motowidlo, S. J. (1993). Expanding the criterion domain to include elements of contextual performance. In N. Schmitt & W. C. Borman (Eds.), *Personnel selection in organizations* (pp. 71–98). San Francisco, CA: Jossey-Bass.

Borman, W. C., & Penner, L. A. (2001). Personality predictors of citizenship performance. In B. W. Roberts & R. Hogan (Eds.), *Personality psychology in the workplace* (pp. 45–61). Washington, DC: American Psychological Association.

Borman, W. C., & Vallon, W. R. (1974). A review of what can happen when behavioral expectation scales are developed in one setting and used in another. *Journal of Applied Psychology, 59*, 197–201.

Borman, W. C., White, L. A., & Dorsey, D. W. (1995). Effects of ratee task performance and interpersonal factors on supervisor and peer performance ratings. *Journal of Applied Psychology, 80*, 168–177.

Boswell, W. R., & Boudreau, J. W. (2000). Employee satisfaction with performance appraisals and appraisers: The role of perceived appraisal use. *Human Resource Development Quarterly, 13*, 283–299.

Boswell, W. R., & Boudreau, J. W. (2002). Separating the developmental and evaluative performance appraisal uses. *Journal of Business and Psychology, 16*, 391–412.

Bouskila-Yam, O., & Kluger, A. N. (2011). Strength-based performance appraisal and goal setting. *Human Resource Management Review, 21*, 137–147.

Bowen, C., Swim, J. K., & Jacobs, R. (2000). Evaluating gender biases on actual job performance of real people: A meta-analysis. *Journal of Applied Social Psychology, 30*, 2194–2215.

Bowen, D. E., & Ostroff, C. (2004). Understanding HRM-firm performance linkages: The role of the "strength" of the HRM system. *Academy of Management Review, 29*, 203–221.

Bowman, J. (1999). Performance appraisal: Verisimilitude trumps veracity. *Public Personnel Management, 28*, 557–576.

Box, G. E. P., & Tiao, G. C. (1973). *Bayesian inference in statistical analysis.* Reading, MA: Addison-Wesley.

Bozeman, D. P. (1997). Inter-rater agreement in multisource performance appraisal: A commentary. *Journal of Organizational Behavior, 18*, 313–316.

Bracken, D. W., Dalton, M. A., Jako, R. A., McCauley, C. D., & Pollman, V. A. (1997). *Should 360-degree feedback be used only for developmental purposes?* (pp. 11–22). Greensboro, NC: Center for Creative Leadership.

Bracken, D. W., & Rose, D. S. (2011). When does 360-degree feedback create behavior change? And how would we know it when it does? *Journal of Business & Psychology, 26*, 183–192.

Bracken, D. W., Rose, D. S., & Church, A. H. (2016). The evolution of and devolution 360° feedback. *Industrial and Organizational Psychology: Perspectives on Science and Practice, 9*, 761–794.

Bracken, D. W., Timmreck, C. W., & Church, A. H. (2001). *The handbook of multisource feedback: The comprehensive resource for designing and implementing MSF processes.* San Francisco, CA: Jossey-Bass.

Brett, J. F., & Atwater, L. E. (2001). 360° feedback: Accuracy, accuracy, reactions, and perceptions of usefulness. *Journal of Applied Psychology, 86*, 930–942.

Bretz, R. D., Milkovich, G. T., & Read, W. (1992). The current state of performance appraisal research and practice: Concerns, directions, and implications. *Journal of Management, 18*, 321–352.

Brewer, M. B. (1979). In-group bias in the minimal intergroup situations: A cognitive-motivational analysis. *Psychological Bulletin, 86*, 307–324.

Brouer, R., Badaway, R., Gallagher, V., & Haber, J. (2015). Political skill dimensionality and impression management choice and effective use. *Journal of Business and Psychology, 30*, 217–233.

Brown, M., & Benson, J. (2005). Managing to overload? Work overload and performance appraisal processes. *Group and Organization Management, 30*, 99–12.

Brown, M., Kulik, C. T., & Lim, V. (2016). Managerial tactics for communicating negative performance feedback. *Personnel Review, 45*(5), 969–987.

Brutus, S. (2010). Words versus numbers: A theoretical exploration of giving and receiving narrative comments in performance appraisal. *Human Resource Management Review, 20*, 144–157.

Brutus, S., Derayeh, M., Fletcher, C., Bailey, C., Velazquez, P., Shi, K., . . . Labath, V. (2006). Internationalization of multi-source feedback systems: A six-country exploratory analysis of 360-degree feedback. *International Journal of Human Resource Management, 17*, 1888–1906.

Brutus, S., & Fleenor, J. W. (1999). Demographic and personality predictors of congruence in multi-source ratings. *Journal of Management Development, 18*, 417–436.

Brutus, S., Fleenor, J. W., & London, M. (1998). Does 360-degree feedback work in different industries?: A between-industry comparison of the reliability and validity of multi-source performance ratings. *Journal of Management Development, 17*, 177–190.

Brutus, S., Fleenor, J. W., & McCauley, C. D. (1999). Demographic and personality predictors of congruence in multi-source ratings. *Journal of Management Development, 18*, 417–435.

Brutus, S., Fletcher, C., & Baldry, C. (2009). The influence of independent self-construal on rater self-efficacy in performance appraisal. *International Journal of Human Resource Management, 20*, 1999–2011.

Buckingham, M., & Goodall, A. (2015). Reinventing performance management. *Harvard Business Review, April, 93*, 40–50.

Buckley, M. R., Beu, D. B., Frink, D. D., Howard, J. L., Berkson, H., Mobbs, T. A., & Ferris, G. R. (2001). Ethical issues in human resource systems. *Human Resource Management Review, 11*, 11–29.

Budworth, M., Latham, G. P., & Manroop, L. (2015). Looking forward to performance improvement: A field test of the feedforward interview for performance management. *Human Resource Management, 54*, 45–54.

Burchett, S. R., & DeMeuse, K. P. (1985). Performance appraisal and the law. *Personnel, 62*, 29–37.

Bureau of National Affairs. (1974). Management performance appraisal programs. *Personnel Policies Forum Survey*, 104.

Burke, R. J., & Wilcox, D. S. (1969). Characteristics of effective employee performance review and development interviews. *Personnel Psychology, 22*, 291–305.

Burke, R. J., Weitzel, W., & Weir, T. (1978). Characteristics of effective employee performance review and development interviews: Replication and extension. *Personnel Psychology, 31*, 903–919.

Busemeyer, J. R., & Townsend, J. T. (1993). Decision field theory: A dynamic-cognitive approach to decision making in an uncertain environment. *Psychological Review, 100*, 432–459.

Caligiuri, P. M., & Day, D. V. (2000). Effects of self-monitoring on technical, contextual, and assignment-specific performance. *Group and Organization Management, 25*, 154–174.

Callister, R. R., Kramer, M. W., & Turban, D. B. (1999). Feedback seeking following career transitions. *Academy of Management Journal, 42*, 429–438.

Campbell, D. J., Campbell, K. M., & Ho-Beng, C. (1998). Merit pay, performance appraisal, and individual motivation: An analysis and alternative. *Human Resource Management, 37*, 131–149.

Campbell, J. P. (1990). Modeling the performance prediction problem in industrial and organizational psychology. In M. D. Dunnette & L. M. Hough (Eds.), *Handbook of industrial and organizational psychology* (Vol. 1, pp. 687–732). Palo Alto, CA: Consulting Psychologists Press.

Campbell, J. P., McCloy, R. A., Oppler, S. H., & Sager, C. E. (1993). A theory of performance. In N. Schmitt & W. C. Borman (Eds.), *Personnel selection in organizations* (pp. 35–70). San Francisco, CA: Jossey-Bass.

Campbell, J. P., & Wiernik, B. (2015). The modeling and assessment of performance at work. *Annual Review of Organizational Psychology and Organizational Behavior, 2*, 47–74.

Cannon-Bowers, J., & Bowers, C. (2011). Team development and functioning. In S. Zedeck (Ed.), *Handbook of industrial and organizational psychology* (Vol. 1, pp. 597–650). Washington, DC: American Psychological Association.

Cappelli, P., & Neumark, D. (1999). *Do "high-performance" work practices improve establishment-level outcomes.* NBER Working Paper 7274, JEL No. M11, M12, J50. Washington, DC: National Bureau of Economic Research.

Capelli, P., & Tavis, A. (2016). The performance management revolution. *Harvard Business Review*, October, pp. 58–67.

Cardy, R. L., & Dobbins, G. H. (1986). Affect and appraisal accuracy: Liking as an integral dimension in evaluating performance. *Journal of Applied Psychology, 71*, 672–678.

Cardy, R. L., & Dobbins, G. H. (1994). *Performance appraisal: Alternative perspectives.* Cincinnati, OH: SouthWestern Publishing.

Cardy, R. L., Dobbins, G. H., & Carson, K. P. (1995). TQM and HRM: Improving performance appraisal research, theory and practice. *Canadian Journal of Administrative Sciences, 12*, 106–115.

Carr, A. E. (2016). *Executive and employee coaching: Research and best practices for practitioners.* Society for Industrial and Organizational Psychology White Paper Series. Bowling Green, OH: Society for Industrial and Organizational Psychology.

Carterucci, C. (2017, April 3). The Fox News sexual harassment scandal is looking worse by the minute. *Slate.* Retrieved from http://www.slate.com/blogs/xx_factor/2017/04/03/the_fox_news_sexual_harassment_scandal_is_looking_worse_by_the_minute.html

Caruso, A. (2015). *Statistics of U.S. business employment and payroll summary: 2012.* Washington, DC: U.S. Census Bureau.

Carver, C. S., & Scheier, M. F. (1981). *Attention and self-regulation: A control theory approach to human behavior.* New York, NY: Springer-Verlag.

Cascio, W. F. (1987). *Applied psychology in personnel management* (3rd ed.). Englewood Cliffs, NJ: Erlbaum.

Cascio, W. F., & Bernardin, H. J. (1981). Implications of performance appraisal litigation for personnel decisions. *Personnel Psychology, 34*, 211–226.

Cawley, B. D., Keeping, L. M., & Levy, P. E. (1998). Participation in the performance appraisal process and employee reactions: A meta-analytic review of field investigations. *Journal of Applied Psychology, 83*, 615–633.

Chadwick-Jones, J. K, Brown, C., Nicholson, N., & Sheppard, A. (1971). Absence measures: Their reliability and stability in an industrial setting. *Personnel Psychology, 24*, 463–470.

Chadwick-Jones, J. K, Nicholson, N., & Brown, C. (1982). *The social psychology of absenteeism.* New York, NY: Praeger.

Chao, G. T. (1988). The socialization process: Building newcomer commitment. *Career Growth and Human Resource Strategies*, 31–47.

Chen, Z., Lam, W., & Zhong, J. A. (2007). Leader-member exchange and member performance: A new look at individual-level negative feedback-seeking behavior and team-level empowerment climate. *Journal of Applied Psychology, 92*, 202–212.

Cheng, H. C., & Cascio, W. (2009). Performance-appraisal beliefs of Chinese employees in Hong Kong and the Pearl River Delta. *International Journal of Selection and Assessment, 17*, 329–333.

Cheng, M. D., Luckett, P. F., & Mahama, H. (2007). Effect of perceived conflict among multiple performance goals and goal difficulty on task performance. *Accounting and Finance, 47*, 221–242.

Cheramie, R. (2013). An examination of feedback-seeking behaviors, the feedback source and career success. *Career Development International, 18*, 712–731.

Chiang, F. F. T., & Birtch, T. A. (2010). Appraising performance across borders: An empirical examination of the purposes and practices of performance appraisal in a multi-country context. *Journal of Management Studies, 47*, 1365–1393.

Chory, R. M., & Hubbell, A. P. (2008). Organizational justice and managerial trust as predictors of antisocial employee responses. *Communication Quarterly, 56*, 357–375.

Chrisler, J. C., Bacher, J. E., Bangali, A. M., Campagna, A. J., & McKeigue, A. C. (2012). A quick and dirty tour of misogynistic bro culture. *Sex Roles, 66*, 810–811.

Church, A. H., Rogelberg, S. G., & Waclawski, J. (2000). Since when is no news good news? The relationship between performance and response rates in multi-rater feedback. *Personnel Psychology, 53*, 435–451.

Church, A. H., & Waclawski, J. (2001). A five-phase framework for designing a successful multisource feedback system. *Consulting Psychology Journal: Practice & Research, 53*, 82–95.

Cianci, A. M., Schaubroeck, J. M., & McGill, G. A. (2010). Achievement goals, feedback, and task performance. *Human Performance, 23*,131-154.

Claus, L., & Briscoe, D. (2009). Employee performance management across borders: A review of relevant academic literature. *International Journal of Management Reviews, 11*, 175–196.

Cleveland, J. N., Gunnigle, P., Hearty, N., Morley, M., & Murphy, K. (2000). Human resource management practices of U.S.-owned multinational corporations in Europe: Accommodation or imposition? *Irish Business Administrative Research, 21*, 9–28.

Cleveland, J., Lim, A., & Murphy, K. (2007). Feedback phobia? Why employees do not want to give or receive it. In J. Langan-Fox, C. Cooper, & R. Klimoski (Eds.), *Research companion to the dysfunctional workplace: Management challenges and symptoms* (pp. 168–186). Cheltenham, U.K.: Edward Elgar Publishing.

Cleveland, J. N., Morrison, R., & Bjerke, D. (1986). *Rater intentions in appraisal ratings: Malevolent manipulation or functional fudging.* Paper presented at the first annual conference of the Society for Industrial and Organizational Psychology, Chicago.

Cleveland, J. N., & Murphy, K. R. (1992). Analyzing performance appraisal as goal-directed behavior. In G. Ferris & K. Rowland (Eds.), *Research in personnel and human resources management* (Vol. 10, pp. 121–185). Greenwich, CT: JAI Press.

Cleveland, J. N., & Murphy, K. R. (2016). Organizations want to abandon performance appraisal: Can they? Should they? In D. L. Stone & J. H. Dulebohn (Eds.), *Human resource management theory and research on new employment relationships* (pp. 15–46). Charlotte, NC: Information Age Publishing.

Cleveland, J. N., Murphy, K. R., & Colella, A. (2017). Who defines performance, contribution and value. In J. L. Farr & N. T. Tippins (Eds.), *Handbook of employee selection* (rev. ed., pp. 535–571). New York, NY: Routledge.

Cleveland, J. N., Murphy, K. R., & Williams, R. (1989). Multiple uses of performance appraisal: Prevalence and correlates. *Journal of Applied Psychology, 74*, 130–135.

Cocheu, T. (1986). Performance appraisal: A case in points. *Personal Journal, 65*, 48–55.

Cohen-Charash, Y., & Spector, P. E. (2001). The role of justice in organizations: A meta-analysis. *Organizational Behavior and Human Decision Processes, 86*, 278–321.

Colella, A., DeNisi, A. S., & Varma, A. (1998). The impact of ratee's disability on performance judgments and choice as partner: The role of disability-job fit stereotypes and interdependence of rewards. *Journal of Applied Psychology, 83*, 102–111.

Colquitt, J. A., Conlon, D. E., Wesson, M. J., Porter, C. O., & Ng, K. Y. (2001). Justice at the millennium: A meta-analytic review of 25 years of organizational justice research. *Journal of Applied Psychology, 86*, 425–445.

Combs, J. G., Ketchen, D. J., Jr., Hall, A. T., & Liu, Y. (2006). Do high performance work practices matter? A meta- analysis of their effects on organizational performance. *Personnel Psychology, 59*, 501–528.

Conway, J. M. (1996). Additional construct validity evidence for the task/contextual performance distinction. *Human Performance, 9*, 309–331.

Conway, J. M. (1998). Understanding method variance in multitrait-multirater performance appraisal matrices: Examples using general impressions and interpersonal affect as measured method factors. *Human Performance, 11*, 29–55.

Conway, J. M., & Huffcutt, A. I. (1997). Psychometric properties of multisource performance ratings: A meta-analysis of subordinate, supervisor, peer, and self-ratings. *Human Performance, 10*, 331–360.

Conway, J. M., Lombardo, K., & Sanders, K. C. (2001). A meta-analysis of incremental validity and nomological networks for subordinate and peer rating. *Human Performance, 14*, 267–303.

Conway, M. A. (1997). *Recovered Memories and False Memories.* Oxford University Press.

Cooper, M. J., Gulen, H., & Rau, P. R. (2016). Performance for pay? The relation between CEO incentive compensation and future stock price performance (November 1, 2016). http://dx.doi.org/10.2139/ssrn .1572085

Cooper, W. H. (1981a). Conceptual similarity as a source of illusory halo in job performance ratings. *Journal of Applied Psychology, 66*, 302–307.

Cooper, W. H. (1981b). Ubiquitous halo. *Psychological Bulletin, 90*, 218–244.

Copus, D., Uglow, R. S., & Sohn, J. (2005). A lawyer's view. In F. J. Landy (Ed.), *Employment discrimination litigation: Behavioral, quantitative, and legal perspectives.* San Francisco, CA: Pfeiffer.

Costa, P. T., & McCrae, R. R. (1997). Longitudinal stability of adult personality. *Handbook of Personality Psychology,* 269–290.

Coward, W. M., & Sackett, P. R. (1990). Linearity of ability-performance relationships: A reconfirmation. *Journal of Applied Psychology, 75,* 297–300.

Cox, C., & Beier, M. (2014). Too old to train or reprimand: The role of intergroup attribution bias in evaluating older workers. *Journal of Business and Psychology, 29,* 61–70.

Cron, W. L., Slocum, J. W., VandeWalle, D., & Fu, Q. (2005). The role of goal orientation on negative emotions and goal setting when initial performance falls short of one's performance goal. *Human Performance, 18,* 55–80.

Cronbach, L. J. (1955). Processes affecting scores on "understanding of others" and "assumed similarity." *Psychological Bulletin, 52,* 177–193.

Cronbach, L. J. (1990). *Essentials of psychological testing.* New York, NY: Harper and Row.

Cronbach, L. J., Gleser, C. C., Nanda, H., & Rajaratnam, N. (1972). *The dependability of behavioral measurements: Theory of generalizability for scores and profiles.* New York, NY: Wiley.

Cropanzano, R. S., & Kacmar, K. M. (1995). *Organizational politics justice and support: Managing the social climate of the workplace.* Westport, CT: Quorum Books.

Cropanzano, R. S., & Mitchell, M. S. (2005). Social exchange theory: An interdisciplinary review. *Journal of Management, 31,* 874–900.

Culbert, S. A., & Rout, L. (2010). *Get rid of the performance review: How companies can stop intimidating, start managing—and focus on what really matters.* New York, NY: Business Plus.

Culbertson, S. S., Henning, J. B., & Payne, S. C. (2013). Performance appraisal satisfaction: The role of feedback and goal orientation. *Journal of Personnel Psychology, 12,* 189–195.

Cunningham, L. (2015). In big move, Accenture will get rid of annual performance reviews and rankings. Retrieved from http://www.washingtonpost.com/blogs/on-leadership/wp/2015/07/21/in-big-move-accenture-will-get-rid-of-annual-performance-reviews-and-rankings/?tid=pm_pop_b

Cunningham, T. R., & Austin, J. (2007). Using goal setting, task clarification, and feedback to increase the use of the hands-free technique by hospital operating room staff. *Journal of Applied Behavior Analysis, 40,* 673–677.

Curtis, A. B., Harvey, R. D., & Ravden, D. (2005). Sources of political distortions in performance appraisals: Appraisal purpose and rater accountability. *Group and Organization Management, 30,* 42–60.

Dahling, J. J., Chau, S. L., & O'Malley, A. (2012). Correlates and consequences of feedback orientation in organizations. *Journal of Management, 38,* 531–546.

Dahling, J. J., O'Malley, A. L., & Chau, S. L. (2015). Effects of feedback motives on inquiry and performance. *Journal of Managerial Psychology, 30,* 199–215.

Dansereau, F., Graen, G., & Haga, W. J. (1975). A vertical dyad linkage approach to leadership within formal organization: A longitudinal investigation of the role making process. *Organizational Behavior and Human Performance, 13,* 46–78.

David, E. M. (2013). Examining the role of narrative performance appraisal comments on performance. *Human Performance, 26,* 430–450.

Day, D. V., & Sulsky, L. M. (1995). Effects of frame-of-reference training and information configuration on memory organization and rating accuracy. *Journal of Applied Psychology, 80,* 158–167.

Deadrick, D. L., & Gardner, D. G. (1997). Distributional ratings of performance levels and variability. *Group and Organization Management, 22,* 317–342.

DeCotiis, T., & Petit, A. (1978). The performance appraisal process: A model and some testable propositions. *Academy of Management Review, 3,* 635–646.

Dekker, H. C., Groot, T., & Schoute, M. (2013). A balancing act? The implications of mixed strategies for performance measurement system design. *Journal of Management Accounting Research, 25,* 71–98.

Delaney, J. T., & Huselid, M. A. (1996). The impact of human resource management practices on perceptions of organizational performance. *Academy of Management Journal, 39,* 949–957.

Den Hartog, D. N., Boselie, P., & Paauwe, J. (2004). Performance management: A model and research agenda. *Applied Psychology: An International Review, 53,* 556-569.

DeNisi, A. S. (2000). Performance appraisal and control systems: A multilevel approach. In K. Klein & S. Kozlowski (Eds.), *Multilevel theory, research, and methods in organizations* (pp. 121–156). San Francisco, CA: Jossey-Bass.

DeNisi, A. S. (2006). *A cognitive approach to performance appraisal.* New York, NY: Routledge.

DeNisi, A. S., Cafferty, T., & Meglino, B. (1984). A cognitive view of the performance appraisal process: A model and research propositions. *Organizational Behavior and Human Performance, 33,* 360–396.

DeNisi, A. S., Cafferty, T. P., & Meglino, B. M. (1984). A cognitive view of the performance appraisal process: A model and research propositions. *Organizational Behavior and Human Performance, 33,* 360–396.

DeNisi, A. S., & Murphy, K. R. (2017). Performance appraisal and performance management: 100 Years of progress? *Journal of Applied Psychology, 102,* 421–433.

DeNisi, A. S., & Peters, L. H. (1996). Organization of information in memory and the performance appraisal process: Evidence from the field. *Journal of Applied Psychology, 81,* 717–733.

DeNisi, A. S., & Pritchard, R. D. (2006). Performance appraisal, performance management and improving individual performance: A motivational framework. *Management and Organization Review, 2,* 253–277.

DeNisi, A. S., Robbins, T., & Cafferty, T. P. (1989). Organization of information used for performance appraisals: Role of diary-keeping. *Journal of Applied Psychology, 74,* 124–129.

DeNisi, A. S., & Smith, C. E. (2014). Performance appraisal, performance management, and firm-level performance: a review, a proposed model, and new directions for future research. *Academy of Management Annals, 8,* 127–179.

DeVries, D. L., Morrison, A. M., Shullman, S. L., & Gerlach, M. (1986). *Performance appraisal on the line.* Greensboro, NC: Center for Creative Leadership.

Dierdorff, E. C., & Surface, E. A. (2007). Placing peer ratings in context: Systematic influences beyond ratee performance. *Personnel Psychology, 60,* 93–126.

DiMaggio, P. J., & Powell, W. W. (1983). The iron cage revisited: Organizational isomorphism and collective rationality in organizational fields. *American Sociological Review, 48,* 147–160.

Dipboye, R. L. (1985). Some neglected variables in research on discrimination in appraisals. *Academy of Management Review, 10,* 116–127.

Dipboye, R. L., & de Pontbriand, R. (1981). Correlates of employee reactions to performance appraisals and appraisal systems. *Journal of Applied Psychology, 66,* 248–251.

Dobbins, G. H., Cardy, R. L., Facteau, J. D., & Miller, J. S. (1993). Implications of situational constraints on performance evaluation and performance management. *Human Resource Management Review, 3,* 105–130.

Dobbins, G. H., Cardy, R. L., & Truxillo, D. M. (1986). Effects of ratee sex and purpose of appraisal on the accuracy of performance evaluations. *Basic and Applied Social Psychology, 7,* 225–241.

Dobbins, G. H., & Russell, J. M. (1986). The biasing effects of subordinate likeableness on leaders' responses to poor performers: A laboratory and a field study. *Personnel Psychology, 39,* 759–777.

Dornbusch, S. M., & Scott, W. R. (1975). *Evaluation and the exercise of authority.* San Francisco, CA: Jossey-Bass.

Dorsey, D. W., Cortina, J. M., & Luchman, J. (2010). Adaptive and citizenship-related behaviors at work. In J. Farr & N. Tippins (Eds.), *Handbook of employee selection* (pp. 463–488). New York, NY: Routledge.

Drexler Jr., J. A., Beehr, T. A., & Stetz, T. A. (2001). Peer appraisals: differentiation of individual performance on group tasks. *Human Resource Management, 40,* 333–334.

Drogosz, L. M., & Levy, P. (1996). Another look at the effect of appearance, job type and gender on performance-based decisions. *Psychology of Women Quarterly, 20,* 437–445.

Drucker, P. F. (1954). *The practice of management.* New York, NY: Harper.

Drymiotes, G. (2008). Managerial influencing of boards of directors. *Journal of Management Accounting Research, 20,* 19–45.

Duarte, N. T., Goodson, J. R., & Klich, N. R. (1994). Effects of dyadic quality and duration on performance appraisal. *Academy of Management Journal, 37,* 499–521.

Dulebohn, J. H., & Ferris, G. R. (1999). The role of influence tactics in perceptions of performance evaluations' fairness. *Academy of Management Journal, 42*, 288–303.

Dweck, C. S. (1986). Motivational processes affecting learning. *American Psychologist, 41*, 1040–1048.

Dweck, C. S. (2006). *Mindset: The new psychology of success*. New York, NY: Ballantine Books.

Edwards J. E., & Morrison, R. F. (1994). Selecting and classifying future Naval officers: The paradox of greater specialization in broader arenas. In M. Rumsey, C. Walker, & J. Harris (Eds.), *Personnel selection and classification* (pp. 69–84). Hillsdale, NJ: Sage.

Edwards, J. R. (2010). Reconsidering theoretical progress in organizational and management research. *Organizational Research Methods, 13*, 615–619.

Edwards, W. (1980). Multiattribute utility for evaluation: Structures, uses, and problems. In M. Klein & K. Teilmann (Eds.), *Handbook of criminal justice evaluation*. Beverly Hills, CA: Sage.

Edwards, W., & Newman, J. (1982). *Multiattribute evaluation*. Beverly Hills, CA: Sage.

Ellington, J. K., Dierdorff, E. C., & Rubin, R. S. (2014). Decelerating the diminishing returns of citizenship on task performance: the role of social context and interpersonal skill. *Journal of Applied Psychology, 99*, 748–758.

Elangovan, A. R., & Xie, J. L. (1999). Effects of perceived power of supervisor on subordinate stress and motivation: The moderating role of subordinate characteristics. *Journal of Organizational Behavior, 20*, 359–373.

Endo, K. (1998). "Japanization" of a performance appraisal system: A historical comparison of American and Japanese systems. *Social Science Japan Journal, 1*, 247–262.

Entrekin, L., & Chung, Y. W. (2001). Attitudes towards different sources of executive appraisal: a comparison of Hong Kong Chinese and American managers in Hong Kong. *International Journal of Human Resource Management, 12*, 965–987.

Erdogan, B. (2002). Antecedents and consequences of justice perceptions in performance appraisals. *Human Resource Management Review, 12*, 555–576.

Erdogan, B., Kraimer, M. L., & Liden, R. C. (2001). Procedural justice as a two-dimensional construct: An examination in the performance appraisal context. *The Journal of Applied Behavioral Science, 37*, 205–22.

Erdogan, B., & Liden, R. C. (2002). Social exchange in the workplace: A review of recent developments and future research directions in leader–member exchange theory. In L. L. Neider & C.A. Schriesheim (Eds.), *Leadership* (pp. 65–114). Greenwich, CT: Information Age.

Erez, M. (2011). Cross-cultural and global issues in organizational psychology. In S. Zedeck (Ed.), *APA handbook of industrial and organizational psychology* (Vol. 3, pp. 807–854). Washington, DC: American Psychological Association.

Erez, M., & Kanfer, F. H. (1983). The role of goal acceptance in goal setting and task performance. *The Academy of Management Review, 8*, 454–463.

Ehrnrooth, M., & Björkman, I. (2012). An integrative HRM process theorization: Beyond signaling effects and mutual gains. *Journal of Management Studies, 49*, 1109–1135.

Evans, W. R., & Davis, W. D. (2005). High-performance work systems and organizational performance: The mediating role of internal social structure. *Journal of Management, 31*, 758–775.

Facteau, J. D., & Craig, S. B. (2001). Are performance appraisal ratings from different rating sources comparable? *Journal of Applied Psychology, 86*, 215–227.

Farh, J., & Werbel, J. D. (1986). Effects of purpose of the appraisal and expectation of validation on self-appraisal leniency. *Journal of Applied Psychology, 71*, 527–529.

Farh, J. L., Dobbins, G. H., & Cheng, B. S. (1991). Cultural relativity in action: A comparison of self-ratings made by Chinese and US workers. *Personnel Psychology, 44*, 129–147.

Farndale, E. E., &, Kelliher, C. (2013). Implementing performance appraisal: Exploring the employee experience. *Human Resource Management, 25*, 71–98.

Farr, J. L., & Jacobs, R. (2006). Trust us: New perspectives on performance appraisal. In W. Bennett, D. Woehr, & C. Lance (Eds.), *Performance measurement: Current perspectives and future challenges* (pp. 321–337). Mahwah, NJ: Lawrence Erlbaum Associates.

Farr, J. L., O'Leary, B. S., & Bartlett, C. J. (1971). Ethnic group membership as a moderator of the prediction of job performance. *Personnel Psychology, 24*, 609–636.

Feild, H. S., & Holley, W. H. (1982). The relationship of performance appraisal system characteristics to verdicts in selected employment discrimination cases. *Academy of Management Journal, 25*, 392–406.

Feldman, J. M. (1981). Beyond attribution theory: Cognitive processes in performance appraisal. *Journal of Applied Psychology, 66*, 127–148.

Feldman, J. M. (1986). Instrumentation and training for performance appraisal: A perceptual cognitive viewpoint. In K. Rowland & J. Ferris (Eds.), *Research in personnel and human resources, Vol. 4*. Greenwich, CT: JAI Press.

Feldman, J. M., & Ng, T. (2008). Motivation to engage in training and career development. In R. Kanfer, G. Chen, & R. Pritchard (Eds.), *Work motivation: Past, present and future* (pp. 401–431). New York, NY: Routledge.

Ferguson, A. J., Ormiston, M. E., & Moon, H. (2010). From approach to inhibition: The influence of power on responses to poor performers. *Journal of Applied Psychology, 95*, 305–320.

Ferris, G. R., Davidson, S. L., & Perrewé, P. L. (2005). *Political skill at work: Impact on work effectiveness*. Mountain View, CA: Davies-Black.

Ferris, G. R., Munyon, T. P., Basik, K., & Buckley, M. R. (2008). The performance evaluation context: Social, emotional, cognitive, political, and relationship components. *Human Resource Management Review, 18*, 146–163.

Ferris, G. R., & Treadway, D. C. (2012). *Politics in organizations: Theory and research challenge* New York, NY: Routledge/Taylor and Francis Publishing.

Ferris, G. R., Treadway, D. C., Perrewé, P. L., Brouer, R. L., Douglas, C., & Lux, S. (2007). Political skill in organizations. *Journal of Management, 33*, 290–320.

Finkelstein, L. M., Burke, M. J., & Raju, N. S. (1995). Age discrimination in simulated employment contexts: an integrative analysis. *Journal of Applied Psychology, 80*, 652–663.

Fisher, C. D. (1986). Organizational socialization: An integrative review. In K. Rowland & C. Ferris (Eds.), *Research in personnel and human resources management*, Vol. 4. Greenwich, CT: JAI Press.

Fiske, S. T., Bersoff, D. N., Borgida, E., Deaux, K., & Heilman, M. E. (1991). Social science research on trial: The use of sex stereotyping research in *Price Waterhouse v. Hopkins. American Psychologist, 46*, 1049–1060.

Fiske, S. T., Harris, L. T., Lee, T. L., & Russell, A. M. (2016). The future of research on prejudice, stereotyping, and discrimination. In T. D. Nelson (Ed.), *Handbook of prejudice, stereotyping, and discrimination* (2nd ed.; pp. 487–498). New York, NY: Psychology Press.

Fitzgibbons, J., & Moch, A. (1980). *Employee absenteeism: A summary of research*. Washington, DC: Educational Research Service.

Flanagan, J. C. (1949). Critical requirements: A new approach to evaluation. *Personnel Psychology, 2*, 419–425.

Fleenor, J. W., & Brutus, S. (2001). Multisource feedback for personnel decisions. In D. W. Bracken, C. W. Timmreck, & A. H. Church (Eds.), *The handbook of multisource feedback* (pp. 335–351). San Francisco, CA: Jossey-Bass.

Fleenor, J. W., Fleenor, J. B., & Grossnickle, W. F. (1996). Interrater reliability and agreement of performance ratings: A methodological comparison. *Journal of Business and Psychology, 10*, 367–438.

Flint, D. H. (1999). The role of organizational justice in multi-source performance appraisal: Theory-based applications and directions for research. *Human Resource Management Review, 9*, 1–20.

Folger, R., & Cropanzano, R. S. (1998). *Organizational justice and human resource management*. Thousand Oaks, CA: Sage.

Folger, R., & Konovsky, M. A. (1989). Effects of procedural and distributive justice on reactions to pay raise decisions. *Academy of Management Journal, 32*, 115–130.

Folger, R., Konovsky, M. A., & Cropanzano, R. (1992). A due process metaphor for performance appraisal. *Research in Organizational Behavior, 14*, 129–129.

Ford, D. K. (2004). Development of a performance appraisal training program for the Rehabilitation Institute of Chicago. *Journal of European Industrial Training, 28*, 550–563.

French, J., & Raven, B. (1959). The bases of social power. In D. Cartwright (Ed.), *Studies in social power*. Ann Arbor: Institute for Social Research, University of Michigan.

Fried, Y., Levi, A. S., Ben-David, H. A., & Tiegs, R. B. (1999). Inflation of subordinates' performance ratings: Main and interactive effects of rater negative affectivity, documentation of work behavior, and appraisal visibility. *Journal of Organizational Behavior, 20*, 431–444.

Galford, R. M., & Drapeau, A. S. (2003). The enemies of trust. *Harvard Business Review,* February. https://hbr.org/2003/02/the-enemies-of-trust

Ganzach, Y. (1995). Negativity (and positivity) in performance evaluation: three field studies. *Journal of Applied Psychology, 80*, 491–499.

Geddes, D., & Baron, R. A. (1997). Workplace aggression as a consequence of negative performance feedback. *Management Communication Quarterly, 10*, 433–454.

Geddes, D., & Konrad, A. M. (2003). Demographic differences and reactions to performance feedback. *Human Relations, 56*, 1485–1513.

Gerhart, B., & Fang, M. (2015). Pay, intrinsic motivation, extrinsic motivation, performance, and creativity in the workplace: Revisiting long-held beliefs. *Annual Review of Organizational Psychology and Organizational Behavior, 2*, 489–521.

Gerhart, B., Rynes, S. L., & Fulmer, I. S. (2009). Pay and performance: Individuals, groups and executives. *Academy of Management Annals, 3*, 251–315.

Gerstner, C. R., & Day, D. V. (1997). Meta-analytic review of leader–member exchange theory: Correlates and construct issues. *Journal of Applied Psychology, 82*, 827–844.

Gibson, K. J., Zerbe, W. J., & Franken, R. E. (1993). The influence of rater and ratee age on judgments of work-related attributes. *Journal of Psychology: Interdisciplinary and Applied: Interdisciplinary and Applied, 127*, 271–280.

Giles, W. F., Findley, H. M., & Feild, H. S. (1997). Procedural fairness in performance appraisal: Beyond the review session. *Journal of Business and Psychology, 11*, 493–506.

Gioia, D. A, & Sims, H. P. (1985). Self-serving bias and actor-observer differences in organizations: An empirical analysis. *Journal of Applied Social Psychology, 15*, 547–563.

Giumetti, G. W., Schroeder, A. N., & Switzer, F. S. (2015). Forced distribution rating systems: When does 'rank and yank' lead to adverse impact? *Journal of Applied Psychology, 100*, 180–193.

Golden, T. D., Barnes-Farrell, J. L., & Mascharka, P. B. (2009). Implications of virtual management for subordinate performance appraisals: A pair of simulation studies. *Journal of Applied Social Psychology, 39*, 1589–1608.

Goldstein, L., & Mobley, W. H. (1971). Error and variability in the visual processing of dental radiographs. *Journal of Applied Psychology, 55*, 549–553.

Goodman, J. S., & Wood, R. E. (2004). Feedback specificity, learning opportunities, and learning. *Journal of Applied Psychology, 89*, 809–821.

Goomas, D. (2007). Electronic performance self-monitoring and engineered labor standards for 'man-up' drivers in a distribution center. *Journal of Business and Psychology, 21*, 541–558.

Goomas, D. T., & Ludwig, T. D. (2009). Standardized goals and performance feedback aggregated beyond the work unit: Optimizing the use of engineered labor standards and electronic performance monitoring. *Journal of Applied Social Psychology, 39*, 2425–2437.

Gordon, M. E., & Stewart, L. P. (2009). Conversing about performance: Discursive resources for the appraisal interview. *Management Communication Quarterly, 22*, 473–501.

Gorman, C. A., Cunningham, C. J. L., Bergman, S. M., & Meriac, J. P. (2016). Time to change the bathwater: Correcting misconceptions about performance ratings. *Industrial and Organizational Psychology, 9*, 314–322.

Gorman, C. A., Meriac, J. P., Roch, S. G., Ray, J. L., & Gamble, J. S. (2017). An exploratory study of current performance management practices: Human resource executives' perspectives. *International Journal of Selection and Assessment, 25*, 193–202.

Gorman, C. A., & Rentsch, J. R. (2009). Evaluating frame-of-reference rater training effectiveness using performance schema accuracy. *Journal of Applied Psychology, 94*, 1336–1344.

GAO. (2016). *Federal employee performance ratings.* GAO-16-520R. Washington, DC: Government Accounting Office.

Graen, G. (1976). Role-making processes within complex organizations. In M. Dunnette (Ed.), *Handbook of industrial and organizational psychology.* Chicago, IL: Rand-McNally.

Graen, G. B., & Uhl-Bien, M. (1995). The relationship-based approach to leadership: Development of LMX theory of leadership over 25 years: Applying a multi-level, multi-domain perspective. *Leadership Quarterly, 6*, 219–247.

Greenberg, J. (1991). Using explanations to manage impressions of performance appraisal fairness. *Employee Responsibilities and Rights Journal, 4,* 51–60.

Greenwald, A. G., Banaji, M. R., & Nosek, B. A. (2015). Statistically small effects of the Implicit Association Test can have societally large effects. *Journal of Personality and Social Psychology, 108,* 553–561.

Greenwald, A. G., McGhee, D. E., & Schwartz, J. L. K. (1998). Measuring individual differences in implicit cognition: The implicit association test. *Journal of Personality and Social Psychology, 74,* 1464–1480.

Gregory, J. B., & Levy, P. E. (2010). Employee coaching relationships: Enhancing construct clarity and measurement. *Coaching: An International Journal of Theory, Research, and Practice, 3,* 109–123.

Gregory, J. B., & Levy, P. E. (2011). It's not me, it's you: A multilevel examination of variables that impact employee coaching relationships. *Consulting Psychology Journal: Practice and Research. 63,* 67–88.

Gregory, J. B., & Levy, P. E. (2015). *Using feedback in organizational consulting.* Washington DC: American Psychological Association.

Greguras, G. J. (2005). Managerial experience and the measurement equivalence of performance ratings. *Journal of Business and Psychology, 19,* 383–397.

Greguras, G. J., Ford, J. M., & Brutus, S. (2003). Manager attention to multisource feedback. *Journal of Management Development, 22,* 345–360.

Greguras, G. J., & Robie, C. (1998). A new look at within-source interrater reliability of 360-degree feedback ratings. *Journal of Applied Psychology, 83,* 960–968.

Greguras, G. J., Robie, C., Schleicher, D. J., & Goff, M. (2003). A field study of the effects of rating purpose on the quality of multisource ratings. *Personnel Psychology, 56,* 1–21.

Grote, D. (2005). *Forced ranking: Making performance management work.* Boston, MA: Harvard Business School Press.

Grund, C., & Sliwka, D. (2009). The anatomy of performance appraisals in Germany. *International Journal of Human Resource Management, 20,* 2049–2065.

Gueutal, H. G., Luciano, J., & Michaels, C. A. (1995). Pregnancy in the workplace: Does pregnancy affect performance appraisal ratings. *Journal of Business and Psychology, 10,* 155–167.

Guilford, J. P. (1954). *Psychometric methods* (2nd ed.). New York, NY: McGraw-Hill.

Gunnigle, P., Murphy, K., Cleveland, J., Hearty, N., & Morley, M. (2002). Localization in human resource management: Comparing American and European multinational corporations. *Advances in International Management, 14,* 259–284.

Gupta, A. K., Govindarajan, V., & Malhotra, A. (1999). Feedback-seeking behavior within multinational corporations. *Strategic Management Journal, 20*(3), 205–222.

Guralnik, O., Rozmarin, E., & So, A. (2004). Forced distribution: Is it right for you? *Human Resource Development Quarterly, 15,* 339–345.

Guzzo, R. A., & Dickinson, M. W. (1996). Teams in organizations: Recent research on performance and effectiveness. *Annual Review of Psychology, 47,* 307–338.

Hackett J. D. (1928). Rating legislators. *Personnel, 7,* 130–131.

Hackman, J. R. (1976). Group influences on individuals. In M. Dunnette (Ed.), *Handbook of industrial and organizational psychology.* Chicago, IL: Rand-McNally.

Hackman, J. R., & Oldham, C. R. (1980). *Work redesign.* Reading, MA: Addison-Wesley.

Hackman, J. R., & Porter, L. W. (1968). Expectancy predictions of work effectiveness. *Organizational Behavior and Human Performance, 3,* 417–426.

Haines, V. Y., & St-Onge, S. (2012). Performance management effectiveness: practices or context? *International Journal of Human Resource Management, 23,* 1158–1175.

Hall, J. L., Leidecher, J. K., & DiMarco, C. (1996). What we know about upward appraisals of management: Facilitating the future use of UPAs. *Human Resource Development Quarterly, 7,* 209–226.

Hammond, K. R., McClelland, G. H., & Mumpower, J. (1980). *Human judgment and decision making: Theories, methods, and procedures.* New York, NY: Praeger.

Hamner, W. C., Kim, J. S., Baird, L., & Bigoness, W. J. (1974). Race and sex as determinants of ratings by potential employers in a simulated work-sampling task. *Journal of Applied Psychology, 59,* 705.

Harris, K. J., Kacmar, K. M., Zivnuska, S., & Shaw, J. D. (2007). The impact of political skill on impression management effectiveness. *Journal of Applied Psychology, 92,* 278.

Harris, L. (2001). Rewarding employee performance: Line managers' values, beliefs and perspectives. *International Journal of Human Resource Management, 12,* 1182–1192.

Harris, M. M. (1994). Rater motivation in the performance appraisal context: A theoretical framework. *Journal of Management, 20,* 737–756.

Harris, M. M., & Schaubroeck, J. (1988). A meta-analysis of self-supervisory, self-peer, and peer-subordinate ratings. *Personnel Psychology, 41,* 43–62.

Harris, M. M., Smith, D. E., & Champagne, D. (1995). A field study of performance appraisal purpose: Research- versus administrative-based ratings. *Personnel Psychology, 48,* 151–160.

Harris, T. C., & Barnes-Farrell, J. L. (1997). Components of teamwork: Impact on evaluations of contributions to work team effectiveness. *Journal of Applied Social Psychology, 27,* 1694–1715.

Harrison, D. A., Johns, G., & Martocchio, J. J. (2000). Changes in technology, teamwork, and diversity: New directions for a new century of absenteeism research. *Research in Personnel and Human Resources Management, 18,* 43–92.

Hastie, R. (1980). Memory for behavioral information that confirms or contradicts a personality impression. In R. Hastie et al. (Eds.), *Person memory: The cognitive basis of social perception.* Hillsdale, NJ: Erlbaum.

Hastie, R., & Park, B. (1986). The relationship between memory and judgment depends on whether the judgment task is memory-based or on-line. *Psychological Review, 93,* 256–268.

Hauenstein, N. M. (1992). An information-processing approach to leniency in performance judgments. *Journal of Applied Psychology, 77,* 485–493.

Hauenstein, N. M. (1998). Training raters to increase the accuracy of appraisals and the usefulness of feedback. *Performance Appraisal: State of the Art in Practice,* 404–442.

Hauenstein, N., Brown, R., & Sinclair, A. (2010). BARS and those mysterious, missing middle anchors. *Journal of Business and Psychology, 25,* 663–672.

Haynes, M. E. (1986). Partnerships in management: Employee involvement gets results. *Personnel Journal, 65,* 46–55.

Hays, J. C., & Williams, J. R. (2011). Testing multiple motives in feedback seeking: The interaction of instrumentality and self protection motives. *Journal of Vocational Behavior, 79,* 496–504.

Hedge, J. W., & Teachout, M. S. (2000). Exploring the concept of acceptability as a criterion for evaluating performance measures. *Group and Organization Management, 25,* 22–44.

Hedge, J. W., & Kavanagh, M. J. (1988). Improving the accuracy of performance evaluations: Comparison of three methods of performance appraiser training. *Journal of Applied Psychology, 73,* 68.

Heidemeier, H., & Moser, K. (2009). Self-other agreement in job performance ratings: A meta-analytic test of a process model. *Journal of Applied Psychology, 94,* 353–370.

Heilbroner, R. L. (1953). *The unworldly philosophers.* New York, NY: Simon & Schuster.

Heilman, M. E. (1983). Sex bias in work settings: The lack of fit model. *Research in Organizational Behavior, 5,* 269–298.

Heilman, M. E., Block, C. J., & Stathatos, P. (1997). The affirmative action stigma of incompetence: Effects of performance information ambiguity. *Academy of Management Journal, 40,* 603–625.

Heilman, M. E., & Chen, J. J. (2005). Same behavior, different consequences: reactions to men's and women's altruistic citizenship behavior. *Journal of Applied Psychology, 90,* 431–441.

Heneman, R. L. (1986). The relationship between supervisory ratings and results-oriented measures of performance: A meta-analysis. *Personnel Psychology, 39,* 811–826.

Heneman, R. L. (1992). *Merit pay.* Reading, MA: Addison-Wesley.

Hennessey, H. W. Jr., & Bernardin, H. J. (2003). The relationship between performance appraisal criterion specificity and statistical evidence of discrimination. *Human Resource Management, 42,* 143–158.

Heron, A. (1956). The effects of real-life motivation on questionnaire response. *Journal of Applied Psychology, 40,* 65–68.

Heslin, P. A., Latham, G. P., & VandeWalle, D. (2005). The effect of implicit person theory on performance appraisals. *Journal of Applied Psychology, 90,* 842–856.

Heslin, P. A., & VandeWalle, D. (2011). Performance appraisal procedural justice: The role of a manager's implicit person theory. *Journal of Management, 37*, 1694–1718.

Heslin, P. A., VandeWalle, D., & Latham, G. P. (2006). Keen to help? Managers' implicit person theories and their subsequent employee coaching. *Personnel Psychology, 59*, 871–902.

Higgins, E. T., & Stangor, C. (1988). A "change-of-standard" perspective on relations among context, judgment and memory. *Journal of Personality and Social Psychology, 54*, 181–192.

Ho, A. K., Thomsen, L., & Sidanius, J. (2009). Perceived academic competence and overall job evaluations: Students' evaluations of African American and European American professors. *Journal of Applied Social Psychology, 39*, 389–406.

Hochwarter, W. A., Ferris, G. R., Zinko, R., Arnell, B., & James, M. (2007). Reputation as a moderator of political behavior-work outcomes relationships: A two-study investigation with convergent results. *Journal of Applied Psychology, 92*, 567–576.

Hochwarter, W. A., Witt, L. A., & Kacmar, K. M. (2000). Perceptions of organizational politics as a moderator of the relationship between conscientiousness and job performance. *Journal of Applied Psychology, 85*, 472–478.

Hoffman, B. J., Blair, C. A., Meriac, J. P., & Woehr, D. J. (2007). Expanding the criterion domain? A quantitative review of the OCB literature. *Journal of Applied Psychology, 92*, 555–566.

Hoffman, B. J., Gorman, C. A., Blair, C. A., Meriac, J. P., Overstreet, B., & Atchley, E. K. (2012). Evidence for the effectiveness of an alternative multisource performance rating methodology. *Personnel Psychology, 65*, 531–563.

Hoffman, B. J., Lance, C. E., Bynum, B., & Gentry, W. A. (2010). Rater source effects are alive and well after all. *Personnel Psychology, 63*, 119–151.

Hoffman, B. J., & Woehr, D. J. (2009). Disentangling the meaning of multisource performance rating source and dimension factors. *Personnel Psychology, 62*, 735–765.

Hofmann, D. A., Jacobs, R., & Baratta, J. E. (1993). Dynamic criteria and the measurement of change. *Journal of Applied Psychology, 78*, 194–204.

Hofstede, G. (1980). *Culture's consequences: International differences in work-related values.* Beverley Hills, CA: Sage.

Hofstede, G. (2001). *Culture's consequences: Comparing values, behaviors, institutions and organizations across nations.* Thousand Oaks, CA: Sage.

Hofstede, G., Hofstede, G. J., & Minkov, M. (2010). *Cultures and organizations: Software of the mind* (revised and expanded 3rd ed.). New York, NY: McGraw-Hill.

Hofstede, G., Neuijen, B., Ohayv, D. D., & Sanders, G. (1990). Measuring organizational cultures. *Administrative Science Quarterly, 35*, 286–316.

Holbrook, R. L. (1999). Managing reactions to performance appraisal: The influence of multiple justice mechanisms. *Social Justice Research, 12*, 205–221.

Holbrook, R. L. (2002). Contact points and flash points: Conceptualizing the use of justice mechanisms in the performance appraisal interview. *Human Resource Management Review, 12*, 101–121.

Hollenbeck, J. R., Beersma, B., & Schouten, M. E. (2012). Beyond team types and taxonomies: A dimensional scaling conceptualization for team description. *Academy of Management Review, 37*, 82–106.

House R. J. et al. (2004). *Culture, leadership, and organizations: The GLOBE Study of 62 societies.* Thousand Oaks, CA: Sage.

Howard, M. C. (2016). The relationship between the number of raters and the validity of performance ratings. *Industrial and Organizational Psychology, 9*, 361–367.

Huang, G. H., Zhao, H. H., Niu, X. Y., Ashford, S. J., & Lee, C. (2013). Reducing job insecurity and increasing performance ratings: Does impression management matter? *Journal of Applied Psychology, 98*, 852.

Hunt, S. T. (1996). Generic work behavior: An investigation into the dimensions of entry-level, hourly job performance. *Personnel Psychology, 49*, 51–83.

Huselid, M. A. (1995). The impact of human resource management practices on turnover, productivity, and corporate financial performance. *Academy of Management Journal, 38*, 635–670.

Ilgen, D. R. (1983). Gender issues in performance appraisal: A discussion of O'Leary and Hansen. In F. Landy, S. Zedeck, & J. Cleveland (Eds.), *Performance measurement and theory.* Hillsdale, NJ: Erlbaum.

Ilgen, D. R., Barnes-Farrell, J. L., & McKellin, D. B. (1993). Performance appraisal process research in the 1980s: What has it contributed to appraisals in use? *Organizational Behavior and Human Decision Processes, 54,* 321–368.

Ilgen, D., & Davis, C. (2000). Bearing bad news: Reactions to negative performance feedback. *Applied Psychology, 49,* 550–565.

Ilgen, D. R., & Feldman, J. M. (1983). Performance appraisal: A process focus. In L. Cummings & B. Staw (Eds.), *Research in organizational behavior* (Vol. 5). Greenwich, CT; JAI Press.

Ilgen, D. R., Fisher, C. D., & Taylor, S. M. (1979). Consequences of individual feedback on behavior in organizations. *Journal of Applied Psychology, 64,* 347–371.

Ilgen, D. R, & Hollenback, J. H. (1977). The role of job satisfaction in absence behavior. *Organizational Behavior and Human Performance, 19,* 148–161.

Ilies, R., & Judge, T. A. (2005). Goal regulation across time: The effects of feedback and affect. *Journal of Applied Psychology, 90,* 453–467.

Ilgen, D. R., Mitchell, T. R., & Frederickson, J. W. (1981). Poor performers: Supervisors and subordinates responses. *Organizational Behavior and Human Performance, 27,* 386–410.

Imada, A. S. (1982). Social interaction, observation and stereotypes as determinants of differentiation in peer ratings. *Organizational Behavior and Human Performance, 29,* 397-415.

Interagency Advisory Group Committee on Performance and Recognition. (1993). *Evaluating team performance: A report of the working group on evaluating team performance.* Washington, DC: U.S. General Accounting Office.

Ivancevich, J. M. (1982). Subordinates' reactions to performance appraisal interviews: A test of feedback and goal-setting techniques. *Journal of Applied Psychology, 67,* 581–587.

Jako, R. A., & Murphy, K. (1990). Distributional ratings, judgment decomposition, and their impact on inter-rater agreement and rating accuracy. *Journal of Applied Psychology, 75,* 500–505.

Jackson, S. E., Schuler, R. S., & Jiang, K. (2014). Strategic human resource management: A review and aspirational framework. *Academy of Management Annals, 8,* 1–56.

Jacobs, R., Kafry, D., & Zedeck, S. (1980). Expectations of behaviorally anchored rating scales. *Personnel Psychology, 33,* 595–640.

James, L. (1973) Criterion models and construct validity for criteria. *Psychological Bulletin, 80,* 75–83.

Janssen, O., & Prins, J. (2007). Goal orientations and the seeking of different types of feedback information. *Journal of Occupational and Organizational Psychology, 80,* 235–249.

Janssens, M. (1994). Evaluating international managers' performance: Parent company standards as control mechanism. *International Journal of Human Resource Management, 5,* 853–873.

Jawahar, I. M. (2005). Do raters consider the influence of situational factors on observed performance when evaluating performance? Evidence from three experiments. *Group and Organization Management, 30,* 6–41.

Jawahar, I. M. (2006). Correlates of satisfaction with performance appraisal feedback. *Journal of Labor Research, 27,* 213–236.

Jawahar, I. M. (2010). The mediating role of appraisal feedback reactions on the relationship between rater feedback-related behaviors and ratee performance. *Group and Organization Management, 35,* 494–526.

Jawahar, I. M., & Williams, C. R. (1997). Where all the children are above average: The performance appraisal purpose effect. *Personnel Psychology, 50,* 905–925.

Jennings, T., Palmer, J. K., & Thomas, A. (2004). Effects of performance context on processing speed and performance ratings. *Journal of Business and Psychology, 18,* 453–463.

Jensen, M. C., & Meckling, W. (1976). Theory of the firm, managerial behavior, agency costs and capital structure. *Journal of Financial Economics, 3,* 305–360.

Jhun, S., Bae, Z., & Rhee, S. (2012). Performance change of managers in two different uses of upward feedback: a longitudinal study in Korea. *International Journal of Human Resource Management, 23,* 4246–4264.

Johnson, D. A. (2013). A component analysis of the impact of evaluative and objective feedback on performance. *Journal of Organizational Behavior Management, 33,* 89–103.

Johnson, J. W. (2001). The relative importance of task and contextual performance dimensions to supervisor judgments of overall performance. *Journal of Applied Psychology, 86,* 984–996.

Johnson, J. W., & Ferstl, K. L. (1999). The effects of interrater and self-other agreement on performance improvement following upward feedback. *Personnel Psychology, 52,* 271–303.

Johnson, S., Holladay, C., & Quinones, M. (2009). Organizational citizenship behavior in performance evaluations: Distributive justice or injustice? *Journal of Business and Psychology, 24,* 409–418.

Jonason, P. K., Slomski, S., & Partyka, J. (2012). The Dark Triad at work: How toxic employees get their way. *Personality and Individual Differences, 52,* 449–453.

Jones, A. P, Tait, M., & Butler, M. C. (1983). Perceived punishment and reward values of supervisory actions. *Motivation and Emotion, 1,* 313–329.

Jones, C. (2017). Walmart layoffs just the latest cuts in retail industry. *USA Today* (January 11). http://www.usatoday.com/story/money/2017/01/11/walmart-layoffs-just-latest-retail-cuts/96450196/

Jones, E., & Nisbett, R. (1971). The actor and the observer: Divergent perceptions of the causes of behavior. In E. Jones et al. (Eds.), *Attribution: Perceiving the causes of behavior.* Morristown, NJ: General Learning Press.

Jordan, A. H., & Audia, P. G. (2012). Self-enhancement and learning from performance feedback. *Academy of Management Review, 37,* 211–231.

Jourden, F. J., & Heath, C. (1996). The evaluation gap in performance perceptions: Illusory perceptions of groups and individuals. *Journal of Applied Psychology, 81,* 369–379.

Judge, T. A., & Ferris, G. R. (1993). Social context of performance evaluation decisions. *Academy of Management Journal, 51,* 709–732.

Jundt, D. K., Shoss, M. K., & Huang, J. L. (2015). Individual adaptive performance in organizations: A review. *Journal of Organizational Behavior, 36,* 53–71.

Kacmar, K. M., & Baron, R. A. (1999). Organizational politics: The state of the field, links to related processes and an agenda for future research. In G.R. Ferris (Ed.) *Research in personnel and human resource management* (Vol. 17, pp. 1–39). Stamford, CT: JAI Press.

Kacmar, K. M., & Whitfield, J. M. (2000). An additional rating method for journal articles in the field of management. *Organizational Research Methods, 3,* 392–406.

Kacmar, K. M., Witt, L. A., Zivnuska, S., & Gully, S. M. (2003). The interactive effect of leader-member exchange and communication frequency on performance ratings. *Journal of Applied Psychology, 88,* 764–772.

Kahneman, D. (2011). *Thinking fast and slow.* New York, NY: Farrar, Straus & Giroux.

Kahneman, D., & Tversky, A. (1979). Prospect theory: An analysis of decision under risk. *Econometrica, 47,* 263–291.

Kane, K. F. (1993). Situational factors and performance: An overview. *Human Resource Management Review, 3,* 83–105.

Kane, J. S. (1983). Performance distribution assessment: A new breed of performance appraisal methodology (pp. 325–341). In H. J. Bernardin & R. W. Beatty (Eds.), *Performance appraisal: Assessing human behavior at work.* Boston, MA: Kent.

Kane, J. S. (1986). Performance distribution assessment. In R. Berk (Ed.), *The state of art in performance assessment.* Baltimore, MD: John Hopkins University Press.

Kane, J. S. (1994). A model of volitional rating behavior. *Human Resource Management Review, 4,* 283–312.

Kane, J. S. (1996). The conceptualization and representation of total performance effectiveness. *Human Resource Management Review, 6,* 123–145.

Kane, J. S., Bernardin, H. J., Villanova, P., & Peyrefitte, J. (1995). Stability of rater leniency: Three studies. *Academy of Management Journal, 38,* 1036–1051.

Kane, J. S., & Freeman, K. A. (1997). A theory of equitable performance standards. *Journal of Management, 23,* 37–50.

Kane, J. S., & Lawler, E. E. (1978). Methods of peer assessment. *Psychological Bulletin, 85,* 555–586.

Kane, J. S., & Lawler, E. E. (1980). In defense of peer assessment: A rebuttal to Brief's Critique. *Psychological Bulletin, 88,* 80–81.

Kanungo, R. N., & Jaeger, A. M. (1990). Introduction: The need for indigenous management in developing countries. In A. M. Jaeger & R. N. Kanungo (Eds.), *Management in developing countries* (pp. 1–23). London: Routledge.

Kasten, R., & Nevo, B. (2008). Exploring the relationship between interrater correlations and validity of peer ratings. *Human Performance, 21*, 180–197.

Katz, D., & Kahn, R. (1978). *The social psychology of organizations* (2nd ed.). New York, NY: Wiley.

Kaufman, L. (2014). Google got it wrong: The open-office trend is destroying the workplace. *Washington Post,* December 30, https://www.washingtonpost.com/posteverything/wp/2014/12/30/google-got-it-wrong-the-open-office-trend-is-destroying-the-workplace/

Kay, E., Meyer, H., & French, J. (1965). Effects of threat in a performance interview. *Journal of Applied Psychology, 49*, 311–317.

Keeney, R. L., & Raiffa, H. (1976). *Decisions with multiple objectives: Preferences and value tradeoffs.* New York, NY: Wiley.

Keeping, L. M., & Levy, P. E. (2000). Performance appraisal reactions: Measurement, modeling, and method bias. *Journal of Applied Psychology, 85*, 708–723.

Kehoe, R. R., & Wright, P. M. (2013). The impact of high performance human resource practices on employees' attitudes and behaviors. *Journal of Management, 39*, 366–391.

Kenny, D. A, & Berman, J. S. (1980). Statistical approaches to the correction of bias. *Psychological Bulletin, 88*, 288–295.

Kidd, J. S., & Christy, R. T. (1961). Supervisory procedures and work-team productivity. *Journal of Applied Psychology, 45*, 388–392.

Kiker, D. S., & Motowidlo, S. J. (1999). Main and interaction effects of task and contextual performance on supervisory reward decisions. *Journal of Applied Psychology, 84*, 602–609.

Kikoski, J. F. (1999). Effective communication in the performance appraisal interview: Face-to-face communication for public managers in the culturally diverse workplace. *Public Personnel Management, 28*, 301.

Kim, E., & Glomb, T. M. (2014). Victimization of high performers: The roles of envy and work group identification. *Journal of Applied Psychology, 99*, 619–634.

Kim, M., & Rosenberg, S. (1980). Comparison of two structural models of implicit personality theory. *Journal of Personality and Social Psychology, 38*, 375–389.

Kingsbury, F. A (1922). Analyzing ratings and training raters. *Journal of Personnel Research, 1*, 377–382.

Kingsbury, F. A. (1933). Psychological tests for executives. *Personnel, 9*, 121–133.

Kinicki, A. J., Hom, P. W., & Trost, M. R. (1995). Effects of category prototypes on performance-rating accuracy. *Journal of Applied Psychology, 80*, 354–370.

Kinicki, A. J., Hom, P. W., Trost, M. R., & Wade, K. J. (1995). Effects of category prototypes on performance-rating accuracy. *Journal of Applied Psychology, 80*, 354–370.

Kinicki, A. J., Prussia, G. E., Wu, B. J., & McKee-Ryan, F. M. (2004). A covariance structure analysis of employees' response to performance feedback. *Journal of Applied Psychology, 89*, 1057.

Kirkpatrick, D. L. (1967). Evaluation of training. In R. L. Craig & L. R. Bittel (Eds.), *Training and development handbook.* New York, NY: McGraw-Hill.

Klein, H. J. (1989). An integrated control system theory of human motivation. *Academy of Management Review, 14*, 150–172.

Kluger, A. N., & DeNisi, A. S. (1996). The effects of feedback interventions on performance: A historical review, meta-analysis and a preliminary feedback intervention theory. *Psychological Bulletin, 119*, 254–284.

Kluger, A. N., & Nir, D. (2010). The feedforward interview. *Human Resource Management Review, 20*, 235–246.

Knowles, D. (2013). Al Qaeda leaders lash out at lazy terrorist in 10-page letter over insubordination, failure to file expense reports. *New York Daily News*, May 29. http://www.nydailynews.com/news/world/al-qaeda-reprimands-lazy-terrorist-article-1.1357873

Kolb, K. J., & Aiello, J. R. (1997). Computer-based performance monitoring and productivity in a multiple task environment. *Journal of Business and Psychology, 12*, 189–204.

Kolodinsky, R. W., Treadway, D. C., & Ferris, G. R. (2007). Political skill and influence effectiveness: Testing portions of an expanded Ferris and Judge (1991) model. *Human Relations, 60*, 1747–1777.

Korn, C. W., Rosenblau, G., Rodriguez Buritica, J. M., & Heekeren, H. R. (2016). Performance feedback processing is positively biased as predicted by attribution theory. *PloS one, 11*, e0148581.

Korsgaard, M. A., & Roberson, L. (1995). Procedural justice in performance evaluation: The role of instrumental and non-instrumental voice in performance appraisal discussions. *Journal of Management, 21*, 657–669.

Kostova, T. (1999). Transnational transfer of strategic organizational practices: A contextual perspective. *Academy of Management Review, 24*, 308–324.

Kozlowski, S. W. J., Chao, G. T., & Morrison, R. F. (1998). Games raters play: Politics, strategies, and impression management in performance appraisal. In J. W. Smither (Ed.), *Performance appraisal: State of the art in practice* (pp. 163–205). San Francisco, CA: Jossey-Bass.

Kraiger, K., & Ford, J. K. (1985). A meta-analysis of ratee race effects in performance ratings. *Journal of Applied Psychology, 70*, 56–65.

Krasman, J. (2013). Putting feedback-seeking into "context": Job characteristics and feedback-seeking behaviour. *Personnel Review, 42*, 50–66.

Kuckartz, U. (2014). *Qualitative text analysis: A guide to methods, practice and using software.* Newbury Park, CA: Sage.

Kuvaas, B. (2006). Performance appraisal satisfaction and employee outcomes: Mediating and moderating roles of work motivation. *International Journal of Human Resource Management, 17*, 504–522.

Kuvaas, B. (2011). The interactive role of performance appraisal reactions and regular feedback. *Journal of Managerial Psychology, 26*, 123–137.

Kuvaas, B., & Dysvik, A. (2009). Perceived investment in employee development, intrinsic motivation and work performance. *Human Resource Management Journal, 19*, 217–236.

Kwak, W. J., & Choi, S. B. (2015). Effect of rating discrepancy on turnover intention and leader-member exchange. *Asia Pacific Journal of Management, 32*, 801–824.

Lacho, K. J., Stearns, G. K., & Villere, M. F. (1979). A study of employee appraisal systems of major cities in the United States. *Public Personnel Management, 8*, 111–125.

Lam, L. W., Peng, K. Z., Wong, C., & Lau, D. C. (2015). Is more feedback seeking always better? Leader-member exchange moderates the relationship between feedback-seeking behavior and performance. *Journal of Management, 25*, 1–23.

Lance, C. E. (1994). Test of a latent structure of performance ratings derived from Wherry's (1952) theory of rating. *Journal of Management, 20*, 757–771.

Lance, C. E., Baranik, L. E., Lau, A. R., & Scharlau, E. A. (2009). If it ain't trait it must be method: (mis)application of the multitrait-multimethod design in organizational research. In C. E. Lance & R. L. Vandenberg (Eds.), *Statistical and methodological myths and urban legends* (pp. 227–360). New York, NY: Routledge.

Lance, C. E., LaPointe, J. A., & Stewart, A. M. (1994). A test of the context dependency of three causal models of halo rater error. *Journal of Applied Psychology, 79*, 332–340.

Lance, C. E., Teachout, M. S., & Donnelly, T. M. (1992). Specification of the criterion construct space: An application of hierarchical confirmatory factor analysis. *Journal of Applied Psychology, 77*, 437–452.

Landy, F. J. (1985). *Psychology of work behavior* (3rd ed.). Homewood, IL: Dorsey.

Landy, F. J. (2010). Performance ratings: Then and now. In J. L. Outtz (Ed.), *Adverse impact: Implications for organizational staffing and high-stakes selection* (pp. 227–248). New York, NY: Routledge.

Landy, F. J., Barnes, J., & Murphy, K. R. (1978). Correlates of perceived fairness and accuracy of performance appraisals. *Journal of Applied Psychology, 63*, 751–754.

Landy, F. J., Barnes-Farrell, J., & Cleveland, J. (1980). Perceived fairness and accuracy of performance appraisals: A follow-up. *Journal of Applied Psychology, 65*, 355–356.

Landy, F. J., & Farr, J. L. (1980). Performance rating. *Psychological Bulletin, 87*, 72–107.

Landy, F. J., & Farr, J. L. (1983). *The measurement of work performance.* New York, NY: Academic Press.

Landy, F. J., Shankster, L. J., & Kohler, S. S. (1994). Personnel selection and placement. *Annual Review of Psychology, 45*, 261–296.

Langer, E. J., Fiske, S., Taylor, S. E., & Chanowitz, B. (1976). Stigma, staring, and discomfort: A novel-stimulus hypothesis. *Journal of Experimental Social Psychology, 12*, 451–463.

Larson, E. L., Patel, S. J., Evans, D., & Saiman, L. (2013). Feedback as a strategy to change behaviour: The devil is in the details. *Journal of Evaluation in Clinical Practice, 19*, 230–234.

Larson, J. R. (1986). Supervisors' performance feedback to subordinates: The impact of subordinate performance valence and outcome dependence. *Organizational Behavior and Human Decision Processes, 37*(3), 391–408.

Latest Telecommuting Statistics. http://globalworkplaceanalytics.com/telecommuting-statistics

Latham, G. (1986). Job performance and appraisal. In C. Cooper & I. Robertson (Eds.), *International review of industrial and organizational psychology*. Chichester, UK: Wiley.

Latham, G. P., & Pursell, E. D. (1975). Measuring absenteeism from the opposite side of the coin. *Journal of Applied Psychology, 60,* 369–371.

Latham, G., & Wexley, K. (1977). Behavioral observation scales. *Journal of Applied Psychology, 30,* 255–268.

Latham, G. P., Wexley, K. N., & Pursell, E. D. (1975). Training managers to minimize rating errors in the observation of behavior. *Journal of Applied Psychology, 60,* 550–555.

Lawler, E. E. (1971). *Pay and organizational effectiveness A psychological view.* New York, NY: McGraw-Hill.

Lawler, E. E. (2012). Performance appraisals are dead: Long live performance management. *Forbes,* Retrieved from http://www.forbes.com/sites/edward lawler/2012/07/12/performance-appraisals-are-dead-long-live-performance-management/

Lawler, E. E., Benson, G. S., & McDermott, M. (2012). What makes performance appraisals effective? *Compensation and Benefits Review, 44,* 191–200.

Lawler, E. E., & Jenkins, C. D. (1992). Strategic reward systems. In M. D. Dunnette and L.M. Hough (Eds.), *Handbook of industrial and organizational psychology* (Vol. 3, 2nd ed., pp. 1009–1055). Palo Alto, CA: Consulting Psychologists Press.

Lawrence, H. V. (1992). *The effects of training in feedback on managers' attributional bias and perceived effectiveness of their work groups* (Doctoral dissertation). Retrieved from Virginia Polytechnic Institute and State University.

Lazer, R. I., & Wikstrom, W. S. (1977). *Appraising managerial performance: Current practices and future directions* (Conference Board Rep. No. 723). New York, NY: Conference Board.

LeBreton, J. M., Scherer, K. T., & James, L. R. (2014). Corrections for criterion reliability in validity generalization: A false prophet in a land of suspended judgment. *Industrial and Organizational Psychology: Perspectives on Science and Practice, 7,* 478–500.

Ledford, G. E., Benson, G., & Lawler, E. E. (2016). Aligning research and the current practice of performance management. *Industrial and Organizational Psychology: Perspectives on Science and Practice, 9,* 253–260.

Lee, H., & Dalal, R. S. (2011). The effects of performance extremities on ratings of dynamic performance. *Human Performance, 24,* 99–118.

Lee, J. S. Y., & Akhtar, S. (1996). Determinants of employee willingness to use feedback for performance improvement: cultural and organizational interpretations. *International Journal of Human Resource Management, 7,* 878–890.

Lee, M., & Son, B. (1998). The effects of appraisal review content on employees' reactions and performance. *International Journal of Human Resource Management, 9,* 203–214.

Lee-Hoffmann, P. (2011). Discover the secrets of becoming a great place to work. *Leader To Leader, 2011,* 17–22.

Lefkowitz, J. (2000). The role of interpersonal affective regard in supervisory performance ratings: A literature review and proposed causal model. *Journal of Occupational and Organizational Psychology, 73,* 67–85.

Lefkowitz, J., & Battista, M. (1995). Potential sources of criterion bias in supervisor ratings used for test validation. *Journal of Business and Psychology, 10,* 389–441.

LePine, J. A., & Van Dyne, L. (1998). Predicting voice behavior in work groups. *Journal of Applied Psychology, 83,* 853.

Leung, K., Su, S., & Morris, M. W. (2001). When is criticism not constructive? The roles of fairness perceptions and dispositional attributions in employee acceptance of critical supervisory feedback. *Human Relations, 54,* 1155–1187.

Levy, P. E., Silverman, S. B., & Cavanaugh, C. M. (2015). The performance management fix is in: ow practice can build on research. *Industrial and Organizational Psychology: Perspectives on Science and Practice, 8,* 80–85.

Levy, P. E., & Thompson, D. J. (2012). Feedback in organizations: Individual differences and the social context. In R. Sutton, M. Hornsey, & K. Douglas (Eds.), *Feedback: Handbook of praise, criticism, and advice* (pp. 217–232). New York, NY: Peter Lang.

Levy, P. E., & Williams, J. R. (2004). The social context of performance appraisal: A review and framework for the future. *Journal of Management, 30,* 881–905.

Lewicki, R. J., & Bunker, B. B. (1996). *Trust in organizations: Frontiers of organizational research.* Newbury Park, CA: Sage.

Lewis, M. (1989). *Liar's poker: Rising through the wreckage on Wall Street.* New York, NY: W. W. Norton.

Li, N., Harris, T. B., Boswell, W. R., & Xie, Z. (2011). The role of organizational insiders' developmental feedback and proactive personality on newcomers' performance: An interactionist perspective. *Journal of Applied Psychology, 96,* 1317–1327.

Li, W., Alam, P., & Meonske, N. (2013). Performance measure properties and efficacy of incentive contracts: perceptions of U. S. employees. *International Journal of Human Resource Management, 24,* 3378–3392.

Liden, R. C., & Graen, G. (1980). Generalizability of the vertical dyadic linkage model of leadership. *Academy of Management Journal, 23,* 451–465.

Liden, R. C., & Mitchell, T. R. (1983). The effects of group interdependence on supervisor performance evaluations. *Personnel Psychology, 36,* 289–300.

Liden, R. C., Wayne, S. J., Judge, T. A., Sparrowe, R. T., Kraimer, M. L., & Franz, T. M. (1999). Management of poor performance: A comparison of manager, group member, and group disciplinary decisions. *Journal of Applied Psychology, 84,* 835–850.

Linna, A., Elovainio, M., Van den Bos, K., Kivimäki, M., Pentti, J., & Vahtera, J. (2012). Can usefulness of performance appraisal interviews change organizational justice perceptions? A 4-year longitudinal study among public sector employees. *International Journal of Human Resource Management, 23,* 1360–1375.

Linville, P. W., & Jones, E. J. (1980). Polarized appraisals of out-group members. *Journal of Personality and Social Psychology, 38,* 689–703.

Lizzio, A., Wilson, K., & MacKay, L. (2008). Managers' and subordinates' evaluations of feedback strategies: The critical contribution of voice. *Journal of Applied Social Psychology, 38,* 919–946.

Locke, E. A., & Latham, G. P. (1990). *A theory of goal setting & task performance.* Upper Saddle River, NJ: Prentice-Hall.

Locke, E. A., Shaw, K. N., Saari, L. M., & Latham, G. P. (1981). Goal setting and task performance: 1969–1980. *Psychological Bulletin, 90,* 125–152.

Loftus, E. (2005). Planting misinformation in the human mind: A 30-year investigation of the malleability of memory. *Learning & Memory, 12,* 361–366.

London, M. (2001). The great debate: Should multisource feedback be used for administration or development only. In D. W. Bracken, C. W. Timmreck, & A. H. Church (Eds.), *The handbook of multisource feedback* (pp. 335–351). San Francisco, CA: Jossey-Bass.

London, M. (2003). *Job feedback: Giving, seeking and using feedback for performance improvement* (2nd ed.). Mahwah, NJ: Lawrence Erlbaum.

London, M., Larsen, H. H., & Thisted, L. N. (1999). Relationships between feedback and self-development. *Group & Organization Management, 24,* 5–27.

London, M., & Smither, J. W. (2002). Feedback orientation, feedback culture, and the longitudinal performance management process. *Human Resource Management Review, 12,* 81–101.

London, M., Smither, J. W., & Adsit, D. J. (1997). Accountability: The Achilles' heel of multisource feedback. *Group and Organization Management, 22,* 162–184.

Longenecker, C. O., & Gioia, D. A. (1988, Winter). Neglected at the top: Executives talk about executive appraisal. *Sloan Management Review,* 41–47.

Longenecker, C., & Ludwig, D. (1990). Ethical dilemmas in performance appraisals revisited. *Journal of Business Ethics, 9,* 961–969.

Longenecker, C. O., Sims, H. P., & Gioia, D. A. (1987). Behind the mask: The politics of employee appraisal. *Academy of Management Executive, 1,* 183–193.

Lopez, F. M. (1968). *Evaluating employee performance.* Chicago, IL: Public Personnel Association.

Lopez, S. J., & Snyder, C. R. (2009). *The Oxford handbook of positive psychology.* New York, NY: Oxford University Press.

Lord, F. M., & Novick, M. R. (1968). *Statistical theories of mental test scores.* Reading, MA: Addison-Wesley.

Lord, R. G. (1985). An information processing approach to social perceptions, leadership and behavioral measurement in organizations. *Research in Organizational Behavior, 7,* 87–128.

Lukas, C. (2010). Optimality of intertemporal aggregation in dynamic agency. *Journal of Management Accounting Research, 22*, 157–174.

Lyness, K. S., & Heilman, M. E. (2006). When fit is fundamental: Performance evaluations and promotions of upper-level female and male managers. *Journal of Applied Psychology, 91*, 777–785.

Mabe, P. A., & West, S. G. (1982). Validity of self-evaluation of ability: A review and meta- analysis. *Journal of Applied Psychology, 67*, 280–290.

MacDonald, H. A., Sulsky, L. M., Spence, J. R., & Brown, D. J. (2013). Cultural differences in the motivation to seek performance feedback: A comparative policy-capturing study. *Human Performance, 26*, 211–235.

Maley, J. (2013). Hybrid purposes of performance appraisal in a crisis. *Journal of Management Development, 32*, 1093–1112.

Malos, S. (2005). The importance of valid selection and performance appraisal: Do management practices figure in case law. In F. Landy & E. Salas (Eds.), *Employment discrimination litigation: Behavioral, quantitative and legal perspectives* (pp. 373–409). San Francisco, CA: Jossey-Bass.

Manners, I., & Cates, S. (2016). Bullying in the workplace: Does it exist in United States organizations? *International Journal of Business & Public Administration, 13*, 99–114.

Manoharan, T. R., Muralidharan, C., & Deshmukh, S. G. (2011). An integrated fuzzy multi-attribute decision-making model for employees' performance appraisal. *International Journal of Human Resource Management, 22*, 722–745.

March, J. G., & Simon, H. A. (1958). *Organizations.* New York, NY: Wiley.

Markus, H. R., & Kitayama, S. (1991). Culture and the self: Implications for cognition, emotion, and motivation. *Psychological Review, 98*, 224–253.

Martell, R. F., & Evans, D. P. (2005). Source-monitoring training: Toward reducing rater expectancy effects in behavioral measurement. *Journal of Applied Psychology, 90*, 956–963.

Martell, R. F., Guzzo, R. A., & Willis, C. E. (1995). A methodological and substantive note on the performance-cue effect in ratings of work-group behavior. *Journal of Applied Psychology, 80*, 191–195.

Martin, D. C., & Bartol, K. M. (2003). Factors influencing expatriate performance appraisal system success: An organizational perspective. *Journal of International Management, 9*, 115–132.

Martin, D. C., Bartol, K. M., & Kehoe, P. E. (2000). The legal ramifications of performance appraisal: The growing significance. *Public Personnel Management, 29*, 379–406.

Martin, J., & Siehl, C. (1983). Organizational culture and counter culture: An uneasy symbiosis. *Organizational Dynamics, 12*, 52–64.

Martocchio, J. J., & Dulebohn, J. (1994). Performance feedback effects in training: The role of perceived controllability. *Personnel Psychology, 94*, 357–373.

Massey, D. J. (1975). Narrowing the gap between intended and existing results of appraisal systems. *Personnel Journal, 54*, 522–524.

Maurer, T. J., Mitchell, D. R. D., & Barbeite, F. G. (2002). Predictors of attitudes toward a 360-degree feedback system and involvement in post-feedback management development activity. *Journal of Occupational & Organizational Psychology, 75*, 87–107.

Maurer, T. J., Palmer, J. K., & Ashe, D. K. (1993). Diaries, checklist, evaluations, and contrast effects in measurement of behavior. *Journal of Applied Psychology, 78*, 226–231.

Maurer, T. J., Raju, N. S., & Collins, W. C. (1998). Peer and subordinate performance appraisal measurement equivalence. *Journal of Applied Psychology, 83*, 693–702.

Maurer, T. J., & Tarulli, B. A. (1996). Acceptance of peer/upward performance appraisal systems: Role of work context factors and beliefs about managers' development capability. *Human Resource Management, 35*, 217–241.

Mayer, R. C., & Davis, J. H. (1999). The effect of the performance appraisal system on trust for management: A field quasi-experiment. *Journal of Applied Psychology, 84*, 123–136.

Mayhew, B. H. (1983). Hierarchical differentiation in imperatively coordinated associations. *Research in the Sociology of Organizations, 2*, 153–229.

McArthur, L. (1980). What grabs you? The role of attention in impression formation in causal attribution. In E. Higgins, C. Herman, & M. Zanna (Eds.), *Social cognition: The Ontario symposium on personality and social psychology.* Hillsdale, NJ: Erlbaum.

McCarthy, A. M., & Garavan, T. M. (2001). 360° feedback process: Performance, improvement and employee career development. *Journal of European Industrial Training, 25,* 5–32.

McCormick, I. A., Walkey, F. H., & Green, D. E. (1986). Comparative perceptions of driver ability: A confirmation and expansion. *Accident Analysis and Prevention, 18,* 205–208.

McEvoy, G. M., & Buller, P. F. (1987). User acceptance of peer appraisals in an industrial setting. *Personnel Psychology, 40,* 785–797.

McEvoy, G. M., & Cascio, W. F. (1990). The United States and Taiwan: Two different cultures look at performance appraisal. *Research in Personnel and Human Resources Management, 2,* 201–219.

McGregor, D. (1960). Theory X and theory Y. *Organization Theory,* 358–374.

McIntyre R. M., & Salas E. (1995). Measuring and managing for team performance: Emerging principles from complex environments. In R. Guzzo & E. Salas (Eds.), *Team effectiveness and decision making in organizations* (pp. 9–45). San Francisco, CA: Jossey-Bass.

McIntyre, R. M., Smith, D., & Hassett, C. E. (1984). Accuracy of performance ratings as affected by rater training and perceived purpose of rating. *Journal of Applied Psychology, 69,* 147–156.

McKay, P. F., & McDaniel, M. A. (2006). A reexamination of black-white mean differences in work performance: more data, more moderators. *Journal of Applied Psychology, 91,* 538–554.

McNabb, R., & Whitfield, K. (2001). Job evaluation and high performance work practices: Compatible or conflictual? *Journal of Management Studies, 38,* 293–312.

Mechanic, D. (1962). Sources of power of lower participants in complex organizations. *Administrative Science Quarterly, 7,* 349–364.

Mercer. (2013). Global performance management survey report: Executive summary. Retrieved from http://www.mercer.com/content/dam/mercer/attachments/global/Talent/Assess-BrochurePerfMgmt.pdf

Meier, R. A., & Feldhusen, J. F. (1979). Another look at Dr. Fox: Effect of stated purpose of evaluation lecturers expressiveness and density of lecture content on student ratings. *Journal of Educational Psychology, 71,* 339–345.

Mero, N. P., & Motowidlo, S. J. (1995). Effects of rater accountability on the accuracy and the favorability of performance ratings. *Journal of Applied Psychology, 80,* 517–524.

Mero, N. P., Motowidlo, S. J., & Anna, A. L. (2003). Effects of accountability on rating behavior and rater accuracy. *Journal of Applied Social Psychology, 33,* 2493–2514.

Meyer, H. H. (1980). Self appraisal of job performance. *Personnel Psychology, 33,* 291–295.

Meyer, H. H., Kay, E., & French, J. (1965). Split roles in performance appraisal. *Harvard Business Review, 43,* 123–129.

Miceli, M. P., Jung, I., Near, J. P., & Greenberger, D. B. (1991). Predictors and outcomes of reactions to pay-for-performance plans. *Journal of Applied Psychology, 76,* 508.

Michael, D. F. (2014). The impact of leader-member exchange, supportive supervisor communication, affective commitment, and role ambiguity on bank employees' turnover intentions and performance. *International Journal of Business and Science, 5,* 8–21.

Milkovich, G. T., & Wigdor, A. K. (1991). *Pay for performance.* Washington, DC: National Academy Press.

Miller, B. K., & Werner, S. (2005). Factors influencing the inflation of task performance ratings for workers with disabilities and contextual performance ratings for their coworkers. *Human Performance, 3,* 309–329.

Miller, D. L., & Karakowsky, L. (2005). Gender influences as an impediment to knowledge sharing: When men and women fail to seek peer feedback. *Journal of Psychology: Interdisciplinary and Applied, 139,* 101–118.

Miller, D. T., & Ross, M. (1975). Self-serving biases in the attribution of causality: Fact or fiction? *Psychological Bulletin, 82,* 213–225.

Miller, M. (2017). Threatened pension cuts will test Trump ties to U.S. Rust Belt voters. Retrieved from http://www.reuters.com/article/us-column-miller-pensions-idUSKBN16G1KO

Milliman, J., Nason, S., Zhu, C., & De Cieri, H. (2002). An exploratory assessment of the purposes of performance appraisals in North and Central America and the Pacific Rim. *Human Resource Management, 41,* 87–102.

Minter, H. (2017). How to tackle bro-culture in tech startups. *The Guardian* (March 13). Retrieved from https://www.theguardian.com/careers/2017/mar/13/sexism-tech-startups-women-workplace

Mintzberg, H. (1983). *Power in and around organizations.* Englewood Cliffs, NJ: Prentice-Hall.

Mishra, V., & Roch, S. (2013). Cultural values and performance appraisal: assessing the effects of rater self-construal on performance ratings. *Journal of Psychology: Interdisciplinary and Applied, 15*, 2911–2926.

Mitchell, T. R. (1983). The effects of social, task, and situational factors on motivation, performance, and appraisal. In F. Landy, S, Zedeck, & J. Cleveland (Eds.), *Performance measurement and theory* (pp. 39–59). Hillsdale, NJ: Erlbaum.

Mitchell, T. R., Green, S. G., & Wood, R. E. (1981). An attributional model of leadership and the poor performing subordinate: Development and validation. In B. Staw & L. Cummings (Eds.), *Research in organizational behavior,* Vol. 3 Greenwich, CT: JAI Press.

Mitchell, T. R., & Liden, R. C. (1982). The effects of the social context on performance evaluations. *Organizational Behavior and Human Performance, 29*, 241–256.

Mitchell, T. R., & O'Reilly, C. A. (1983). Managing poor performance and productivity in organizations. In K. Rowland & G. Ferris (Eds.), *Research in personnel and human resources management,* Vol. 1. Greenwich, CT: JAI Press.

Mitra, A., Gupta, N., & Jenkins, C. D. (1997). A drop in the bucket: When is a pay raise a pay raise? *Journal of Organizational Behavior, 18*, 117–137.

Mitra, A., Tenihälä, A., & Shaw, J. D. (2016). Smallest meaningful pay increases: Field test, constructive replication, and extension. *Human Resource Management, 55*, 69–81.

Mohrman, A. M., & Lawler, E. E. (1983). Motivation and performance appraisal behavior. In F. Landy, S. Zedeck, & J. Cleveland (Eds.), *Performance measurement and theory.* Hillsdale, NJ: Erlbaum.

Morgeson, F. P., Mumford, T. V., & Campion, M. A. (2005). Coming full circle: Using research and practice to address 27 questions about 360-degree feedback programs. *Consulting Psychology Journal: Practice and Research, 57*, 196–209.

Morse, S. (2010). Utilising a virtual world to teach performance appraisal. *Journal of European Industrial Training, 34*, 852–868.

Moss, S. E., Sanchez, J. I., Brumbaugh, A. M., & Borkowski, N. (2009). The mediating role of feedback avoidance behavior in the LMX-performance relationship. *Group and Organization Management, 34*, 645–664.

Moss, S. E., Valenzi, E. R., & Taggart, W. (2003). Are you hiding from your boss?: The development of a taxonomy and instrument to assess the feedback management behaviors of good and bad performers. *Journal of Management, 29*, 487–510.

Mossholder, K. W., & Bedian, A. G. (1983). Cross-level inference and organizational research: Perspectives on interpretation and application. *Academy of Management Review, 8*, 547–558.

Motowidlo, S. J., & Peterson, N. G. (2008). Effects of organizational perspective on implicit trait policies about correctional officers' job performance. *Human Performance, 21*, 396–413.

Motowidlo, S. J., & Van Scotter, J. R. (1994). Evidence that task performance should be distinguished from contextual performance. *Journal of Applied Psychology, 79*, 475–480.

Mount, M. K., Judge, T. A., Scullen, S. E., Sytsma, M. R., & Hezlett, S. A. (1998). Trait, rater, and level effects in 360-degree performance ratings. *Personnel Psychology, 51*, 557–576.

Mowday, R. T., Porter, L. W., & Steers, R. M. (1981). *Employee-organizational linkages: The psychology of commitment, absenteeism, and turnover.* New York, NY: Academic Press.

Muchinsky, P. (1977). Employee absenteeism: A review of the literature. *Journal of Vocational Behavior, 10*, 316–340.

Murphy, K. R. (1982a). Assessing the discriminant validity of regression models and subjectively weighted models of judgments. *Multivariate Behavioral Research, 17*, 354–370.

Murphy, K. R. (1982b). Difficulties in the statistical control of halo. *Journal of Applied Psychology, 67*, 161–164.

Murphy, K. R. (1989a). Is the relationship between cognitive ability and job performance stable over time? *Human Performance, 2*, 183–200.

Murphy K. R. (1989b). Dimensions of job performance. In R. Dillon & J. Pelligrino (Eds.), *Testing: Applied and theoretical perspectives* (pp. 218–247). New York, NY: Praeger.

Murphy, K. R. (1993). *Honesty in the workplace.* Monterey, CA: Brooks/Cole.

Murphy, K. R. (2002). Can conflicting perspectives on the role of "g" in personnel selection be resolved? *Human Performance, 15*, 173–186.

Murphy, K. R. (2008a). Explaining the weak relationship between job performance and ratings of job performance. *Industrial and Organizational Psychology: Perspectives on Science and Practice, 1*, 148–160.

Murphy, K. R. (2008b). Perspectives on the relationship between job performance and ratings of job performance. *Industrial and Organizational Psychology: Perspectives on Science and Practice, 1*, 197–205.

Murphy, K. R. (2009). Validity, validation and values. *The Academy of Management Annals, 3*, 421–461.

Murphy, K. R., & Anhalt, R. L. (1992). Is halo error a property of the rater, ratees, or the specific behaviors observed? *Journal of Applied Psychology, 77*, 494–500.

Murphy, K. R., & Balzer, W. K. (1986). Systematic distortions in memory-based behavior ratings and performance evaluations: Consequences for rating accuracy. *Journal of Applied Psychology, 71*, 39–44.

Murphy, K. R., & Balzer, W. K. (1989). Rater errors and rating accuracy. *Journal of Applied Psychology, 74*, 619–624.

Murphy, K. R., Balzer, W. K., Kellam, K. L., & Armstrong, J. (1984). Effect of purpose of rating on accuracy in observing teacher behavior and evaluating teaching performance. *Journal of Educational Psychology, 76*, 45–54.

Murphy, K. R., Balzer, W. K., Lockhart, M., & Eisenman E. (1985). Effects of previous performance on evaluations of present performance. *Journal of Applied Psychology, 70*, 72–84.

Murphy, K. R., & Cleveland, J. N. (1991). *Performance appraisal: An organizational perspective.* Needham Heights, MA: Allyn & Bacon.

Murphy, K. R., & Cleveland, J. N. (1995). *Understanding performance appraisal: Social, organizational and goal-oriented perspectives.* Newbury Park, CA: Sage.

Murphy, K. R., Cleveland, J. N., & Mohler, C. (2001). Reliability, validity and meaningfulness of multisource ratings. In D. Bracken, C. Timmreck, & A. Church (Eds.), *Handbook of multisource feedback* (pp. 130–148). San Francisco, CA: Jossey-Bass.

Murphy, K. R., Cleveland, J. N., Skattebo, A. L., & Kinney, T. B. (2004). Raters who pursue different goals give different ratings. *Journal of Applied Psychology, 89*, 158–164.

Murphy, K. R., & Constans, J. I. (1987). Behavioral anchors as a source of bias in rating. *Journal of Applied Psychology, 72*, 523–579.

Murphy, K., & Davidshofer, C. (2005). *Psychological testing: Principles and applications* (6th ed.). Upper Sadddle River, NJ: Prentice Hall.

Murphy, K., Deckert, P., & Hunter, S. (2013). What personality does and doesn't predict and why: Lessons learned and future directions. In N. Christiansen & R. Tett (Eds.), *Handbook of personality at work* (pp. 633–650). New York, NY: Taylor & Francis.

Murphy, K. R., & DeNisi, A. S. (2008). A model of the appraisal process. In A. Varma, P. S. Budhwar & A. S. DeNisi (Eds.), *Performance management systems: A global perspective* (pp. 81–94). London: Routledge.

Murphy, K. R., & DeShon, R. (2000). Interrater correlations do not estimate the reliability of job performance ratings. *Personnel Psychology, 53*, 873–900.

Murphy, K. R., Gannett, B., Herr, B., & Chen, J. (1986). Effects of subsequent performance on evaluations of previous performance. *Journal of Applied Psychology, 71*, 427–431.

Murphy, K. R., Garcia, M., Kerkar, S., Martin, C., & Balzer, W. K. (1982). Relationship between observational accuracy and accuracy in evaluating performance. *Journal of Applied Psychology, 67*, 320.

Murphy, K. R., Herr, B. M., Lockhart, M. C., & Maguire, E. (1986). Evaluating the performance of paper people. *Journal of Applied Psychology, 71*, 654–661.

Murphy, K. R., Jako, R. A., & Anhalt, R. L. (1993). Nature and consequences of halo error: a critical analysis. *Journal of Applied Psychology, 78*, 218–225.

Murphy, K. R., Martin, C., & Garcia, M. (1982). Do behavioral observation scales measure observation? *Journal of Applied Psychology, 67*, 562–567.

Murphy, K., Philbin, T., & Adams, S. (1989). Effect of purpose of observation on accuracy of immediate and delayed performance ratings. *Organizational Behavior and Human Decision Processes, 43*, 336–354.

Murphy, K. R., & Russell, C. J. Mend it or end it: Redirecting the search for interactions in the organizational sciences. *Organizational Research Methods* 2017/*20*, 549–573.

Murphy, K. R., & Shiarella, A. (1997). Implications of the multidimensional nature of job performance for the validity of selection tests: Multivariate frameworks for studying test validity. *Personnel Psychology, 50,* 823–854.

Nae, E. Y., Moon, H. K., & Choi, B. K. (2015). Seeking feedback but unable to improve work performance? Qualified feedback from trusted supervisors matters. *Career Development International, 20,* 81–100.

Napier, N. K., & Latham, G. P. (1986). Outcome expectancies of people who conduct performance appraisals. *Personnel Psychology, 39,* 827–837.

Nathan, B. R., & Tippins, N. (1989). The consequences of halo "error" in performance ratings: A field study of the moderating effect of halo on test validation results. *Journal of Applied Psychology, 74,* 290–296.

National Research Council. (2012). *Education for life and work: Developing transferable knowledge and skills in the 21st century* (Committee on Defining Deeper Learning and 21st Century Skills, J. W. Pellegrino & M. L. Hilton, Eds.). Washington, DC: The National Academies Press.

Neary, D. B. (2002). Creating a company-wide, on-line, performance management system: A case study at TRW Inc. *Human Resource Management, 41,* 491–498.

Neck, C. P., Stewart, G. L., & Manz, C. C. (1995). Thought self-leadership as a framework for enhancing the performance of performance appraisers. *The Journal of Applied Behavioral Science, 31,* 278–302.

Neubert, J. C., Meinert, J., Kretzschmar, J., & Greiff, S. (2015). The assessment of 21st century skills in industrial and organizational psychology: Complex and collaborative decision making. *Industrial and Organizational Psychology: Perspectives on Science and Practice, 8,* 238–268.

Neville, L., & Roulin, N. (2016). Genius or folly? It depends on whether performance ratings survive the "psychological immune system." *Industrial and Organizational Psychology: Perspectives on Science and Practice, 9,* 281–288.

Newcomb, T. (1931). An experiment designed to test the validity of a rating technique. *Journal of Educational Psychology, 22,* 279.

Ng, I., & Maki, D. (2008). Trade union influence on human resource management practices. *Industrial Relations: A Journal of Economy and Society, 33,* 121–135.

Ng, K. Y., Koh, C., Ang, S., Kennedy, J. C., & Chan, K. Y. (2011). Rating leniency and halo in multisource feedback ratings: Testing cultural assumptions of power distance and individualism-collectivism. *Journal of Applied Psychology, 96,* 1033–1044.

Ng, T. W., & Feldman, D. C. (2008). The relationship of age to ten dimensions of job performance. *Journal of Applied Psychology, 93,* 392–423.

Niemann, J., Wisse, B., Rus, D., Yperen, N., & Sassenberg, K. (2014). Anger and attitudinal reactions to negative feedback: The effects of emotional instability and power. *Motivation and Emotion, 38,* 687–699.

Nieminen, L. R. G., Rudolph, C. W., Baltes, B. B., Casper, C. M., Wynne, K. T., & Kirby, L. C. (2013). The combined effect of ratee's bodyweight and past performance information on performance judgments. *Journal of Applied Social Psychology, 43*(3), 527–543.

Nieva, V. E., & Gutek, B. A. (1980). Sex effects on evaluations. *Academy of Management Review, 5,* 267–276.

Nisen, M. (2015). How millennials forced GE to scrap performance reviews. *The Atlantic* (August 18). http://fortune.com/2013/11/18/microsoft-ge-and-the-futility-of-ranking-employees/

Nishii, L. H., Lepak, D. P., & Schneider, B. (2008). Employee attributions about the "why" of HR practices: Their effects on employee attitudes and behaviors, and customer satisfaction. *Personnel Psychology, 61,* 503–545.

Northcraft, G. B., Schmidt, A. M., & Ashford, S. J. (2011). Feedback and the rationing of time and effort among competing tasks. *Journal of Applied Psychology, 96,* 1076–1086.

Nurse, L. (2005). Performance appraisal, employee development and organizational justice: Exploring the linkages. *International Journal of Human Resource Management, 16,* 1176–1194.

O'Boyle Jr., E., & Aguinis, H. (2012). The best and the rest: Revisiting the norm of normality of individual performance. *Personnel Psychology, 65,* 79–119.

Ock, J. (2016). Construct validity evidence for multisource performance ratings: Is interrater reliability enough? *Industrial and Organizational Psychology, 9,* 329–333.

Odiorne, G. S. (1965). *Management by objectives: A system of managerial leadership.* London: Pitman.

Ogunfowora, B., Bourdage, J., & Lee, K. (2010). Rater personality and performance dimension weighting in making overall performance judgments. *Journal of Business and Psychology, 25,* 465–476.

...son, E. G. (2013). Microsoft, GE and the futility of ranking employees. *Fortune* (November 18). http://fortune.com/2013/11/18/microsoft-ge-and-the-futility-of-ranking-employees/

O'Neill, T. A., McLarnon, M. J. W., & Carswell, J. J. (2015). Variance components of job performance ratings. *Human Performance, 32*, 801–824.

Ones, D. S., Viswesvaran, C., & Schmidt, F. L. (2008). No new terrain: Reliability and construct validity of job performance ratings. *Industrial and Organizational Psychology: Perspectives on Science and Practice, 1*, 174–179.

Organ, D.W. (1988). *Organizational citizenship behavior: The good soldier syndrome.* Lexington, MA: Lexington Books.

Organ, D. W. (1990). The motivational basis of organizational citizenship behavior. In B. M. Staw & L. L. Cummings (Eds.), *Research in organizational behavior* (Vol. 12, pp. 43–72). Greenwich, CT: JAI Press.

Organ, D. W. (1997). Organizational citizenships behavior: It's construct cleanup time. *Human Performance, 10*, 85–97.

Organization for Economic Cooperation and Development (OECD). (2012). *Better skills, better jobs, better lives. A strategic approach to skills policies.* Paris: OECD Publishing.

Osgood, C. E. (1962). Studies of the generality of affective meaning systems. *American Psychologist, 17*, 10–28.

Oswald, F. L., Mitchell, G., Blanton, H., Jaccard, J., & Tetlock, P. E. (2013). Predicting ethnic and racial discrimination: A meta-analysis of IAT criterion studies. *Journal of Personality and Social Psychology, 105*, 171–192.

Paik, Y., Vance, C. M., & Stage, H. D. (2000). A test of assumed cluster homogeneity for performance appraisal management in four Southeast Asian countries. *International Journal of Human Resource Management, 11*, 736–750.

Palaiologos, A., Papazekos, P., & Panayotopoulou, L. (2011). Organizational justice and employee satisfaction in performance appraisal. *Journal of European Industrial Training, 35*, 826–840.

Palmer, J. K., Maurer, T. J., & Feldman, J. M. (2002). Context and prior impression effects on attention, judgment standards, and ratings: contrast effects revisited. *Journal of Applied Psychology, 87*, 2575–2597.

Palmer, M. G., Johnson, C. M., & Johnson, D. A. (2015). Objective performance feedback: Is numerical accuracy necessary? *Journal of Organizational Behavior Management, 35*, 206–239.

Park, B., & Rothbart, M. (1982). Perception of outgroup homogeneity and levels of social categorization: Memory for subordinate attributes of in-group members. *Journal of Personality and Social Psychology, 42*, 1051–1068.

Park, G., Schmidt, A. M., Scheu, C., & DeShon, R. P. (2007). A process model of goal orientation and feedback seeking. *Human Performance, 20*, 119–145.

Pascale., R., & Athos, A. (1981). *The art of Japanese management applications for American executives.* New York, NY: Simon & Schuster.

Patten, T. H., Jr. (1977). *Pay: Employee compensation and incentive plans.* London: The Free Press.

Paulhus, D. L., & Williams, K. M. (2002). The dark triad of personality. *Journal of Research in Personality, 36*, 556–563.

Pearce, J. L., & Porter, L. W. (1986). Employee responses to formal performance appraisal feedback. *Journal of Applied Psychology, 71*, 211–218.

Peiperi, M. A. (1999). Conditions for the success of peer evaluation. *International Journal of Human Resource Management, 10*, 429–458.

Peretz, H., & Fried, Y. (2012). National cultures, performance appraisal practices, and organizational absenteeism and turnover: A study across 21 countries. *Journal of Applied Psychology, 97*, 448–459.

Pesta, B. J., Kass, D. S., & Dunegan, K. J. (2005). Image theory and the appraisal of employee performance: To screen or not to screen? *Journal of Business and Psychology, 19*, 341–360.

Peters, L. H., & O'Connor, E. J. (1980). Situational constraints and work outcomes: The influences of a frequently overlooked construct. *Academy of Management Review, 5*, 391–397.

Peters, L. H., O'Connor, E. J., & Eulberg, J. R. (1985). Situational constraints: Sources. consequences, and future considerations. In K. Rowland & G. Ferris (Eds.), *Research in personnel and human resource management*, Vol. 3. Greenwich, CT: JAI Press.

Peters, L. H., O'Connor, E. J., & Rudolph, C. J. (1980). The behavioral and affective consequences of performance-relevant situational variables. *Organizational Behavior and Human Performance, 25*, 79–96.

Peters, T., & Waterman, R. H. (2004). *In search of excellence: Lessons from America's best run companies.* New York, NY: Harper Collins.

Peterson, N. G., Mumford, M. D., Borman, W. C., Jeanneret, P. R., & Fleishman, E. A. (Eds.). (1999). *The occupation information network (O*NET).* Washington, DC: American Psychological Association.

Petrie, F. A. (1950). Is there something new in efficiency rating? *Personnel Administrator, 13*, 24.

Pettijohn, L. S., Parker, R. S., Pettijohn, C. E., & Kent, J. L. (2001). Performance appraisals: usage, criteria and observations. *Journal of Management Development, 20*, 754–772.

Pettijohn, C., Pettijohn, L. S., Taylor, A. J., & Keillor, B. D. (2001). Are performance appraisals a bureaucratic exercise or can they be used to enhance salesforce satisfaction and commitment? *Psychology & Marketing, 18*, 337–364.

Pfeffer, J. (1981). *Power in organizations.* Belmont, CA: Pitman.

Pfeffer, J., & Salancik, G. (1978). *The external control of organizations A resource dependence perspective.* New York, NY: Harper and Row.

Pfeffer, J., & Sutton, R. I. (2006). Evidence-based management. *Harvard Business Review, 84*, 62–74.

Piening, E. P., Baluch, A. M., & Salge, T. O. (2013). The relationship between employees' perceptions of human resource systems and organizational performance: Examining mediating mechanisms and temporal dynamics. *Journal of Applied Psychology, 98*, 926–947.

Phillips, J. S., & Freedman, S. M. (1984). Situational performance and constraints and task characteristics: Their relationship to motivation and satisfaction. *Journal of Management, 10*, 321–331.

Pierce, J. R., & Aguinis, H. (2013). The too-much-of-a-good-thing effect in management. *Journal of Management, 39*, 313–338.

Piotrowski, M., Barnes-Farrell, J., Esrig, F. (1989). Behaviorally anchored bias: A replication and extension of Murphy and Constans, *Journal of Applied Psychology, 74*, 823–826.

Ployhart, R. E., & Hakel, M. D. (1998). The substantive nature of performance variability: predicting interindividual differences in intraindividual performance. *Personnel Psychology, 51*, 859–901.

Ployhart, R. E., Wiechmann, D., Schmitt, N., Sacco, J. M., & Rogg, K. (2003). The cross-cultural equivalence of job performance ratings. *Human Performance, 16*, 49–79.

Podsakoff, N. P., Whiting, S. W., Podsakoff, P. M., & Blume, B. D. (2009). Individual- and organizational-level consequences of organizational citizenship behaviors: A meta-analysis. *Journal of Applied Psychology, 94*, 122–141.

Podsakoff, N. P., Whiting, S. W., Welsh, D. T., & Mai, K. M. (2013). Surveying for artifacts: the susceptibility of the OCB-performance evaluation relationship to common rater, item, and measurement context effects. *Journal of Applied Psychology, 98*, 863–874.

Polanyi, M. (1966), *The tacit dimension.* Chicago, IL: University of Chicago Press.

Porter, M. E. (1985). *Competitive advantage.* New York, NY: The Free Press.

Posner, M. I. (1978). *Chronometric explorations of the mind.* Hillsdale, NJ: Erlbaum.

Posthuma, R. A. (2000). The dimensionality of supervisor evaluations of job performance. *Journal of Business and Psychology, 14*, 481–487.

Posthuma, R. A., Campion, M. C., Masimova, M., & Campion, M. A. (2013). A high performance work practices taxonomy: Integrating the literature and directing future research. *Journal of Management, 39*, 1184–1220.

Potter, L. W., Allen, R. W., & Angle, L. L. (1981). The politics of upward influence in organizations. *Research in Organizational Behavior, 3*, 109–149.

Prince, J. B., & Lawler, E. E. (1986). Does salary discussion hurt the developmental performance appraisal. *Organizational Behavior and Human Decision Processes, 37*, 357–375.

Pritchard, R. D., Harrell, M. M., DiazGrandos, D., & Guzman, M. (2008). The productivity measurement and enhancement system: A meta-analysis. *Journal of Applied Psychology, 93*, 540–567.

Pritchard, R. D., Jones, S. D., Roth, P. L., Steubing, K. K., & Ekeberg, S. E. (1988). Effects of group feedback, goal setting, and incentives on organizational productivity. *Journal of Applied Psychology* (Monograph), *73*, 337–358.

Privitera, C., & Campbell, M. A. (2009). Cyberbullying: The new face of workplace bullying? *Cyberpsychology and Behavior, 12*, 395–400.

Prowse, P., & Prowse, J. (2009). The dilemma of performance appraisal. *Measuring Business Excellence, 13*, 69–77.

Putka, D. J., Le, H., McCloy, R. A., & Diaz, T. (2008). Ill-structured measurement designs in organizational research: Implications for estimating interrater reliability. *Journal of Applied Psychology, 93*, 959.

Pulakos, E. D. (1984). A comparison of rater training programs: Error training and accuracy training. *Journal of Applied Psychology, 69*, 581–588.

Pulakos, E. D. (1986). The development of training programs to increased accuracy in different rating tasks. *Organizational Behavior and Human Decision Processes, 38*, 76–91.

Pulakos, E. D. (2004). *Performance management: A roadmap for developing, implementing and evaluating performance management systems.* Alexandria, VA: SHRM Foundation.

Pulakos, E. D. (2009). *Performance management: A new approach for driving business results.* Maiden, MA: Wiley-Blackwell.

Pulakos, E. D., Arad, S., Donovan, M. A., & Plamondon, K. E. (2000). Adaptability in the workplace: Development of a taxonomy of adaptive performance. *Journal of Applied Psychology, 85*, 612–624.

Pulakos, E. D., Mueller-Hanson, R. A., Arad, S., & Moye, N. (2015). Performance management can be fixed: An on-the-job experiential learning approach for complex behavior change. *Industrial and Organizational Psychology: Perspectives on Science and Practice, 8*, 51–76.

Pulakos, E. D., Mueller-Hanson, R. A., O'Leary, R. S., & Meyrowitz, M. M. (2012). *Building a high-performance culture: A fresh look at performance management.* SHRM Foundation Effective Practice Guidelines Series, Alexandria, VA: SHRM Foundation.

Pulakos, E. D., & O'Leary, R. S. (2010). Defining and measuring the results of workplace behavior. In J. L. Farr & N. Tippins (Eds.), *Handbook of employee selection* (pp. 512–530). New York, NY: Routledge.

Pulakos, E. D., & O'Leary, R. S. (2011). Why is performance management so broken? *Industrial and Organizational Psychology: Perspectives on Science and Practice, 4*, 146–164.

Pulakos, E. D., White, L. A., Oppler, S. H., & Borman, W. C. (1989). Examination of race and sex effects on performance ratings. *Journal of Applied Psychology, 74*, 770–780.

Quattrone, C. A., & Jones, E. E. (1980). The perception of variability within in-groups and outgroups: Implications for the law of small numbers. *Journal of Personality and Social Psychology, 38*, 141–152.

Quinn, R. E., & Rohrbaugh, J. (1983). A special model of effectiveness criteria: Toward a competing values approach to organizational analysis. *Management Science, 29*, 363–377.

Raver, J. L., Jensen, J. M., Lee, J., & O'Reilly, J. (2012). Destructive criticism revisited: Appraisals, task outcomes, and the moderating role of competitiveness. *Applied Psychology: An International Review, 61*, 177–203.

Raymark, P. H., Balzer, W. K., & DeLaTorre, F. (1999). A preliminary investigation of the sources of information used by raters when appraising performance. *Journal of Business and Psychology, 14*, 319–339.

Rayner, C., & Cooper, C. L. (1997). Workplace bullying: Myth or reality? Can we afford to ignore it? *Leadership and Organization Development Journal, 18*, 211–214.

Rayner, C., & Cooper, C. L. (2006). Workplace bullying. In E. Kelloway, J. Barling, & J. Hurrell Jr. (Eds.), *Handbook of workplace violence* (pp. 47–90). Thousand Oaks, CA: Sage.

Reb, J., & Greguras, G. J. (2010). Understanding performance ratings: Dynamic performance, attributions, and rating purpose. *Journal of Applied Psychology, 95*, 213–220.

Ree, M. J., Carretta, T. R., & Teachout, M. S. (2015). Pervasiveness of dominant general factors in organizational measurement. *Industrial and Organizational Psychology: Perspectives on Science and Practice, 8*, 409–427.

Reeves, J. (2015). The rise of the employee-centric workplace. *Workforce Solutions Review, 6*, 15–17.

Rehg, M. T., Miceli, M. P., Near, J. P., & Van Scotter, J. R. (2008). Antecedents and outcomes of retaliation against whistleblowers: Gender differences and power relationships. *Organization Science, 19*, 221–240.

Reilly, R. R., Smither, J. W., & Vasilopoulos, N. L. (1996). A longitudinal study of upward feedback. *Personnel Psychology, 49*, 599–612.

Reilly, S. P., Smither, J. W., Warech, M. A., & Reilly, R. R. (1998). The influence of indirect knowledge of previous performance on ratings of present performance: The effects of job familiarity and rater training. *Journal of Business and Psychology, 12*, 421–436.

Reinke, S. J. (2003). Does the form really matter? Leadership, trust, and acceptance of the performance appraisal process. *Review of Public Personnel Administration, 23*, 23–37.

Ren, L. R., Paetzold, R. L., & Colella, A. (2008). A meta-analysis of experimental studies on the effects of disability on human resource judgments. *Human Resource Management Review, 18*, 191–203.

Rees, W. D., & Porter, C. (2003). Appraisal pitfalls and the training implications—Part 1. *Industrial and Commercial Training, 35*, 280–284.

Robbins, T. L., & DeNisi, A. S. (1993). Moderators of sex bias in the performance appraisal process: A cognitive analysis. *Journal of Management, 19*, 113–126.

Robbins, T. L., & DeNisi, A. S. (1994). A closer look at interpersonal affect as a distinct influence on cognitive processing in performance evaluations. *Journal of Applied Psychology, 79*, 341–353.

Roberson, L., Galvin, B. M., & Charles, A. C. (2007). When group identities matter: Bias in performance appraisal. *The Academy of Management Annals, 1*, 617–650.

Roberson, L., Torkel, S., Korsgaard, A., Klein, D., Diddams, M., & Cayer, M. (1993). Self-appraisal and perceptions of the appraisal discussion: A field experiment. *Journal of Organizational Behavior, 14*, 129–142.

Roberts, G. E. (2003). Employee performance appraisal system participation: A technique that works. *Public Personnel Management, 32*, 89–98.

Roberts, T. A., & Nolen-Hoeksema, S. (1989). Sex differences in reactions to evaluative feedback. *Sex Roles, 21*, 725–747.

Robertson, B. J. (2015). *Holacracy: The new management system for a rapidly changing world.* New York, NY: Holt.

Robinson, S. L., & Bennett, R. J. (1995). A typology of deviant workplace behaviors: A multidimensional scaling study. *Academy of Management Journal, 38*, 555–572.

Roch, S. G., Ayman, R., Newhouse, N., & Harris, M. (2005). Effect of identifiability, rating audience, and conscientiousness on rating level. *International Journal of Selection and Assessment, 13*, 53–62.

Roch, S. G., McNall, L., & Caputo, P. M. (2011). Self-judgments of accuracy as indicators of performance evaluation quality: Should we believe them? *Journal of Business and Psychology, 26*, 41–55.

Roch, S. G., Paquin, A. R., & Littlejohn, T. W. (2009). Do raters agree more on observable items? *Human Performance, 22*, 391–409.

Roch, S. G., Sternburgh, A. M., & Caputo, P. M. (2007). Absolute versus relative rating formats: Implications for fairness and organizational justice. *International Journal of Selection and Assessment, 15*, 302–316.

Roch, S. G., Woehr, D. J., Mishra, V., & Kieszczynska, U. (2012). Rater training revisited: An updated meta-analytic review of frame-of-reference training. *Journal of Occupational and Organizational Psychology, 85*, 370–395.

Rodgers, R., & Hunter, J. E. (1991). Impact of management by objectives on organizational productivity. *Journal of Applied Psychology, 76*, 322–336.

Roe, R. M., Busemeyer, J. R., & Townsend, J. T. (2001). Multialternative decision field theory: A dynamic connectionist model of decision making. *Psychological Review, 108*, 370–392.

Rosch, E. (1977). Human categorization. In N. Warren (Ed.), *Studies in cross-cultural psychology*, Vol. l. New York, NY: Academic Press.

Rosch, E., Mervis, C. G., Gray, W. D., Johnson, D. M., & Boyes-Braem, P. (1976). Basic objects in natural categories. *Cognitive Psychology, 8*, 382–439.

Rosen, B., & Jerdee, T. H. (1976). The nature of job-related age stereotypes. *Journal of Applied Psychology, 61*, 180–183.

Rosen, C. C., Levy, P. E., & Hall, R. J. (2006). Placing perceptions of politics in the context of the feedback environment, employee attitudes, and job performance. *Journal of Applied Psychology, 91*, 211–220.

Rosen, M. A., Bedwell, W. L., Wildman, J., Fritzsche, B., Salas, E., & Burke, C. S. (2011). Managing adaptive performance in teams: Guiding principles & behavioral markers for measurement. *Human Resource Management Review, 21*, 107–122.

Ross, L. (1977). The intuitive psychologist and his shortcomings: Distortions in the attribution process. In L. Berkowitz (Ed.), *Advances in experimental social psychology*, Vol. 10 (pp. 173–220). New York, NY: Academic Press.

Roth, P. L., Huffcutt, A. I., & Bobko, P. (2003). Ethnic group differences in measures of job performance: A new meta-analysis. *Journal of Applied Psychology, 88*, 694–706.

Rothe, H. F. (1946a). Output rates among butter wrappers: 1. Work curves and their stability. *Journal of Applied Psychology, 30*, 199–211.

Rothe, H. F. (1946b). Output rates among butter wrappers: 11. Frequency distributions and hypotheses regarding the "restriction of output." *Journal of Applied Psychology, 30*, 320–327.

Rothe, H. F. (1947). Output rates among machine operators: I. Distribution and their reliability. *Journal of Applied Psychology, 31*, 384–389.

Rothe, H. F. (1951). Output rates among chocolate dippers. *Journal of Applied Psychology, 35*, 94–97.

Rothe, H. F., & Nye, C. T. (1958). Output rates among coil workers. *Journal of Applied Psychology, 42*, 182–186.

Rothe, H. F., & Nye, C. T. (1959). Output rates among machine operators: II. Consistency-related methods of pay. *Journal of Applied Psychology, 43*, 417–420.

Rothe, H. F., & Nye, C. T. (1961). Output rates among machine operators: III. A nonincentive situation in two levels of business activity. *Journal of Applied Psychology, 45*, 50–54.

Rotundo, M., & Spector, P. E. (2010). Counterproductive work behavior and withdrawal. In J. Farr and N. Tippins (Eds.), *Handbook of employee selection* (pp. 489–512). New York, NY: Routledge.

Rousseau, D. M. (1988). The construction of climate in organizational research. In C. Cooper & I. Robertson (Eds.), *International review of industrial and organizational psychology*, Vol. 3. Chichester, UK: Wiley.

Rudd, H. (1921). Is the rating of human character practicable? *Journal of Educational Psychology, 12*, 425–438.

Rupp, D. E., Vodanovich, S. J., & Credé, M. (2006). Age bias in the workplace: The impact of ageism and causal attributions. *Journal of Applied Social Psychology, 36*, 1337–1364.

Russell, J. S., & Goode, D. L. (1988). An analysis of managers' reactions to their own performance appraisal feedback. *Journal of Applied Psychology, 73*, 63–67.

Russell, T. L., Sparks, T. E., Campbell, J. P., Handy, K., Ramsberger, P., & Grand, J. A. (2017). Situating ethical performance in the nomological network of job performance. *Journal of Business and Psychology, 32*(3), 253–271.

Saal, F. E., Downey, R. C., & Lahey, M. A. (1980). Rating the ratings: Assessing the quality of rating data. *Psychological Bulletin, 88*, 413–428.

Saal, F. E., & Knight, P. A. (1988). *Industrial organizational psychology: Science and practice*. Pacific Grove, CA: Brooks-Cole.

Saavedra, R., & Kwun, S. K. (1993). Peer evaluation in self-managing work groups. *Journal of Applied Psychology, 78*, 450–462.

Sanchez, J. I., & De La Torre, P. (1996). A second look at the relationship between rating and behavioral accuracy in performance appraisal. *Journal of Applied Psychology, 81*, 3–10.

Saffie-Robertson, M. C., & Brutus, S. (2014). The impact of interdependence on performance evaluations: The mediating role of discomfort with performance appraisal. *International Journal of Human Resource Management, 25*, 459–473.

Schall, M. S. (1983). A communication-rules approach to organizational culture. *Administrative Science Quarterly, 28*, 557–581.

Schaubroeck, J., Shaw, J. D., Duffy, M. K., & Mitra, A. (2008). An under-met and over-met expectations model of employee reactions to merit raises. *Journal of Applied Psychology, 93*, 424–434.

Schein, E. H. (1967). *Organizational socialization and the profession of management*. Cambridge, MA: Massachusetts Institute of Technology.

Schleicher, D. J., Bull, R. A., & Green, S. G. (2009). Rater reactions to forced distribution rating systems. *Journal of Management, 35*, 899–892.

Schmid, S., & Kretschmer, K. (2010). Performance evaluation of foreign subsidiaries: A review of the literature and a contingency framework. *International Journal of Management Reviews, 12*, 219–258.

Schmidt, F. L., & Hunter, J. E. (1981). Employment testing: Old theories and new research findings. *American Psychologist, 36*, 1128–1137.

Schmidt, F. L., & Hunter, J. E. (1998). The validity and utility of selection methods in personnel psychology:

Practical and theoretical implications of 85 years of research findings. *Psychological Bulletin, 124*, 262–274.

Schmidt, F. L., Hunter, J. E., McKenzie, R. C., & Muldrow, T. (1979). The impact of valid selection procedures on work force productivity. *Journal of Applied Psychology, 64*, 609–626.

Schmidt, F. L., Viswesvaran, C., & Ones, D. S. (2000). Reliability is not validity and validity is not reliability. *Personnel Psychology, 53*, 901–912.

Schmitt, N., & Lappin, M. (1980). Race and sex as determinants of the mean and variance of performance ratings. *Journal of Applied Psychology, 65*, 428–435.

Schneider, B., Ehrhart, M. G., & Macey, W. H. (2011). Perspectives on organizational climate and culture. In S. Zedeck (Ed.), *APA handbook of industrial and organizational psychology* (Vol. 1, pp. 373–414). Washington, DC: American Psychological Association.

Schneider, B., Ehrhart, M. G., & Macey, W. H. (2013). Organizational climate and culture. *Annual Review of Psychology, 64*, 361–388.

Schneider, B., & Reichers, A. E. (1983). On the etiology of climates. *Personnel Psychology, 36*, 19–40.

Schneider, C. E. (1977). Operational utility and psychometric characteristics of behavioral expectation scales. *Journal of Applied Psychology, 62*, 541–548.

Schrader, B. W., & Steiner, D. D. (1996). Common comparison standards: An approach to improving agreement between self and supervisory performance ratings. *Journal of Applied Psychology, 81*, 813–820.

Schuler, R. S., & Jackson, S. E. (1987). Organizational strategy and organizational level as determinants of human resource management practices. *Human Resource Planning Journal, 10*, 125–143.

Schwartz, S. H. (1999). A theory of cultural values and some implications for work. *Applied Psychology: An International Review, 48*, 23–47.

Scott, W. R. (1975). *Institutions and organizations*. Los Angeles, CA: Sage.

Scott, S. G., & Einstein, W. O. (2001). Strategic performance appraisal in team-based organizations: One size does not fit all. *Academy of Management Executive, 15*, 107–116.

Scott, W. D., Clothier, R C., & Spriegel, W. R. (1941). *Personnel management*. New York, NY: McGraw-Hill.

Scullen, S. E., Bergey, P. K., & Aiman-Smith, L. (2005). Forced distribution rating systems and the improvement of workforce potential: A baseline simulation. *Personnel Psychology, 58*, 1–31.

Scullen, S. E., Mount, M. K., & Goff, M. (2000). Understanding the latent structure of job performance ratings. *Journal of Applied Psychology, 85*, 956–970.

Seifert, C. F., Yukl, G., & McDonald, R. A. (2003). Effects of multisource feedback and a feedback facilitator on the influence behavior of managers toward subordinates. *Journal of Applied Psychology, 88*, 561–569.

Seligman, M. E. P., & Csikszentmihalyi, M. (2000). Positive psychology: An introduction. *American Psychologist, 55*, 5–14.

Seo, M., & Barrett, L. F. (2007). Being emotional during decision making--Good or bad? An empirical investigation. *Academy of Management Journal, 50*, 923–940.

Sewell, G., Barker, J. R., & Nyberg, D. (2012). Working under intensive surveillance: When does 'measuring everything that moves' become intolerable? *Human Relations, 65*, 189–215.

Shadish, W. R., Cook, T. D., & Campbell, D. T. (2001). *Experimental and quasi-experimental designs for generalized causal inference*. Boston, MA: Houghton-Mifflin.

Shadur, M. A., Rodwell, J. J., & Bamber, G. J. (1995). The adoption of international best practices in a Western culture: East meets West. *International Journal of Human Resource Management, 6*, 735–757.

Shapira, Z., & Shirom, A. (1980). New issues in the use of behaviorally anchored rating scales: Level of analysis, the effects of incident frequency and external validation. *Journal of Applied Psychology, 65*, 517–523.

Sharma, R., & Sahoo, C. K. (2013). Regenerating organizational strength the employee centric way. *Strategic HR Review, 12*, 61–69.

Sharon, A. (1970). Eliminating bias from student rating of college instructors. *Journal of Applied Psychology, 54*, 278–281.

Sharon, A., & Bartlett, C. (1969). Effect of instructional conditions in producing leniency on two types of rating scales. *Personnel Psychology, 22*, 252–263.

Shaw, J. D., Duffy, M. K., Mitra, A., Lockhart, D. E., & Bowler, M. (2003). Reactions to merit pay increases: A longitudinal test of a signal sensitivity perspective. *Journal of Applied Psychology, 88*, 538.

Sherif, M., & Sherif, C. W. (1969). *Social psychology*. New York, NY: Harper and Row.

Shibata, H. (2000). The transformation of the wage and performance appraisal system in a Japanese firm. *International Journal of Human Resource Management, 11*, 294–313.

Shibata, H. (2002). Wage and performance appraisal systems in flux: A Japan–United States comparison. *Industrial Relations, 41*, 629–652.

Shiffrin, R. M., & Scheider, W. (1977). Controlled and automatic human information processing: II. Perceptual learning, automatic attending and a general theory. *Psychological Review, 84*, 127–190.

Shore, T. H., Adams, J. S., & Tashchian, A. (1998). Effects of self-appraisal information, appraisal purpose, and feedback target on performance appraisal ratings. *Journal of Business and Psychology, 12*, 283–298.

Si, S., & Li, Y. (2012). Human resource management practices on exit, voice, loyalty, and neglect: Organizational commitment as a mediator. *International Journal of Human Resource Management, 23*, 1705–1716.

Shin, D., & Konrad, A. M. (2017). Causality between high-performance work systems and organizational performance. *Journal of Management, 43*, 973–997.

Siegel, S. R. (1993). Relationships between current performance and likelihood of promotion for old versus young workers. *Human Resource Development Quarterly, 4*, 39–50.

Simons, D. J., & Charbris, C. F. (2011). What people believe about how memory work: A representative survey of the U.S. population. *Plos One, 6*, e22757.

Sims, R. R. (2000). Changing an organization's culture under new leadership. *Journal of Business Ethics, 25*, 65–78.

Sinclair, R. C. (1988). Mood, categorization, breadth, and performance appraisal: The effects of order of information acquisition and affective state on halo, accuracy, information retrieval, and evaluations. *Organizational Behavior and Human Decision Processes, 42*, 22–46.

Sisson, E. D. (1948). Forced-choice: The new Army rating. *Personnel Psychology, 1*, 365–381.

Sisson, K., & Storey, J. (2000). *The realities of human resource management: Managing the employment relationship*. Maidenhead, UK: Open University Press.

Six, F., & Sorge, A. (2008). Creating a high-trust organization: An exploration of organizational policies that stimulate interpersonal trust building. *Journal of Management Studies, 45*, 857–884.

Slaughter, J. E., & Greguras, G. J. (2008). Bias in performance ratings: clarifying the role of positive versus negative escalation. *Human Performance, 21*, 414–426.

Smith, A., & Fortunato, V. (2008). Factors influencing employee intentions to provide honest upward feedback ratings. *Journal of Business and Psychology, 22*, 191–207.

Smith, B., Hornsby, J. S., & Shirmeyer, R. (1996). Current trends in performance appraisal: An examination of managerial practice. *SAM Advanced Management Journal, 61*, 10–15.

Smith C. A., Organ, D. W., & Near, J. P. (1983). Organizational citizenship behavior: Its nature and antecedents. *Journal of Applied Psychology, 68*, 653–663.

Smith, P. C. (1976). Behaviors, results, and organizational effectiveness. In M. Dunnette (Ed.), *Handbook of industrial and organizational psychology*. Chicago, IL: Rand-McNally.

Smith, P. C., & Kendall, L. M. (1963). Retranslation of expectations: An approach to the construction of unambiguous anchors for rating scales. *Journal of Applied Psychology, 47*, 149–155.

Smith, S. (2016). Military urinalysis (drug testing) program. Retrieved from https://www.thebalance.com/military-urinalysis-drug-test-program-4054324

Smither, J. W. (2015). The fate of performance ratings: Don't write the obituary yet. *Industrial and Organizational Psychology: Perspectives on Science and Practice, 8*, 77–80.

Smither, J. W., London, M., & Reilly, R. R. (2005). Does performance improve following multisource feedback? A theoretical model, meta-analysis, and review of empirical findings. *Personnel Psychology, 59*, 33–66.

Smither, J. W., Reilly, R. R., & Buda, R. (1988). Effect of prior performance information on ratings of present performance: Contrast versus assimilation revisited. *Journal of Applied Psychology, 73*, 487–496.

Snape, E., Thompson, D., Yan, F. K., & Redman, T. (1998). Performance appraisal and culture: Practice and attitudes in Hong Kong and Great Britain. *International Journal of Human Resource Management, 9*, 841–861.

Snyder, C. R., & Lopez, S. J. (2007). *Positive psychology: The scientific and practical explorations of human strengths*. Thousand Oaks, CA: Sage.

Society for Human Resource Management. (2017). SHRM practice guidelines on performance management.

Society for Industrial and Organizational Psychology. (2017). Introduction to coaching. Retrieved from http://www.siop.org/Workplace/coaching/introduction.aspx

Solomonson, A. L., & Lance, C. E. (1997). Examination of the relationship between true halo and halo error in performance ratings. *Journal of Applied Psychology, 82*, 665–674.

Sommer, K. L., & Kulkarni, M. (2012). Does constructive performance feedback improve citizenship intentions and job satisfaction? The roles of perceived opportunities for advancement, respect, and mood. *Human Resource Development Quarterly, 23*, 177–201.

Sorcher, S. (2013). How the military's 'bro' culture turns women into targets. *National Journal, 2*.

Sparr, J. L., & Sonnentag, S. (2008). Feedback environment and well-being at work: The mediating role of personal control and feelings of helplessness. *European Journal of Work and Organizational Psychology, 17*, 388–412.

Spector, P. E., Bauer, J. A., & Fox, S. (2010). Measurement artifacts in the assessment of counterproductive work behavior and organizational citizenship behavior: Do we know what we think we know? *Journal of Applied Psychology, 95*, 781–790.

Spence, J. R., & Keeping, L. M. (2010). The impact of non-performance information on ratings of job performance: A policy-capturing approach. *Journal of Organizational Behavior, 31*, 587–608.

Spence, J. R., & Keeping, L. (2011). Conscious rating distortion in performance appraisal: A review, commentary, and proposed framework for research. *Human Resource Management Review, 21*, 85–95.

Spriegel, W. R. (1962). Company practices in appraisal of managerial performance. *Personnel, 39*, 77.

Sridharan, V. G., & Bui, J. (2015). Mismatch in the design of performance measures: A solution for managing conflicting organisational goals. *Journal of Applied Management Accounting Research, 13*, 49–62.

Stamoulis, D. T., & Hauenstein, N. M. (1993). Rater training and rating accuracy: Training for dimensional accuracy versus training for ratee differentiation. *Journal of Applied Psychology, 78*, 994–1003.

Stanton, J. M. (2000). Reactions to employee performance monitoring: Framework, review, and research directions. *Human Performance, 13*, 85–113.

Starbuck, W. H. (2004). Performance measures: Prevalent and important but methodologically challenging. *Journal of Management Inquiry, 14*, 280–286.

Stauffer, J. M., & Buckley, M. R. (2005). The existence and nature of racial bias in supervisory ratings. *Journal of Applied Psychology, 90*, 586–591.

Stevenson, W. J. (2015). *Operations management* (12th ed.). New York, NY: McGraw Hill.

Stone, D., & Heen, S. (2014). *Thanks for the feedback: The science and art of receiving feedback well (even when it is off base, unfair, poorly delivered, and, frankly, you're not in the mood)*. New York, NY: Viking.

St-Onge, S. (2000). Variable influencing the perceived relationship between performance and pay in a merit pay environment. *Journal of Business and Psychology, 14*, 459–480.

Steel, R. P., & Ovalle, N. K. (1984). Self-appraisal based on supervisory feedback. *Personnel Psychology, 37*, 667–685.

Steelman, L. A., Levy, P. E., & Snell, A. F. (2004). The Feedback Environment Scale: Construct definition, measurement, and validation. *Educational and Psychological Measurement, 64*, 165–184.

Steers, R. M., & Rhodes, S. R. (1978). Major influences on employee attendance: A process model. *Journal of Applied Psychology, 63*, 391–407.

Steiner, D. D., Rain, J. S., & Smalley, M. M. (1993). Distributional ratings of performance: further examination of a new rating format. *Journal of Applied Psychology, 78*, 438–442.

Stetz, T. A., & Chmielewski, T. L. (2016). Efficiency ratings and performance appraisals in the United States federal government. *Industrial and Organizational Psychology: Perspectives on Science and Practice, 9*, 270–275.

Stewart, S. M., Gruys, M. L., & Storm, M. (2010). Forced distribution performance evaluation systems: Advantages, disadvantages and keys to implementation. *Journal of Management and Organization, 16*, 168–179.

Sturman, M. C., Cheramie, R. A., & Cashen, L. H. (2005). The impact of job complexity and performance measurement on the temporal consistency, stability, and test-retest reliability of employee job performance ratings. *Journal of Applied Psychology, 90,* 269–283.

Sully de Luque, M. F., & Sommer, S. M. (2000). The impact of culture on feedback-seeking behavior: An integrated model and propositions. *Academy of Management Review, 25,* 829–849.

Sulsky, L. M., & Balzer, W. K. (1988). Meaning and measurement of performance rating accuracy: Some methodological and theoretical concerns. *Journal of Applied Psychology, 73,* 497–506.

Sulsky, L. M., & Kline, T. J. (2007). Understanding frame-of-reference training success: a social learning theory perspective. *International Journal of Training and Development, 11,* 121–131.

Sumer, H. C., & Knight, P. A. (1996). Assimilation and contrast effects in performance ratings: effects of rating the previous performance on rating subsequent performance. *Journal of Applied Psychology, 81,* 436–442.

Sutton, A. W., Baldwin, S. P., Wood, L., & Hoffman, B. J. (2013). A meta-analysis of the relationship between rater liking and performance ratings. *Human Performance, 26,* 409–429.

Szilagyi, A. D., & Wallace, M. J. (1983) *Organizational behavior and performance* (3rd ed.). Glenview, IL: Scott Foresman.

Taylor, E., & Wherry, R. (1951). A study of leniency of two rating systems. *Personnel Psychology, 4,* 39–47.

Taylor, M. S., Masterson, S. S., Renard, M. K., & Tracy, K. B. (1998). Managers' reactions to procedurally just performance management systems. *Academy of Management Journal, 41,* 568–579.

Taylor, M. S., Tracy, K. B., Renard, M. K., Harrison, J. K., & Carroll, S. J. (1995). Due process in performance appraisal: A quasi-experiment in procedural justice. *Administrative Science Quarterly,* 495–523.

Taylor, S. E. (1985). *Employee resourcing.* London: Institute of Personnel and Development.

Taylor, S. E., & Fiske, S. T. (1978). Salience, attention, and attributions: Top of the head phenomena. In L. Berkowitz (Ed.), *Advances in experimental social psychology* (Vol. 11). New York, NY: Academic Press.

Taylor, S. N., & Bright, D. S. (2011). Open-mindedness and defensiveness in multisource feedback processes: A conceptual framework. *Journal of Applied Behavioral Science, 47,* 432–460.

Tesser, A., & Conlee, M. C. (1973). Recipient emotionality as a determinant of the transmission of bad news. In *Proceedings of the Annual Convention of the American Psychological Association.* American Psychological Association.

Tesser, A., & Rosen, S. (1975). The reluctance to transmit bad news. *Advances in Experimental Social Psychology, 8,* 193–232.

Tetlock, P. E. (1985). The impact of accountability on judgment and choice: Toward a social contingency model. *Advances in Experimental Social Psychology, 25,* 331–376.

Thomas, G. E. (1999). Leaderless supervision and performance appraisal: A proposed research agenda. *Human Resource Development Quarterly, 10,* 91–94.

Thompson, J. D. (1967). *Organizations in action.* New York, NY: McGraw-Hill.

Thorndike, E. L. (1920). A constant error in psychological ratings. *Journal of Applied Psychology, 4,* 25–29.

Thornton, C. C., III. (1980). Psychometric properties of self-appraisals of job performance. *Personnel Psychology, 33,* 263–271.

Toegel, G., & Conger, J. A. (2003). 360-degree assessment: Time for reinvention. *Academy of Management Learning and Education, 2,* 297–311.

Tolli, A. P., & Schmidt, A. M. (2008). The role of feedback, causal attributions, and self-efficacy in goal revision. *Journal of Applied Psychology, 93,* 692.

Tornow, W. W. (1993). Perceptions or reality: Is multi-perspective measurement a means or an end? *Human Resource Management, 32,* 221–229.

Treadway, D. C., Duke, A. B., Ferris, G. R., Adams, G. L., & Thatcher, J. B. (2007). The moderating role of subordinate political skill on supervisors' impressions of subordinate ingratiation and ratings of subordinate interpersonal facilitation. *Journal of Applied Psychology, 92,* 848–855.

Treadway, D. C., Ferris, G. R., Hochwarter, W., Perrewé, P., Witt, L. A., & Goodman, J. M. (2005). The role of age in the perceptions of politics—job performance relationship: A three-study constructive replication. *Journal of Applied Psychology, 90,* 872.

Tsui, A. S., & Gutek, B. A. (1999). *Demographic differences in organizations: Current research and future directions.* Lanham, MD: Lexington Books.

Tuytens, M., & Devos, G. (2012). The effect of procedural justice in the relationship between charismatic leadership and feedback reactions in performance appraisal. *International Journal of Human Resource Management, 23*, 3047–3062.

Tziner, A. (1999). The relationship between distal and proximal factors and the use of political considerations in performance appraisal. *Journal of Business and Psychology, 14*, 217–231.

Tziner, A., Joanis, C., Murphy, K. R. (2000). A comparison of three methods of performance appraisal with regard to goal properties, goal perception, and ratee satisfaction. *Group and Organization Management, 25*, 175–190.

Tziner, A., Kopelman, R. E., & Livneh, N. (1993). Effects of performance appraisal format on perceived goal characteristics, appraisal process satisfaction, and changes in rated job performance: A field experiment. *Journal of Psychology: Interdisciplinary and Applied: Interdisciplinary and Applied, 127*, 281–291.

Tziner, A., Latham, G. P., Price, B. S., & Haccoun, R. (1996). Development and validation of a questionnaire for measuring perceived political considerations in performance appraisal. *Journal of Organizational Behavior, 17*(2), 179–190.

Tziner, A., & Murphy, K. R. (1999). Additional evidence of attitudinal influences in performance appraisal. *Journal of Business and Psychology, 13*, 407–419.

Tziner, A., Murphy, K. R., & Cleveland, J. N. (2005). Contextual and rater factors affecting rating behavior. *Group and Organization Management, 30*, 89–98.

Tziner, A., Murphy, K. R., Cleveland, J. N., Beaudin, G., & Marchand, S. (1998). Impact of rater beliefs regarding performance appraisal and its organizational context on appraisal quality. *Journal of Business and Psychology, 12*, 457–468.

Tziner, A., & Roch, S. G. (2016). Disappointing interventions and weak criteria: Carving out a solution is still possible. *Industrial and Organizational Psychology: Perspectives on Science and Practice, 9*, 350–356.

Uggerslev, K. L., & Sulsky, L. M. (2002). Presentation modality and indirect performance information: Effects on ratings, reactions, and memory. *Journal of Applied Psychology, 87*, 940–950.

Uggerslev, K. L., Sulsky, L. M. (2008). Using frame-of-reference training to understand the implications of rater idiosyncrasy for rating accuracy. *Journal of Applied Psychology, 93*, 711–719.

Uggerslev, K. L., Sulsky, L. M., & Day, D. V. (2003). *Effects of performance theory characteristics and training protocols on frame-of-reference training.* In 63rd Annual Meeting of the Academy of Management, Seattle, WA.

Unger-Aviram, E., Zwikael, O., & Restubog, S. L. D. (2013). Revisiting goals, feedback, recognition, and performance success: The case of project teams. *Group and Organization Management, 38*, 570–600.

U.S. Office of Personnel Management. (1998). *Performance appraisal for teams: An overview.* Washington, DC: U.S. Government Printing Office.

U.S. Office of Personnel Management. (2017). Implementing FCAT-M performance management competencies: Performance coaching and feedback. Retrieved from https://www.opm.gov/policy-data-oversight/performance-management/performance-management-cycle/developing/performance-coaching-and-feedback/

Valle, M., & Bozeman, D. (2002). Interrater agreement on employees' job performance: Review and directions. *Psychological Reports, 90*, 975–985.

Vancouver, J. B., Weinhardt, J. M., & Schmidt, A. M. (2010). A formal, computational theory of multiple-goal pursuit: Integrating goal-choice and goal-striving processes. *Journal of Applied Psychology, 95*, 985–1008.

VandeWalle, D. (2003). A goal orientation model of feedback-seeking behaviour. *Human Resource Management Review, 13*, 581–604.

VandeWalle, D., Cron, W. L., & Slocum, Jr., J. W. (2001). The role of goal orientation following performance feedback. *Journal of Applied Psychology, 86*, 629–640.

Van Der Geht, G. S., Emans, B. J. M., & Van Der Vriert, E. (2001). Patterns of interdependence in work teams: A two-level investigation of the relations with job and team satisfaction. *Personnel Psychology, 54*, 51–69.

van der Heijden, B. I. J. M., & Nijhof, A. H. J. (2004). The value of subjectivity: Problems and prospects for 360-degree appraisal systems. *International Journal of Human Resource Management, 15*, 493–511.

van der Rijt, J., van de Wiel, M. W. J., Van den Bossche, P., Segers, M. S. R., & Gijselaers, W. H. (2012). Contextual antecedents of informal feedback in the workplace. *Human Resource Development Quarterly, 23,* 233–257.

van der Vegt, G. S., de Jong, S. B., Bunderson, J. S., & Molleman, E. (2010). Power asymmetry and learning in teams: The moderating role of performance feedback. *Organization Science, 21,* 347–361.

Van Dyne, L., & LePine, J. A. (1998). Helping and voice extra-role behaviors: Evidence of construct and predictive validity. *Academy of Management Journal, 41,* 108–119.

Van Scotter, J. R., & Motowidlo, S. J. (1996). Interpersonal facilitation and job dedication as separate facets of contextual performance. *Journal of Applied Psychology, 25,* 577–600.

Van Scotter, J. R., Motowidlo, S. J., & Cross, T. C. (2000). Effects of task performance and contextual performance on systemic rewards. *Journal of Applied Psychology, 85,* 526–536.

van Woerkom, M., & de Bruijn, M. (2016). Why performance appraisal does not lead to performance improvement: Excellent performance as a function of uniqueness instead of uniformity. *Industrial and Organizational Psychology: Perspectives on Science and Practice, 9,* 275–281.

Vara, V. (2015, August). The push against performance reviews. *The New Yorker.*

Varma, A., DeNisi, A. S., Peters, L. H. (1996). Interpersonal affect and performance appraisal: A field study. *Personnel Psychology, 49,* 341–360.

Vecchio, R. P., & Gobdel, B. C. (1984). The vertical dyadic linkage mode of leadership: Problems and prospects. *Organizational Behavior and Human Performance, 34,* 5–20.

Verma, A. (2005). What do unions do to the workplace? Union effects on management and HRM policies. *Journal of Labor Research, 26,* 415–449.

Vest, M. J., Scott, K. D., & Tarnoff, K. A. (1995). When accuracy is not enough: The moderating effect of perceived appraisal use. *Journal of Business and Psychology, 10,* 207–220.

Vest, M. J., Scott, K. D., Vest, J. M., & Markham, S. E. (2000). Factors influencing employee beliefs that pay is tied to performance. *Journal of Business and Psychology, 14,* 553–562.

Villanova, P., & Bernardin, H. J. (1989). Impression management in the context of performance appraisal.

In R. A. Glacalone & P. Rosenfeld (Eds.), *Impression management in the organization.* Hillsdale, NJ: Lawrence Erlbaum Associates.

Villanova, P., Bernardin, H. J., Dahmus, S. A., & Sims, R. L. (1993). Rater leniency and performance appraisal discomfort. *Educational & Psychological Measurement, 53,* 789–799.

Viswesvaran, C. (1993). *Modeling job performance: Is there a general factor?* (Unpublished doctoral dissertation). University of Iowa.

Viswesvaran, C., Ones, D. S., & Schmidt, F. L. (1996). Comparative analysis of the reliability of job performance ratings. *Journal of Applied Psychology, 81,* 557–574.

Viswesvaran, C., Schmidt, F. L., & Ones, D. S. (2002). The moderating influence of job performance dimensions on convergence of supervisory and peer ratings of job performance: Unconfounding construct-level convergence and rating difficulty. *Journal of Applied Psychology, 87,* 345–354.

Viswesvaran, C., Schmidt, F. L., & Ones, D. S. (2005). Is there a general factor in ratings of job performance? A meta-analytic framework for disentangling substantive and error influences. *Journal of Applied Psychology, 90,* 108–131.

Vranjes, I., Baillien, E., Vandebosch, H., Erreygers, S., & De Witte, H. (2017). The dark side of working online: Towards a definition and an Emotion Reaction model of workplace cyberbullying. *Computers in Human Behavior, 69,* 324–334.

Walker, A. G., & Smither, J. W. (1999). A five-year study of upward feedback: What managers do with their results matters. *Personnel Psychology, 52,* 393–423.

Wagner, R. K. (1986). Tacit knowledge in everyday-intelligent behavior. *Journal of Personality and Social Psychology, 52,* 1236–1247.

Waite, M. L., & Stites-Doe, S. (2000). Removing performance appraisal and merit pay in the name of quality. An empirical study of employees' reactions. *Journal of Quality Management, 5,* 187–206.

Waldman, D. A., & Avolio, B. J. (1991). Race effects in performance evaluations: Controlling for ability, education, and experience. *Journal of Applied Psychology, 76,* 897–901.

Waldman, D. A., & Bowen, D. E. (1998). The acceptability of 360 degree appraisals: A customer-supplier relationship perspective. *Human Resource Management, 37*, 117–132.

Wanberg, C. (2012). *The Oxford handbook of organizational socialization.* New York, NY: Oxford University Press.

Wang, M., Burlacu, G., Truxillo, D., James, K., & Yao, X. (2015). Age differences in feedback reactions: The roles of employee feedback orientation on social awareness and utility. *Journal of Applied Psychology, 100*, 1296–1308.

Wang, X. M., Wong, K. F. E., & Kwong, J. Y. (2010). The roles of rater goals and ratee performance levels in the distortion of performance ratings. *Journal of Applied Psychology, 95*, 546–561.

Wanous, J. P. (1980). *Organizational entry: Recruitment, selection, and socialization of newcomers.* Reading, MA: Addison-Wesley.

Waung, M., & Jones, D. R. (2005). The effect of feedback packaging on ratee reactions. *Journal of Applied Social Psychology, 35*, 1630–1655.

Waung, M., & Highhouse, S. (1997). Fear of conflict and empathic buffering: Two explanations for the inflation of performance feedback. *Organizational Behavior and Human Decision Processes, 71*, 37–54.

Wax, A., Asencio, R., & Carter, D. R. (2015). Thinking big about big data. *Industrial and Organizational Psychology, 8*, 545–550.

Wayne, S. J., & Liden, R. C. (1995). Effects of impression management on performance ratings: A longitudinal study. *Journal of Management, 20*, 232–260.

Wayne, S. J., Liden, R. C., Graf, I. K., & Ferris, G. R. (1997). The role of upward influence tactics in human resource decisions. *Personnel Psychology, 50*, 979–1006.

Wayne, S. J., Shore, L. M., & Liden, R. C. (1997). Perceived organizational support and leader–member exchange: A social exchange perspective. *Academy of Management Journal, 40*, 82–111.

Wegner, D. M., & Schneider, D. J (2003). The white bear story. *Psychological Inquiry, 14*, 326–329.

Wegner, D. M., & Vallecher, R. (1977). *Implicit psychology.* New York, NY: Oxford University Press.

Weiss, H. M. (1978). Social learning of work values in organizations. *Journal of Applied Psychology, 63*, 711–718.

Welch, J., & Byrne, J. A. (2001). *Jack: Straight from the gut.* New York, NY: Warner Business Books.

Wells, D. L., Moorman, R. H., & Werner, J. M. (2007). The impact of the perceived purpose of electronic performance monitoring on an array of attitudinal variables. *Human Resource Development Quarterly, 18*, 121–138.

Wendelken, D., & Inn, A. (1981). Nonperformance influences on performance evaluations: A laboratory phenomenon? *Journal of Applied Psychology, 66*, 752–758.

Werner, J. M. (1994). Dimensions that make a difference: Examining the impact of in-role and extrarole behaviors on supervisory ratings. *Journal of Applied Psychology, 79*, 98–107.

Werner, J. M., & Bolino, M. C. (1997). Explaining U.S. courts of appeals decisions involving performance appraisal: Accuracy, fairness, and validation. *Personnel Psychology, 50*, 1–24.

West, J. A. (1998). *Do performance standards reflect conceptions of competence? The relationship between implicit theories of competence and standard-setting judgments* (January 1, 1998). ETD Collection for Fordham University. Paper AAI9825852. http://fordham.bepress.com/dissertations/AAI9825852

Wexley, K. N., & Klimoski, R. J. (1984). Performance appraisal: An update. In K. M. Rowland & G. R. Ferris (Eds.), *Research in personnel and human resources management* (Vol. 2; pp. 35–79). Greenwich, CT: JAI Press.

Wexley, K. N., & Youtz, M. A. (1985). Rater beliefs about others Their effects on rating errors and rater accuracy. *Journal of Occupational Psychology, 58*, 265–275.

Wherry, R. J., & Bartlett, C. J. (1982). The control of bias in ratings: A theory of rating. *Personnel Psychology, 35*, 521–555.

Whetten, D. A (1987). Organizational growth and decline processes. *Annual Review of Sociology, 13*, 335–358.

Whisler, T. L., & Harper, S. F. (1962). *Performance appraisal: Research and practice.* New York, NY: Holt, Rinehart and Winston.

Whitaker, B. G., Dahling, J. J., & Levy, P. (2007). The development of a feedback environment and role clarity model of job performance. *Journal of Management, 33*, 570–591.

Whitener, E. M. (2001). Do "high commitment" human resource practices affect employee commitment?

A cross-level analysis using hierarchical linear modeling. *Journal of Management, 27*, 515–535.

Whiting, S. W., Podsakoff, P. M., & Pierce, J. R. (2008). Effects of task performance, helping, voice, and organizational loyalty on performance appraisal ratings. *Journal of Applied Psychology, 93*, 125–139.

Whitman, M. V., Halbesleben, J. B., & Holmes, O. I. (2014). Abusive supervision and feedback avoidance: The mediating role of emotional exhaustion. *Journal of Organizational Behavior, 35*, 38–53.

Whyte, W. F. (1943). *Street corner society: The social structure of an Italian slum.* Chicago, IL: University of Chicago Press.

Wiggins, J. S. (1973). *Personality and prediction: Principles of personality measurement.* Reading, MA: Addison-Wesley.

Williams, J. R., & Johnson, M. A. (2000). Self-supervisor agreement: The influence of feedback seeking on the relationship between self and supervisor ratings of performance. *Journal of Applied Social Psychology, 30*, 275–292.

Williams, J. R., & Levy, P. E. (2000). Investigating some neglected criteria: The influence of organizational level and perceived system knowledge on appraisal reactions. *Journal of Business and Psychology, 14*, 501–514.

Williams, J. R., & Lueke, S. B. (1999). 360° feedback system effectiveness: Test of a model in a field setting. *Journal of Quality Management, 4*, 23–49.

Williams, K. J., DeNisi, A. S., Blencoe, A. G., & Cafferty, T. P. (1985). The role of appraisal purpose: Effects of purpose on information acquisition and utilization. *Organizational Behavior and Human Performance, 35*, 314–339.

Williams, K. J., DeNisi, A. S., Meglino, B. M., & Cafferty, T. P. (1986). Initial decisions and subsequent performance ratings. *Journal of Applied Psychology, 71*, 189–195.

Williams, L. J., & Anderson, S. E. (1991). Job satisfaction and organizational commitment as predictors of organizational citizenship and in-role behaviors. *Journal of Management, 17*, 601–617.

Wilson, J. P., & Western, S. (2000). Performance appraisal: an obstacle to training and development? *Journal of European Industrial Training, 6*, 93–99.

Wilson, K. Y. (2010). An analysis of bias in supervisor narrative comments in performance appraisal. *Human Relations, 63*, 1903–1933.

Wiswell, A. K., & Lawrence, H. V. (1994). Intercepting managers' attributional bias through feedback-skills training. *Human Resource Development Quarterly, 5*, 41–53.

Woehr, D. J. (1994). Understanding frame-of-reference training: The impact of training on the recall of performance information. *Journal of Applied Psychology, 79*, 525–534.

Woehr, D. J., & Feldman, J. (1993). Processing objective and question order effects on the causal relation between memory and judgment in performance appraisal: The tip of the iceberg. *Journal of Applied Psychology, 78*, 232–241.

Woehr, D. J., & Huffcutt, A. I. (1994). Rater training for performance appraisal: A quantitative review. *Journal of Occupational and Organizational Psychology, 67*, 189–205.

Woehr, D. J., & Miller, M. J. (1997). Distributional ratings of performance: More evidence for a new rating format. *Journal of Management, 23*, 705–720.

Woehr, D. J., & Roch, S. G. (2016). Of babies and bathwater: Don't throw the measure out with the application. *Industrial and Organizational Psychology: Perspectives on Science and Practice, 9*, 357–361.

Woehr, D. J., Sheehan, M. K., & Bennett, W. (2005). Assessing measurement equivalence across rating sources: A multitrait-multirater approach. *Journal of Applied Psychology, 90*, 592–600.

Wong, K. F., & Kwong, J. Y. (2005). Between-individual comparisons in performance evaluation: a perspective from prospect theory. *Journal of Applied Psychology, 90*, 284–294.

Wong, K. F. E., & Kwong, J. Y. (2007). Effects of rater goals on rating patterns: Evidence from an experimental field study. *Journal of Applied Psychology, 92*, 577.

Wu, C., Parker, S. K., & de Jong, J. P. J. (2014). Feedback seeking from peers: A positive strategy for insecurely attached team-workers. *Human Relations, 67*, 441–464.

Youndt, M. A., Snell, S. A., Dean, J. W., & Lepak, D. P. (1996). Human resource management, manufacturing strategy and firm performance. *Academy of Management Journal, 39*, 836–866.

Young, S. F., & Steelman, L. A. (2014). The role of feedback in supervisor and workgroup identification. *Personnel Review, 43*, 228–245.

Youngcourt, S. S., Leiva, P. I., & Jones, R. G. (2007). Perceived purposes of performance appraisal: Correlates of individual-and position-focused purposes on attitudinal outcomes. *Human Resource Development Quarterly, 18*, 315–343.

Yu, J., & Murphy, K. (1993). Modesty bias in self ratings of performance: A test of the cultural relativity hypothesis. *Personnel Psychology, 46*, 357–363.

Yukl, G. A., & Latham, G. P. (1975). Consequences of reinforcement schedules and incentive magnitudes for employee performance: Problems encountered in an industrial setting. *Journal of Applied Psychology, 60*, 294–298.

Zajonc, R. B. (1980). Feeling and thinking: Preferences need no inferences. *American Psychologist, 35*, 151–175.

Zaleznik, A., Christensen, C. R., & Roethlisberger, F. J. (1958). *The motivation, productivity, and satisfaction of workers: A production study.* Cambridge, MA: Harvard University Press.

Ziguang, C., Wing, L., & Jian, A. Z. (2007). Leader–member exchange and member performance: A new look at individual-level negative feedback-seeking behavior and team-level empowerment climate. *Journal of Applied Psychology, 92*, 202–212.

Zivnuska, S., Kacmar, K. M., Witt, L. A., Carlson, S., & Bratton, V. K. (2004). Interactive effects of impression management and organizational politics on job performance. *Journal of Organizational Behavior, 25*, 627–640.

Zyphur, M. J., Chaturvedi, S., & Arvey, R. D. (2008). Job performance over time is a function of latent trajectories and previous performance. *Journal of Applied Psychology, 93*, 217–224.

INDEX